Professional's Guide to Value Pricing

by Ronald J. Baker

Highlights

Professional's Guide to Value Pricing shows you how to price your professional services for greater profit. Ronald Baker provides CPAs, attorneys, and other professionals with the information they need to evaluate the economics and ethics of a wide variety of alternative pricing methods, select among them with regard to their individual practices and for specific customer situations, implement the switch from hourly billing to alternative pricing methods, and both monitor and perfect value pricing in their firms.

Sixth Edition

The Sixth Edition of *Professional's Guide to Value Pricing* has been updated throughout with information on managing the firm, human capital issues, the art of business development, and evaluating prospective customers. Included is a new chapter on the subject of using—and not using—timesheets. Further, you will find expanded coverage in these areas:

- Why you're losing money every hour and don't know it
- Why hourly billing defies the law of supply and demand

- Why the market for professionals has changed dramatically
- How pricing decisions should really be made
- How to charge premium prices for your services
- Value pricing consulting
- Why your firm should establish a pricing cartel
- Case studies of actual practitioners who have implemented value pricing

11/04

For questions concerning this shipment, billing, or other customer service matters, call 1-800-248-3248.

Sixth Edition

Professional's Guide To VALUE PRICING

Ronald J. Baker

CCH INCORPORATED
Chicago
A WoltersKluwer Company

ISBN: 0-7355-4806-4

4025 W. Peterson Ave.
Chicago, IL 60646-6085
1 800 248 3248
http://tax.cchgroup.com

Portions of this work were published in prevous editions.

Value Curve, from William C. Cobb, "The Value Curve and the Folly of the Billing-Rate Pricing," in *Beyond the Billable Hour: An Anthology of Alternative Billing Methods*, Richard C. Reed, ed., Chicago: American Bar Association, 1989, p. 18, reprinted by permission of the author and the American Bar Association.

"Surgical Procedures Bought Online," by Anne Naujeck, is reprinted with the permission of The Associated Press.

Printed in the United States of America

CONTENTS

To my father, Sam Baker,
who genetically encoded me to
challenge the conventional wisdom

ଓଓ ଓଓ ଓଓ

I bargained with Life for a penny,
And Life would pay no more,
However I begged at evening
When I counted my scanty store.
For Life is a just employer,
He gives you what you ask,
But once you have set the wages,
Why, you must bear the task.
I worked for a menial's hire,
Only to learn, dismayed,
That any wage I had asked of Life,
Life would have willingly paid.

—Jessie B. Rittenhouse, "My Wage,"
The Door of Dreams (1918)

That is a good book which is opened with expectation,
and closed with profit.

—Amos Bronson Alcott
American teacher and philosopher, 1877

FOREWORD

Let me be very blunt with you.

You are now holding the most significant book ever written on the accounting and legal professions. No other book I am aware of has the potential to impact your practice like this one. I know that is a bold claim. To help you see why I make such a claim, picture the following scene:

I'm presenting a seminar in Australia. I'm talking in part about Fixed Price Agreements and the way in which implementing them leads unquestionably to running a far better practice. I mention this book. I describe it as "the best book that's been written on the accounting profession in the last 18 months." Then one of the participants raises his hand and his voice. "I take serious issue with that comment," he says.

"Oh," I say, "and you've read the book?" I ask.

"Yes I have." The participant pauses almost as if to wait until the entire audience is looking his way.

"Baker's book is not the best book written on the profession in the last 18 months. It's the best book that's *ever* been written on the profession."

My seminar participant is right. I cannot recall a book that gives so much—so much research, so much sound theory, and, at the same time, so much downright valuable, right-on-the-point practical material—material you can use the moment you read about it. Yes, you're right, I like this book!

When I first spoke with Ron Baker about his book, I asked him what his mission was in life. "To get rid of the Almighty Hour," he said. He went on to talk about how the "professional" (whether lawyer or accountant) absolutely and categorically knows that pricing based on time does not equate to value: In mathematical terms, we know that Time multiplied by Rate does not equal Value.

Yet we behave as if we did not understand that truth. We see the timesheet, we multiply the hours by the rate and we know that the number we get does not value the job appropriately. So we add on some more time units to "make up the value." As my friend and former colleague Ric Payne observes, "We add a few units on for each walk past the photocopier." It's dishonest, isn't it? Yet it happens. Frequently.

Using the ideas in this book will change that for you. Let me give you one more important perspective—that of the customer.

In the past ten years in particular, I have been face-to-face with literally thousands of first-class customers of accounting firms. When you ask them about pricing they universally (and I do mean that literally) decry the Rate × Time method of pricing things. They loathe it. In the book, Ron tells you about major companies that won't have a bar of it either.

So when you move to the Value Pricing methodologies in this book, you're doing your customers a huge favor too—you're responding to what they want.

I began by talking about a seminar. Let me mention another one. I well remember a man came up to me before a program in Detroit thinking (I don't know why) that I was Ron Baker. "Love your book," he said. And before I could explain who I was he said, "Just last week I used the book to move a $2,000 customer to a $27,000 customer. I could never have done it without using the ideas."

The real key to that is in the last three words . . . "using the ideas." I urge you to do that.

Be like an accountant in New Zealand who used this book to lift his price from $5,000 to $150,000 only to be surprised by the customer telling him "you haven't charged me enough." And yet the accountant would have (before this book) charged one-thirtieth of the value the customer received. Value, as you'll learn in this book, is like beauty—it is only ever in the eye of the beholder (or customer).

I've heard enough success stories to know that what Ron Baker has to say in this book is right on target *and,* most importantly, real-world. And I've come to know Ron better and better—through presenting seminars with him and dialoguing with him frequently via e-mail. I've come to know that Ron not only likes wine, he is in some ways like the finest wine—he gets better with age. You'll see that in this latest edition of his work.

Yet unlike fine wine, Baker does not remain bottled up, as it were. He's courageous enough to spend most days each week out on the speaking circuit hammering and refining his ideas—listening and learning. Again, he doesn't bottle it up. He's audacious enough to take a classic document like the *Declaration of Independence* and paraphrase it (see www.verasage.com as well as the Conclusion to this book) to firmly make the point about finally proclaiming our rightful independence from time accounting and everything that manifests itself with it.

I am, like many, many others, convinced that Ron is the best thing to happen to professional practices for years. I know the hard work Ron has put into this new edition of the book. I know it didn't come easy. But one truth remains in all of this—as great as Ron Baker has made this book, it needs you to actually implement the ideas.

Take a tip from Nike—just do it. I know thousands of people who've gone before you who've done that. Not a single solitary one of them regrets taking these ideas and making them work. I know that you won't either. Have the courage that comes with commitment for the better way that Ron Baker advocates so wonderfully. I promise you you'll never look back.

Paul Dunn

Founder, Results Accountants' Systems

Co-Founder, Renew Group (www.renewgroup.com)

Co-Author, *The Firm of the Future: A Guide for Accountants, Lawyers, and Other Professional Services*

PREFACE

People of the same trade seldom meet together, even for merriments and diversion, but the conversation ends in a conspiracy against the public, or in some contrivance to raise prices.

—Adam Smith, *The Wealth of Nations*

I conduct seminars around the world on the shift from hourly billing to value pricing, and if an observer from outside the profession were to attend, Adam Smith's charge would certainly ring true. In a sense, this book is about how to raise your prices. But it is not a conspiracy against the public. In fact, the main message of this book is that the customer is the ultimate judge of the value that we, as professionals, provide. We should charge the customer only for the value received from our services. If we don't provide something of value to the customer, we have no business being in business.

This book has been a personal odyssey for me. In June 1989 I attended a four-day seminar titled "Increasing CPA Firm Profitability." In the tranquil setting of Lake Tahoe, Nevada, I learned three major lessons on how to increase my firm's profitability:

1. Raise my hourly billing rate by at least $10.
2. Grade my customers "A," "B," and "C," and fire all the "Cs."
3. Offer my customers fixed fees on all services.

Inspired, I immediately shared all of these ideas, and more, with my new partner. We talked about becoming a "winning firm," the term the instructor used throughout the seminar, which meant, by today's standards, a world-class firm. The course provided me with the tools I needed to put some of these ideas into place immediately. In other words, it taught me *how* to do it.

What it didn't teach me is *why* I should do it. It was all case studies and examples, but had absolutely no theory. So when I returned to my firm I had a hammer—the tool I needed to implement some of these concepts—and I started hitting things. I raised my rates but didn't convince the customer that my value rose commensurately with that increase. I began grading my customers, and ridding my firm of the "Cs," but it wasn't until I began researching the ideas behind total quality service that I learned that *my customers weren't going to get better until I did.* Without the solid theoretical foundation of *why* I was doing these things, I failed miserably.

This is the single biggest weakness of most management ideas, CPE seminars, and business books: They're all practice with no theory. Pick up a business book today and one of the first things the author will say is how this book is not some "ivory tower" theory, but practical, real-world ideas that you can use Monday morning at the office.

All learning starts with theory. Therefore, the book you are about to read is more theoretical than you may be used to if you're an avid reader of business books or attend many practice management seminars. I make no apologies, for that is the best way to learn. I am skeptical of consultants and self-professed management gurus who have claimed to discover the next paradigm shift or even what the future will bring. While this book draws from many sources—some of them even the better known gurus—I have always tried to have the theory drive the ideas, and not the other way around. While I do claim that the hourly billing method will continue to die out in the next decade or so, the observation is rooted in empirical evidence.

In their piercing book *The Witch Doctors: What Management Gurus Are Saying and Why It Matters*, John Micklethwait and Adrian Wooldridge, two staff editors for *The Economist*, level this charge against the immature discipline of management theory:

> Management theory, according to the case against it, has four defects: it is constitutionally incapable of self-criticism; its terminology usually confuses rather than educates; it rarely rises above basic common sense; and it is faddish and bedeviled by contradictions that would not be allowed in more rigorous disciplines. The implication of all four charges is that management gurus are con artists, the witch doctors of our age, playing on business people's anxieties in order to sell snake oil. The gurus, many of whom have sprung suspiciously from the "great university of life" rather than any orthodox academic discipline, exist largely because people let them get away with it. Modern management theory is no more reliable than tribal medicine. Witch doctors, after all, often got it right—by luck, by instinct, or by trial and error. (Micklethwait and Wooldridge, 1996: 12)

I have tried to avoid these four defects, because I see them in almost every business book I have read that professes to offer you the surest way to stay ahead of the competition or achieve superior financial results, or whatever the latest fad is.

My goal is not to have you think *like* me, but to have you think *with* me. I want you to be skeptical about the concepts in this book, to subject them to your own rigorous analysis and experience. Do not accept anything at face value. Be wary of anyone who considers himself or herself an expert, for, as Harry Truman said, "An expert is someone who doesn't want to learn anything new, because then he wouldn't be an expert."

I have been working on this topic for over a decade, and I still consider myself a student of price theory. Price is an issue that all businesses grapple with every day, and it is one of the most complex components of marketing.

Price is a major marketing decision for any business. That is why it is one the four "Ps" of marketing—product, place, promotion, and price. While professionals have become more sophisticated with respect to the other three "Ps," price has been largely ignored. As professionals and experts in law, auditing, taxes, and internal control systems, we know our product like no one else. We have even become more sophisticated with respect to promotion. Twenty years ago it was rare to find a professional firm that spent even 1 percent of its gross revenue on marketing and promotion; today it is not uncommon to find firms spending between 2 and 8 percent. Many firms have their own in-house marketing consultants. This is a dramatic change from the attitude that "professionals don't advertise." We are doing better on place too, by niching ourselves and specializing in various markets.

But we have ignored price. Most of the literature within the legal and accounting professions—with the exception of the ABA books I have cited throughout—has little to say with respect to price, and unfortunately what is said is often wrong. Some literature treats pricing as nothing more than an administrative task, with little discussion of how a pricing strategy communicates a marketing message. We have let price be determined by the number of hours that we spend working on various projects. It is my fervent hope that, upon completing this book, you will begin to *price on purpose*, rather than using an antiquated paradigm no longer relevant to a knowledge-based economy.

The stakes are high. Failure to take pricing seriously—and to maintain its exalted position in the four "Ps" of marketing—results in lower profit margins. Too many professionals have surrendered their pricing to their competitors or their worst customers, neither of whom have a vested interest in the financial success of the firm. Professionals must begin to make a serious commitment to pricing strategies in order to capture the value of their services, not to lower their value. Out of the four "Ps" of marketing, three deal with costs and only one with revenue, and it is far more complex and requires more intellectual rigor than we have heretofore understood.

Chapters 1 through 5 of the book cover a history of the accounting profession and move into why people buy what they buy, and how much they will pay.

Chapters 6 and 7 analyze—which in Greek means "cut to pieces"—the 50-year-old practice of hourly billing. If you apply the rigorous economic theory of price and value to this practice, you will understand the risk-reward trade-off you have made by using hourly billing: In exchange for a minimum floor, you have placed an artificial ceiling over your head.

Chapter 8 looks at price psychology and at why professionals suffer from write-downs.

In Chapters 9 through 13 you will find alternatives to the hourly billing method that are superior in obtaining the value for the services provided. Far too many professionals are so attached to the hourly rate that they end up working 16-hour days, charging for eight hours, and getting paid for four. There is a better way.

Chapter 14 reinforces the importance of customer service and loyalty. Chapter 15 is about making the transition from a compliance CPA to a consultant.

Chapter 16 discusses the morality of hourly billing vs. value pricing, along with some of the ethical quandaries that attorneys are struggling with as they shift away from hourly billing.

Chapter 17 explores the critical link between a professional's level of self-esteem and the ability to value price.

Chapters 18 and 19 delve deeper into theory and law and cover antitrust policy and advanced price theory.

Chapter 20 discusses making the transition to a timeless culture.

Chapter 21 contains an editorial on the diffusion of both the ideas of value pricing and eliminating timesheets in the professions. Responses to the editorial from various consultants and my responses to them are included in the chapter.

Chapter 22 includes case studies written by firm leaders who have made the transition to value pricing, and some who have trashed their timesheets.

Chapter 23 concludes with thoughts regarding the death of the Almighty Hour and whether value pricing is a fad that will disappear or a portentous "paradigm shift" that will permanently alter the way in which professionals price their services.

All businesspeople live the ultimate contradiction: We spend our nights praying for the ability to charge monopoly prices, and we spend our days engaged in the very activity that drives those prices downward—that is, increasing the market supply of our services. We will examine why we price the way we do. For too long, our prices have been set by our competitors—those who gauge the value of what they do only by the time they spend.

The theories and concepts in this book are passed on to you in the hope that your transition from hourly billing to value pricing will be easier—and less prone to failure—than mine was. CPAs and attorneys add tremendous value to the lives of their customers, and an inordinate amount of empirical evidence backs this up. It is time we start to receive what our customers already believe we are worth.

How To Use This Book

I have tried to follow the wisdom of an inspiring little book by John Milton Gregory, *The Seven Laws of Teaching*, first published in 1884. Gregory's book offers the seven pillars necessary in order to educate effectively, and they will act as my covenant with the reader (I am indebted to Larry Lucas, of Moscow, Idaho, for recommending Gregory's book):

1. A *teacher* must be one who *knows* the lesson or truth or art to be taught.

2. A *learner* is one who *attends* with interest to the lesson.

3. The *language* used as a *medium* between teacher and learner must be *common* to both.

4. The *lesson* to be mastered must be explicable in the terms of truth already known by the learner—the *unknown* must be explained by means of the *known.*
5. *Teaching* is *arousing* and *using* the *pupil's mind* to grasp the desired thought or to master the desired art.
6. *Learning* is *thinking* into one's own *understanding* a new idea or truth or working into *habit* a new art or skill.
7. The *test* and *proof* of teaching done, the finishing and fastening process, must be a *reviewing, rethinking, reknowing, reproducing*, and *applying* of the material that has been taught, the knowledge and ideas and arts that have been communicated. (Gregory, 1995: 18–19)

That being said, it is my wish not only that you learn from this book but that the ideas, concepts, and practices become part of your firm's culture. It is only by applying these ideas that you will begin to really make them part of your tacit knowledge base. Gregory tells the story of a boy, "having expressed surprise at the shape of the earth when he was shown a globe." The boy was asked, "Did you not learn that in school?" To which the boy replied, "Yes, I learned it, but I never knew it." (Gregory, 1995: 88)

ABOUT THE AUTHOR

Ronald J. Baker started his accounting career in 1984 with KPMG Peat Marwick's Private Business Advisory Services in San Francisco. Today, he is the founder of VeraSage Institute, a think tank dedicated to teaching Value Pricing to professionals around the world.

As a frequent speaker at CPA events and conferences, and an educator to CPA firms on implementing Total Quality Service and Value Pricing, Mr. Baker's work takes him around the world. He has been an instructor with the California CPA Education Foundation since 1995 and has authored nine courses for them: *How to Build a Successful Practice with Total Quality Service*; *The Shift From Hourly Billing to Value Pricing*; *Value Pricing Graduate Seminar*; *You Are What You Charge For: Success in Today's Emerging Experience Economy* (with Daniel Morris); *Alternatives to the Federal Income Tax*; *Trashing the Timesheet: A Declaration of Independence*; *Everyday Economics*; *The Firm of the Future*; and *Everyday Ethics: Doing Well by Doing Good.*

He is the author of the best-selling marketing book ever written specifically for the CPA profession, *Professional's Guide to Value Pricing, Sixth Edition*, published by CCH INCORPORATED. The book has been ranked number 1 on amazon.com in Australia and New Zealand. Mr. Baker is also the author of *Burying the Billable Hour*, *Trashing the Timesheet*, and *You Are Your Customer List*, published by The Association of Chartered Certified Accountants in the United Kingdom. His most recent book, *The Firm of the Future: A Guide for Accountants, Lawyers, and Other Professional Services*, co-authored with Paul Dunn, was published in April 2003 by John Wiley & Sons, Inc.

Ron has shared his Value Pricing vision to over 70,000 professionals around the world. He has been appointed to the AICPA's Group of One Hundred, a think tank of leaders to address the future of the profession, named on Accounting Today's 2001, 2002, 2003, and 2004. Top 100 Most Influential People in the profession, and he received the 2003 Award for Instructor Excellence from the California CPA Education Foundation.

He graduated in 1984 from San Francisco State University with a Bachelor of Science in accounting and a minor in economics. He is a graduate of Disney University, Cato University, and the University of Chicago Graduate School of Business course: *Pricing: Strategy and Tactics*. He is a member of the Professional Pricing Society and presently resides in Petaluma, California.

For more information on the California CPA Education Foundation Courses offered by VeraSage Institute, contact the California CPA Education Foundation at (800) 922-5272 or visit its Web site at www.educationfoundation.org.

For more information on the dates and locations of the events, conferences and CPE seminars presented by VeraSage Institute, please visit our Web site at www.verasage.com.

To contact Ron Baker:

VeraSage Institute
Phone: (707) 769-0965
Fax: (707) 781-3069
E-mail: BandBRJB@aol.com
E-mail: Ron@verasage.com
Web site: www.verasage.com

ACKNOWLEDGMENTS

No book is written in a vacuum. I have relied upon the wisdom and ideas of many seminal thinkers, and if I have been able to gain a better insight into pricing beyond some, it is because I have stood on the shoulders of these giants. After all, it has been said that new ideas are old ideas in new places.

I had the great pleasure of meeting David Friedman in 1996 at a lecture he gave on his book *Hidden Order: The Economics of Everyday Life*. His ideas permeate this book and I thank him, again, for offering a vision of the world that is impossible to find anywhere else. He, like his mother and father (Rose and Milton Friedman), is truly thought-provoking.

I was fortunate to meet Steven Landsburg at Cato University—in beautiful Montréal in October 2000—another innovative and thought-provoking economist, who has taught me more about price theory and economics in everyday life than nearly anyone else. Landsburg's textbooks are an invaluable resource, as are his books for the general reader, *The Armchair Economist* and *Fair Play*. His "Everyday Economics" articles in *Slate* (www.slate.com) are necessary reading for anyone who believes that the "dismal science" applies only to money and business.

Thomas Nagle and Reed Holden, authors of arguably the best pricing book ever written specifically for businesspeople (*The Strategy and Tactics of Pricing: A Guide to Profitable Decision Making*, now in its third edition), advanced my knowledge tremendously of how the theoretical aspects of pricing are applied in the real world. Their course at the University of Chicago Graduate School of Business, "Pricing: Strategy and Tactics," is among the best pricing education you can receive anywhere. Nagle and Holden are both pioneers in the field of pricing, and have made this position respectable and prominent on the organizational charts in corporations around the world, rather than letting it be relegated to being the last of the four Ps of marketing.

Michael Novak, of the American Enterprise Institute, and Richard John Neuhaus, editor of *First Things: A Monthly Journal of Religion and Public Life*, introduced me to the encyclicals of the various popes, which aided me tremendously in formulating my views with respect to the morality of value pricing, as shared in Chapter 16. The idea of business as a moral calling—that is, serving others first before you receive anything in return—is finally gaining the attention and acceptance it deserves from theologians, economists, politicians, and the general public, thanks in large measure to these two individuals.

Other prominent authors have also influenced my thinking on economics and human behavior, and I feel I owe them all a debt of gratitude: Thomas Sowell, Walter Williams, Charles Adams, Martin Anderson, Mark Skousen, Jude Wanniski, Bruce Bartlett, Robert Bartley, Warren Brookes, Paul Craig Roberts, Arthur Laffer, Nicholas Eberstadt, Charles Murray, James Payne, and Virginia Postrel, among others too many to name.

A very special mention is owed to George Gilder. I believe he is truly the Adam Smith of the twentieth (and twenty-first) century. So much of his thinking and ideas have become part of my being that I am forever in his debt. I have just begun to catch up with his treatises, *Wealth and Poverty* and *Recapturing the Spirit of Enterprise*, two profound works written in the 1980s that permanently altered my vision of the way the world works. Gilder, more than any other author, has clarified the role of profits in a free market economy, and made the moral case for capitalism.

I would also like to thank Allan Boress for being the first to give me a forum to express my views on total quality service and value pricing.

Thank you August Aquila, editor of *Partner Advantage Advisory*, who has written his own pioneering book on this topic, *Breaking the Paradigm: New Approaches to Pricing Accounting Services*, published by the AICPA. I admire August greatly and believe his work will have a salutary effect on our profession.

Timothy J. Beauchemin, who passed away in February 1997, also contributed immensely to my thinking about our profession. Although I never had the good fortune to meet him, he was one of a few truly gifted consultants, able to focus on the right things, rather than just doing things right. Tim convinced me of the value of self-esteem, which became the genesis for Chapter 17, which may be the most important portion of the book.

Troy Waugh, another excellent consultant to CPAs, helped shape my thinking about the profession. He is keeping the spirit of Timothy Beauchemin alive by building on his seminal work.

Christian Frederiksen, who reviewed the first edition of this book in manuscript form and was initially skeptical about the ideas it contained, has become a proponent of value pricing.

To Bob Gaida, the dean of the BDO Seidman Advanced Sales College, for giving me many opportunities to present my ideas to his pupils. He provided the inspiration for my second book, *The Firm of the Future*, with his question, "Does the client have the ability to pay a premium price and do they have a thirst for knowledge?" If I ever get a Top 10 firm to trash its timesheets, I have a feeling it will be because of Bob's vision and leadership.

Thank you Eric Mitchell, President of Professional Pricing Society, for creating a forum where businesspeople involved in pricing can share their intellectual capital, and for providing me with the opportunity to present at your wonderful conferences.

Thank you to all of my colleagues from seminars and readers of prior editions of this work, those with whom I have privately consulted and those who have implemented these ideas and who have shared their triumphs as well as their admonishments when they failed. Those failures, too, have made me sharpen my thinking and have contributed substantially to my knowledge of price theory and how it works at the practice level. There is no greater joy than to watch my "students" surpass their instructor.

I would also like to thank Daryl Golemb, Michael McCulloch, Arthur Jacob, Shirley Nakawatase, Ron Crone, Ed Miller, and Larry Lucas, CPAs who constantly keep me engaged professionally and whose friendship I am grateful for.

To my British Trusted Advisor and Web Master for my new web site, Paul O'Byrne, whose Monty Pythonian sense of humor is refreshing, and whose ceaseless wit is cutting. I truly cherish our friendship.

Thank you, William Cobb, for giving me permission to use the beloved value curve, which is simply the best graphical depiction of the professions I have ever seen.

Ric Payne, founder and chairman of Principa, is a mentor to me. Despite our disagreement on the issue of timesheets, I admire his accomplishments and contribution to the profession, not to mention his continuous intellectual challenge to me to prove that my ideas work not only in theory but also in practice. Thomas Malthus once wrote to David Ricardo, "I should not like you more than I do if you agreed in opinion with me." I couldn't have said it better. Thanks, Thugger.

The accounting profession owes an enormous debt of gratitude to Paul Dunn, founder of Results Accountants' Systems, for his trailblazing work. He has been an indefatigable supporter of this work and I want to express my thanks to him for all of the intellectual capital—and tacit knowledge—he has contributed to me over the years. Having the opportunity to work closely with Paul has been nirvana—especially since I learned that in Zen, *nirvana* literally means a complete sense of timelessness. I know the best is yet to come.

I am indebted to the California CPA Education Foundation's entire team for continuing to take risks by letting me develop and teach my courses, which continue to aid me in clarifying my thinking and the presentation of this material. I marvel at the efficiency, and effectiveness, of that group and would like to thank John Dunleavy, Kurtis Docken, Kay Phelan, Laura Ritter, and Nancy Heubach for all of their support and encouragement.

My friend and partner (and co-founder of VeraSage Institute) for over fifteen years, Justin Barnett, successfully implemented many of these concepts, even though it took me a few years to convince him of their validity. Thanks, Justin, for holding down the fort and putting up with my schedule that took me out of the office so much. I can't express it any better than Justice Cardozo, who once wrote, "There is no greater loyalty than a partner's to his fellow partner."

To Dan Morris, my colleague, fellow Cognitor, and co-founder of VeraSage Institute. Collaborating with you has truly been a pleasure, with each location providing not only intellectual growth, but also a deeper friendship. It is truly a blessing to find someone with the same dream, and passion, to better the profession.

Thank you Anita Rosepka, Tony Powell, and Jennifer Crane, my editors at CCH INCORPORATED, for taking the ultimate risk and publishing this work. While the substance of what we think is born in thought, it must live in ink. One of my favorite authors, Mark Skousen, gives this advice to any writer, "The editors are always right. Don't argue with them." Sage advice I have taken to heart, and which all of you have proved correct by improving every page of this book.

My brother, Ken Baker, put up with this material over many late night dinners. His marketing insights, and forensic coaching, helped me tremendously to clarify my thinking and improve upon the presentation of these concepts to my colleagues. One could not ask for a better coach, or brother.

My mother, Florence Baker, instilled in me the tenacity and perseverance to forge ahead in the face of the odds. Her mother, Angelina Zimmerman, provided me with a home to hibernate in while I put the finishing thoughts into the first edition of this work. Not a day passes that I don't think of her.

I would not be where I am today without the inspiration of my father, Sam Baker. He has spent many absorbing hours with me recounting the days of the British Invasion in the late 1960s and the impact it had on his chosen profession, barbering. His embrace of hairstyling, chemical services, retail, continuing education, and the "unisex salon," long before they became commonplace in his profession, truly inspired me to push forward with the ideas in this book. He accomplished back then what for me would be the equivalent of tripling my prices in a few years, while challenging the conventional wisdom of colleagues. His is a story I treasure, both for the lessons it teaches and the pride it gives me. Goethe wrote, "*Was du ererbt von deinen Vätern hast, / Erwirb es, um es zu besitzen*," which translated reads, "What you have inherited from your father, you must earn in order to possess." I hope I have earned his legacy.

Ronald J. Baker

Petaluma, California
August 1, 2004

INTRODUCTION

Whoever desires constant success must change his conduct with the times.

—Niccolò Machiavelli, Florentine statesman and philosopher

My father is a barber. One night over dinner, he told me a fascinating story about his profession in the late 1960s. I repeat it here because what is happening today in the law and accounting professions is similar, and dramatic change usually takes us by surprise.

In the late 1960s, something was going on in this country that had a profound impact on barbers: The British Invasion. To this day, if you talk to old-time barbers, they still curse the Beatles. Men growing their hair long meant fewer trips to the local barber. The profession that had always done well, both in good economic times and bad, was taking it on the chin, and the barbers didn't know what to do about it.

In the fall of 1969, my father ran for president of the Santa Rosa, California, local barber union. At the election meeting my father and his opponent gave their "campaign" speeches. His opponent went first and ran on the following three platform items:

1. Haircut prices would be increased from $2.50 to at least $2.75, if not $3 (as the San Francisco barber union had just increased their prices to $3);
2. Hours of operation would be standardized for all members—9:00 a.m. to 6:00 p.m., Tuesday through Saturday; and
3. The local union would codify the above into a new union contract.

These three items were very serious to the barbers, and my father's opponent generated a lot of excitement by promising to work hard to achieve them.

Then it was my father's turn. He got to the platform and asked the assembled barbers what was happening to their incomes? They all grumbled, for incomes were dropping precipitously throughout the industry. Even during the Great Depression, barbers didn't experience the decline they were now suffering. My father began to exhort the crowd on what they had to do to meet the challenge that was being thrust upon them. And it had nothing to do with the three items that his opponent was clamoring for. He started talking to them about how barbers had to get into hairstyling, retail sales, chemical services, and even hiring cosmetologists and bringing them into the barber shop to form unisex salons. Understand that this was all very radical in those days—there was no such thing as a unisex salon, and the barbers protested against this change the loudest. Now my father is the first to admit that he was no sage; he didn't have a crystal ball that allowed him to peer further into the future than his colleagues. He gives the credit to his continual learning with Roffler and Redken Laboratories, two leaders in the industry that were helping the participants cope with the systemic changes taking place.

My father won the election, which teaches us that while people may not like change, they will elect leaders they trust to lead them through it. A leader takes people where they would not go themselves. Under my dad's presidency, the barbers increased their prices to $2.75, they standardized the hours of operation, and they codified all of it in their new union contract. But my father was conducting a radical experiment in his shop. He partitioned off a chair in the back and started booking hairstyles in the evenings, by appointment only, for $7.50. He knew that he could sell the men on this new style of haircut and teach them how to blow dry and care for it, because it would reduce the frequency with which they had to visit him (from every two to three weeks to every four to six), and as a result he could command more than two-and-a-half times the price of a clipper cut.

After a few months, my father was astonished to learn that approximately 80 percent of his revenue came from these new hairstyles, and that he was making more in four hours than his fellow barbers were making in eight. He decided he needed to pursue this full-time, so he closed up his traditional barbershop, moved across town, and opened the Hairistocrat. This was one of the first unisex salons in the area. My father started doing permanent waves and hair coloring and he became more actively involved with retail sales. In 1972, while most of the barbers in the union were still working at $3, my father had increased his haircut prices to $10, and by 1975 he was charging $15. It doesn't sound like momentous change now, but back then this was a radical approach for a very staid profession. In fact, visit any town, and you will still find a few traditional barbershops—the last few holdouts that resisted change and are still charging less than $10 for a haircut.

As I listened to my dad tell this story, I was astonished at how similar it was to the accounting profession. After all, I had been giving a total quality service seminar for the California CPA Education Foundation and had encountered my share of CPAs who were resistant to change. A revolution is going on in the business world today, and it is one of customer service. If you look at the history of management movements, in the big picture, here are the stages of thought it has gone through:

1960s = Marketing

1970s = Manufacturing

1980s = Total Quality Management

1990s = Total Quality Service (Final Frontier)

In the 1960s, marketing was the model that businesses embraced. It was the Proctor & Gamble model: Manufacture a product and sell it to as many people as you can; capture market share through marketing. The 1960s was a seller's paradise, so this model worked well. In the 1970s, companies coming off of their successes in the 1960s became arrogant. They began to diversify and added manufacturing capacity, on the assumption they could sell everything they produced. This was the age of the big conglomerates. It did not matter what business you bought; business was business, so ITT could do communications *and* sell Wonder Bread.

This horizontal and vertical integration began to fall apart in the 1980s. Businesses discovered that it *did* matter what business you were in (core competencies, to use today's parlance), and with the adoption of the total quality management movement, they began to divest themselves of divisions that they really did not know how to run effectively. By then, the Japanese, and other global competitors, had taken a large chunk of the automobile and electronics markets, and U.S. businesses finally heeded the message from management thinkers such as W. Edwards Demming and Joseph Juran and began to focus on quality.

Today, quality is not enough. It has become a table stake, the minimum you need to be in the game. For professionals, quality is no longer an effective competitive differentiation. In the eyes of the customer, our quality is all the same. Who would stay with an incompetent CPA? Thus, the only way we can differentiate ourselves in today's marketplace is through total quality service, or what I call the final frontier. All CPAs have lost customers, even though they did outstanding technical work, because customers do not evaluate CPAs on the basis of technical work. They would not know a good audit or tax return from a bad one. But what they do know is how CPAs treat them—our bedside manner, so to speak.

Total quality service is not the main topic of this book, but it is an essential prerequisite to value pricing. The only way to get full value for the services your firm offers is to provide your customers with total quality service, and that means entering into monogamous partnerships with them. It means moving beyond *doing* business with them to *being in* business with them. This is a difficult concept for us as CPAs, because we are trained to be objective and independent and to look at our customers with a jaundiced eye. If all a CPA firm does is audits, this attitude may work, but not if you are interested in performing value-added services. The Roman statesman and philosopher Seneca once said "The mind is slow in unlearning what it has been long in learning."

We have a lot of unlearning to do as a profession. We can no longer look back to the halcyon days of our predecessors and assume that what they did will work for us. Consider the predicament of Mikhail Gorbachev when he took over the Soviet Union. Here was a man whose entire world paradigm—Communism—was swept onto the ash heap of history. He immediately blamed his predecessors for all his problems. In fact, the running joke in the Soviet Union at the time went something like this:

> A new manager of a collective farm finds two letters from his predecessor, with instructions to open the first when difficulties begin. When the farm fails to meet its quotas, the manager opens the first letter, which says, "Blame me."

> He does. It buys some time. But the farm fails again and he comes under fresh criticism, so he opens the second letter. It says: "Prepare two letters." (Will, 1992: 67)

It is time to stop emulating our predecessors blindly and instead embrace the opportunities that the dramatic changes taking place in our profession present. Let us now turn to what some of those changes are.

Sixth Edition

Professional's Guide To

VALUE PRICING

1 A BRIEF HISTORY OF THE ACCOUNTING PROFESSION

Nothing stops an organization faster than people who believe that the way they worked yesterday is the best way to work tomorrow. To succeed, not only do your people have to change the way they act, they've got to change the way they think about the past.

—John Madonna, Chairman, KPMG International

Italian Fra Luca Pacioli published his *Summa de Arithmetica Geometria, Proportioni et Proportionalita* in 1494, representing the collected knowledge of mathematics at that time. In the portion of the work titled *Particularis de Computis et Scripturis*, he introduced double-entry bookkeeping, a creation for future accountants that was as big as the invention of zero for mathematicians. Unfortunately, one could also make the argument that it was significant for being the last revolutionary idea to come from the accounting profession. In *Intellectual Capital*, David Wilson, CPA and partner at Ernst & Young, wrote: "It has been 500 years since Pacioli published his seminal work on accounting and we have seen virtually no innovation in the practice of accounting—just more rules—none of which has changed the framework of measurement" (Stewart, 1997: 58).

The balance sheet dates from 1868, the income statement from before World War II. Generally accepted accounting principles (GAAP) fit an *industrial* enterprise, not an *intellectual* one. Currently, GAAP measure the cost of everything, and know the value of nothing. As Robert K. Elliott pointed out in an essay titled "The Third Wave Breaks on the Shores of Accounting":

> [GAAP] focuses on tangible assets, that is, the assets of the industrial revolution. These include inventory and fixed assets: for example, coal, iron, and steam engines. And these assets are stated at cost. Accordingly, we focus on *costs*, which is the *production* side, rather than the *value created*, which is the *customer* side (Stewart, 1997: 58).

Accounting Today

The profession of public accounting as it is known today came into existence in Great Britain in the 1850s with the introduction of the Companies Acts and the Bankruptcy Acts, legislation designed to protect shareholders and promote capital accumulation during the early stages of the Industrial Revolution. In the decades following the American Civil War, British chartered accountants came to the United States to monitor the capital investments of the Old World in the New World.

The city directories of New York, Chicago, and Philadelphia showed an increase in the number of public accountants, from 81 in 1884 to 322 in 1889. During the 1890s, the predecessors of at least three of the Big Eight were established, and on April 17, 1896, New York became the first state to pass legislation establishing the title of certified public accountant. By 1899, the New York Stock Exchange had initiated steps to require financial statement reports on a regular basis from listed companies.

After the turn of the century, the Progressive Era ushered in another wave of growth for the public accounting profession. This was a natural fit for the public accountant, as the profession gained considerable visibility and recognition through its work in the governmental sector. As the "disinterested expert," the public accountant would command a central role for many of the Progressive reformer's policies: Increased efficiency in government and business, regulation of large businesses and trusts, and the passage of the income tax in order to redistribute and equalize wealth.

The United States' adoption of the income tax, along with the announcement of official accounting standards and guidelines by the Federal Trade Commission and the Federal Reserve Bank, led to an increased demand for accounting services. In the aftermath of the stock market crash of 1929, the most significant legislation was the Securities Act of 1933 and the Securities Exchange Act of 1934, which produced the largest growth in demand for public accounting. Subsequently, the rules promulgated by the predecessor to the American Institute of CPAs were known as ARBs (Accounting Research Bulletins).

During the 1930s and 1940s, CPAs experienced high growth and high incomes. In 1945, Milton Friedman and Simon Kuznets published a fascinating study of five different professions, titled *Income from Independent Professional Practice*. This study, which was the basis of Friedman's Ph.D.

dissertation at Columbia University in 1946, was actually completed in 1941, but its publication was delayed because of the controversy it created. Friedman concluded in this study that the medical profession had monopolistic powers that enabled it to raise physicians' incomes above a competitive level. Since then, Friedman has been one of the most articulate spokesmen against all forms of occupational licensure, a position he has expanded upon in his later works, especially *Capitalism and Freedom* and *Free to Choose*. A majority of economists who have studied the topic find Friedman's position compelling.

The astonishing results of the study are as follows:

Arithmetic mean annual income (dollars)	Average 1929–34
CPAs	$5,311
Physicians	$4,081
Dentists	$3,081

(Friedman and Kuznets, 1945:104)

How could this be? How did CPAs make more money than doctors and dentists? It's an interesting question, and while there may have been some supply-side effects, due to the licensure requirements for CPAs, the answer is found on the demand side. Between 1929 and 1934, the United States was in the throes of the Great Depression, so doctors and dentists were probably among the last to be paid (and were most likely receiving a lot of barter payments as well). This was before the introduction of employer-paid health insurance.

During World War II, businesses wanted to attract talented employees. The government had frozen wages and prices, while at the same time, the labor pool was limited, as most men were off fighting the war. Businesses came up with the idea of offering tax-free health insurance. The IRS ruled that this was, indeed, a tax-free benefit, and ever since, companies have provided health insurance for their employees. After health insurance was introduced, the economics of healthcare spending changed dramatically. Prior to health insurance, individuals paid their own healthcare expenses, and thus doctors and dentists had to satisfy one customer at a time. Now individuals were spending someone else's money—namely, that of the insurance companies—on themselves, which is not a motivation to be economical. One of the main reasons healthcare costs have been increasing faster than the rate of inflation in the United States is that third-party payments account for some 76 percent of all healthcare spending. Almost half of that is from the government and the remaining portion is from insurance companies. Economists are fond of pointing out that if consumers spent only 25 cents on the dollar (of their own money) for food, clothing, and housing, costs would skyrocket in each of those markets. This is the economic rationale for the Medical Savings Account: Have people spend their own money on themselves and competition will drive down prices. Chapter 4 looks more closely at the different ways that one can spend money.

Meanwhile, CPAs were mainly performing attest services during this period and were benefiting from the effects of the new SEC regulations. They weren't doing tax returns at this point, because only about 10 percent of the population filed returns during this time. The country didn't pull most citizens into tax return filing until the Current Tax Payment Act, which was signed into law by President Franklin D. Roosevelt in June 1943.

One more point on CPAs' income being higher than that of doctors and dentists: This was *before* the profession engaged in hourly billing. During this time, CPAs charged fixed prices for their services. They sometimes charged by the day. An article in *Fortune* magazine in 1932 states that the rate for Juniors was $20 a day; Semi-seniors earned $15 to $30 a day; Seniors earned $35 a day; Supervisors brought in $50 to $75 a day; and Partners earned $100 to $1,000 a day.

This is not to say that they made more because they did not use hourly billing, but only that not using hourly billing did not prevent them from being more profitable. The reasons outlined above are closer to the real explanation.

In 1954, all of the existing tax laws were codified into the Internal Revenue Code of 1954. Most Americans had been drawn inside the tax system through the Withholding Act of 1943. Since CPAs were well-versed in tax law, they naturally and enthusiastically entered the tax preparation market, much to the chagrin of the attorneys. Almost immediately, attorneys brought lawsuits against the CPAs for practicing law—meaning tax law—without a license. They lost in courts around the country that basically said they should have sued the CPAs back in 1913, with the passage of the 16th Amendment. It is an interesting analogy to the lawsuits involving American Express Tax and Business

Services (AmEx), which the Florida and Texas State Boards of Accountancy had charged with violating professional standards by holding themselves out as CPAs. Because the free market will ultimately prevail against government regulation, AmEx prevailed in these suits.

In 1955, Henry Bloch borrowed $5,000 from his aunt and launched a one-man bookkeeping company for small businesses. He later took his brother, Richard, into the business at his mother's insistence. By 2001, H&R Block was preparing and filing more than 17 million tax returns, 13 percent of all individual tax returns filed that year. It has 10,400 offices worldwide (80 percent of Americans can find an H&R Block office within 10 miles of their homes), employs 90,000 people during tax season, and earns approximately 200 million dollars on nearly 2 billion dollars gross revenue, half of which is derived from tax preparation. CPAs scoffed at H&R Block when it entered the market, charg-ing it with being incompetent and unprofessional. The marketplace prevailed, and most economists would argue that the biggest beneficiaries are the 19 million consumers worldwide, who received economical tax services.

In 1960, the computer made its debut. This allowed CPAs to perform write-up work more efficiently and to begin consulting on computer hardware and software. The computer also allowed hourly billing to take hold in the profession. With the computer, billing became nothing more than a clerical task—input the hours spent, the computer grinds hours times the rates, and a bill is sent to the customer—all done with low-cost administrative staff and very little partner or manager time. It took all the *art* out of pricing and turned it into an *administrative task.*

Then the Tax Reform Act of 1969 (Public Law 91–172) was passed, allowing companies to claim Investment Tax Credits and, more important from the CPA's point of view, instituting one of the most complex provisions of the tax code that exists to this day: the Alternative Minimum Tax. This section was placed in the Code largely due to the efforts of Joseph Barr, Secretary of the Treasury during the Johnson administration, who testified before Congress in January 1969 that 155 taxpayers with adjusted gross incomes over $200,000 paid zero tax in 1966. Congress heard the outrage from the citizenry and placed what many called at the time "the Accountant's and Lawyer's Retirement Act" into the Code. The tax laws became so complex that even small business owners needed a CPA.

Seven years later, Congress passed the Tax Reform Act of 1976 (Public Law 94–455), which created what soon replaced baseball as America's favorite pastime: tax shelters. Americans from across the political spectrum rushed to reduce their ever-increasing tax bills. These people included Barry Goldwater, George McGovern, Norman Lear, Barbara Streisand, Lorne Greene, Eddie Murphy, Sydney Poitier, and many well-known athletes.

It was also during the 1970s that a large number of baby boomers entered the CPA profession. It was easier to enter than other professions, such as medical or legal professions, and it offered high status and a good living. In 1977 the Supreme Court ruled, in *Bates & O'Steen v State Board of Arizona*, 433 U.S. 350 (1977), that attorneys could market their legal services. This had a profound effect on both the legal and accounting professions.

Prior to this landmark Supreme Court decision, the AICPA Code of Professional Conduct for CPAs explicitly proscribed advertising, stating:

> Solicitation to obtain clients is prohibited under the Rules of Conduct because it tends to lessen the professional independence towards clients which is essential to the best interests of the public. . . Advertising, which is a form of solicitation is prohibited. . . Promotional practices such as solicitation and advertising, tend to indicate a dominant interest in profit.

In 1978, the profession responded to the *Bates* decision by amending this rule to read:

> A member shall not seek to obtain clients by advertising or other forms of solicitation in a manner that is false, misleading, or deceptive.

Despite the accounting profession's reluctance to advertise, due to the traditional belief that advertising accounting services was unprofessional, the consumer welcomed the change as both appropriate and helpful in disseminating information about the capabilities of the profession. In today's highly competitive environment, the idea that

CPAs should not advertise seems preposterous, indicating the pace of change that the profession has had to deal with.

In the 1980s, the single biggest revolution since double-entry bookkeeping, the introduction of the personal computer, took place in the accounting profession. This machine changed the profession like nothing else up to this point. The PC liberated ordinary workers and businesses, putting more computing power in their hands, which lessened the leverage of the "experts." Now many tasks that were once the private domain of professionals were taken over by the customer or outsourced to others vying for a piece of the market once taken for granted by CPAs.

The Tax Reform Act of 1986 (Public Law 99–514) simplified the Code for many taxpayers and eliminated the tax shelter industry, but it also added the passive loss provisions, which complicated the preparation of returns even beyond the capabilities of CPAs. Enter low-cost tax preparation software and accounting systems such as Quicken and QuickBooks, and a myriad of consultants and Certified Financial Planners, and CPAs discovered that work they used to get automatically was now being lost to this increasingly competitive field of players.

Summary and Conclusions

This brings us to today. How will the actions taken today by the profession affect the future? This chapter looked at where CPAs have been; the next chapter looks at where the profession is headed.

2 THE ACCOUNTING PROFESSION IN THE NEW MILLENNIUM

Whom the gods would destroy,
they first grant forty years of business success.

—Peter F. Drucker

Life is a series of collisions with the future.

—José Ortega y Gasset

An astute observer of the retail industry would be the first to notice that within the last decade or so, *inventory* has been replaced by *information*. When you study the success of Wal-Mart, you realize this was the exact formula by which Sam Walton dealt a knockout blow to Sears, once America's preeminent retailer. Sears didn't even see it coming; it wasn't until the late 1980s that internal position papers of Sears even mentioned Wal-Mart as a competitor. The store that once sold the equivalent of one percent of America's Gross National Product and held a 50 percent market share of the household credit card market was suddenly brought to its knees by a man from Arkansas with a better idea. Some believe that Wal-Mart eliminated the Mom and Pop stores. Nonsense. Wal-Mart did not eliminate these stores; the American consumer did. Today, more than 100 million Americans shop at Wal-Mart stores throughout the country every week. And why shouldn't they, if that is where they receive the most value for their dollar?

The same trend is found in bookstores. Visit a Borders or a Barnes & Noble and you'll see over 100,000 titles. Log on to Amazon.com and you can browse (by author, topic, keyword) through 3,000,000 titles. Amazon doesn't have expensive brick-and-mortar stores. It relies on databases and the Internet, whose costs are continuing to fall, and thus Amazon poses the biggest threat to the traditional bookstore. It has changed the playing field on selling books, and if the megastores do not start offering similar conveniences to their customers, they, like Sears, will watch their market shares continue to erode. This is precisely why Borders has joined forces with Amazon.

Because of the plummeting cost of information storage and retrieval, the artificial boundaries between professions will dissolve. In the past, professions held all of the trade secrets and specialized information, and the consumer was forced to seek out these experts and pay relatively high prices for their wisdom. Today this is no longer the case. Information that was once available only to lawyers, doctors, and accountants is now available to anyone with a computer and an Internet connection. A patient suffering from a specific medical affliction can download from various medical databases the most recent studies and latest treatment regimes, and chances are the patient will know more about the condition than the doctor does. The economic value of memorization as a skill is falling, and the importance of locating the right information is increasing. To be a professional, which means to "profess" something, was always considered to be several notches above a businessman. This thinking is obsolete. Now that information is available to anyone, what is professed is not as important as how information is synthesized and used in its most creative applications to add value to customers.

What is happening in the accounting industry is similar to the stage in which the retail industry currently finds itself—that is, a mature industry. This is a stage in the product life cycle, which all products and services eventually pass through. The four stages of the product life cycle are as follows:

1. Introduction
2. Growth
3. Maturity
4. Decline

The accounting profession has entered stage 3, and some would even argue that certain services in accounting, such as audits, are in stage 4. During the period between 1989 and 1995, Gross Domestic Product (GDP) grew 28 percent, yet audit revenue has been flat since 1989 and has declined as a portion of GDP. This trend will continue, albeit perhaps at slower pace, because as a result of the Enron and other accounting scandals of 2002, the financial community will start to recognize the value of an independent audit. Consulting work will continue to increase as a percentage of smaller firm revenues, as it is in the introduction and growth stages of the product life cycle. As August J. Aquila, Ph.D., points out in his book *Breaking the Paradigm: New Approaches to Pricing Accounting Services*, the signs that the accounting profession is in the maturity stage are many:

- Consolidation
- Brand-name recognition
- Price competition
- Increased involvement in marketing
- Competition from outside the profession
- Sophisticated buyers

(Aquila, 1995: 33–34)

A more detailed look at each of these trends will show they are permanently changing the market conditions in the accounting profession.

Consolidation

Since 1987, the Big Eight has gone to the Big Four. Many CPAs say this has occurred because the big players want to reduce the level of competition among themselves. But every business wants to reduce competition. This is confusing cause and effect. Consolidation takes place in a mature industry in order to eliminate redundancies in overhead, and this very rarely happens in the introduction or growth stages of the product life cycle. What is happening can be referred to as *dinosaurs mating*. As Tom Peters once humorously pointed out with respect to a particular bank merger: "Why anybody thinks that they will produce a gazelle by mating two dinosaurs is beyond me." This trend will continue not just with the big firms, but with regional and local firms as well.

In addition to the consolidation taking place in the profession, CPAs also seem destined to replace insurance agents and brokers as their customer's primary financial advisor. Further, a majority of states now allow commissions and contingency pricing as well as non-CPA ownership. These ideas were anathema a decade ago, but now even the AICPA has accepted the realities of the marketplace exerting its sovereignty, and it has become an agent for change, rather than defending the status quo.

Brand-Name Recognition

Obviously, the Big Four already possess brand-name recognition, and many other firms are forming alliances throughout the United States and the rest of the world to achieve the same recognition. Before the Coopers Price merger, H&R Block ranked Number 7 among the top 100 accounting firms. This is the firm that many CPAs said would not last and was unprofessional, reflecting a repeat of Sears's attitude with respect to Wal-Mart. More recently, AmEx has caused a major controversy in the accounting world by buying up practices throughout the country. Because competition is the lifeblood of the free enterprise system, this is a good thing. No industry should be allowed to control who enters. Although various state societies tried to erect barriers against AmEx in the name of "protecting the consumer," economic evidence shows that occupational licensure does not protect the consumer but rather protects the profession from the consumer. AmEx is here to stay, as long as it adds value to the customer. Customers will be won by the firm that offers more value than the competition. CPAs who fail at this deserve to fail at business as well.

Price Competition

At the inception of accounting firms and for many years thereafter, the way to make money was to leverage *people*. With the introduction of computers, accounting firms leverage *technology*. This has caused a flattening of the traditional pyramid structure, and the folks getting squeezed out tend to start their own firms, with low overhead, intensifying price competition. According to the AICPA membership database, in 1998, "of the 47,751 public practice units, 41,252, or 86%, have 10 or fewer professionals and thus are considered to be small firms. Just over 21,166, or about 44%, are sole practitioners."

For the past several years, the "virtual office" has provided an excellent advantage, because business opportunities exist in the customer's offices, not the CPA's. Here is a story about a CPA who wants to start a virtual office but does not know how to go about it, so he sets off to get advice at the feet of the Master.

> The [CPA] slowly climbed toward the summit of the mountain, hand over hand, pulling upwards toward the guru's cave.

> The [CPA] reached the top, fingers raw and clothing tattered. He beheld the master: long white hair, wearing a flowing robe, indeterminate age. The master sat in the lotus position and seemed completely detached from worldly concerns.
>
> The pilgrim knew he could ask only one question. A question for which there were no answers in the books, the journals, or the consultancies. He approached the master and asked: "Master, what is the secret of virtual operations?"
>
> The Master was still for a long time, considering this question. At last he spoke: "You could have sent e-mail." (Grenier and Metes, 1995: 99)

More and more CPAs are taking advantage of the "virtual office," something easy to achieve given a laptop computer, Internet and e-mail access, cellular phone, pager, and FedEx. This doesn't involve much overhead, and CPAs who work in this manner tend to have very low "hourly rates," which is baffling since their low overhead does not translate into low value to the customer. As a result of start-ups and small firms, price competition has intensified and will continue to intensify for all services, not just the so-called commodities (audits, reviews, compilations, and tax returns).

Increased Involvement in Marketing

CPAs have been forced into this arena, kicking and screaming all the way. In the past, especially after watching the experience of the attorneys, CPAs had the attitude that marketing and advertising were unprofessional. Good firms did not need to stoop that low; it was unbecoming of a true professional. This attitude today will bring nothing but early, involuntary retirement. Marketing is an essential ingredient, perhaps the most essential, to running a successful firm. According to August Aquila, "Whereas ten years ago accounting firms spent very little on marketing, today it is not unusual for them to spend from 2 percent to 8 percent of their net fees on marketing" (Aquila, 1995: 34). It is not uncommon for a firm today to have in-house a non-CPA marketing professional, either full- or part-time. All professions have had to become more sophisticated in this area, as it's no longer a seller's market but a buyer's market.

Competition from Outside the Profession

Some work that once automatically went to the professional firm can now be performed by a myriad of outside consultants—financial planners, employee benefit consultants, paralegals, and computer specialists—not to mention inexpensive software products that can produce tax returns, wills and trusts, and legal contracts. It is no longer possible to make money selling paper. More and more the choice for the customer is not just which of various professional firms to employ, but also whether to hire a professional firm, hire a consulting firm, do it themselves, or not do it at all. Firms have seen their "share of customer" decrease. Because of outsourcing and increased competition, the typical firm's share of the entire accounting, tax, and consulting dollar of the average customer has declined. Part of this is due to CPAs having the wrong focus. Many pursue market share, which is selling one service to as many customers as possible, rather than pursuing share of customer, which is selling as many services as possible to one customer from cradle to grave. Since the only real monopoly CPAs have is in the attest service, and this market is in its mature phase (if not decline), it behooves the CPA to focus on each customer's need for value-added consulting services and not take for granted that work will be rewarded by virtue of being a company's auditors. The CPA must earn a customer's business, proving to be better than the alternatives. Competition is not going away; in fact, it will increase dramatically as AmEx, H&R Business Services, Century Business Services, and others enter the market, and competition will come from out-of-state and around the world, due to the Internet, which is rapidly erasing geographical boundaries.

Sophisticated Buyers

Today's customer is more *value*-conscious (though not necessarily *price*-conscious) than ever before. It is not unusual for a customer to come into a firm knowing exactly what he wants with a good idea of the value of the service desired. Over time, customers become more sophisticated, especially when they have instant access to information that in the past would have taken a prodigious amount of time to gather and assimilate.

According to Kevin Davis, in his book *Getting into Your Customer's Head*, today's buyers are:

- More demanding
- More value-conscious
- More knowledgeable about buying
- Less loyal
- Deluged by choices
- More uncertain about the future
- More at risk if a mistake is made
- Much more cautious

(Davis, 1996: 3)

Customers are also becoming less tolerant of poor service. Many organizations provide outstanding service, from FedEx and Marriott to Disney and Lexus, and once customers experience this level of service, they want more, and they become less tolerant of bad service from their local restaurant, dry cleaner, hairstylist, CPA, or lawyer. Their expectations are being raised constantly. The final frontier of business—total quality service—is explored in Chapter 14.

All of the aforementioned signs of a mature industry force firms to seek out services that are in the growth stage or design innovative new services to launch into the introduction stage of the product life cycle. The profession has moved away from merely manipulating financial information and attesting to it and has taken on a full-service financial advisory role, as customers gravitate to CPAs as the most trusted and respected of all business advisors.

The Value Curve

The value curve is a model for analyzing which services add relatively high value and thus command higher prices in the marketplace, compared with other services that add relatively little value and thus are more price-sensitive. The value curve, which to the trained eye is really an indifference curve, was developed by William C. Cobb, who approaches pricing in the classical economics tradition. This curve was published in the seminal work by the American Bar Association Section of Economics of Law Practice, *Beyond the Billable Hour*, edited by Richard C. Reed. This is what Cobb had to say about value, as perceived by the customer:

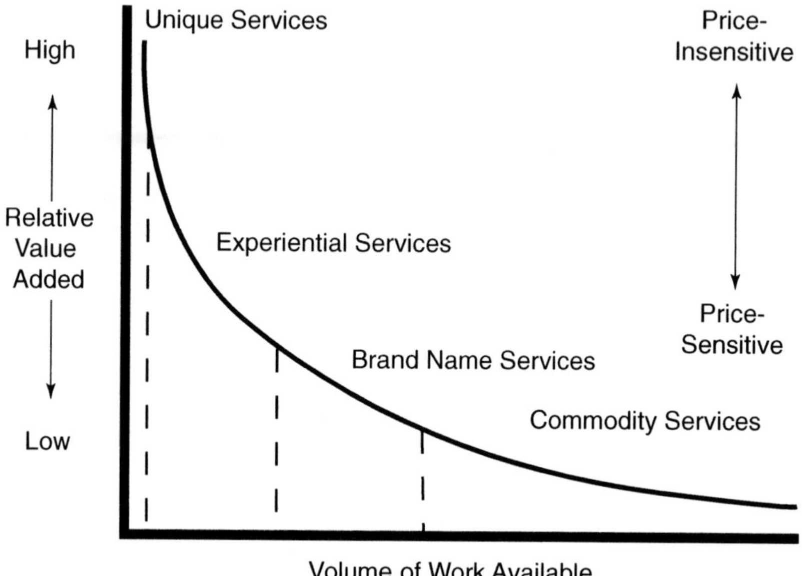

© William C. Cobb
SOURCE: Adapted from William C. Cobb, "The Value Curve and the Folly of the Billing-Rate Pricing," in *Beyond the Billable Hour: An Anthology of Alternative Billing Methods.* Richard C. Reed, ed. Chicago: American Bar Association, 1989, p. 18.

> Sophisticated clients do not tie benefits to hours; they tie benefits to the impact on their business. Some services are lifesaving. Other services are mundane, commodity services that must be performed in the course of getting the client's product produced and sold. In such situations, value has no real relationship to the hours involved. . . . Legal services do not escape the laws of economics (Reed, 1989: 17).

Let's examine each one of the categories on Cobb's curve:

1. **Unique Services** These services are typically distinctive to a particular customer and add high value because either they avert a major catastrophe or they have a significant impact upon the cus-

tomer's future. Examples are succession planning, major tax litigation, a merger or acquisition, and bankruptcy. It is estimated that less than 4 percent of work in any given market is unique.

2. **Experiential Services** This is work of high-risk or high-impact nature, and the customer typically selects the professional perceived as best able to handle the matter effectively. Such services include real estate services, litigation support, and divorce planning (as one CPA humorously advertises). Approximately 16 percent of work in any given market fits this category.
3. **Brand-Name Services** This work, while perhaps routine, is important to the customer and tends to go to firms that have well-established reputations in a particular area. The Big Four, for example, get a share of their work simply based upon their reputation in the marketplace, and they are the major players in SEC and initial public offering work. National, regional, and local firms who may have a reputation for a particular niche, such as healthcare, construction, or automobile dealerships, tend to earn brand-name recognition over time. About 20 percent of work is of this nature.
4. **Commodity Services** This includes write-up, tax return compliance (income, payroll, sales, etc.), compilations, and basically any other work that customers expect their CPA to be able to provide. This is the largest slice of work in any market, approximately 60 percent.

Implications of the Curve

Ample opportunities exist to engage in value pricing no matter where a firm is on the curve. A firm that does nothing other than provide "commodity" services is still able to engage in the value pricing techniques discussed in this book. Any firm that has a downward-sloping demand curve—what economists call market power—can be, to some extent, a price *maker* and not merely a price *taker*. Engaging in value pricing is not predicated on where a firm is on this curve, so if a firm profile fits the low end, this is no cause for despair.

A firm's position on the value curve can change. Many professionals, when they examine the curve for the first time, tend to sell themselves short, seeing the majority of what they do as "commodity," or low-end, types of services. The empirical evidence does not support these self-assessments. Practically all but the most low-end compliance-driven firms perform some experiential services, such as IRS audits or divorce work, and at one time or another, some customers will demand a unique service, tailored to their particular situation. The secret to value pricing is recognizing these opportunities, at the margin, and pricing accordingly.

Despite the conventional wisdom, audits are not "commodities," although practically every CPA firm will say that audits are just a commodity at some time when discussing the curve. The customer–CPA relationship is a personal one, commanding an immense amount of trust and respect. In fact, CPAs are trusted business advisors, as ranked by occupational standing polls on public respect. If Enron has taught the profession one lesson, it is that the audit is certainly not a commodity—how could a commodity wreak so much havoc?

There is no such thing as a commodity in today's marketplace, only commodity thinking. Anything from a chocolate bar to a haircut to a taxi cab ride can be differentiated, as the following story from *The Tom Peters Seminar* illustrates:

> Transformation. Breaking the mold. Anything—ANYTHING—can be made special. Author Harvey Mackay tells about a cab ride from Manhattan out to La Guardia Airport: First, this driver gave me a paper that said, "Hi, my name is Walter. I'm your driver. I'm going to get you there safely, on time, in a courteous fashion." A mission statement from a cab driver! Then he holds up a *New York Times* and a *USA Today* and asks would I like them? So I took them. We haven't even moved yet. He then offers a nice little fruit basket with snack foods. Next he asks, "Would you prefer hard rock or classical music?" He has four channels. (Peters, 1994: 235–236)

This cab driver made between $12,000 and $14,000 extra per year in tips (in the early 1980s). If he can build a rapport with a passenger in the short period of time from downtown New York to the airport, what can a professional do with long-term customers over a lifetime? Peters further expands on this in his book *The Pursuit of Wow!*:

> The idea of professional-service delivery becoming "commoditized" is ludicrous. That's as true for the two-person firm as for the Big Six accountancy. Professional services

> are inherently personal. They are commodities only if you are a commodity—that is, if you don't have anything special to offer, if you're just another accountant, engineer, trainer, or professional whatever. . . . I always try to personalize: Can I imagine saying, "Opened a management book today. Couldn't be sure whether it was mine or Peter Drucker's"? (Peters, 1995: 102–103)

Traditional auditors do not provide a commodity service. First of all, many small CPA firms—the majority of the practice units, as cited above—do not even perform audits, and that limits competition from the start. Second, all of the ancillary services that surround an audit—the management letter, board meetings, and internal control analysis, to name just a few—are tremendously valuable services in the eyes of the customer. These need to be differentiated and priced according to their value and actuarial risk, rather than the time spent to produce them. Finally, with the consolidation of the Big Four, which intensifies concentration at the very upper end of the market, the gap left—the middle market—is wide open for other large national, regional, and local firms. Do not discount the value of an audit; it is still of significant help in obtaining other value pricing opportunities.

To promote a firm's value, and move up the curve, a firm must develop partnerships with its customers. Without a partnership, the firm very well may sell a commodity. With a partnership, however, it will have the ultimate monopoly—itself. Even though many businesses today deal with more than one firm, they would probably rather deal with just one, as it would be easier, more profitable, and less risky, and it would provide more opportunity for a value-added relationship to develop. Witness the trend of outsourcing, especially in the automotive industry, where the Big Three—following the lead of the Japanese—have chosen to form long-term partnerships with their outside suppliers and get them involved in the engineering and designing process of building cars. This practice might appear to be more risky because it means putting all your eggs in one basket, but its advantages clearly outweigh the risks; otherwise many of these firms would not be cutting back their supplier networks.

One of the main reasons businesses switch CPA firms, not to mention hiring outside consultants, is that the CPAs have not done an adequate job convincing the customers that they can perform the work and that they are a better choice than the competition. In other words, cross-selling efforts have not been as successful as they could be. This is why it is so important to focus on share of customer, rather than on market share, to ensure that a firm does not miss those opportunities to climb up the curve. Too many CPAs spend their time cranking out the work at the lower end of the curve, which should be delegated to someone else in the firm. Thus they miss myriad opportunities to cross-sell other value-added services to their customers. When customers talk with their CPAs and ask how business is, CPAs tend to complain about the next impending deadline, planting the notion in the customer's head that they are too busy to take on additional work from them or from others, thus discouraging referral sources from them. Chris Frederiksen, an internationally known consultant to CPAs, has a wonderful slogan: "Business is great and we're looking for more." That sends the right message.

Another implication of the value curve is what economists call umbrella pricing. For example, in an oligopoly setting, such as American automakers, it is a known fact that when General Motors raises its prices, it puts an "umbrella" over Ford and Daimler-Chrysler and allows them enough shelter to increase their prices as well. Walt Disney World, in Orlando, Florida, under the leadership of Michael Eisner, engaged in a series of price increases at the theme parks, and the surrounding competition—Busch Gardens, Sea World, Universal Studios—followed with their own increases. Likewise, within a firm, when value-added consulting services are offered, this serves to place an umbrella over the prices of the more traditional tax and attest services. If the focus is on the totality of the value that a firm provides the customer, and the services are bundled, commanding prices at the top of the curve becomes easier.

The CPA Vision Project

It is worth taking a look at the implications and trends the AICPA's CPA Vision Project set forth for the future of the profession. Here is how its report begins:

> This unprecedented Vision Process was a profession-wide effort involving the contribution of approximately 3,400 CPAs from all states, Washington, D.C., Puerto Rico, and the Virgin Islands to craft the CPA Vision. A series of 177 profession-

> ally facilitated, day-long "Future Forums" were conducted to gather input from CPAs working in public practice, business and industry, government, and education. Participants evaluated global forces and scenarios that could emerge from the interplay of those forces using a visioning framework known as PESTHR, an acronym for the following categories of global forces: Political, Economic, Social, Technological, Human Resources, and Regulation (AICPA, 1998: 8–9).

The project identified eight major forces affecting the profession:

1. **Non-CPA Competitors** The number of new, non-CPA competitors, not bound by the profession's code of standards and ethics, is increasing at an alarming rate.
2. **Decline of New CPAs** The number of students and young people electing to join the CPA profession has dramatically declined.
3. **Technology Displacement** Many of the traditional essential skills of CPAs are being replaced by new technologies that are being rapidly developed, often from unexpected sources.
4. **Borderless World** As the world becomes borderless, the marketplace is demanding more complex, real-time advice and services, presenting unlimited opportunities for CPAs to expand their skills, competencies, and services.
5. **Leadership Imperative** Corporations are conducting business in a world of commerce that is global, technological, instantaneous, and increasingly virtual. The leadership they require from both internal and external advisors requires new insights, new skills, and extraordinary agility.
6. **Technological Advances** Technology will continue to challenge and reshape our lifestyles, work patterns, educational experiences, and communication styles and techniques. Technology will rewrite the rules of business, leaving those far behind who do not harness it and effectively integrate it.
7. **Market Value Shifts** The perceived value of some of the profession's cornerstone services—accounting, auditing, and tax preparation—is declining in the marketplace.

8. **Pressure to Transform Finance from Scorekeeper to Business Partner** The CPA in business is being challenged to deliver value to the organization and help create a sustainable competitive advantage. (AICPA, 1998: 3)

The AICPA's report also pointed out that CPAs must become market-driven and not dependent upon regulations to keep them in business; the market demands less auditing and accounting and more value-adding consulting services. Specialization is critical for the future of the CPA profession. This is essentially a move away from the traditional number-crunching image toward interpretation and value-added services. (AICPA, 1998: 11)

The report also set forth the Economic Platforms model, as follows:

Economic Platform	*Scope of Knowledge*	*Distribution of Knowledge and Effect*	*Time Span of Impact*
Platform 7	Global	Ability to determine the rules of the game at an international level	50 years
Platform 6	National	Ability to influence the rules of the game at a national level	20 years
Platform 5	Industry	Ability to conceptualize the the multiple realities that exist within the environment and capitalize on them	10–15 years
Platform 4	Market	Ability to create and manage multiple, parallel outcomes based on market needs and internal competencies	3–5 years
Platform 3	Value Chain	Ability to identify and improve alternative systems to achieve predetermined goals	1–2 years
Platform 2	Process	Ability to conform and adhere to linear and technical processes	3 months
Platform 1	Product	Ability to perform given tasks and focus on immediate, tangible tasks	Immediate

According to the report, the path to success is moving from information services on Platforms 1 and 2 to services in the emerging knowledge industry of Platform 3 and beyond. Of course, it is emphasized that the services with higher value are built on the base of traditional CPA services. (AICPA, 1998: 22–23)

In effect, the Vision Project confirms what many CPAs have already discovered in the trenches of the marketplace: The customer is demanding more and more value-added consulting services and is turning to the most trusted and respected of all business advisors to perform that role—the CPA. But the transition from a traditional, conservative paradigm to one that is innovative, entrepreneurial, and risk-seeking does not happen overnight. The profession has built up an enormous amount of human capital in the role of financial historian, and it now finds itself in the position of being forced into the more ambiguous and less rule-bound atmosphere of the business advisor. How does one make that transition?

What the CPA Offers Today

According to Stuart Kessler, former AICPA chairman, the new "CPA" designation might be defined as *certified professional advisor*, a "forward-looking assurer of the integrity of real-time, customized data." Customers tend to judge CPAs as members of a profession rather than individually. Making the transition to advisor is one way to differentiate your firm from the competition.

According to consultants, various state societies, customers of CPA firms, and surveys conducted by the AICPA, the following services tend to be located at the top of the value curve and have significant growth potential. This list is not meant to be comprehensive; it is a way to get you to think differently about the future, which has already arrived:

- Benchmarking
- Business valuations
- Mergers and acquisitions
- International services
- Buy-sell agreements
- Key person insurance

- Mission statement development
- Marketing analysis and planning
- Customer retreats as annual events
- Business planning
- Cash flow analysis
- Choice of entity
- TQM/ISO 9000 consulting
- Business process reengineering
- Information technology
- Personal financial planning
- Estate and succession planning
- Consulting on pricing (using the concepts discussed in this book)
- Continuing professional education (Peter Drucker believes this is the growth industry of the future.)
- Economic analysis
- Activity-based costing
- Eldercare (Individuals age 65 and over control approximately $11 trillion to $13 trillion in wealth.)
- Negotiation
- Forensic accounting
- Business turnaround
- Dispute resolution
- Regulatory compliance
- Ethics attestation and implementation
- Internet and electronic commerce
- School performance (As the United States shifts more and more to private choice schools, CPAs can attest to their performance standards.)

One last point with respect to the future of the profession: The debate between the generalist and the specialist is over, and the specialist has won. The majority of successful firms specialize in a few industries or niche markets. CPAs are one of the last businesses to specialize. Doctors, dentists, lawyers, auto mechanics, and even retail stores have all carved out a particular expertise. You can no longer be everything to everybody. The difference between a generalist and a specialist is the difference between an incandescent light and a laser beam. Each requires the same amount of energy to operate, but one can burn a hole through metal because of its intense focus. As Confucius said, "The man who chases two rabbits catches neither."

Summary and Conclusions

Members of the accounting profession no longer have the luxury of launching a practice and having an automatic ticket to prosperity. The seller's market is over, and the customer is sovereign, demanding more and more every day. Accounting is a profession rich in history and traditions. Some of those traditions have served CPAs well for the past century or so. Others, such as government regulations and psychological attachment to hourly billing, are beginning to hinder the ability to service customers adequately.

Recall that the accounting profession is in the maturity stage of the product life cycle and that this alone alters the marketplace. Combine this with the increasing expectations of customers, who now demand that their CPA be a total financial advisor and business consultant, and the environment CPAs operate in has been permanently altered.

Study William C. Cobb's value curve and commit it to memory. Its lessons are many and vital, rooted deep in economic theory. The lesson embedded in the curve—and it is not obvious at first—is that no matter where a firm is on the curve, opportunities are available to value price its services.

This chapter was not written to predict the future, but because CPAs need to think differently about the future and the customer's ever-changing needs. Nobody can keep up with the market. The best anyone can do is to be on the lookout for changes in direction and trends and be among the early adopters of change in order to capitalize on emerging opportunities. Forecasts about the future of the profession are interesting, but leadership requires decisions in the present. Even if one knew exactly what the future held, that would only be half the battle. To take advantage of this knowledge, a firm would have to be formed, which leads to the question: Why are professionals in business?

3 WHY PEOPLE ARE IN BUSINESS

If you aim to profit, learn to please.

—Winston Churchill

When participants in a course for the California CPA Education Foundation were asked why they are in business, more than 75 percent answered: "To make a profit." Even the father of double-entry accounting, Fra Luca Pacioli, began the second chapter of his book with the following proposition:

> Begin with the assumption that a businessman has a goal when he goes into business. That goal he pursues enthusiastically. That goal, the goal of every businessman who intends to be successful, is to make a lawful and reasonable profit. (Pacioli, 1494: 4)

But is the answer really that simple?

Any business needs to earn a profit to survive; indeed, profit is the measurement of how much value an organization adds to the lives of others. However, to think that a business exists solely to make a profit is to confuse cause and effect, putting the cart before the horse. As Peter Drucker indefatigably points out, not only is the notion that businesses exist to make a profit false, it is irrelevant. Profit is a *result* of customer behavior. More accurately, profit is a *lagging indicator* of customer behavior. The real results of any organization take place in the hearts and minds of its customers. The central purpose of any business organization is to *create a customer*. This is a difficult concept to understand, especially for accountants and attorneys who have been trained to focus on the financial and transactional side of business life. Nonetheless, it is definitely true, as is shown in this chapter.

The Economist's Definition of Profit

The economics profession has a different definition of profit from that of the typical GAAP financial statement. Economists consider both parties to a transaction, because both parties must receive more value than each is giving up; otherwise no transaction would take place in the first place (assuming no fraud or coercion). United States Representative Samuel Barrett Pettengill (1886–1974) gave an excellent definition of *profit* from an economist's perspective:

> The successful producer of an article sells it for more than it costs him to make, and that's his profit. But the customer buys it only because it's worth more to her than she pays for it, and that's her profit. No one can long make a profit producing anything unless the customer makes a profit using it.

That is a good definition of profit because it focuses the organization on the customer and ensures that the customer, too, earns a profit from using your services. A most articulate expression of the above definition came from Stanley Marcus, chairman emeritus of Neiman-Marcus, the ultimate authority on customer service:

> You're really not in business to make a profit, but you're in business to render a service that is so good people are willing to pay a profit in recognition of what you're doing for them.

That is the ultimate mission statement for any business. The focus is right where it belongs—on the customer. This was common practice in the dark days of the Great Depression when Stanley Marcus ran the store founded by his father, Herbert Marcus. Back then, business owners understood the value of a customer and how hard it was to find one. Sometime after World War II, when businesses enjoyed a seller's market, this attitude was forgotten. Businesses had the attitude that customers were easily replaced, and not much attention was given to customer service and customer-loyalty economics. It wasn't until the mid-1980s that extensive research began to appear on the importance of customer service and how critical customer loyalty is to any organization.

Forgotten Lessons from the Past

They say that you can't turn back the clock and go back to the old days. Nonsense. This is exactly what is happening with the total quality service movement, the customer loyalty movement, and other concepts that put the customer at the center of the business organization. Millions of dollars are being spent on consultants to relearn what was once common sense, practiced by the great entrepreneurs from the turn of the century to the mid-1950s—individuals such as Stanley Marcus, Walt Disney, J.W. Marriott, and Ray Kroc. The movie *Miracle on 34th Street* is a testament to the importance of customer service and the value of loyalty. When the Macy's Santa Claus sends the customers to the competition because it has the toy the child desires—and it is on sale—management gets upset, but the customers love it and do the rest of their Christmas shopping at Macy's. Somewhere along the line, this common sense practice was lost, and just recently professionals have begun to recognize what their ancestors knew so well. Wisdom is timeless, and sometimes turning back the clock is the wisest course of action. Two books by Stanley Marcus, *Minding the Store* and *Quest for the Best*, are recommended reading.

Today's excellent customer service organizations have not only learned the value of customer service, they have put the concepts into practice, and are obtaining superior financial performance as a result. Organizations such as Disney, FedEx, Marriott, Lexus, Nordstrom, and Cadillac all have corporate cultures that are driven by the customer. Even though a customer may have had a bad experience with any of these organizations, recovery systems are in place to make good on errors, retain the customer, and in the process actually increase customer loyalty and goodwill. They also all understand that profit is a lagging indicator of customer behavior.

FedEx has an internal mission statement that sums up the importance of focusing on the customer in order to earn a profit: "People. Service. Profits." If FedEx takes care of its internal associates, they in turn will provide excellent service to its external customers, who in turn will pay FedEx a profit in recognition of what they are doing for them. That exact order comports with the real world of business, and it is also the reason a business does not exist solely to make a profit. A lot of work is done long before the bottom line on the income statement is black.

Businesses talk about profit centers, but this term, as Peter Drucker points out, is a misnomer. In any organization, from a for-profit business to a not-for-profit charity to a governmental agency, *all* results exist externally. Inside any organization all you have is *costs* and *efforts*. The result of a hospital is a well patient. The result of a school is an educated student. And the results of a business organization is a satisfied customer. As Stanley Marcus pointed out: "You achieve customer satisfaction when you sell merchandise that doesn't come back to a customer that does." If the focus is on the internal "profit centers," the firm is misguided. The only profit center is a customer's check that doesn't bounce.

At the Disney Institute Professional Development Program (formerly the Disney University), a course is offered titled *The Disney Approach to Customer Loyalty: Creating Service That Keeps Your Customers Coming Back.* The course emphasizes customer loyalty and what a business has to do to earn that loyalty. Better yet, the participants get to see first-hand how Walt Disney World puts these theories into practice and achieves the astonishing result of 75 percent of its guests (Disney parlance for customers) at the Walt Disney World Resort being repeat guests in 1996. This is impressive, considering that Walt Disney World's annual attendance is approximately 31.5 million.

The Walt Disney World Success Formula is as follows:

Quality Cast Member (employee) Experience

plus

Quality Guest Experience

plus

Quality Business Practices

equals

Future

Disney achieves this formula by focusing on its employees and their needs first. Employees are encouraged to set customer satisfaction as a priority. Out of this grows customer loyalty. The ultimate goals—profits and growth—follow naturally.

For Disney and other successful companies, profit follows an entire process of adding value both internally and externally. Focusing solely on profit is analogous to playing tennis by focusing on the scoreboard rather than keeping your eye on the ball.

When presented with these ideas, one CPA responded: "That's all well and good, but if I don't make a profit, first and foremost, I can't survive in order to serve." The obvious retort is that you must serve in order to survive. But CPAs are a tougher sell than that. So he was asked to perform this exercise: Figure out the lifetime value of each customer in your firm, multiply that amount by how many years you intend to practice, and compute the result. Then go to your balance sheet and make the following entry:

	Debit	Credit
Accounts Receivable	$XX	
Deferred Revenue		$XX

Then he was asked, "How do you intend to convert that to cash?" This focuses on the right area, i.e., the customer. Everything else is merely effort, and as they say, effort will be rewarded in Heaven—but customers want results.

Discovering the "P" in CPA

As a profession, CPAs find it much easier to focus on the "A" in the acronym rather than the "P." They focus on the "A" because they understand accounting and have been trained and certified in it; quite honestly, dealing with "A" is easier than dealing with the customer relationship. As Joan Baez once remarked: "The easiest kind of relationship for me is with 100,000 people. The hardest is with one." When CPAs give any thought at all to serving the public they think of processing tax returns, attesting to financial statements, or, worse yet, racking up billable hours.

It's certainly easy for a CPA to sit in an office, surrounded by a customer's files, and believe he or she is serving the customer well. This attitude will handicap efforts to climb up the value curve, however. The CPA needs to focus on the customer, or on *who* benefits, rather than on *what* to do. This places the customer relationship at the center and puts the emphasis on the *outcome* of effort, not on the *activity*. The old joke about how CPAs are easily suited to be morticians because of their disdain for customer contact may have some truth to it, but no longer can a CPA be successful based exclusively upon backroom technical competence. The best professionals, in any of the professions, are those who care deeply about their customers as fellow humans. As David H. Maister says in his book *True Professionalism*, "The opposite of the word *professional* is not *unprofessional*, but rather *technician*. Professionalism is predominantly an attitude, not a set of competencies. A real professional is a technician who cares." (Maister, 1997: 16)

An inspiring story of excellent service comes from my father, whom you met in the Introduction. While giving a haircut, my dad learned that his customer had recently, and unexpectedly, lost his job. During the course of the usual barber chair banter, the customer explained that he was financially strapped and having a difficult time. After the haircut, as the customer pulled out his wallet to pay, my father held up his hand, refused to take his money, and told him it was on the house, as all future haircuts would be, until the customer had a chance to get back on his feet.

That is compassion. That is empathy. That is actively listening to customers and hearing what they say. It is responding to the *person*, not just to the *need*. It was a small investment—a few 45-minute haircuts, and lost revenue of $50 to $100, for a customer who is so enamored with my father that he will stay with him for life. From the perspective of loyalty economics, it was a worthwhile investment, because it can cost *five* times more to obtain a new customer than it does to keep an existing one. (CPAs take note: The AICPA states that it costs *eleven* times more.) Imagine increasing advertising and marketing effectiveness by a factor of between five and eleven by investing in your existing customers.

This story is the embodiment of the spirit of service. In his trailblazing book, *The Only Thing That Matters: Bringing the Power of the Customer into the Center of Your Business*, Karl Albrecht defines the spirit of service as follows:

> *The Spirit of Service*: An attitude based on certain values and beliefs about people, life, and work, that leads a person to willingly serve others and take pride in his or her work.
>
> It's an element of giving—a spirit of generosity that makes people give something of themselves in addition to just doing the job. It's going beyond the bare minimum or the standard actions. It's being attentive to the *person* behind the need, and responding to the *person* more than just responding to the

> need. It's being there psychologically and emotionally as well as being there physically. (Albrecht, 1992: 88)

Rewards follow service, and so does profit. Henry Ford said it this way: "The man who will use his skill and constructive imagination to see how much he can give for a dollar, instead of how little he can give for a dollar, is bound to succeed." George Gilder, author, economist, and technologist, defines the spirit of enterprise:

> It is a world where service of others—solving their problems and taking on new ones for yourself—is the prime source of leadership and wealth. . . . "Do unto others as you would have them do unto you" and "give and you will be given unto" are the central rules of the life of enterprise. (Gilder, 1992: 298, 308)

Is All This Just So Much "Fluff"?

Business is about serving others and adding value to their lives in excess of payment in cash. If an organization doesn't succeed in that mission, the market should squeeze it out of existence unmercifully, because such an organization is merely wasting society's resources by not deploying them to the advantage of others. Business is not about survival of the fittest (i.e., only the strong survive), as if social Darwinism ruled the world of enterprise. This notion can be disproved simply by looking at where all of the growth and innovation come from in a free-market economy—the small business sector. If social Darwinism ruled business life, only the *Fortune* 500 would exist, since all the money is there.

Another preposterous notion found in many business books is that business is *war*. Popular novelists such as Michael Crichton and Tom Clancy have added to this myth. If business were war, everyone would be dead. In a $11 trillion plus economy, literally billions of transactions are taking place every day. The only way to win in a war is to annihilate the enemy or overwhelm the enemy with such force that they surrender. In business, the only way to win against competition is to add more value to the customer. That's not *war*, it's *peace*. It puts all of the advantages into the hands of the customer, where they should be. Business is all about volitional acts under no threat of coercion, fraud, or duress. Certainly illegal acts take place, and that is why contract law and the court system exist, to enforce restitution and award damages to injured parties. But the majority of business transactions happen without dishonest intent, based upon mutual trust and respect. Economists focus their attention on the customer, not the business sector, because they, too, profit from each transaction.

So much of business terminology is borrowed from the battlefield that it has been ingrained into the average person since college. Even everyday business attire has its roots in the battlefield, as was pointed out by Adam M. Brandenburger and Barry J. Nalebuff in their book *Co-opetition*:

> Drawing on the work of Anne Hollander, Eric Nash points out that the clothing people wear to work also comes from war: the tie was long called a cravat, after the seventeenth-century Croatian mercenaries who wore them on French battlefields; the vestigial brass loops on trench coats are actually grenade hooks; the tailored suit can be traced back to the linen padding worn under a suit of armor; men's coats unbutton from the left so that a right-handed man might draw a sword or gun quickly. (Brandenburger and Nalebuff, 1996: 267)

Despite this attitude, economists, sociologists, theologians, and even Pope John Paul II have spoken on the morality of capitalism and the vital role profits perform in its functioning.

The theory of total quality service is grounded in empirical evidence: It works. Organizations whose cultures are driven by the customer outperform those that are not. It is both that simple and that complex. Total quality service enables a business to charge premium prices, just like FedEx, Disney, and Nordstrom. Do people turn away at the gate at Disneyland or Walt Disney World when they discover that prices are higher than the local competition? Hardly. Disney practices total quality service—or what they call Disney Quality Service (DQS)—because it's the right thing to do both morally and ethically, and it has the salutary effect of tremendously increasing profitability.

The purpose of this book is to help you make more money. The book focuses on the *top line* (i.e., pricing policies) with the sole purpose of increasing the *bottom line*. You will not be able to do that unless you provide your customers total quality service, emanating from a firm possessing the spirit of service, which is cultural and attitudinal. Once total quality service and the spirit of service are the driving forces of a firm, value pricing can be implemented.

Customer vs. Client

Many organizations have tried to call their customers something other than a customer. Here is what Albrecht had to say with respect to the words businesses use:

> In an organization, the language that people use when referring to customers, or when describing service-quality programs, signals very clearly how they view their customers and how they see themselves as relating to them. Many organizations have evolved a special terminology that enables them to *avoid* referring to people as customers. (Albrecht, 1992: 9)

If you have read this far, you have already noticed the use of the word *customer* rather than *client* when referring to the people served by professionals. This is deliberate and is done for several reasons.

Where Does the Word *Client* Come From?

Professionals tend to substitute the word *client* for *customer*. However, the word *client*, when you look at its etymology, is an inappropriate word to describe the person the professional serves in today's marketplace. *Client* is derived from the Latin word *cliens*, which is a follower, retainer, one who hears his patron.

According to the dictionary, "among the ancient Romans a client was a citizen who placed himself under the protection of a patrician, who was called his patron; a dependent; one under the protection or patronage of another."

In the legal profession in the early Roman Empire, individuals learned in the law provided legal services without compensation. According to William G. Ross, in his book *The Honest Hour: The Ethics of Time-Based Billing by Attorneys*:

> Early Roman lawyers were . . . obliged to advise and defend their clients, because these were duties which lawyers, as patrons, owed to those who were dependent upon them. Later, as clients ceased to be the dependents of their lawyers, persons who performed legal services often continued to work without pay because they were wealthy and hoped to achieve public recognition and political benefit from pleading the cases of their clients. (Ross, 1996: 9)

The dictionary also describes a client as "a person or company for whom a lawyer, accountant, advertising agency, etc. is acting; loosely, a customer; a person served by a social agency." Visit any governmental agency that dispenses aid to individuals and you will soon discover that it uses the term "client." The welfare state may have clients but the same term does not need to be used to describe the relationship professionals desire to have with those they are privileged to serve.

Today the word "client" is used simply because that's what professionals have always called their customers. It is time to question the appropriateness of this word.

Use of the Word *Customer* Provides a Competitive Differentiation

Professionals have attempted to elevate themselves above the "crass commercialism of the marketplace," as if something is inherently wrong with professionals having to compete for customers, although auto companies, grocery stores, malls, airlines, and all other businesses in the free market do so.

What has happened to the word *customer*, and why do so many businesses attempt to describe the people they serve as something else? After all, *customer* is derived from the word *custom*, which is something done regularly. Therefore, a customer is a person who buys, especially one who buys regularly. Why businesses, and particularly the professions, have adopted other terms is an interesting question, and one worth thinking about. Doctors see "patients," which is a Latin word for "suffering" or "endurance" (*patientia*). Thus a patient is by definition "long-suffering."

Airlines carry "passengers." Taxi drivers transport "fares." Utility companies have "ratepayers." Insurance companies service "policyholders." Newsletters solicit "subscribers." The IRS deals with "taxpayers."

Businesses have replaced the word *customer* with other terms. Albrecht offers an explanation:

> These labels signal that the company sees the customer as a passive figure, an object to be acted upon, or something to be processed through a system. The choice of these words makes the customer into a thing rather than a person. The words make it easier to obscure the fact that customers are *people*, entitled to judge the quality of the delivered experience and who make the ultimate decision about doing business with the organization.
>
> Apparently we don't like giving the customer that much power. We don't like the feeling of having to earn the customer's approval. We want to change customers into things we can manipulate, statistics we can analyze, or wild animals we have to capture to gain 'market share.'
>
> The loss of this focus on the customer as a human being is probably the single most important fact about the state of service and service management in the Western world today. (Albrecht, 1992: 10)

Walt Disney insisted that his customers be called "guests." His attitude, which still permeates the entire culture of all Disney theme parks, is that the role of employees ("Cast Members") is to entertain the guests and show them a good time. The words used to describe the people served by a business are a good indication of the attitude of the firm.

Customers will develop a deeper respect for professionals if they are treated like *people*, rather than viewed as *tasks* to be processed through the firm. Customers are much more sophisticated with respect to other services offered them by professionals, and they have access to more information than ever before. With the dramatically increased level of competition over the past decade, professionals must strive to serve and please the customer to win their continued patronage. *The customer is sovereign. Period.* Professionals may not like it; they may wax nostalgic for the old days, when customers lined up like sheep to be fleeced once every year, but those days are gone, forever. Professionals can no longer place themselves above the "crass marketplace." They must participate in it and differentiate themselves from the competition if they are to succeed.

For professionals who do start referring to clients as "customers," this will have a salutary effect on the attitude, firm culture, customer loyalty and respect, and ultimately, on the professional's bottom line.

Summary and Conclusions

The seller's market, which existed after World War II up until the end of the 1970s, is over. Today, the customer is sovereign, and businesses are "turning back the clock" to learn the lessons their predecessors knew so well from the turn of the century up until the 1950s—that each customer wants quality service and wants to be treated individually. The total quality service leaders of today—companies such as Disney, FedEx, Marriott, Lexus, Nordstrom, Cadillac, L.L. Bean, and Ritz-Carlton—are studying the lessons from the entrepreneurs of a bygone age—Herbert and Stanley Marcus, Ray Kroc, J.W. Marriott, and Walt Disney—who understood the importance of treating customers well.

Serving people is what being a professional is, or should be, all about. Focus on your customers, and continually solve an ever-increasing share of their problems and burdens. Give as much as you can for a dollar, rather than as little as you can. The profits and rewards you seek will be yours.

4 WHAT AND HOW PEOPLE BUY

The secret of staying afloat in business is to create something people will pay for.

—Thomas Edison

To engage in value pricing, a professional must understand exactly *what* customers are buying, and it helps to understand *how* they are buying as well. Ask any group of professionals what their customers are paying them for and the result is a wide range of answers that unfortunately focuses on what the professional thinks the customer needs, not what the customer actually buys. Here are the most frequent responses:

- Preparation of financial statements, tax returns, and tax planning
- Management advisory services
- Expertise, knowledge, and experience
- Time

All of these answers emphasize the technical aspect of what a CPA does, rather than the benefits perceived by the customer. With the exception of time, most of the answers are subjects emphasized in college and CPE courses, and any relationship to what customers pay for is truly coincidental. Other industries do not suffer from this dilemma; they have an excellent understanding of exactly what their customer is buying. Automobile salesmen know that they aren't selling utilitarian transportation; they are selling status, personality, performance, fun, and image. Booksellers do not sell books; they sell information and reading enjoyment. Insurance salesman are not selling policies (who reads them?); they are selling peace of mind.

So, What Do People Really Buy?

It is the old marketing axiom that people are not buying *drill bits*, which are small and easily misplaced; they are buying *holes*. One doesn't buy *golf clubs* but the *activity* they allow the customer to engage in. Gillette is selling *shaves*, not *razors*. 7-Eleven is selling *convenience.* McDonald's is selling *fast*, not *food.* An owner of a Roto-Rooter business would quickly discover that a good percentage of business comes not from unplugging drains but from retrieving wedding rings, which is useful information to place in a Yellow Pages ad for the customer in a panic. The manufacturer of Rogaine is not selling hair but is really selling *hope*. Charles Revson, who created the cosmetic empire Revlon, said, "When it leaves the factory, it's *lipstick.* But when it crosses the counter in the department store, it's *hope*."

In his book *How to Win Customers and Keep Them for Life*, Michael LeBoeuf, Ph.D., states:

> Despite all of the untold millions of products and services for sale in today's market place, customers will exchange their hard-earned money for only two things:
>
> 1. Good feelings
> 2. Solutions to problems
>
> (LeBoeuf, 1989: 39)

Professionals are excellent at solving problems. Sometimes they are even too good, because they tend to jump right into the solution without first discovering what the customer really wants and expects, almost completely ignoring the creation of the good feelings that are so essential to developing long-term relationships. Simply offering solutions to problems isn't enough. The customer automatically expects problems to be solved, which is why they seek out a professional, but more emphasis should fall on creating good feelings.

The Dynamics of Customer Expectations

There is a difference between getting what you pay for and what you hope for.

—Malcolm Forbes (1919–90), American publisher

Theodore Levitt, retired marketing professor at Harvard Business School, simplified LeBoeuf's two factors by observing that customers are really buying only one thing: expectations. This view focuses on the utility that the customer is trying to maximize. All consumers are out to maximize their own utility, measured either by happiness, pleasure, or something similar. No two customers are alike; each one is trying to maximize something different.

Marketing brochures of CPA firms all claim to offer outstanding service and customer satisfaction. It is important to understand, however, just how customer satisfaction is measured, which is as follows:

$$\text{Customer Satisfaction} = \frac{\text{Perceived Performance}}{\text{Customer Expectations}}$$

The *customer's* perceptions and expectations of CPA performance are what matter. The customer satisfaction equation drives home the importance of ascertaining, prior to starting each engagement, exactly what the customer's expectations are, since that is how, ultimately, the firm will be judged. Meeting a customer's expectations is hard enough when they are known. To exceed those expectations is nearly impossible if they are unknown. Customer satisfaction is no longer enough. Customer *satisfaction* must move on to customer *delight.* According to the *Harvard Business Review*, 65 to 85 percent of customers who chose a new supplier said they were satisfied or very satisfied with their former supplier. That is an astonishing statistic, one that should strike fear into the hearts and minds of all of us.

Prior to every single engagement, it is essential to ask the customer: What are your expectations? Asking this gives a CPA the ability to manage and control the outcome. For instance, if a millionaire anticipates paying no taxes, he has an unrealistic outlook. The options are to educate him, to lower his expectations, or to refuse the engagement altogether. The onus is on the CPA to discover what the customer is counting on, then to control and educate the customer. The CPA is then able to exceed the customer's expectations.

Customers arrive at a professional's office with preconceived ideas of what can be done for them. These ideas have been created by professionals through marketing, advertising, and promotional material. Some expectations have been created by others—referral sources and existing customers who rave about the service they received. Managing and controlling what the customers anticipate is critical. Southwest Airlines does this well. Many people see flying on this airline as a cattle call. The passengers are fed peanuts and it is strictly no-frills. This is intentional. Expectations are lowered and it becomes much easier for Southwest to exceed those expectations when they arrive on time, with the passengers' luggage, crack jokes, and do other irreverent things that make the airline so much fun to fly on. Compare that to buying a first-class ticket on another airline, say, United Airlines. What are a customer's expectations then? If any inconvenience were to occur on that flight, the customer would be less satisfied because expectations started out higher. The higher the customer's expectations are from the start, the higher the probability of being dissatisfied.

By always asking the customers what they expect, you can discover value pricing opportunities. A CPA met for the first time with the CEO of two companies. Due to banking covenants, the CEO was required to prepare a full-disclosure compiled financial statement. During the meeting, the CPA asked, "What do you expect from us?" The CEO sat back and replied: "Obviously I need the compilations, but what I really want from you is for you to develop a relationship with my banker. You see, during the year I tend to fall out of compliance with my loan covenants, and if my banker were comfortable with you it would make my life much easier." When the CPA heard that, he knew exactly what the customer expected. Upon returning to his office he immediately called the banker to set up a lunch. He also priced the services at three times his "standard hourly rate," based upon what he knew the engagement, and the relationship with the banker, was worth to the CEO.

In order to discover what the customer really wants, the professional must treat each customer individually, with custom-designed services (and pricing) delivered on every engagement. In her book *Measuring and Managing Customer Satisfaction*, Sheila Kessler recounts the following story:

> Motorola noticed a radical increase in its pager revenues in Korea. When investigating how people there were using them, Motorola found that young women sometimes carried as many as seven pagers tucked into their waistband. Each pager represented a different boyfriend who was paging the woman—an exclusive communication link. The numbers of pagers a young woman wore was a status symbol. (Kessler, 1996: 179)

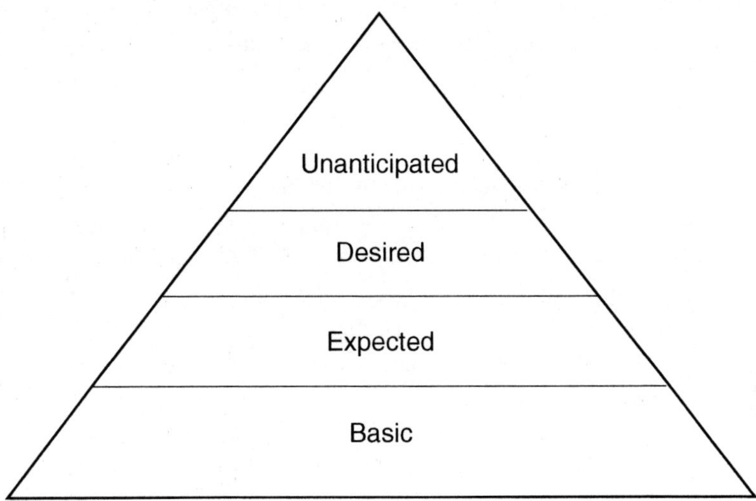

Customers should not be treated *equally*; they should be treated *individually*. One characteristic of customer expectations is that they are *dynamic*, not *static*. Over time, customers get spoiled as competition progresses from *features* to *cost* to *quality* to *service*. Karl Albrecht describes this phenomenon with a hierarchy of customer value, similar to Maslow's hierarchy of needs. (Albrecht, 1992: 113)

Because of the dynamic nature of a customer's expectations, it is imperative that a professional continually ask what is expected. Customers judge CPAs not only against other professionals in the same trade, but *against any organization that has the ability of raising customer expectations.*

What does this mean? It means that CPAs compete against Disney, FedEx, L.L. Bean, Lexus, Marriott, and Amazon.com. While CPAs do not run amusement parks or overnight services, their customers frequent these businesses. Once customers receive good service, they want more.

The lesson is vital, and it is this: Either the professional raises the customer's expectations or these other organizations will. Instead of comparing a professional service firm's level of service with that of another professional firm, compare it to Disney or Ritz-Carlton or FedEx. If the firm's level of service isn't up to that of these other organizations, then the customer may legitimately ask: Why should I do business with you?

You will find a valuable checklist, "Discovering Customer Expectations," in "Useful Checklists" at the end of this book and on the CD-ROM.

Focus On What You Do, Not What You Are

Ask professionals what they do, and they almost always respond: "I'm an attorney," or "I'm a CPA." However, that is what they *are*, not what they *do*. Telling people what they are leaves the judgment open about what they do, and that probably means the questioner will conjure up the stereotype of the profession. At the Results Accountants' Systems Boot Camp, they taught professionals not to refer to themselves as a CPA, because this is too restricting. They encouraged their participants to say they are business development specialists, and that they help business owners develop businesses that work so that the owners don't have to.

The customer cares about the *results*, not how the results are achieved. Yet most professionals will tell customers not *what* they do, but *how* they do it. Firm brochures boast about use of the latest technology or explain that they process tax returns in-house for greater efficiency. To a customer, this is boring.

An effective ad for Ernst & Young showed a picture of a very nice two-story house, all white, with a spacious lawn and front porch in a decent looking neighborhood. Next to that was a picture of a castle, not too ostentatious, but certainly much nicer than the two-story house. Underneath the house was the caption: "Your house." Underneath the castle was the caption: "Your competitor's." And underneath that: "Why?" This ad pulled at the emotion of the potential customer, addressing the question of whether he could be doing better, along with the fear that he is falling behind the competition.

Customers want to hear the *benefits* that are available. By focusing on the value to the customer, a professional will discover how to move up the value curve.

How People Buy

I like best the wine drunk at the cost of others.

—Ascribed to Diogenes The Cynic, c. 380 B.C.

People buy *emotionally* and justify *intellectually*. A customer may walk into a Porsche dealership, take a test drive, and sign on the dotted line. This is an emotional purchase. When the customer goes home, and has to justify the purchase to his wife, the intellectualizing begins. "Honey, we deserve this. We had a good year. We didn't even take a vacation."

The best time for earthquake insurance sales is right after an earthquake. This is curious, especially from an actuarial point of view. If customers are willing to assume the risk prior to a quake, why would they not be willing to assume the risk after one strikes? The probability of another earthquake striking simply because one just did is no greater, as fault lines don't have memories. The purchase is not made based upon the intellectual calculation of the statistical odds, but on the emotional desire for peace of mind. The customer is attempting to maximize serenity.

One application of this principle of emotions is that people don't like to be *sold* something, but they do like to *buy* (and own). People do not like to be sold something, because that makes them feel like they are out of control. The best salesperson in the world actually empowers the customers to buy and helps customers envision the future with their product or service. Forget *selling*; focus on what the customer *buys.*

This leads to *how* people buy. In any economy, according to Milton and Rose Friedman in *Free to Choose*, people can spend money in four ways (Friedman and Friedman, 1990: 116–17):

Whose Money	**On Whom Spent**	
	You	Someone Else
Yours	I	II
Someone Else's	III	IV

Category I: When you spend your money on yourself, you will do everything in your power to maximize your utility. For example, if you are in the market for a car, you will shop around, talk to friends, visit dealerships, take test drives, and read consumer reports to get the best value for your dollar.

Category II: Perhaps you are buying a gift for a spouse, friend, or colleague. You still want to maximize your utility and theirs. You will still shop around to get the best value for your dollar.

Category III: The greatest luxury of all is to spend someone else's money on yourself. An expense account is a perfect example. Little incentive to economize exists. You might fly first class, upgrade your rental car, not eat all of your dinner, and remove items from the minibar. This is why airlines, hotels, and rental car agencies discriminate in their pricing against business travelers; they know these people are not paying their own bills. They are, by definition, less price sensitive. The airlines would be missing a wonderful opportunity if they did not charge these passengers higher prices.

When you encounter customers who are in Category III, you have an opportunity to value price, even if your firm is on the low end of the value curve.

Category IV: When you spend someone else's money on strangers there is virtually no incentive to economize. Government programs are a perfect example, and that is why government spending is out of control. This also explains the paradox explored in the Introduction of how CPAs once made more money than doctors and dentists. Healthcare spending has moved from Category I and II to III (health insurance) and IV (government spending on healthcare). Representative Dick Armey has this axiom: "Three groups spend other people's money: children, thieves, politicians. All three need parental supervision." (Armey, 1995: 316)

These categories hold many lessons about how other businesses value price their goods and services and are referred to throughout this book.

Summary and Conclusions

Understanding exactly what a customer buys—expectations—will help a firm to exceed those expectations and thus be able to charge premium prices for services. Understanding the customers themselves—that they buy *emotionally* and justify *intellectually*, and that they don't like to be *sold* but they like to *buy*—helps the professional focus on the true needs of the customer and makes cross-selling the firm's services more effective.

5 WHY IS MOVIE THEATER POPCORN SO EXPENSIVE?

The economist's greatest passion is not to change the world but to understand it.

—Steven E. Landsburg, *The Armchair Economist*

Why Study Economics?

Economists take the intellectual high ground when it comes to price theory, defined as how prices coordinate economic activity. If a business book supposedly dealing with pricing a product or service does not mention economic theory, or cite any economists, it is intellectually bankrupt. To understand how prices are set, what signals they send, how they distribute income, and a given society's resources, one *must* study economics. This is the starting point to understanding the theoretical underpinning of value pricing.

Economists are often seen as people who try to predict (and measure) macroeconomic activity—the stock market, inflation, unemployment, the budget deficit, monetary policy, and so forth. This is far too parochial a view of what economists do. The really fascinating economists are engaged in the study of *human behavior*. The most fertile minds in economics today, the likes of Gary S. Becker, Thomas Sowell, Walter Williams, Milton and Rose Friedman, David Friedman, and Steven E. Landsburg, to name just a few, deal with observing the world and trying to understand it, not with predicting it.

They all start with the basic assumption that human behavior is, overall, rational. This assumption has been challenged because it seems people do many irrational things. It is true that not all human behavior is rational, but that is not what the economists are saying. Here is how David Friedman (Milton Friedman's son), in his book *Hidden Order: The Economics of Everyday Life*, defined economics and how it may be used to observe human behavior:

> Economics is based on the assumption that people have reasonably simple objectives and choose the correct means to achieve them. Both assumptions are false—but useful.
>
> Suppose someone is rational only half the time. Since there is generally one right way of doing things and many wrong ways, the rational behavior can be predicted but the irrational cannot. If we assume he is rational, we predict his behavior correctly about half the time—far from perfect, but a lot better than nothing. If I could do that well at the racetrack I would be a very rich man. (Friedman, 1996: 4)

The theory of rationality is a paradigm, a mental model of the way the world works. Economists are reluctant to part with this theory because it serves them well. Here is how the consummate economist Steven E. Landsburg explained it in his textbook *Price Theory and Applications*:

> Economists insist on seeking explanations that are grounded in rational behavior. There are two reasons for this insistence. First, on the basis of his past experience, the economist is aware of the power and wide applicability of economic analysis, which presumes rationality. Second, by attempting to extend such analysis into realms where it first appears inapplicable, the economist tests the limits and the durability of his theories.
>
> If physicists abandoned their theories so easily, physics could never progress. The first physicist to have observed a helium-filled balloon would have admitted that there was no gravity, and the true physics of the situation would not have been discovered. By attempting to fit unfamiliar phenomena into familiar patterns, we arrive at deeper understandings of both the patterns and the phenomena. (Landsburg, 1996: 690–691)

Price theory is grounded in the theory of rationality. For example, take 99-cent pricing. Why do businesses price their products this way, making the consumer give and take those useless pennies? The common answer is, "It's a sales gimmick. The customer perceives $2.99 being cheaper than $3.00." From an economic approach, this contradicts the theory of rationality, because it implies that consumers, over the long run, are too ignorant to tell the difference between $2.99 and $3.00. Might there be a better explanation? How is 99-cent pricing serving the interests of someone?

Here is how Landsburg explained the phenomenon of 99-cent pricing, in his book *The Armchair Economist: Economics and Everyday Life*:

> The phenomenon of "99-cent pricing" seems to have first become common in the nineteenth century, shortly after the invention of the cash register. The cash register was a remarkable innovation; not only did it do simple arithmetic, it also kept a record of every sale. That's important if you think your employees might be stealing from you. You can examine the tape at the end of the day and know how much money should be in the drawer.
>
> There is one small problem with cash registers: They don't actually record *every* sale; they record only those sales that are rung up. If a customer buys an item for $1 and hands the clerk a dollar bill, the clerk can neglect to record the sale, slip the bill in his pocket, and leave no one the wiser.
>
> On the other hand, when a customer buys an item for 99 cents and hands the clerk a dollar bill, the clerk has to make change. This requires him to open the cash drawer, which he cannot do without ringing up the sale. Ninety-nine-cent pricing forces clerks to ring up sales and keeps them honest. (Landsburg, 1993: 15–16)

Upon reflection, this appears a more adequate explanation than "sales gimmick," doesn't it? And that epitomizes the advantages of the economic way of viewing the world and assuming that behavior is rational.

Another interesting phenomenon is movie theater popcorn. To the outsider, a good question to ask might be, Wouldn't they sell more popcorn if they lowered the price? You never see any movie theater popcorn price wars, as you do with airlines or automobiles. Why is that? Why is movie theater popcorn so expensive? This question, asked in value pricing seminars, elicited these answers, ranked from most common to least common:

- Captive audience (represents 90 percent of the answers)
- Limited selling time

- Part of the experience
- High fixed cost of concession stand
- It's where the theater makes all of its profit
- Higher clean-up costs imposed on theater
- Tastes and smells better than you make at home
- You feel guilty if you sneak food in

These answers seem reasonable at first glance, but they are all wrong if you view the world through the eyes of an economist. Indeed, theater owners have a captive audience and thus no other competition in the sale of popcorn. However, they also have a monopoly on bathrooms and don't have pay toilets. If they did, this would make the theater less attractive to customers and what the owner made from the pay toilets would be lost at the box office. The limited selling time seems to be a plausible explanation, but now with mega-theaters that are open practically 24 hours, popcorn prices still haven't dropped.

That popcorn is part of the experience is certainly true, as you are buying a set of opportunities when you purchase a theater ticket—one to watch a movie, and the other, if you desire, to eat popcorn. However, that doesn't explain the high price. The fixed cost of the concession stand is a plausible reason, but that cost is probably a small percentage of the premium charged for the popcorn, so that explanation, too, is inadequate. That it is where the theater makes all of its profits is certainly true, but that doesn't answer the riddle of why the theater owner doesn't just raise the price of admission tickets and make the profit there. The higher clean-up cost, again, cannot be anywhere near the premium charged. And the popcorn certainly tastes and smells better, and is more fattening, than what you could make at home, but that still doesn't explain the high price.

To the economist, all of the answers are inadequate. Something else must be happening to explain the phenomenon. What does the theater owner know that the above answers ignore? Landsburg explains:

> I believe he knows this: *some moviegoers like popcorn more than others*. Cheap popcorn attracts popcorn lovers and makes them willing to pay a high price at the door. But to take advantage of that willingness, the owner must raise ticket prices so high that he drives away those who come only to see

> the movie. If there are enough nonsnackers, the strategy of cheap popcorn can backfire.
>
> The purpose of expensive popcorn is not to extract a lot of money from customers. *That* purpose would be better served by cheap popcorn and expensive movie tickets. Instead, the purpose of expensive popcorn is to extract *different* sums from *different* customers. Popcorn lovers, who have more fun at the movies, pay more for their additional pleasure. (Landsburg, 1993: 159)

This is an excellent explanation, and many lessons can be learned from the practice of the theater owners. They know that some moviegoers like popcorn more than others, and they have no way to identify who these folks are when they purchase their admission tickets. They don't stand outside in the queue and ask people if they plan to purchase popcorn upon entering; if they did, how many people would tell the truth, especially if discounts were offered to popcorn lovers? Once in the theater, the popcorn lovers identify themselves by walking up to the concession stand, and that is where the owner extracts the "consumer surplus" from their pockets. By keeping the admission price low, and separate from the price of popcorn, the theater is not turning away starving students, parents with a large number of children, and other financially challenged patrons.

Price Discrimination

Charging different prices to *different* customers is the definition of *price discrimination*. The term was coined in 1920 by Arthur Cecil Pigou in *The Economics of Welfare*. Other terms for the same concept are *revenue management* and *segmented pricing*. Price discrimination occurs when a good or service is sold at different prices that do not reflect differences in production costs. Firms engage in price discrimination to extract the consumer surplus from the customer. Consumer surplus is defined as the amount by which consumers value a product over and above what they pay for it. The traditional economic graph of supply and demand shows the customers that a firm is trying to identify in order to capture the consumer surplus.

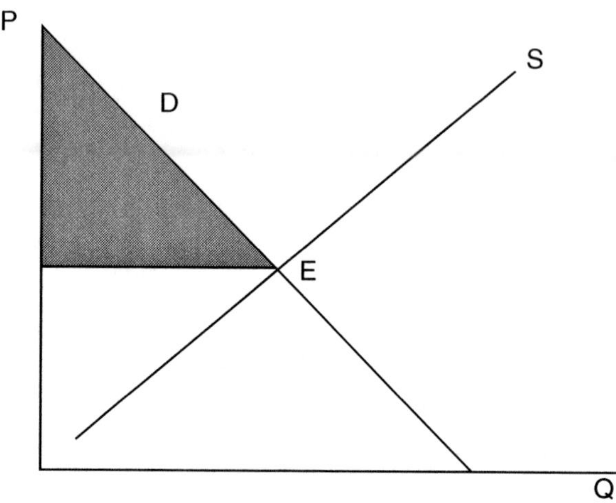

P = Price; *D* = Demand; *S* = Supply;
E = Equilibrium price; and *Q* = Quantity.

To be included on a demand curve, customers must meet two requirements: (1) They have to be *willing* to buy the product; and (2) They have to be *able* to buy the product. For instance, a customer may not be on the demand curve for a Rolls-Royce because, although the customer is *willing* to buy the car, the customer is not *able* to buy it. The shaded area of the graph depicts the consumer surplus, and represents the individuals who are *willing* and *able* to pay more for the product than they are being charged at the equilibrium (i.e., market) price. On any downward sloping demand curve, certain customers are willing and able to pay more for a product than they are being charged.

To measure the elasticity of demand for professional services, use the following coefficient of elasticity:

$$E = \frac{\text{Percentage change in quantity demanded}}{\text{Percentage change in price}}$$

Elastic demand exists when *E* is greater than 1. Conversely, an inelastic demand curve exists when *E* is less than 1. The traditional example of an elastic demand curve, one that is more horizontal than that shown above, but downward sloping nevertheless, is a bale of hay. If the bale of hay is a true commodity, meaning farmer John's bale is no different from farmer Joe's, it wouldn't make sense for a customer to pay a higher price for one than the other (unless, of course, there was some other way to differentiate the two farmers—location, delivery, service, personality, etc.). In other words, if farmer John increased the price of his hay relative to farmer Joe, the quantity demanded would drop, thereby lowering his gross revenues overall. Elastic demand exists in markets with many competitors and many substitutes, such as chewing gum or groceries.

Inelastic demand, on the other hand, exists when a firm can raise the price, and the quantity demanded, while it will decrease, will not fall enough to lower revenues overall. The classic example is gasoline. When oil companies increase prices, demand falls, but not enough to offset the price increase, because not many substitutes for gasoline can be found, and each consumer needs a certain amount for necessities (commuting, grocery shopping, etc.). Blood is an example of a perfectly inelastic demand curve—at least in an emergency situation—meaning that the customer would demand a fixed quantity at any price, represented by a perfectly vertical demand curve.

What is the elasticity of demand for professional services? There is ample evidence that the demand curve for the legal and accounting professions is relatively inelastic. Many firms that have increased their prices find that their top lines have increased concomitantly, even though they are selling to fewer customers. There is no doubt that the elasticity of demand differs not only for the type of service being offered, but also the value the particular customer places on a particular service. For instance, a customer who is 25 years old will have a much more elastic demand curve for estate planning than a customer who is 75 years old.

The goal of a firm owner is to try to place a customer on the firm's demand curve. This is a difficult process, but it can be achieved. Ample evidence comes from other industries that it is worth the effort to engage in price discrimination and thereby capture a portion of the consumer surplus.

Price discrimination is demand-motivated, not cost-motivated, as Kenna C. Taylor points out in *Puzzles and Paradoxes in Economics*:

> In a single-price market there is a great deal of consumer surplus because the price in the market for all units derives from the value attributed by consumers to the last unit consumed, thus making for consumer surplus on the earlier more

> valuable units consumed. This reflects the fact that the desire for any good or service is subject to the law of diminishing marginal satisfaction, so that the more valuable first units are consumed earlier and less valuable ones are consumed later as the price declines. (Skousen and Taylor, 1997: 57–58)

This is the answer to the famous diamond-water paradox, as pointed out by Adam Smith (1729–1790) in Chapter 4 of Book I of *The Wealth of Nations*: "Nothing is more useful than water: but it will purchase scarce anything. . . . A diamond, on the contrary, has scarce any value in use; but a very great quantity of other goods may frequently be had in exchange for it." (Skousen and Taylor, 1997: 27). Most people believe the answer to this paradox is scarcity—that is, diamonds are far less abundant than water. But that is not the answer. Imagine signing your name on a piece of paper in pink crayon. How much would a stranger be willing to pay for this autograph? Even though it may be the only signature of yours in pink crayon, it is not going to bring a high price. Scarcity does not automatically lend value. So what is the answer to the diamond-water paradox?

Besides being abundant, water tends to be priced based upon the marginal satisfaction of the last quantities consumed. Therefore, while the first several gallons of water may be imperative for your survival, the water used to shower, flush the toilet, and wash the dishes is less valuable. And even less valuable is that quantity used to wash your dog, wash your car, and clean your driveway. The price of water reflects the last uses of the good for the aggregate of all consumers of water. On the other hand, the marginal satisfaction of one more diamond tends to be very high (except, perhaps, for Elizabeth Taylor).

If water companies knew that you were dehydrated in the desert, then they would be able to charge you a higher price for those gallons of water consumed, and then they would gradually adjust the price down the demand curve to coincide with exactly what you were using the water for. However, they don't possess that information, and thus, water is priced in the aggregate based upon its *marginal* value.

Think back to the value curve introduced in Chapter 2. Moving up the curve, the marginal value of the service is higher, and this certainly comports to the evidence in the market. The marginal value of one more audit is lower than the marginal value of a business valuation or of a merger and acquisition engagement. If professionals are to engage in value pricing, they must understand the marginal value of their services from the perspective of customers (and not from their own internal costs).

In a perfect market (from the seller's perspective), consumers would each pay their reservation price for each product or service. The reservation price is defined as the maximum amount a customer would be willing and able to pay for a product or service. This would be the ultimate expression of pure price discrimination. Unfortunately, the market is not perfect from a seller's perspective, and other methods must be devised to ascertain how much different buyers value their offerings, such as popcorn lovers valuing popcorn. Sellers who are successful in constructing price discrimination strategies that induce consumers to reveal their reservation prices will increase their profits.

To achieve price discrimination, four requirements must be met:

1. **The firm must have market power**—Not monopoly power, but a downward-sloping demand curve.
2. **Buyers with different demand elasticities must be separable into submarkets**—Differences arise from income disparities, preferences, locations, etc.
3. **The transaction cost is less than the potential profit**—Costs associated with separating buyers with differential demands must be lower than the differential gain in profit expected from the multiple-price as compared with the one-price strategy.
4. **The seller must separate buyers to avoid arbitrage**—Otherwise, products sold more cheaply in one location can be purchased there and transported to a higher-price location (Skousen and Taylor, 1997: 58–59).

How well do professional service firms meet these conditions?

First, firms must have market power, meaning a downward-sloping demand curve. Even if this requirement is met, the degree of elasticity of demand for professional services is a factor. However, no one would argue with the conclusion that the demand curve was other than downward-sloping.

Number two, separating buyers with different demand elasticities, is easily achievable by attorneys and CPAs, who possess a great deal of information about their customers. They know exactly the motivations of their customers for each purchase of service, how it will be used, and how the customers will benefit by it; therefore, professionals are able to judge marginal value to the customer. Professionals also have the luxury of knowing the financial backgrounds and preferences of their customers, which aids in assessing demand elasticities. This second requirement is certainly easier for professionals to meet than it is, say, for car salesmen or manufacturers of appliances.

The third requirement, that the transaction costs associated with separating the buyers be less than the potential profit from doing so, is also met by the professional service provider. All customers are met with individually, and professionals can easily develop a psychological, as well as financial, profile of them. The marginal cost to the professional of doing this is negligible, and it is far less than the potential profit.

A case in which the third requirement was *not* met was Disneyland's A–E ticket system (E stood for *exciting*), used to price its attractions. From a pure economic perspective, this was the perfect price discrimination strategy, whereby the park charged the highest prices to those guests who simply had to ride the most exciting rides many times. It was similar to theater owners extracting the consumer surplus from the popcorn lovers. Take it from a card-carrying member of American Coaster Enthusiasts (ACE): If amusement parks were to charge admission prices for their top roller coasters, over and above the basic admission price, no doubt they would maximize revenue. ACE members will ride a coaster 30 to 50 times in a row. If each ride cost, say, $3, ACE members may not ride that many times but they would probably still ride more than ten times. However, the problems with the A–E ticket system outweighed the benefits. Disney had to print the tickets, its guests had to wait in long lines to purchase them (thus diminishing the fun and experience of the park), and the Cast Members at each ride had to handle and police the tickets. The costs of engaging in this type of customer segregation exceeded the profits derived from it. In 1982 Disneyland changed to a fixed-price, all-day pass.

Another example in which requirement number three has forced a change is automobile pricing. Saturn's no-haggling price policy, and General Motors' value pricing campaign, are instances where the auto companies have discovered that customers prefer a hassle-free, nonadversarial relationship when purchasing their cars. The old method of the sticker price and the eventual negotiation was a tactic the dealers used because they knew some customers would pay the sticker price (maybe even a markup beyond it) with no questions asked. It was their way of getting at each customer's reservation price. It worked, and it works to this day.

However, Saturn and General Motors believe that the customer satisfaction generated with a no-hassle pricing policy outweighs the benefits of the more discriminatory (but adversarial) method.

The fourth, and final, requirement, avoiding arbitrage, is much easier for service providers to meet than product sellers. If a bakery were to sell pies in two nearby towns, and price them $10 in one town and $5 in the other, eventually customers would buy in the lower price location. Some customers would even buy pies in the lower priced location and transport them back to the higher price location and sell them, thus keeping the consumer surplus for themselves. This is known as arbitrage. But one cannot engage in arbitrage with services. You can't send your butler, who may be charged on a sliding scale based on his income, to get your kidney transplant. And your customer can't sell his audit or tax return to someone else. Services consumed on the spot, such as movie theater popcorn or medical and dental services, are not susceptible to arbitrage.

It should be evident that attorneys and CPAs (and engineering, consulting, and medical companies) have the capability to engage in price discrimination.

Now that we've looked at the requirements necessary to price discriminate, let's examine the three degrees of price discrimination:

1. **First-degree price discrimination**—Charging each customer the most that he would be willing to pay for each item that he buys, thereby transferring all of the consumer surplus to the seller.
2. **Second-degree price discrimination**—Charging the same customer different prices for identical items.
3. **Third-degree price discrimination**—Charging different prices in different markets.

   (Landsburg, 1996: 363–365)

Due to the high transaction cost of determining what each and every buyer is willing to pay, auctions and negotiable price markets are the closest approximations to first-degree price discrimination. Whether it's Princess Diana's dresses or articles from the Kennedy estate, buyers line up and identify the maximum amount they are willing to pay, and thus the item ends up being sold to that individual who *values* it the most. Some of the more famous examples from the Kennedy estate were JFK's golf irons and woods, which sold for $387,500 and $772,500, respectively, to Arnold

Schwarzenegger. A $100 necklace of fake pearls went for $211,500. Even the Lunokhod 2 vehicle, which sits on the moon's surface and can never be brought back to earth, secured a bid of $68,000. (Lacey, 1998: 11, 301)

Auctions make interesting studies in human behavior, because no matter how much you pay for an item, you can console yourself that you only overpaid by one bid. Auctions have been a popular method of selling estates due to today's litigious atmosphere. Because heirs can bring a suit against a trustee for failing to obtain the maximum value for the property in their charge, lawyers tend to consign estates to auction houses, rather than to dealers, to ensure they get the maximum market value for the property.

Other than in auction houses, perfect first-degree price discrimination rarely exists, because more knowledge is required than most producers can ever have. However, this knowledge can be approximated, as is pointed out by Landsburg:

> In the ancient days when people spoke with their computers through the medium of gigantic stacks of "computer cards," IBM required users of its computers to buy all of their cards from IBM. The cards were priced above marginal cost. This strategy was widely misinterpreted as an attempt to extend IBM's monopoly power from the market for computers to the market for cards. However, this explanation makes no sense. If buyers of computers are required to pay more for cards, their willingness to pay for computers is reduced and IBM loses on the computers what it makes on the cards. In actuality, *the card strategy enabled IBM to charge different prices to different customers*. In effect, those who used more cards were charged more for their computers.
>
> IBM's ideal strategy was to require each buyer of a computer to pay the amount that a computer was worth to him. This was well-approximated by charging a higher price to the heavier users. The card strategy accomplished this. (Landsburg, 1996: 365)

Why not have the attitude that what you are doing in your firm is auctioning off a limited number of services, and you want them to go to the highest bidder? Obviously people will not line up and reveal the true value that you are worth to them, but many will reveal more than you may initially believe, a topic included in the discussion of a fixed price agreement in Chapter 10. It is a splendid analogy, and one that is important to your firm's pricing culture.

Second-degree price discrimination exists when businesses charge the same customer different prices for identical items, such as Proctor & Gamble giving Wal-Mart a discount on Pampers for larger quantity orders. Another example is utility companies and cellular phone companies charging different rates for peak and off-peak use. Some CPA firms use this tactic in their hourly rate pricing by having a rate of, say, $225 per hour between February 1 and April 15, and beginning April 16 the rate changes to $175. This effort should be applauded since this is a form of price discrimination and proves that the firm is on the right track. However, the partners can be asked this: "What happens at midnight on April 15 that causes you to lose nearly 30 percent in value to your customers?" Again, this is CPAs being internally focused on *their* work flow and *their* time pressures, with no regard to the external value of what they are providing the customer. In addition, it is not good customer relations to discriminate based upon a government-imposed deadline and to imply that a professional's value is at all contingent upon the time of year he or she performs a service. This notion comes from the law of supply and demand that basically says to raise prices when demand exceeds supply, which can be quite rational in some markets. However, in the professional service firm, who says you have to be at full capacity to demand a premium price? There is a big difference between working harder and working smarter, and the two tend not to be synonymous.

An example of third-degree price discrimination—charging different prices in different markets—is coupons. If Proctor & Gamble can make a profit selling a box of Tide soap with a 50-cents off coupon, what are they making when a customer buys a box without a coupon? Coupons are a way in which manufacturers attract those customers whose demand is more elastic. Not everyone redeems coupons and that is the point, for if everybody did, they would be superfluous. The manufacturer would simply discount the price of the product by the coupon amount and be done with it, saving the costs of printing, distributing, and redeeming the coupons.

Professional firms engage in third-degree price discrimination when they charge lower rates to not-for-profits, for instance, or when lawyers engage in pro bono or sliding-scale work. Also, when firms are entering a new market or industry, they will sometimes reduce their prices simply to climb the learning curve and gain a foothold in that particular area.

While second-degree and third-degree price discrimination are used by professional firms, first-degree discrimination is less common. This is likely because professionals spend far too little time building (and explaining) the value of what they are accomplishing for the customer, and they do not price in accordance with *external value*. Instead, they focus on *internal cost*, using the cost-plus pricing method of standard hourly rates.

In terms of degree, professionals, more than any other business, have the capability of implementing first-degree price discrimination, since they don't inhabit a single-price market, such as water or food. They have the potential to meet with every customer to determine each one's particular demand elasticity. It merely takes asking the right questions and educating the customer about the value of what they do. Professionals inhabit a market that most sellers would die for, with the ability to negotiate each price for each service, at a non-prohibitive cost. The professions need to start taking advantage of this enormous opportunity to achieve first-degree price discrimination.

Make no mistake about it, no two customers are created equal. Consider these astonishing statistics:

- Lexus accounts for 3 percent of unit sales for Toyota, yet contributes approximately 30 percent of Toyota's total profits;
- The top third of credit card holders account for 66 percent of credit card charges;
- Only 21 percent of moviegoers account for 80 percent of the attendance;
- The top third of personal long-distance callers account for 68 percent of long-distance billing;
- Blockbuster Video earns half of its profits from late charges;
- A study of the revenues of 300 movies released over an 18-month period found that four (1.3 percent) accounted for 80 percent of box office receipts and the other 296 movies (98.7 percent) earned 20 percent of box office receipts;
- The top third of diners at family restaurants account for almost 90 percent of the visits;
- The top third of shoppers account for 80 percent of the grocery spending in any particular supermarket;
- 5 percent of households buy 85 percent of Levi's blue jeans;

- 3 percent of households buy 82 percent of L'eggs pantyhose; and
- 60 percent of Delta Air Lines' profits comes from 6 percent of its customers.

Not only do economists understand the consumer surplus, so do marketers. They spend an inordinate amount of time "building fences" around these high value customers, trying to segregate them from the rest of the pack and extract the consumer surplus from them in very creative ways. As the above statistics prove, the profits of mass-market brands do not come from the mass market. The majority of the profits in your firm do not come from the majority of your customers, but, more likely, the top 5 percent generate 50 percent of your profit, or the top 20 percent generate 80 percent of your profit.

Professionals understand this, just as they understand that 5 percent of their customers account for more than 50 percent of their headaches or their liability risk. If that is the case, the Pareto Principle is at work in your firm. Named after the Italian economist and sociologist Vilfredo Pareto (1848–1923), the Pareto Principle is this: *In any phenomenon, only a few of the contributors account for the bulk of the effect.* He was referring to the distribution of income. If this rule applies to your firm, then why do all of your customers get charged the same standard rate regardless of the work you are performing for them? As Don Peppers and Martha Rogers point out in their book *The One to One Enterprise*:

> The truth is, it's actually *more fair* to treat different customers differently. A customer who invests more in your firm is certainly owed a greater level of service and attention, and by treating customers individually the enterprise can usually raise the general level of service for nearly *all* customers.
>
> Customers don't *want* to be treated equally. They want to be treated *individually* … Any company that treats a customer the same as "everybody" is treating that customer like nobody. (Peppers and Rogers, 1997: 127, 133, 321)

The mistake made by most firms is treating each customer like an "average customer." In reality, there's no such thing as an *average* customer. There are only *individual* customers, and therefore you should set an appropriate, customized price for each of them.

Here are examples of price discrimination in various industries. Notice the creativity, ingenuity, and thought that has gone into these practices, and compare this to the level of thought you have given to pricing in your firm. You may never look at pricing the same way again.

Hardcover vs. Paperback Books

John Grisham and Tom Clancy novels are priced at nearly $30 in hardback, and around $10 in paperback. Would you be shocked to discover that the production cost to the publisher is approximately the same for both books? What the publisher is doing is having those fans of Grisham or Clancy who simply cannot wait for the paperback version, due out in six to twelve months, identify themselves and buy the hardcover. The publisher extracts the additional $20 of consumer surplus from them. The fact that serious book lovers prefer hardcover books to paperbacks (they last longer, look more impressive in one's library) is simply icing on the cake, and merely adds to the perceived value of the hardcover. The real goal is *charging different prices to different customers* based upon their individual demand elasticities.

Bookstore owners (or, if you have customers who own bookstores) take note. There is a lesson here, and Amazon.com has already learned it. Owners should inform their best customers when certain books are due to be published, those written by the customer's favorite author, and perhaps ship the books to them automatically upon arrival (in hardcover, of course).

Senior Discounts

The one demographic group in the United States least in need of discounts is seniors. As a group, they are the wealthiest people in society. They have worked all their lives, have had longer to save, and thus have more to show for their accumulated efforts. So why do businesses offer these wealthy individuals discounts? Seniors have one thing on their hands that a lot of other consumers lack: time. They tend to seek out establishments that offer them discounts, even if they must arrive at certain times or clip coupons. If a restaurant can make a profit serving a senior citizen a prime rib dinner at $7.95, what are they making off a customer who will pay $12.95? Restaurants engage in the same practice with "early bird" dinners and by charging much higher prices on the dinner menu than on the lunch menu for the same food.

Children's Prices

At the fair, Disneyland, and the movies, and on trains, planes, and buses, kids take up one seat, yet they are charged a lower price than an adult. This is done to prevent discouraging parents from bringing their families, and because of the fact that children have a more elastic demand curve than their parents. But from a cost standpoint, is it any cheaper for the airline to fly a child?

Kodak Film at Disneyland

Part of the opportunity of visiting Disneyland is taking pictures, and if you're unlucky enough to run out of film, you will pay a premium to get some inside the park. This is Kodak's way of charging the heavy users of film—and thus those customers who place a higher value on pictures—a premium, and extracting the consumer surplus from the photo bugs. (Note the "Kodak Picture Spots" throughout the park.)

Nightclubs

Arrive early and admission is free and happy hour drink prices are less—tactics used by the owner to attract crowds early so that by nighttime it is a happening place, when the owner will be able to extract a cover price from the nightclub crowd. The concept of a cover charge is discussed later in the chapters on the fixed price agreement. An economist calls it a two-part tariff—that is, charging a customer a price in exchange for the right to purchase more of your product.

Newspapers

This one is obvious: Newsstand purchasers pay more for their newspapers than subscribers, who pay a cheaper, subsidized rate, covered by the advertisers. The cheaper subscription rate helps boost circulation, thereby increasing the advertising rates that can be charged. *Different customers, different prices.*

General Motors

Many cars from the five divisions of GM—Chevrolet, Pontiac, Buick, Cadillac, and GMC—are produced in the same plant, with little variance in cost (albeit some in material). Yet when those cars arrive at the showroom, the sticker price of a Cadillac is far higher than that of a Buick, and no doubt higher, as a percentage, than the variance in the cost of production. This is GM's way of having a car for each location on the demand curve, the theory being you'll be loyal to GM from your first car (a Chevy) to your last (a Cadillac). A car for "every purpose and purse," as Alfred Sloan used to say.

Intel 386 and Other High-Technology Products

The 386 was introduced in two versions: with and without a math coprocessor. Both contained the math coprocessor, but the less expensive chip merely disabled the coprocessor. What was the cost difference? Whenever a new generation computer, printer, or chip is put on the market, the manufacturers know that a certain segment of the population—known as early adopters—will rush to buy the latest and greatest. These individuals are price-insensitive when it comes to technology. Thus, the product is put on the market and a high price is set, allowing the technology mandarins to identify themselves, and shortly thereafter, the price makes its way down the demand curve until everyone else can afford it. This happens with computers, and it happened with car phones, CDs, laser discs, VCRs, DVDs, and camcorders. The early adopters transfer the consumer surplus to the manufacturer.

Trade-In Discounts

Hewlett-Packard and Canon sometimes offer trade-in allowances for your old printer if you purchase a new one. Jewelers do the same with watches. They will discard the item as soon as they get it. Why do they do this? Because if you already own what they are trying to sell you, chances are good that your demand curve is more elastic than someone who doesn't own the product. Thus, people who already have printers are charged less than those who do not.

Cosmetics

My brother, Ken Baker, was formerly in marketing for a large cosmetics firm. He spent most of his time trying to price products just right for each particular market. He demonstrated to me a particular example of price discrimination.

He sent me down to a drugstore to buy L'Oréal eye shadow. For $5 I got four colors and one brush (no compact, no mirror), a net weight of 0.17 oz. of eye shadow. My brother then instructed me to go to Macy's and buy Lancôme eye shadow. This eye shadow comes in an attractive gold leaf box, has a compact with a mirror, and has two brushes. It has only three colors, with a net weight of 0.15 oz. The price was $35.

I called my brother back, perturbed about being out $40 for eye shadow that I have no use for, and asked him what the point was. He told me to check the ingredients on the back of each box. They were identical. The only difference, according to my brother, is less than $1 in chemicals and about $3.50 in packaging; the contents are 95 percent the same. I protested that my team member who uses Lancôme says it lasts longer, doesn't smear. She swears it's a better product. My brother replied, "Of course she does; how do you think we get the extra $30 out of her purse?"

The two eye shadows are made in the same vat, with virtually the same ingredients, and at almost identical cost. Yet one sells for $5 and the other for $35. It's the four "Ps" of marketing coming together creatively to segregate the customers and extract the consumer surplus. The first P, product, is segregated into two different quality markets, the low-price drugstore line and the upscale department store line. Marginal quality improvements to Lancôme and different color pallets are combined to enhance the perceived quality. The second P, place, is how the manufacturer, Cosmair, is able to segregate the two different buyers, the one in drugstore distribution and the other in fine department stores such as Macy's and Nordstrom—excellent distribution segmentation. The third P, promotion, is actually quite curious because L'Oréal does most of the advertising and has many expensive models who represent the product line. Lancôme, on the other hand, has very limited advertising (mostly print, hardly ever television) and has only one official spokesmodel to represent the entire line.

Based on true cost-plus pricing, perhaps CPAs would price Lancôme at $10 (because of the compact and the mirror and one extra brush). Perhaps some would suggest $15. Few would be bold enough to price it at a $30 differential.

Airlines: Leaders in the Art of Price Discrimination

Once the airlines were placed into open competition by the Airline Deregulation Act of 1978, pricing decisions were no longer set by government fiat. Southwest Airlines perfected a two-tier pricing system—peak and off-peak—that basically applied the economics of price elasticity to passenger flight, and charged passengers based upon their price sensitivity to a given fare. Other airlines soon followed, and the pricing of tickets became very sophisticated, not to mention complicated, as the United States airline industry changes its prices 12 million times a day.

A fascinating book by Robert G. Cross, *Revenue Management*, candidly reveals the secrets of airline pricing. Cross, a lawyer, accepted a position in the legal department of Delta Air Lines at the time of airline deregulation. In the mid 1980s, he found himself in the marketing division in a "free-formed position designed to identify problems and new opportunities on the marketing side."

He explains that airline performance is measured by two basic standards:

1. Yield—the amount of money the airline gets per passenger mile
2. Load—the percentage of seats filled by paying passengers

Cross estimated that if Delta were simply discounting one seat unnecessarily on every flight, it would cost the company *$52 million in annual revenue*. Delta operates approximately 1,500 daily flights for a total of 86 million seats on an annual basis. Here is the dilemma Cross faced in looking into Delta's pricing policies:

> Some flights that had been loaded with discount seats sold out well in advance of the departure. But on these flights, Delta would also turn away significant last-minute, full-fare traffic. This added up to a lot of lost revenue. Also, on numerous occasions we had severely limited discount fares and ended up

> sending flights out with empty seats that could have been filled with discount passengers . . . . I estimated that Delta was leaving as much as 200 million dollars a year on the table, just from misallocating discount seat availability on its flights. This number was so mind-boggling, I didn't dare tell anyone. No one would have believed it!
>
> In one year's time, Delta realized an incremental revenue gain of *$300 million* solely from the new seat inventory control process. This 300 million dollars accounted for half the 600 million dollar turnaround Delta reported in fiscal 1984. (Cross, 1997: 42, 45)

Have you ever noticed that you can sit next to someone on an airplane who paid five times more than what you did? Does it cost the airline any more (or less) to fly that passenger than to fly you? Does it cost the airline four to eight times more to fly a first-class passenger? Oh, sure, they give you edible food, Starbucks coffee, miniature drinks, and a Mrs. Fields cookie, but could that possibly justify the price differential between first class and coach fare? One passenger made the observation that he recently had flown to Europe first-class, and all of the passengers were reading hardcover books. Coincidence?

How do the airlines identify the business traveler and the leisure traveler? They do it by determining when you are booking your ticket—the closer you get to the flight, the less price-sensitive you are because you need to go, no matter what—and if you are laying over Saturday night. If you are not, statistically, you are a businessperson and chances are you are not paying for your ticket anyway (remember Category III from Chapter 4, spending someone else's money on yourself), and thus you will be charged a premium. This is precisely how Delta derives 60 percent of its profits from 6 percent of its (business) passengers.

The lessons here are many, but perhaps the biggest one is the declining importance of the demographics and psychographics of your customers, at least in terms of pricing. In the 1960s, marketing managers paid a lot of attention to segregating their customers based on demographics—income, race, neighborhood, gender, and so forth. This is well and good for narrowing target markets. Then in the early 1970s, an article was published asking if you would treat Tricia Nixon Cox the same as Grace Slick (former lead singer with Jefferson Starship). Demographically, these two ladies (at the time) were indistinguishable—both were 25 to 34 years old, family size of three, urban residents, and college educated. Psychographics opened up a whole new way of thinking about consumer behavior, and many firms started to pay attention to it.

Demographics and psychographics play an important role in pricing professional services. Think of the former as shedding light on the customer's *ability* to pay, and the latter as indicating the customer's *willingness* to pay. But pricing is more complicated than that. For instance, a customer who is buying a ticket for a business trip may not be at all price-sensitive about airfare. He may wait until close to the trip to call for fares and put very little effort into trying to find a bargain rate. But when this customer flies on vacation, he will stay up until 3:00 a.m. trying to get one of the $99 special rates on Southwest Airlines. Demographically and psychographically, the customer is the same person, but his approach to buying tickets is not consistent.

The final lesson with respect to the examples presented and how they relate to pricing your firm's professional services is this: *Price on the margin.*

The margin is what happens next. Everyone lives on the margin. Life itself is a marginal adventure. It really doesn't much matter what you did yesterday, what counts is what you do next (i.e., on the margin). When you price on the margin, what you charged in the past for the same service to another customer, or even, perhaps what you charged in the past to this customer, does not matter. *Measure that customer's demand elasticity at that time, for that particular service, one service at a time, every time.* Don't let the past guide your marginal pricing decisions, and don't let your cost influence your price (except as a minimum). If you begin to price in this manner, you will be surprised how many opportunities arise for you to climb up the value curve, even with a so-called commodity service.

How Much Money Is Your Firm Leaving on the Table?

You can think of your firm as an airplane—you have first-class customers, business-fare customers, and coach customers. How do you identify them? If you cannot identify what your customers are willing and able to pay for a given service (and hourly billing will not help you), you are leaving between **20 and 50 percent** of your *gross* revenue on the table, if not more.

Several years ago, I received a referral from an attorney who was working on the estate of one of his deceased customers. The decedent hadn't filed his last three years' income tax returns. To get duplicate 1099s and other records meant tracking down the third parties. I proceeded to file the returns, get the penalties waived, etc. The time came for the U.S. Income Tax Return for Estates and Trusts (Form 1041) to be filed (no Form 706 was required because the estate was less than $600,000). I was not going to be in town very much over the following two months because I would be away teaching seminars and consulting. A CPA friend referred me to someone who would do this work for me. I sent her the information and a letter asking her to get back to me with a fixed price.

A week later she called and said she got the material, and the return would be no problem to prepare. She also said she had received a flyer listing the three courses I would be teaching, and she thought the value pricing course looked interesting. She quoted her fixed price for the job as $500 (the tax return was relatively simple and no longer than a four-hour project). When she said this, I knew I had just made $1,500, because I charged my customer $2,000 for the return. Had she asked more questions, she would have quickly discovered that I was not very price-sensitive. In fact, she possessed the one piece of information that should have tipped her off: My schedule of classes for the next several months (18 in all).

Had she priced on the margin, rather than simply multiplying her rate times hours, she would have asked herself why I came to her in the first place (either I do not have the expertise or the time to do the work). Second, she knew that I made my money filing the prior three years' tax returns, and this return was more of a nuisance to me than anything. Third, she could have asked what I was willing to pay, which was up to $2,000.

This sad story is an example of how CPAs underprice their services. In my seminars, I pick one person, give him or her the facts as outlined above (including the flyer showing all the dates I would be away from my office), and send that person out of the room with instructions to return in five minutes, ask me anything, and quote me a price. While the CPA is out of the room, I bet the class that he or she won't even consider the fact that I'm out of the office so many days, and that the CPA won't quote me a price higher than $1,000. I have yet to lose. The participants come back and ask questions such as: "When does this need to be completed?" "Who is signing the return?" "Will you refer them other work?" When the participants are asked what was learned from the flyer, the response is usually, "Nothing, except that you teach three courses." Other savvy businesspeople would consider other factors, but CPAs are so focused on hours spent, rather than on value delivered, that they miss many opportunities to capture the consumer surplus.

The Use of Knowledge in Society

Friedrich A. von Hayek, a Nobel Prize winner and perhaps one of the best economists of the twentieth century, addressed the American Economic Association in 1945 on the occasion of his retirement as its president. The title of his address was "The Use of Knowledge in Society," wherein he called attention to the important social role of prices as carriers of information and contrasted this knowledge with so-called scientific knowledge. In this address he articulated the theoretical justification for price discrimination, whereby firms can take advantage of "special knowledge of circumstances of the fleeting moment not known" to their competitors:

> Today it is almost heresy to suggest that scientific knowledge is not the sum of all knowledge. But a little reflection will show that there is beyond question a body of very important but unorganized knowledge which cannot possibly be called scientific in the sense of knowledge of general rules: the knowledge of the particular circumstances of time and place. It is with respect to this that practically every individual has some advantage over all others in that he possesses unique information of which beneficial use might be made, but of which use can be made only if the decisions depending on it are left to him or are made with his active cooperation. To know of and put to use a machine not fully employed, or somebody's skill which could be better utilized, or to be aware of a surplus stock which can be drawn upon during an interruption of supplies, is socially quite as useful as the knowledge of better alternative techniques. And the shipper who earns his living from using otherwise empty or half-filled journeys of tramp-steamers, or the estate agent whose whole knowledge is almost exclusively one of temporary opportunities, or the *arbitrageur* who gains from local differences of commodity prices, are all performing eminently useful functions based on special knowledge of circumstances of the fleeting moment not known to others.

> It is a curious fact that this sort of knowledge should today be generally regarded with a kind of contempt, and that anyone who by such knowledge gains an advantage over somebody better equipped with theoretical or technical knowledge is thought to have acted almost disreputably. To gain an advantage from better knowledge of facilities of communication or transport is sometimes regarded as almost dishonest, although it is quite as important that society make use of the best opportunities in this respect as in using the latest scientific discoveries. (von Hayek, 1945: 521–22)

This observation has far-reaching implications for the pricing policies of for-profit entities. What von Hayek is basically saying is that it is perfectly normal—and beneficial—for firms to take into account special circumstances in order to provide the most value, and hence receive the highest price, in the delivery of its services.

A lot of the knowledge that exists in the economy today is so-called tacit knowledge—that is, knowledge that is specific to time, place, and circumstance. Travelers in unfamiliar cities will befriend a local in order to discover good restaurants, sightseeing locations, etc. Think of the advantage a golfer has who played on the course many times and is said to have "local knowledge."

Summary and Conclusions

The economic way of explaining human behavior has many lessons to teach the willing student. The fact that management gurus, consultants, and members of the professions ignore economics as some sort of ivory tower babbling is negligence at best, malpractice at worst. There is simply no better profession to look to for explaining how and why prices are set the way they are, and that is the reason for this theoretical exploration of the world through the economist's paradigm.

Now that you possess the paradigm of the economist, observe how the consumer surplus is being captured by using price discrimination. Once you start looking for the many creative ways in which other businesses engage in price discrimination, you soon discover it is a ubiquitous practice.

How do professional firms use this theory? How do they identify and segregate different customers to obtain a portion of the consumer surplus? What pricing methods help them achieve this goal? The short answer is that professionals have not paid conscious attention to these theories, and their pricing method—hourly billing—offers absolutely no guidance in capturing the consumer surplus. After all, when a customer buys a product or service at a price less then he or she is willing to pay, and thereby keeps the consumer surplus for themselves, this makes the customer *happy*. On the other hand, when a seller sells a product or service for a price over and above the minimum price the seller was willing to accept—called *economic rent* by economists—this is what makes people *rich*. An understanding of the genesis of hourly billing, discussed in the next chapter, will help you to understand how professionals were led to price in this manner.

6 THE GENESIS OF HOURLY BILLING

Custom is the whole of equity for the sole reason that it is accepted. That is the mystical basis of its authority. Whoever tries to trace this authority back to its origin, destroys it.

—Blaise Pascal, *Pensées*

You can tell a lot about a culture by the way it views time. Anthropologist Edward Hall labeled rules of social time the "silent language." The pace of our lives determines our views about the passage of time. J. T. Fraser, the founder of the International Society for the Study of Time summed it up well: "Tell me what to think of time, and I shall know what to think of you." (Levine, 1997: XV, XIX)

Robert Levine points out in his fascinating book, *A Geography of Time*, that before the first mechanical clocks had been invented, the idea of coordinating people's activities was almost impossible. Appointments usually took place at dawn. "It is no coincidence that, historically, so many important events occurred at sunrise—duels, battles, meetings." (Levine, 1997: 60)

The first known mechanical timepieces appeared in Europe in the fourteenth century. These clocks had a specific purpose: "to inform pious monks when it was time to pray." (Levine, 1997: 56) Throughout history, clocks have come progressively closer to the person. We have progressed from the public clocks of the Middle Ages to clocks inside the home to pocket watches to those attached to our bodies. The wristwatch appeared around 1850 (referred to by some as "the handcuff of our time"). In fact, some would argue that it is the clock, not the steam engine, that is the key machine of the industrial age. Active economies all over the world place great emphasis on time, and economics certainly drives the pace and tempo of modern life:

> As proof of this, it was the railroads that exerted pressure to coordinate time zones because as late as the 1860s, the United States alone had approximately 70 different time zones. In 1883, the railroads established the four time zones used in the

> country today. In 1918, the federal government codified these time zones into law. It's also interesting to note that IBM initially sold time clocks in order to "save money, enforce discipline and add to the productive time." (Levine, 1997: 68)

The Labor Theory of Value

Ideas have consequences. As John Maynard Keynes wrote in the final passage of his *General Theory*:

> The ideas of economists and political philosophers, both when they are right and when they are wrong, are more powerful than is commonly understood. Indeed, the world is ruled by little else. Practical men, who believe themselves to be quite exempt from any intellectual influences, are usually the slaves of some defunct economist. Madmen in authority, who hear voices in the air, are distilling their frenzy from some academic scribbler of a few years back. . . . Soon or late, it is ideas, not vested interests, which are dangerous for good or evil. (Buchholz, 1989: 219)

1998 was the 150th anniversary of an idea that changed the history of civilization and has affected the lives of billions of people. For over a century, it was the leading intellectual paradigm on several continents and commanded an enormous amount of influence on the destiny of nations.

The Communist Manifesto, the famous revolutionary treatise published in 1848 by Karl Marx and Friedrich Engels, still wields considerable power over the world's political systems and even over the professional's pricing strategies.

Marx is far from dead. Even though Marxist ideology and Marx's theory have been thoroughly repudiated by empirical evidence, his ideas are so deeply ingrained into our value paradigm that we don't even notice them, let alone analyze their validity. In the nineteenth century, Marx posited a definition of value that has been subsequently called the "labor theory of value." In its simplest form it says that the price of an item is determined by the amount of labor used in its production. This theory is so deeply ingrained that it is essential to explore it somewhat at length, in order to prove its speciousness. Here is how Marx explained his labor theory of value in *Value, Price and Profit*, first published in 1865:

> A commodity has a *value*, because it is a *crystallization of social labour*. The *greatness* of its value, or its *relative* value, depends upon the greater or less amount of that social substance contained in it; that is to say, on the relative mass of labour necessary for its production. The *relative values of commodities* are, therefore, determined by the *respective quantities or amounts of labour, worked up, realized, fixed in them*. The *correlative* quantities of commodities which can be produced in the *same time of labour* are *equal*. (Marx, 1995: 31)

This sounds reasonable, and in fact this misconception deceived many great economists, such as Adam Smith and David Ricardo. It is not uncommon throughout history to measure the value of a product or service as a function of labor time. The word *acre* in medieval English meant the amount of land that could be ploughed in one day.

The problem with the labor theory of value is that it does not comport with human behavior. It fails to explain how land or raw materials have value, since they contain no labor input. The Army, for instance, can order soldiers to dig trenches and refill them, day after day, which is precisely why there is no such thing as unemployment in the Army (or in former Marxist countries, for that matter). But certainly, in the private marketplace, there must be a demand for a good (or service) in order for it to possess any value whatsoever.

Taken to its extreme, the labor theory of value would mean that countries that work longer and harder should have higher standards of living. This is demonstrably false, since China should have the highest standard of living—given its large amount of labor hours available. In fact, what we see throughout the world is that countries with less labor input and more entrepreneurship have vastly higher standards of living, including shorter hours for workers.

If the labor theory of value was correct, a diamond found in a mine would be of no greater value than a rock found right next to it, since each took an equal amount of "billable hours" to locate. Yet how many rocks do you see in your local mall's jewelry store display cases?

Look around your office. Do you have any pictures of your spouse, family, or friends? Under the labor theory of value, someone should, theoretically, be able to replace each one of those pictures with a picture of a perfect stranger. The value of the strangers' pictures should be the same as your original pictures, because the new pictures most likely took the same amount of "billable hours" to produce.

When you go to lunch today, perhaps you'll have pizza. Under the labor theory of value, you must necessarily value the fifteenth slice just as much as you valued the first, since each took the same amount of "billable hours" to produce. The labor theory of value doesn't take into account the well-established law of diminishing marginal utility, which states that the value to the customer declines with additional consumption of the good in question.

Marx tried to circumvent these dilemmas by proclaiming that only "socially necessary labor" creates value:

> It might seem that if the value of a commodity is determined by the *quantity of labour bestowed upon its production*, the lazier a man, or the clumsier a man, the more valuable his commodity, because the greater the time of labour required for finishing the commodity. This, however, would be a sad mistake. You will recollect that I used the word "social labour," and many points are involved in this qualification of "social." In saying that the value of a commodity is determined by the *quantity of labour* worked up or crystallized in it, we mean *the quantity of labour necessary* for its production in a given state of society, under certain social average conditions of production, with a given social average intensity, and average skill of the labour employed.
>
> If then the quantity of socially necessary labour realized in commodities regulates their exchangeable values, every increase in the quantity of labour wanted for the production of a commodity must augment its value, as every diminution must lower it. (Marx, 1995: 33–34)

How does one determine what is "socially necessary labor"? That is where the consumer enters the theory, and in a competitive market it is ultimately the consumer who determines value—bringing Marx right back to the values of the free market that he so vehemently abhorred. Marx derived his definition of value from the assumption that there must be an equality in two goods that are exchanged—namely, labor hours. But the nature of exchange is the exact opposite—it is based on an inequality in the subjective value of the good received and the good exchanged. In order for any transaction to take place, both the buyer and the seller must profit from the exchange, and receive more value—in their perception—than what they are giving up. Were this not so, we could simply exchange five-dollar bills with each other and achieve a Marxian Utopia.

Marx claimed that the number of hours of "socially necessary working time" that goes into the production of a commodity determines its comparative value in the marketplace, and any profit that goes to an employer above his payroll is in effect stolen from his "exploited" workers. One is left to the conclusion that the true Marxian exploitation is the exploitation of people's misunderstanding of economics. Perhaps this is why President Ronald Reagan made this statement on September 25, 1987: "How do you tell a Communist? Well, it's someone who reads Marx and Lenin. And how do you tell an anti-Communist? It's someone who understands Marx and Lenin."

For the historical record, it should be pointed out that although Karl Marx spent his entire life writing about finance and industry, he never set foot in a mill, factory, mine, or any other workplace, and he knew only two people connected with financial and industrial matters. His uncle in Holland, Lion Philips, was one of these individuals, who created what eventually became Philips Electric Company. Marx was also a profligate spender and an irresponsible debtor, rarely paying back what he borrowed and getting angry when the creditor asked for payment. He never seriously attempted to get a job, thinking his family should support his important work. This attitude caused his mother to cut him off completely, wishing that "Karl would accumulate capital instead of just writing about it" (Johnson, 1990: 60, 74).

In all fairness, it must be stated that even Adam Smith posited his own false theory of value, and it too has held sway over a large majority of businesspeople. Smith's "cost of production" theory basically said that all of the costs of production—including depreciation of equipment, interest, and Marx's dreaded profit—determined the value of a commodity in the marketplace. The flaw in this theory is that "costs of production" are also prices and reflect their own calculus of value. This cost-plus pricing mentality can lead to serious errors in value pricing goods and services because it ignores the external value to the customer.

One can find this error in the writing of accountants after World War I. One of the twentieth century's most influential accounting theorists was William Paton, who in a 1922 treatise described what he thought was the cost accountant's chief activity:

> The essential basis for the work of the cost accountant—without it, there could be no costing—is the postulate that the value of any commodity, service, or condition, utilized in production, *passes over into* the object or product for which the original item was expended and *attaches to* the result, giving it its value (quoted in Johnson and Kaplan, 1991: 135–36).

This "cost attach" idea was later repudiated by Paton in a speech he gave at a conference in 1970:

> The basic difficulty with the idea that cost dollars, as incurred, attach like barnacles to the physical flow of materials and stream of operating activity is that it is at odds with the actual process of valuation in a free competitive market. The customer does not buy a handful of classified and traced cost dollars; he buys a product, at prevailing market price. And the market price may be either above or below any calculated cost figure. (Johnson and Kaplan, 1991: 139)

This statement is a profound recognition of the correct theory of value articulated in the late 1800s and early 1900s. Mr. Marx, Mr. Smith, Mr. Paton, and the entire cost accounting profession, meet the Austrian school of economics.

The Correct Theory of Value

The alternative to an incorrect theory is not to do away with the theory and simply rely on "common sense." The alternative to an *incorrect* theory is a *correct* theory. All learning starts with theory. The alternative to the labor theory of value is the theory that value is subjective—goods and services have no inherent value but are valuable only to the extent that there is a valuer desiring them.

The subjective theory of value was well understood by both the Spanish Scholastics and the French laissez-faire school of economic thought. The theory was widely advanced, and became accepted as the way the world works, by the Austrian school of economics, in the tradition of Eugene von Bohm-Bawerk, Carl Menger, Ludwig von Mises, and Friedrich A. von Hayek.

Ever since Ben Franklin wrote, "Time is money," professionals have taken this statement literally, believing that time is value. However, effort—that is, hours spent—emphatically does not equate with value. Results are what counts to the customer. Value is in the eye of the beholder, not the labor time of the seller. There is no doubt that time is a nonrenewable, precious resource. But even resources are useless until a purpose is found for them that people will value. Oil, for example, was worthless until the invention of the combustion engine.

Why the Professions Adopted Hourly Billing

Why did the professions adopt pricing based upon the hour? What is the historical context in which the practice arose? Old habits die hard, but understanding how the habit started in the first place is imperative before it can be replaced with a better practice. Replacement is easier if the original circumstances for adopting the habit no longer exist.

In a sense, Karl Marx is the father of the billable hour. His labor theory of value certainly caused a stir among economists. Earlier, Adam Smith, with his "cost of production" theory, may have had a better grasp on the reality of the marketplace, since he recognized the importance of entrepreneurship and profits. In terms of incorporating these theories into the actual operations of an enterprise, the railroads, textile manufacturers, and merchandising companies—headed by the likes of Andrew Carnegie, Pierre du Pont, Donaldson Brown, Alfred Sloan, and other engineers of the scientific management movement—were the leaders in developing cost accounting.

Prior to World War I, the Du Pont Powder Company was using nearly all of the management accounting principles for operating a company known today: cost accounting for labor, material, and overhead; cash, income, and capital budgets; and flexible budgets, sales forecasts, standard costs, variance analysis, transfer prices, and operating division performance measures. Perhaps the most important contribution Du Pont made to management accounting theory was the invention of the return on investment (ROI) measure. In their enlightening book on the rise and fall of management accounting, *Relevance Lost*, H. Thomas Johnson and Robert S. Kaplan provide the history of the ROI measure:

> The idea for the Du Pont return on investment formula originated, as far as we know, with F. Donaldson Brown, a college-trained electrical engineer and one-time electrical equipment salesman who joined the Powder Company's sales department in 1909 and became assistant treasurer of the company in 1914. None of Brown's surviving records indicates how he hit upon the idea for his return on investment formula. Interestingly, Brown had no formal training or experience in accounting.
>
> His experience in selling no doubt gave him an appreciation for the effect of turnover and distribution costs on a company's profits. Evidently, his mathematical, engineering, and marketing skills gave Brown a unique perspective on the determinants of company performance that was not understood by most contemporary accountants. Brown's idea about financial planning and control had a profound impact on the Du Pont organization and later on General Motors. Yet his ideas did not become widely known among professional accountants until the 1950s, when a new generation of management accounting textbooks introduced them into the standard MBA curriculum. (Johnson and Kaplan, 1991: 86–87)

The importance of the ROI cannot be overestimated; it certainly had a profound effect upon the manufacturing world, but it also had a major impact on professional services firms. The engineers, and later cost accountants, who worked in the manufacturing sector, started to migrate into the services firms and carried with them certain cost accounting principles. If the labor theory of value is the father of the billable hour, the ROI is its cousin. Deriving a particular return on investment from all the costs of operating a practice shows exactly how much per hour must be charged by everyone within the firm. This led to the keeping of timesheets within law firms.

Hourly billing is a practice that dates back to the 1940s, when large Wall Street law firms adopted timesheets. The practice was advocated by business school graduates who entered the professions conversant in cost-accounting techniques used by the railroads, textile, chemical, and auto industries.

The most comprehensive history of the billable hour is William G. Ross's *The Honest Hour: The Ethics of Time-Based Billing by Attorneys*. Here is what Ross says with respect to the antecedents of time-based billing:

> During the 1950s and early 1960s, various studies indicated that attorney compensation was failing to keep pace with inflation and was lagging behind that of other professionals, particularly physicians. Starting as early as the 1940s, management experts concluded from various studies that lawyers who kept time records earned more than attorneys who did not. Management experts advised lawyers to raise their compensation by selecting a target annual salary and dividing that figure by the number of hours that they could bill to a client during a year and factoring in overhead costs in order to arrive at an hourly billing rate.
>
> Although many commentators have suggested that time-based billing dates from the 1960s, it was actually being used by many attorneys during the previous decade. While even so large a firm as New York's Shearman and Sterling did not keep time records until 1945, timekeeping had become much more common by the 1950s than is now usually supposed.
>
> Between the 1950s and the middle 1970s, management experts extolled the benefits of timekeeping and exhorted law firms to institute time-based billing. As one commentator exclaimed in 1960, "lawyers who *do* keep personal time records have a *net* income which is almost equal to the *gross* income of lawyers who *do not* keep time records. Need more be said!" (Ross, 1996: 16–17)

Indeed, what better motivation existed than the opportunity to make more money with the hourly billing method?

Prior to billing by the hour, attorneys (and CPAs) charged fixed rates for everything they did. According to Ross:

> During the late 1930s and 1940s, more and more state and local bar associations adopted fee schedules because they

> provided a more objective means for attorneys to justify their fees to clients. Left to their own devices, many attorneys were uncertain about how to charge clients or were embarrassed to charge for minor work or to request a reasonable compensation for their services. Fee schedules gave lawyers the courage to charge higher fees. . . . By the 1950s, fee schedules existed in virtually every state.
>
> Fee schedules were not obligatory, since bar associations recognized that mandatory fees might run afoul of the antitrust laws and that such fees would fail to take account of the special expertise of individual attorneys. (Ibid., 14–15)

With fixed fees, billing was an *art*—not the administrative task hourly billing ultimately turned it into. The professional always asked, "What results have we achieved?" and "What is the value to the customer?" That is a much more daunting task than merely multiplying hours spent by an arbitrary rate and cranking out a bill. During the 1950s and 1960s, when the management experts were extolling the virtues of hourly billing, studies put out by the American Bar Association also documented other discoveries besides the one that lawyers who tracked their time made more than those who didn't that seemed to lend even more support to hourly billing. For example, the studies claimed that customers valued *efforts* over *results*. What better way to document every minute of effort than the timesheet?

In fact, this effort vs. results debate continues to this day. One of the primary reasons that lawyers bill for every single fax, copy, phone call, and quarter hour is to convince the customer of all the effort expended on his behalf. In his book *How to Draft Bills Clients Rush to Pay*, J. Harris Morgan advocates that lawyers follow this practice, and he cites a 1960 Prentice-Hall Missouri Motivational Study: ". . . 47 percent of the respondents listed effort as the most important single element in setting a fee and creating a bill." Morgan added: "The clients said that effort is the most important element in a lawyer's bill! No subsequent research has disproved this conclusion." (Morgan, 1995: 2) There is no better illustration of the power of the entrenched labor theory of value than this statement. Customers emphatically do not buy *efforts,* they buy *results.* Despite Mr. Morgan's assertion to the contrary, there is plenty of empirical evidence to support this conclusion.

Hourly billing also converted major overhead costs into "profit centers" allowing firms to leverage their capital and human investments. For instance, paralegal salaries, fax machines, word processing, and copies could all be charged out at a multiple of their cost, adding to the firm's bottom line. This was one reason beginning salaries for Ivy League law school graduates increased so much in the late 1980s, up to around $80,000. The firms could simply pass the cost through to the customer in terms of marking up the hourly rate of the new associate, usually by a factor of three to five times their cost.

Another factor that accelerated the adoption of hourly billing by the professions was the computer. It became very easy to input timesheets and have the computer crunch out the invoice, freeing up the professional's time to bill even more hours.

The final nail in the coffin of fixed-fee pricing was the Supreme Court's decision in 1975 that the fee schedules published by the ABA and local courts violated the Sherman Antitrust Act, in *Goldfarb v. Virginia State Bar*, 421 U.S. 773 (1975), *rehearing denied*, 423 U.S. 886 (1975). But by then, both the legal and the accounting professions billed predominantly by the hour.

What buried the coffin was the *Bates* decision, as explained in *Win-Win Billing Strategies: Alternatives That Satisfy Your Clients and You*, the second book published by the ABA Section of Law Practice Management:

> Until the late 1970s, most lawyers gave little thought to the pricing of their services. This lack of concern stemmed in part from the prosperity that many lawyers enjoyed and the lack of competition.
>
> To understand why the concept of pricing is new and sometimes difficult for lawyers to understand, it is helpful to review the nature of the legal profession before the landmark United States Supreme Court decision in *Bates & O'Steen v. State Bar of Arizona*, 433 U.S. 350 (1977), which enabled lawyers to market legal services. [In the past], the fees lawyers charged their clients were determined by minimum-fee schedules authorized by state and local bar associations and some courts. Because marketing was restricted before the *Bates* decision, most clients were unaware of the scope, availability, and cost of legal services. (Reed, 1992: 31)

The Customer's Role in the Adoption of Hourly Billing

What was the customer's role in the shift from fixed-fee to hourly billing? Did customers ask for hourly billing or was it imposed on them because the professions enjoyed a seller's market? The opinions on this point vary.

Ross quotes Professor Herbert M. Kritzer of the University of Wisconsin Law School, who contends:

> The current form of hourly billing was not "foisted off onto an unsuspecting business community by a bunch of sharp-eyed lawyers" but rather "probably results largely from the accounting culture, produced by elite business schools, that came to dominate the senior management circles of the American corporations." Kritzer explains that "as the offices of corporate general counsel became professionalized (in a business sense, not a legal sense), there was a need to apply business principles to their operation, including the purchase of outside services. Hours and rates could be easily measured and compared, and general counsel began to demand that their outside law firms provide detailed bills with this information." (Ross, 1996: 21)

Perhaps since all lawyers started to bill by the hour, the customer began to use hours as a basis for comparing one firm to another, and historical revisionists assume that the customer demanded it be done this way. Another plausible explanation for the shift to hourly billing is that customers were complaining about the high price of legal services, under the minimum fee schedules and prior to the 1975 Supreme Court decision ruling them unconstitutional, and embraced hourly billing as a consumer-protection measure, thinking they would be better off. The flaw in this argument is that hourly billing started in the 1950s, well before the Supreme Court ruling.

Is Hourly Billing a Cost-Accounting Tool?

What was ignored by all of the attorneys was that tracking one's time was originally intended to be a *cost-accounting* tool, not a *pricing* method.

Timekeeping was viewed as a guideline that would allow a firm to measure the *profitability* of an engagement, not as the means of *pricing* that engagement. The timesheet was originally developed to control the "inventory" of the professional, but since hourly billing became endemic, it *became* the inventory. The focus changed from how much value a professional added to how many hours were spent. It was the ultimate quantification of Abraham Lincoln's utterance: "Time is an attorney's stock in trade." Mary Ann Altman, a lawyer and principal in the consulting firm of Altman & Weil, discusses this in *Beyond the Billable Hour: An Anthology of Alternative Billing Methods*, published by the ABA, Section of Economics of Law Practice (one of three seminal books published by the ABA on the death of the billable hour):

> Because I was involved personally in the introduction of time records to the legal profession approximately thirty years ago, I can attest to the fact that one of the reasons that time records were instituted originally was to determine the cost of providing legal services. At that time, lawyers had, for many decades, produced bills to clients that were based on the value of the services rather than on the time involved, although time certainly was a mental factor in determining value. Once time records became available to lawyers, lawyers quickly began to use these time records as billing, rather than as a cost-accounting tool. It was much easier to ask the bookkeeping department to multiply the time record by a dollar factor and prepare a bill than it was for the lawyer to exercise judgment in a determination of the value of the case. (Reed, 1989: 11)

When professionals today are asked to consider eliminating timesheets from their firms, most of them protest that they wouldn't know whether or not they were making money on any one engagement. This is a valid point, but not as valid as you may, at first, think. The problem with the current "standard rates" is that the "desired net income" is loaded on top of the overhead amount, then divided by expected billable hours. That is not *cost accounting*, but *profit forecasting*, and it is an especially egregious error for CPAs who, for all their fastidiousness when it comes to GAAP and attesting to financial statements, should know better. The hourly rate is really nothing more than the adaptation of Du Pont's ROI formula from the early 1900s and Karl Marx's labor theory of value from the 1800s.

Summary and Conclusions

In the years since hourly billing was adopted, the Berlin Wall has fallen, the Soviet Union has imploded, China has embraced free markets and taken back Hong Kong, and the personal computer and the Internet have changed the world. Amidst all of this tumultuous change, CPAs (and to a lesser extent, attorneys) still price by the hour.

The market has changed. Customers are demanding fixed prices, set up front, from their attorneys and accountants. The inside legal counsel in a number of American corporations will no longer accept hourly billing from their outside attorneys. Ford Motor Company, for example, demands fixed price agreements with all of their outside counsel. Wal-Mart is at 60 percent and is moving toward 100 percent as well. As Jay D. Logel, In-House Counsel for Ford Motor Company, said at an ABA seminar titled *Alternative Billing: The Sequel*, "Billable hours don't win lawsuits." That basically sums up the attitude of today's customer with respect to the Almighty Hour and it is the reason that the method, among the largest firms in the legal profession, for all practical purposes, is already dead. And just as CPAs followed attorneys into the method, lagging by about ten years, it is their destiny to follow the attorneys right back out of it. In the final analysis, time is not money and customers do not buy hours. Pricing by the hour is causing professional service firms to focus on the wrong things, with deleterious consequences—the subject of our next chapter.

7 THE DELETERIOUS EFFECTS OF HOURLY BILLING

Custom doth make dotards of us all.

—Thomas Carlyle, *Sartor Resartus, III,* 1836

A foolish consistency is the hobgoblin of little minds.

—Ralph Waldo Emerson

The preceding chapter explored the fallacy of Karl Marx's labor theory of value and how it fails to explain human behavior in the real world. The reader is justified in asking the following questions: If people are supposedly rational—the assumption of rationality as discussed in Chapter 5 is the bedrock assumption of economists—why is it that intelligent members of various professions have continued to apply the wrong theory to the value of their services? Doesn't this disprove the economist's assumption of rationality? If Marxism is an incorrect theory at the macroeconomic level, what are the ramifications of implementing this incorrect theory at the microeconomic level—that is, in the professional service firm?

The fact that hourly billing is so deeply entrenched and has been widely used for decades proves that it has some advantages. This is a case of cognitive dissonance—two completely contradictory ideas exist at the same time in one's mind. The only way to eradicate this paradox is to prove that hourly billing is a rational policy. Therefore, before showing that the disadvantages exceed the advantages, this chapter explores what is right about hourly billing and why it is a rational pricing policy for the professional.

The Advantages of Hourly Billing

Hourly Billing Is a Relatively Easy and Efficient Pricing Method

Hourly billing is easy and efficient and can be handled simply with an appropriate software program that prepares bills, generates reports, and calculates work-in-progress and realization rates, all with minimal partner and manager time. Administrative personnel are usually responsible for this task, and that allows the professional team member to take care of what is more important—customer relations. This was one of the major reasons firms began using the method, especially once the computer was introduced. What is proposed in this book—customized pricing—is more complex and requires more thought, creativity, and interaction with the customer. More attention is paid to value created rather than to hours spent, and this attention must come from those who have the relationship with the customer—the professional team member, not the administrative team member.

Richard C. Reed, in *Billing Innovations*, discusses what may become a new career in the law firm: "the position of estimator, a specialist who will have expertise in cost accounting and in determining the price to be charged." (Reed, 1996: 140) This would be, however, a grave mistake. The person best equipped to set a price is the one who is in charge of the relationship. From the customer's perspective, an estimator has no perceived value. However, customers see enormous value in the relationship with their attorney or CPA. Nevertheless, it makes sense for larger firms to establish pricing cartels, a topic we will explore in Chapter 21.

Sometimes the Customer Demands Hourly Billing

No doubt, some customers demand to be billed by the hour, or at the least demand to know how many hours a given task will take the firm, especially alumni of accounting and law firms who now work in private industry. It is also true that sometimes a customer just wants to buy your time (perhaps to ask a multitude of questions), and the only benchmark of value in that instance is the time spent. This is not the type of customer you want to do business with, because the customer really has no idea of the value you are providing.

Hourly Billing Documents Effort in Case of Litigation

In a lawsuit, the attorneys are undoubtedly going to want to see time reports to support the tasks performed, and if you believe this is a serious concern, then by all means document the hours for the file. However, this does *not* preclude your firm from pricing its services on an alternative basis, and as long as you have an explicit agreement with the customer (preferably in writing) of the price being charged and the services being performed, then the only place hours might be logged is in the file.

Further, one could produce the three seminal books published by the ABA that encourage attorneys to use alternative pricing methods (a.k.a. value pricing or value billing) in a court of law to justify why hours were not the criteria for pricing. If firms were run under the constant assumption that they were going to be sued, they would not get anything accomplished. Slowly, but surely, the rules of the game are changing, and hours are becoming superfluous in the pricing of professional services. Eventually value pricing will be common practice in the professions, and the threat of litigation as justification for tracking every minute will wane.

Hourly Billing Is a Cost-Accounting Tool

This is probably the single biggest advantage of hourly billing. People wonder, "If you did not keep time reports, how would you know if you are making money on a particular job? How would you measure the productivity of your staff?" These are valid questions that go right to the heart of why lawyers began tracking time back in the 1950s—to measure *efficiency* and *profitability*. However, as mentioned earlier, what started as a method to control and measure the inventory (i.e., the professional's time) *became* the inventory. The other problem with the cost accounting defense is that hourly billing isn't really about cost accounting, but rather *profit forecasting*, as it includes the "desired net income" of the owners of the firm in the cost-plus formula. Other businesses, except for regulated utilities and government-owned operations such as Amtrak and the post office, do not use the cost-plus formula to set their prices. Examine your manufacturing customer's books, and ask the CEO or CFO how costs are allocated, or how they price their products. It is probably not based solely on cost-plus accounting.

Does this mean the elimination of timesheets from your firm? Yes. I have worked with firms anywhere in size from five to 30 who do not keep timesheets at all. The partners couldn't tell you how many hours they billed, nor could the team members, nor does anyone care. These firms are the models to emulate since they are making more money by pricing smarter than firms with timesheets.

However, the cause and effect should not be confused. It is not true that if you eliminate your timesheets you will become more profitable. In fact, the causation runs in the opposite direction. These firms eliminated their timesheets *because* they became profitable as a result of value pricing. When partners in these firms are asked how they know if they are making money, they all respond with the same answer, "We look at our income statement." Managing from the income statement by looking at cost of labor as a percentage of gross revenue is a different mind-set from poring over hourly time reports.

I have also worked with firms that retain their time and billing program, but they have converted it into a true *cost-accounting system*, rather than a *pricing* method. The attorneys who began tracking their time made more money in net income than those who didn't, but they were using the tracking solely for cost-accounting purposes, *not* as a pricing method.

This topic is discussed in more detail in the section later in this chapter on the deleterious effects of hourly billing and in Chapters 20 through 22.

Hourly Billing Transfers Risk to the Customer

This advantage is truly a double-edged sword, for while the professional prefers that the risk be with the customer, which is what happens with hourly billing, the customer prefers the exact opposite. For the professional, however, this advantage is the answer to the question of why hourly billing is rational.

With hourly billing, generally the customer must bear the entire risk of the job going over budget, or of unforeseen circumstances arising. This comforts CPAs, because at least they are assured of receiving the "standard rate." CPAs have paid a reverse risk premium to the customer, the customer assumes the risk, and CPAs will only ask for their hourly rate; no more, usually less.

This is quite rational, if you are adverse to risk, and many professionals are. It puts a nice, comfortable floor beneath professionals, because a decent net income is inserted into the cost-plus formula. But in exchange for the comfort of this floor, professionals have created an artificial ceiling, and they cannot seem to rise above it. This is demonstrated by the fact that average realization rates in CPA firms across the country are between 70 and 95 percent of the standard rate.

Another example of removal of risk is the practice of labor unions. Talk with union members, and you quickly discover that they credit the union for their standard of living. Certainly, they are paid an above-market wage (Milton Friedman, again, has proved this point) and receive good benefits, a healthy pension, and generous time off. But have you ever met a wealthy rank-and-file union member? The trade-off they made for their union compensation package is an artificial ceiling that they can never rise above, at least not while employed in a union job. Seniority and other restrictions limit their potential.

Profits come from *risk*. No risk, no reward. Indeed, the word "entrepreneur" comes from the French word *entreprendre*, which means "to undertake" and also forms the basis of the English word "enterprise." The French economist—and father of supply-side economics—J.-B. Say invented the word to mean "venture capitalist" or "adventurer." The entrepreneur is society's perennial risk taker. Bill Gates, Larry Ellison, and other members of *Forbes* 400 did not become wealthy by charging hourly rates. Some entrepreneurs win, some lose, but any profits are the result of giving to others, filling their needs first. A professional puts his fate into the hands of others—customers—and provides them with a service that is so good they willingly pay a profit in recognition of what is being done for them.

A business organization that doesn't take risks is doomed to mediocrity, and perhaps extinction. When risk is transferred to customers, they will implicitly limit the professionals' rewards, for that is how a free market works. The bigger the risk, the greater the potential reward (and potential failure). By adopting value pricing, you assume more risk. However, it's an intelligent and calculated risk, and one that is worth assuming because the gains exceed the losses. In fact, the risk is quite small compared with the rewards. As Peter Drucker pointed out:

> A business always saws off the limb on which it sits; it makes existing risks riskier or creates new ones ... Risk is of the

> essence, and risk making and risk taking constitute the basic function of enterprise ... This risk is something quite different from risk in the statistician's probability; it is risk of the unique event, the irreversible qualitative breaking of the pattern. (Quoted in Kehrer, 1989: 53)

Drucker is expressing the basic economic theory known as Boehm–Bawerk's Law, which states, "Existing means of production can yield greater economic performance only through greater uncertainty; through taking greater risks." (Kehrer, 1989: 298) Businesses, and CPAs in particular, have very sophisticated means of measuring the costs and benefits of risks, *once they have been taken*. But the risk occurs only *before* the event, and cannot be accurately measured until *after* it has occurred. There is no theory—either in economics or finance—that measures the costs of *not* taking a risk. Yet, it is precisely these losses that cost the business the most.

Risk and uncertainty are the twin banes of human existence. Consider what people will sacrifice to avoid them. Risk avoidance has created a $1.5 trillion worldwide insurance industry. Risk is the reason rental car companies make more from the "collision damage waiver" insurance they sell than from renting cars and why buyers of appliances (e.g., microwaves and stereos) will spend large sums on extended warranties for products that could be replaced more cheaply. Risk causes criminals and prosecutors to plea bargain, each being uncertain about what a jury is going to do. It even explains why some Americans will eat at McDonald's in France—they are fearful of making a bad choice on a local restaurant, and thus settle for the certainty of a known brand.

Economists estimate that risk and uncertainty cost Americans roughly $575 billion each year. Such costs estimate the amount of money people would give up in order to reduce the following uncertainties: Macroeconomic fluctuations (recessions); job insecurity; retirement uncertainty; and fear of future supply-demand shifts. Economists distinguish between uncertainty and risk in the following manner: An economic decision is "risky" if you can assign a numerical probability to each possible outcome (e.g., 50 percent chance that a coin will come up heads). By contrast, a decision has "uncertain" consequences when you do not know enough even to assign probabilities to the different outcomes. (Mandel, 1996: 147)

By linking your fate to your customer's, and sharing in the risk, you will also avail yourself of the opportunity to share in the rewards. That is what free enterprise is all about. As Walter Wriston, former CEO of Citibank, makes clear in his book *Risk and Other Four-Letter Words*:

> It is almost impossible to exaggerate the importance to the general welfare of the willingness of individuals to take a personal risk. The worst thing that can happen to a society, as to an individual, is to become terrified of uncertainty. Uncertainty is an invitation to innovate, to create; uncertainty is the blank page in the author's typewriter, the granite block before a sculptor, the capital in the hands of an investor, or the problem challenging the inventive mind of a scientist or an engineer. In short, uncertainty is the opportunity to make the world a better place. (Wriston, 1987: 230)

The more professionals understand about risk taking, and the better they become at risk analysis, the more it can be minimized. In his exhaustive study of risk, *Against the Gods: The Remarkable Story of Risk*, Peter L. Bernstein explains why risk management plays a vital role in a society's progress:

> The ability to define what may happen in the future and to choose among alternatives lies at the heart of contemporary societies. Risk management guides us over a vast range of decision-making, from allocating wealth to safeguarding public health, from waging war to planning a family, from paying insurance premiums to wearing a seatbelt, from planting corn to marketing corn flakes.
>
> Without a command of probability theory and other instruments of risk management, engineers could never have designed the great bridges that span our widest rivers, homes would still be heated by fireplaces or parlor stoves, electric power utilities would not exist, polio would still be maiming children, no airplanes would fly, and space travel would be just a dream. (Bernstein, 1996: 2)

Professionals should take greater risks in pursuit of gain. Though hourly billing carries the advantage of placing the risk with the customer, that advantage is really small in comparison with the potential profit made possible when a professional shoulders more of the risk and prices based on value.

This Book Summed Up in Two Words

One day I entered my office and found my partner agitated. He had just finished a telephone conversation with a customer he had been auditing for several months. He had a fixed price agreement with this customer, including the audit, but the customer's books were not in the best of shape, adjustments were mounting, and the prepared by customer (PBC) schedules were not tying to the general ledger, all contributing to the audit taking longer than he originally estimated.

He called one of the owners to discuss the situation and was trying to extract a few extra thousand dollars for the cost overruns. He explained to the customer that he had already spent the hours, and the customer replied, "**Hours schmours**." This did not make my partner happy.

The customer was right not to equate hours spent with value. The firm had given him a fixed price and should stick to it. The fact that my partner underestimated the job is really not any of the customer's concern. The moral of the story, and the reason it sums up this book, is that when you and your customer see things differently, *you change*. (Better ways of dealing with cost overruns are discussed in Chapter 11.) A professional who clings to hourly billing and ignores the psychology of it from the customer's perspective may cause irreparable injury to the health of a firm.

The Disadvantages of Hourly Billing

Here, in no particular order, is a list of the deleterious effects of hourly billing for you to consider.

Hourly Billing Misaligns the Interests of Professional and Customer

Even ardent supporters of hourly billing, such as William G. Ross, will admit that there exists, right from the start, a conflict between the professional's interest and the customer's. In *The Honest Hour*, Ross writes:

> The first step toward more ethical billing practices is for both attorneys and clients to frankly admit the harsh truth that hourly billing creates an inherent conflict of interest between the client's needs for expeditious work and the attorney's

> desire to bill time. Only by recognizing that this tension tends to create abuses can attorneys begin to cultivate ethical standards for billing. (Ross, 1996: 6)

When you make hours important, then the customer is bound to focus on hours. Those professionals caught "padding" timesheets because they believe the value of what they did exceeded the price measured in hours will lose the respect of their customers.

This conflict of interest also exists because in a cost-plus pricing system one way to increase a firm's revenue is to increase its costs. This explains the willingness of law firms to raise beginning associate's salaries in the late 1980s. The cost was passed right through to the customer. Hospitals and defense contractors used to have this perverse incentive as well. The market has changed. Cost-plus pricing is rarely used by hospitals, building contractors, and defense contractors (except for Strategic Defense Initiative work). In fact, cost-plus pricing is really thriving in only three industries: regulated utilities, government-owned operations (Amtrak and the post office), and professional service firms. Probably no one will benchmark the post office to learn world-class customer service. The professions need to turn away from using the same pricing method as the post office and associate with more practical and forward-looking industries.

In an age of corporate downsizing, reengineering, and businesses (and government) trying to do *more with less*, cost-plus pricing is the antithesis of efficiency. Customers are beginning to recognize this, which explains why the *Fortune* 500 companies, such as Ford Motor Company and Wal-Mart, will not even discuss "billable hours" with their outside counsel, as they no longer want to be the sole risk bearer, but they want their law firms to participate in their uncertainty. The whole objective of the total quality service movement is to become partners with your customers and to link your fate to theirs. This goal is difficult enough to achieve without the added burden of an inherent conflict of interest in how you price your services.

Hourly Billing Focuses on Hours, Not Value

Today's sophisticated customers understand the subjective theory of value; they do not automatically correlate value with billable hours. Remember when online services were priced according to the amount of time the customer was connected to the system? Is it any wonder customers devised methods to get the information in the least time possible? Pricing by the time they were connected had no value to the customer because what they were really purchasing—and hence what they valued—was the information. This would be the equivalent of shoppers trying to minimize the amount of time shopping for a product or trying to maximize the number of products they purchase within a given period of time, neither of which would affect the value of the purchases.

Whenever professionals have to justify price to a customer, they inevitably resort to discussing hours spent. Marketers would never do this, as they always try to create value in the minds of the customer first, and talk price last. By having a billing rate that is anywhere from four to ten times what customers make per hour, you are putting them in a psychological frame of mind to focus on how long it will take you.

Imagine learning from a doctor that you have a condition that is difficult to diagnose, possibly a rare disease, and saying, "Well, doctor, please don't think about my case *too* long and don't consult with your colleagues, since I want to keep the billable hours down."

Richard C. Reed points out in *Billing Innovations:* "If you are buying an automobile, do you really care how much time it took to install the hood of the car?" (Reed, 1996: 103)

If the customers focus on hours, they are constantly trying to calculate whether or not they can afford what you are doing for them and they ignore the value you are providing. The multidimensional value that professionals provide is turned into a one-dimensional, commoditized billing rate. You have to wonder how much of what is referred to as customers being price-resistant is actually the customers simply doubting the value they are asked to pay for, because the professionals have not discussed this aspect of their service.

A few years back, a customer leased me a car as part of my compensation. He reasoned that he wasn't hiring me for my ability to do his tax return, but for my brain power and perspective on his business. He said, "Whose business will you think about every time you get into that car?" He was right—I thought about his problems and opportunities everywhere I drove.

Ultimately, in a free market economy, "all prices and quantities are determined by just two things: the technology available to firms and the tastes of individuals." (Landsburg, 1996: 549) If that is the case, then professionals need to educate the customer regarding the value they provide, including factors such as the resources of their firm, the experience and judgment of their team members, the risk they are assuming, and the convenience they are providing.

Hourly Billing Places the Risk on the Customer

As discussed earlier in this chapter, if you offer your customers fixed prices you will be able to charge a premium because you are reducing their risk. If this sounds counterintuitive, look at the mortgage market. Which commands a higher interest rate, a fixed rate or an adjustable rate mortgage? Surveys conducted by the American Bar Association Section of Litigation's Committee on Corporate Counsel "indicate that most clients are willing to pay a premium in exchange for a predictable fee." (Reed, 1996: 89)

Hourly Billing Fosters a Production Mentality, Not an Entrepreneurial Spirit

Over the years, the professions have lost sight of the all-important question: What did you accomplish? It has been replaced with: How many hours did you bill? Firms have rewarded production, measured in hours, and have been slow to recognize customer service, retention, loyalty, and other yardsticks of long-term profitability. As Ross states in *The Honest Hour*:

> Although associate compensation has increased tenfold during the past thirty years, the billing rates of associates have increased only about fourfold. Since law firm profitability has generally increased rather than fallen, law firms have paid for the higher salaries by increasing billable hours rather than charging higher rates. (Ross, 1996: 2)

Hourly billing has the pernicious effect of de-emphasizing marketing, especially at the lower levels of the firm, because the professional doesn't want to forgo billable hours, since most compensation plans are based on them. Over time, the professional becomes production oriented, becoming adept at solving problems but lethargic at pursuing opportunities. This is a costly mediocrity, as the professional is simply living off existing skills and not taking any risks in order to become more valuable to customers. Again, Ross sums up this attitude:

> During my nine years of practice in law firms in New York City, I rarely heard a fellow lawyer boast of resolving a problem, settling a dispute, or developing an elegant legal theory. Instead, I found that all too many attorneys seemed to evaluate their accomplishments solely in terms of the sheer number of hours that they had billed. (Ross, 1996: 3)

Developing an entrepreneurial culture is the responsibility of the firm's leadership, as team members do not automatically become outstanding producers simply because they get promoted to the partnership. On the contrary, an entrepreneurial attitude has to be developed in associates from day one, rather than just training for technical competence. As Allan S. Boress points out in his book *Building Entrepreneurial People*:

> Although most colleges today claim to be producing more well-rounded accounting school graduates, I have yet to meet a single person who has taken a course in a School of Accountancy on managing and improving client relationships, managing a CPA firm, or building a practice. This largely one-sided, technically oriented education has prepared accounting graduates for entry-level positions at most CPA firms, but has not prepared them for the real world. It is up to accounting firms to shift new graduates away from total concentration on technical competence. (Boress, 1995: 4)

The Almighty Hour is nothing but a hindrance to cultivating this environment.

Hourly Billing Creates a Subsidy System

If all customers are charged the same hourly rate, it is a safe bet that some will be overcharged and others will be undercharged in order to meet hourly quotas. This is true for individual professionals and thus must be true for firms as a whole.

An example of this effect is a tax research project that is billed to one customer for, say, $5,000. If a different customer then has the exact same issue, how much would be billed? Attorneys are still trying to resolve the question. Is a firm justified in charging the second customer $5,000, even if the time spent was only 20 percent of what was billed to the first customer?

If the hours logged were equal to the first customer's billing, one could certainly argue that the first customer underwrote the R&D costs, and the majority of the second customer's bill was pure profit to the firm. If the second customer was charged less than the first, perhaps due to ethical considerations, or a feeling of guilt, then certainly the first customer subsidized the second.

These are the kinds of issues that arise in any pricing method, as good customers will always, to some extent, subsidize poorer (or, more accurately, less valuable) ones. But the subsidy is especially pronounced with hourly billing because it is an internal cost method. If all customers were charged what they perceived as the value of the service, an argument could be made that no one customer is being subsidized. This is not one of hourly billing's more severe consequences, but it certainly has generated its share of ethical arguments within the legal profession.

Hourly Billing Transmits No Useful Information

One of the most useless pieces of information is everybody's billable hours. It transmits little information of value, except perhaps to separate the "finders" (rainmakers), the "minders" (managers), and the "grinders" (technicians). Far more significance is found in a person's customer service attitude, customer retention (and defection) rates, customer loyalty, profitability and collection, ingenuity, imagination, experience, productivity, effectiveness, ability to delegate, mentoring skills, risk taking, and practice development activities—in short, all the virtues necessary to build a successful practice. Billable hours, in and of themselves, shed no light in any of these areas. Consider this scenario:

> Assuming two lawyers within the same firm with identical year-end statistics, how often do firms then go on to measure the relative profitability of those two fee producers? One lawyer's practice may have required a high level of staff sup-

> port, high-level advance of costs, and delayed collection of fees. The other lawyer, with the same total statistics, may have had substantially lower cost of production and hence greater profitability. For the most part, law firms using hourly billing tended to charge an established hourly rate (or possibly more than one rate) pretty much across the board without regard to differences in cost of production of certain services, including benefits conferred or the exposure to malpractice risks. (Reed, 1996: 137)

This is a valid point, and proves that hourly billing rates are not truly a cost-accounting tool. If an outside consultant can enter a firm and make an assessment of its performance without considering billable hours, then the question becomes, What kinds of decisions are being made internally by collecting hourly information? In other words, if it is not the right question to ask from an outside perspective, why is it so important on the inside?

Is it possible that internal measurements are being assembled simply because that's the way it has always been done? Most of the decisions that are made in a professional firm regarding personnel, hiring, firing, productivity, and raises are based on information that is discovered long before it is seen on an hourly billing report. How many major, profit-enhancing decisions have you made as a result of hourly information? It is considered sacrosanct simply because it is so closely correlated to how professionals price their services. If you begin to price based upon external value, you will soon discover that hours are superfluous. You may come to agree that counting hours is, as Fra Luca Pacioli said in his treatise on double-entry accounting, *De minimis no curat Praetor,* "one of the little items that doesn't contribute knowledge of the business to its owner." (Pacioli, 1494: 47)

Hourly Billing Encourages Hoarding of Hours

Due to compensation, bonuses, and performance reviews being based on billable hours, professionals have a tendency to hoard work to fulfill their hourly quotas. This results in low-level work being performed by high-level associates, which is terribly inefficient. Just as surgeons should not pierce ears, managers and partners should not spend their time on compliance work that could be more efficiently completed by lower-level associates. Effective delegation not only provides lower- level associates with the experience and on-the-job training they require, it frees the upper echelon of the firm to focus on offering value-added consulting services, thus moving up the value curve.

Hoarding hours also lessens the advantages of a diversified firm by not delegating the work to the person(s) who can most efficaciously complete it. This results in a constant reinventing of the wheel, instead of using systems and procedures based on work that has been done before. One of the goals of every firm is to increase productivity and effectiveness. Hoarding hours is the antithesis of this.

Another negative effect of hoarding hours deals with write-offs. Who decides when time should be written off? And whose time is usually discounted? Partners and managers usually decide that write-offs are due to team member inefficiency, and concomitantly compensation and bonuses are reduced, lowering the morale of the associates.

Hourly Billing Focuses on Effort, Not Results

Who buys efforts in the marketplace? One brilliant epiphany that occurs while driving may be worth more to the customer than 1,000 plodding, inefficient hours spent researching and pondering an issue. You may come up with an idea that saves a customer thousands of dollars, and yet you spend only one hour developing the solution. What do you do when it comes to completing the timesheet? Hourly billing simply doesn't reward creativity and ingenuity. On the contrary, it rewards inexperience, inefficiency, and even incompetence.

This is precisely why professionals pad their timesheets. Not only is it the perfect crime, it is the logical and rational course to take if you believe that what you did is worth more than the time you spent. By focusing on the hourly rate, you are forced into a Hobson's choice: Either be honest and undervalue your services, or lie on your timesheet to collect your just compensation. Is it any wonder that many professionals choose the latter option?

In his book *Start Consulting*, William L. Reeb made some interesting observations with respect to tracking time. Reeb's book is all about consulting, the new growth area for the accounting profession, and one would expect new ideas and approaches in marketing and pricing that type of service. Unfortunately, the Almighty Hour is firmly embedded in his thinking. Notwithstanding the fact that he discusses pricing—one of the essentials of marketing—in a section of the book that deals with administrative and organizational issues, here is what he has to say regarding tracking time:

> Accounting for hours and minutes has to be the most tedious and boring task associated with our profession. . . . So making an effort to record *all of your time* is essential if you want consulting to be profitable.
>
> Consulting is different. Because the client is usually very comfortable with the objectives and implementation plan of most management projects, he or she is more likely to scrutinize the manner in which the time was spent. By providing an itemized bill, you give your client an easy way to review your efforts and progress.
>
> When there is price sensitivity, an itemized bill gives the client an opportunity to satisfy his or her concerns by reviewing the detailed time. Detailed billing is especially helpful in the worst-case scenario, in which the client challenges the value of some specific portion of your work. It's advantageous because, at this point, instead of arguing about the overall fee, you are now only discussing a few line items on the bill. This helps resolve issues expeditiously and, if concessions are made, they are based on smaller numbers.
>
> Immediately after our "we bill for our time" explanation, we would likely continue with, "Would you like for us to remove that line item from the bill?" (Reeb, 1998: 285–287)

This approach leads to all of the deleterious effects listed in this chapter. It is as if the professional is setting herself up for write-downs right from the start, and she is trying to convince the customer that efforts and value are equated. Rather than taking on these issues at the beginning of the engagement and discussing value, the professional should simply capitulate when the customer expresses "price sensitivity" (or is it value-doubting?) and write down the price. The profession makes the same mistake over and over, and professionals wonder why they are not even receiving the "standard rate." This issue is discussed in more detail in Chapter 8.

Professionals have done a poor job at ascertaining exactly what it is that its customers are buying. While customers are focusing on the results provided (not to mention service, that is, *how* professionals provide those results), professionals are counting hours. Other businesses don't make this fatal mistake when it comes to their customers and their pricing.

After the Gulf War, when the oil wells in Kuwait were on fire, the pundits agreed that it would take at least six months, if not longer, to extinguish the fires. Red Adair (and others) went over to the Middle East and performed the job in about three months. Do you think Red Adair charged by the hour? What would have been the result if he had?

If efforts—and thus, hours—were the sole determinant of value, then perhaps CPA firms should scrap their computers and complete tax returns with manual typewriters and carbon paper. This would certainly require more effort, but who in his right mind would pay for it?

This is not such an obsolete and Luddite attitude. In *A History of Accountancy in the United States*, Gary John Previts and Barbara Dubis Merino point out the following:

> Accounting reports rendered during this period [the 1880s] were prepared and submitted in longhand, since the popular acceptance of the typewriter did not occur until the mid-1890s. One of the requisite skills of the accountant was to have "an accomplished hand" in penmanship and a modicum of patience: when multiple copies were required they had to be produced in the same tedious and exacting longhand.
>
> Some accountants, then as now, were skeptical as to the advantages of new office technologies, such as the typewriter when it first appeared. "Why should I pay $125 for a machine when I can buy a pen for two cents?" some asked. (Previts and Merino, 1998: 134)

Only two things determine prices in today's market: preferences and technologies. A customer will be reluctant to pay for anything that doesn't utilize the latest technologies. Even a handmade Rolls Royce is subject to this reality.

David Friedman humorously (but profoundly) illustrates the point in *Hidden Order: The Economics of Everyday Life*:

> When I was very young, I used to amuse myself by shooting stalks of grass with a BB gun. That is an expensive way of mowing the lawn, even at a nine-year-old's wage. I think it

> unlikely that anyone would pay a correspondingly high price to have his lawn mowed in that fashion. (Friedman, 1996: 23)

Many professionals object that if you do not focus on efforts, corners may be cut in quality to meet the fixed price of the service and not lose money. However, due to the perverse incentives inherent in hourly billing, many argue that corners should be cut. Second, quality is a table stake—the minimum you need to play the game. Cut corners on quality long enough, and you will not survive in a free marketplace. What customer is going to stay with an incompetent professional?

By focusing (and pricing) on efforts, professionals are fulfilling the prophetic vision of C. Northcote Parkinson, who developed Parkinson's Law: Work expands so as to fill the time available for its completion. Any professional who has performed work according to a predetermined budget can attest to this law and that it is not a prescription for success.

Hourly Billing Penalizes Technological Advances

This is perhaps the most egregious effect of the hourly billing method. Every year, professional firms make substantial investments in technology (computer hardware, software, printers, broadband, etc.) that allow any given task to be performed in less time. Technology investments are being made, yet professional firm revenue would then decline under hourly pricing. How can this be? Economists refer to this as the *productivity paradox*.

When businesses invest in technology, usually the result is higher profits—either due to increased internal efficiencies (thus lowering costs) or by price reductions to the customer resulting in increased sales (as in the high-tech industry). You do not need to reduce the price of your services when you invest in technology, although that is certainly a strategy if your firm is on the lower end of the value curve. Firms should reap some of the cost savings that result from investments in technology. Does a doctor's revenue *decrease* after the purchase of an MRI machine? Hardly. That is because the price for using that machine is determined by its value to the patient, not by the time it takes (or saves) the doctor in diagnosing the medical problem.

Under hourly billing, however, revenues drop as a result of technological advances. Professionals who use hourly billing have a tendency to reinvent the wheel rather than develop systems, procedures, and methods to perform routine tasks. They have little incentive to implement more efficient methods to complete work, because by doing so they would forgo billable hours. The exception, perhaps, to the productivity paradox is professionals who are trying to meet billable hour quotas.

Hourly Rates Are Set by Reverse Competition

Hourly rates are often set by *reverse competition*. This means that you look at the rates of your fellow professionals operating in your geographical market, make a decision on where you want to fit in on the competitive spectrum, and set your rates accordingly. Unfortunately, most pick a rate that is somewhere in the middle. What kind of message does this send to your customers? "We are not the most expensive, but we are not the cheapest either; we are right in the middle." In other words, you have chosen to compete with everybody.

It is little wonder some professionals think of themselves as commodities—they act like it. Professionals should not let competitors dictate price. Me-too pricing leads to serious pricing errors for any one customer in your firm. Professionals are not *price takers*. Professionals need to learn the art of becoming *price makers*.

Be honest. Did you set your hourly billing rate by crunching the numbers? You know, the rate equals overhead plus desired profit divided by expected billable hours. Only 10 percent of the CPAs I've asked admitted they did it in this manner. The rest confessed that they never performed any numerical analysis. This is an astonishing confession from a profession of proverbial number crunchers. Ardent defenders of the hourly billing method claim that it is an excellent cost-accounting tool. Yet, the majority concede that they have not even run the numbers.

This makes the notion of a "standard" hourly rate a pure fiction. Professionals have varied hourly rates since they've been adopted, charging a lower hourly rate for more volume or charging different rates for different types of work. Since professionals haven't taken the rate seriously, neither have their customers. Pricing policies need to be more sophisticated than this, based upon an assessment of value to the customer rather than on conjured-up standard rates set by competitors.

Pricing policy needs to be reevaluated continuously; it is not simply a one-time event whereby you set an hourly rate and increase it every few years by an inflation factor. When a professional changes jobs from one firm to another, why is it possible for his or her hourly rate to increase anywhere from $25 to $100 per hour? Has the professional become more valuable merely by changing work locations? Worse yet, the hourly rate selected at the launching of your firm is not necessarily the right one once you become adequately profitable. After you are comfortable that you can meet your overhead and payroll and provide yourself with an adequate living, your prices should be adjusted upward. Low prices at the beginning of a business may make sense in order to attract customers, though this is doubtful, but that same policy could prevent you from succeeding in the long term. As business conditions change and as you enter new markets, offer new services, become more proficient, develop larger networks, and gain more experience, your pricing policies need to be changed. This is an ongoing process, as any marketing person will tell you. Yet professionals sometimes set a rate and stick to it for years, paying inadequate attention to price, one of the most fundamental elements of marketing—and the most critical driver of profitability.

Hourly Billing and Net Income

Customers do not believe that it is their job to provide the professional with a decent profit. They see it as the professional's job to provide them with a service that is so good they willingly pay the professional a decent profit. Professionals must learn to accept the cause and effect that these different attitudes generate. The move toward activity-based costing offers a solution to this dilemma. While cost-accounting measures the cost to do something, activity-based costing captures the cost of not doing something, such as down-time, inventory shortages, and rework.

Usually, the cost of not doing something far exceeds the cost of doing something, and cost accounting does not capture the former. Activity-based costing always asks, Does this process have to be done? If so, what is the most efficient way of doing it? This costing method has provided manufacturers with the information they need to cut costs substantially, but the real promise of activity-based costing may rest with service industries. Peter Drucker makes this observation in his book *Managing in a Time of Great Change*:

> Activity-based costing shows us why traditional cost accounting has not worked for service companies. It is not because the techniques are wrong.

> It is because traditional cost accounting makes the wrong assumptions. Service companies cannot start with the cost of individual operations, as manufacturing companies have done with traditional cost accounting. They must start with the assumption that there is only *one* cost: that of the total system. And it is a fixed cost over any given time period. The famous distinction between fixed and variable costs, on which traditional cost accounting is based, does not make much sense in services.
>
> But that all costs are fixed over a given time period and that resources cannot be substituted for one another, so that the *total* operation has to be costed—those are precisely the assumptions with which activity-based costing starts. By applying them to services, we are beginning for the first time to get cost information and yield control.
>
> Banks, for instance, have been trying for several decades to apply conventional cost-accounting techniques to their business—that is, to figure the costs of individual operations and services—with almost negligible results. Now they are beginning to ask, Which one *activity* is at the center of costs and of results? The answer: Serving the customer. The cost per customer in any major area of banking is a fixed cost. Thus it is the *yield* per customer—both the volume of services a customer uses and the mix of those services—that determines costs and profitability. Retail discounters, especially those in Western Europe, have known that for some time. They assume that once a unit of shelf space is installed, the cost is fixed and management consists of maximizing the yield thereon over a given time span. Their focus on yield control has enabled them to increase profitability despite their low prices and low margins. (Drucker, 1995: 124–125)

This is precisely the method that airlines began to use after deregulation. Recall from Chapter 5 how Delta Air Lines began focusing on yield (the amount of money the airline gets per passenger mile) and load (the percentage of seats filled by paying passengers) in order to price its tickets and balance supply and demand (and capture the consumer surplus). It should be no different with a professional service firm. Yet, professional firms spend an inordinate amount of time trying to allocate fixed costs to *one* particular customer, and even more absurd, to *one* particular job for that one customer. Activity-based costing, on the other hand, would look at the total revenue yield from that one customer and compare it to an allocation of the total fixed cost to that customer.

This raises an interesting question: How should a firm allocate its fixed costs to any one customer? Labor hours certainly seem a logical way to achieve this. But if labor hours are used as the designated allocation, then the cost per labor hour should be a true cost and should *not* include a desired profit for the firm's owners. This is based on the logic that a professional firm's fixed costs, over a given period of time, cannot be changed. In fact, they are sunk costs. And here is the advice David Friedman received from his father, Milton, with regards to such costs:

> When, as a very small child, I quarreled with my sister and then locked myself in my room, my father would come to the door and say, "Making a mistake and not admitting it is only hurting yourself twice." When I got a little older, he changed it to "Sunk costs are sunk costs." (Friedman, 1996: 181)

CPA firms know their fixed costs, to the penny. It would be logical to manage the firm from the income statement, analyzing the ratio of labor and overhead costs to gross revenue, spotting trends, and making adjustments accordingly. Further, by using Key Performance Indicators (discussed in Chapter 20), the firm can begin to rely on leading indicators of profitability, rather than the lagging indicator that is the timesheet. This is precisely how the firm's manufacturing customers manage their businesses, but it seems a foreign concept to CPAs. This is strange; they assist their customers in managing their businesses this way, and yet they do not follow these same procedures when running their firms.

You may try changing your firm's time and billing program standard hourly rates to a true cost-accounting number. If you continue to keep timesheets, then by all means plug in the correct cost per labor hour. Take out the desired net income from the cost-plus formula and measure the cost and profitability based on true cost-accounting principles. This one simple change will have a dramatic impact on your attitude regarding pricing, because no longer will you assume that the price charged is calculated by your time and billing program. That alone is enough reason to make the change.

The question always arises of what to do about the firm's partner draws. Should salaries (or guaranteed draws) be included in this formula? An economist would say this is a legitimate cost to the firm. After all, if the partner were not there, the firm would have to go into the labor market and hire a replacement; thus the replacement cost of the partner should be used. Another method would be to include the partner's opportunity cost, that is, the minimum the partner has to make to keep him or her employed at the firm. However, this confuses cost with price. Price is not determined by cost; it is determined by the value the customer places on the service. Any method of costing that obfuscates that fundamental economic law is not useful in determining a value price.

For this reason, I prefer not to include any partner draw or opportunity cost, on the theory that if an amount is put in for that cost, the partners will be less aggressive in pricing the firm's services, because they will feel that a cushion is built in to the cost. Remember, the focus is cost accounting, not profit forecasting. Some firms use both methods (many time-and-billing software programs accommodate multiple rates to be used), but it is simply too early to tell which method produces better pricing decisions. If you do use the partner draw in the formula, make sure it is understood to be the absolute minimum price that should be charged, with a good justification for doing so. The hourly billing method, to the extent it is used at all (if your time-and-billing program allows multiple rates), should always be the floor below which the firm will *never* price, known as the "reservation" (or walk-away) price.

Talk it over with your partners, agree on a method, and then monitor it to see if you are making better pricing, costing, and profitability decisions as a result. Force the benefits of maintaining timesheets to justify the costs, an analysis I have found to be nearly impossible once you understand how deleterious and expensive keeping timesheets is in terms of both economical and psychological burdens. Let the income statement, and key performance indicators, play a pivotal role in your firm's hiring, budgeting, and profitability decisions. The attitudinal effects of the costing method are more important than trying to allocate your sunk costs to any one customer. Firms that do not use timesheets at all analyze their income statements to monitor overall results. Asked how they know if they are making money on any one given customer, their response is, "Well, in reality, we do not." Intuitively they do know they are making money, because they serve only customers they can charge a high price to, and therefore they know there is very little subsidizing of low-priced customers taking place. Remember, these firms are not profitable because they have eliminated timesheets; they have eliminated timesheets because they are profitable.

Hourly billing is an *inward-looking* pricing mechanism, focusing on competition and cost. Professional firms need to change to an *outward-looking* pricing mechanism, one that focuses on customer value. By changing your standard hourly rate to a true cost-based amount per labor hour, you will be forced to look to the customer for determining the value of any given service. This is how it should be. The ultimate arbiter of value is the customer, not internal costs.

Hourly Billing Creates Bureaucracy

A CPA firm recently calculated that it could save approximately $30,000 per year by eliminating timesheets, and that was only the direct cost of inputting, producing, and generating the reports. It did not include the countless hours spent by team members tracking every quarter hour, the morale problems of having to account for every single hour, the negative effect of hourly quotas on marketing and practice development, and the other myriad effects that have been discussed.

The next logical question is this: Does the time-and-billing program generate at least $30,000 worth of useful information? Nobody could answer this with any certainty, because it is very hard to quantify whether or not better decisions are being made with time reports than would be made in their absence. One point all the partners agreed upon was that the majority of important decisions that are made—hiring, firing, staffing jobs, and raises—are determined long before they even see the results of the time reports. If, for instance, a particular team member is not performing up to minimum standards, time reports are not going to indicate that as much as the grumbling from other team members, missed deadlines, and customer complaints do. If the firm is operating at maximum capacity, the managers and partners will usually hire an additional person, not as a result of analyzing time reports but because the people who report to them can justify the extra need.

CPAs often ask how they will be able to monitor and control their people if they do not make them account for their time. If they do not trust their people, why did they hire them in the first place? Firms that do not use timesheets have very effective communication between the team, managers, and partners. Methods such as weekly meetings, whereby the team members talk about the work-in-progress and if they are overused or underused, take place, and adjustments are made. You may want to attempt this method on one particular job and see what type of decisions are made in the absence of timesheets. If the results are unfavorable, then by all means bring back the timesheets. But you may be surprised.

Hourly Billing Does Not Set the Price Up Front

The most absurd and economically illogical effect of hourly billing is how it denies the professional the ability to quote a fixed price before work begins. Few products or services in the marketplace are purchased without the customer knowing the price up front. The more common ones are cab rides, medical services, legal services, and accounting services. In most cases, though, before you purchase any item, you know the price. Think how frustrating it must be for a customer to be told, "We cannot give you a price up front because we just do not know how long this will take." When the customer complains, the professional tends to launch into an explanation of how complex the project at hand is and how many unforeseen variables there are. The professional may think to themselves, and sometimes even have the temerity to inform the customer, that the customer obviously does not understand the complexity of the business.

In *Billing Innovations*, Reed quotes the following scenario written by Kevin B. Pratt, a lawyer in Colorado Springs, Colorado:

> **AIRLINES GOING TO BILLABLE HOURS?**
>
> The Denver lawyer stepped up to the airline ticket counter and asked to buy a ticket for a flight to Chicago.
>
> "No problem," said the clerk, "but before I issue the ticket, I should remind you of the new way we charge for tickets. This year we have adopted a 'basic rate' of three dollars a minute for our flights. The clock starts when you check in at the gate and stops when you pick up your luggage. We mail you a bill about two months after the flight."
>
> "Well, I guess that's okay," commented the lawyer.
>
> The clerk continued, "Remember, we call it a 'basic rate' because we sometimes adjust that rate up or down if the flight

is very empty or very full. Too, we may multiply that rate if our expert pilot finds a tail wind. We also adjust the rate according to what you will be doing in Chicago. You look like a lawyer, so I'll assume it's very important that you get there by plane, so we quadruple the basic rate. [Airlines actually do this, sort of—see Chapter 5.] Another thing, how much is your annual income? You see, if you earn a great deal and it turns out the plane crashes, we will have to pay more on your spouse's damage claim, and we have, of course, to consider that increased risk of the airline."

The astounded lawyer choked, "But how much will this trip cost me? How do I know you do not slow down on purpose? How do I know your bill will be correct?"

The clerk stared down over the end of his nose. "I can see you're not familiar with the complexities of airline work. There are so many things we just cannot know in advance—the winds, traffic delays, the weather, the routing. Airlines are a business, and we have to make a profit to stay in business. Now do not worry, we're very honest and sensitive about all this billing business and I am sure you'll be pleased with our fully itemized bill when you get it. If there's any question just call." Then the clerk whispered, "But just so we understand each other, if you do not pay the bill in full and promptly, you'll never fly on this airline again."

"Oh," grunted the Denver lawyer, "is there anything else I should know?"

The clerk smiled thoughtfully and murmured, "On your flight there is a new copilot in training, and we charge an additional 50 cents a mile. Copilots are really very important, you know, to carry the pilot's charts, to fly on clear calm days, even to land the plane if the pilot is busy with other matters. Too, if you fly with us again, your copilot may have become your pilot. Wouldn't that be great? One other thing, if the copilot uses computerized flight routing there will be an additional $75 charge. But of course computerized flight routing is almost standard charge with technologically advanced airlines."

> "But I just wanted to get to my meeting in Chicago and come home. Now I do not even know if I should fly at all," groaned the lawyer.
>
> The clerk smiled again. "Mature passengers come to understand that flying is just a cost of doing business. They never know how much it costs 'til we bill them. But then, there's really no choice, is there?"
>
> "No," conceded the lawyer, "I guess not."
>
> And then the lawyer tried again. "Why can't you just give me a fixed price and I'll decide if I'll go or not?"
>
> The clerk frowned. "But we can't do that. That wouldn't be fair to you. We might overcharge you and then you'd be unhappy. Or we might underestimate and then the airline would lose money and couldn't maintain the planes, and we certainly do not want that."
>
> And so the Denver lawyer came to hate airlines and took his revenge by regaling acquaintances at cocktail parties about the new pitfalls of airline travel. (Reed, 1996: 3–4)

This story illustrates the absurdity of hourly billing from the customer's viewpoint. By not setting a price up front, the customer has no control over the situation, which is not a good position to put your customer in. People like to feel they are in control, especially when they are spending their money. With hourly billing, the only involvement the customers have is paying the bill, and that means they have to make the value judgment after the service is rendered, which is not a good time to discover they do not agree with the price.

Lawyers used to be taught that it was unprofessional to discuss price with the customer during the first meeting, fearing they might get the wrong impression. Today, an overwhelming majority of customers want their professional to discuss price up front, as it relieves them of the burden. The Mobar-Pren-Hall Survey, which was published by Prentice-Hall and the Missouri State Bar Association, found the following results:

- 80 percent of customers want lawyers to discuss their fees up front.
- 88 percent said not to wait until the end of the case.
- 92 percent said to discuss the fee at the start of each matter.
- 78 percent want to know the basis for the fee.

  (Reed, 1992: 74)

The study also found that nearly 36 percent of the lawyers studied did not perform in accordance with the customer's desires. If the only price customers are aware of at the initial meeting is the hourly rate, then they will be forced to consider whether or not they can afford to pay that fee. They will not be considering the value of the service rendered. Mary Ann Altman sums up this predicament:

> The process of discussing the way in which the fee will be charged at the initial meeting with the client again is a prime factor. If "time billing at hourly rates" is the only explanation of the fee-calculation method, the client is making a decision based on the ability of his or her pocketbook to pay a given hourly rate but not on the value of the services in the short or long run. The lawyer should raise the question of the value of services and allow the client to make a determination as to whether or not he or she wishes to receive those services. A great deal of future grief may be avoided by such an initial discussion. (Reed, 1989: 13–14)

Whether or not you discuss price up front rest assured that customers have some price in mind, whether it is what they paid in the past, a quote from a competitor, or a completely unreasonable estimate they have pulled from thin air. The time to find out what they think is *before* your firm has performed any services, rather than after, when you will be on your knees trying to collect a bill from the customer whose value assessment is radically different from yours. The professions ignore the economic law, and customer psychology, of pricing up front at their peril. This is why time is up for the billable hour.

Hourly Billing Does Not Differentiate Your Firm

The vast majority of CPA firms (and to a lesser extent, law firms) charge by the hour, thus converting their crown jewels of experience, expertise, culture, intellectual capital, and relationships into a commodity, codified in an hourly rate. Low pricing is not an effective competitive differentiation, unless you enjoy price wars, since someone, somewhere, is always willing to do what you do for less money. Yet price is one of the most important signals a firm can transmit to the marketplace regarding its services.

Because competition really means conformity, why not get out of the pack and offer fixed prices? This is especially effective with new customers, as they will welcome receiving an up-front quote and it will project confidence and experience on your part, characteristics valued highly by customers, even if subjectively. This strategy is very effective with Yellow Pages customers. If people call your firm from the Yellow Pages they will usually ask what your hourly rate is. If you say you do not charge by the hour, they will be intrigued, probably enough to come in and see you for an initial consultation, during which you can review their needs and offer them a fixed price. The logic is that once they are in your office you will have a better chance of success in making the sale than if you are one of a dozen they are considering from the Yellow Pages herd.

The typical professional firm puts more creativity, mind power, and time into a brochure or an advertisement than in thinking about pricing policies. This is a serious mistake. Pricing is how the firm captures the value it provides to the marketplace. Analyze other industry advertising, and notice that much of it contains the price. Professional advertising, on the other hand, does not. This is a large advantage. Customers don't expect professionals to advertise based upon price; they might even perceive a firm that did as possessing lesser professionalism and dignity. Yet, firms engage in me-too pricing, simply following the herd and using cost-plus pricing or fictional "standard" rates. This is not an effective strategy to differentiate your firm from the competition. Remember, accountants are not commodities. Imagine thinking coffee beans and water are nothing more than commodities, and the effect that thinking might have had on Starbucks. In fact, consider the "Starbucks effect" on coffee sales in the United States. Ten years ago, according to the March-April 2000 *Harvard Business Review*, only 3 percent of all coffee sold in the United States was priced at a premium (that is, at least 25 percent higher than value brands). Today, 40 percent of coffee is sold at premium prices. The lesson: Change the way a product or service is sold and delivered, and the entire category can reap higher prices and profits.

Hourly Billing Diminishes the Quality of Life

There's no doubt that morale in the professions is suffering, and one major cause is the relentless pursuit of the billable hour. In *The Honest Hour*, Ross quotes an associate attorney at a Chicago law firm who billed more than 2,000 hours per year during the prior four years:

> One negative effect of hourly billing is the stressful impact on attorneys—particularly associates who in big firms have target hours of 2000 or more per year. It's not so much the fact that we must work hard but that we're slaves to the clock—almost like piecemeal workers. Perhaps that's why "sweatshop" well describes many firms. A young associate feels that an hour not billed is an hour wasted—an incredibly stressful state of mind. In short, hourly billing is a barrier to the quality of one's professional life. (Ross, 1996: 232)

Not only is one's professional life diminished, but also one's overall sense of well-being. According to the American Bar Association:

> From the lawyers' perspective, total dependency from revenues on hours billed means that compensation also is totally dependent on hours billed, which in turn means long hours, burnout, increased family problems and personal stress, and decreased morale.
>
> Simply put, if billable hour goals prevent a lawyer from having time for things other than work, that person cannot be a truly good lawyer without time to pursue whatever outside interests a lawyer has, be it family or a personal hobby. The lawyer lives to work, rather than works to live. At a certain point, the demand for billable hours on lawyers became so great that initiatives like better training and communication, or part-time work options that only a handful lawyers in fact can actually utilize, no longer make enough of a difference. At a certain point, lawyers may simply have no life outside the office, with a resulting negative impact on the lawyer, the family, and the firm. (deKieffer, 1995: 91)

This lessening in the quality of life results in a high cost to firms, measured in associate turnover, low morale, absenteeism, inefficiencies, and neglect of practice development. These costs should be included in any cost/benefit analysis of maintaining hourly billing; these costs are likely to outweigh any benefits derived.

In reality, the whole notion that professionals don't have enough time may be false, if you follow Pareto's 80/20 principle. Richard Koch, in

The 80/20 Principle: The Secret of Achieving More With Less, explains his unconventional—but compelling—argument this way:

> We have more than enough time. We demean ourselves, both by lack of ambition and by assuming that ambition is served by bustle and busyness. Achievement is driven by insight and selective action. The still, small voice of calm has a bigger place in our lives than we acknowledge. Insight comes when we are feeling relaxed and good about ourselves. Insight requires time—and time, despite conventional wisdom, is there in abundance.
>
> There is no shortage of time. In fact, we are positively awash with it. We only make good use of 20 percent of our time. And for the most talented individuals, it is often tiny amounts of time that make all the difference. The 80/20 Principle says that if we doubled our time on the top 20 percent of activities, we could work a two-day week and achieve 60 percent more than now. This is light years away from the frenetic world of time management. . . . It is our use of time, and not time itself, that is the enemy.
>
> The 80/20 Principle says that we should act less. Action drives out thought. It is because we have so much time that we squander it. The most productive time on a project is usually the last 20 percent, simply because the work has to be completed before a deadline. Productivity on most projects could be doubled simply by halving the amount of time for their completion. This is not evidence that time is in short supply.
>
> It is not shortage of time that should worry us, but the tendency for the majority of time to be spent in low-quality ways. (Koch, 1998: 141, 149)

Hourly Billing Limits Your Income Potential

There are only so many hours in a year. During the early 1990s, net earnings of most professional firms were flat, and costs were increasing at a faster rate than revenue; yet, firms refused to consider their pricing and tend to spend a high percentage of their resources obtaining new customers. Or, they raise their hourly rates, much to the chagrin of their existing customers. Or they may simply try to bill more hours, perhaps by working inefficiently, all of which David H. Maister refers to as the *donkey strategy*—achieving more by pulling a heavier load.

Consider circus elephants. When young, the elephant is chained to a stake, and the elephant learns that its movement is restricted. Once the elephant gets older, the chain around the leg is effective at restraining the elephant, even though the elephant has enough power to rip the stake out of the ground. The barrier is not *physical*, it is *mental*. It is the same with hourly billing. The only way to make more money is to *work harder*. With value pricing, however, you will make more money by *pricing smarter*.

American Bar Association Commission on Billable Hours

The legal profession is once again taking a leadership role in studying the billable hour paradigm. Similar to the Task Force on Alternative Billing Methods that was established in 1987–88 as part of the Law Practice Management Section, the American Bar Association (ABA), under its then-president, Robert E. Hirshon, is once again studying the effects of the billable hour on the profession. In early 2002, the ABA established the Commission on Billable Hours, which issued its report in August 2002. In an article titled "Law and the Billable Hour: A Standard Developed in the 1960s May Be Damaging Our Profession," Hirshon says:

> Studies suggest an unease in our profession, especially among younger lawyers. The causes are varied but all seem to lie in the difference between working in a profession vs. working a job. Mentoring, life-balance, workplace stimulation and innovation are affected when the timesheet reigns. The billable hour is fundamentally about quantity over quality, repetition over creativity. Because a lawyer's time is not an elastic variable, increased billable hour requirements are squeezing out other aspects of what it means to be a lawyer. Although I have a specific interest in how this phenomenon has adversely affected our profession's ability to do pro bono work, the demoralizing consequences of billable hours extend much more broadly. Many believe that if we innovate our billing models, not only are the same revenues attainable, but also lawyering itself will become more enjoyable.

> Firms will have to think differently—not an easy proposition for traditionally conservative, risk-adverse institutions. But for the sake of profitability and the preservation of that wonderful law firm life (one I've spent 30 years enjoying), we must begin to look at value instead of cost when determining fair payment for services rendered. It will mean accepting some risk. It will mean that efficiency and process improvements will increase profits.
>
> Richard Reed, an expert on this issue, offers tips to law firm leaders who seek new ways: "First, gather your best people and think globally about how the practice is changing. Read everything you can about alternative billing methods, but more importantly, become a student of value analysis. Consider small practice areas to pilot new billing strategies. Have your finance people run mock parallel billing strategies on current projects. Think about how your marketing efforts could be enhanced by innovative billing methods."

On the ABA's Web site (www.abanet.org), "Background on the ABA Commission on Billable Hours" enumerates the reasons this issue needs to be reexamined in the profession:

> There is no doubt that new lawyers are feeling the treadmill effect of having to record high levels of billable hours. Many law school graduates are drawn to accept high paying jobs with law firms in order to make meaningful payments on their law school loans. After a few years, many newer lawyers become discouraged with high hours and lack of mentoring, training, collegiality and the opportunity to perform pro bono work. Those who entered law school with the intention of embarking on a career in public service or public interest law are especially disaffected. At the same time, public sector and public interest employers are finding it increasingly difficult to recruit and retain lawyers.
>
> Many experienced practitioners also are concerned that their worth is being judged predominantly in terms of the numbers of hours billed and not on the quality of those hours or on other factors, such as supervision of junior lawyers,

> involvement for the firm in community activities or pro bono contributions.
>
> The unintended consequences of billable hours extend even more broadly than its demoralizing effects. Many clients have fallen into the trap of what President Hirshon refers to as "drill down valuing" where the client values legal services rendered as merely the sum of the micro-specific components. This type of valuing protects the client from padding and other over-charging abuses, but in its effort to micro-manage services rendered, the client loses focus of a larger, more fundamental concept of value. At the same time, incentives are created that run counter to the client's best interest. Many believe that if we innovate our billing models, not only are the same revenues attainable, but lawyering itself will become more enjoyable.
>
> The Commission on Billable Hours will issue its report in August [2002] at the ABA Annual Meeting in Washington. The report will be posted on this Web site. In addition to its report, the Commission created this online toolkit to be used by lawyers, law firms, and bar associations to create discussion, educate lawyers and provide the information necessary to implement alternative billing methods and be more creative in their approach to billable hours (http://www.abanet.org/careercounsel/billable/toolkit/bkrnd.html).

Once again, the CPA profession will be following the legal profession's lead away from the billable hour to value pricing.

The Tyranny of Time

Ever since Abraham Lincoln muttered those infamous words, "Time is an attorney's stock in trade," professionals have been taught that that is all they sell. It has become part of their paradigms—their mental models of the way the world works. But *time is not money*, it is simply a *precious, nonrenewable resource*. And a resource, by itself, is not valuable until one finds a use for it and it produces results that are valuable to others.

The "time is money" attitude is endemic to the professions and is summed up nicely in the following letter that appeared in the Winter 1996 *Outlook* magazine, published by the California Society of CPAs, from an "I only sell my time" CPA:

> I am writing to comment on the tactics of QuickBooks, whose latest ad appears in the fall issue of *Outlook*. QuickBooks and TurboTax, both owned by Intuit, market their products to both consumers and the CPA profession. My concern is the attempt by Intuit to be both the vendor *and* competitor to our profession.
>
> The ad suggests that we counsel our clients to use QuickBooks for their businesses. However, some time after the client purchases QuickBooks, they will receive a direct mailing from Intuit essentially suggesting that they can now also handle their income taxes using TurboTax for business. The mailing uses terms such as *quickly, easily, accurately, fast,* etc. For the timid, they propose having a professional tax preparer review and sign the completed return. There's a tempting proposition: taking responsibility for a return in which I did none of the input, and for which the client expects to pay for about 30 minutes of my time!
>
> I realize that write-up and tax-preparation services are becoming more and more a commodity. We should not be helping it along with the QuickBooks/TurboTax package.

Notwithstanding his attack on the First Amendment right of a business to advertise, consider the letter writer's *mental attitude* that all he has to offer his customer is 30 minutes of his time. If this CPA cannot become more creative in selling value-added services to a TurboTax user—maybe through tax planning, projections, or financing packages—then perhaps he deserves to be treated like a commodity and forced to compete with a $49 tax-preparation program. Another way to look at this scenario is that the customer has freed up his time to focus on the high end of the value curve. If the customer is interested in only 30 minutes of his time, and he cannot sell any additional services, then this is a customer he should not have in the first place.

Summary and Conclusions

Workers of the world . . . forgive me.

—Graffiti on a statue of Karl Marx, Moscow, 1991

Time is precious; it is what professionals are giving up when they are at work, and thus professionals have started to think their lives are divided into *billable* and *nonbillable* hours. But this focus is far too narrow, and professionals need to broaden their view of the value they add to customers' lives. That value is not measured by time but by results. Albert Einstein once wrote, "Our theories determine what we measure." Hourly billing measures the wrong things.

Even the AICPA Vision Project, which was an attempt to map the future for the profession into the year 2050, paid homage to the Almighty Hour on the first page of its report with this sentence: "Approximately 3,400 members of the CPA profession devoted a combined total of 21,456 hours ... to identify both challenges and opportunities for the profession in 2011." They report this statistic proudly and prominently, as if the people reading it will value it more simply because of how much effort was put into it, and not because of the quality of its predictions and prescriptions for the future. It is as if a surgeon paid more attention to how long the surgery took than to whether the patient got well.

Professionals are subject to the same laws of supply and demand and customer psychology that all businesses are. Hourly billing tries to defy those laws by placing the risk on the customer and misaligning the interest of the firm and the customer. Professionals continue to thrust this method of pricing onto their customers, and then they wonder why they get beat up on price. It is an idea for which the French coined the perfect expression: *fausse idée claire*—a terrific idea that doesn't work.

Professionals need to forge a new paradigm of pricing based upon the subjective value of services and stop ritualistically accepting the false labor theory of value proffered by Karl Marx 150 years ago. The billable hour should be relegated to the ash heap of history—along with carbon paper, the manual typewriter, and the slide rule—right next to *The Communist Manifesto*, as an idea whose time has passed.

8 WRITE-DOWNS AND PRICE PSYCHOLOGY

Billing is like golf—
It is a game played on a six-inch course between your ears.

—Charles and Joseph Larson,
Innovative Billing and Collection Methods That Work

Why do professionals suffer from write-downs and write-offs? Statistical surveys of CPAs, such as those conducted by the Missouri Management of an Accounting Practice (MAP) Conference and by the state of Texas clearly prove that write-downs are far more prevalent than write-ups. Studying the many theories for the underlying cause of this phenomenon perhaps gives a better understanding of the actions required to prevent write-downs and write-offs in the future. The role of value pricing is also important and is included in the discussion.

One reason for write-downs is that professionals, by nature, are *loss averse*. They tend to avoid conflict and anything they believe might anger a customer and cause him or her to select another service provider. Not only does this translate into a lack of confidence, it also provides an opportunity for customers to beat up the professional on price, because businesspeople are used to negotiating.

Another reason for write-downs is the low self-esteem that is prevalent among professionals. This is examined in Chapter 17.

One other factor in the prevalence of write-downs is apparent after a look at how other industries price their products and services. Professionals have not given enough attention to the psychological aspects of pricing.

In their book *Innovative Billing and Collection Methods That Work*, Charles Larson and Joseph Larson discuss the results of asking CPAs at MAP conferences to list the reasons they take significant write-downs and write-offs. Here are the major reasons given:

1. Poor time and billing system
2. Changes not anticipated resulting from:
   - Client deficiencies
   - Staff
   - Poor budgeting (or no budgeting)
3. First-time work/one-time work on new engagements
4. Poor engagement management
5. On-the-job training that partners do not feel can be billed
6. Client is surprised by the fee and doesn't think the job is "worth it"
7. Poor results in situations regarding financing, IRS reviews, or similar matters—areas that should be premium billings
8. Delays in billing
9. Bad client—unable to pay

(Larson and Larson, 1994: 6–7)

Most of the conditions listed above can be eliminated with better methods of determining client expectations up front, by setting a fixed price at the beginning of an engagement, and by issuing change orders if the customer is deficient in providing the necessary information or the engagement changes in an unanticipated way. As Larson and Larson point out: "***Most* fee problems occur because of violated client expectations.**" (Larson and Larson, 1994: 31) This is true and is perhaps the main cause of most write-downs. Worse yet, write-downs create a lack of trust and foster disputes between you and the customer, leading to a vicious downward spiral.

Why Customers Don't Pay

Recall the demand curve from Chapter 5. To be included on a demand curve, one must be *willing and able* to pay for the product or service. The experiences of many practicing CPAs, confirmed by Larson and Larson in their research, show only two reasons customers will not pay their professional's bill:

1. They are not *able* (no money); or
2. They are not *willing*.

All write-downs can be traced to these two issues, so it is worth taking time to explore each in detail.

Unable to Pay

A customer who cannot pay you is a sign of a bad qualification process on your part. This is one of the biggest hurdles to overcome for any salesperson—properly qualifying a buyer. According to Tom Hopkins, in his book *How to Master the Art of Selling*, you will close one of every two properly prequalified leads, whereas unqualified leads require ten in order to close just one (Hopkins, 1980: 180).

All professionals need to do a thorough job prescreening customers. Check references with bankers, attorneys, CPAs, and other businesses to determine their reputation, character, and financial ability. This is easier for CPAs and attorneys than, say, salesmen, simply because the former have a wealth of information on their potential customers, and are privy to information that most salesmen would kill for. Can they afford it? What do they pay for the service now? Who are the decision makers?

As the Greeks used to say, character is destiny. Character is the only thing that matters, especially in a professional relationship where trust is the foundation for a value-added partnership. It is a wise idea to pull a credit report on a prospective customer and check as many references as you can—in other words, do your homework. The time to discover potential problems with a customer is *before* your firm commits any resources to the engagement, not *after*. This requires an investment of up-front time, but this can save countless dollars in unpaid work, not to mention the stress, risk, and dissatisfaction of working with people who do not value your firm.

The lesson is this: **Do not take all comers**. In the insurance industry, this is known as *adverse selection,* "the problem that arises when people know more about their own risk characteristics than others do." (Landsburg, 1996: 329) Insurance companies are very cognizant of the fact that the customer in the market for insurance, statistically and actuarially, is most likely to be the worst risk, since they may not be insurable. Therefore, they subject potential policyholders to medical exams or fire inspections. Insurance companies do not take all comers, as they are in the business of managing risk and will avoid taking any unnecessary ones. Professional firms, especially in today's litigious society, should adopt the same attitude and implement methods and procedures that ensure that all new customers have gone through a rigorous prequalification process.

Starting a professional practice entails risk, and turning away business is especially difficult in the early years of building a practice. However, when your intuition tells you a customer is not right, follow it, even though it means sacrificing income. Most people choose a spouse, friends, partners, and acquaintances with an enormous amount of care and attention, and that same level of screening should be part of the customer acquisition process as well. Seriously flawed customer relationships have a pernicious effect, a sort of Gresham's Law: Bad customers drive out good. By holding on to customers who constantly doubt the value your firm is providing or are unable to pay for it, you adversely affect the morale within the entire firm. Life is too short to work with people you do not enjoy. Investing the time required to prequalify all comers makes for better quality customer relationships. Once you use better prequalifying techniques, the customers who are not *able* to pay will virtually disappear from your write-off headaches.

Unwilling to Pay

A customer's unwillingness to pay is much harder to deal with. Essentially, you are colliding with the customer's expectations. If those are violated, the customer is not going to be willing to pay your price, regardless of your technical quality. Therefore, it is critical to find out, *before* any firm resources are committed to the engagement, what the customer's expectations are. Sometimes those expectations are impossible to meet and the customer needs to be educated so that his or her expectations are lowered to a more realistic level. If you are unable to do that, withdraw from the engagement.

The lesson is vital, and it is this: By asking, probing, and listening to customers, you not only will determine their expectations, you will also be able to shape and manage them. Recall how Southwest Airlines manages its customer's expectations by offering no frills, then exceeds the customer's already low expectations by being irreverent, arriving on time, and not losing the customer's luggage. In order to exceed customer expectations in a professional firm, it is vital to invest time ascertaining what exactly the customer thinks he is purchasing and what they expect after the service is delivered. Rest assured that every customer you work for has expectations. Your job is to discover them and then exceed them. Exceeding those expectations is crucial if your goal is to provide total quality service. By ascertaining and managing your customer's expectations at the beginning of each engagement, reason number two for write-offs and write-downs should diminish.

Please refer to "Considerations Before Accepting a New Customer," found in "Useful Checklists" at the end of this book and also on the CD-ROM.

So far, the negatives involved in write-downs have been discussed. Even more beneficial is a study of successful methods firms employ to prevent write-downs.

Do You Learn More from Success or from Failure?

In Peter F. Drucker's autobiography, *Adventures of a Bystander*, he states: "I suddenly realized that the right method, at least for me, was to look for the thing that worked and for the people who perform. I realized that I, at least, do not learn from mistakes. I have to learn from successes." (Drucker, 1994: 75) When participants in my courses were asked whether they learned more from success or failure, 90 percent said failure. When you start really pondering this, however, you realize that success is a far more valuable teacher than failure. Yet people are far more proficient in their rationalizations for failure than in planning for success.

Most people would agree with the statement that there are more wrong ways to do something than there are right ways. If that is true, then certainly it follows that learning the right way to do a particular thing is the best path to success. After all, incompetence is one thing found in abundant and never-ending supply. If you had to study all of life's failures, you would never have enough time to achieve success.

In a business context, studying success is becoming vital to remaining competitive. Witness the process known as benchmarking, which all major world-class firms conduct to improve their operations.

Benchmarking is a continuous search for and application of significantly better practices that lead to superior competitive performance. It is a major criterion for the Malcolm Baldrige National Quality Award, and will likely be one of the growth areas for consultants in the twenty-first century.

No business benchmarks the post office. If the management of the post office were smart, it would benchmark FedEx, but the government is not a learning institution. It does not learn from its mistakes, it simply perpetuates them.

Both success and failure are largely the result of habit. Failure breeds failure and success breeds success. When you program yourself to believe that you learn more from failure than success, you begin to make excuses for your failures. You will make statements such as, "Yes, I really messed that up, but look at the education I got from my mistake." Yet probably not that many people really improve from their mistakes. Examine the list of reasons for write-downs and write-offs; CPAs across the United States experience the same failures, over and over. Recounting them here is not going to assist you in preventing them. Being aware of why failures occur can be, no doubt, helpful. But not until you learn the correct way to achieve your goal will you gain the confidence needed to improve.

For instance, social reformers have been constantly preoccupied with the problem of poverty. However, poverty is the usual condition of man, and in reality, it needs no explanation. What needs an explanation is not poverty, but wealth. Adam Smith took this approach in his *Wealth of Nations*, which enabled countries to make real progress in ameliorating poverty by understanding what attributes create wealth.

Successful sports stars take the same approach. Earl Woods believes that success breeds success and used this principle to teach his son Tiger, at a young age, to shoot below par golf. He took the approach of rewarding success. He would assign Tiger a par higher than regulation par, making it possible for the child to come in often under par. Earl Woods explains the effect of this technique in *Training a Tiger*:

> It was the beginning of a competitive desire that knows no comfort zone. By that I mean when Tiger is five under par, he wants to be six under par. When he's six under par, he wants to be seven. He does not say, "Wow, I'm five under. I'm not supposed to be shooting like this." The truth is

> Tiger has been shooting like that since he was two years old. He's been shooting five, six, seven under par with those assigned pars. (Woods, 1997: 26)

Here is the major point regarding success vs. failure, and it comes, once again, from Drucker: *"Do not solve problems; pursue opportunities."* The difference is critical. A firm should spend at least as much time pursuing opportunities as it does solving problems, if not more. It is imperative to adopt the procedures necessary to avoid the two causes of write-downs and write-offs, but that is not enough. That is merely solving problems. You also want to pursue opportunities and discover how to provide total quality service. You want to gain the ability to charge a premium price for your services. You are more likely to achieve these things by studying the success of others.

Studying Success

Why are some CPAs successful, making anywhere between $400,000 and $1 million per year, per partner? CPAs earning this level of income are not that much different from other CPAs. However, they do tend to work *smarter*, not *harder*. Most of them have capitalized on value pricing and command premium prices for their services. According to Larson and Larson in *Innovative Billing and Collection Methods That Work,* factors that result in favorable CPA profit include:

- Good clients
- Effective engagement planning
- Superior communication
- Adequate performance
- Appropriate administrative support
  (Larson and Larson, 1994: 8)

I would add to this list value pricing, total quality service, high self-esteem, confidence, and continuous learning and development of intellectual capital. Nevertheless, if you study the top achievers in this profession, the preceding five factors are almost always present.

One of the best definitions of *high-quality professional services* was developed by Peter Giuliana, a consultant in Westport, Connecticut, written for attorneys but also relevant to CPAs:

- The ability to perceive client needs or commercial objectives quickly and correctly.
- The expertise and diligence needed to facilitate the satisfaction of client needs or commercial objectives.
- The professionalism, training, and skill to ensure that client needs are satisfied in a manner that conforms to and is in compliance with applicable law and ethical standards.
- The delivery of cost-effective, timely, and responsive service that adds value or achieves a result whose value exceeds the fee charged. (Reed, 1996: 168)

This is an excellent mission statement for any professional service firm, as it puts the focus on providing value to the customer, meeting expectations in the most efficacious manner possible, all the while providing total quality service. Analyze your firm's value proposition and how it differs from that of your competition. Focus on the service aspect and you will discover that price and quality will both increase as a result.

What About Marketing Success?

Another characteristic of successful firms is the way they measure their success in the marketing realm. Most professionals look at revenues, and if they increased, they feel their marketing efforts have succeeded—or at least paid off on their investment. The top rainmakers, by contrast, look at the profitability of the new business generated. As David H. Maister points out in his excellent book, *True Professionalism*:

> Revenues are an insufficient (and potentially misleading) indicator of marketing success. Marketing in a professional firm is (or should be) about getting *better* business, not just *more* business.
>
> *Of course* low-profit work is better than no work—*this year*. But again, this can hardly be called marketing success:

> Taking any work you can get is no way to build a business. To be successful, a firm must win more than its fair share of the profitable work, and marketing-success measures must be established to track this. (Maister, 1997: 185, 187)

Maister also offers a two-prong test to measure marketing success: The Income Statement Test and the Balance-Sheet Test. The Income Statement Test, obviously, is the impact of the marketing efforts on the firm's top and bottom lines. The Balance-Sheet Test, a more challenging test, is the impact of the new work on the firm's asset-building efforts—developing new skills, strengthening customer relationships that will pay dividends in the future, creating a reputation in new markets or segments, etc.

The Balance-Sheet Test is failed by most professional firms, and that is dangerous in the long run. Maister points out that "Too much asset-milking work will leave the firm exposed strategically. Skills and reputation depreciate over time, and only by building new skills, relationships, and reputations can a firm thrive over time." (Maister, 1997: 188)

Price Psychology

It is worth reiterating that pricing is a major marketing decision. And since people tend to buy *emotionally*, and justify *intellectually*, the study of pricing psychology is a worthwhile task. Two sources of wise counsel are Timothy Beauchemin, with his audio cassette program titled *Five-Star Client Service System*, and Troy Waugh, a nationally known CPA consultant.

In his *Five-Star Client Service System*, Beauchemin teaches that CPAs should run their practices like five-star restaurants, pointing out the many similarities between the two businesses. Each relies on word-of-mouth advertising, each values repeat business, each sells a product that is available elsewhere, and each makes money on "dessert" (value-added services). He also identifies the two characteristics of price psychology:

1. Price leverage
2. Pricing emotions

Price Leverage

Price leverage is not so much an advantage possessed by one party over the other as a question of who has the most (or least) price sensitivity at a given time during the transaction. Before an engagement has begun, the professional possesses the price leverage. This is because the customer is able and willing to do business with you (otherwise you would not have made it this far in the process) and desires (or badly needs) the service. Consider the psychological factors when the customer is confronted with an IRS audit. The fear and anxiety of the customer is very serious. The time to negotiate and set the price for your representation is not *after* you have completed the audit, but *before*.

By setting the price up front, you can command a premium because you have assumed some of the risk involved in not knowing exactly how much resources it is going to require. You will also provide the customer with control over the decision of whether or not to engage your services, and this sense of control is very important to customers. Once you complete an engagement (or particular project), the price leverage shifts to the customer and you are left trying to recoup any portion of your price the customer is willing to pay. This puts you at a severe disadvantage and is one of the reasons professionals experience write-offs.

Price leverage also works with change orders, a topic dealt with in Chapter 11. Contractors are notorious for using change orders. If the project is changed in the middle of the job, the contractor will notify the customer and a change order will be issued. At the time of a change order, the pricing leverage is on the side of the contractor, who has already started the job and is familiar with it. The switching costs are usually prohibitive at this stage. Change orders are an extremely effective mechanism for keeping in contact with the customer and retaining your price leverage when projects do not turn out as originally planned. In fact, many contractors will low-ball their bids and sit in their offices praying for a change order to occur, because this is where most of their profit comes from.

Beauchemin offers a wonderful analogy in his program, that of the dessert tray in the five-star restaurant. The restaurant makes a deliberate attempt to sell dessert while the customers are still hungry. This maintains the price leverage to the restaurant's advantage and allows the restaurant to earn more profit from the customer. You always want to establish your price when you possess the leverage, which is *before* the engagement begins. A service that is needed is always worth more than a service that has been delivered.

Pricing Emotions

Customers experience three primary pricing emotions at various times through the purchasing cycle:

1. Price resistance
2. Payment resistance
3. Price anxiety

Price Resistance ("Sticker Shock")

As long as you are dealing with people, you will encounter price resistance, usually at the beginning of the negotiating process and thus it is easy to identify. The best way to overcome it is by educating customers about the value you provide. The purpose of the fixed-price agreement (FPA) meeting with customers (see Chapter 10) is solely to discuss the value you add. This meeting is an excellent opportunity to educate them with respect to this value. By discussing value, rather than price, you lower a customer's price resistance. One major reason for this is that you have changed the customer's focus from each service your firm provides to the totality of what your firm has to offer. When you bundle a group of services into an FPA (see Chapter 11), you have, in a way, "tangibilized" the intangible. Whenever you can turn the intangible into the tangible, you have an advantage. The FPA serves this purpose.

Witness the success McDonald's has had with its Value Meals. Items most frequently purchased are combined, leading customers to consider the value of the total meal, not just its component parts. This has been an unquestionable success for McDonald's, so much so that all of its competitors have emulated the strategy. This same strategy can be used in professional firms through offering, for example, an "entrepreneurial business program" whereby a firm helps a business incorporate, select an entity type, draft the minutes of meetings, perform tax planning, and prepare the tax return, all for one standard price (negotiated with each customer, of course). This is highly successful, because it offers the customer an entire service package and changes their focus from the cost of each service to the value of the total offering.

To overcome sticker shock, the professional must prove to the customer that the value they will derive from the service exceeds the cash price they pay. Value, from a customer's perspective, is computed by dividing the benefits received by the price of the service. If you cannot convince the customer that this ratio is greater than 1.0, you will not effectively overcome sticker shock. If price resistance cannot be conquered through educating the customer, then you should probably not take the engagement. You do not want to work for people who do not understand, or who refuse to pay for, the value you provide.

Never lower your price to acquire a customer who is suffering from price resistance, as this cheats your firm's best customers—those who value what you provide—and subsidizes your worst customers—those drawn to you by price considerations alone. These will be the first customers to defect once they find a service provider willing to do the work for less.

Many people automatically equate high price with high quality. In his fascinating book, *Influence: The New Psychology of Modern Persuasion*, Robert B. Cialdini tells of a friend who had opened an Indian jewelry store in Arizona. She had an allotment of turquoise jewelry that she had not been able to sell, even during the peak tourist season. Before leaving town, she wrote a note to her head saleswoman, "Everything in this display case, price x 1/2," hoping just to be rid of the offending pieces, even if at a loss. When she returned, she was surprised to learn that all of the jewelry had been sold. But the employee had read the "1/2" in the scrawled message as a "2." The entire allotment had sold out at twice the original price. (Cialdini, 1993: 1–2)

No doubt some customers will equate high price with high value, especially when there is very little else to judge your value on. Wise consultants know that if they price their services on the low end of the market, the customers do not have the incentive to take their advice seriously. On the other hand, if rates are at the upper end of the spectrum (say, $10,000 per day), the customers will hang on every word you say and the probability of implementing your suggestions is higher. If they do this, and what you are selling is good advice, they will be more successful and thus will value you that much more. This cycle spirals upward; the more you charge, the more people follow your suggestions, the more profitable they become, and the more valuable you are to them.

Payment Resistance

Payment resistance is simply the customer's unwillingness to cut the check. Who likes to pay their bills? Payment resistance is overcome by involving the customer in the design, price, and payment terms of your service. Because subjective terms such as "fair price" and "prompt payment" can have different meanings to a professional and a customer, these terms should be defined when you meet with the customer to draw up the FPA. An important part of any sale is the payment terms. In this area, professionals have been lackadaisical in realizing exactly how much value they offer their customers by giving them payment terms. Accounts receivable, a major headache in any firm, is largely the result of payment resistance. Customers of professionals do not have problems with the quality of the work, but they do know that there's not much downside to paying the professional last. Once people are committed to a written agreement, they are much less likely not to cut the check.

One effective method to overcome payment resistance, besides using the FPA that details the payment terms, is to deliver all services in person. This provides the customer with a factor to judge your value by, other than the bill you present. The personal relationship has a very salutary effect on lowering a customer's payment resistance and should be used as frequently as possible to speed up accounts-receivable collections.

Sometimes the problem is that the firm failed to get the customer to commit to payment terms. The all-important "ego investment" is missing, whereby the customer will strive to act in accordance with that commitment. The customer may have signed the Engagement Letter, wherein your firm spells out its price, payment terms, and what happens in the event the customer does not pay. But how many of your customers read that letter? How much customer involvement is there when the firm *imposes* payment terms on the customer?

In any other business, when terms are offered, a profit is made. Witness General Motors Acceptance Corporation and General Electric

Credit, among others. These organizations take a risk, and thereby make a profit, by offering credit to customers. Yet professional organizations take a great risk by granting terms and they reap no profit as a result. They have all the downside of write-offs and write-downs but share none of the up side. Most other businesses have converted to cash terms (doctors, dentists). Converting your firm to a COD basis would be difficult, though some CPA firms do it, for instance, with tax returns. However, payment terms are a major bargaining chip when it comes to negotiating a price, as your customers will attest to in running their own businesses.

Make the payment terms an instrumental part of the price negotiation. The old axiom of business valuators is: "I'll let you set the price if you let me set the terms." Put terms on the table as part of the price negotiation. This gets that all important ego investment from the customer. For example, if you are dealing with a retailer who is cash poor in the spring (when most CPA firms are cash rich), they may prefer to make a smaller payment during that time of the year and gradually raise the payment through the last quarter, when they are flush with cash. This flexibility allows the customer to budget accounting or legal fees with the cyclical nature of the specific business, an enormously valuable offering from your firm, and one that should never be discounted. Customers may prefer to pay quarterly, monthly, semiannually, or even a third down at the beginning of the year with the rest paid evenly the following 11 months. As long as they pay the entire agreed-upon price in 12 months (this can be calendar or fiscal), leave them free to choose when they want to pay. For new customers, get a retainer, or a 25 to 50 percent down payment. Always require a deposit from all new customers to gauge their seriousness and commitment to your firm. If customers are not willing to pay a portion *before* the service, they may be reluctant to pay *after* the service is performed.

Once the customer decides how to pay you, this is codified in the FPA and authorized by the customer. As soon as you get this commitment, the customer will usually behave in the manner agreed to. FPA customers simply load the payment terms as set forth in the agreement into their accounting system and a check is cut, like clockwork, at the designated due date. It reduces the administrative burden, as no invoice is required, and it removes the negative moment of truth that a bill creates each month in the mind of the customer. What more could you ask for?

You may also want to consider accepting credit cards or establish electronic fund transfers (EFTs). Try to make paying your firm as easy as possible for the customer.

Price Anxiety

The FPA can help with price anxiety, or buyer's remorse. It is a well-known fact that luxury automobile advertisements are targeted at existing owners, rather than potential owners. This is because after such a large purchase, first-time customers may regret it or at least want reassurance that they made a good decision; price anxiety is less likely to affect repeat customers. Price anxiety is a significant psychological emotion customers experience, especially after entering into an FPA with your firm. Overcome price anxiety by staying in touch with your customers, assuring them that they made the right decision in hiring you, and exceeding their expectations. You can also offer a service guarantee, which dramatically lowers price anxiety.

Summary and Conclusions

This chapter looked at the reasons professionals, as a group, tend to have write-downs and write-offs. Customers do not pay their bills for two reasons: They are *unable* or they are *unwilling*. Professionals can negate the former by becoming more adept at prequalifying all new customers. To lessen the latter, work to ascertain customer expectations at the beginning of each job, exceeding those expectations, setting prices at the beginning of each engagement, and emphasizing the service component. Firms that concentrate on these problems should be able to cut drastically the occurrence of write-downs and write-offs.

9 THE ADVANTAGES OF VALUE PRICING

A cynic is one who knows the price of everything and the value of nothing.

—Oscar Wilde

The successful professional firms of today price their services according to external value, as perceived and determined by the customer, rather than by internal costs. By so doing, they restore pricing to being the strategic marketing decision that it is. One of the first tasks is to define exactly what is meant by "value pricing."

Just as businesses have gone out of their way to replace the word *customer*, they have done away with the word *price*. People pay a postage *rate* to the United States Postal Service; *fees* to professionals; *premiums* to insurance companies; *rent* for apartments; *tuition* for education; *fares* for taxis, airlines, and buses; *tolls* to cross bridges; *admissions* for concerts, movies, and sporting events; *finance charges* for credit cards; and *tariffs* and *duties* for importing goods to another country. All of these euphemisms deal with the strategic marketing decision of price.

The term *value pricing* has a very positive connotation, and this terminology should become part of your firm's culture. Use the term *pricing* with your customers, because it is a more friendly term than *billing*. (Who likes to receive bills?) Consider the word *pricing* in contrast to the word *fee*. Webster's Dictionary describes the word *fee* as "payment, service, or homage due a superior; payment asked or given for professional services, admissions, licenses, tuition, etc.; charge."

The word *value* has an even more specific meaning, especially to an economist. It means: *"The maximum amount that a consumer would be willing to pay for an item."* (Landsburg, 1996: 784) This is the auction market concept, wherein each bidder offers the maximum price he or she is willing to pay for a particular item.

Therefore, *value pricing* can be defined as *the maximum amount a given customer is willing to pay for a particular service, before the work begins.*

Value pricing does not mean a percentage markup on your standard rate, or a contingency arrangement based upon a certain result, or a bonus added to the agreed upon price, though any price negotiation may include any of these factors. Value pricing requires that you price on the margin, for each customer, for each service, disregarding the following:

- What you charge other customers for the "same service"
- What you have charged the customer in the past
- What your competition is willing to charge the customer
- What the competition used to charge the customer

Robert G. Cross, in *Revenue Management,* defines value pricing (he calls it "revenue management") in this manner:

> Revenue Management is the application of disciplined tactics that predict consumer behavior at the micromarket level and optimize product availability and price to maximize revenue growth. In even simpler terms, Revenue Management ensures that companies will sell the right product to the right customer at the right time for the right price. (Cross, 1997: 51–52)

Here is an example of pricing on the margin. A customer's tax return is paid for by his wife's employer, up to a maximum amount of $1,000 each year. He is paid this amount in full, and if he can negotiate a price of less than $1,000, he pockets the difference. At standard rates, his tax return would cost $400. The CPA negotiates a price of $800. The customer is pleased because he pockets $200, and the CPA is happy because he earns twice the "standard rate." That price was determined irrespective of what the CPA had charged the customer in the past (when the wife's employer did not pay for it), and it was set without discussing time involvement, because that entire issue was removed from the consideration. The CPA discovered that the wife's employer paid the bill by asking questions, and the customer volunteered the information. Had the CPA simply focused on hours spent, he would leave approximately $400 on the table. That $400 represents part of the consumer surplus, as discussed Chapter 5, for this particular customer.

Another example of pricing on the margin is the stylist who does the hair and makeup for a bride on her wedding day, and maybe even for the entire wedding party. Do you think the bride values this particular service on this particular day more than any other day? The cosmetologist does not require any more time to do their hair, but she charges more for accommodating the bride on a particular day. And, as proof that even more consumer surplus exists, the customer usually provides a very generous tip for the service.

Some argue that this is immoral or that it is tantamount to taking advantage of someone based upon special circumstances. Nonsense. No transaction would occur if both parties did not derive a benefit from it (in the absence of coercion, duress, or fraud, naturally) and thus what this really represents is *consenting adults engaging in capitalist acts*. It is exactly what Friedrich A. von Hayek discussed when he spoke of "special knowledge of circumstances of the fleeting moment." Super Bowl tickets command a high price, as do apartments during the Olympics or vacation homes during ski season. Different time, different place, different circumstances, *different price.* The only reason professionals have such an ethical and moral problem with this type of pricing is that they treat all of their customers the same, regardless of what they are doing for them or how much the customer may value their service. Customers do not want to be treated *equally*, they want to be treated *individually.* The post office and your local cable company treat you *equally*, and they are not good models to emulate.

Many factors influence the prices of products and services in our $11 trillion-plus economy, and the only reason professionals run into ethical issues is that they live in a one-dimensional world of hours spent multiplied by a "standard rate," where any deviation from that formula is considered immoral. The ethical and moral issues of value pricing and hourly billing are also discussed in Chapter 16.

We Live in a Barter Economy

It may be helpful, for the time being, to suspend talking about absolute price in terms of dollars and cents. *Absolute price* is defined as "the number of dollars that can be exchanged for a specified quantity of a given good." Instead, let's think of price in relative terms. *Relative price* is "the quantity of some other good that can be exchanged for a specified quantity of a given good." (Landsburg, 1996: 34) When you get to the heart of the matter, you really live in a barter economy. By purchasing this book you have traded some of your services as a professional for some of my services as an author. Money is simply a way to eliminate the necessity of a coincidence of wants. Because I did not need your particular service at this time, you were able to exchange money, earned serving others who did require your services, for this book. Money has no value, per se; value is based on what people are willing to give up. Individual demand can be no greater than the ability to supply others with the goods and services they want. Money simply facilitates the myriad of transactions that take place in the economy—its use is more efficient than bartering.

In the final analysis, any time you make a purchase, you are simply exchanging some of your labor for the labor of others. In micro-economics, when the word *price* is used, it always refers to a *relative price*. When you view the world through this paradigm, it is obvious that each individual has a very different relative price for any given product or service.

An interesting example of the effects of relative pricing is oranges that are grown in Florida and shipped to New York. Even though New Yorkers do not grow oranges, they tend, on average, to eat better oranges than the residents of Florida. To understand why, consider relative price. Suppose "good oranges" cost $1 in Florida and "bad oranges" cost 50¢ (not bad per se, but "bad" relative to the "good" oranges). Therefore, the relative price of a good orange in Florida is two bad ones. But for the New Yorker, because of 50¢ in transportation costs, a good orange costs $1.50 and a bad orange costs $1. Therefore, the relative price of a good orange is only 1.5 bad oranges. Since New Yorkers face a lower relative price, they eat, on average, more good oranges.

This explains why high quality goods tend to get exported and why luxuries are disproportionately represented in international trade. Examples are British Rolls Royces, grapes from California, leather goods from Italy, French wines, Texas steaks, Colombian coffee, Idaho potatoes, Hawaiian pineapples, and Washington apples. Whenever a tax, transportation expense, or other fixed cost is added to a variable price of a product, what is known as the Alchian-Allen effect takes place: *Consumers tend to shift their tastes in favor of higher quality products.*

For example, when the U.S. government began taxing packages of cigarettes, king-size and super-king-size were introduced to provide more smoking minutes per pack. The same logic applies to phone calls. In years past, many phones on airplanes charged a flat rate of $15 per domestic call, no matter how long you talked. Charge a flat price for a phone call, and people will talk longer. Put a fixed charge on any product, and it will migrate to where its relative cost is the lowest.

The point is this: The price of anything is influenced by a multitude of factors, and the more you understand about your customer's circumstances, the better able you are to capture the consumer surplus that may exist. One residential contractor who builds spec homes raises the price if a home does not sell within a month of being listed. The contractor discovered that when he raised the price by $50,000, a different type of customer would show interest in the home—perhaps a customer who was trying to roll over a capital gain from the sale of a previous home and had to spend a minimum amount. The contractor operated in an area where people moved in from states with relatively high real estate prices. The contractor understood some of the factors that influenced people's willingness to pay. He was successful selling at the higher price between 80 and 90 percent of the time. This is price discrimination at its finest.

Relative price also has ramifications for pricing based upon opportunity costs. For example, airlines frequently charge a penalty (or fee) to change a travel date. I recently was on a trip and had to move up my departure date by two days. The airline charged me $150 for accommodating this request. Did it cost them anything to do this? No, but they knew I would compare that $150 charge to two nights in a hotel room, two more days of my rental car, and two more days of airport parking. Had the airlines priced that change on a pure cost-plus basis, they would miss those marginal opportunities to tap into the consumer surplus.

The Fixed Price Agreement

Value pricing can effectively be put in writing by meeting with the customer and drawing up a fixed price agreement (FPA). Here is a sample draft of an FPA, so that you can see what is being referred to. This agreement is presented again and discussed in Chapter 11.

Sample Fixed Price Agreement

December 1, 2004

Dear Customer:

In order to document the understanding between us as to the scope of the work that ABC, CPAs will perform, we are entering into this **Fixed Price Agreement** with XYZ, Inc. To avoid any misunderstandings, this Agreement defines the services we will perform for you as well as your responsibilities under this Agreement.

2005 PROFESSIONAL SERVICES

ABC will perform the following services for XYZ during 2005:

- 2004 W-2s/1099s and 4th Quarter Payroll Tax Reports and Workers' Comp Report
- 1st, 2nd, & 3rd Quarter Payroll 2005 Reports and Workers' Comp Reports and Fiscal Year Sales Tax Return
- 2004 Year-End Accounting Adjustments and Closing of 2004 Books
- 2004 XYZ S Corporation Tax Returns
- 2004 Audited Financial Statements with PBCs to be provided by XYZ by March 15, 2005
- Unlimited Access 2005*

TOTAL 2005 PROFESSIONAL SERVICES	$XXX

* Included in the Unlimited Access are the following services to be provided by ABC to XYZ:

- Unlimited meetings to discuss operations of XYZ, business matters, tax matters, and any other topic at the discretion of XYZ or its employees and/or agents.
- Unlimited phone support for XYZ personnel and/or independent contractors and agents regarding accounting assistance, recording of transactions, etc.

Because our Fixed Price Agreement provides ongoing access to the accounting, tax, and business advice you need on a fixed-price basis, you are not inhibited from seeking timely advice by the fear of a clock running endlessly. Our services are designed around fixed prices, as opposed to hourly rates, and offer you access to the accumulated wisdom of the firm through CPAs with substantial experience who can help enhance your company's future and achieve its business goals.

While the fixed price entitles your company to unlimited consultation with us, if your question or issue requires additional research and analysis beyond the consultation, that work will be subject to an additional price before the service is to be performed, and a Change Order will be issued before delivery of the additional service, with payment terms agreed to in advance.

Unanticipated Services

Furthermore, the parties agree that if an unanticipated need arises (such as, but not limited to, an audit by a taxing agency or any other exogenous service not anticipated in this agreement by the parties), ABC hereby agrees to perform this additional work at a mutually agreed upon price *before the service is provided*. This service will be invoiced separately to XYZ, as part of a Change Order, and will be payable upon presentation [or payable upon terms mutually agreed upon].

Service Guarantee

Our work is guaranteed to the complete satisfaction of the customer. If XYZ is not completely satisfied with the services performed by ABC, we will, at the option of XYZ, either refund the price, or accept a portion of said price that reflects XYZ's level of satisfaction. We will assume you are satisfied upon final payment received under the terms of this Agreement.

Price Guarantee

Furthermore, if you ever receive an invoice without first authorizing the service, terms, and price, you are not obligated to pay for that service.

Payment Terms

The following payment plan is hereby agreed to by XYZ and ABC:

• January 31, 2005	XX
• February 28, 2005	XX
• March 31, 2005	XX
• April 30, 2005	XX
• May 31, 2005	XX
• June 30, 2005	XX
• July 31, 2005	XX
• August 31, 2005	XX
• September 30, 2005	XX
• October 31, 2005	XX
• November 30, 2005	XX
• December 31, 2005	XX
TOTAL 2005 PAYMENTS	$ XXX

To assure that our arrangement remains responsive to your needs, as well as fair to both parties, we will meet throughout 2005 and, if necessary, revise or adjust the scope of the services to be provided and the prices to be charged in light of mutual experience.

Furthermore, it is understood that either party may terminate this Agreement at any time, for any reason, with 10 days written notice to the other party. It is understood that any unpaid services that are outstanding at the date of termination are to be paid in full within 10 days from the date of termination.

If you agree that the above adequately sets forth XYZ's understanding of our mutual responsibilities, please authorize this Agreement and return it to our office. A copy is provided for your records.

We would like to take this opportunity to express our appreciation for the opportunity to serve you.

Very truly yours,

BY: ___________________________

Allan Somnolent, Partner
ABC, CPAs

Agreed to and authorized:

By: ____________________________Date: ________________

Customer, President
XYZ, Inc.

The Advantages of the Fixed Price Agreement and Value Pricing

Consider the following advantages of value pricing and an FPA, and contrast them to the disadvantages of the hourly billing method discussed in Chapter 7.

Value Pricing Clarifies the Customer's Expectations

We know how important it is in today's environment to exceed the customer's expectations. This goal is difficult enough without the added burden of not knowing exactly what those expectations are. One of the first questions to ask any customer, new or veteran, is "What do you expect from us?" Simply by asking this question, you will be able to manage and control, to some degree, those expectations, and if you believe the expectations are unreasonable, withdraw from the engagement. No matter how unreasonable those expectations may be, the time to discover them is *before* you commit any of your firm's resources to the customer. If you do not ascertain the expectations up front, no matter how technically brilliant your work may be, your customer will not be satisfied, you will encounter severe payment resistance, and most likely you will suffer write-downs and write-offs.

The other aspect of customer expectations that needs to be understood is that *each* member of the firm who works with a customer needs to be cognizant of those expectations. It does no good for a partner to know exactly what the customer expects if he hoards that information and does not share it with the team members working on the engagement. Every person should understand the expectations of the customer and strive to exceed them. This separates the total quality service firms from the mediocre firms. The entire firm, from receptionist to managing partner, should be involved in delivering excellent service to every customer.

Value Pricing Prequalifies the Customer

Discovering a customer's expectations reduces the danger of the customer being *unwilling* to pay you; prequalifying the customer ensures that the customer is *able* to pay you. To prequalify a customer, check references (bankers, attorneys, CPAs, etc.) and examine credit reports from Dun & Bradstreet, as well as personal credit reports. This method is critical for all new customers. Prequalifying a customer before performing any work takes time but in the long run saves countless hours spent in pricing disputes, write-offs, and other problems that could have been avoided had there been better communication at the beginning of the engagement. Those firms that complain about bad customers are usually firms that don't adequately prequalify their customers, and they also rarely turn down work. If a customer is worth accepting, then they are worth the effort it entails to adequately prequalify them.

Value Pricing Provides the Opportunity to Cross-Sell

By brainstorming with your customers regarding future goals and aspirations, you will inevitably learn of many opportunities to cross-sell your firm's services. During meetings with customers, you may discover plans to sell the business, buy a business, expand a business, or start a new division, just to name a few, and all of these are rich with opportunities for additional services. David H. Maister offers the following reason why cross-selling among professional firms has been less than successful:

> Every professional service firm I have ever encountered has had, and still has, the goal of cross-selling—expanding relationships with existing clients in order to increase the range of services delivered. Yet success in this area has been limited. Few firms, if any, have made cross-selling work on a systematic basis. And there is a simple explanation for this apparent failure: Firms have been going about it in the wrong way.
>
> Cross-selling does little, if anything, for the *client*. . . . If it does not do anything extra for the clients and just benefits you, then it is almost certainly unsustainable, and will fail. (Maister, 1997: 178–179)

Your firm cannot automatically expect to receive additional work from the customer—you have to earn it. After all, if your firm is so adept at the additional service, you should be able to compete in the market against your competitors. By focusing on what the customers want, not on what you want, you have a much better forum for effective cross-selling. This is because you are not *selling* as much as the customers are *buying*; you are helping the customers achieve their vision of the future. A saying from Cicero reads: *Cui bono*? (Who stands to gain?). If you want to be effective at cross-selling your firm's services, you must always make sure the *customer* stands to gain. Stanley Marcus' father, Herbert Marcus, gave his son this advice upon hiring him to work at Neiman-Marcus in 1926: "There is never a good *sale* for Neiman-Marcus unless it's a good *buy* for the customer." Convey the message that you want to help in making the customer's vision come true, and as a result you will be able to cross-sell your services effectively. Empirical evidence shows that you will be more successful in cross-selling services to an FPA customer. You will also command a higher percentage of the customer's "share of wallet," that is, the total amount spent on their tax, accounting, legal services, and consulting services, with less going to your competitors.

Value Pricing Allows You to Gain "Ego Investment" from the Customer

The biggest failure when implementing value pricing is a basic one: Failure to get the customer's ego investment. Your customers' involvement in the design, delivery, and pricing of your firm's services results in a powerful emotional investment on their part. Once an ego investment is made, customers tend to behave in a manner that is consistent with the commitment. This aspect of human psychology is documented in *Influence: The Psychology of Persuasion,* by Robert B. Cialdini. One example Cialdini gives relates to gamblers at a racetrack:

> A study done by a pair of Canadian psychologists uncovered something fascinating about people at the racetrack: Just after placing a bet, they are much more confident of their horse's chances of winning than they are immediately before laying down that bet. Of course, nothing about the horse's chances actually shifts; it's the same horse, on the same track, in the same field; but in the minds of those bettors, its prospects improve significantly once that ticket is purchased. Although a bit puzzling at first glance, the reason for the dramatic change has to do with a common weapon of social influence.... It is, quite simply, our nearly obsessive desire to be (and to appear) consistent with what we have already done. Once we have made a choice or taken a stand, we will encounter personal and interpersonal pressures to behave consistently with that commitment. Those pressures will cause us to respond in ways that justify our earlier decision. (Cialdini, 1993: 57)

A second story told by Cialdini is illuminating from a human behavioral perspective and as a price discrimination strategy. Cialdini was in a toy store in January purchasing a big, electric road-race set for his son. He ran into a neighbor making the same purchase for his son. They recalled that they had run into each other the previous January, too, making rather expensive post-Christmas gift purchases for their sons, and chalked this up to coincidence. Cialdini later recounted this story to a friend who had worked in the toy business, and the following conversation ensued:

> "No coincidence," the friend said knowingly.
>
> "What do you mean, 'No coincidence'?"
>
> "Look," he said, "let me ask you a couple of questions about the road-race set you bought this year. First, did you promise your son that he'd get one for Christmas?"
>
> "Well, yes, I did. Christopher had seen a bunch of ads for them on the Saturday morning cartoon shows and said that was

what he wanted for Christmas. I saw a couple of the ads myself and it looked like fun, so I said okay."

"Strike one," he announced. "Now for my second question. When you went to buy one, did you find all the stores sold out?"

"That is right, I did! The stores said they'd ordered some but did not know when they'd get any more in. So I had to buy Christopher some other toys to make up for the road-race set. But how did you know?"

"Strike two," he said. "Just let me ask one more question. Did not this same sort of thing happen the year before with the robot toy?"

"Wait a minute. . . you are right. That is just what happened. This is incredible. How did you know?"

"No psychic powers; I just happen to know how several of the big toy companies jack up their January and February sales. They start prior to Christmas with attractive TV ads for certain special toys. The kids, naturally, want what they see and extract Christmas promises for these items from their parents. Now here's where the genius of the companies' plan comes in: They undersupply the stores with the toys they've gotten the parents to promise. Most parents find those things sold out and are forced to substitute other toys of equal value. The toy manufacturers, of course, make a point of supplying the stores with plenty of these substitutes. Then, after Christmas, the companies start running the ads again for the other special toys. That juices up the kids to want those toys more than ever. They go running to their parents whining, 'You promised, you promised,' and the adults go trudging off to the store to live up dutifully to their words."

"Where," I said, beginning to see now, "they meet other parents they haven't seen for a year, falling for the same trick, right?"

"Right. Uh, where are you going?"

"I'm going to take that road-race set right back to the store." I was so angry I was nearly shouting.

"Wait. Think for a moment first. Why did you buy it this morning?"

> "Because I did not want to let Christopher down and because I wanted to teach him that promises are to be lived up to."
>
> "Well, has any of that changed? Look, if you take his toy away now, he won't understand why. He'll just know that his father broke a promise to him. Is that what you want?"
>
> "No," I said, sighing, "I guess not. So, you are telling me that they doubled their profit on me for the past two years, and I never even knew it; and now that I do, I'm still trapped—by my own words. So, what you are telling me is, 'Strike Three.'"
>
> He nodded, "And you are out." (Cialdini, 1993: 65–66)

Everyone wants to be in control; this is basic human nature. Think of how you feel in an airport when your plane is delayed, and the gate attendants do not provide you with any information. You feel helpless and out of control. This is precisely why the pilot of an airplane will make an announcement during the flight of where you are, your estimated time of arrival, and how high you are flying. As a passenger, are you going to argue that he's flying too low? The announcement is designed to give you a sense of control in a situation in which you are virtually helpless.

Give customers a sense of ownership over your firm's services by providing them with information, offering them choices, and customizing your delivery to meet their needs. FedEx and UPS, for example, have spent billions of dollars providing customers with computers and software that allow them to track their own shipments. While this has not increased the efficiency or decreased the time of delivery, it has gone a long way toward giving the customers a sense of ownership over their shipping needs. The customer also has been given the power to access the internal workings of these two organizations, making for an "excuseless" culture. Some professionals would be uncomfortable giving their customers complete access to their work-in-progress, yet this is exactly what is beginning to happen among law firms. Customers are demanding instantaneous access to work as it is performed on their case, through Internet and intranet links, a trend that will increase. Imagine for a moment that your customers could track, in real time, exactly where their work was within your firm. Would this change how work-in-progress was allocated and completed in your firm? Would this make your team members more responsible for completing work within the customer's expectations? Why aren't more professional service firms providing this level of service, especially since the Internet makes this possibility virtually costless?

Value Pricing Improves Communication

Effective communication is one of the characteristics of the successful firms when it comes to value pricing. Better communication with the customer leads to fewer write-downs and write-offs, and also lowers the probability of litigation. Keeping the lines of communication open between your firm and the customer is critical in making your climb up the value curve. Offer the customer unlimited phone calls and meetings any time during the year to tear down the time-clock mentality. Nobody likes to be nickeled and dimed for every phone call or meeting.

If customers have an "Unlimited Access" in the FPA offering unlimited phone calls and meetings, they will seek your advice *before* engaging in a significant transaction. Many professionals look at their customers after the fact and say, "Why didn't you contact me before you did this? If we had structured it this way, we could have saved $X?" Customers do not contact you because they want to avoid paying for every call. By removing that negative feeling, you will learn what the customer is planning and have an opportunity to add value *before* a major event, thereby advancing your firm's services up the value curve.

Furthermore, the process of drafting the FPA, with the customer's input, will dramatically improve the communication between the parties. The FPA isn't so much a legal contract as it is a method of communication. Similar to the practice of companies having employees sign a mission (or value) statement, getting the customer's signature on the FPA is an effective way of cementing the relationship. Most people place great emphasis on their signature and take seriously the obligations signed. This is what makes the FPA so valuable, even though it contains a relatively easy exit clause.

Quoting Fixed Prices Projects Confidence and Experience

A most frequent question regarding offering fixed prices is: "How do you know how to set the price before you know how long it will to take to perform the service?" The response to this question is that the price of the service has absolutely nothing to do with how long it takes you.

If you are not yet comfortable with this thinking, consider that you can set a price after a service has been performed, either by writing it up or, more likely, down; then why are you unable to determine the value before you start? Most of the work professionals perform (probably more than 90 percent) is routine, which means professionals have enough experience to quote a fixed price.

Sometimes when you quote a price, the nature of the engagement changes so much that a higher price is warranted. But that does not mean you should not quote a price up front. What it means is that you issue a change order when unexpected events arise that require more resources to be devoted by your firm. Change orders require you to stop working and communicate with the customer that the nature of the engagement has changed, why it has changed, and how much more it is going to cost them. Change orders are discussed more extensively later in this chapter and in Chapter 11. They are a wonderful device for communicating with the customer and extracting a higher price when the original job quoted has changed in scope.

Two other points need to be raised regarding quoting fixed prices up front. First, your competition is probably not doing this, except perhaps for audits and tax returns. Quoting fixed prices gives a significant competitive advantage; but as customers continue to revolt against hourly billing, this advantage will wane.

Second, never quote a range of price. When you are too timid to quote a single price and say something to the effect of: "It will cost between $15,000 and $20,000," the customer heard $15,000 and you heard $20,000. When you submit an invoice for $18,000, thinking you saved the customer $2,000, the customer is going to ask why it cost $3,000 more than you said. Never quote ranges. Straighten your back, push up your shoulders, get up your nerve, and quote the high end of your mental range, every time. This will avoid many disputes at the end of the engagements.

Value Pricing Increases a Customer's Switching Costs

When you enter into an FPA with your customers, you are increasing their switching costs over time. The higher the price of the agreement, the more services you are performing, and the more you know about a customer, the more expensive it will be for the customer to defect. This binds the two of you in "golden handcuffs" and is a prerequisite for creating a long-term partnership.

Think about airlines' frequent flyer programs. Because they impose a switching cost on travelers who might otherwise divide their flying budgets among several airlines, they encourage customers to use only one airline. These programs, which were introduced in 1981, are extremely effective in engendering loyalty among customers.

Creating a partnership with your customers interlinks your destiny and prosperity. When you have a partnership, you are no longer worried about your competition, but you are focused on your customer's competition. Your goal is to climb up the value curve by offering more consultative services.

Also, by bundling a package of services into an FPA, you are making it more difficult for a competitor to enter into the customer relationship, because they won't be able to single out one part of the bundled services in order to offer a lower price (this is the reason you don't want to price each service in the FPA separately, but rather as a whole package). Price bundling also reduces the customer's propensity to haggle over each item and instead focus on the value of all the services being provided.

Value Pricing Forces Your Firm to Be Efficient

Needless to say, if your firm offers fixed prices, you must delegate the work to the level best equipped to handle it— this prevents surgeons from piercing ears. This frees up manager and partner time to cross-sell the firm's services as the firm makes its way up the customer's value curve. By developing efficient internal methods, procedures, and processes to complete routine work, you also lower your internal costs and achieve higher profitability.

Start with a blank page and analyze each procedure, process, and method your firm performs, asking yourself the following questions:

- Why do we do this?
- Do we need to do it at all?
- Does it add value for our customers?
- If so, how can we do it better?

If it does not add value to the customer, there's no need to do it. There is no right way to do the wrong thing. Professional firms charge for everything they can. Focus on those things that the customer values, not on faxes, copies, phone calls, technology fees, or computer processing fees, none of which the customer values. At Milliken & Company, an international textile and chemical firm and a Malcolm Baldrige National Quality Award winner, a sign reads: "Quality is not the absence of defects as defined by management, but the presence of value as defined by customers." If work is delegated to the most effective person, the customer is assured that the person with the most experience is handling the work, a tremendous selling point if your firm is large.

Value Pricing Overcomes Buyer's Emotions

Value pricing works to overcome price resistance, payment resistance, and price anxiety, common emotions experienced by buyers. These emotions are discussed in detail in Chapter 8.

Value Pricing Gives the Customer a Chance to Complain

A "100% Unconditional Money Back Service Guarantee" clause included in the FPA is a covenant with customers that if, for any reason whatsoever, they are not satisfied with your firm's value proposition (quality, service, or price), you agree to give them a complete refund, or let them pay what they believe is the worth of the service(s). Notice this is not based on any type of result or contingency (which may be in violation of various ethical and government laws); rather, it is based upon the customer's level of satisfaction. This involves taking a risk, but that is, after all, where profits come from. Here is what Maister says about the service guarantee:

> Consider the alternative. Without a guarantee, what is a firm saying to its clients? "We're committed to complete satisfaction, but if we fail to please you, we expect to be paid anyway!" (Maister, 1997: 196)

Consider the advantages of this strategy, then decide for yourself if you think the risk is worth the reward.

The service guarantee communicates a commitment to excellence and total quality service on the part of your firm by *showing* your customers—not just *telling* them—how much better you are than your competition. Your entire firm will be driven to exceed the customer's expectations, as everyone, from the receptionist on up, will be cognizant of how important this is because your money is where your mouth is. A guarantee sends the message that there is no profit center in your firm that people can automatically count on, other than a customer's check that does not bounce. Your inferior competition cannot (and will not) offer a guarantee like this, and that gives you an advantage in the marketplace, which is especially effective with new customers. It may be the one element in your request for proposal (RFP) that sways the customer to go with your firm, by eliminating their risk. It also generates word-of-mouth advertising, the most effective advertising known.

A guarantee forces your firm to prequalify new customers more effectively. Because you realize you are liable to give back the money, you want to have a high level of trust with the customer. You must develop a mutually advantageous relationship, understand each other's expectations, and make sure that each party receives value from entering into the transaction.

All things being equal, a service that is guaranteed is worth more than one that is not. You will be able to command a higher price for offering this level of commitment to the customer. Why should the customer bet on you if you will not bet on yourself?

An additional benefit of offering the service guarantee, more important than those listed above, is this: It gives the customer an incentive to complain. Customer complaints, when handled correctly, are actually opportunities in disguise to impress the customer with your great service and increase their loyalty, goodwill, and, ultimately, retention.

Only 4 percent of dissatisfied customers complain. The other 96 percent quietly go away and 91 percent of those will never come back. Further, a typical dissatisfied customer will tell eight to 10 people about his or her problem. One in five will tell 20. This is why it takes 12 positive service incidents to make up for one negative incident. If word-of-mouth advertising can build businesses, think how negative word-of-mouth advertising can destroy them. Generally speaking, customers will not complain for three reasons:

1. They think it will do no good;
2. Complaining is difficult; and
3. Most customers do not want to feel awkward and pushy. Competition is intense and customers find fleeing easier than fighting.

In 1988, more than 450 million people traveled by airplane. Yet, only 21,000 complained. In one month alone, 20,000 passengers had their baggage mishandled (lost, delayed, damaged) and only 156 passengers bothered to file complaints. These results are quite consistent with human behavior.

In total quality service organizations, a complaint represents an opportunity to correct a problem and a second chance to preserve the customer relationship. When a customer complains, firms gain valuable knowledge of areas of service delivery that need improvement. A firm that is unaware of how or where it needs to improve is no better than one that is unable to improve. A complaint is a second chance to gain the customer's business. If corrected to the customer's satisfaction, a complaint can actually increase customer loyalty.

When it comes to defects, the customer will remember the *satisfying outcome*, not the original error. When customers bring errors to your attention, the customers need to be rewarded with fast, positive action. A customer problem represents a gap between what the customer wanted to have happen and what actually happened. When customers are upset enough to complain, their stress level is very high but their expectations are very low (they may even be expecting an argument). If you handle the error correctly, you have a wonderful opportunity to exceed those expectations and quite literally turn customers into raving fans who will tell their spouses, friends, and colleagues what a satisfactory service experience they had with your firm.

The golden rule with respect to customer recovery systems is simple: It is not *who is right;* it is *what is right.* Rather than abdicating personal responsibility for an error, take ownership of it. Hal Rosenbluth, CEO of Rosenbluth Travel, returns the commissions earned on any travel arrangements his company makes incorrectly, in effect, working for free whenever a mistake is made in the customer's travel itinerary. Now that is a service guarantee. According to Rosenbluth in his book *The Customer Comes Second and Other Secrets*:

> It's better to spend money refunding clients when they are not satisfied than to forfeit money in lost accounts for the same reason.
>
> Many of our service-guarantee refunds have been because of supplier error [airlines, hotels, rental car agencies, etc.], but we returned our commissions to our clients because we hold ourselves responsible for the entire process. (Rosenbluth, 1992: 135, 204)

That is a practice that is virtually nonexistent in the travel agency industry. It is a commitment to total quality service. No amount of marketing can purchase the loyalty that results from that type of treatment. *If you wouldn't charge your best friend for the service, do not charge your customer*. It is a very high standard to live by, but that is what total quality service is all about—constantly raising the bar of customer expectations.

Will customers take advantage of you? Perhaps. But at least they will identify themselves as problem customers, and you will refund their money *once*, then drop them from your customer base. The customers who try to take advantage of you are not the type of customers you want. Of the many CPAs I've met who offer service guarantees, very few have ever given a full refund. More have given partial refunds—and admit that the customer was entitled to them because the CPA was at fault. Most customers are not out to take advantage of you, but if you believe they are and this attitude prevents you from implementing a policy that has such tremendous advantages, then you are too involved in trying to solve problems. You are forgoing wonderful opportunities.

Studies conducted by Marriott on guest return rates found the following astonishing results: If the guest had no problems during their stay, the return rate was 89 percent. If the guest encountered a problem during the stay and it was not corrected to their satisfaction, the return rate dropped to 69 percent. However, if guests had problems that were solved to their satisfaction, the return rate jumped to 94 percent. This explains Marriott's zealousness to make sure that no guest leaves any of its properties unsatisfied. So even when you have defects—and you will never achieve zero defects in a professional firm because to err is human—you can turn them into zero *defections* by correcting the problem to the customer's delight.

Consider Nordstrom, world-renowned for taking any item back, anytime, for any reason. Does the company get burned? Sometimes, but typically only by 2 to 3 percent of their customers. It's the other 97 to 98 percent that they are concerned with. And those customers appreciate and pay a premium for Nordstrom's no-hassle return policy. Wal-Mart, Embassy Suites, and Hampton Inns all offer the same guarantee and have nothing but praise for the policy.

Another point with respect to client complaints is to be wary if you are not receiving any. Nobody is ever completely satisfied with the level of service you are performing; there is always room for improvement. Either your customers are not being candid, or, more likely, they are not being asked for feedback. In fact, according to the U.S. Office of Consumer Affairs, 37 to 45 percent of all service customers are dissatisfied but do not complain. This is an astonishing statistic that should alert you to encourage complaints and view each one as an opportunity to build customer loyalty and goodwill.

A last consideration is this: **You already offer a service guarantee.** If customers complain loudly enough, you write down or write off their bills. But you are doing this after the fact, when you receive no benefit from it. You already have the policy in place but it is *covert*, not *overt*. By placing the guarantee in your marketing literature, firm brochure, on your letterhead, fax coversheet, and in your FPAs, you will derive a tangible benefit. Not only will you be valued more highly and command a greater level of respect in the eyes of the customer, but this also will assist you in value pricing by removing more risk from the customer.

In addition to the service guarantee, the price guarantee included in the FPA is designed to ensure that your firm sets the price when you have the leverage, which is before the work begins. At this point, you will command the highest value price possible. By offering the customer the price guarantee—insisting they do not have to pay for work they did not pre-authorize—you are further reducing their risk and instilling a "no surprises" culture in your firm, thereby enhancing your climb up the value curve.

Value Pricing Prices Can Be Increased Each Year

When was the last time you raised your hourly rate? What did your customers think? (Did you even ask them?) Most customers do not like it because they do not equate your hourly rate with any tangible value. But with an FPA, on the other hand, the totality of your firm's value proposition is right in front of them, and they had a hand in designing it. Therefore, every year, even if no services are added to the FPA, you will be able to increase the price by a cost-of-living factor. How much should a no-change FPA be raised? Consider that your customers are used to most of their business costs increasing every year. Look at a customer's income statement, talk about major vendors, and try to ascertain how much the customer's costs went up. If you learn that a customer's major supplier, which makes up 20 percent of the cost of goods sold, increased prices by 8 percent, you will use that as a benchmark. You may increase your price by 5 percent. Other factors to consider are your relationship with the customer, whether you are getting a larger share of the customer's wallet, whether you are able to cross-sell them additional services in the upcoming year, and the payment terms.

It is a fact that you will be able to increase your prices every year with a customer who has entered into an FPA with less resistance than with one who did not. This is easier than trying to raise your hourly billing rate.

Value Pricing Provides a Competitive Differentiation

Since each FPA is *customized* to the customer, the perceived value of your firm increases. In contrast, by using hourly billing, you are simply treating all customers the same, which is not a prescription for success in today's marketplace. Innovation is important in the business world today. Customers want their professionals to be creative and innovative in helping them solve their problems and pursue opportunities. Being innovative with respect to designing and pricing your firm's services, and customizing them to each customer, is a truly effective competitive differentiation in the marketplace.

Your close rate will increase when you offer fixed prices combined with a service guarantee to new customers. Customers love this type of pricing, and that alone will ensure increases in the years ahead. The competitive window of advantage will slowly close as customers come to *expect* fixed prices, so the time to adopt the practice is before the rest of the crowd does. The early adopters almost always benefit the most by taking a new risk. Once the method is fully proven, and the rest of a population adopts it, the profit opportunities will diminish.

Value Pricing Specifies Conditions for Change Orders

Auto mechanics are sued principally over the quality of their work. You take your rough-running car to a mechanic, get it back, and it still runs rough. The issue is never how long it took the mechanic to perform the job, despite standard shop rates and estimated times to perform each job, which are used as a benchmark to provide prices. Then consider why professionals have pricing and collection problems. The reason rarely concerns the quality of the work, but rather how much time it took, the most popular question from the customer being, "How could it have taken that long?" This is an interesting contrast and leads to the question, "What are the mechanics doing that professionals are not?" The answer is that they are issuing change orders. Various state laws force mechanics to give the customer an estimate before each job is done, and this imposes on them the legal requirement to contact the customer and explain how the scope of the job has changed and provide an estimate of the cost. But why should you wait for a law to be passed to engage in a practice that is obviously highly effective? Part of being "professional" means that you are self-regulating and do not look to government licensing bodies to promulgate business practices that make sense for your customers (not to mention for you).

Value Pricing Lowers Asymmetrical Information

Customers will always try to conceal from you how much they are willing to pay for your services. Economists refer to *asymmetrical information* as information concerning a transaction that is unequally shared between the two parties to the transaction.

The FPA provides a venue for a meeting of the minds to take place between customer and professional when it comes to designing and valuing a firm's services. This is a tremendous opportunity to discover exactly what a customer values. The next chapter discusses questions you can ask the customer to lower the level of asymmetrical information that naturally exists between any buyer and seller.

Value Pricing Provides an Opportunity for a Two-Part Tariff

Steven E. Landsburg, in his textbook *Price Theory and Applications*, describes the two-part tariff:

> It occurs when a firm charges an initial fee in exchange for the right to purchase its services. For example, an amusement park might charge an entrance fee, followed by a price for each ride. Private dining clubs require yearly membership fees that entitle the member to buy meals. Polaroid pictures provide a less obvious example. No consumer wants a camera for its own sake; the good that you actually purchase from the Polaroid company is Polaroid pictures. You pay for these pictures in two steps: First you pay for the camera, which then makes it possible for you to buy film and take pictures. (Landsburg, 1996: 376)

How can you apply this pricing strategy to your professional firm? One way is to start charging new customers a setup price for setting up the customer file, performing due diligence research, contacting the predecessor CPA (or attorney), and generally everything else that is entailed in taking on a new customer. This is a very effective strategy for tapping into the consumer surplus.

Second, your firm can establish a minimum price that you will never go below to serve a customer. Setting this price requires some creative thought on your part. One percent of gross revenue is sometimes used, and this appears to be a reasonable benchmark. For instance, if your book of business is $300,000, you should not spend your time on any one customer with less than $3,000 in revenue opportunity. One advantage of the percentage method is that it grows with your firm. As you grow, your customer base changes, you gain more experience, and you want to move up the value curve. By establishing a minimum price, you are ensuring that your firm will not devote its precious resources (and fixed costs) to customers who do not value them highly enough.

Another advantage of a minimum price is it allows your referral network to screen potential customers for you. If a referral source sends you a potential customer, he or she will already know about your minimum price, and you can start the negotiations from that point. If the customer is turned away by the minimum price, your referral source just did you an enormous favor—prequalified a price-sensitive customer on your behalf, without you spending any time whatsoever.

Value Pricing Opens Lines of Communications

The "Unlimited Access" service provides all FPA customers with unlimited phone calls and meetings for an annual charge. This is similar to attorneys being paid a retainer whether they earn it or not and is very effective. Customers are guaranteed that you are always on call for them, willing to meet to discuss important issues affecting their businesses and personal lives. This breaks down that Berlin Wall of communication between you and the customer, you discover events *before* they happen, which is precisely the time when you can add the most value, and you can cross-sell additional services and value price them accordingly by issuing change orders.

This service will obviously be priced at different levels depending on the size of the customer, what is happening in their lives, how involved you are with them, and, of course, what they are willing to pay for it. And recall from the discussion of absolute versus relative price, any time you put a fixed cost on a product or service, customers will gravitate to the higher quality goods.

By paying for an Unlimited Access service, the customer is more likely to climb up the value curve of your firm and purchase the more expensive services you offer.

Summary and Conclusions

Overwhelming empirical evidence from inside and outside the professions proves that the advantages of value pricing outweigh the disadvantages. However, if you are still skeptical of value pricing, it is a hypothesis that can be tested in the marketplace. Begin to implement value pricing in incremental steps, allowing your firm to take the calculated risk of offering customers fixed prices. Once you begin to experience success, this will bolster your confidence enough that you will want to implement it on a wider range of services and engagements. It may take one to three years to get 80 percent of your firm's revenue under the aegis of value pricing. Move at a pace that is comfortable for your firm and for your customers. Creativity and intelligence will enable you to put these concepts into practice and to be successful in making the transition from hourly billing to value pricing, one customer at a time.

10 PREPARING FOR THE FIXED PRICE AGREEMENT MEETING

When I am getting ready to reason with a man I spend one-third of my time thinking about myself and what I am going to say, and two-thirds thinking about him and what he is going to say.

—Abraham Lincoln

Now that you have a good theoretical understanding of the advantages of a fixed price agreement (FPA), this chapter discusses how to negotiate a fixed price agreement as you meet with your customer. Ideally, the resulting FPA will be tailored to a customer's needs as well as to the personality and culture of your firm.

My Early Failures with Value Pricing

In 1989, I began implementing fixed-fee engagement letters (what I called them at the time). I selected a few good customers (based on my relationship with them, not necessarily the size of their revenues), and offered to enter into a fixed-fee arrangement with them. They were receptive to the idea, as it allowed them to budget exactly their accounting and tax costs. I had no idea why I was doing this (e.g., to remove the risk), so I did not engage in any price discrimination or charge a premium for the risk I was assuming.

Worse yet, I drafted these agreements in a vacuum, without any customer involvement. This was my biggest mistake, and it caused most of my early attempts at value pricing to fail. I would meet with the customer, explain the concept, and say something to the effect of, "I'll go back to my office and draft the agreement with what your accounting and tax needs will be in the forthcoming year, price it out, and send it to you for your approval." For every five agreements drafted in this manner, four were rejected. I did so many things wrong that recounting my errors would be of little benefit. I want to share what I have since learned is a more effective way to negotiate and prepare the fixed price agreement (FPA), namely *with* the customer's involvement.

The FPA Meeting

The sole purpose of the FPA meeting is to discuss with the customers the value that you add to their business and their lives. Naturally the subject of price will come up, but you should build your value first—the many services that you can offer the customer that both of you believe are needed—and price should be the last topic on the agenda. In the beginning I did not involve the customer in the design and nature of the services I was offering, and this was my biggest failure. Customer involvement is crucial to any sale.

Involvement refers to the level of mental and physical effort exerted by a customer in selecting a good or service. Would you buy an automobile without test driving it? Would you purchase a stereo without listening to it? The more involved the customer is, the more positive emotions are evoked, and positive emotions lead directly to more sales. Recall that nobody likes to be *sold* anything. When was the last time you purchased a big ticket item (car, house, appliance, etc.) and told your spouse or friends, "Guess what I was just *sold*?" The true sales professional involves the customers to the extent that they convince themselves on the sale; the sales professional merely helps rationalize what the customers want.

The major benefit of an FPA meeting is that the focus is on giving the customers exactly what they want and expect. This is an opportunity for you and a customer to create a shared vision of the future, to analyze where the customer is at this point, and to develop the necessary action plan to move them to where they want to be. The best salesmen in the world—from Tom Hopkins to Zig Ziglar—understand the power of getting the customer to envision a preferred future, and if you can assist the customer in attaining that vision, then you have made a tremendous move up the value curve.

Hold the meeting away from your office or the customer's, if possible. By getting out of your respective environments, you are less susceptible to distractions and interference. Avoid holding the meeting in the customer's office, where the customer will feel in control. Another disadvantage of meeting in the customer's office is that the customer may be less candid—the walls have ears—than in neutral territory.

Before the FPA meeting, refer to "Items to Consider Before Conducting a Fixed Price Agreement (FPA) Meeting with a Customer," found in the

"Useful Checklists" at the end of this book and on the CD-ROM, to make sure you have researched and analyzed your customer adequately.

Listen to the Customer

When you meet with a customer, let the customer talk. Try to maintain a ratio of the customer talking twice as much as you. This is difficult and requires self-restraint. Hardly anyone can achieve this ratio, even after several attempts, although it is desirable if you are to build value into your services. Listening is difficult because you think much faster than people talk. While someone is talking, you are usually listening with one-half of your brain and formulating your answer with the other. Active listening is a skill that needs to be developed. Professionals are fairly good at this, at least better than most salespeople. But you need to be even better.

Talkers may *dominate* a conversation but the listener *controls* it. In *The "I Hate Selling" Book*, Allan S. Boress says the best salesmen are good listeners:

> The best business producers listen much more than they talk. They know that by being quiet they'll learn more about other individuals and their needs. Also, clients and others greatly appreciate being listened to, which helps establish a good relationship and leads to more business. If you do more than 20 percent of the talking in a selling situation, you are doing something wrong. You must do whatever it takes to keep yourself from dominating the conversation. Instead of blabbering away, ask relevant questions, and then sit back and take notes while the client gives you the information you need to make the sale. (Boress, 1994: 16)

One of the best ways to get somebody to talk in more detail is to take notes. Taking notes conveys to the customer that what he is saying is important and that you care enough to record it. It also helps you remember exactly what was said. But most important, and this is precisely why psychiatrists and psychologists take notes, the person will provide much more detail. The more you know, the more value you will be able to add, and the higher the prices you will command.

Avoid the ever-present temptation to provide solutions to the customer's problems. That is not the purpose of the FPA meeting, at least in the initial stages. Your role at this point is to ask questions and have the customer formulate—or at least articulate—a vision of the future. Resist what William Reeb, in *Start Consulting,* has called "premature speculation." (Reeb, 1998: 92) Before doctors can prescribe, they must diagnose, which is the role you assume at this stage in the FPA meeting.

Focus on Wants, Not Needs

Think of listening with having no preconceived notions of what the customer really wants. Karl Albrecht, in his book *The Northbound Train,* offers this axiom that is true of professionals: "The longer you've been in business, the greater the probability you do not really understand what's going on in the minds of your customers" (Albrecht, 1994: 138). Professionals are so skilled at solving problems that they begin to believe they know what the customer needs better than the customer. And this may be true with respect to needs. A lawyer certainly knows how to draft a contract to avoid future problems, and a CPA knows how to structure a tax-free exchange in order to defer paying tax. However, the focus is on *needs.* Customers want to know if you have a solution to their need and, if so what will be the cost? What is the risk of using your service vs. not using it? This is a rather straightforward process when dealing with a tax return, audit, or routine legal service. In contrast, when you are holding the FPA meeting, with the goal of building value, focus on the customer's *wants*. If you want to command premium prices, solving the customer's needs is not enough; you have to improve the customer's condition. Moving up the value curve is easier when people get what they want rather than what they need.

As Werner Erhard used to say, "The access to people is through their concerns." Be confident in your professional abilities to solve people's problems, but focus on their wants, desires, goals, and visions for the future. Professionals need to devote more time learning as much about the customer as they know about accounting, tax, and law.

The FPA meeting is the venue for exploring these areas, and sometimes more than one meeting is needed to determine exactly what the customer wants and desires from your firm. What better reason exists to meet with a customer than to discuss the value you are adding to the relationship?

In the old days when professionals enjoyed a seller's market, it was relatively easy to get the respect and trust of customers. In today's market, with a more sophisticated customer, this is no longer true. The FPA meeting is a means of earning the respect of customers because it aligns your interest with theirs and sends the signal that your firm is interested in their welfare and prosperity, not just billing hours. This type of face-to-face encounter is one of the most underused marketing tools of the professional, and yet it is one of the most effective ways to build perceived value in the mind of the customer. And since no seller imposes a price on a customer—after all, the customer is the one with the money—you must build up your value in the minds of your customers before you are able to prove your value with the results of your work.

You have to understand the importance of your existing customers, and how much more profitable they are than new ones. You also have to invest in those relationships—give something back, in effect—to *earn* people's loyalty. People want to be loyal, but only if you give them a reason. Long-term relationships are not static, they are dynamic. Either they are growing stronger or they are getting weaker. Far too many firms spend all of their marketing and advertising budgets chasing after new customers while ignoring their existing customers. You have no business getting new customers if you are not pleasing your existing ones. At least half of your marketing budget should be devoted to retention marketing—investing in current customer relationships, geared toward the top 20 to 30 percent of your customer base, which most likely represents 80 percent of your gross revenue and profits.

Questions to Ask Yourself Before You Set a Price

The premise is that the more you know about your customers, the better able you will be to approximate their position on your firm's demand curve (not necessarily the value curve). For example, even if you are setting a price for a "commodity" service such as an audit or tax return, you know that because you have a downward-sloping demand curve, customers exist who are willing and able to pay more than you would have charged them if you used a market price as a benchmark. Some businesses are fortunate in that the customers identify themselves. First-class passengers on an airline and hardcover book buyers come to mind. But how does a professional firm go about discovering which customers are at the top of its demand curve? For starters, by merely agreeing to enter into an FPA with your firm, such customers are, most likely, your least price sensitive, because they tend to recognize the value of the services being performed. The most effective method to discover your "first-class passengers" is by lessening the amount of asymmetrical information that exists between the buyer and seller, and that is accomplished through extensive questioning and listening to the customer to find out their true wants (and needs). The following are questions and issues you should consider, either on your own or with your associates who serve the customer, prior to establishing a price.

The first group of issues to consider comes from the American Bar Association's Model Rules of Professional Conduct, which set forth the ground rules governing all fees. Rule 1.5, which deals with lawyers' fees, states, "A lawyer's fee shall be reasonable." That is a highly subjective definition and is certainly subject to debate between the lawyer and the customer. The rule has eight factors to be considered in determining the reasonableness of a fee:

1. The time and labor required, novelty and difficulty involved, and the skill needed to perform the services.
2. The likelihood, if apparent to the client, that acceptance of the assignment will preclude other employment.
3. The customary fee charged for similar services in the locality.
4. The amount involved and results obtained.
5. Time limits imposed by the client or circumstances.
6. The nature and length of the professional relationship with the client.
7. The experience, reputation, and ability of the lawyers performing the services.
8. Whether the fee is fixed or contingent.

"Rule 1.5 recommends that the fee agreement be in writing unless the lawyer regularly represents the client. If the fee is contingent, then the agreement *must* be in writing." (Reed, 1992: 15)

You can certainly advance the argument that this is a self-serving list of factors drawn up by a special interest group representing attorneys. But the point is not that these factors are self-serving as much as that these factors are considered *at all* in determining a price. In other words, more is being considered than just the time spent. The ABA showed creativity and sagacity in discussing factors other than time that add value to the customer. CPAs have no such rule and have for too long considered time as the main benchmark for their prices. However, attorneys consider several other factors, and CPAs should do the same.

A look at the eight factors shows how they contribute to the value professionals provide their customers. Number one is obvious but number two is interesting. For CPAs, this is not as common an occurrence as for attorneys, but it certainly can happen. If acceptance of an assignment precludes acceptance of other assignments, a premium price should be charged since you are forgoing other opportunities, especially if a particular customer does not want you to work with a competitor and you have built up substantial industry experience.

Number three is just a way to gauge what the local market charges for similar services and is not a reliable indicator of how much any one customer values your services.

Number four is important in a contingency or results-based price, which is only allowed for certain services and only in states that allow this type of pricing.

Number five is charging for convenience, which is not done enough by CPAs.

Number six proclaims an important law of customer loyalty economics: The longer you have a relationship with customers, the more highly they value your services. This is due in part to their switching costs being higher, but also because they are familiar with your firm, understand your capabilities, and are less likely to be lured away simply to save a few dollars. Also, your cost of serving veteran customers is much less than the cost of serving a new customer, as the latter tend to demand a lot of hand-holding from partners and managers and are less receptive to various team members working on their engagement. Veterans, by contrast, are more familiar with your firm and its personnel and may even demand to have a particular team member work on their engagement. All these factors mean that a veteran customer will pay higher prices than a new one, on average.

Number seven is particularly important if your firm offers experiential and unique services, as indicated on the value curve, such as litigation support, real estate, business valuations, divorce planning, succession planning, major tax litigation, and mergers and acquisitions. This type of work is performed by professionals who are seen by their customers as having extensive experience and skill in these areas; and by their nature, these services are valued more highly than services located lower on the value curve.

Number eight deals with contingent fees, and this is becoming a major issue for CPAs, especially since more than half of the states now allow this type of pricing.

Charles and Joseph Larson, in their book *Innovative Billing and Collection Methods That Work*, list the following factors that influence the value of your services, which should be premium priced accordingly:

- Special expertise or knowledge
- Special resources, such as software and access to similar engagements completed for other clients
- Special contacts that facilitate a transaction
- Opportunity to achieve unique results
- Risk assumption, credit liability, or otherwise
- Extra effort based on deadlines or any form of accommodation for the client
- Potential profit or loss to the client
- "No one else can do it" factor
- Convenience
- Comfort level

(Larson and Larson, 1994: 140)

Keep this checklist handy to see if any of these factors are present on a particular engagement. If so, you should be able to command a higher price. For instance, in our firm we have developed a good working relationship with various agents who work on the IRS Practitioner Priority Service. Usually we are able to get special accommodations for our customers, such as stays on collection activities, with a simple phone call. These relationships took years to develop and they are worth a great deal to the customers, especially to one who is about to have a bank account levied. We would be leaving substantial sums of money on the table by pricing according to the time involved. The same is true for networks you may refer customers to for various business deals—bankers, insurance agents, and attorneys. All of these relationships are part of your firm's unique human and social capital and should command a price in accordance with the value the customer receives, not the time it takes to place a phone call.

Before determining a price for any customer, it is a good idea to brainstorm with the team that serves the customer and at least one individual who does not even know the customer (if you have a large enough firm), just to have an outsider who is not familiar with the personalities who can be objective. Here are questions that are useful in establishing a price:

- Who on the organizational chart am I dealing with?
- Who referred the customer to me?
- What is the nature of the relationship with the referral source?
- What is the time line on the customer's decision to select a CPA?
- What are the impending deadlines driving the decision to engage a CPA?
- Who is paying for the service?
- Are any competitors in the arena with me? Who?
- Do I have any price information from those competitors (bids, RFPs, etc.)?
- How profitable is the organization? How long has it been in business?
- Who was the prior CPA and what is the reason for the change?
- If the business is new, who is the banker, the attorney, etc.?
- How sophisticated is the customer with respect to my services?
- What is the relative price the customer would pay for the service?
- Is the service I am providing a want or a need?
- Does this customer add to the firm's skills, or am I simply using existing skills?
- Does this customer open up a new niche or market segment for the firm?
- Do I like this customer? Is it a business I am interested in?
- Ideally, what price would we consider commensurate with the value the firm is providing?

Three internal prices should be established: (1) a *reservation* price (a price that will provide a *normal* profit to the firm and one you will not go one nickel below), (2) a *hope for* price (a price that will return a *supernormal* profit to the firm), and (3) a *pump fist* price (a price that will return a *windfall* profit to the firm). Obviously, you should quote the pump fist price first because you will never get it if you do not ask for it. Remember, only talk price after discussing with the customer their needs, wants, and the value of your services.

Several years ago I got a call from a bookkeeper who works with one of my FPA customers and who has been a good referral source over the years. She had recently picked up a new customer, a limited liability corporation (LLC), that was in its first half-year of operations, had a fiscal year-end, and had a tax return due in approximately six weeks. The LLC was 25 percent owned by a company located in France and 75 percent owned by a local woman. The company needed a tax return, and the French company's CPA firm—one of the then Big Five—had quoted a price that the bookkeeper was asked to see if she could improve upon.

When the bookkeeper called, my mind raced to the above questions. First, this was a warm referral source, who knows me quite well, and therefore I am probably presold to the owner, as my abilities had already been testified to by the bookkeeper. Also, I would be dealing with the CEO of the company. The higher on the organizational chart the employee you are dealing with is, the less price sensitive that employee will be. A CEO does not have time to interview multiple CPAs, so if you are at that level, your chances are fairly good of landing the customer. A CEO also has other concerns, such as productivity, profitability, and value, that a CFO, or accounting manager might not consider as important.

Also, the company had an impending deadline. In six weeks the company had to file its first tax return. The owner would be traveling to France in two weeks to stay for another three weeks. Therefore, she was ready to make a decision immediately. The French company had infused some working capital into the company, which was a consideration because when spending someone else's money you are less price sensitive.

The bookkeeper told me that the then Big Five firm quoted $5,400 and the owner thought that was a little steep. This was a new business and not very profitable, so I had to come in at less than $5,400. In this case, the prior CPA was not an issue (there was no prior CPA), but that is always a consideration in your prequalifying routine. Checking references is also important, but since this came from a person I knew and trusted, I did not check any other references.

The owner was a first-time business owner, so she was not a sophisticated buyer of CPA services. Part of my job would consist of educating her about what a CPA can offer and the value of these services. This particular customer would add to my firm's skills because LLCs were relatively new at the time, and this was a customer with some interesting issues that needed to be explored. I did not do a personality grading, because I did not get a chance to meet the customer before I priced the service. I relied solely on what the bookkeeper told me, and did not learn anything that would prevent me from wanting to work with the people involved.

The bookkeeper faxed me the financial statements, which consisted of a one-page balance sheet and a one-page income statement (this was a new business, only in operation for six months). Looking at the financials, I knew the tax return would take me no longer than four hours. At a theoretical "standard hourly rate" of $200, I would quote this job at $800.

A partner once told me that, in a situation that was numerically similar to mine, he felt that the customer was being ripped off at $5,400, and he quoted the job at $1,000. He did not get it. He told me he learned a valuable lesson from that: Low prices command low respect. In the mind of the customer, his service could not be of equal quality at less than one-fifth the price. If all customers have is price to judge a service on, they will naturally assume that high price equals quality service.

Based on my answers to the above questions, I put together an FPA priced at $3,500 (my *hope for* price), and the owner signed it and faxed it back immediately. And I left money on the table. Realistically, I could have bid $4,000 and perhaps as high as $4,500 (my *pump fist* price). I simply did not have the courage at the time (this changes; over time your courage increases dramatically). Nevertheless, with hourly billing I would have left $2,700 on the table—more than three times standard. This is what is meant by pricing on the margin and turning pricing into the art that it is, rather than an administrative task involving hours times rate.

You may ask: "What would happen if she goes to another CPA next year and discovers that the job is worth $1,000?" The answer is: "You do not let her go to another CPA next year." You meet with her, educate her, and sell her more services, thereby increasing her switching cost and creating a partnership with her so that she will not go out looking for another provider. The value of any product or service is what someone is willing to pay for it. A CPA can command $3,500 for a tax return some competitors may be willing to perform for $1,000—if the CPA provides $2,500 more value through total quality service and developing a partnership with the customer.

Questions You Should Ask the Customer

There are questions you should ask the customer in order to lower the level of asymmetrical information and assist you in determining just where on the demand curve your customer is. The more information you seek from customers, the better equipped you will be to assess their price sensitivity. Always ask open-ended questions to engage the customer in discussing goals, aspirations, fears, and desires. This has a tremendous psychological impact, because most people's favorite topic is themselves. Once you have determined the customer's needs, focus on *wants,* because that is where the value pricing opportunities are. Start with the following questions (I am indebted to Troy Waugh for some of these questions):

- What do you expect from us?
- What is your current plan?
- What keeps you awake at night?
- How do you see us helping you address these challenges and opportunities?
- What growth plans do you have?
- Do you expect capital needs? New financing?
- Do you anticipate any mergers, purchases, divestitures, recapitalizations, or reorganizations in the near future?
- We know you are investing in total quality service. What are the service standards you would like for us to provide you?
- How important is our service guarantee to you?
- How important is rapid response on accounting and tax questions? What do you consider rapid response?
- Why are you changing professionals? What did you not like about your former firm that you do not want us to repeat?*
- How did you enjoy working with your former firm?**

---

* Do not denigrate the predecessor CPA (or attorney). First, this insults customers and reminds the customer of a poor decision. Second, this diminishes respect and confidence in the profession as a whole.

** Even though the customer is changing firms, almost certainly the customer liked some characteristics of the predecessor. Find out what these were and exceed them. For instance, if the prior CPA always returned phone calls within one day, return them within 4 hours.

- Do you envision any other changes in your needs?
- Are you particularly concerned about any of your asset, liability, or income statement accounts?
- What are the best ways to learn about your business so we can relate your operations to the financial information and so we can be more proactive in helping you maximize your business success?
- Would you be comfortable if we were to attend certain of your internal management meetings as observers?
- May our associates tour your facilities?
- What trade journals do you read? What seminars and trade shows do you regularly attend? Would it be possible for us to attend these with you?
- What is your budget for this type of service?

Here is one of the most effective questions that you can ask during the FPA meeting, as suggested by Allan Boress in *The "I Hate Selling" Book*:

> If price was not an issue, what role would you want your CPA to play in your business? (Boress, 1994: 68)

The customer's answers to the foregoing questions will lower the level of asymmetrical information. The importance of this is illustrated by my experience several years ago while I was wandering around in a used bookstore and came across an out-of-print book. I had been searching for this book for a few years and was shocked to discover, upon opening it, that it was signed by the author. I would have gladly paid the owner $100 for that book and I was delighted to turn to the next page and learn that it was priced at $10. I did not say to the owner: "I was willing to pay $100 for this, but you have priced it at $10, so I'll split the $90 difference with you." Hardly. From an economist's viewpoint I walked out of that store $90 wealthier because I kept the entire consumer surplus in my pocket. Bookstore owners do not have the luxury of knowing all of their individual customer's wants, and perhaps the transaction costs of discovering what those wants are would be prohibitive. But would this owner have been better off had he known that I was searching for this particular book? Had he simply talked with me, he could have learned that I very much *wanted* this book, and he could have captured a portion of *my* consumer surplus. Professionals have the ability to ascertain their customers' wants and goals.

Let me reiterate, when a customer buys a product or service at a price less then he or she is willing to pay, and thereby keeps the consumer surplus for themselves, this makes the customer *happy*. On the other hand, when a seller sells a product or service for a price over and above the minimum price the seller was willing to accept—called *economic rent* by economists—this is what makes people *rich*. Simply by engaging your customer in a dialogue, you will learn all sorts of useful information that will assist you in setting a value price for your services.

In my seminar *The Shift from Hourly Billing to Value Pricing*, with a group of between 50 and 60 colleagues, I use the following experiment. I ask them to pretend that I have come to them as a customer who has spent his off-hours researching, writing, and developing a seminar. I have a business that provides me with a good living, but this is a serious avocation for me and the topic is in great demand. I have worked for years on my material and may someday write a book. The question is: "How should I price my seminar?"

These CPAs usually ask how much was spent in R&D for the course. The answer is approximately $20,000, including books, seminars, travel costs to benchmark with firms, etc. This does not include the opportunity cost of my time, which is what I could have made in my business had I spent the time working on it. But is this question even relevant? Sunk costs are sunk. Obviously I want to recover my costs and I hope to make a profit, but what I really want to know is how to price my seminar when someone from a professional firm calls me on the phone asking how much it would cost to bring me in for a day. What factors should I consider before quoting a price?

Here is a list of questions that my colleagues have advised me to ask before pricing the seminar (assume that all travel costs will be paid for by the customer):

- How many will be attending?
- How is the total number of attendees divided among partners, managers, professionals, and clerical staff?
- What is the location of the firm?
- What type of firm is it (CPA, PA, EA, or attorneys)?
- How long has the firm been in business? How profitable is it?
- What is the firm willing to pay?
- What is the firm's opportunity cost of coming to you?

This is a good group of questions. Notice how none of the questions has to do with time. These questions are designed to ascertain what the seminar is worth to this particular firm, at this particular time. The last question is especially good, because if a firm wanted to attend the one-day California CPA Education Foundation course, employees would incur travel costs, hotel and lodging, meals, and other incidentals. Those costs naturally would be compared to the cost of bringing the instructor to them. Should I not compute what that opportunity cost is for them before setting my price?

The questions from my colleagues prove that they intuitively understand value pricing. Yet many of them will go back to their offices and multiply time spent by an hourly rate. How much money will they leave on the table by not pricing in accordance with these questions? In some cases, a firm would have to pay more than $10,000 to send personnel to the course. This is why there are no "standard prices" for my services. As Napoleon Hill said, "There is no standard price on ideas. The creator of ideas makes his own price, and, if he is smart, gets it." (Hill, 1937: 99) These are words to live—and price—by.

Ascertaining Customer Loyalty

Although the FPA meeting is a venue to determine what the customer's expectations are, and how they have changed, it is just as important to continue to meet with the customer face-to-face to ascertain satisfaction with your firm's service. This is an integral part of providing total quality service and exceeding your customer's expectations, and these two components are essential to value pricing. What you want is a loyal, repeat customer. The goal should be zero defections.

In today's business world, the conventional wisdom is that only those things that are measured are managed. This may be true when you are producing widgets, but it is an absurd view when you are dealing with human beings and all of their flaws, foibles, and emotions. When it comes to customer loyalty, the most important things cannot be measured; they are simply what is in the hearts and minds of your customer. After all, the most important things in life—love, beauty, friendship—cannot be precisely defined, let alone measured. Attempts to ascertain customer satisfaction may be common, but because of the intangibles involved, these efforts may spring hidden traps you should be aware of.

Many businesses conduct customer satisfaction surveys, either by mail, over the phone, or with on-site questionnaires. However, customer surveys are an abused tool, especially in professional firms, where the relationship with the customer should be a partnership. Imagine placing a customer satisfaction survey, a #2 pencil, and a self-addressed, stamped envelope next to your spouse's coffee in the morning, with a note reading, "Honey, here is a survey on the state of our marriage. Please fill it out and send it back to me in the enclosed SASE, and then we'll talk (maybe)." You would not behave this way toward a spouse; why would you want to do this with your best customer?

Written surveys to gauge customer satisfaction have many design and implementation problems. The questions are naturally biased by how you formulate them and might not measure accurately how a customer truly feels about a particular service. You might leave out an issue (or questions) that a customer is particularly affected by and therefore have a service defect that goes undetected through this type of feedback. Also, most people do not like to write, and they certainly do not spend the waking hours of their lives cogitating on the nuances of your firm's service delivery.

Another problem with a written survey is that you are not going to get a representative sample of your firm's customers, because most likely your response rate will not be anywhere near 100 percent. How many people get excited about filling out a customer satisfaction survey? Customers may actually become annoyed with a long, 4 to 6 page survey, or a 15 to 30 minute telephone interview. You are most likely to get complete surveys from customers who either love you or who have just had a very rotten experience with your firm. Written surveys *will not* generate a representative sample of your customers.

The biggest problem with customer satisfaction surveys concerns what economists call *revealed preference*: what people *do* counts, not what they *say*. The entire point of customer satisfaction surveys is to determine whether or not your customers will continue to patronize your firm. What you want is customer loyalty, revealed by the customer returning, over and over, to your firm, rather than increases in your customer satisfaction scores. You could earn very high customer satisfaction scores and still lose customers. According to *Harvard Business Review*, 65 to 85 percent of customers who chose a new supplier said they were satisfied or very satisfied with their former supplier. Satisfaction is not enough—you must delight the customer.

In fact, this is exactly what happened to General Motors and other automobile companies in the 1980s. While GM was earning very high marks on dealer customer satisfaction surveys, the company was losing market share, and profits were anemic. Associates rewarded for high customer satisfaction surveys can raise their scores up by using methods such as bribing the customer with a free detail or oil change. Some associates will even change the answers. Thus the written surveys did not reflect reality.

You see this same phenomenon with Saturn, a company that receives very high customer satisfaction scores and is ranked very high in the J.D. Powers surveys. However, Saturn is not getting many repeat customers. The problem is that Saturns are usually sold to first-time car buyers, and once they own one for several years, they trade up to a more expensive line. So while Saturn has done a terrific job with customer satisfaction scores, it is not getting enough repeat business. The company figured this out and began manufacturing an upscale line.

What is a better way than written surveys to measure customer satisfaction? Try informal feedback, which includes face-to-face meetings in which you ask the customer open-ended questions such as How are we doing? How could we service you better? How do you feel? Another tool is customer advisory boards. Assemble your best customers and solicit their advice on serving them even better. These techniques may be informal, and not as quantitative as written surveys, but they are absolutely more effective.

Marriott, a total quality service organization whose entire culture is driven by the customer, discovered that its in-room satisfaction surveys were often being filled out by children (who usually checked off "poor" in every category). So Marriott developed several other listening posts where they solicit customer feedback. One of the most effective has been its cocktail parties on the concierge floor. Managers mingle and informally interview the customers, and they claim to have learned more vital information from this technique than almost any other.

CPAs meet with all of their customers at least once a year anyway; they should be meeting with the large ones quarterly, at least. Ask your customers at each meeting "How are we doing?" and "How could we serve you better?" and "How do you feel about our service?" You will be amazed by the amount of information your customers willingly give you in an informal encounter. By asking the customers how they *feel*, you elicit their true perceptions of your firm's service. This is better than asking them what they *think* because that is a question of intellect and can be challenged.

They may be unwilling to express their true thoughts because they feel intimidated; thinking can be challenged, feelings cannot. Asking how they feel gets to the truth of what the customer is thinking.

Professionals often object to this approach for two reasons, both of which have a false basis. First, they claim it is prohibitively expensive to meet this way with *every* customer and take the time to ask these questions. The answer to the objection is this: if you can't do it, have your team do it. Focus on the top 20 to 30 percent of your customers, who generate 80 percent of your business, and let the team members informally interview the others. Actually, it is prohibitively expensive *not* to do this because only 4 percent of customers complain, 96 percent just walk away, and 91 percent of those who walk away never come back.

The second objection to informal meetings is that by asking the customer for feedback you are raising the bar of their expectations. If you do not provide a higher level of service as a result, you have put the customer at risk. This is certainly possible, but research shows that just by asking your customers these questions, their satisfaction with you as a service provider actually increases.

Summary and Conclusions

It is important to understand that customers are not necessarily trying to minimize their legal and accounting costs; what they are trying to accomplish is maximizing the net value they receive from those costs. And net value is measured by taking the gross value of the service less its price. By engaging the customer, and getting an ego investment, you are offering a form of "participatory pricing" that in today's market customers expect. They can decide to fly first class or coach, shop at a department store or a discount store, and even place bids for airline travel at the price they desire through an online service such as priceline.com. Customers make these and a myriad of other decisions in which they have total control over the price/value equation.

Value pricing provides you with competitive differentiation that allows you to stand out from the crowd. Competition means *seeking together*. It means conformity, and the biggest gains are to be made not from playing the game differently, but from changing the game itself. The shift from hourly billing to value pricing changes the game completely, and the firms that adopt value pricing first, before it becomes adopted by the majority, stand to gain the most.

11 THE FIXED PRICE AGREEMENT AND CHANGE ORDERS

The goal of meeting with the customer is the fixed price agreement (FPA). This chapter focuses on the agreement itself and the elements that can be included. A sample agreement is reproduced and then discussed in detail to assist you in writing your own. Please take all of the numerical examples with a grain of salt because professional practices differ in size, type of customer served, experience, market, and length of time in business. Prices for any given service are only stated to illustrate the relative percentage of value that is being left on the table if you do not engage in value pricing.

A Sample Agreement

An FPA that is drafted between your firm and a customer is the result of a negotiating process. This is your chance to provide the customer with a customized list of services to meet specific needs and wants, to offer a fixed price for those services, and to specify the payment terms. No two FPAs should look alike—they should be as unique and individual as your customers. One of the biggest advantages of the FPA is that it allows you to treat customers *individually*. The more customized the FPA is, the higher its perceived value.

Some of the firms that engage in value pricing do not use written FPAs but rely instead on oral agreements. These firms are also self-insured when it comes to malpractice, so this procedure cannot be used by everyone. They also have long-term customers and a very high level of trust exists between the parties. These firms are admirable, and from a financial standpoint, they are among the top 5 percent in terms of annual partner income. However, use of written FPAs is still recommended. Also, if you have liability insurance, you must have written agreements, which leads to one final caveat regarding the sample FPA: The FPA does not replace your firm's standard engagement letter. You still must use engagement letters for each major service you provide, in accordance with your professional liability carrier's guidelines. (For CPAs, this means an engagement letter for each audit, review, compilation, tax return, and management advisory service.)

The only modification you need to make to your standard engagement letter is in the discussion of price (or, more likely, fees). In that section, simply refer to the fixed price agreement, dated xx/xx/xx, and that seems to satisfy the insurance carrier's requirements. The engagement letter is where you maintain all of the legal language (such as mediation and arbitration clauses in the event of a dispute, interest charged on past due amounts, the right to stop work for nonpayment of services). Nothing in your firm's present engagement letter should change as a result of using an FPA, with the exception of the price clause.

In the FPA you can discuss the value of your services that the customer will receive. You can tailor the FPA to build value in the eyes of the customer, without resorting to all of the legal language that must be contained in the engagement letter. The standard engagement letter has to comply with your liability carrier's requirements; it is not the vehicle for a discussion of value. The FPA, however, provides a venue to be as creative and imaginative as you'd like with respect to your services.

The following sample FPA is for use by CPAs; if you are an attorney, refer to the American Bar Association books edited and authored by Richard C. Reed that are listed in the Suggested Reading section; they contain many sample engagement agreements used by law firms.

Sample Fixed Price Agreement

December 1, 2004

Dear Customer:

In order to document the understanding between us as to the scope of the work that ABC, CPAs will perform, we are entering into this **Fixed Price Agreement** with XYZ, Inc. To avoid any misunderstandings, this Agreement defines the services we will perform for you as well as your responsibilities under this Agreement.

2005 PROFESSIONAL SERVICES

ABC will perform the following services for XYZ during 2005:

- 2004 W-2s/1099s and 4th Quarter Payroll Tax Reports and Workers' Comp Report
- 1st, 2nd, & 3rd Quarter Payroll 2005 Reports and Workers' Comp Reports and Fiscal Year Sales Tax Return

- 2004 Year-End Accounting Adjustments and Closing of 2004 Books
- 2004 XYZ S Corporation Tax Returns
- 2004 Audited Financial Statements with PBCs to be provided by XYZ by March 15, 2005
- Unlimited Access 2005*

TOTAL 2005 PROFESSIONAL SERVICES	$XXX

---

* Included in the Unlimited Access are the following services to be provided by ABC to XYZ:
  - Unlimited meetings to discuss operations of XYZ, business matters, tax matters, and any other topic at the discretion of XYZ or its employees and/or agents.
  - Unlimited phone support for XYZ personnel and/or independent contractors and agents regarding accounting assistance, recording of transactions, etc.

Because our Fixed Price Agreement provides ongoing access to the accounting, tax, and business advice you need on a fixed-price basis, you are not inhibited from seeking timely advice by the fear of a clock running endlessly. Our services are designed around fixed prices, as opposed to hourly rates, and offer you access to the accumulated wisdom of the firm through CPAs with substantial experience who can help enhance your company's future and achieve its business goals.

While the fixed price entitles your company to unlimited consultation with us, if your question or issue requires additional research and analysis beyond the consultation, that work will be subject to an additional price before the service is to be performed, and a Change Order will be issued before delivery of the additional service, with payment terms agreed to in advance.

Unanticipated Services

Furthermore, the parties agree that if an unanticipated need arises (such as, but not limited to, an audit by a taxing agency or any other exogenous service not anticipated in this agreement by the parties), ABC hereby agrees to perform this additional work at a mutually agreed upon price *before the service is provided.* This service will be invoiced separately to XYZ, as part of a Change Order, and will be payable upon presentation [or payable upon terms mutually agreed upon].

Service Guarantee

Our work is guaranteed to the complete satisfaction of the customer. If XYZ is not completely satisfied with the services performed by ABC, we will, at the option of XYZ, either refund the price, or accept a portion of said price that reflects XYZ's level of satisfaction. We will assume you are satisfied upon final payment received under the terms of this Agreement.

Price Guarantee

Furthermore, if you ever receive an invoice without first authorizing the service, terms, and price, you are not obligated to pay for that service.

Payment Terms

The following payment plan is hereby agreed to by XYZ and ABC:

• January 31, 2005	XX
• February 28, 2005	XX
• March 31, 2005	XX
• April 30, 2005	XX
• May 31, 2005	XX
• June 30, 2005	XX
• July 31, 2005	XX
• August 31, 2005	XX
• September 30, 2005	XX
• October 31, 2005	XX
• November 30, 2005	XX
• December 31, 2005	XX
TOTAL 2005 PAYMENTS	$ XXX

To assure that our arrangement remains responsive to your needs, as well as fair to both parties, we will meet throughout 2005 and, if necessary, revise or adjust the scope of the services to be provided and the prices to be charged in light of mutual experience.

Furthermore, it is understood that either party may terminate this Agreement at any time, for any reason, with 10 days written notice to the other party. It is understood that any unpaid services that are outstanding at the date of termination are to be paid in full within 10 days from the date of termination.

If you agree that the above adequately sets forth XYZ's understanding of our mutual responsibilities, please authorize this Agreement and return it to our office. A copy is provided for your records.

We would like to take this opportunity to express our appreciation for the opportunity to serve you.

Very truly yours,

By: ____________________________

Allan Somnolent, Partner
ABC, CPAs

Agreed to and authorized:

By: ____________________________Date: ________________

Customer, President
XYZ, Inc.

Explaining the Sample FPA

A close look at each clause in the agreement will provide further clarification of the reason for its design.

Date of the FPA

The date of the agreement is, for most firms, usually in the last quarter of the year, as most FPAs are on a calendar year basis. It is advantageous to meet to draft the FPA in the last quarter of the prior fiscal (or calendar) year, to clarify the customer's expectations before the new year begins, as well as to learn of opportunities that may be present to offer the customer additional services. Do not feel the need to rush this process. If it takes multiple meetings with the customer, as sometimes it does to overcome price resistance and anxiety, do not panic and feel the need to draft something. *The FPA is not a request for proposal (RFP).* There are no surprises in an FPA, as there can be in an RFP, because the customer is instrumental in the design and is involved every step of the way. The more customer involvement you obtain, the higher the level of commitment you will get, and the more likely the customers will act consistent with their commitment.

Professional Services Provided

Obviously, you will describe each service to be provided by your firm, and you may provide additional detail to the degree necessary to have no misunderstandings between you and your customer. For example, with the audit service you are specifying that the customer is responsible for providing you with PBC (prepared by customer) schedules by March 15, 2005. If the customer does not deliver by this date, the scope of the audit changes, then a change order should be issued. The customer will understand that the scope has changed, and that is the time to issue a change order—*before* the work is performed.

You will have to exercise your professional discretion as to the level of detail necessary to avoid misunderstandings regarding the level of responsibility being assumed by both parties. If you are entering into an FPA with a new customer, and one that may not be as sophisticated with respect to your services as a veteran customer, then a higher level of detail is required. Always adapt the FPA to the customer's level of sophistication and experience with your services. This level will become apparent as you meet with them and begin to design (and price) the services. The old rule still applies to the FPA: The greater the written detail, the less chance for misunderstanding between the parties.

Unlimited Access

The Unlimited Access service is your firm's two-part tariff as discussed in Chapter 9—charging the customer a price for the privilege of purchasing more services from you. Notice that this annual service offers the customer unlimited phone calls and meetings for the customer and the customer's support personnel. This is done on the theory that since you are on call for the customer at any time during the year, you should be compensated accordingly. Also, this breaks down the communication barrier that may arise if you charge for each meeting and phone call. The more you talk with the customer throughout the year, the better able you will be to provide the customer with additional, value-added services that facilitate your climb up the value curve.

I am always asked if customers abuse this service. The answer is no. Any customer who enters into an FPA with your firm, first of all, is usually an "A" customer, and a high level of mutual trust, respect, and understanding already exists. Second, because they are such good customers, if they do need to call you at home on Saturday evening at 11:00 p.m. it is usually for a very good reason (a death in the family, an accident, etc.), and you *want* to talk to them. Third, unlimited phone calls and meetings does not imply that any additional work you have to perform as a result is free. A change order should be issued before you take on an additional project as a result of a phone call or meeting with the customer. Fourth, if after a period of time you find that the customer is putting inordinate (or unreasonable) demands on your firm, increase the price of this service. If the customer is using you that much, you are obviously adding value to them, and they should be willing to pay a higher price for this service.

Finally, if the customer becomes abusive and disrespectful of your time, you always have the option of withdrawing from the engagement. In fact, with FPA customers the opposite usually occurs—the customer is reluctant to contact you. Therefore, be sure to stay in touch whether you think the customer needs you or not. One of the dangers of the FPA is that you are increasing the customer's expectations, and when you do that you are also increasing the probability of defection if your performance fails to live up to those increased expectations. Constant communication with good customers is something you should strive for, with or without an unlimited access clause. By charging for it, you will capture a portion of the consumer surplus, sell more services to customers, and have a higher perceived value in their eyes.

Unanticipated Services

Unanticipated services are discussed in the change order clause, which basically says that if a service arises that is not specified in the FPA, then your firm agrees to provide that service at a mutually agreed upon price, in advance of performing the service. You do this by issuing a change order, a sample of which is found later in this chapter. This clause offers many advantages. By specifying the services that you are aware of at the time of drafting the FPA, you are leaving many opportunities for providing additional services, and because customers are paying you the unlimited access price, they are more likely to select you to provide those additional services, thereby effectively locking out your competition. Another advantage is that change orders are priced before the service is delivered, when you have the leverage, a critical advantage to have when establishing a price. Also, whenever a change order arises, value pricing opportunities exist because, by their nature, change orders deal with marginal services that the customer *wants*, rather than what the customer *needs* (because the FPA has taken care of their basic needs). Lastly, the change order can also be used in conjunction with a loyalty program—similar to the airlines frequent flyer programs.

Service Guarantee

You may want to highlight the service guarantee clause, or place it at the beginning (or end) of the FPA to build up its value to the customer. If you are reluctant to include this in your FPAs, you can always implement it gradually, perhaps providing it to new customers at first, and then, once you are convinced of its advantages, offering it to all customers.

The gradual implementation strategy for new customers has been used by many firms that are reluctant to adopt the guarantee for all customers, but there is one caveat: That strategy is backward. Your existing customers are far more valuable to your firm than any new ones you may acquire (recall the AICPA statistic that it costs a firm 11 times more to attract a customer than to retain one). Customer *retention* is far more important than customer *acquisition;* therefore, if you are going to discriminate with the service guarantee, you should discriminate in favor of existing customers. However, either way you implement it, you will discover that its advantages outweigh its disadvantages and, eventually, you will offer it to *all* of your customers.

Price Guarantee

The price guarantee is designed to ensure that your firm sets the price when you have the leverage, which is before the engagement begins. This is precisely the time when you can command the highest price. If you wait till the engagement begins, or worse, till it ends, the leverage is with the customer and your price will be lower. The price guarantee instills a "no surprises" culture within your firm, and customers will value it highly. It is an excellent competitive differentiation, and an outstanding complement to the service guarantee.

Payment Terms

The sample FPA shows 12 payments, but this clause can be designed for quarterly payments or semiannual payments, or with a deposit (or retainer) made upon signing the FPA. The important point is to get customers to design the payment terms, usually in accordance with the cyclical nature of their business, in order to remove payment resistance (the unwillingness on the part of the customer to cut the check). Again, if customers design and commit to the payment terms, they will act consistently with that commitment. Get a deposit (or retainer) for all new customers, as this demonstrates commitment on their part. Lawyers are excellent at demanding this; CPAs need to be just as insistent on receiving retainers *before* work is performed for a new customer.

Revisions to the FPA

This is a good clause to add, especially for new customers, or if you do not feel totally comfortable with your established price, because it reduces the risk the customer is taking. It also ensures that you remain in communication with the customer and continuously solicit feedback on their level of satisfaction. Constant customer feedback is a critical component of offering total quality service and enables you to exceed customer expectations as well as become aware of when those expectations change. Of course, this clause is optional and its use will depend upon the nature of the relationship your firm has with the customer.

Termination Clause

This clause removes risk from the customers. If they know, in advance, that they can always cancel the agreement for any reason, they will suffer less from price anxiety. This is an additional way, combined with the service guarantee, to overcome this pricing emotion. If the FPA is terminated before the term expires, then both parties will have to compute the value of the services delivered by the firm, less the amount already paid by the customer, and someone will owe someone a refund.

By drafting an FPA, rather than pricing each individual service, you offer one total price. If the customer should cancel the FPA before its term expires, then you will have to agree on the allocated value of the services already performed. However, FPA customers are the least likely to defect from your firm, so you probably will not encounter this problem. The potential disadvantages are not great enough to stop you from offering one total price. Again, pursue opportunities rather than attempting to solve every problem that may arise in the course of dealing with customers.

The Words You Should Use

Just as the word *price* is better than the word *fee*, you should make it a habit to say, "The services are valued at $X," not "the services cost $X." Your goal is to build up the gross value of your firm's services, not to have the customer focus solely on cost. If you have broken down the FPA into a monthly or quarterly payment, the terminology should be, "Your monthly investment is $X," not "your monthly cost is $X."

The word *agreement* is preferable to the word *contract*. *Contract* conjures up images of disputes, lack of trust, courts, and lawsuits, but *agreement* has a much more positive connotation to the customer. Also, when the agreement is ready to be signed, ask the customer to authorize the agreement rather than sign the contract. Again, the word *authorize* is far more positive than *sign*, because it puts the control with the customer.

Package Pricing Clause

The more you focus the customer's attention on the totality of your firm's service offering, the higher the price you can command. For new customers, for instance, the following clause could be used in the first-year FPA:

> **The Entrepreneurial Business Program**
>
> ABC created its Entrepreneurial Business Program in 1990 to assist customers in establishing their new ventures on an optimal foundation, based upon the owner's goals and objectives, tax considerations, and future direction of the business. For a fixed price of $X,XXX, ABC will incorporate a new venture and provide basic corporate legal [or accounting] services (tax preparation, planning, accounting setup) for 12 months. Under the Program, our customer can get the right start in structuring his or her corporation, have available the resources of a full-service CPA firm, and be able to predict basic accounting prices and budget for these.

The point of this clause is not to market one specific price for this bundle of services, but to get the customer to sign up for all of the services offered. You should still price each customer *on the margin*.

Handling Price Objections

One of the questions professionals always ask about quoting a value price is what happens when the customer objects that it is simply too high. First, realize that price is always a consideration, and naturally every business-person is going to attempt to get the best price possible. Consequently, if you are to succeed in getting full value for your services, you must learn how to handle price objections. As Tom Hopkins says in *How to Master the Art of Selling*:

> I think I'm safe in saying that money is an objection you are going to encounter frequently as long as you are in sales. That being so, can you reach your full potential without learning how to cope with it? (Hopkins, 1980: 232)

It helps to keep in mind the following equation when dealing with price:

$$\text{Value} = \frac{\text{Benefits Received}}{\text{Price}}$$

If the customer is objecting to your price, perhaps you have not done an adequate job in educating the customer about the benefits of your services. The customer may not be objecting to the price as much as doubting the value of the services. This is a critical distinction because the majority of a professional's customers are not price-sensitive. This is precisely why it is so important to discuss value first and set price last. The more you can build up the benefits offered, the higher the perceived value of your firm, and thus the higher the price you can command. One way to achieve this is to focus the customer on the objectives they want to achieve rather than the price to be paid. In so doing, the customer will focus on how to maximize the objectives rather than minimize the price.

With new customers, most price objections are due to inadequate pre-qualifying. When meeting with new customers, the following may occur:

- **The customer's only consideration is price**—This is, most likely, a customer you should not deal with at all. These customers are attracted to you solely because of price and they will be the first to defect when they can locate a cheaper service provider. Be wary of these customers, and do not waste your precious marketing resources on them. You are better off spending those resources on existing customers, who are more loyal and more valuable to your firm.

- **The customer never asks about your price**—Although this may sound ideal, the reality is quite different. Price is always a consideration, especially with businesspeople. The person who never asks about your price is also the person who probably does not intend to pay your price. Always ask these customers for a large retainer up front to test level of commitment.
- **The customer says price is no object**—Again, this is probably because the customer has no intention of paying you anyway. Price is *always* important.
- **The customer asks a lot of questions, seeking your advice**—If customers are unwilling to commit to an FPA, they are merely using you as an unpaid consultant. Avoid them.
- **The customer complains about the predecessor professional**—In another year, you will be the subject of this customer's wrath. Employ adverse selection. If this is such a great customer, why doesn't one of your competitors have this customer already?

Allan Boress has an effective question to use to save time when meeting with potential customers: "We are not the cheapest CPA firm in town. Should we continue talking?" This projects confidence and lets the customer know that you think highly of yourself (you are what you charge for), as well as giving you the ability, early on, to judge the customer's price sensitivity and whether or not the customer is a good fit for your firm.

Price objections with existing customers require a different approach. Most likely, these customers will require a good deal of educating on the value of the FPA. Always remember that the FPA lowers the customer's risk and uncertainty, and that is one of its major value-added benefits that should be emphasized. If you are still encountering many price objections utilizing this approach, this is not a good sign. The popular view is that price objections are a good sign (who would object to your price if they were not serious about doing business with your firm?). Neil Rackham points out in his classic sales book, *SPIN Selling*, a different viewpoint:

> No, make no mistake about it, the more objections you get in a call, the less likely you are to be successful. It's a comforting myth for trainers to tell inexperienced salespeople that

> professionals welcome objections as a sign of customer interest, but in reality an objection is a barrier between you and your customer. However skillfully you dismantle this barrier through objection handling, it would be smarter not to have created it in the first place.
>
> When I was new to selling I thought that, next to closing, objection-handling skills were the ones most crucial to sales success. Looking back, I can now see that my concern was motivated by the large number of objections I was facing from my customers. I didn't ask myself what caused the objections—but just knew that there were lots of them, so I'd better improve my objection handling. I now understand that the majority of objections I faced were only a symptom caused by poor selling. By improving my probing skills, I've become more successful at objection prevention. (Rackham, 1988: 133)

Despite the best probing questions, development of a future vision, and a focus on the customer's wants, it is inevitable that you will receive at least some price objections. While getting many may be a sign of a deficient sales approach, a few can usually be handled using some of the more common objection-handling techniques. Troy Waugh offers this seven-step strategic method for handling objections:

1. **Listen carefully; hear the customer out**—Avoid the temptation to talk or try to solve the objection right then and there.
2. **Confirm your understanding of the objection**—Repeat it back to the customer to ensure that you understand exactly what the objection is.
3. **Acknowledge the customer's point of view**—Practice empathy; do not try to impose your view on the customer, but help the customer become convinced of your view. As Benjamin Franklin said: "Men are best convinced by reasons that they themselves discover." You will only succeed when you see things from your customer's point of view, not the other way around.
4. **Select a specific technique**—No one technique works best for all customers, and you must select one that fits your personality as well as the customer's.

5. **Answer the objection**—Ultimately, you must answer the customer's objection if the FPA is to be authorized. You may postpone the price objection to the end of the meeting if you are still trying to build your firm's value, but in the end, price must be dealt with.
6. **Confirm that your answer satisfied the concern.**
7. **Attempt to get authorization for the FPA**—If the customer still objects, continue with the meeting until you reach an agreement on your value.

If price objections occur late in the sales process, find out what underlying interest is causing the concern. Two typical causes trigger a concern over price late in the sales cycle: (1) fear and (2) the desire to get a better deal.

Once you know the underlying reason for the price objection, you have two choices:

1. If the underlying concern is fear, adopt the role of a therapist and draw the fear out into the open. Remember, traditional objection-handling techniques [such as those discussed below] are not effective with fear. They move too quickly to a logical conclusion and do not get to the heart of the problem. Fear is emotional, not logical.
2. If your prospect's price objection is caused by the desire to get a better deal, adopt the role of a negotiator and create a win-win agreement. (Davis, 1996: 200)

Here are specific methods from Troy Waugh for overcoming objections to price:

1. Postpone the price objection.
2. Use the lowest denominations.
3. Use comparison.
4. To get volume up, sell down.

Postpone the Price Objection

You cannot intelligently discuss price until you know exactly what the customer needs and wants. A car salesman would never walk you over to a car and say, "This one is $40,000." Before price is mentioned, the salesman will discuss your needs, features preferred, and desires. He will also be attempting to gauge your price sensitivity and the value you place on dealing with this particular dealership by asking you questions about your occupation, what the car will be used for, where you live, and whether you currently own a car. Here are two responses that postpone the price objection until you have had a chance to build your firm's value:

- I can appreciate that you would be interested in the price, and I assure you we will discuss it completely, but before we even consider the price, I want to be sure that our service can satisfy your needs. Will that be all right?
- Mr. Smith, your concern for price is quite understandable. The actual amount paid for the service, however, will depend upon the nature of the services you ultimately select. Let's consider the price for the services after we establish the specific services you will require. Is that fair?

If you discuss price at the beginning, the customer may think you have nothing else to talk about. Sometimes, a customer is insistent in knowing a ballpark amount, and in these cases you will not be able to postpone the objection. If you try, the customer may stay so focused on your reluctance to talk price that everything else you say regarding value will be mentally blocked out. If you have to mention price, err on the high side, for reasons that will become apparent.

Use the Lowest Denominations

One of the advantages of setting the payment terms in accordance with the customer's desires is that this breaks down the price into the lowest denominations, usually monthly. A monthly price is a much more manageable number to deal with than the total FPA price. Also, this is the time to reiterate your service guarantee and the fact that you will be available any time to respond to the customer's needs, if you include an unlimited access clause in the FPA.

Use Comparison

An effective comparison to make is that of your customer's pricing policies, with a statement such as the following:

> Mr. Becker, your own company makes a high-grade product that commands an exceptionally high price, and deservedly so. Your tool-and-die products warrant their outstanding reputation because of the top-quality materials used to make them. Our high level of service and attention to helping you create more value in your business are naturally suited for you. Sure, you can buy less expensive financial help than ours, but you would not be satisfied with the performance.

This approach achieves a level of parity between your firm and your customer's business, which makes considerable sense, as all business owners are convinced of *their* product's superiority. Testimonials from other customers can also help prove your case.

To Get Volume Up, Sell Down

All customers have a price they are *able* to pay and a price they are *willing* to pay. Do not project your own apprehensions about price resistance onto the behavior of your customer. Never assume that a customer is only willing to spend, for example, what you would spend in similar circumstances. A fascinating study conducted by Macy's of New York illustrates this lesson:

> Macy's gave ten professional shoppers $1,000 each with instructions to enter one of Macy's departments to buy merchandise without mentioning price. The shopper was to buy whatever was offered by the salesperson up to $1,000. Not one of the shoppers was able to get rid of more than $350. For example, when one shopper asked about ladies' hats, the salesperson brought out a hat within her own price range—$75; the buyer could have bought a $200 hat.

You should always present your most expensive price first, and then move down. Men's clothing is sold in such a manner. The salesman will first show you a $1,000 suit, make you try it on, and when you choke, he'll then move down, gradually, to your price level. Once he has sold you the suit, he will then move down to sweaters, shoes, shirts, ties, and socks. It is easier to buy a $99 sweater after you have decided to purchase a $375 suit. Psychologically, this is a very effective method.

Tom Hopkins offers another effective technique called the "Bracket-up for money" strategy. Here's how it works. You say, "Most customers who desire this level of service are prepared to invest $12,000. A fortunate few can invest between $15,000 and $20,000. Then there are those on a limited or fixed budget who cannot go higher than $10,000. Which of these categories does your company fit into most comfortably?" (Hopkins, 1980: 184)

Most likely, the customer will not want to be in the bottom category, and will opt for the middle amount. Make sure you begin your pricing at a level that is approximately 20 percent above your price ($12,000). Then, continue by quoting a price 50 percent to 100 percent above your price ($15,000–$20,000). Finally, give your actual price ($10,000). Psychologically, you are tapping into the instinct of the customer that says: **Expensive = Good**. This is the good, better, and best strategy, and it works.

If price is still an objection, focus on the difference. Perhaps you are trying to price the FPA at $20,000, but the customer wants to pay $15,000. Do not focus on the $20,000; focus instead on the $5,000 difference. That is the real problem, and that puts the focus on the smaller, more manageable amount.

If price is still an objection, be slow to cut it, as you will lose credibility with the customer if you do not get a concession in return. Instead, work on the other terms of the FPA first. Perhaps you can change the payment terms; perhaps you can cut some services or add additional services. Remember the Pareto analysis: 20 percent of the issues will account for 80 percent of the value. Customers will want to win some points, even trivial ones. Concede on those 80 percent of the points that make up 20 percent of the value and chances are you will reach a more satisfactory negotiation for both parties.

Most people think that the final decision in the buying process is one of risk—either the risk of not buying or of not making the right decision on a service provider. However, the very last buying decision is ensuring that you get the best deal. This is a separate issue from the value of the service; the customer is already convinced of the value or you would not be this far along in the buying process.

When customers are trying to ascertain whether they've gotten the best price, they will test you. As Michael Bosworth says in his excellent book, *Solution Selling*:

> At negotiation time, in the buyer's mind, the seller is a washcloth. . . . And if that buyer has an IQ over 80, he's going to take at least one wrenching squeeze to see what happens. Am I right? And the squeezing will continue until the seller stops dripping. As long as the seller drips, the buyer squeezes.
>
> How does a seller stop the squeezing? By resolving to stop dripping, by resolving to walk out if the business is not right, and by resolving to walk away from the business. The seller must take his stand with conviction—enough conviction to convince the buyer he is getting the best possible deal. (Bosworth, 1995: 147)

If the buyer sees you panic—as most CPAs do—this reinforces their fear that they have not yet negotiated the best price. This is an emotional process, not a logical one; standing your ground is very important. Think of purchasing a car. When you have finally come to the decision to buy, you will attempt to get the best price from the salesman. Once he is willing to let you walk off the lot without the car, you know you made the best deal. That is exactly what you need to do—be willing to let customers walk out the door. Only then will they realize they have made the best deal possible.

Bosworth also suggests using the word "fair," such as "Is this a fair price to you?" People have an innate desire to be fair and it is a very powerful word. In fact, it is so powerful that you should use it sparingly.

Also, it is important to remember, after you state your price, to shut up. Don't talk, as the ball is now in the customer's court. Do not panic just because the customer is silent—they may be experiencing "sticker shock," for instance—as most people do go through a moment of silence before spending a relatively large amount of money. Think about the moment of hesitation you have experienced before agreeing to purchase a car, buy a piece of jewelry, and so forth. This is simple human nature. Don't interfere with it by, in effect, showing your cards too early (or worse yet, folding by cutting your price). In this business, it costs nothing to see all of the cards.

Learn to accept price objections for what they are—opportunities in disguise. They can be a sign of an interested customer, and with practice and skill, you will be able to overcome them without cutting your price. Reading the books mentioned in this chapter will help you develop the skills you need to work with price objections and become an effective value pricer.

Change Orders

Change orders should be used whenever the scope of a service changes, or when a service need arises that was not anticipated in the FPA. This is a very effective tool for keeping in constant communication with the customer, giving the customer control over any and all changes in your services, and allowing you to set a price when you possess the leverage. The cardinal rule with respect to value pricing is *no surprises*; the change order is a tested method of adhering to that rule.

In a typical CPA firm when problems are encountered (with for instance, the state of the customer's records), the lowest-level team member keeps right on working, spending time, without anyone's knowledge or consent. Managers and partners are guilty of this pattern as well, and this creates nothing but collection problems once the job is completed. Think of taking your car to an auto mechanic to get a bid for a tune-up. You return to the shop only to find that he performed additional services, without your prior consent, and he is now attempting to charge you. Not a very pleasant or effective way to cross-sell additional services, is it?

It is critical that all personnel assigned to a particular engagement understand the scope of the engagement that has been set forth in the FPA, the responsibilities of the customer, and the price of the service. When a problem is spotted, the team should communicate to the supervisor, manager, or partner that a change order should be issued. Otherwise, they will unilaterally commit firm resources to complete the work with no commensurate increase in the customer's price.

Change orders also present opportunities for value pricing and innovative pricing methods. Since the FPA has covered the basic services (i.e., those services on the lower end of the value curve), change orders usually represent opportunities to climb up the curve and should be priced accordingly. By issuing change orders at the earliest possible time, and *before* the work is performed, your firm possesses the leverage—precisely when you want to set a price. You are also involving the customer and keeping the customer in control of the decision either to help solve the problem (if the change order is being issued due to their internal problems) or to partake in the design of the service. As Larson and Larson point out in *Innovative Billing and Collection Methods That Work*:

> Clients are more likely to respond favorably to an additional charge if they still have the opportunity to be part of the

decision-making process in resolving the unanticipated problem. (Larson and Larson, 1994: 91)

Think of the example of the mechanic. If he's got your car on the rack to perform a tune-up and discovers another problem and calls you to inform you of what it will cost to fix, at least you feel empowered to make the decision to proceed. In the majority of cases, you will simply agree to the additional charge because the mechanic possesses the leverage. You are not likely to pick up the car and take it to another shop. State laws require mechanics to do this; but why should professionals have to be compelled by law to do something that is clearly in the best interest of both the professional and the customer?

The following pages contain sample change orders. As with the FPA, this is nothing but an outline that should help your firm develop its own change order based upon your culture, personality, and the type of customer you serve. If you service auto mechanics or contractors, you may even want to obtain one of their change orders to help you design your own. They are well written, and your customer will be impressed that you are implementing this technique.

SAMPLE CHANGE ORDER

Customer:

Date:

Project Description [and estimated completion date, customer responsibilities, if appropriate, and any other level of detail needed]:

____

____

____

____

____

Price: $____________

Terms: ____________

We believe it is our responsibility to exceed your expectations. This Change Order is being prepared because the above project was not anticipated in our original Fixed Price Agreement, dated xx/xx/xx. The price for the above project has been mutually agreed upon by Customer XYZ and ABC, CPAs. It is our goal to ensure that XYZ is never surprised by the price for any ABC service, and therefore we have adopted the Change Order policy. The price above is due and payable upon completion of the project described [or, payable up front, if agreed upon, or in installments, etc., whatever you and the customer agree to].

If you agree with the above project description and the price, please authorize and date the Change Order below. A copy is enclosed for your records. Thank you for letting us serve you.

Sincerely,

Allan Somnolent, Partner
ABC, CPAs

Agreed to and authorized:

By: ________________________

Customer, President
XYZ

Date: ________________________

SAMPLE CHANGE ORDER—SERVICE NOT SPECIFIED IN THE FPA

Customer: XYZ, Inc.

Date: November 10, 2004

Project Description: ABC, CPAs will hereby represent XYZ, Inc. before the Internal Revenue Service for the audit of their 2002 Corporate Tax Return, for the issues as described in the IRS letter dated November 1, 2004.

XYZ, Inc. hereby agrees that its accounting department will provide all records, documentation, and schedules as deemed necessary by ABC, CPAs.

Based upon ABC, CPAs knowledge of the IRS's concerns and issues to be examined, we hereby agree to represent XYZ, Inc. for the fixed price stated below.

If, in the course of the audit, other issues are raised that are outside the scope of the IRS letter mentioned above, ABC, CPAs and XYZ, Inc. hereby agree to enter into another Change Order at that time, at a mutually agreed upon price.

Price: $X

Terms: 50% payable upon commencement of the IRS audit.
50% payable upon completion of the audit.

We believe it is our responsibility to exceed your expectations. This Change Order is being prepared because the above project was not anticipated in our original Fixed Price Agreement, dated xx/xx/xx. The price for the above project has been mutually agreed upon by XYZ, Inc. and ABC, CPAs. It is our goal to ensure that XYZ, Inc. is never surprised by the price for any ABC, CPAs service, and therefore we have adopted the Change Order policy.

If you agree with the above project description and the price, please authorize and date the Change Order below. A copy is enclosed for your records. Thank you for letting us serve you.

Sincerely,

Allan Somnolent, Partner
ABC, CPAs

Agreed to and authorized:

By: ______________________

Customer, President
XYZ, Inc.

Date: ______________________

SAMPLE CHANGE ORDER—SERVICE SPECIFIED IN THE FPA; SCOPE CHANGE DUE TO CUSTOMER NOT FULFILLING AN OBLIGATION

Customer: XYZ, Inc.

Date: August 20, 2004

Project Description: During fieldwork of the audit for the year ended June 30, 2003 ABC, CPAs discovered that the Prepared By Customer (PBC) Schedules were not accurately completed, in a timely manner, by the accounting staff of XYZ, Inc.

In order to complete the audit in a timely manner, both parties agree that ABC, CPAs will hereby complete the PBC schedules.

Since this service was not originally anticipated by ABC, CPAs in its fixed price for the audit, both parties agree to the mutually acceptable price for this service as stated below.

Price: $X

Terms: Payable upon authorization of this Change Order.

We believe it is our responsibility to exceed your expectations. This Change Order is being prepared because the above project was not anticipated in our original fixed price for the audit, as outlined in our Fixed Price Agreement, dated xx/xx/xx. The price for the above project has been mutually agreed upon by XYZ, Inc. and ABC, CPAs. It is our goal to ensure that XYZ, Inc. is never surprised by the price for any ABC, CPAs service, and therefore we have adopted the Change Order policy.

If you agree with the above project description and the price, please authorize and date the Change Order below. A copy is enclosed for your records. Thank you for letting us serve you.

Sincerely,

Allan Somnolent, Partner
ABC, CPAs

Agreed to and authorized:

By: ______________________

Customer, President
XYZ, Inc.

Date: ______________________

Innovative Price Methods You Can Use with the Customer

Outside-In Pricing

One of the most innovative ways to capture the consumer surplus is simply to ask the customers what they think the service is worth. This method, which can be referred to as outside-in pricing, starts with the theory that, ultimately, a service is worth only what someone is willing to pay for it. Therefore, why not ask directly what it is worth? It sounds radical, but remember that *radical* is Latin for *getting back to the root.*

Consider this excerpt from a story in from *People* magazine (February 15, 1999) titled "Priceless," with the tag line reading "London Restaurateur Michael Vasos lets diners pay what they choose—but woe unto those who choose cheap":

> Here's one worry that patrons of the London restaurant Just Around the Corner will never have—being stuck with a bill

> too big for their budget. That's because it's the customers themselves who decide how much to pay. "When I came up with the idea," says owner Michael Vasos, "everyone thought I was crazy."
>
> Turns out, Vasos's little marketing concept, begun in 1986, has been insanely successful. Most regulars who pack the pink-tableclothed, 85-seat eatery fork over about 25 pounds (around $41), fairly standard in pricey London, for three-course meals featuring such pre-nouvelle noshes as lemon sole with hollandaise sauce. "If the food wasn't any good," says diner Mandip Phlora, "the novelty would wear off pretty quickly."
>
> Cheapskates are rare, says Vasos, 42, but the worst get their just desserts. "One guy put down a fiver," recalls waitress Liz Noonan, "and Michael went over to the table and gave him back the five pounds. Then everyone in the restaurant stood up and applauded." In fact, patrons tend to overpay rather than underpay. One night, four American government officials handed over nearly $1,000 for a meal worth less than $200. "They asked me if they had left enough," recalls Vasos, who was too diplomatic, he says, to set them straight. "You can't tell people they've left too much—it's like putting them down."
>
> Vasos, who left his native Cyprus at 18, credits Londoners' generosity for his success. Some diners beg to differ. "It's fear of embarrassment. If you don't pay enough, there might be a scene, and the English hate that more than anything," says Rob Gillies, 26. "This kind of place would never work in Scotland," chimes in native Scotsman Danny Easton, 30. "We'd feel no guilt at all about paying you just a pound."

This is a wonderful story, and perhaps the most poignant point made by Vasos was this: "Trust people and they will trust you." That is a perfect attitude for professionals to have toward the people they serve. After all, if you don't trust your customers, why are they customers in the first place? I had the great good fortune of dining in Mr. Vasos's London restaurant and having a long talk with him about his unique pricing philosophy. He is passionate about providing an excellent dining experience to each customer, and his entire team offers total quality service. It was an outstanding experience, and I am sure I paid an above-market price for the meal. It was worth every [British] pound, and I would certainly go back

The outside-in pricing method has many advantages. First, it has the potential to identify your first-class passengers, because your firm has some customers who are *willing* and *able* to pay more than you are charging them. Second, it involves the customer in your pricing and gets that all important "ego investment." Third, it lowers price and payment resistance; what customer will dispute a price he set? Fourth, if the customer quotes a ridiculously low price you do not have to accept it. At least you have a chance to educate the customer with respect to the service's value and you still have the opportunity to decline the engagement if you believe the customer does not value you highly enough. When do you want to learn what the customer's value perception is—*before* or *after* you do the work?

Lastly, outside-in pricing allows you to build customer loyalty and goodwill. You need not always capture 100 percent of the consumer surplus. Invest in the relationship by letting the customer retain a portion of it. A customer once quoted a price of $3,000 as what he expected to pay for a certain project that he demanded on very short notice (over the weekend). At "standard rates," the job would have been priced at $1,200. The CPA told him what a valuable customer he was, and expressed a willingness to help him with this particular project. The CPA said he would do it for $2,500. The customer was happy; the CPA was happy. No amount of marketing or advertising can build that type of loyalty and goodwill. That is what total quality service, customer loyalty, and developing partnerships with your customers is all about. A substantial amount of consumer surplus is still available for you to tap into, and you should at least get a portion of it when you can identify its existence.

Consider this testimonial on the effectiveness of the outside-in pricing method, which I received from a colleague on April 20, 2000:

> Hello Ron,
>
> I hope the tax season finds you well. I was fortunate enough to be at the Atlanta conference when you spoke and I picked up an autographed copy of your book, which I devoured on the plane trip back.
>
> The engagement which I refer to ($150,000 price) had already started a month or two before, and I had used the old standard rate x hours routine and billed about $2,000 at a

standard rate of $180/hour. After listening to you and reading the book, I was determined to reevaluate the price structure and simply went back to my customer and said, "Guys, this is what I am bringing to the table. It brings a lot of value which is etc., etc. I don't believe hourly rates based upon time is appropriate. I am unable to place a value on this. I need your help. You tell me what the value of all this is to you. You are the customer and only you can truly establish the value. I know I'll be happy with what ever you come up with." This is almost an exact quote.

I left it at that two months ago. I was handed a check for the first installment of $50,000 on the way out at the end of the engagement. I guess this is what you call "outside-in pricing." I like it.

Gus Stearns, CPA

This story from Gus gets even better, and it not only illustrates the advantage of outside-in pricing, but also the retrospective price clause, discussed next.

Retrospective Price ("TIP" Clause)

Recall the principle of *pricing on the margin*, that is, pricing each service to each customer according to its value at that point in time, regardless of what that customer may have paid in the past or what you charge other customers for the same service. Perhaps my father, the barber, can best illustrate this economic concept. I was sitting in his shop one day waiting for him to finish his last customer. As this new customer got out of his chair, he opened his wallet and asked how much his haircut was. My father replied "$20." The customer handed him $40, thanked my dad, and walked out. Turning to me, my father asked, "Ron, do you know what that tells me? My prices are too low." Despite my reluctance to disagree with my father's teachings, I responded, "No, Dad, that's not what that teaches you. What that teaches you is your price is too low to *that customer*. The next customer who sits in your chair is not influenced by what that customer just paid." Since then, my father has not offered fixed prices for his haircuts but has engaged in price discrimination, at least with new customers, by asking how much they think the service is worth. Unfortunately, the perception is that professionals cannot rely on the custom of a tip in order to capture a portion of the consumer surplus. Or can they?

The retrospective price is an innovative way to get at an approximation of what the customer thinks the full value of the service is worth. Others have called it the "to insure performance (TIP)" clause. A sample of this clause, which can be used in an FPA or a change order, is the following:

Sample Fixed Price Agreement Clause Retrospective Price (Non-Attest Customer)

In the event that we are able to satisfy your needs in a timely and professional manner, you have agreed to review the situation and decide whether, in the sole discretion of XYZ, some additional payment to ABC is appropriate in view of your overall satisfaction with the services rendered by ABC [and/or the financial results achieved by XYZ for this transaction].

For CPAs, this applies only for a nonaudit customer, and your particular state might not allow contingency fees. If so, simply remove the "financial results" portion, and base the price on the customer's satisfaction alone. By predicating the price on the customer's level of satisfaction with your service, you are not charging a contingency.

As a follow-up to the prior letter sent to me from Gus Stearns, here is how he was able to use the TIP clause in order to capture the value from the service he was providing:

> Hello Ron,
>
> Basically the large engagement was for a previous client that I had hired a controller for. He took over the tax work, at my suggestion, as he was a CPA. The engagement was an exit and management succession strategy which involved some fairly hefty income tax savings as well. The total time expended was about 100 hours, although a lot of the time was on unrelated things that I did not want to charge for due to the magnitude of the price (we quit using timesheets some time

ago and have substituted "daily activity sheets" to make sure our clients get billed, based upon our perceived value of each engagement).

I used a flip chart in the presentation, pointing out the value of what they were getting. At the end of the presentation I asked how much they thought it was worth, and suggested $300,000, $500,000, a million? I wanted them to think in big numbers. The CEO was rather excited and said a million. Knowing that this would be difficult to obtain in one fell swoop I suggested $400,000 down and a retainer of $4,000 per month. They agreed but asked that I serve on the board of directors and attend quarterly meetings through 2008, when the note to the previous owners would be paid off. They were also kind enough to put me on salary so I could participate in their pension plan which is a 25% direct contribution from the company. This all adds up to a little bit over $1 million.

Never once was the word time used or referred to by myself, or my client. They could care less about time. In all of our engagements, I never use the word. By concentrating on value and encouraging the client to participate in the valuation of the engagement our prices have skyrocketed. You were absolutely on target when you said that accountants are terrible at valuing our services (myself included).

Keep up the wonderful work.

Gus Stearns, CPA

The point of this story is not to suggest everyone can obtain a $1 million tip, but rather to point out how professionals tend to undervalue their own work. I am sure Gus would have never placed a value of $1 million on his contribution in his wildest dreams, but his customer did, which proves the subjective theory of value we discussed in Chapter 6. Had he not used the TIP clause he would have simply realized his hourly rate and would have never been the wiser with respect to how much money was left on the table. Professionals make this pricing error all of the time, as the following stories illustrate.

Value Pricing Opportunities

Recall the "hours, schmours" story in Chapter 7. Two years after the audit, the owners sold their business. The acquiring company's auditors (a Big Four firm) started looking over the books. As the financials had not been audited for two years, and the controller was less than competent, the auditors became skittish about the reliability of the numbers on which they were basing the business valuation. The price of the business dropped from $10 million to $7 million as a result. My partner got actively involved in this process, met with the auditors and the attorneys for the buyers and sellers, and worked almost exclusively for this company for approximately a week and a half. Through his efforts he was able to save the sale and maintain the price at $7 million. Everyone acknowledged that he did a great job, from the auditors to the attorneys. My partner was the hero who saved the day.

Unfortunately, my partner had an FPA with the customer that had a "frequent flyer" clause which said that "any service that is not anticipated in the FPA will be performed at 80 percent of the *standard hourly rate*." The firm has since removed any reference to an hourly rate and replaced it with the following: "We will perform the service at a discount of 10 percent [or sometimes 20 percent] of the *agreed-upon price*." Sadly, my partner was still enamored with the hourly billing method and was not ready to let go of it entirely.

The work he did was billed at $10,000 at standard rates, and he was under obligation to discount it to $8,000 based on the frequent flyer clause included in the FPA. When he met with the customer to go over the final sale documents, he learned that the attorney was paid $108,000 and the controller (whose incompetence caused the sale price to drop from $10 million to $7 million) received a bonus of $35,000. My partner was devastated. The customer even asked him: "Did we not pay you enough?" My partner is a moral person with impeccable character, and he stayed true to his commitment of 80 percent of the standard hourly rate, and thus he got paid $8,000.

It is precisely opportunities such as this that professionals let slip by, at the margin, at a significant loss in profits with the use of hourly billing. While my partner would not have been compensated as much as the attorney, he certainly would have been paid more than the controller. If he had had a retrospective price clause in a change order prepared before he performed the work, in all likelihood the customer would have paid him $75,000 for the results he achieved.

According to an illustration in Larson and Larson, my partner had made the ultimate accounting entry:

	Debit	Credit
Experience	$67,000	
Cash		$67,000

Another example comes from a CPA who assisted his customer in selling a business and was able to make a $15 million difference in the purchase price, which directly accrued to his customer. He billed $38,000 for his services. When he was later asked what he thought the customer would have paid had he used a change order with a retrospective price clause, he said—to his chagrin—$500,000. In other words, he left $462,000 on the table.

These stories are the exception, rather than the rule, in terms of the opportunities that arise daily in your practices. However, opportunities such as these *do* present themselves, and by using change orders you should become more cognizant of them. The retrospective price clause is obviously going to be used only with a customer with whom you have developed a high level of trust and respect. But this is precisely the customer who is going to value your services the most. Had my partner and the other CPA mentioned above simply issued a change order, with perhaps a minimum price to cover their efforts, and left it up to the customer to decide what the value of the service (or result) was worth, they would have been much better off, and the customer would have been just as happy with them. Good customers are not out to take advantage of their professionals, especially when a professional has helped them achieve a major goal.

A CPA from Southern California accompanied his customer to Las Vegas to negotiate the purchase of some real estate. They worked for about six hours, gambled a bit, played a round of golf, and then returned home. When he got back to his office to prepare the bill, he had no idea how much to charge the customer for his time. So he came up with a variation of retrospective price. He sent out a bill that read: "Professional Services Provided in Las Vegas, $X,XXX." He felt he couldn't possibly get $10,000 or more for the day, but the CPA decided to leave it to the sole discretion of his customer. The customer sent him a check the following week for $8,000, far more than he would have billed even for 24 hours at his standard rate. It would have been better to discuss the price before leaving for Las Vegas because the customer may have valued the service even more highly at that time. However, this appears to be an effective strategy to use when you find yourself in a position where you did not adequately discuss price up front.

Beware: In order to retain your price leverage, you must discuss the TIP clause *before* providing the service in question. I have seen many professionals attempt to get a TIP after the engagement has begun, or worse, after it has ended. Almost every time, this has not been successful. The customer must agree to and sign off on the TIP clause *before* you begin the work.

Consider the stories discussed in this chapter illustrating the TIP clause. In the absence of a TIP, all the firms realize is their standard hourly rate, which looks like a success if you analyze realization reports based upon billable hours. The difficult aspect of pricing, however, is that lost opportunities—and mistakes—do not show up anywhere in the firm's traditional metrics. The CPA in the business sale example has no idea he left $462,000 on the table because it does not show up on the firm's income statement or realization reports. This is precisely why pricing will always be an *art*, not a *science*.

Yogi Berra was once asked by a reporter how his team could have lost to the Pirates, and he replied, "We made too many wrong mistakes." (Berra, 2001: 75) There is enormous wisdom in that statement when it comes to pricing. The pricing mistakes illustrated above are precisely the *wrong* types to make because very few firms will learn from them and improve on the next pricing decision (we learn more from success than failure, remember). In fact, the conventional metrics used—hourly realization rates compared to standard rates—will reinforce the *wrong* error. In a value pricing culture, the firm is constantly assessing its pricing policies and striving to improve upon them in order to capture the value it creates. Also, because the firm is using innovative pricing strategies, such as the FPA, change orders, outside-in pricing, and the TIP clause, it is better able to correlate the value created and the price obtained. Will mistakes still be made in a value-pricing environment? Absolutely. But here is the difference: they will be the *right* types of mistakes because the firm will learn from them. Pricing is an iterative process, and the more you analyze each engagement to determine where value pricing opportunities reside, the more sophisticated you will become in capturing the value of your services.

These stories also illustrate that firms skilled at value pricing do not have to maintain time records. How many hours is $462,000 worth at standard rates? Again, these firms are not profitable because they do not use time sheets; they do not use timesheets *because* they are so profitable. It takes only one or two opportunities such as these each year to add tremendously to your bottom line.

Summary and Conclusions

Value pricing offers tremendous rewards to enhance your bottom line. By entering into a fixed price agreement with your customers, you will be able to communicate the value your firm is providing, command premium prices, and reduce price resistance, anxiety, and payment resistance.

Change orders are another excellent device for communicating the value of your firm's services and receiving premium prices for them. By using change orders effectively, you empower customers in the decision to continue an engagement or begin a new one, all the while gaining their ego investment and commitment to the process. Change orders usually represent services at the top of the value curve, since most of the essential compliance services have already been covered in the fixed price agreement. Change orders help ensure that your firm is not committing resources without the customer's agreement as to the value and terms of those additional services. Widely used by contractors and auto mechanics, the change order should become standard operating procedure within your firm's pricing culture. With creativity and ingenuity, change orders can be combined with innovative pricing methods, such as outside-in pricing and retrospective pricing, which allow your firm to capture a portion of the consumer surplus for any given customer.

12 VALUE PRICING ENGAGEMENTS AND METHODS

The following is a discussion on the pricing of various services. It also addresses issues that are emerging in the professional services area, such as electronic commerce, financial services, alliances, contingency pricing, and menu pricing.

Audits

The financial statement audit is the flagship of the accounting profession. It is the reason CPAs have been granted their monopoly status, as they are the only professionals who can provide this service. The audit also serves as the main justification for the rules of objectivity and independence that are the hallmarks of the CPA designation.

The English word *audit* comes from the Latin *audire*, which means "to hear," or more accurately, "that which is heard." There was a lot of discussion in the 1990s about the obsolescence of the audit, and the AICPA's Special Committee on Assurance Services even proposed that the financial statement audit be replaced by an information audit. With the advent of bar code scanners, it has even been suggested that financial statements could be updated in real time.

Given the gap that exists between the investor's need for accurate and timely financial information and how accountants see the role of the audit, the profession can either educate the public on what the audit means (and what it doesn't) or develop an entirely new product that better serves investors' needs. One of the problems with the way the current audit is designed is that the average investor—who the audit is designed to serve and protect—can't understand it. This causes the investor to place a blind faith dependence on the auditing firm, which of course leads to the litigation problems that have plagued the profession in recent decades.

One of the issues that must be confronted when pricing an audit is the actuarial risk assumed by the auditor in performing the service. Unfortunately, this risk has been ignored by the profession for too long. As one member of the profession observed, "Society is asking the CPA profession to do a $500 paint job for $300 and then to indemnify the job!" (Previts and Merino, 1998: 399)

In a free market economy a correlation exists between risk and reward. In a typical IPO, however, an *inverse* relationship exists between the risk assumed by the various service providers and the price they receive. The investment bankers make the most, and they assume practically no risk. The attorneys earn the second highest income, and they assume relatively little risk. Next, the printers are paid, and they have virtually no risk at all. And then there's the CPAs—the lowest income earners in the group, yet the most exposed, liabilitywise, if something goes wrong. While CPAs suffer in all of the downside risk if a particular IPO does not go through, as do the investment bankers and attorneys, they share none of the upside reward in a successful IPO. Audits are considered "commodities" by a lot of CPAs and this is unfortunate, because it contributes to the low price they command. Following the logic of the value curve and marginal pricing, an audit for the purposes of an IPO is worth more than a regular annual audit, say, for the bankers. Yet the price does not reflect the added risk.

In his book, *The Circle of Innovation*, Tom Peters makes this point:

> I've had Big Six accountants tell me that the audit is "becoming commoditized." I've had engineering-services professionals tell me that their business is being determined "entirely by price." I've had trainers lament that "leadership training" is now a commodity.
>
> Is the person you see when you look in the mirror at 6:00 a.m. a "commodity"? No! It's Tom Peters. It's Mary Jones. It's Jeff Smith. It's Jane Doe. It is a person. Singular. With character. Unique skills. The delivery of professional services is the delivery of . . . Jane Doe, Tom Peters, and so on.
>
> If professional services become "commoditized," it means that you and I have become commoditized. I say again: The delivery of a professional service is the delivery of who you are, who I am. (Peters, 1997: 324)

From a marketer's perspective, the notion of a commodity is anathema. Brand names are one method marketing departments deploy in order to overcome the "commodity mentality" that afflicts so many in the professional service world. This is explained by former Harvard Business School professor Theodore Levitt in his article in the *Harvard Business Review* titled, "Marketing Success through Differentiation—of Anything":

> There is no such thing as a commodity. . . On the commodities exchange, for example, dealers in metals, grains, and pork bellies trade in totally undifferentiated products. But what they "sell" is the claimed distinction of their execution—the efficiency of their transactions in their clients' behalf, their responsiveness to inquires, the clarity and speed of their confirmations and the like. In short, the *offered* product is differentiated, though the *generic* product is identical. (Shapiro, 1995: 164)

The audit is no doubt in the decline stage of the service life cycle (see Chapter 2). Today, fewer than 10 public firms account for more than 90 percent of the auditing services offered to publicly traded companies. According to classical marketing price theory, there are three strategies a firm can take when it finds its service in the decline phase:

- Retrenchment
- Harvesting
- Consolidation

A retrenchment strategy involves partial or complete capitulation of some market segments, and refocusing resources on where the firm's strengths and core competencies lay. This requires the firm to relinquish market share, but the trade-off is better concentration in a segment in which the firm has a competitive advantage. Many CPA firms in the 1990s, for instance, focused their audit services on industries they selected as their niche—banking, healthcare, etc. The increased efficiencies generated by this strategy allowed the firms to compete against low-priced providers who attempted to invade their niche without the same competitive and cost advantages.

The harvesting strategy is a planned withdrawal from a market entirely. It may start out like the retrenchment strategy, whereby the firm divests itself of its weakest links. The harvesting firm does not price to defend its existing market share but rather to maximize its revenues until it completes its withdrawal. Many CPA firms have adopted this strategy for audits, deciding to forego offering the service altogether and outsourcing the work to other firms.

In a consolidation strategy, the firm attempts to strengthen its position in a declining market. This strategy is effective when a firm has adequate resources to weather the storm that forces its competitors from the market. After the shakeout, the firm is well positioned, with a larger market share and less competition.

One recurring pricing error is that of pricing the audit low in the hopes of securing the more lucrative tax—and, better yet, consulting—work. The customer has learned how to hold out the carrot of more work once you get past this audit proposal. For the customer, it has been a very successful negotiation tactic. Unfortunately for the firm, it is rarely a successful practice.

The problem with the low introductory price is that it serves as a reference price for evaluating all other services. And because customers tend to be more sensitive to perceived price increases, this strategy locks the firm into low-balling the other supposedly more lucrative services, if they are lucky enough to get them, that is.

Caution is called for when pricing an audit. Do not discount all of the other services that surround the service—the management letter, internal control reviews, etc.—that provide value to the customer. In December 1991, Arthur Andersen developed its global best practices knowledge base because it noticed it was spending a lot of time inside customers' businesses performing audits. The company determined that if it could compare one company's performance to its competitors, it would add significant value to the audit service. This proved to be a very successful differentiation strategy that separated Arthur Andersen from its competitors and also combated the "commodity" mentality.

A California two-partner CPA firm found themselves in the position of having to bid on an audit for one of its customers whose business was being acquired by a large company in New York. The company's CPAs in New York would actually sign the audit and be in charge of filing the audit report as part of an SEC filing and, in effect, would hire the California firm. The audit would cover three years for two companies; the opportunity was presented in late September, and the deadline was November 30. The partners, at first, estimated the price, based upon "standard hourly rates," at $25,000. However, once the partners asked themselves the questions discussed in Chapter 10, they became aware of the convenience factor (a two-month deadline): the specific knowledge of the customer they had and the relationship with the owner; the fact that the audit was instrumental to the closing of a $30 million deal; the relative price to the CPA firm of doing it in-house (and sending a team from New York to California to accomplish it); the fact that the New York CPAs were struggling with capacity issues and were not a member of an accounting firm association, among various other factors.

The partners discussed these issues with me at length, and I advised that the $25,000 was far too low (even though it was 100 percent realization on an audit and conducted in the off season). They worried that if they submitted a price that was too high, the New York CPAs would balk or, worse, select another firm. This is typical, in that accountants project their own price sensitivity onto the customer, a serious mistake. We phoned a senior manager in a Big Four firm and asked him how much he would price the audit. His answer was $60,000. Now, I am not a fan of letting your competition set your price, but if you are curious about the competition, at least go to those who place an umbrella over your prices.

Now the partners were facing the Russian proverb: "There are two fools in every market, one asks too little, one asks too much." I asked the partners what price they would desire in a perfect world; they responded "$30,000." This is not a frivolous question, as I have come to believe that any engagement should have its own internal "reservation price" set by the team member(s) in charge of the engagement (we discuss minimum prices later in this chapter). I felt they should have priced the job at $45,000, based on everything that was known; they decided on $40,000. The New York firm didn't blink, accepted the price, and never asked "how many hours." This was an additional $15,000 premium, over and above "standard hourly rates," arrived at simply by our focusing on the pricing issue. Would you agree that the time we invested in thinking about the price was well worth it? This is precisely what is meant by price being one of the most complex of the four Ps of marketing; it requires thought, analysis, and creativity. Further, the firm got a $3,500 change order out of the engagement as well. Please understand, this was an audit, a so-called commodity service in the marketplace. Nonsense. Almost every engagement has "value drivers" surrounding it, time of delivery being a good example in this case. Look for those value drivers, examine as many factors as you can, think long and hard about the price you are offering.

The question is almost never "Will we make money on this engagement?" On most jobs, a firm would have a hard time losing money because the gross profit in a service firm is relatively high, especially once you remove the "desired net income" from the hourly rate and change it to a real cost-accounting number. The relevant question is "Are we optimizing the profit from this engagement?" Focusing on this question leads to a 60 percent price premium. One final point: How important are timesheets on this engagement? Are they necessary? What valid information would they convey? How would they help price in the future? Would they provide the team members any disincentives to stretch out the hours on the job given the premium price, thus fulfilling Parkison's Law? Should the firm measure hours or its progress on meeting the deadline? We discuss the necessity of timesheets in Chapters 20 and 21. This is a classic example of pricing on the margin, and it illustrates the validity of pricing for value, not hours.

Reviews and Compilations

Like the audit, review and compilation services are only provided by CPAs. While it may be true that the marginal value of one more review or compilation is not as high as the value of an audit, these services still need to be priced based on their value. Most customers need one of these services to comply with their bank covenants and maintain their lines of credit and other financing arrangements. These services also need to be priced at the margin. To most businesspeople, the cost of a review or compilation is simply an additional interest premium for securing their loan. CPAs should never underestimate the value of this service, especially since they are the only professionals who can offer it.

Tax Services

Tax services are on the high end of the value curve. Given the average taxpayer's fear of the IRS (more Americans would choose to be mugged rather than face an IRS audit), tax services, from compliance to planning, offer value pricing opportunities. Now that contingency fees are allowed in various states, you will begin to see innovative tax-planning products that offer customers tax savings of gigantic proportions. The price for these services will be a percentage of the savings.

Some have argued that low-level tax compliance work will increasingly become a paraprofessional activity, while the professional spends his or her time structuring and researching complex scenarios. This rings true, because it's very hard to compete with a $39 tax program or a Web site that allows individuals to access forms and advice in preparing their taxes. This may affect a new customer's reference price, but your old customers are more likely to value your services enough to pay more. For many firms, the pricing of the tax services will represent a reference price for all other services. For the same reasons discussed in the audit section earlier, these services should not be discounted with the hope of receiving more lucrative work.

Never discount your tax services. Customers come to CPAs expecting to pay more. Otherwise they would have gone to a PA, an EA, or H&R Block. Do not offer discounts for filing early; do not tier your prices based on your internal work flow. All of this is completely irrelevant to the value of the service to the customer. When dealing with IRS issues such as collection problems, offers in compromise, and audits, price in accordance with your abilities and experience. Keep in mind the relationships that you have developed with various government officials that may enable you to perform services more efficiently for the customer than someone else. With respect to estate taxation, remember that many people are spending other people's money on themselves or on others. Be on the lookout for these opportunities.

Some consultants distribute price sheets for a service, such as preparing tax returns. However, no one but the customer should decide the value of any service. Do not use price lists from a tax preparation program or from a standard list published by some other organization. These tools can be used as guidelines, but never delegate your pricing to some external force. You and your customers should decide on the value of any given service. That is what is meant by pricing on purpose.

There has been a lot of talk about radical tax reform in the Congress and at the grassroots level throughout the country. This talk was fueled by the Republican takeover of the Congress in 1994, and it has quelled quite a bit since then, due to good economic times. However, at the next downturn in the economy, this issue will come back on the national scene. Depending on the political makeup of the Congress and White House in the year 2005, major tax reform will certainly make its way into the national discussion. A lot of talking heads predict a national sales tax, a value added tax, or a personal consumption tax; others advocate a flat tax. The flat tax would do the most to transform the tax side of the CPA profession, as it would simplify the compliance required, though not completely eliminating it. A VAT would likely never pass in the United States (European tax systems hold lessons of failure, not success), and a national sales tax would also not pass once the economic realities of the rate required for revenue neutrality were well understood. The flat tax appears to be the ultimate direction the Congress will take with respect to reform.

An issue lays buried beneath tax reform, however, and needs to be considered by professionals who do a lot of work in this area. This is the issue of estate and gift taxation, which generates less than 1 percent of all federal revenues and has been criticized by both sides of the political spectrum as costing more than it is worth. As a redistribution policy, it is an abject failure. This tax will probably come under serious assault in the next decade and may just be wiped away with the stroke of a pen.

Management Advisory Services (MAS)

Management advisory services (MAS) are usually at the top of the value curve and should be among the highest-priced services your firm offers. By pricing on the margin, you will be able to set the value in accordance with the particular circumstances of the moment, and the customer will often value the services even more highly than your standard prices. By using the retrospective price clause you will be able to capture more of the consumer surplus.

Outside-in pricing, whereby you ask the customers what the value of the service is worth to them, is also custom-made for MAS services. Many times, you may not know all that is involved with offering a particular MAS service (a computer installation with training of the accounting personnel, for instance), in which case you may want to set a minimum price and have the customer review the results and pay a premium based on satisfaction. By asking customers what they perceive the value to be, you are gaining their ego investment, giving them control over the decision, and involving them in determining the value after the engagement is over.

If you have entered into a fixed price agreement (FPA) with a customer, and a MAS arises, issue a change order priced at the high end of the value curve. Because the basic services are already covered in the FPA, a MAS service, most likely, is contributing to the profitability of the business or directly benefiting the owner(s).

A former customer presented my partner with a MAS engagement in December 1999. The customer had left our firm approximately two years earlier, mostly due to personality clashes with various personnel. In December, they were about to enter into a merger agreement with a larger company, a deal of approximately $2.5 million. One of the principals of the company, who was a good friend of my partner's and had never wanted to leave our firm, asked for a price on merger consulting. After reviewing the engagement parameters and examining the prior two years' tax returns, my partner found many errors in the filings. After we discussed the issue at length, he submitted the following FPA to the customer on December 10, 1999:

- We will provide general advice in negotiating the merger agreement.
- We will perform document review for all documents in the process (proposed and final).
- We will file final 1999 corporate tax returns, federal and state.
- We will file final 1999 personal tax returns for the three shareholders, federal and state.
- We will amend the 1998 corporate tax returns, federal and state.
- We will amend the 1998 personal tax return for [one of the owners].
- We will provide unlimited phone and meeting support for the merger, tax returns, and tax and general questions for all the above issues, both corporate and personal.
- The total price for the foregoing will be $25,000.
- This price is payable at the closing of the merger or by March 1, 2000, whichever is earlier.

The first question we asked ourselves was "Why aren't they using their existing CPA for this work?" The friend of my partner felt the existing CPA lacked the expertise in this area, as he was unable to answer questions about the tax ramifications of the proposed merger. That alone indicates a lack of price sensitivity. Once we submitted the above FPA, the customer came back and wanted to know the breakdown between the tax work and the consulting services. In our experience, this is an unusual request, especially when you bundle your proposals in the above manner. However, we knew there were other firms being considered, so my partner used a very ingenious pricing strategy. He knew the tax work would be put out to bid, so he priced the tax work at a competitive $7,500 price and the consulting services at $17,500. He got the engagement, and the owners later said he was the only one who offered unlimited phone support and meetings, which tilted their preference toward us. In fact, the customer was so impressed with the FPA, my partner won them back, as well as the other owners of the company. Further, he was able to cross-sell additional services utilizing change orders, one of which was the establishment of a trust at a price of $700 per month.

Management advisory services are an excellent way to differentiate your firm from the competition, especially when you bundle them into an FPA. As Ric Payne, founder of Principa, is fond of pointing out, "It is harder to differentiate your firm at a price of $2,000 than at $25,000. We lose customers because our price is too low—i.e., we are not offering enough high-level services to our customers." Many Principa firms offer a business valuation every other year to their best customers, which is positioned in the marketplace as a way to help the owners work "on" the business rather than "in" the business. This allows these firms to advertise statements such as: "In the past five years, ABC, CPAs has helped its clients grow their businesses by $xxx. If you'd like to find out how, call us." This is a very effective competitive differentiation, not to mention advertising.

Government Audits and Bankruptcy Work

Unfortunately, government audits and bankruptcy work are two areas where value pricing will take longer to become standard practice. Most government agencies require RFPs to include hourly budgets and rates. Bankruptcy work requires professionals to charge by the hour, and even round to the nearest tenth of an hour. Bankruptcy courts will look to the "lodestar" method to determine the fairness of a price. This method is described in Chapter 13. If these two services make up the majority of your practice, you are limited in your ability to move away from the Almighty Hour. Nonetheless, add-on work should be priced based on value. CPAs who specialize in these two areas always have opportunities arise in which the firm can command prices in accordance with value, not hours.

Litigation Support

Courts are still tied to hourly billing, but this area offers more opportunities for innovative pricing, such as contingency pricing and retrospective pricing. If you are ever questioned about an innovative pricing method by a court, point out that the American Bar Association itself is a proponent in the forefront of moving away from hourly billing. Cite the three books edited by Richard C. Reed (see the references section). Courts are going to have to accept the fact that a price is "reasonable" as long as it is agreed to by the parties voluntarily. Further, there are encouraging signs that some court jurisdictions are beginning to recognize that a price agreed to by two parties—especially in advance of the work performed—is by definition a fair and reasonable price. This is discussed more in Chapter 16.

New Customers

When making the transition from hourly billing to value pricing, starting with new customers is always easier because they will be the most receptive to the approach. It is also an effective marketing differentiation that attracts customers who are, more and more, demanding fixed prices from their professionals.

The Juran Institute has found that less than 10 percent of customers defect because of price. Yet, most CPAs say they feel compelled to charge the same as, or even less than, their predecessor. This is a mistake. Consider the study performed by the Rockefeller Corporation, which discovered the following reasons for customer defections:

1% The customer dies.
3% The customer moves away.
5% The customer has a friend who provides the same service.
9% The customer is lost to a competitor.
14% The customer is dissatisfied with the service provided.
68% **The customer believes you do not care about them.**

In other words, two-thirds of customers defect because of the way they were *treated*. The Rockerfeller Corporation's study has been corroborated by another study conducted by August J. Aquila and Allan D. Koltin, published in the *Journal of Accountancy* in May 1992. The article, titled "How to Lose Clients Without Really Trying," is excellent, earning them the 1992 Annual Literary Award for the best article of the year from the *Journal*. Here are the top seven reasons CPAs lose customers:

1. "My accountant just does not treat me right."
2. CPAs ignore clients.
3. CPAs fail to cooperate.
4. CPAs let partner contact lapse.
5. CPAs do not keep clients informed.
6. CPAs assume clients are technicians.
7. CPAs use clients as a training ground.

(Aquila and Koltin, 1992: 67–70)

Customers would not be in your office if they were satisfied with your predecessor. They defected over service issues—the way *they* were handled, not the way their *work* was handled—and not price. What the predecessor charged should be the minimum baseline for your price, and you should add a premium. The value proposition of every firm is price, service, and quality. Because you cannot compete on quality alone, and price is not why new customers come to you, you can command premium prices only for quality service. Many CPAs disagree with me on this point. They have created their own self-fulfilling prophecy. By thinking that they gain new customers only by low-balling the price, they attract the undesirable customers who are price sensitive, not service sensitive. When these customers locate another professional who will do the work for less, they defect, even though good service was provided.

Quality service commands a premium price in other industries, and the empirical evidence is clear that most customers will pay more for better service. Witness Disney, FedEx, Marriott, and Cadillac. They do not compete on price; they compete on service.

Years ago a customer was referred to me by another CPA. In looking over the prior CPA's work, I found it to be in order and completed in a timely manner. When asked why she was leaving her CPA of more than 20 years, the new customer said four memorable words: "*He showed no compassion.*" Earlier that year, her husband had passed away, and the prior CPA did not attend the funeral or send a sympathy card. The CPA lost this customer not because of deficient work, but because of the way he treated her. When I informed the woman that my price was *four* times that of her prior CPA, she did not blink, and she has been an excellent customer ever since.

When you are setting a price for new customers, start high. It is the *service* they are after, not the *price*. If they are interested only in price, it is better to find that out before they become customers.

Another variant in pricing is known as *phasing*. This is when a project (or a group of projects) is broken down into smaller segments that can be identified with starting and completion points. For example, Phase I could cover those items that are needed immediately—accounting assistance, tax compliance issues, and a financial statement review. Phase II could deal with assistance on securing new financing, high-end tax planning, and other general business consulting. Phase III could deal with the unique services located at the top of the value curve.

This innovative pricing method is effective for several reasons: It allows the customer to pick and choose a level of commitment to the relationship; it reduces the customer's perceived risk by allowing the customer to test drive the firm to determine their satisfaction; it lowers the level of price resistance—sticker shock—for a new customer not familiar with the level of services offered by a CPA firm; and it proves to the customer that the firm is interested in doing more than just solving its basic accounting and tax needs.

Phased pricing has been adopted in legal firms, although with a slight variance in the method. Usually, a budget is negotiated for each phase. As the phases are completed, any excess price (or savings) is put into a suspense account. The firm can recoup the amount in the suspense account if it comes in under budget for the entire engagement. Even though this method has been used in conjunction with hourly billing, it does illustrate another way in which the risk is being shared between professional and customer.

The last point with respect to pricing for new customers involves using a retainer. Getting a retainer does more than reduce the risk of not getting paid; it demonstrates serious commitment on the part of the customer. No one is willing to pay in advance for services that he or she does not value. Payment of a retainer also increases the ego investment of customers, which enhances their commitment to the relationship. Another advantage of retainers is that they set a precedent that the firm expects to get paid, in a timely manner, for services provided.

The amount of the retainer is based on the perceived risk, commitment, and financial ability of the customer. A good rule of thumb is to set the retainer amount somewhere between 25 percent and 50 percent of the total FPA.

Veteran Customers

Your long-term customers will require a little more time and education to convert them to value pricing. You will have to outline the benefits of converting to this new method. One of the biggest benefits, and you should never forget to mention this, is that the risk is removed from them and placed on your firm. When drafting an FPA for the first year, it is always easier to include more services and change the focus to the totality of your firm's offering. By including the unlimited access clause, you are dramatically changing the scope of the service, and if you are able to deliver more services, put them into the FPA and you should command a higher price from the customer.

One caveat with the strategy of adding as many services as you can applies to both new and old customers: Price services as they arise, using the change order, because, at the margin, you will command a higher price for them. A business owner is less price sensitive for help with his SBA loan one month before he attempts to secure it rather than 12 months in advance, when he is naturally more price sensitive. So when you draft an FPA, try to stick to the basic, compliance-oriented services, and let the value-added services be handled with change orders. You will command a higher price because you will possess more leverage.

Alumni Customers

An alumnus situation arises when your prospective customer once worked for your firm and is a CPA too (or an attorney). These folks know how the game is played and most likely will demand to know the amount of hours that will be spent providing the service. Here is a solution offered by a partner from a national firm: "You tell them the game has *changed* and we do not discuss hours anymore; we discuss value."

This tremendous answer cuts right to the heart of the issue: Does the customer care more about time spent or value derived? Most would answer, of course, value, and this is a good approach to take with your colleagues who may be, at some point, your customers.

Colleagues

Naturally, most colleagues will force you to discuss hours (unless they, too, have made the transition to value pricing). A good response is that the game has changed and that now you discuss value. Fellow professionals may be more receptive to the idea of paying for value than you may at first think. An interesting trend began in the mid-1980s. Public accountants in private industry began to outnumber those in public accounting. Over half of CPAs now work in private industry, and you are likely to find a CPA in the controller position in smaller companies. In other words, it is more and more likely that the person who will exert tremendous influence on hiring your firm in the future will be a CPA.

Chapter 9 discusses the fact that we really live in a barter economy, and it is the relative price that is important, as opposed to the nominal price. One important relative price when dealing with CPAs who work in the customer's company is the price of performing the work internally. When pricing for various services, especially consulting engagements, always take into account how much work can be done internally vs. that which can be done by your firm.

In today's marketplace it is not uncommon to find many firms outsourcing some of their work to per diem professionals, for example, in India. One Chartered Accountant in Australia said something I will always remember: "I outsource to people who are stupid enough to charge me by the hour." When you think about how much money is being left on the table when you pay someone solely by the hour, the validity of value pricing becomes apparent. If your firm does per diem-type work, use the same principles we have been discussing, and it is a fairly safe bet you will achieve higher prices.

Request for Proposal

Never forget that your weapon is made by the lowest bidder.

—Law #20 of Murphy's Laws of Combat

In their book, *The Strategy and Tactics of Pricing*, Thomas Nagle and Reed Holden explain the economic anomaly known as the winner's curse—that is, in a bidding situation with many bidders, the winning bidder is often a loser. Here's why:

> The more bidders there are, the more likely you will lose money on every job you win, even if on average you estimate costs correctly and both you and your competitors set bids that include a reasonable margin of profit. This is because the bids you win are not a random sample of the bids you make. You are much more likely to win jobs for which you have underestimated your costs and are unlikely to win those for which you have overestimated your cost. Consequently, the expected profitability of a job, conditional on the fact that you have won it, is much less than the expected profitability before winning. The difference between the conditional and unconditional probabilities increases with the number of competitors against whom you must bid. (Nagle and Holden, 1995: 205)

In today's marketplace, competitive bidding is an alternative to negotiation for price buyers. Also, many companies use the RFP as an effective method to lower their professional services price, with no intention of switching providers. Be careful before committing firm resources to preparing RFPs. Make sure you understand the reason the company is asking for one, and try to develop an internal advocate who can help steer your RFP through the channel and keep you informed of the process.

In their book *Co-opetition*, Adam Brandenburger and Barry Nalebuff offer this sage advice with respect to RFPs:

> There seems to be a natural impulse to offer competition for free. After all, that is what business people are supposed to do, is not it? You want a bid? I'll give you a bid . . . .
>
> The right question to ask is: How important is it to the customer that you bid? If bidding is so important, then you should get compensated for playing the game. If it is not so important, then you are unlikely to get the business and even less likely to make money. You might want to reconsider bidding at all. (Brandenburger and Nalebuff, 1996: 84)

What they are saying is that competition is valuable and not to be given away. An effective method of testing the customer's commitment is to engage in outside-in pricing. Ask him to offer you a price that he would be willing to pay to engage your services. Car dealers have used this technique for years. It prevents you from spending precious resources preparing proposals. Test the customer's commitment; find out how serious the customer is before you prepare a proposal. Ask for a guaranteed engagement letter for the project if you agree with the customer's price. Find out if you can propose on more of the company's business.

Another strategy with proposals follows the same principles as value pricing: *No surprises*. Your potential customer should know everything in your proposal—there should be no new knowledge. This means you have already determined your customer's expectations (and how to exceed them). Just by doing this, you will increase your chances of getting the business. If customers are worth bidding on, they are worth investing time up front to determine expectations, needs, and wants. In your pre-proposal meetings, if these issues are discussed, your proposal will stand out from the competition's and you should also command a higher price. Do not be shy about value pricing in a proposal situation. Differentiate your firm based on service. Why attract customers who do not value you anyway?

Once you submit a proposal, you lose all control (and leverage). All you can do then is call every week and ask, "Have you made a decision yet?" This is not a good position to be in. If you are going to surprise customers, do it by exceeding their expectations, perhaps by offering a service you know they want (or need) or by thinking of an innovative strategy or plan. Change the game; ignore the old rules.

Brandenburger and Nalebuff point out these eight hidden costs of bidding:

1. **There are better uses of your time.** Keeping your current customers happy is smarter than chasing after other people's customers. (The AICPA says that attracting a new customer is 11 times more costly than keeping an existing one. By investing in existing customer relationships, you are, in effect, increasing the effectiveness of your marketing and advertising 11 times.)

2. **When you win the business, you lose money.** A customer you win on price alone is telling you he has no loyalty. If you think that getting the customer gives you an opportunity to make money later by raising price, think again. By coming to you, this customer has just revealed himself as someone who will switch suppliers to get a lower price. [Employ adverse selection.]

3. **The incumbent can retaliate.** If this is a good customer, then your win is someone else's loss. (If it is a bad customer, then you have already made a mistake.) The incumbent supplier is likely to respond. He can go after one of your customers. He may not get your customer, but he can surely force you to lower the price. If he succeeds in snagging your customer, then you and your rival have turned two high-margin accounts into two low-margin accounts. The end result: lose-lose.
4. **Your existing customers will want a better deal.** This is not a big problem, because a professional's customers can't compare service and price with others as easily as a job shop or other businesses.
5. **New customers will use the low price as a benchmark.** A bigger concern is that a professional would use the low price as a benchmark with other new customers.
6. **Competitors will also use the low price as a benchmark.** Even if you were willing to risk charging a higher price again in the future, your rivals might expect you to come in with a low price, and these expectations become a self-fulfilling prophesy. [This illustrates the importance of not letting your competitors who do not price based on value determine your prices.]
7. **It does not help to give your customer's competitors a better cost position.** Your future and that of your customer are naturally linked. If your future is tied to Coke, you do not want to help Pepsi get a lower price. Unless you have very good reason to believe that you can get Pepsi's business and keep Coke's, bidding for Pepsi's business is costly. You help your competitor's customer and thereby hurt your own.
8. **Do not destroy your competitors' glass houses.** The view that you win if competitors lose is simplistic and potentially dangerous. Remember to think co-opetition. If you lower your rival's profits, he then has less to lose and every reason to become more aggressive. He can go after your existing accounts with abandon. In contrast, the more money your rival is making, the more he has to lose from getting into a price war. (Brandenburger and Nalebuff, 1996: 86–88)

Keep these hidden costs in mind when preparing a proposal. Make sure that customers are worth the trouble of bidding by testing their commitment, and do not waste your firm's fixed resources submitting bids that may be being used merely as leverage against a customer's existing professional.

Write-Up Work

Write-up work is another area that has been encroached on by businesses from outside the profession. Intuit, makers of QuickBooks, has a commanding 70 percent share of the North American small business accounting software market. What Intuit learned through market research was that 85 percent of companies in the United States were too small to employ an accountant. Most of the owners themselves, or members of their families, took care of the company's books, and they had no formal knowledge of debits and credits, let alone an audit trail. Intuit immediately spotted an opportunity in that most of the makers of software for small businesses had overshot the market, with programs that offered more functionality than the average small business required.

In fact, Intuit developers had a profound insight. The double-entry accounting method, so eloquently written about by Fra Luca Pacioli in 1494 (see Chapter 1), was devised in order to catch mistakes within the recorded entries. Computers typically don't make mistakes in addition and subtraction, and this fact allowed Intuit's software developers to simplify both its Quicken and QuickBooks products.

Write-up work is certainly another candidate for services in your firm's market niche. It still requires that you price it on value, and be sure to differentiate your firm from the software product. Emphasize the value of your being available to oversee the use of the software and your expertise and handling of the accounting records.

Write-up work is certainly on the low end of the value curve. Also, you will face competitive price pressure as well as the ever-present threat that the customer will bring the task in-house. However, you should still include the service as part of a comprehensive FPA, making sure you price it according to the totality of the firm's service offering.

Pricing Authority

Many professional firms now employ a marketing manager either full-time or part-time. In the past, this was unheard of—a nonprofessional selling professional services; today, it is relatively common, and the trend is increasing. It is worth taking some time to formulate your pricing strategy when you employ marketing and salespeople to sell your firm's services.

How much authority should they have over pricing decisions? When is it appropriate for them to decide unilaterally to cut a price? Should there be minimum prices? These types of issues are very common in most other businesses and thus there is much experience to tap into when it comes to whether or not your pricing authority should be centralized or decentralized.

Normally, there are three types of pricing authority:

1. The sales force (or other decentralized unit) has full authority over all pricing decisions.

Advantages:

- The morale of the sales force is boosted because they have more authority and responsibility within the company.
- Because the sales force is closest to the marketplace and the customer, it has the information regarding a specific transaction and is best able to evaluate where on the demand curve the customer is positioned and the customer's willingness to pay. This allows the firm to capture the consumer surplus.
- The sales force can quickly react to marketplace changes and competitive threats.
- In negotiations with the customer, level of services and pricing are interrelated, and if the salesperson has no authority, the process can be hindered and unnecessarily stalled.
- Decentralization leads to the optimum price when the salesperson's commission is based on the contribution margin of the sale.

2. The sales force has limited authority. Down to a set minimum price level members of the sales force can make a decision. If the price is below that level, they must obtain approval from superiors.

Advantages:

- The sales force is always tempted to cut the price to make the sale, even though a commission is based on the contribution margin. This can seriously hinder the firm's marketing strategy and position in the marketplace, as pricing affects both dramatically.

- By having pricing decisions centralized, the sales force is relieved of the psychological pressures of discussing price, which most sales people are afraid of getting beat up over.
- Centralization can also reduce the pressure from the buyer for price concessions. One of the axioms of purchasing agents is, "find out if the salesperson can cut the price. If he can, insist he does."
- Only top management is in the position to look at each market segment and decide on the optimal pricing strategy that capitalizes on their strengths while minimizing their weaknesses.

3. The sales force has no authority over pricing. Any changes from those prescribed by management must be approved.

Although each business must decide for itself how to split pricing authority, most marketing managers, who are experts in pricing literature, seem to agree that the centralization of pricing authority results in a higher probability of profit enhancing pricing.

Chapter 7 mentions that in the legal profession a new job of "estimator" might be created. However, it would be better if all pricing authority rested with the partners, or, at the least, with the person who has the best relationship with the customer. Professional services are valued largely because of the personal relationship, and a sales or marketing force cannot convey that sense of value, no matter how good they may otherwise be.

With respect to marketing managers, a disturbing trend is appearing, at least in CPA firms. Because there is so much pressure on them to pay off on the investment the firm is making in their position, they tend to undercut price with alacrity in too many situations, simply to bring in the business and look successful. Cutting price is a very effective way to increase demand; it is not an effective profit-maximizing strategy for a firm with a sophisticated view of its marketplace and niche. There are no easy answers when it comes to price, and each firm must develop its own strategy.

A group of partners and managers should establish the price on all new engagements, ideally with a full understanding of the customer and after meeting with them. Furthermore, someone who is unfamiliar with the customer—but who is adept at pricing decisions and ascertaining value—should be present to ensure that the overall objectives of the firm are not lost in the adrenaline rush that comes from the potential of bringing in new business. In fact, some firms have established a pricing cartel, responsible for reviewing all pricing decisions before and after each engagement to ensure the firm learns from its mistakes and capitalizes on its opportunities. So far, the results have been impressive, and forming a pricing cartel within your firm is strongly suggested if your firm is large enough. We will explore the pricing cartel further in Chapter 20.

Financial Services

Financial services and commissions have entered the CPA profession. The major consolidators—from American Express to H&R Block—are buying up CPA firms in the hope of tapping into the most trusted and respected business advisor relationship. For American Express, it's an alternative distribution channel marketing strategy; for the CPA profession, it is an enormous opportunity. And, most important of all, the customer is demanding it.

Financial services have become a growth industry for the profession because of the regulatory and legislative changes, customer demands, and profit potential. According to *Millionaire Next Door*, the number of estates valued at more than $1 million was 40,921 in 1996 and is expected to be 100,650 by 2005, while the estimated number of millionaires will be 5,626,409, or 5,239 per 100,000 households, in 2005. (Stanley and Danko, 1996: 213, 225) As the baby boom generation passes on its trillions of dollars of wealth to its kids, the nature and scope of the profession will be permanently altered.

As Chris Frederiksen pointed out at a 1999 conference: "CPAs probably control half the wealth of the nation and yet are involved in less than one tenth of 1 percent of the transactions." This strikes at the heart of the independence and objectivity on which the profession has built its illustrious reputation. But the notions of independence and objectivity may just be obsolete for all but those involved in financial statement auditing. The fact of the matter is that customers don't want the CPA to be independent and objective. They want you to help them achieve their goals. They trust their CPA more than a financial advisor or a stockbroker. The successful firm, Charles Schwab, started with the strategy of noncommissioned brokers. Then, in the 1980s, the company's market research showed that customers did want advice relating to investments and managing financial affairs.

This required sending investors into the world of commissioned salespeople, what Charles Schwab himself termed "the lion's den." In response, the company created Schwab Institutional, a network of independent fee-based financial advisors to whom Schwab could refer its customers. Today, more than $100 billion in invested Schwab accounts is managed by these advisors. (Berry, 1999: 146)

Many practitioners posit the theory that this trend will not work for the profession, because customers are not really interested in "one-stop shopping." They point to the disaster of Sears' financial supermarket as an example of why it won't work. This example is not what it seems, however. When Sears entered into the financial services market in the 1980s—with Allstate, Dean Witter, and the Discover Card—it wasn't long before the strategy backfired and the company was forced to retreat. Former Sears CEO Arthur C. Martinez diagnosed the real problem:

> What was wrong was that too much of the strategic focus, management energy, and financial capital [had gone] to building the financial supermarket side of the business and no attention, or let's say insufficient attention, was paid to the retail side, which was the mother lode of the whole thing. If you didn't have customers coming into your store, happy with their relationship with the store, they weren't necessarily going to be interested in anything else you had to offer. Strategically, the idea [of the financial supermarket] was sound. The problem was, while they were building another floor on the house, the foundation was rotting. (O'Shea and Madigan, 1998: 121–122)

Moving into the financial services market will dramatically affect a firm's pricing strategies. One trend that has been taking place throughout the United States is that of life insurance salespeople selling policies to estates, earning the commission, and from that paying the CPA or attorney for the estate planning and other services. Something is terribly wrong when a salesman can earn enough to pay the person with the expertise for his or her work. Obviously, this imbalance will be brought to parity as more and more CPAs offer insurance services themselves.

There are enormous profits to be made from selling products on a commission, especially if one breaks it down into earnings per hour. How many hours does it take to sell an estate's life insurance vs. doing its tax compliance and strategy? If partners bring the same paradigm of hourly rates into this new arena, they are likely to undervalue their traditional work in order to get the commission. This would be a serious mistake.

There is no doubt that some CPA services will become loss leaders in order to attract the customer's portfolio, pension plan, and so on. It may make sense to give away, or significantly reduce, the price of tax compliance services in order to get this type of work; this trend is already taking place. But as the level of service moves up the value curve—where the customer is relatively price insensitive—the firm should not discount its price just to secure a life insurance sale. This is why it is so important to understand that price is based on value, not on internal cost, and certainly not on time.

Minimum and Setup Pricing

One way to ensure that your firm maintains a consistent pricing message within its marketplace is to establish a minimum price, as well as a setup price, for all new customers. By establishing a minimum price, the firm is sending a message to all involved that they cannot be all things to all people. One of the first things any new marketing manager should ascertain is who the firm should serve. A minimum price ensures that the firm won't spend its limited resources on customers who don't value its offering. One effective minimum price is 1 percent of a firm's (or office's) gross revenue; no customer should be accepted whose price does not rise to that level. This pricing policy is dynamic, it grows with your firm.

A setup price is, in effect, one method of implementing a two-part tariff, as discussed in Chapter 9. Start by charging new customers a setup price, ranging, for example, from $500 to $1,000, simply for setting up the customer file, performing due diligence research, contacting the predecessor CPA (or attorney), and performing everything else that taking on a new customer entails. This is a very effective strategy for tapping into any consumer surplus that may exist. It also develops customer buy-in and ego investment at the beginning of the engagement, thereby committing the customer to your firm. If you are too shy to ask for a retainer, the setup price is an effective alternative.

Menu Pricing

Menu pricing has a long and successful history among marketers. This is the bundling of a certain group of products or services into one price. Think of a restaurant pricing a full, prix fixe meal vs. à la carte; or American Express offering different levels of service to its Green, Gold, Platinum, and Black Card members (American Express's "Centurion Card," the black card, is offered by invitation only); or an auto manufacturer offering a myriad of options on a car. Menu pricing enables a business to differentiate its products in the minds of its buyers, a classic segmentation strategy. It also encourages buyers to trade up to a higher-priced product. Kent B. Monroe explains this in *Pricing: Making Profitable Decisions*:

> Bundling is ubiquitous and thus seemingly escapes notice. However, because it is so commonplace it has not received recognition as an important marketing strategy. Yet if properly developed and implemented, a price bundling strategy can enhance a customer's perceptions of value, provide competitive advantage, lead to cost economies, and effect a profitable pricing strategy. If bundling is improperly done, it can lead to lost sales, reduced profits, and a deterioration of customer satisfaction.
>
> Essentially, bundling is a segmentation strategy based on the theory that different segments value different combinations of products or services differently. Unless the firm's managers understand customer segmentation, it is likely that a successful strategy will not be developed. Some customers find a one-stop purchasing source desirable. Full-service banks attempt to capture such customers by offering full financial services at one institution. However, other customers want a simple checking and savings service only. If the bank forced all customers to pay for full financial services which they neither need nor want, or priced each service separately, neither customer segment would be satisfied. In either situation, the bank would be treating very different customers in a similar manner. (Monroe, 1990: 319)

The movie industry once practiced the strategy known as *block booking*. Individual films were not rented to theaters; theaters were required to rent a block of films. Many thought this was a way for the distributors to force theaters to take the good along with the bad films. Economist George Stigler in 1963 proposed another reason this strategy was rational. He used the example of *Gone with the Wind* and *Getting Gertie's Garter*, two movies with widely different popularity. Stigler proposed what two theaters, A and B, would pay for the films individually:

	Gone with the Wind	*Getting Gertie's Garter*
Theater A	$8,000	$2,500
Theater B	$7,000	$3,000

Both theater owners are willing to pay substantially more for *Gone with the Wind.* The bundling strategy is effective if the distributor can reverse the relative value of the two theaters. *Gone with the Wind* is more valuable to Theater A than to Theater B, but the reverse is true for *Getting Gertie's Garter.* To rent both films separately at fixed prices, the distributor could charge no more than $7,000 for *Gone with the Wind* and $2,500 for *Getting Gertie's Garter*, for a total of $9,500 for the pair. But Theater A values the pair at $10,500 and Theater B at $10,000. Thus, by selling both films in a bundle at $10,000, the distributor is able to obtain $500 more for the pair than if they sold the films individually. This is segmented pricing because each theater pays the difference between the price of the films when sold separately ($9,500) and the price when sold together ($10,000). Theater A pays the extra $500 for *Gone with the Wind* while Theater B pays it for *Getting Gertie's Garter* (Nagle, July 1983: 17).

How has the strategy been employed in professional service firms? One firm in Australia offers its customers three levels of services, each presented in menu form: compliance level, management accounting level, and business advisory level. A partner in the firm has developed, with the assistance of his Professional Development Advisor from Results Accountants' Systems, the following explanation of each level, along with other characteristics of a total quality service firm, to form a menu pricing structure:

The COMPLIANCE SERVICE incorporates . . .

Interim Financial Statements You will receive a set of financial accounts during the year, which gives important information about how your business is operating during the year. This will give you the chance to make changes during the rest of the year if necessary.

Year-End Tax Planning Review We agree, no one likes paying taxes. So that your share is fair and equitable, we will do everything we can within the guidelines. So that you avoid the need for last-minute tax strategies, you will have your options reviewed in the last quarter of the financial year.

Taxation Audit Protection You will not incur any professional costs from us if you are selected for taxation audit. And we will cover up to $3,000 of specialist legal advice as part of your service. You will, of course, be liable for any tax or penalties that arise from an audit.

An Analysis of Where Your Money Came From and Where It Went You will receive an analysis that shows just where money came from during the year and where it went to. And we do this in a graphical way so that it is easy for you to see how the government still has their hand out for their share when you may not have any money in the bank. (But we will be working together to ensure this is never the case.)

Trend Analysis You will receive an analysis of the most important trends in the progress of your business. We do this in a graphical way so that the trends become clear to you.

An Annual Cash Flow Projection and Profit Plan This assures that your business performs to the expectation that you commit to at your strategic meeting at the beginning of the year. We will review this together when we review your interim financial accounts. And we adjust for variances to get a realistic view for the rest of the year.

Guaranteed Turnaround Time for your Work of Less than 20 Working Days We guarantee your work will be completed within 20 working days of you providing all materials to us. This will enable you to make proactive decisions, rather than reacting to historical data. If we fail to deliver on our promise we will pay you $100 for every day the work is not completed in the time frame. This is our guarantee to you.

Guaranteed Completion of Taxation Returns All of your statutory requirements will be completed by 30th November of the new financial year. If all the materials required have been supplied and we fail to deliver on our promise, we will pay you $100 per day for every day the work is not completed in the time frame. This is our guarantee to you. And no, you won't be penalized for early lodgment. You don't have to pay earlier for early lodgment.

Guaranteed Response Time to Return Your Telephone Calls If for some reason your account manager is not able to take your call and no one else is able to immediately assist you, your call will be returned before the end of the next working day.

A Fixed Investment The value of this service is established with you in advance and you can select a payment plan which suits your budget. This way there are no surprises for you.

Our Work Is Guaranteed You rightly deserve quality work completed in a timely manner. If you are not delighted with the work we do for you, we respect your right to withhold your fee.

The MANAGEMENT ACCOUNTING SERVICE incorporates . . .

Quarterly Financial Statements You will receive a set of financial accounts during the year, which gives important information about how your business is operating during the year. This will give you the chance to make changes during the rest of the year if necessary.

Year-End Tax Planning Review We agree, no one likes paying taxes. So that your share is fair and equitable, we will do everything within the guidelines so that your share is fair and equitable. So that you avoid the need for last minute tax strategies, you will have your options reviewed in the last quarter of the financial year.

Unlimited Access to Advice on Ad Hoc Matters You can phone your account manager at any time for advice on ad hoc matters in the knowledge that we will not be charging you for that advice. This is subject to the understanding that if an occasion of service exceeds 15 minutes, you will be charged, but only after we have consulted with you and only if you feel that you got value from the consultation.

Taxation Audit Protection You will not incur any professional costs from us if you are selected for taxation audit. And we will cover up to $3,000 of specialist legal advice as part of your service. You will of course be liable for any tax or penalties that arise from an audit.

An Analysis of Where Your Money Came From and Where It Went You will receive an analysis that shows just where money came from during the year and where it went to. And we do this in a graphical way so that it is easy for you to see how the government still has their hand out for their share when you may not have any money in the bank. (But we will be working together to ensure this is never the case.)

Trend Analysis You will receive an analysis of the most important trends in the progress of your business. We do this in a graphical way so that the trends become clear to you.

A Quarterly Cash Flow Projection and Profit Plan This assures that your business performs to the expectation that you commit to at your strategic meeting at the beginning of the year. We will review this together when we review your quarterly financial accounts. And we adjust for variances to get a realistic view for the rest of the year.

Your Business Compared to That of Your Peers We have access to key financial performance indicators of businesses within your industry. Your business will be compared to these, so that you are aware of your progression toward business excellence.

Net Worth Change Are you in business to improve your net worth? If not, we suggest that you should be. And to help you stay committed to this path, your asset base will be broken up into each economic sector and examined for economic return. Your results will be graphically represented, so that you can see for yourself your increasing net worth. And exactly where it is coming from.

Guaranteed Turnaround Time for Your Work of Fewer than 15 Working Days We guarantee your work will be completed within 15 working days of you providing all materials to us. This will enable you to make proactive decisions, rather than reacting to historical data. If we fail to deliver on our promise we will pay you $100 for every day the work is not completed in the time frame. This is our guarantee to you.

Guaranteed Completion of Taxation Returns All of your statutory requirements will be completed by 31st October of the new financial year. If all the materials required have been supplied and we fail to deliver on our promise, we will pay you $100 per day for every day the work is not completed in the time frame. This is our guarantee to you. And no, you won't be penalized for early lodgment. You don't have to pay earlier for early lodgment.

Guaranteed Response Time to Return Your Telephone Calls If for some reason your account manager is not able to take your call and no one else is able to immediately assist you, your call will be returned before the end of the next working day.

A Fixed Investment The value of this service is established with you in advance and you can select a payment plan which suits your budget. This way there are no surprises for you.

Our Work Is Guaranteed You rightly deserve quality work completed in a timely manner. If you are not delighted with the work we do for you, we respect your right to withhold your fee.

The BUSINESS ADVISORY SERVICE incorporates . . .

Monthly Financial Statements You will receive a set of financial accounts during the year, which gives important information about how your business is operating during the year. This will give you the chance to make changes during the rest of the year if necessary.

Year-End Tax Planning Review We agree, no one likes paying taxes. So that your share is fair and equitable, we will do everything within the guidelines so that your share is fair and equitable. So that you avoid the need for last minute tax strategies, you will have your options reviewed in the last quarter of the financial year.

Unlimited Access to Advice on Ad Hoc Matters You can phone or visit your account manager at any time for advice on ad hoc matters in the knowledge that we will not be charging you for that advice. This is subject to the understanding that if an occasion of service exceeds 15 minutes, you will be charged, but only after we have consulted with you and only if you feel that you got value from the consultation.

Taxation Audit Protection You will not incur any professional costs from us if you are selected for taxation audit. And we will cover up to $3,000 of specialist legal advice as part of your service. You will of course be liable for any tax or penalties that arise from an audit.

An Analysis of Where Your Money Came From and Where It Went You will receive an analysis that shows just where money came from during the year and where it went to. And we do this in a graphical way so that it is easy for you to see how the government still has their hand out for their share when you may not have any money in the bank. (But we will be working together to ensure this is never the case.)

Trend Analysis You will receive an analysis of the most important trends in the progress of your business. We do this in a graphical way so that the trends become clear to you.

A 12-Month Cash Flow Projection and Profit Plan This assures that your business performs to the expectation that you commit to at your strategic meeting at the beginning of the year. We will review this together when we review your monthly financial accounts. And we adjust for variances to get a realistic view for the rest of the year.

Your Business Compared to That of Your Peers We have access to key financial performance indicators of businesses within your industry. Your business will be compared to these, so that you are aware of your progression toward business excellence.

Net Worth Change Are you in business to improve your net worth? If not, we suggest that you should be. And to help you stay committed to this path, your asset base will be broken up into each economic sector and examined for economic return. Your results will be graphically represented, so that you can see for yourself your increasing net worth. And exactly where it is coming from.

Your Key Performance Indicator Reviewed Monthly And what is a KPI? This is a measurement of the performance of those activities within your business that you absolutely MUST get right. How do you know which activities you must get right? Your business's governing economic purpose will be identified and from this we will extract those activities which are most critical to its success. Let them know that you will be working with them proactively each month to review the results. It's not "coaching"—this comes with the BD work. But it will help add value.

Guaranteed Turnaround Time for Your Work of Fewer than 10 Working Days We guarantee your work will be completed within 10 working days of you providing all materials to us. This will enable you to make proactive decisions, rather than reacting to historical data. If we fail to deliver on our promise we will pay you $100 for every day the work is not completed in the time frame. This is our guarantee to you.

Guaranteed Completion of Taxation Returns All of your statutory requirements will be completed by 31st October of the new financial year. If all the materials required have been supplied and we fail to deliver on our promise, we will pay you $100 per day for every day the work is not completed in the time frame. This is our guarantee to you. And no, you won't be penalized for early lodgment. You don't have to pay earlier for early lodgment.

Guaranteed Response Time to Return Your Telephone Calls If for some reason your account manager is not able to take your call and no one else is able to immediately assist you, your call will be returned before the end of the next working day.

A Fixed Investment The value of this service is established with you in advance and you can select a payment plan that suits your budget. This way there are no surprises for you.

Our Work Is Guaranteed You rightly deserve quality work completed in a timely manner. If you are not delighted with the work we do for you, we respect your right to withhold your fee.

This type of pricing is not without its disadvantages, however. One issue is that the customers might not perceive the options as tailored to their specific situations, and thus they may feel as if they are being sold an off-the-shelf bundle of goods. They may not want or need many of the items included. Another problem with this type of pricing is that firms offer a fixed price, set in advance—with no customer involvement—for each level of service. This is a serious mistake. Pricing should never take place in a vacuum, and because the customer is the final arbiter of value, one should always establish a price with the input of the customer. Finally, this type of pricing may give the marketing manager and the partners a false sense of security. They will think that they have covered anything that a business owner may want or need, but this is rarely the case. Packaging services into groups is an excellent strategy, but not if doing so is at the expense of creatively customizing services in order to meet any one customer's specific circumstances.

Notwithstanding the problems with the bundling method, it carries many advantages. A thoughtfully crafted menu pricing strategy does allow your firm to respond to (or forestall) certain competitive threats. It can enhance your revenues while minimizing your revenue loss due to price fluctuations. This method can also help you manage the cost of delivering services to a particular niche as well as capitalize on marginal price changes for any one customer. One last important advantage is that customers seem to approve of the policy.

Electronic Commerce

Like the personal computer, the Internet has changed the world. It has torn down geographical boundaries and has provided the average individual with more information than government leaders or industrialists ever dreamed imaginable at the start of the Industrial Revolution. When the Internet first arrived on the scene, many dismissed it as a fad—the citizens band radio for computer geeks. They couldn't have been more wrong. What separates the Internet from, say, television, is that one can make money with it, because it enhances human capital. Rather than turning people into the online equivalent of mindless couch potatoes, the Internet can be used to get what you want, when you want it, exactly the way you want it. It is the difference between taking a train—and being held at the whim of fixed schedules and destinations—and taking a car, going at your own pace, stopping when you want and leaving when you wish.

The amazing power of the Internet is destined to alter—forever—the face of commerce. Estimates on the size of e-commerce vary, because it is difficult to measure this new phenomena. One survey conducted by ActiveMedia, using data collected in early 1998 from Web site executives and business managers worldwide, showed that $1 million in sales per month was not uncommon among leading sites, such as Dell Computer, Cisco, and Boeing. An Ernst & Young study for the National Retail Federation found 32 percent of consumers with Internet access had purchased goods online. The percentage of Internet users making purchases more than doubled in a year. Cyberdialogue found that 48 percent of online buyers were satisfied and 48 percent were very satisfied with the experience, and 19 percent indicated they were shopping in stores less. (Gilder, May 1998: 5)

Certainly the Internet has already eclipsed the U.S. Postal Service as a carrier of mail. By one estimate, one trillion e-mail messages are sent, compared with 180 billion postal deliveries. What is interesting about the Internet is not the predictions of its future, but the implications the technology will have on the future.

Nothing but Net

Scott McNealy of Sun Microsystems started saying in 1996 that "The network is the computer." The personal computer was optimized for the desktop. All of the complexity sat in the PC through its processor and operating system software. However, with the 200-fold rise in Internet traffic between 1996 and 2001, most users spend more time accessing remote memories than they do their own desktop data storage. The day may come when, as long predicted by technology expert George Gilder, television dies. Television, after all, forces the viewer to adhere to a broadcaster's schedule while the Internet delivers—through fiber optics or satellites—the user's first choice, when and where the user wants it. You don't need 500 television channels. You need only one, as long as you can get your first choice. That is the promise of the Internet acting as your computer.

Think for a moment of the implications this will have on the entertainment industry, to pick just one example. As George Gilder explains:

> The key thing computer networking does to any business is change vertical systems into horizontal systems. It eliminates middlemen—middle executives—of all descriptions. And the heart of Hollywood today is intermediation. About 70 percent of the cost of making a movie is in areas such as distribution and advertising, and about 30 percent goes to the people involved in making the movie.
>
> Most of that 70 percent will be collapsed by a truly pervasive fiber-optic network system. It will collapse when you can make it available to the entire world, and you don't need to attract miscellaneous audience to theaters in Des Moines, San Jose, Seattle, and Pittsfield [Massachusetts] at once. The 70 percent cost of the film drops to 5 percent, or even less for some.
>
> Meanwhile, the remaining 30 percent of the cost of a film is getting these people whose star properties come from their lowest-common-denominator appeal and from their monopoly position of being able to finance those 70 percent costs. Those costs can be drastically reduced. (Gregorsky, 1998: 80)

Although the Internet will shift more power to the customer and make it harder for the seller to capitalize on asymmetrical information, there are compelling advantages to e-commerce from the vendor's perspective, according to John Hagel III and Arthur G. Armstrong, in *Net Gain: Expanding Markets through Virtual Communities*:

- **Reduced search costs** Vendors and likely customers will be able to locate one another more easily.
- **Increased propensity for customers to buy** Similar to the introduction of automatic teller machines in the 1980s, once customers become familiar with using the Internet to transact business, the probability of other purchases made online will increase.

- **Enhanced ability to target** Not only will customers be able to find exactly what they want, vendors will also be able to target specific communities, based upon membership profiles, to locate their specific niche.
- **Greater ability to tailor and add value to existing products and services** Known as one-to-one marketing, firms will be able to customize products and services, even to a mass market. Also, because of the interactive feedback dynamic of the Internet, vendors will be able to learn more about each customer with every purchase, and will be better equipped to market and sell additional products and services to them.
- **Lower capital and investment in bricks and mortar** Just like Amazon.com, which replaced inventory with information, the Internet allows communities to exist without expensive buildings in fixed locations that people must wait in traffic to get to. This creates a significant advantage for banks, retail outlets, and even professional service firms.
- **Broader geographic reach** The Internet tears down geographical boundaries effectively, opening the entire world to both vendor and customer.
- **Disintermediation potential** Vendors will be in a better position to deal directly with their customers, as Gilder pointed out in the entertainment industry example above. This will enable one link—the middleman—to be removed from the value chain, lowering overall price to the customer. (Hagel and Armstrong, 1997: 10–12)

All of these forces, combined, will shift the demand curve to the right for any one particular vendor. The lower costs associated with transactions via the Internet will put downward pressure on prices in some markets. In fact, the notion of a fixed price may well be obsolete in the virtual community. This will take place largely as the result of customers being better informed; having more information means having more power. Lowering the amount of asymmetrical information that exists will put customers—and businesses, for that matter—in a better position to bargain and get exactly what they want, at the price they want it. While one could look at this and say that the consumer surplus will, more and more, be kept by the customer, that may be a premature conclusion. It is also very possible that the vendors will be able to tap into the consumer surplus more readily because they too will have more information on the customer's perceived value at their disposal.

The Internet is the perfect medium in which to price on the margin. Sites such as Priceline.com allow customers to set their own price for airline and hotel reservations. Mortgages, cars, and even energy are now sold in the same manner over the Internet. Does this negate the theory of value pricing? Not at all. Airlines, for instance, offer discounts only to leisure travelers, with advance purchase and other restrictions or based upon load capacities. Airlines still discriminate against the business traveler, but they are now better able to offer empty, last-minute seats to customers seeking a deal.

This is not to say that the Internet doesn't create pricing challenges. It does. Customers naturally gravitate to the lowest price, at first. But customer service and loyalty are still very important, in the long run, to any successful Internet business. The Internet is a dynamic medium and allows customer loyalty, finally, to be a two-way street, rather than the one-way street most businesses have viewed it as in the past. Now that customers have a number of options available at their fingertips—shelf space is not a restriction in a virtual world—why should they deal with you? Answering that question involves more than offering the cheapest price, especially for professional service providers. After all, would you choose your heart operation from a doctor who gave you the lowest bid? The answer lies in total quality service, which is still critical over the Internet, especially when you consider how fast word-of-mouth can spread online.

The Internet allows businesses to experiment with pricing to select groups of customers, and thus pricing is likely to become much more volatile in this environment. It also allows vendors to customize packages and menu pricing to the various needs of specific market segments.

Business Process Outsourcing (BPO)—Offshoring

One trend on the increase is outsourcing professional work overseas for processing, work such as tax returns, bookkeeping, etc. This has been taking place in banking, insurance, software code, call-centers, and the medical and legal professions for decades, it is nothing new. Outsourcing has, however, received a lot of publicity in the accounting profession lately, in particular because sensitive client information—in the form of bookkeeping and tax records—usually is included in the information available to overseas workers.

In the early 1980s, Japan was considered a serious threat to the United States' manufacturing jobs. In the 1990s, NAFTA supposedly was going to decimate U.S. jobs. Presently, China and India have replaced both of these countries as the biggest threats to employment in the highly paid service sector.

The facts do not fit the theory however. Between 1982 and 2003, the U.S. created a net 42 million new jobs. In fact, between 1993 and 2002, the U.S. created almost 328 million new jobs and lost nearly 310 million, for a net gain of 18 million new jobs. The idea that the U.S. is a victim of foreign trade is absurd.

Forrester Research, in a much-cited report, estimated that 3.3 million service-industry jobs will go overseas by 2015, barely noticeable against the over 30 million jobs lost, on average, every year since 1993. The U.S. leads the world in employment precisely *because* people can lose their jobs. A job is a means to an end; if we could maintain our same standard of living without working many people would choose that option. We could easily create, or "save," jobs by assigning a guard to every mailbox. Yet jobs are only created when they produce something of value to customers. Expect this trend of outsourcing jobs overseas to continue if it adds value to the firms that engage in it, which it appears to be doing.

That said, there are many professional issues involved in outsourcing jobs overseas—i.e., "offshoring"—but the most contentious debates revolve around the following issues:

- Technical quality standards and assurance thereof
- Security of data
- Identity theft threat
- Disclosure of offshoring to the client
- Effect on prices

The issue of technical quality will work itself out because of market pressures. Who will continue to patronize incompetent foreign accountants? Because accountants in other countries tend to be trained in U.K. and/or U.S. colleges, their credentials generally are the same as ours. Risks to the security of the data and of identity theft also appear to be minimal. If the risks were large, we would have already heard numerous such stories in the press, yet there have been relatively few. Furthermore, insurance companies—the people who have to price risk, not just have opinions about it—have not been charging higher premiums to firms that engage in offshoring.

The issue of disclosure is more contentious, as there are no specific legal requirements to do so, and many firms have decided not to disclose the practice of offshoring to their customers. State Boards of Accountancy might change the disclosure requirements, on a state-by-state basis, as might the federal government. One school of thought seems to be that it is better for a firm to engage in full disclosure so that if the customer were to somehow find out, another (albeit small) accounting scandal would not ensue. Other firms choose not to disclose, comparing offshoring to the tax processing services of yesteryear, when sensitive information was outsourced domestically and no disclosure was made. Firms that are part of a global network tend to follow the latter policy. Either way, it should be noted that the firm that signs the returns assumes ultimate responsibility for accuracy of the returns, safety of customer information, etc.

It is likely that firms will begin to sort themselves into two categories: those who engage in offshoring and those who don't. You may even begin to see "compensating differences"—that is, a lower price or perhaps no price increases—being offered as incentives to the customer in return for the customer's authorization to outsource. The market will sort this out through the pricing mechanism, as the insurance companies will through premiums with respect to the actual risks of this practice.

Alliances

In the future, global alliances will become one of the predominant methods used to compete in the professional marketplace. Witness, for example, United Airlines' Star Alliance program, whereby they share flights, gates, pricing, frequent flyer miles, and other infrastructure with specific partners. Today, automobile and oil companies are increasingly entering into alliances with their competitors around the world. What's interesting, from a historical perspective, is that the leaders of the alliance movement have been accounting firms. Because of professional regulations in most countries requiring partnerships to be national (that is, owned by a citizen of that country), the problem of global businesses having to hire a firm in each country with the same level of service, quality, and consistency became a formidable obstacle. As a result, the major accounting firms—in order to be more responsive to their customers—globalized through forming alliances.

Ric Payne, in a two-part article published in the Australian business magazine *BRW*, discussed the increasing importance of network alliances in the future for the accounting profession:

> As long as smaller independently owned firms are able to deliver all the services that their larger competitors can offer, they will thrive in this environment and will carve out, and in my view retain, a very profitable niche.
>
> The key here can be found in the words "are able to deliver all the services that their larger competitors can offer." One way to do that is to align your firm with a network that gives you access to a broader range of services so that you can position yourself as a multidisciplinary firm. In the future, I believe the most viable form of structure for professional service firms will be through formal networks. To put that another way, if you are not in a network you will be competing against one.
>
> And if you are in a network you had better avail yourself of all the benefits that that offers, because simply offering your clients what you have provided them in the past will not cut it.

There are many networks in the accounting profession today that firms can join in order to offer a wider range of services in an expanded geographical market—networks such as BDO Seidman, BKR International, McGladrey Network, CPAmerica, The Enterprise Network, and so on. Cyrus Freidheim, a consultant with Booz-Allen and author of *The Trillion-Dollar Enterprise: How the Alliance Revolution Will Transform Global Business*, succinctly states why alliances are successful:

> Alliances can be a profitable way to expand a business. In an acquisition or merger, the partners take all—the good and the bad, the pretty and the ugly, businesses that fit and the baggage, the profitable and the unprofitable, the core capa-

> bility, and the unwanted branch in Somalia. Any problems, liabilities, warts, and unfinished business of the acquired company are yours, for better or for worse, from this day forward.
>
> In an alliance, you can carve out the piece you like. You can take the prime cuts of meat and leave the liver and the hooves behind. Alliances are about combining capabilities of two or more partners. We take advantage of your strength in the market and my technology, or your cost position and my distribution. We do as Pepsi and Lipton did with iced tea—Pepsi's distribution and Lipton's product. (Freidheim, 1998: 42)

This is not to say that mergers and acquisitions will be replaced by alliances but rather that alliances will be an effective competitive strategy for the smaller firms in order to offer the same array of services that their larger competitors can provide. Consider Freidheim's "seven main reasons that companies choose alliance over acquisition or internal action":

1. **Risk sharing** Companies cannot afford the potential downside of the investment opportunity alone. Airbus Industries, an alliance of German, French, British, and Spanish aerospace companies, was created exactly for this reason. The oil industry has long used alliances to share exploration risks in such locations as the North Sea, the South China Sea, and Azerbaijan.

2. **Acquisition barriers** Companies cannot acquire the right partner because of price, size, unwanted businesses, government resistance, reluctance of owners, or regulatory restrictions. The GM-Toyota alliance fits almost every one of those reasons.

3. **Market-segment access** Companies don't understand their customers or don't have the relationships or infrastructure to distribute their products to a particular market. Lipton chose PepsiCo for this reason.

4. **Technology gaps** Companies don't have all the technology they need and can't afford the time or resources to develop it themselves.

5. **Geographic access** Companies aren't where they want to be and don't have the resources to get there. Corning joined forces with Samsung to enter and compete in the Asian market. In many cases, government regulations inhibit direct access. China is a good example. Few companies have the resources, commitment, or permission to go it alone in China. Most companies welcome the government's encouragement (or mandate) to get a local partner.
6. **Funding constraints** Individual companies can't afford to develop or launch the venture alone.
7. **Management skills** Companies need more talent to be successful. Oracle and Microsoft have several alliances with start-up technology companies to which they contribute management talent and access to their resources in exchange for proprietary access to the start-up technology. (Freidheim, 1998: 42–44)

It is apparent that several of the factors above apply to the smaller professional firm. If your firm presently is not in an alliance, you may want to seriously consider the advantages of belonging to one. The investment will pay off, as it will provide your firm another competitive differentiation in the marketplace.

Summary and Conclusions

This chapter discussed, among other trends, pricing strategies that can be used when pricing particular services for a customer. When it comes to new customers vs. long-term customers, firms must understand the importance of their long-term customers and how much more profitable these are than the new ones. You have no business getting new customers if you are not pleasing your existing ones. The goal should be obtaining *better* business, not just *more* business.

Examine some closed files in your office (a checklist is included in "Useful Checklists" at the end of the book and on the CD-ROM). They contain a wealth of information—who performed the work, how much was spent, what technology was used, how much was charged, and ultimately, collected. Try to determine whether any consumer surplus existed that could have been tapped into. This is a good exercise to perform with your fellow partners, managers, and team members to develop a value pricing culture in your firm.

13 ALTERNATIVE METHODS OF PRICING BY ENGAGEMENT

The fixed price should be used as often as possible. Other pricing methods need to be considered, however. One reason is that the transition to value pricing may be gradual and you may wish to use other pricing methods along with value pricing until you build your confidence and pricing skills. Also, value pricing may be used in combination with other pricing methods, such as retrospective price or a contingent price.

The following are the prevalent pricing methods in the accounting and legal professions, with the exception of fixed price and hourly billing, which are covered in detail in earlier chapters. Advantages and disadvantages are cited, along with suggestions on when to use them. I do not endorse the use of any hourly rate method: They are shown here simply because they are so prevalent in the marketplace.

At the end of this chapter is a list of pricing methods appropriate for specific engagements, such as estate planning, payroll services, and tax planning.

Contingent Pricing

Contingent prices depend upon the results achieved for the customer and require a clear agreement on what the desired results should be. The AICPA's Code of Professional Conduct (AICPA, Professional Standards, vol. 2, ET sec. 302) defines a contingent fee as follows: "A fee established for the performance of any service pursuant to an arrangement in which no fee will be charged unless a specified finding or result is attained, or in which the amount of the fee is otherwise dependent upon the finding or result of such service."

Bans on CPA advertising and the acceptance of commissions and contingent fees date back to 1918. With the passage of the wartime excess profits tax, many unqualified tax practitioners were attracted to the profession and proclaimed to be "tax experts," charging a contingency for any tax savings they were able to provide. This got the attention of the Treasury Department, which insisted that the American

Institute of Accountants (AIA) pass rules prohibiting contingent fees and "unseemly" advertising, and in 1919 the AIA did just that.

Here is an explanation of the situation from *A History of Accountancy in the United States*:

> In 1919, the institute's council responded, banning contingent fees after a heated debate. The rule read as follows: "No member shall render professional services, the anticipated fee for which shall be contingent upon his findings and results thereof. (This rule shall be construed as inhibiting only services in which the accountant's findings or expert opinion might be influenced by consideration of personal financial interest)." The sentence in parentheses was deleted in 1920 because some practitioners contended that it permitted tax work by accountants on a contingency fee. This new rule proved ineffective and was widely ignored. In 1923, the AIA passed a yet more stringent rule, banning contingent fees absolutely: "Members and associates should neither render nor offer to render services for which the fees are contingent." Practitioners could accept no contingent fees for any type of service.
>
> Even institute members rebelled against the ban. Robert H. Montgomery, a past president of the American Association of Public Accountants and one of the most influential members of the AIA, and Walter Staub mentioned the rule in their 1923 edition of *Auditing Principles* but concluded it was too strict to be enforceable. The authors suggested that tax practitioners might ignore the rule and accept work on a contingent fee basis. Normally, influential members of an organization are expected to comply with its norms; when they do not it becomes clear that the organization does not have the authority to enforce its sanctions. The American Society of Certified Public Accountants condemned the ban on contingent fees; these restrictions provided support for the society's claims that the institute sought to protect the elite in the profession. The institute's efforts to restrict advertising simply added more fuel to the fire. (Previts and Merino, 1998: 247)

Today, despite the resistance of various state societies, and even the AICPA at one point, the marketplace has asserted its sovereignty and deregulation of the profession—as in so many industries since the late 1970s—has begun. Many believe contingent pricing is the death knell for the profession; others believe it is a tremendous opportunity for those firms that take the lead and march the profession toward its inevitable destiny.

Advantages

- Price is dependent on results achieved, not on time spent, allowing firms to capitalize on internal efficiencies.
- Contingent pricing can be used with other pricing methods to ensure that the firm receives some minimum price for its efforts.
- The professional can reap "supernormal" profits because of the additional risk assumed.
- The customer's expectations are determined prior to the engagement, thereby clarifying the firm's value-added services.
- The customers who can't afford to pay have access to professional services.

Disadvantages

- Resources devoted to the engagement can exceed the original estimates with no commensurate increase in price.
- The firm assumes the risk of the engagement and the potential loss of not achieving the desired outcome.
- Uneven cash flow can result.
- Contingent pricing cannot be used in conjunction with attest services where independence is a requirement.

When to Use

- The engagement has a high probability of success.
- A firm has developed expertise in handling similar contingent-priced engagements.

- A customer might be otherwise unable to afford the firm's services unless the desired outcome is achieved.
- Regulatory agencies allow for a contingent price to be charged.

Recommended Engagements

- Mergers and acquisitions
- Negotiating the buying or selling of a business
- Representation before governmental taxing authorities or obtaining private letter rulings
- Engagements that influence the drafting or promulgation of a regulation or statute
- Innovative tax strategies that provide substantial tax savings to the customer
- Personal financial planning where a percentage of the total portfolio is the contingent price
- Other engagements that lend themselves to a specific and desirable outcome

Blended Hourly Rates

Blended hourly rates are used when the firm knows the mix of personnel needed to complete the engagement but does not know exactly how long the project will take. Thus, one hourly rate is billed for all hours worked on a particular engagement, regardless of who does the work. For example, if a particular engagement calls for a partner at $200 per hour, a senior as-sociate at $150 per hour and a staff person at $100 per hour, and the firm is not sure how long the project will take, a blended rate might be computed for the entire project. Suppose the partner will spend 25 percent of the total time, the senior associate 35 percent, and the staff person 40 percent; the blended rate is computed as follows:

$200 x 25% =	$50.00
$150 x 35% =	52.50
$100 x 40% =	40.00
Blended rate	$142.50

The firm might quote a rate of $145 per hour in this example. Every hour worked on the project, no matter who performs it, is priced at that rate. If the firm is able to manage the engagement more efficiently, perhaps by delegating more of the work to the staff person, the realization rate will increase.

Advantages

- Generally, the advantages are the same as those of the hourly rate.
- Negotiating a single rate with the customer is easier when numerous professionals are involved.
- The firm has the potential to realize more profit if work is performed more efficiently than estimated.

Disadvantages

- All of the disadvantages of the hourly rate method apply.

When to Use

- The customer absolutely demands it.
- The firm declines to assume any risk from the pricing of the engagement.
- A third party demands hourly billing—e.g., government agencies and courts, which recognize only hourly billing.

Recommended Engagements

- One-time consultations when no other benchmark of value can be agreed upon.
- Engagements in which the uncertainties are so prevalent that no estimate can be made as to the effort required.

Fixed Price Plus Hourly Rates

With this hybrid method, the portions of the engagement that can be defined are priced on a fixed-price basis and those aspects that cannot be defined, due to variables or uncertainties, are priced on an hourly basis. For instance, in an estate-planning engagement, during the initial phase when the strategy is being formulated and preliminary information is being gathered, an hourly rate might apply. Then, once the plan has been agreed upon, a fixed price might be negotiated for implementation.

Advantages

- The professional and the customer share the engagement risk.
- The customer is aware of the fixed-price portion in advance.
- The advantages of the fixed price and the hourly rate methods are combined.

Disadvantages

- The firm assumes some risk by using the fixed price method for a portion of the engagement.
- The disadvantages of the fixed price and the hourly rate methods apply.

When to Use

- Engagements that have many unknown variables at the outset and when the firm is not comfortable quoting a fixed price for the entire project.
- The customer demands it.

Recommended Engagements

- Complex estate planning
- Litigation services
- Compliance services (audits, reviews, compilations, and tax) when any add-on services would be performed on an hourly rate basis
- Complex IRS audits, offers in compromise, and private letter rulings

Hourly Rates Plus a Contingency

Combining an hourly rate and a contingency based upon a determinable outcome is a way for the professional to share the risk of the downside of a transaction, such as a merger or acquisition, while also sharing in the upside potential. Because the professional will receive at least the hourly rate agreed upon, that portion of the risk is borne by the customer. However, if the transaction is a success, the professional will also share in the rewards. Usually, this method requires the firm to discount its "standard" hourly rate in order to share in the upside potential.

Advantages

- The professional and the customer share in the risks and the rewards.
- The hourly rate might cover the firm's internal cost of servicing the engagement.
- The customer will not pay the "standard" hourly rate if the project is unsuccessful and will share the benefits proportionately if it is.
- The customer acquires professional services not otherwise affordable.
- The advantages of both the hourly rate and the contingent price apply.

Disadvantages

- The professional must make an accurate assessment of the probability of a successful engagement because he or she assumes more of a risk by discounting the "standard" rate.
- Disagreement can result if the contingent portion of the price is not clearly agreed to or understood by the customer.
- The disadvantages of the hourly rate and contingent methods apply.

When to Use

- Situations are at the top of the value curve involving large dollar amounts, a high probability of a successful (and therefore value-added) outcome, and a willingness to share in the risks with the customer. If the successful outcome is absolutely guaranteed, it may be wise to forego the hourly rate and simply use a contingent price based on the outcome.

- The customer has an excellent relationship with the firm.
- The regulatory agencies allow for a contingent price to be charged.

Recommended Engagements

- Unique services (those custom-designed to a particular customer)
- Mergers and acquisitions
- Estate planning
- Innovative tax strategies and governmental audits
- Business buy/sell
- Financing packages (SBA loans, lines of credit, etc.)
- Divorce proceedings
- Litigation support

Percentage Pricing

Usually, percentage prices are based on schedules related to the amount involved in the matter being handled. These amounts may be predetermined or ultimately determined by a future outcome. Examples would include a percentage of the estate being probated or a percentage of the dollar amount of a real estate transaction or a bond issue. The percentage rate may be constant or graduated. Traditionally, legal services have been more suited to this type of pricing than accounting services.

Advantages

- Provides ease in delineating to the customer the terms of the engagement and the price to be charged.
- The firm's liability exposure should be covered adequately because the price is determined by the dollar amount involved.
- The price is not dependent upon the time spent.
- If the percentages and the amount of the transaction are known beforehand, the advantages of the fixed price apply.

- If the percentages and the amount of the transaction are unknown beforehand, the advantages of the contingent price apply.

Disadvantages

- Too high a percentage might not be competitive in the marketplace.
- Too low a percentage might not cover the firm's internal costs.
- If complications arise during the engagement, the risk is borne by the firm, unless a change order has been agreed to by the customer and is provided for in the engagement agreement.
- If the percentage and the amount of the transaction are known, the disadvantages of the fixed price apply.
- If the percentage and the amount of the transaction are unknown, the disadvantages of the contingent price apply.

When to Use

- A large dollar amount is involved and the customer and professional are willing to share in the risks and the rewards of outcome.

Recommended Engagements

- Real estate transactions
- Business sales and purchases
- Personal financial planning, where a percentage of the portfolio managed is charged
- Sales of life insurance and investment products (becoming increasingly popular among CPAs moving into these lines of businesses)
- Tax strategies, governmental audits
- Financing packages

Retrospective Pricing

This method is appropriate for engagements that have several possible outcomes. Nevertheless, the factors that ultimately determine the value of the project should be included in the fixed price agreement or change order. This method can be combined with a minimum or maximum fixed price. The price, ultimately, is determined by the *customer* (not the professional). This method is sometimes referred to as a "TIP" clause.

Advantages

- Because the price is set at the end of the engagement, all of the uncertainties and unknowns no longer exist. This allows the customer and professional to agree upon the actual value of the services provided.
- The price is based upon the value of the service, not the time spent performing it.
- Because the customer sets the price, disputes and slow payments are eliminated.
- It allows the firm to capture a portion of the consumer surplus.

Disadvantages

- The customer does not know what the price will be beforehand.
- The professional's perception of value might differ from the customer's.
- If no progress payments are received from the customer, the firm will suffer cash flow consequences.

When to Use

- A trusting, long-term relationship exists between the professional and the customer, with each being aware of the value-added nature of the relationship.
- The professional believes that a better-than-expected benefit will accrue to the customer.
- A professional has rendered a high value-added service, but may not have adequately discussed price beforehand.
- The professional has performed outstanding work, above and beyond the customer's expectations.

- Engagements are at the top end of the value curve.
- Contingent prices are not allowed and price can be based on customer satisfaction rather than any specific financial outcome.

Recommended Engagements

- Business sales and purchases
- Financing packages
- Litigation, arbitration, and mediation services
- Divorce planning and mediation
- Tax strategies, governmental audits and hearings
- Any project involving the professional in negotiations involving large dollar amounts or significant consequences to the customer
- One-time engagements in which the firm can easily perform the service and the value perceived by the customer is large

Availability-Only Retainer

Sometimes referred to as a "pure retainer" or "right-to-call retainer," this is a payment to the professional for no specific services (or limited services, as specified) performed, in return for the professional's commitment to be available when requested, and to refrain from servicing other parties that may pose a conflict to the customer (e.g., a competitor or adverse party). This type of arrangement is rare in an accounting firm.

Advantages

- The professional might not have to perform any services.
- The customer is assured of access (or representation) by the professional.
- The customer is assured that the professional will not perform work or represent any party who is adverse to the customer.
- The customer may perceive that the professional association is prestigious.

Disadvantages

- The professional will be unable to accept work from similar customers in the market.
- The customer may determine that the amount paid does not justify the value received from the retainer.
- The professional's loss of additional work may exceed the amount of the retainer.

When to Use

- The benefits to both parties exceed the costs.
- The monetary amount involved justifies being restricted from obtaining additional work.

Recommended Engagements

- When the professional's expertise or high visibility in the marketplace can lend prestige to the customer (e.g., an expert witness)
- Executive search for a customer
- Acquiring or selling a business on behalf of a customer

Retainer as a Deposit Against Future Services

Although not technically a pricing method, the retainer as a deposit against future services is a way for the firm to ensure payment from the customer. Use this method whenever possible because it greatly enhances cash flow except for attorneys, who usually must put such funds in a trust account. This method can be combined with any of the pricing methods discussed and is very effective for new customers whose credibility has not yet been established.

Advantages

- The customer makes an "ego investment" and commits up front to the relationship.

- Accounts receivable collection problems are minimized and cash flow is maximized.
- The firm is assured of payment.

Disadvantages

- The client must pay up front before receiving any benefit from the services to be rendered.
- If the retainer balance at the end of the engagement is insufficient to cover the price charged, a potential collection problem arises.
- Because the customer is paying before receiving any services, expectations *will* rise and if the firm does not deliver total quality service, the customer might be dissatisfied and defect.

When to Use

- The integrity of the customers or their willingness or ability to pay the prices charged by the firm is in question.
- You want to set a precedent with new customers that the firm expects to be paid (even if just partially) up front.

Recommended Engagements

- Tax collection representations, especially delinquent customers
- Tax audits
- Insolvent customers

Unit Pricing

Unit pricing is a fixed price charged for a specific service without regard to the time spent. This is sometimes referred to as task-based billing. For example, an accounting firm might price tax returns by the form, although this policy does not allow the firm to capture the consumer surplus that might exist for any one customer.

Advantages

- Time recordkeeping is simplified.
- Potential for pricing premiums exists if time for performing the task can be minimized.
- Customer and professional can determine the price up front.

Disadvantages

- Unit pricing might cause confusion if the customer believes the firm is pricing by the hour.
- This requires adequate representation of the unit price for each service.
- The firm is not allowed to capture the consumer surplus.

When to Use

- The professional has accurate knowledge of the internal cost of providing the service.
- The customer demands this type of pricing method.

Recommended Engagements

- Tax compliance work (charge per schedule)
- Bookkeeping and write-up work
- Budgeting and cash flow projections
- Payroll services

Lodestar Pricing

Richard C. Reed explains "lodestar" in *Billing Innovations*:

> The lodestar method of setting fees originated in the federal case of *Lindy Brothers Builders, Inc. v. American Radiator & Standard Sanitary Corp.*, 487 F.2d 161 (3d Cir. 1973) and has been adopted in some states. The

> method involves multiplying the hours spent by a reasonable billing rate per hour to determine the "lodestar." Then that amount is multiplied by a factor, e.g., 1.4, 1.7, 3.0, or 0.8, for considerations other than time spent.
>
> Court decisions have restricted the factors that can be considered as a multiplier, contending that those factors are subsumed in the hourly billing rate. For example, "expertise" originally was a factor in determining the amount of the multiplier, but now is generally considered to be reflected in the hourly billing rate. Uncertainty of payment remains a factor for the multiplier. (Reed, 1996: 24)

Advantages

- The hourly rate may be increased or decreased based on criteria other than time spent.
- This method has the same advantages as the hourly rate method.

Disadvantages

- This method has the same disadvantages as the hourly rate method.
- The courts tend to disallow a portion of the hours spent.
- The court is second-guessing what was required from the professional.
- The lodestar formula might not reflect the value of the services provided.

When to Use

- The court system requires it.

Guaranteed Pricing

The guaranteed price is secured by a 100-percent-money-back service guarantee clause in the fixed price agreement that states: "If you are not completely satisfied with the services performed by ABC, CPAs, we will, at the option of [customer's name], either refund the price or accept a portion of said price that reflects [customer's name] level of satisfaction. We will assume you are satisfied upon final payment received under the terms of this Agreement."

Advantages

- Guaranteed pricing communicates a commitment to excellence and total quality service.
- Every member of the firm is cognizant of the importance of exceeding the customer's expectations.
- Most likely, the competition is not offering this type of guarantee, conferring to the firm an enormous competitive advantage.
- Price resistance and buyer's remorse are overcome.
- The firm will do an adequate job of prequalifying customers, since a high level of trust is required in order to provide a guarantee.
- All things being equal, a service that is guaranteed is more valuable than one that is not, and thus a premium can be charged.
- It gives the customer an incentive to complain and gives the firm a second chance to resolve issues and earn continued trust and loyalty.
- It identifies customers who are out to take advantage of the firm and allows for them to be dropped from the customer base.
- By offering an overt guarantee (i.e., by publicizing it in the firm's marketing and advertising material), your firm enhances its competitive position in the market and increases the value perceived by the customer.

Disadvantages

- Firms are set up for failure if they cannot deliver total quality service that exceeds customer expectations.
- Refunds (partial or full) will be required when the customer has a legitimate complaint about the firm's service.

When to Use

- Customers are new.
- Customers are long-time customers.
- This method, set forth in the response to the request for proposals, is a way to distinguish your firm from the competition.

Outside-In Pricing

One of the most innovative pricing methods, outside-in pricing, starts from *outside* the firm and is based on the premise that the ultimate arbiter of value is the person paying—the customer. Price negotiations are started by asking the customer what they believe the service is worth.

Advantages

- It allows the professional and the customer to discover their perception of value.
- It has the potential of identifying the firm's "first-class passengers," that is, those who are *willing* and *able* to pay more than the market price.
- It involves the customers in pricing the firm's services, gaining their "ego investment."
- It allows the firm to build customer relationship and goodwill based upon a mutually advantageous partnership.
- It transfers some of the customer's consumer surplus to the firm without diminishing the value received by the customer.

Disadvantages

- Customers may quote a price that is unreasonably low and may be reluctant to change their minds. (In that case, withdraw from the engagement.)

- Customers and professionals are put in a negotiating position, which many professionals find distasteful. However, many customers negotiate on a daily basis in running their businesses and are completely comfortable negotiating price with a trusted and respected professional.

When to Use

- The *value* (not the price) of the service has been discussed but no work has yet been performed.
- The firm is working on a marginal engagement for an existing customer who has an excellent relationship with the firm.
- The professional knows that the value of the service exceeds the price that would be charged based upon the time spent.

Possible Pricing Methods to Use for Specific Engagements

The following chart lists several possible pricing combinations. Any number of combinations of pricing methods may be used, depending on the nature of the engagement, the relationship with the customer, the dollar amount involved, the risks being assumed by the parties, and a myriad of other factors. Remember, in almost every engagement, the outside-in price (whereby the customer proclaims the value of the service) is possible as a starting point to negotiating a value price. Also, a 100-percent-money-back service guarantee clause can be used with any of the pricing methods mentioned. Finally, these engagements may present themselves in the standard fixed price agreement or in a change order.

Engagement	Suggested Pricing Method(s)
Arbitration/Mediation Support	Fixed Price Plus a Contingency; Hourly Rate Plus a Contigency; Retrospective Price

Engagement	Suggested Pricing Method(s)
Bookkeeping and Write-Up Work	Fixed Price; Unit; Outside-In Price
Budgets and Cash-Flow Projections	Fixed Price; Unit; Outside-In Price
Buy/Sell Businesses	Contingent Price; Hourly Rate Plus a Contingency; Fixed Price Plus a Contingency; Percentage; Retrospective Price
Buy/Sell Business (on behalf of customer)	Availability-Only Retainer; Contingent Price; Fixed Price Plus a Contingency; Percentage
Divorce Planning/Engagements	Hourly Rate Plus a Contingency; Fixed Price Plus a Contingency; Retrospective Price
Estate Planning (simple)	Fixed Price; Contingent Price
Estate Planning (complex)	Fixed Price Plus Hourly Rate; Hourly Rate Plus a Contingency; Fixed Price Plus a Contingency
Executive Search	Availability-Only Retainer; Percentage
Experiential Services	Fixed Price Plus a Contingency; Hourly Rate Plus a Contingency; Retrospective Price; Outside-In Price
Financial Statement Audits, Reviews, Compilations	Fixed Price

Engagement	Suggested Pricing Method(s)
Financial Statement Audits, Reviews, Compilations (and Add-On Services)	Fixed Price; Fixed Price Plus Hourly; Fixed Price and Change Orders
Financing Packages	Hourly Rate Plus a Contingency; Fixed Price Plus a Contingency; Percentage; Retrospective Price
Governmental Tax Audits (simple)	Fixed Price; Contingent Price
Governmental Tax Audits (complex)	Fixed Price Plus Hourly Rate; Percentage; Retrospective Price
Insolvent Customer	Retainer as a Deposit Against Future Services
Investment Product Sales	Percentage
Litigation Support	Fixed Price Plus Hourly; Fixed Price Plus a Contingency; Hourly Rate Plus a Contingency; Retrospective Price; Lodestar (when required)
Meetings and Telephone Calls	Fixed Price, included as an Unlimited Access Clause; any resulting engagements should be priced using a Change Order
Mergers & Acquisitions	Contingent Price; Fixed Price Plus a Contingency; Hourly Rate Plus a Contingency; Percentage
Offers in Compromise, Private Letter Rulings	Fixed Price Plus Hourly; Percentage; Retrospective Price

Engagement	Suggested Pricing Method(s)
One-Time Consultations; Second Opinions	Fixed Price; Hourly Rate; Blended Hourly Rate
Payroll Services	Unit; Fixed Price
Personal Financial Planning	Contingent Price; Percentage
Real Estate Transactions	Percentage; Fixed Price Plus a Contingency; Retrospective Price
Request For Proposals (RFPs)	100 percent-Money-Back-Service Guarantee Clause
Special Expertise	Availability-Only Retainer
Tax Collections	Retainer as a Deposit Against Future Services; Fixed Price; Fixed Price Plus Hourly; Contingent Price; Retrospective Price
Tax Compliance (simple)	Fixed Price; Unit
Tax Planning & Strategies	Contingent Price; Hourly Rate Plus a Contingency; Fixed Price Plus a Contingency; Percentage; Retrospective Price
Unique Services (customer-tailored)	Fixed Priced Plus a Contingency; Hourly Rate Plus a Contingency; Outside-In Price; Retrospective Price

14 TOTAL QUALITY SERVICE

We try to remember that medicine is for the patient. We try to never forget that medicine is for the people. It is not for the profits. The profits follow, and if we have remembered that, they have never failed to appear. The better we have remembered it, the larger they have been.

—George W. Merck, president of Merck & Co., 1932–1957

There is only one boss: the customer. And he can fire everybody in the company, from the chairman on down, simply by spending his money somewhere else.

—Sam Walton (1918–1992), founder, Wal-Mart Stores

Comedian Steven Wright once remarked that he stayed in a hotel that was so old, the wake-up call was a letter slid under his door. This joke depicts the state of professional service businesses today. The customer service revolution has been slow in coming to the accounting and law professions, but it has definitely arrived and it is time for the professions to take notice of the economics of customer loyalty, and the service principles needed to obtain that loyalty.

The world today is a service economy. In fact, the traditional distinction between "manufacturing industries" and "service industries" is obsolete. All businesses are in the service business—the only difference is the relative degree of tangible and intangible product delivered to the customer. The act of manufacturing a car, computer, television, or toaster is a way of serving others just as much as drafting a will, giving a haircut, or providing medical care.

In reality, over half of the dollars spent in any developed economy buy nothing tangible. Healthcare accounts for more than 10 percent of the GNP in advanced economies, and so do entertainment and travel (the world's largest industry). General Motors' largest supplier is not a steel or glass factory, but a healthcare provider.

Why is good, quality service so rare in a service economy? Everyone has favorite restaurants, hairstylists, tailors, and stores. The main reason people continue to patronize a particular establishment is that the business continually provides outstanding service. Many of the most cherished service stories come from cottage-type industries. But then customers will patronize a grocery or department store and have to wait ten minutes for the privilege of handing over their money or being treated rudely by a surly clerk.

Chapter 3 discusses why you are in business and the spirit of service, and noted the FedEx mission statement: People. Service. Profits. This chapter discusses some of the more prevalent customer service philosophies and principles that are vital to creating a culture embodying the spirit of service. Much of the customer service revolution taking place today is really an attempt to turn back the clocks, to the days of the Great Depression, when businesses knew the value of each customer and how important their loyalty was. To say that one cannot turn back the clock is to be a prisoner of the moment. The things of highest value are not affected by the passage of time; otherwise the very concept of truth becomes impossible.

Total quality service (TQS) is an essential prerequisite to value pricing. After all, the reason for innovative and customized pricing is to enhance customer relationships and engender loyalty. Because service companies really sell a promise, the customer's confidence and trust in the professional is the most precious asset a firm has. Due to the intangible nature of professional services, the customer constantly looks for items of tangibility to assess the skills and competence of a firm. Trust is an essential ingredient in this process because it reduces the risk and vulnerability of the customer.

Professionals, especially CPAs, have very high trust among their customers, something the profession is very proud of and works diligently to maintain. Unfortunately, that work tends to focus on the technical aspects of the job rather than on the interpersonal skills required to provide outstanding service to customers.

Just as a firm cannot specifically measure the spirit of service within its culture, trust is difficult to measure with customers. Trust is not a matter of legality; it is a matter of the heart. Countless surveys of customers of CPAs, for instance, report they are very satisfied with the service they are receiving, because they believe their CPA is "doing a good job." However, very few could articulate exactly what they meant by "doing a good job."

This is difficult for most professionals to deal with because it appears to be based on emotions and feelings, rather than on logic and calculation.

At least information is available on how customers tend to select their CPAs and why they remain loyal to them. (Chapter 12 explores why customers tend to leave CPA firms.) Selection and loyalty have little to do with characteristics that can be measured quantitatively, such as the following:

- Interpersonal skills
- Aggressiveness
- Interest in the customer
- Ability to explain procedures in terms the customer can understand
- Willingness to give advice
- Perceived honesty

(Winston, 1995: 170)

Service quality is certainly less consistent than product quality, making services a high-risk purchase. Also, services are usually not as enjoyable as purchasing products. All this needs to be taken into account when developing relationships with customers. Pondering the characteristics mentioned in the survey above, one is left with the conclusion that obtaining and keeping customers is more a matter of seduction than competence. This is not to say that technical quality and trust are not important, but it now takes more to keep customers loyal.

The Value Proposition

All businesses, no matter what they do, provide a value proposition to their customers, consisting of the following three components:

1. Quality
2. Price
3. Service

Think of businesses that compete almost entirely on quality. Certainly professional firms come to mind, but so do Intel, Ford (Quality is Job #1), and perhaps most predominantly Mercedes-Benz (before the Chrysler acquisition). During the late 1980s, in fact, Mercedes became quite arrogant about its automobiles and their position in the marketplace. After all, Daimler-Benz AG invented the auto industry, and everyone knew that German engineering was the finest in the world. Then Lexus arrived and the Mercedes share of the German market sank from 11.6 percent in 1985 to 6.4 percent in 1992, while the number of cars Mercedes sold in the United States dropped from about 100,000 in 1986 to 59,000 in 1991.

What happened? Why didn't the customer realize that Mercedes made the finest quality cars in the world? Wasn't quality alone enough to ensure Mercedes a share of the market? The answer, of course, is no. Customers tend to ask, "What have you done for me lately?" Lexus came on the market and provided a better value for the dollar and didn't rely on what it had accomplished in the past (because it didn't have a past). Note that Lexus owners are not necessarily price sensitive, but they are value conscious, and it appeared Lexus offered superior value.

Think about the number one complaint in the restaurant industry: poor service. Not lousy food (quality), but lousy service. Quality among professionals is similar, in that it meets certain minimum standards (which tend to be very high). Therefore, you cannot compete on quality alone, because in the customer's eyes all professionals are equally qualified. Even if you are in a niche, unless you have absolutely no competitors, anywhere, then rest assured the customer views your quality as no different than your competitor in the same niche.

Nothing is fascinating about competing based upon price, unless you want to be a low-cost provider like Wal-Mart, Costco, or Southwest Airlines. No doubt some professionals have selected this strategy—Jacoby & Meyers and H&R Block come to mind—and it is viable, as the success of the companies mentioned testifies. Especially when quality is considered to be constant among professionals, price can no doubt become a key indicator of buying preference.

In fact, the very lack of perceived quality differences among professionals from the customer's viewpoint leads managers and partners to utilize price as their main marketing tool. They frequently cut price because it is something that can be implemented quickly, targeted to a specific customer, and is cheap to perform. But as Leonard Berry points in *Discovering the Soul of Service*:

> One of the biggest mistakes managers make is assuming that value and price mean the same thing to customers. They do not. Price is part of value but not its equivalent. To customers, value is the benefits received for the burdens experienced; it is what customers receive in exchange for what they must endure to receive it. Burdens have both a monetary component (price) and a nonmonetary component (for example, unknowledgeable service providers, inconvenient service locations or hours of operation, busy telephone lines). (Berry, 1999: 12)

Cutting price to attract new business sends the message to the marketplace that your firm is willing to compete on price alone. If you are interested in pricing at above-market levels, than this is not a prudent strategy. In the days of e-commerce, some professional, somewhere, is always willing to perform the work you do for less money, and the price-conscious buyer will find them. Don't fall into the trap of believing that all customers care about is the price; it is clear they care about more. They care about the perceived benefits, relative to the price, and service quality is certainly among the attributes they look at to gauge the reasonableness of any price.

Now think of businesses that compete based on service excellence: American Express, Cadillac, Disney, FedEx, Lexus, Marriott, Nordstrom, and Ritz-Carlton. All of these companies have one thing in common: quality service. FedEx has a commanding share of the overnight delivery market because it provides unsurpassed customer service. The empirical evidence is in, and it shows that customers are more than willing to pay premium prices for outstanding service.

The beauty of competing based on service is that it is invisible to your competition. A competitor can match your technical quality. If the competitor doesn't possess it in-house, it can be outsourced or offshored. The competitor can also match, and cut, your price. But your service quality cannot be seen at all. Your relationship and interpersonal skills are something the competitor cannot monitor. All of the service leaders mentioned above understand this and use it to their advantage. Donald E. Petersen, former chairman of Ford Motor Co., initiated the Ford Taurus and Total Quality Management (TQM) improvements that brought the company back from the edge of a precipice.

He began to realize the importance of being focused on customer service and stated, "If we aren't customer-driven, our cars won't be either."

Even as customers have become more sophisticated and better informed, service value is still largely a visceral reaction; it is hard to measure, but you know it when you experience it. A professional's value is based on a myriad of factors, the most important of which are the relationship with the customer and the customer's perception of the level of interest and concern for his or her well-being. Department store owners or auto dealers, whose product offerings are considered fairly generic or easily substitutable, have a tougher time creating loyal customers than professionals do. Professionals have a monopoly on themselves. Professionals need to understand this concept and to value price based upon service excellence accordingly.

The Moment of Truth

We talk a lot about making the best first impressions. Now let's run ahead and think about making the best last impression. The last impression people have of us will stay with them until we have a chance to change it—if we ever have another chance!

—Ron Willingham

The moment of truth is a phrase that has its origins in *the hour of truth,* a term used in bullfighting to signal the third and final hour, the killing of the bull. In a business context, the moment of truth is far more prosaic, but to the life of an organization, it is potentially just as fatal as to the bull.

As president of Scandinavian Airlines, Jan Carlzon led the money-losing airline into the transformation to one of the leading customer service organizations, and hence, one of the most profitable airlines in Europe. He did it by focusing the entire organization on the moment of truth. In his book, *Moments of Truth,* Carlzon explains his philosophy:

> Each of our 10 million customers came in contact with approximately five SAS employees, and this contact lasted an average of 15 seconds each time. Thus, SAS is "created" 50

> million times a year, 15 seconds at a time. These 50 million "moments of truth" are the moments that ultimately determine whether SAS will succeed or fail as a company. They are the moments when we must prove to our customers that SAS is their best alternative. (Carlzon, 1987: 3)

Most business people have heard about the moment of truth (MOT) business philosophy, but misconceptions about the MOT remain. Some define it as any time the company is called on the carpet to answer a complaint or settle a dispute. But others see the MOT as much broader than a recovery system for customer complaints. According to Karl Albrecht's definition, the moment of truth is

> Any episode in which the customer comes into contact with the organization and gets an impression of its service. (Albrecht, 1992: 116)

Therefore, from the customer's perspective, a MOT might be a phone call, an office visit, receipt of an invoice from the firm, a chance meeting on the street or at a social event, and even receipt of a letter from the IRS (who will the customer think of first?). By itself, each MOT is pretty minor. However, over time, the accumulated effects of thousands of MOTs are like placing grains of sand on a scale, one side being mediocrity and the other outstanding service. Over time, the scale will definitely tip in one direction or the other.

There are generally only three possible outcomes for each MOT:

1. Neutral experience
2. Positive experience (moments of magic)
3. Negative experience (moments of misery)

The neutral experience is the most rare; it's not often a customer comes into contact with a company and is left completely indifferent about its service experience. Many companies, from Disney to Saturn, have reengineered the way they do business based upon the MOT philosophy. Disney, for example, learned that in its Epcot park at Walt Disney World, children would complain about the lack of characters roaming the park as they do in the Magic Kingdom. Since then, Disney has turned the characters loose in Epcot, creating millions of moments of magic for its guests. Saturn took a look at the process of purchasing a car (usually the first) from the customer's perspective, and they were not happy with what they found—confrontational, pushy salesman, surly service managers, and incomprehensible finance and insurance people. Saturn changed each MOT with the customer and ended up implementing a very pleasant sales experience for what should be an exciting purchase for any customer.

A positive experience with a company can result in 100 percent faithfulness to them. When a CPA's customer was confined to a wheelchair and could not mail his tax return information, FedEx was called and asked if they could go to the man's apartment and pick up the information and package it for the CPA. The reply was "no problem." Not only did they do that, but when the driver arrived at the customer's apartment, he retrieved the documents, phoned the CPA, read off the documents, and asked if there was anything else needed. This was all done for the regular delivery price. Can you imagine the U.S. Postal Service offering that level of service? It would take an act of Congress, and it still wouldn't be done right.

These examples illustrate the power of using the MOT philosophy to structure your business, always thinking from the customer's perspective and making it a delight for them to do business with your firm. By focusing on the MOT, the attention of the firm changes from the *activity* to the *outcome* of the service experience. The professional is focusing more intently on the outcome of the encounter with the customer than on the technical aspects of the project. While attention is paid to the technical aspects of what is being done, the customer encounter isn't being ignored in the process. It is not so much what the customers get; it's how they are treated when they get it that counts.

Even when customers experience moments of misery, there is an underlying opportunity to turn the experience into a moment of magic. Before the days of the check-off box on the tax return, one innovative CPA firm filed powers of attorney for all of its customers, every year, to ensure that the firm received all correspondence from the IRS. Usually, the CPA firm opened the letter before the customer and thus was able to begin to settle whatever the issue might have been. If the customer received a phone call from the firm indicating that the problem had been solved, or was being handled, imagine how good the customer must have felt having such a proactive CPA looking out for them.

The phenomenon of the MOT is also why it is so important to deliver work face-to-face to customers and even take the time to explain it to them. It may be an impossible task to do this with all customers, but it certainly can be done with the top 20 percent of your customers. Face-to-face encounters are perhaps the most underused marketing tool in any firm's strategy, and delivering work in person not only gives the customer something other than the invoice and price to gauge value, it can also lead to additional work.

Each MOT is an opportunity to unleash the firm's creativity in making the customer feel appreciated and special. Cherish each and every one of them, never take them for granted, and insist that your firm's personnel commit all the energy and resources required in order to gain the right to future MOTs with the customer. Nordstrom's policy is TLC—Think Like a Customer. No MOT, no matter how small, is ever insignificant.

The Importance of Customer Loyalty

How much are you willing to spend to acquire a new customer? You should be willing to spend at least that much to retain one. The obsession with customer acquisition rather than customer retention is a holdover from the professional's fat and lazy days, when the supply of customers was plentiful and competition was slim. Those days are gone. In today's world, the big money is made not in winning new customers but in retaining existing ones.

Too often people think of success in business in terms of financial statistics and ratios. Yet these are nothing more than the results of customer behavior. Reward the customer, encourage him to come back, provide him with more value than he pays in cash, and you'll retain him. Realistically, all that management in any business can do is manage the internal resources—land, labor, and capital. As one lady remarked to a rude clerk, "I believe you have things backward. You are overhead. I am profit." (LeBoeuf, 1989: 26)

Unfortunately, customer loyalty and its economic effects were largely ignored until the late 1980s, and they were ignored by the professions until even later than that. Pick up any business book today and one of the first things you'll read is that customer loyalty is dead. According to studies conducted by Bain & Co. the average U.S. corporation loses 50 percent of its customers in five years, half of its employees in four, and half of its investors in less than one. In the last 20 years, banks have gone from holding 40 percent of customer's assets to 20 percent.

Brand loyalty is also said to be dead, especially with the rise of generic products. And now with the Internet, the dynamics of loyalty are undergoing another radical change.

Is customer loyalty actually dead? Are people really less loyal today than in the past? There may be some truth to this perception, given the fact that the children of the baby boomers are starting to take over their parents' businesses. These young people don't follow the traditions of their parents, and they are not at all tolerant of poor or slow service. They use e-mail, not snail-mail. They demand instantaneous results and put far less emphasis on efforts. And, as professionals are discovering, much to their chagrin, one of the first acts they perform upon taking the helm is to change bankers, lawyers, and CPAs.

However, loyalty is not dead. Most people would choose loyalty over the alternative if for no other reason than that it lowers search and transaction costs. People tend to be loyal to their spouses, families, neighborhoods, and the nonprofit agencies where they volunteer considerable time and effort. What is dead in the business world today—or at least largely ignored until recently—is a *reason* to be loyal. One has to earn loyalty—you don't get it by just showing up and doing the job (no matter how well you may perform). The frequent flyer programs that the airlines adopted in 1981, followed by reward points from hotels and rental car agencies, have proven quite successful in earning a customer's continued loyalty. It is time for professional firms to recognize the importance of customer loyalty—and the dramatic impact it can have on their profitability—with the goal of retaining their best appreciating social capital: their customers.

The Economic Effect of Customer Loyalty

Perhaps another reason the economics of customer loyalty have been ignored is that traditional accounting methods fail to capture the information necessary to measure its effect. Generally accepted accounting principles are woefully inadequate for this task because they fail to distinguish between sales to old and new customers; they don't allow acquisition costs to be amortized over the customer's life—and thus hide the value of any one customer's loyalty in aggregates—and they completely ignore social capital on the balance sheet (which is a measure of relationships).

For these reasons many businesses perform customer retention accounting, with the insurance companies leading the way. According to Frederick F. Reichheld, in *Loyalty Effect*, loyalty-based models explain the success or failure of a particular business better than market share, economies of scale, and cost position. Bain & Co. has conducted studies showing that by raising customer retention rates a mere 5 percentage points, a business could increase profits by 25 to 100 percent.

Firms in the top quartile of marketing success usually generate anywhere from 25 to 40 percent of their new business from sales of additional services to existing customers. If you are a smaller firm, or a sole practitioner, you can generate anywhere from 50 to 80 percent of growth from existing customers.

According to Reichheld, existing customers are more profitable for the following reasons:

- Acquisition cost—Acquiring a customer, according to the AICPA, can cost 11 times more than retaining one, lowering the return on new customers from the beginning of the relationship.
- Base profit—The longer you retain the customer, the more base profit, the better return on your acquisition investment.
- Per-customer revenue growth—Accelerates over time, as veteran customers utilize more of your services than do new customers (they are familiar with your firm's capabilities and trust you).
- Operating costs—Over time, customers become more efficient in dealing with your firm; you've both climbed the learning curve; less research is required on your part, the customer is more familiar with your team members, and so on.
- Referrals—Long-term customers are much more likely to refer additional business to your firm, and those referrals are usually of a better quality; veteran customers can communicate a more accurate picture of your firm (who knows better then they do?).

- Price premium—Veteran customers are less price sensitive than new customers, and they value not only your services but also the relationship, because they have an ego investment in it. (Reichheld, 1996: 42–50)

There are primarily three ways to maximize the net present value of your firm's customer base: (1) Cut costs without reducing your firm's value proposition; (2) Improve value at a greater rate than you increase your costs; and (3) Adjust your pricing to capture the consumer surplus. One example of the first strategy is the virtual office, which can lower a professional's overhead without reducing the value the professional offers. The second strategy is employed by entering into new markets or niches or by offering existing customers a wider array of services. And, of course, the third strategy is what this book is concerned with—pricing your services on value, not hours.

Given all of this empirical evidence that customer retention is much more profitable than customer acquisition, it is interesting to ponder why the professions have ignored this trend. As Theodore Levitt explained in a 1983 *Harvard Business Review* article:

> The sale . . . merely consummates the courtship, at which point the marriage begins. How good the marriage is depends on how well the seller manages the relationship. The quality of the marriage determines whether there will be continued or expanded business, or troubles and divorce. The era of the one-night stand is gone. Marriage is both necessary and more convenient. (Quoted in Hart and Bogan, 1992: 182)

The marriage analogy isn't perfect. The onus is not shared equally between the partners; it falls disproportionately on the firm to maintain continuous customer delight.

Examples of the loyalty effect are widespread. Companies began to recognize the power of retention in the late 1980s. McDonald's, for instance, builds relationships with kids—by providing birthday parties, toys, and playgrounds—because children influence a parent's choice of where to eat.

Certainly hotels and car rental companies have learned the loyalty lesson. Rapid checkouts and concierge floors are examples of these companies providing their "A" customers with a higher level of service, while extracting a premium price. These strategies have the added bonus of holding out carrots to the "B" and "C" customers with the message: Patronize us more and you too can share in these perks.

Perhaps the most successful of the loyalty programs is the frequent flyer program, started by American Airlines in May 1981. American Airlines essentially combined three things to create this tremendous value: plastic cards embossed with the member's frequent flyer account number, a record of the member's travel history (which American was able to capture through its successful SABRE reservation system), and empty seats on airplanes. One measure of the program's success is delay tolerance: prior to 1981, the typical traveler would only wait a half hour before trying to switch carriers owing to a delay; today, after over 20 years of frequent flyer programs, that tolerance has increased to over three and a half hours. Frequent flyer programs generated approximately $10 billion of revenue for the airline industry in 2001, because they receive between .01 and .03 cents per mile from alliance programs with credit cards, hotels, and rental cars (half of all the miles rewarded are on the ground).

From a pricing perspective, the frequent flyer programs are pure marketing genius. If you're a frequent flyer with United Airlines and pay $2,000 for a ticket to the East Coast, you perceive it as less than that price because you accrue miles toward free flights. However, if you take a competitor carrier and pay the same $2,000, you receive no benefit in terms of miles, and thus you pay full fare. This strategy enables the airlines to avoid serious price wars, because they are charging their competitor's customers higher prices while charging their loyal customers less (from the customer's viewpoint).

Many law firms have started a "frequent litigation" program, offering discounts for utilizing the firm's services more. Professional service firms should consider rewarding existing customers, perhaps through a discount off of a change order, for marginal services provided to existing FPA customers (usually, among the most loyal in the firm). This discount can be thought of as retention marketing, which usually generates higher returns than acquisition marketing and doesn't suffer from the problem expressed in department store magnate John Wannamaker's quip: "I am certain that half of what I spend on advertising is money wasted. But I don't know which half." Anytime you invest in a current relationship, you are bound to reap rewards that are greater than those you will get by chasing after new business.

Professionals have the advantage of creating what is known as possessive loyalty in their customers—that is, when the customer uses a possessive pronoun to describe his attorney or accountant (e.g., my CPA). Possessive loyalty exhibits confidence, trust, and perhaps even dependency on the professional. This is a form of loyalty any other business would love to engender.

Following the focus during the 1980s on the total quality management movement and the zero defects movement, TQS changes the focus. Zero defects and zero defections are not mutually exclusive goals. Certainly the former can be managed through TQM, technical training, proper supervision, and so on. But TQS can only be brought about by possessing the spirit of service within your firm's culture. Because even if you were to achieve zero defects in your firm—where absolutely everything you do is perfect—you would not be immune from customer defections. TQS puts the emphasis where it should be: Customer perception of value and customer loyalty.

Customers will continue to patronize businesses where they are invited and remain where they are appreciated. Your firm will get the behavior it rewards. Customer loyalty is worth rewarding. Professional services are based on personal relationships. People don't hire firms, they hire individuals within those firms. A Nordstrom employee sums up the attitude best: "We are trained to make the customer, not the sale. We are trained to make customers."

Firing Customers

Some people are puzzled about how to reconcile TQS with firing customers. It is a good idea to fire customers who do not value your firm's services. However, your customers are not going to improve until you do. This is why TQS is necessary in order to provide service excellence.

Once you have traveled down that road, firing customers becomes essential to your firm's success. This is driven in part by the continuing specialization of the marketplace; firms can no longer be everything to everyone. The era of the general practitioner is over. Another driving force behind firing customers is the lack of capacity. In the past, professional firms could always rely on easy access to a qualified labor pool. Those days are gone. The percentage of the population aged 25 to 34 has been declining since 1985, and it will continue to drop in the twenty-first century, from 23 percent of the population to 17 percent. David Maister sums up the predicament well:

> Educated people with a few years of business experience are in increasing demand by businesses of all types, and will have many more options in building their careers than their baby-boom elders. To place the potential impact of this in perspective, consider the following statistic: the "oil shock" of the early 1970s was caused by only a 5 percent shrinkage in worldwide supply. Professional firms are facing a 25 percent shrinkage in their nonpartner labor force. There is going to be a huge people shortage and its effects will be major. (O'Shea and Madigan, 1998: 300)

This labor shortage is forcing firms to focus on specialized areas and certain customer segments. Firms are learning the Pareto Principle: less is more. Cutting the 80 percent of customers who don't value your firm enables you to focus on the 20 percent who do. Many professionals protest that cutting up to 80 percent of their customer base would be suicidal, making the firm too dependent on a small group of customers, and, anyway, even the customers in the 80 percent category contribute to the firm's overhead.

There are many retorts to this argument, one of the best being that you are already dependent on a small number of customers. By not concentrating on them adequately, you put them at a higher risk of defection. Remember the corollary to Gresham's Law: Bad customers drive out good customers. Through rewarding customer loyalty and providing TQS, your goal is zero defections. You can't focus on 100 percent of your customer base, giving them the attention and services they require; but you can focus on 20 percent of your customers. By trimming your customer base, you remove complexity from your firm and thereby operate more effectively.

Do not immediately fire 80 percent of your customer base; you need to do this incrementally. First run a Pareto analysis of your customers and divide your customers accordingly. You will discover another corollary to the Pareto Law: the 50/5 principle, meaning 5 percent of your customers generate 50 percent of your revenue and profits. Start by getting rid of the low-end customers.

CPA firms employ many tactics to fire customers. Some write letters explaining that their market focus has changed, and they are of the opinion they can no longer adequately serve the needs of the customer, and perhaps refer them to preselected competitors. Other firms send out letters raising the upcoming year's prices, anywhere from a factor of two to four. These firms have discovered an interesting phenomena when they raise prices: over half of the customers chose to stay. This shows the amount of consumer surplus that exists in the relationship. You have to deploy the strategy that is right for your firm and your customers.

Another way to ensure you are following the Pareto Principle is to take on only those customers who understand and are willing to pay for your firm's value proposition. Be up front with prospective customers and tell them you are interested in developing long-term relationships, and you want to be the sole source for their company's needs. This will weed out the price buyers from truly valuable customers. And remember the loyalty effect: you are much better off keeping existing customers than chasing after new ones. It is acceptable not to do business, but it is unacceptable to do bad business. Growing simply for the sake of growth is bad business. Not only does it force your firm to scramble and hire undesirable people, but it takes your attention away from your most profitable customers.

It is also helpful to take into account David Maister's personality grading system, as described in his book *True Professionalism*. Essentially, this means grading customers not on the traditional measures of revenue such as speed of payment and referral quality, but on whether or not you like the business they are in and you like them personally. This may seem naïve to some, but in fact you will be a more successful professional if you work with people you truly care about rather than just chasing the Almighty Dollar.

One innovative CPA firm implemented its firing strategy in a unique way. As a holiday bonus one year, each team member was allowed to select two customers to fire. Not only did this boost the morale in the office, but it also increased cross-selling efforts to existing customers and put more money on the firm's bottom line. Terminating personal relationships is never easy, especially when they are with customers who have been with you since you started. But in order to move forward you must leave some things behind. You can't fight the Pareto Principle. It is much easier to harness its power and focus on those few customers who value your firm the most.

Summary and Conclusions

The paradigm shift that needs to take place in the professions today is a shift not only in how professionals view the world, but also the way they live in it. The TQS train has already left the station, and you have two choices: Be on it or be under it.

The enlightened firms that have adopted TQS will continue to grow, improve, and prosper in the coming decades. If you were to examine all of the great sources of wealth creation throughout the history of the world, from the titans of the Industrial Revolution in the nineteenth century to Bill Gates today, you would notice this profoundly important truth: In every era, the businesses that succeeded and achieved excellence took a clear stand for the customer. Being a professional is more than doing outstanding technical work. The central purpose of professionals is to serve.

It is impossible to maintain value pricing over the long run without offering TQS. Immerse your firm in the philosophies and practices of TQS. Benchmark other businesses—not just other professional service firms—in order to learn what they are doing to offer better, more consistent service. Don't believe you can't learn from FedEx or Disney just because being a "professional" is different from these businesses. All businesses exist solely to serve others. TQS offers a vision, a new way of thinking and operating, emphasizing customer value and a sense of service to others first.

15 THE CPA AS CONSULTANT

Andersen Consulting's battle with Andersen Worldwide has become the soap opera of the business world. What has evolved might be called "The War of the Butterflies and the Bean Counters." These companies hire MBA graduates in remarkable numbers. But who wants to commit to a career at a company going through such public and painful troubles? Won't clients, too, think twice before seeking advice from an institution that is itself confused and conflicted?

—James O'Shea and Charles Madigan, *Dangerous Company*

Making the transition from traditional CPA to business consultant is something that many practitioners will be struggling with in this new century. More and more, customers are demanding expanded services from their CPAs in addition to the traditional accounting and tax services; they want advice on how to run their businesses better—not just their accounting systems—and information about what their competition is doing. In other words, customers want their CPA to stop playing financial historian and instead help them prepare for the future. One customer said that the financial statement compilation provided to him on an annual basis to run his business and make decisions is tantamount to using his smoke alarm to time his cookies. It's a valid point.

Chapter 2 discussed the AICPA's Vision Project and how important it will be for CPAs to make the transition from historians to "certified professional advisors," also known as consultants. Many fine books cover this topic. This chapter focuses on a different perspective of the accounting profession in transition—the customer's perspective. Although the market is demanding more and more consulting services from accountants, the profession has tended to focus on its own needs rather than those of the customer.

In recent years, a backlash has begun against the management consulting industry. Books such as *Dangerous Company*, *The Witch Doctors*, and *Fad Surfing in the Boardroom* have sounded the clarion against this infantile—and often self-contradictory—profession. Much of the criticism resonates with customers. Just as in every other industry, the customer is becoming more sophisticated with respect to hiring "management gurus." To say the least, there is mendacity in the consulting profession, and CPAs need to be aware of how they should counteract these charges and not fall prey to the disadvantages that plague this industry.

The Kennedy Research Group, which closely tracks the management consulting industry, estimates that the global consulting market is over $100 billion. There are myriad reasons for this incredible growth, including the following:

- The global economy is healthy and companies flush with cash seem eager to purchase advice to grow even bigger with more efficiency.
- Management consulting companies have not been shy about marketing their services.
- The reluctance to bring in outsiders for help, once quite strong, has diminished.
- Technology is changing so rapidly it is almost impossible to stay abreast and consulting firms that have built a reputation as technology leaders have gained an edge.
- With the death of communism around the world, and the rise of free markets and privatization, consulting companies have helped to smooth the transition from planned economies to market economies, bringing in much needed human and intellectual capital.
- Deregulation has taken away the privileged status of once-safe industries and opened the door to heavy levels of competition, forcing companies to search for how to do more with less.
- A certain amount of the alacrity to hire consultants is due to internal management figuring if a bold new initiative fails, they can always blame the outside consultants.

In the 1980s and 1990s, many accounting firms saw the percentage of revenue earned from consulting increase at a faster pace than any other category of service offering. Offering consulting services not only helps firms retain customer loyalty, earn a larger percentage of the customer's budget, and capture some of the consumer surplus, but it also helps ensure that the customers remain a viable enterprise themselves. As pointed out by Ric Payne, president of Principa, according to results from several hundred client advisory boards from around the world, three recurring themes come from customers of CPA firms:

1. We don't *want* an accountant, but we *need* one.
2. We are generally happy with our accountant, but we're sure there are other things the firm could be doing for us.
3. If our accountant could show us a better way to run our business, we would be willing to pay for that advice. We are not concerned about fee levels, but we are concerned about service levels (specifically, the timely response to our requests for assistance, and proactivity in relation to matters we should be aware of, but aren't) and the tangible value we derive (cash flow, profit, and value improvement).

   (Payne, October 1998: 10)

This is proof that customers are yearning for their CPAs to take a more proactive role in their business, and price is not an issue. If one listens closely enough, the market will tell you the price it is willing to pay. Perhaps the biggest strength the profession has as it makes this transition is its position as the most trusted and respected of all business advisors. This is an asset the typical management consultant longs for, even among the major consulting firms. Capitalizing on this strength will make the transition a lot less tumultuous.

Consulting requires a dramatic change in mind-set. Accountants have always been regarded as experts, whether in GAAP or tax law. Ask a CPA a question, and he or she will give you an accurate response. This type of knowledge is crucial to the practice of traditional accounting but can become a hindrance in consulting. As William Reeb points out in his book *Start Consulting*, "In the business advisory role *coming up with the solutions is often not nearly as important as asking the client the right questions.*" (Reeb, 1998: 71)

To become consultants, CPAs have to adopt this approach, and the customer's thinking must change as well. The old stereotype of the meek and diffident accountant wearing a green eyeshade has to make way for the comprehensive business advisor. In several airports around the Untied States an ad appeared that read something to the effect of "Who counts beans for Starbucks?" The ad was for Deloitte & Touche and it perpetuated the stereotype of accountants as bean counters, albeit in a humorous way. It is doubtful that the ad inspired anyone to place a call to the firm to count his beans. It's that type of marketing that does the profession no favors and earns CPAs their reputation as put forth in the following passage from Reid Buckley's book, *Sex, Power, and Pericles* (Reid is William F. Buckley, Jr.'s younger brother and presently runs the Buckley School of Public Speaking, in Camden, South Carolina):

> Straight logical progression is the ticket when what one wants is the facts and nothing but the facts, ma'am. This is what you desire when you ask your accountant or CFO for the financial status of your company. Is it operating at a profit or a loss? Period. The good Lord spare anyone a CPA who draws up an emotional or mystical/religious presentation of his company's financial shape, or who indulges in poetic flights of the imagination when what a person needs to know is how much boodle he must part with to meet his payroll taxes.
>
> The accountant may validly analyze the numbers advanced in support of vision, but his report on past performance is never predictive, and his opinion on the validity of the vision itself is worthless. Past performance may be a commentary on current performance, never a harbinger of future performance. It can't be.
>
> Yesterday's profit and loss statement is as useful in foretelling what tomorrow may bring as poking about in the entrails of birds or dipping tea leaves. (Buckley, 1996: 38–39)

Unfortunately, this stereotype has persisted despite all of the advertising and promotion to the contrary by the profession in the past two decades. In an AICPA survey conducted after an image campaign, only 47 percent of respondents felt "CPAs can help individuals and businesses plan for the future," while only 44 percent agreed that "CPAs see more than the numbers, they see opportunities." (Reeb, 1998: 233)

According to Reeb, "We have done a horrible job letting our clients know what we are capable of doing. Clearly, not only do we not understand our market, but our market doesn't understand us either." (Reeb, 1998)

Fortunately, customers are beginning, even if slowly, to regard their CPA as a sort of financial psychiatrist. When they ask for business advice, they are not necessarily looking for a "right" or "wrong" answer but rather the perspective of the CPA. This makes the typical CPA uncomfortable, because too many variables could sway the decision one way or the other. Not only are CPAs afraid of being wrong, with the accompanying fear of failure, but they are also afraid of rejection. CPAs are afraid that if they speak their peace, the customer may get upset and defect or lose confidence in the CPA as a trusted business advisor. But customers don't expect your suggestions to be perfect. Do not let the best become the enemy of the good.

As a group, CPAs have incredible knowledge and wisdom, not to mention practical business experience, but they are also so caught up in the fear of being sued, in GAAP rules and pronouncements, and in tax laws and regulations, that they sometimes lose sight of why the customer is paying them in the first place. Customers expect CPAs to add to their intellectual capital, and as the Payne survey mentioned above shows, they are willing to pay dearly for it.

However, a perusal of any CPE catalog from any state society reveals that most of the courses relate to technical topics, such as taxes, accounting, and auditing. Very little effort is put into the more consultative aspects of the business. The August 1997 issue of the *Journal of Accountancy* published an interesting graphical representation of the composition of revenue of the nine largest firms. Andersen Worldwide derives 65 percent of its revenues from management consulting services, approximately 19 percent from accounting and auditing, and the remaining 16 percent from tax. If one were to examine those ratios 20 years ago, probably they would have been approximately the opposite, meaning that more than 50 percent of revenues came from auditing, 35 percent from tax, and the rest came from consulting. For the past decade or so, Andersen was the largest accounting firm in the world. That is why today, Accenture (and other major consulting firms) spends 6 percent of its gross revenue on employee education and the average team member spends 135 hours each year in a classroom, compared to the average company's 1.8 percent of payroll spent on educating the workforce.

The late Timothy J. Beauchemin, in his fascinating article "Thinking About the Future," published in the December 1995 issue of the *CPA Profitability Monthly* newsletter, stated that the only long-term growth opportunity for accountants would be in consulting. He then offered this profound question as a test of a true consultant:

> Unfortunately, consulting is something that most firms are not that good at. To see whether this comment describes your firm, answer this simple question: If your biggest client fell dead today, could you go in tomorrow and run the client's business well enough to grow it at a 15 percent compounded annual growth rate? If, like most firms, you couldn't, you should not be giving business advice other than on accounting or tax issues. The bad news is that most CPAs are doing an adequate job in the tax and accounting area, but if you can consistently grow companies in a particular industry, and everyone in that industry knows it, you will find people begging for your services. Few CPA "business consultants" meet this 15 percent growth criteria. The ones that can do extremely well.
>
> The way to become a true business consultant is to develop a "positive frame." You have to talk about what to do, rather than what *not* to do. CPAs typically have a "negative frame." (Beauchemin, December 1995: 10–11)

That is a high standard to meet, but certainly a worthwhile goal to strive for, not with all customers, but definitely with the top four or five, who probably make up a large percentage of the gross revenue. If it does qualify, the firm is suddenly in the profit column of the customer's income statement and therefore is able to add more value and command higher prices for all of its services.

Customer Fears in Hiring a Consultant

Howard Shenson conducted a survey of 600 companies that had used, or were planning to use, consultants, and asked them their major fears. As pointed out in *High Income Consulting*, by Tom Lambert, "the following fears are presented in order of importance, with the first being regarded as most important by most respondents":

- Consultant incompetence
- Lack of management control

- Continued dependency
- Excessive fees
- Lack of time
- Need for a consultant seen as an admission of management failure
- Fear of disclosing sensitive data
- Improper diagnosis or needs analysis
- Pushing a product

(Lambert, 1997: 213–16)

This is by no means a comprehensive list, but it is representative of the fears most customers have in hiring consultants. A closer examination of these fears will show CPAs how they can assuage them for their customers.

Consultant incompetence Usually, a business hires a consultant because they don't have the internal expertise, so it is no wonder that they doubt their ability to judge the competence of a specialist. This concern is aggravated by consulting firms that send fresh-out-of-school kids in their twenties to tell management how to run their businesses. As A. Michael Noll, a professor at the Annenberg School for Communications at the University of Southern California and former Bell Labs employee, said: "How do you know if they are the world's best? What businesses have they managed? Look at the people they send, all under thirty and fresh out of business school, where they are mouthing whatever crazy ideas their professors threw at them in class." (O'Shea and Madigan, 1998: 9)

In fact, youth is being used in various (and quite humorous) advertising campaigns. In her book, *Fad Surfing in the Boardroom*, Eileen Shapiro defines child labor as: "That mass of freshly minted BAs and MBAs who have no operating experience and who are therefore assembled by consulting firms into the teams to turn around client companies or otherwise instruct and enlighten senior people within client companies." (Shapiro, 1995: 214)

The issue is deeper than young MBAs trying to tell senior management how to run their businesses. The issue goes right to the heart of consulting in general, and that is that there are no easy answers, no one-size-fits-all solutions in the messy world of human interactions known as business. Most of the knowledge customers have of their businesses has been developed over many decades and generations, and it is the ultimate form of hubris for anyone—including a consultant or CPA—to come in and think he or she could operate the place any better.

The majority of the most important knowledge in any field of endeavor, be it sports, entertainment, or business, is tacit knowledge. This form of knowledge is extremely difficult to articulate and relatively expensive to transfer, often traveling only through apprenticeship and trial and error. Your local coffeehouse knowing exactly how you like your morning ritual, a barber understanding exactly how his customer likes his haircut, the local hotel understanding how the college football schedule influences the demand for rooms—all point to the fluctuating value of location, location, location.

The chemist and philosopher Michael Polanyi explains tacit knowledge in his 1958 book, *Personal Knowledge*:

> Maxims are rules, the correct application of which is part of the art which they govern. The true maxims of golfing or of poetry increase our insight into golfing or poetry and may even give valuable guidance to golfers and poets; but these maxims would instantly condemn themselves to absurdity if they tried to replace the golfer's skill or the poet's art. Maxims cannot be understood, still less applied by anyone not already possessing a good practical knowledge of the art. They derive their interest from our appreciation of the art and cannot themselves either replace or establish that appreciation. (Quoted in Postrel, 1998: 90.)

The fear of incompetence, therefore, is highly justified. A consultant must know the art in question before he or she can understand it, much less render any advice about it. This is why it is so important to approach each consulting engagement as a learning experience and not assume you are the expert. Perhaps the greatest management consultant who has ever lived, Peter Drucker, summed it up best: "My greatest strength as a consultant is to be ignorant and ask a few questions."

Lack of management control You have read horror stories of consultants who run amok among various businesses, seemingly oblivious to the wealth of tacit knowledge that exists among the firm's personnel. Policies and procedures that were implemented produced dismal failures. In the past, management gave their consultants great autonomy. The consultants weren't necessarily accountable to anyone but to whom they issued their final report before moving on to the next victim.

This has changed. Management has asserted their autonomy and let it be known that the consultant works for (and with) the firm and will be held accountable for the results—good or bad—their advice produces. Management, and consultants, have gotten much better about defining the scope of the project, agreeing on benchmarks of performance, and knowing which party will be responsible for various stages in the project. Part of this improvement was brought about because of the perverse incentives inherent in hourly billing, but more importantly because customers want to feel in control of their purchase decisions.

Reeb has this practical approach to letting management control the scope and involvement of the engagement:

> We start by discussing the cash, capacity, and capability technique. It always seems to comfort clients when they understand that—*we offer various degrees of involvement* [and] *they control our degree of involvement.* (Reeb, 1998: 163)

This is why it is vital to get the customer's ego investment at the beginning of the relationship and to let the customer design and scope out the project. Using Reeb's technique will not only lead to a more harmonious relationship but will also give the consulting project a higher probability of success because the customer had a strong role in developing and implementing it based upon the customer's own assessment and resources.

Continued dependency No doubt some consultants will construct a device that no one else can comprehend, with the goal of trying to create lifetime employment. Consultants are, in effect, change agents. And in the past, they have paid very little attention to the consequences of their prescriptions. But any good consultant should be able to communicate the advantages and disadvantages of an innovation before introducing it to customers. Unfortunately, this is seldom done, or if it is done, the disadvantages are often trivialized or, worse yet, ignored altogether.

According to Everett Rogers, in *Diffusion of Innovations*, "seven roles can be identified for the change agent in the process of introducing an innovation in a client system":

1. **To develop a need for change** The change agent helps identify needs, points out alternatives to existing problems, and they may also create needs.
2. **To establish an information-exchange relationship** The change agent must enhance his relationship with the customer by being perceived as credible, competent, trustworthy, and empathizing with the customer's needs and problems. Customers must accept the change agent before they will accept any innovations or solutions they propose.
3. **To diagnose problems** The consultant must determine why existing alternatives are not meeting the customer's needs.
4. **To create an intent in the client to change** Once the consultant has ascertained the various actions required in order for the customer to achieve their goals, they must seek to motivate the customer's interest in their proposed innovation.
5. **To translate an intent to action** This is where interpersonal network influences can help the consultant effectuate change. Altering the opinion of a group's leaders, for instance, is one effective strategy.
6. **To stabilize adoption and prevent discontinuance** Consulting programs have a habit of dying, out of apathy or simple disinterest. The consultant must help the customer "stay the course" until the results of the innovation can be assessed based on a fair trial.
7. **To achieve a terminal relationship** This is perhaps the biggest challenge of all for most consultants—getting the customer to the point of coping with the problem, or solving it completely, whereby they no longer need the consultant. (Rogers, 1995: 337)

The last role is the most difficult, but it refers to the termination of one specific engagement rather than to the termination of the relationship. There will always be other issues and problems to tackle, but the mark of a good consultant is his or her ability to effectuate the needed changes inside the customer's business until the organization is self-sufficient.

Excessive fees The fear of excessive fees is well justified, given the perverse and much abused incentives of hourly billing. From lawyers to consultants, nothing causes customers as much angst and anxiety as getting billed for every minute, especially when they don't know the price before the engagement starts. By using fixed price agreements, change orders, and the other methods explored in this book, you will be able to sell based on value—rather than on hours—and you will see this fear rapidly diminish.

Lack of time As the consulting business has been in a boom cycle these last couple of decades, many have entered the profession without adequate resources, taking on jobs that cannot be completed. Combine that with undercutting price in order to secure the job (because small firms have low overhead) and you have a prescription for disaster in the eyes of the customer.

CPAs can easily overcome this fear by assuring their customers that they have adequate resources and training to complete the job, by pricing based on value, and by relying on the internal expertise of the customer. Reeb points out:

> The tradition of the CPA performing all of the work has evolved from years of practical real world experience. Why? Because CPA firms first focused on large SEC-regulated companies. As time passed, that support has filtered down into smaller and smaller companies. Now CPAs provide services from the *Fortune* 100 companies to the start-up mom-and-pop shops. However, many CPAs attempt to use the same methodology for delivering services to all sizes of businesses. The problem is . . . *the one-approach-fits-all method just doesn't work.* (Reeb, 1998: 111)

Sufficient knowledge of the engagement, and proper supervision, are among the cornerstones of the profession's code of conduct, so this fear should not be a major roadblock for customers of CPA firms.

Need for a consultant is seen as an admission of failure This point of view is bound to be held by at least some in the customer's organization, and while they may not be the decision-makers with respect to hiring the consultant, they can certainly block programs of change and lower the probability of a successful engagement. So much of what a consultant does is facilitate change. It is important to be aware of those within the management structure who may sabotage your efforts. Also, with the necessity to specialize in today's rapidly changing environment, most management teams understand that they simply can't keep up with everything, and thus it always helps to reiterate to the customer that your firm is a specialist in this area and can assist them rapidly and add value to their business.

Fear of disclosing sensitive data This is one area CPAs don't have a problem with compared to the average consultant. Businesses trust their CPAs with all sorts of sensitive information, so this is not a major concern. CPAs should, of course, always follow the professional rules of client confidentiality.

Improper diagnosis or needs analysis The management consultant industry is bedeviled by fads and new programs they pass off as the cure to all ills, which is why they've earned the reputation of being modern day witch doctors. Programs such as TQM and re-engineering have had their share of failure, and yet some consultants insist on pushing a one-size-fits-all solution to any problem. Diagnosing the situation of the customer, through a proper needs analysis, is an important step in any consulting engagement. Imagine a doctor who prescribed medication or treatment without first diagnosing the patient—a sure invitation to malpractice.

However, there is an important caveat to this step in the process. Unlike traditional CPA services, in which the diagnosis is usually done early on and is not a significant part of the engagement, consultants are paid to diagnose problems, and thus CPAs need to avoid what Reeb calls "premature speculation." Resist the temptation to jump right into the conclusion, even if it is readily apparent to you, because the problem you've identified may only be the tip of the iceberg and not the real concern of the customer.

Consulting engagements should be unbundled, according to Reeb, and "a clear distinction made between the costs for *advice, direction and vision, and human resources required to complete the work.*" (Reeb, 1998) Unbundling also makes it easier to value price the engagement, as each step required will have specific benchmarks and any results can be determined in these stages.

Pushing a product With CPAs entering into relationships with software companies—even becoming value-added resellers—and now selling financial products, the fear that you are pushing products on your customers has the potential to be significant. Nobody likes to have a product pushed at them without a clear understanding that it is the best choice among the available alternatives. If you happen to sell a particular product, your fear can be overcome by staying true to your product's niche market and not trying to force it onto a customer whose situation doesn't fit the problem or solution your product was meant to solve.

The idea that just because you sell a particular product you won't take into account the special needs of the customer is anarchistic thinking. Just as automobile salesmen sell particular makes, the free market has a way of allocating customers and vendors based upon mutual advantage and desire. If your firm has developed, for example, a proprietary software program for the medical profession, chances are you won't be able to sell it to all interested parties. As long as you are honest about the product's capacity—and limitations—selling a product does not, per se, block you from being an effective consultant.

Words to Avoid

Consultants have the reputation, whether justified or not, of offering up solutions to all problems, and at times their marketing and advertising can promise more than they are realistically able to deliver. As Warren Burger, then Supreme Court Chief Justice, said on the introduction of lawyer ads: "Some of the advertising would make a used-car dealer blush." And *Consultant News* pointed out, "We've never seen a winning proposal that says 'Maybe we can solve your problem. How much is too much?'" (Quoted in O'Shea and Madigan, 1998: 100.) The courts have begun to answer that question. *Consultant News*, in its review of the *UOP v. Andersen Consulting* case, concluded that Andersen had presented a "Litany of Language to Avoid in

Proposals. Here's some of what could get you into trouble: . . . We continually deliver success . . . We are able to respond to customer needs up to 50 percent faster . . . We know how to manage risk . . . We are prepared to assume responsibility for the price and quality of the solution . . . We can create an environment in which all team members work cooperatively . . . We deliver on scope, schedule, quality, and cost commitments . . . Our project manager will have ultimate responsibility for ensuring successful development . . . Our philosophy is to get the job done, not excusing the responsibilities." (O'Shea and Madigan, 1998 99–100)

The Consultant Customer's Bill of Rights

In their book *Dangerous Company*, James O'Shea and Charles Madigan end with a list of questions that potential employers of consultants should ask themselves and include advice to heed before they hire anyone. It is a thought-provoking list and it may become necessary for CPAs to be able to answer these questions in the coming transition from compliance to consulting. In a sense, it is a Customer's Bill of Rights:

1. Why are you doing this? What do you want to achieve? The more clearly the goal is defined, the greater the chance of reaching it. If you don't know what you want to do, don't make the call.
2. That being achieved, do you need outsiders to help reach this goal? Don't forget to assess the brilliance within your own company before you go trying to buy some from outside. Maybe you don't need an army of consultants. Maybe you just need your very own MBA, whom you can easily steal from a consulting company.
3. If you hire a consulting company, which characters will they send? Be ruthless in this part of the process. If you know the reputations of the partners, or if they display a special, tested expertise, demand that they pay good and frequent attention to your needs. Make it a part of the contract. If they are promising the best, make certain that is what shows up. Do not be meek about sending away people who make you uncomfortable.

4. What will it cost? (And how long will it take?) Avoid open-ended arrangements and vague promises. Demand specificity in contracts, including the dark parts about what happens if the consulting engagement doesn't work. Be tight with your money. Base payments on performance and on your satisfaction. If the task involves high risk, make certain the consulting company is sharing in the risk, not just in the rewards, of the relationship.
5. Never give up control. The best consulting engagements do not take over operations, they complement them. Make certain your own managers retain control over everything, share in decision-making, and understand that for the duration of the contract, they are responsible and in charge.
6. Don't be unhappy for even a day. Ignored consultants can shower down all kinds of havoc on a company. If you sense something is going wrong, confront it immediately and demand repairs. Consultants do not answer to boards of directors, but you do. At these prices, happiness should be assumed.
7. Beware of glib talkers with books. The fact that someone can stack up case after case in which a practice seemed to work is no guarantee that it will work for you. Insist on tailor-made consulting engagements that recognize the unique nature of your business. If you are buying into the book pitch, ask how much time the actual author will be on-site working through his philosophies, then listen closely to the response. Don't be afraid to trim elegant proposals right down to their essence.
8. Value your employees. One of the most common complaints about consultants is that they talk down to the locals or ignore their ideas. Long after the consultants leave, your staff will be on board. How they feel about the outsiders has a lot to do with whether the engagement will work. The best consulting companies know this and will go to great lengths to avoid morale problems. You are buying intelligence, not arrogance.
9. Measure the process. Make certain you have your own internal measure of how a procedure is progressing. Consulting companies do, and they generally try to make this a part of the process. But there is a big conflict of interest in this area and their inclination is to make you happy and stay fully engaged. Find someone you trust

who knows what a devil's advocate is and let him or her monitor the consulting process. Listen frequently to the advocate's report.

10. If it's not broke, don't try to fix it. It is in the consulting company's interest to find trouble where you see calm waters. The consultants' goal will be to sell much broader involvement than you might want or need. They can't help it. It is part of their nature. But it doesn't have to be part of yours.

Perhaps the best advice is the oldest. Niccolò Machiavelli had this to say about seeking advice: "Here is an infallible rule: a prince who is not himself wise cannot be wisely advised. . . Good advice depends on the shrewdness of the prince who seeks it, and not the shrewdness of the prince on good advice." (O'Shea and Madigan, 1998: 302–303)

Summary and Conclusions

In order to ascend the value curve, CPAs must enter the consulting arena. Like the financial services market, the consulting profession does not have the best of reputations. CPAs will elevate the level of professionalism and competence in consulting, as long as they always consider the customer's best interest to be paramount.

Most of the fears of customers who engage consultants can be allayed by implementing total quality service, value pricing, fixed price agreements, change orders, and a service guarantee, as discussed throughout this book.

Entering consulting is an enormous opportunity for the accounting profession, one to look forward to with anticipation and alacrity. It is part of the transformation from compliance worker to certified professional advisor, enabling the profession not only to report on their customer's financial history but also to help make it.

16 ETHICS, HOURLY BILLING, AND VALUE PRICING

Market competition leads a self-interested person to wake up in the morning, look outside at the earth and produce from its raw materials, not what he wants, but what others want. Not in the quantities he prefers, but in the quantities his neighbors prefer. Not at the price he dreams of charging, but at a price reflecting how much his neighbors value what he has done.

—Friedrich A. von Hayek

Capitalism offers nothing but frustrations and rebuffs to those who wish—because of claimed superiority of intelligence, birth, credentials, or ideals—to get without giving, to take without risking, to profit without sacrifice, to be exalted without humbling themselves to understand others and meet their needs.

—George Gilder

Throughout history, the issue of the morality of profits has been debated endlessly, as it should be. Richard John Neuhaus, in his book *Doing Well and Doing Good: The Challenge to the Christian Capitalist*, discusses the ancient debate of a "just" price:

> The idea that there is a right amount or a "just" amount always runs up against the question, Compared to what? The conventional answer is that one pays what the market demands, or what the market will bear. From Athens to Elizabethan England to the Great Terror of the French Revolution, societies have experimented with "sumptuary laws" setting limits on people's income and expenditures. The experiments have never worked out very well, the obvious reason being that it is almost impossible to agree on standards. Few egalitarians, even among the well-to-do, propose a top income limit that is less than what they themselves receive. (Neuhaus, 1992: 193)

If a price is going to be judged based on whether or not it is "just," the first question to ponder is, Who will decide what is "just"? One of the proclivities of professionals is to believe that solutions to these sorts of issues are best solved outside the parameters of the marketplace. For instance, they will turn to governing bodies, such as the American Bar Association or the AICPA, or they will turn to the various government organizations that control the licensure of the profession. This is a serious mistake. The free market already provides an answer to the question of a "just" price—*whatever someone is willing to pay.* That may sound heretical, but it's not. An old legal maxim says: *Emptor emit quam minimo potest, venditor vendit quam maximo potest.* (The buyer buys for as little as possible; the seller sells for as much as possible.) The customer is sovereign and in the long run will make the best choices on how to spend his or her money to maximize utility.

To believe the market is imperfect with regard to fairness is to underestimate your own sovereignty as a customer and put your faith in some third party—usually the government or the courts—to determine what is "fair." No third party has access to all of the relevant information that is contained in a price. This is precisely why wage and price controls have failed *everywhere* they have been tried. If it is immoral for a person—or a firm—to charge premium prices to customers, does it follow that it is immoral for buyers to seek out low prices? Moreover, why is an oil company condemned for earning windfall profits when market conditions change, while an individual homeowner who realizes a tidy profit off of a hot real estate market is applauded? Why are individuals and companies held to different standards?

The solution to the problem of a "just" price lies in the conflict of interest that is inherent between buyers and sellers—the seller is seeking the highest price and the buyer is seeking the lowest. The $11 trillion plus economy is evidence that most price issues are resolved, without the aid of a third party, between the buyer and seller.

Perhaps it is not so much *price* that bothers people as it is *profits.* Profits have a bad reputation because most people simply do not know where they come from. Profits come from *risk.* For example, when the state of Florida entered into a settlement with various major tobacco companies whereby the state would receive a multi-billion-dollar settlement, the attorneys who litigated the case for the state agreed to accept a 25 percent contingency for assuming all of the risks of taking the engagement. Some of the attorneys even mortgaged their homes to finance the investigative research and other expenses that were necessary. The attorneys' share of the settlement worked out to be something on the order of thousands of dollars per hour. A judge ruled that the fee was unconscionable. However, the attorneys assumed all of the *risk*, and since that is where profits come from, they are entitled to the agreed-upon percentage. The state had no business claiming, *in retrospect*, that the fee was unreasonable. All parties entered into the contract, and except in cases of fraud or coercion, they should be required to abide by their commitment.

Are such supernormal profits moral? In his seminal book, *Wealth and Poverty*, George Gilder, a senior fellow at the Discovery Institute, in Seattle, Washington, had this reply to economist John Kenneth Galbraith's long-standing criticism of business firms seeking large profits:

> Galbraith maintains that businesses, far from giving without predetermined returns, actually seek to control their markets, often with aid of government, to "administer" prices and quantities of production and exclude all rivals. This revelation is sometimes offered in the spirit of a child discovering that his parents indulge in sexual intercourse. But we must grant that the child is right. For all their ideological commitment to free enterprise, businesses are primarily devoted to successful enterprise, pursue it any way they can, and are delighted to benefit when government blocks the competition. In precisely the same way that many "liberal" economists can profess egalitarian socialism while waxing rich on the capitalist system, corporations can feed off of government while celebrating free markets. (Gilder, 1993: 47–48)

Profits are a sign that a useful social purpose is being filled and needs are being met. In a free market, no profit could exist without people voluntarily entering into a transaction where each receives more than they give up. Otherwise, everyone could simply exchange $5 bills. What could be more equal? This isn't done, because while it may be equal, it would also be completely pointless. For an exchange to make any sense, each party must receive a *gain* from the exchange. That being said, here is how economists define various profits that are earned in the marketplace:

> **Normal Profits**—The return to the owner of a firm that operates in a perfectly competitive market, in long-run equilibrium. In a perfectly competitive market, when a firm maximizes profits, each factor of production will receive a per unit payment exactly equal to what it produces at the margin. The market price, or the cost of a factor, is equal to the value of its marginal product. . . . When firms are earning normal profits, net *economic* return is zero, since revenues exactly equal costs, where costs include the cost of capital, which is the market rental rate of capital.
>
> **Supernormal Profits**—Profits in excess of normal profits. [These] occur when revenues exceed costs, again including the cost of capital. [They] are often identified with monopoly profits.
>
> **Rents**—When an agent owns a good that has a special characteristic which, through no effort of the agent, is valuable. Professional athletes or musicians are often given as examples of recipients of rents.
>
> **Profits from Immoral Activities**—[Profits from] extortion, theft, blackmail, etc.
>
> **Windfall Profits**—When the event causing the profits is a complete surprise to the profit maker. An example is the OPEC oil embargo of 1974 and its effect on oil companies. (Cowan and Rizzo, 1995: 3–6)

All businesses strive to earn supernormal or windfall profits. Nothing is unusual about this universal desire, and the fact that professionals or industries organize licensing boards and cartels should convince you that these types of profits are actively sought after. When people charge that a corporation is making too much money, the first thing to ask is this: "If you believe that is so, why don't you purchase its stock?"

Profits come from *risk*, and that includes, as economist Joseph A. Schumpeter so poetically phrased it, the entrepreneurial innovations that make up the "perennial gale of creative destruction." Entire industries have been eliminated due to this characteristic of free markets. Horse-drawn buggy manufacturers didn't invent the automobile and slide rule manufacturers did not invent the calculator. Both of these innovations rose up and decimated existing stocks of infrastructure.

In a free market the income that is earned, the prices that are set, and the profits that are made are all the result of volitional acts—*capitalist acts between consenting adults*, as one commentator put it. Nobody has written more eloquently on wealth and poverty, capitalism, and the spirit of enterprise than George Gilder. Here is what he wrote in *Forbes ASAP* (December 2, 1996):

> Barbarian intellectuals in the United States complain of widening gaps between rich and poor. What in fact is happening is a rising trajectory of lifetime incomes. In an economy dominated by a few large companies, entry-level work may be well paid, but lifetime incomes and productivity are capped. In an entrepreneurial economy, where large corporations downsize and new companies proliferate, individuals can more readily fulfill their potentials. Thus their ultimate incomes are higher.
>
> In the past, capital equipment was costly and production complex and dominated by large firms. Bill Gates might have spent his life working his way up the chain of command at IBM or General Electric, thus avoiding an immense contribution to income inequality in America. Instead, he began a new company at a poverty-level entry income with capital goods costing a few thousand dollars.
>
> The income floor, after all, will always be zero, while the ceiling in a free economy is effectively infinite. As more people fulfill their potential, the ostensible "gap" increases. But it is not chiefly a horizontal gap between individuals. It is a gap between people's earnings in entry jobs and their peak earnings later in life. It is morally desirable that this gap increase.
>
> The key to the moral superiority of capitalism is that people get rich by imaginatively serving the needs of others. The key to the productive superiority of capitalism is that the people who have proven their ability to create wealth gain the right to reinvest it.

> Demonstrably a brilliant investor and creator of wealth, Bill Gates gains the burden and opportunity to reinvest it. Socialist economies fail because they tax away and institutionalize the fruits of invention and creativity. (Gilder, 1996: 280–82)

This view of capitalism being a moral system is certainly not one that is propagated in the mainstream. Most popular culture and institutions, from movies and television shows to research organizations, villainize busi-nesspeople and business firms, endlessly portraying them as power-hungry, stop-at-nothing-to-get-ahead, ruthless members of society. This view is pernicious, not to mention completely out of touch with how the world works. A business, in its essence, is a moral institution, because it requires moral conduct to succeed in the long run. Michael Novak, in *Business as a Calling: Work and the Examined Life* lists seven moral requirements for business success, which he labels "Internal Responsibilities":

1. **To satisfy customers with goods and services of real value** Like other acts of freedom, launching a new business is in the beginning an act of faith; one has to trust one's instincts and one's vision and hope that these are well enough grounded to build success. It is the customers who, in the end, decide.
2. **To make a reasonable return on the funds entrusted to the busi-ness corporation by its investors** [Is it moral to lose other people's money?]
3. **To create new wealth** This is no small responsibility. If the business corporation does not meet it, who else in society will?
4. **To create new jobs** You cannot create employees without creating employers.
5. **To defeat envy through generating upward mobility and putting empirical ground under the conviction that hard work and talent are fairly rewarded** The founders of the American republic recognized that most other republics in history had failed and that the reason they failed was envy: the envy of one faction for another, one family for another, one

clan for another, or of the poor toward the rich. . . . The best way to conquer this is to generate economic growth through as many diverse industries and economic initiatives as possible, so that every family has the realistic possibility of seeing its economic condition improve within the next three or four years. Poor families do not ask for paradise, but they do want to see tangible signs of improvement over time. When such horizons are open, people do not compare their condition with that of their neighbors; rather, they compare their own position today with where they hope to be in three or four years. They give no ground to envy. . . . Only then can people see that hard work, goodwill, ingenuity, and talent pay off. When people lose their faith in this possibility, cynicism soon follows.

6. **To promote invention, ingenuity, and in general, "progress in the arts and useful sciences" (Article I, Section 8, U.S. Con-stitution)** The great social matrix of such invention, discovery and ingenuity is the business corporation.
7. **To diversify the interests of the republic** The interests of road builders are not those of canal builders, or of builders of railroads, or of airlines companies. The sheer dynamism of economic invention makes far less probable the coalescing of a simple majority, which could act as a tyrant to minorities. The economic interests of some citizens are, in an important sense, at cross-purposes with the economic interests of others, and this is crucial to preventing the tyranny of a majority. (Novak, 1996: 138–45)

Fra Luca Pacioli, in *Particularis de Computis et Scripturis*, his treatise on double-entry bookkeeping, emphasized religious and moral teachings. Pacioli's Chapter 2, "Inventory," states the following:

> Begin with the assumption that a businessman has a goal when he goes into business. That goal he pursues enthusiastically. That goal, the goal of every businessman who intends to be successful, is to make a lawful and reasonable profit.
>
> Therefore, businessmen should begin their business records with the date AD, marking every transaction so that they

> always remember to be ethical and, at work, always act mindful of His Holy name.
>
> Among Christian businessmen, it is also common to mark the initial account books with the sign of the cross. (Pacioli, 1494: 4, 12)

When Pope John Paul II introduced an encyclical titled *Centesimus Annus* on May 1, 1991, he said "Economic freedom is an aspect of human freedom, which cannot be separated from its other aspects and which must contribute to the full realization of people in order to construct an authentic human community." (Neuhaus, 1992: 184) The Pope's encyclicals are not addressed solely to the Catholic faithful but "to all people of goodwill." They are the Church's "social doctrine." This particular encyclical is remarkable, for the Pope is basically saying that the new capitalism is a moral system, and that prosperity is dependent upon economic freedom. Here are some of the more interesting passages, as they relate to economic freedom and the role of profits in society (references are to the paragraph number of the encyclical):

> Man, who was created for freedom, bears within himself the wound of original sin. Man tends toward good, but he is also capable of evil. He can transcend his immediate interest and still remain bound to it. The social order will be the more stable the more it takes this fact into account and does not place in opposition personal interest and the interests of society as a whole, but rather seeks to bring them into fruitful harmony (¶ 25) . . .
>
> At one time, the *natural fruitfulness of the earth* was the primary factor of wealth. In our time, *the role of human work* is increasingly the productive factor both of nonmaterial and material wealth. Also, more than ever is *work with others* and *work for others*; it is a matter of doing something for someone else (¶ 31) . . .
>
> In our time, another form of ownership is becoming no less important than land: *the possession of know-how, technology, and skill.* The wealth of the industrialized nations is based much more on this kind of ownership than on natural resources. A person produces something so that others

may use it after they have paid a just price, mutually agreed upon through free bargaining. It is precisely the ability to foresee both the needs of others and the combination of productive factors most adapted to satisfying those needs that constitutes another important source of wealth in modern society. In this way, the role of disciplined and creative *human work* and *initiative and entrepreneurial ability* become increasingly decisive (¶ 32) . . .

The Church acknowledges the legitimate *role of profit* as an indication that a business is functioning well. When a firm makes a profit, this means that productive factors have been properly employed and corresponding human needs have been satisfied. But profitability is not the only indicator of a firm's condition. It is possible for the financial accounts to be in order, and yet for the people—who are the firm's most valuable asset—to be humiliated and their dignity offended. This is morally inadmissible [and] will eventually have negative repercussions on the firm's economic efficiency. The purpose of a business firm is to be a *community of persons* endeavoring to satisfy basic needs at the service of the whole of society (¶ 35).

Hourly Billing: The Perfect Crime?

While keeping in mind the above precepts of how a free market economy works in the real world, and why it is a moral system, let's examine the ethical issues attorneys are dealing with as they make the transition from hourly billing to value pricing. CPAs and other professionals can learn from the experience of attorneys about the problems they will likely encounter.

Lawyers have a much bigger public relations problem than do CPAs. A review of rankings of respected occupations shows CPAs right up there with members of the clergy and doctors. Attorneys have not earned the same reputation. The percentage of Americans who gave lawyers high ratings for honest and ethical standards fell from 27 percent in 1985 to 17 percent in 1994. According to the ABA, "One major contributing factor to the discouraging public opinion of the legal profession appears to be the billing practices of some of its members." (Ross, 1996: 5)

Legal auditors and ethics professionals have devoted substantial amounts of time and energy trying to diffuse these types of problems. In fact, every state except Massachusetts and California has adopted some form of mandatory reporting requirement whereby an attorney has an express legal duty to report to supervising attorneys or the appropriate bar authority another attorney who is engaging in unethical billing practices. As Professor William G. Ross points out, in his book *The Honest Hour*, Rule 8.3(a) of the Model Rules of Professional Conduct provides that:

> A lawyer having knowledge that another lawyer has committed a violation of the Rules of Professional Conduct that raises a substantial question as to that lawyer's honesty, trustworthiness or fitness as a lawyer in other respects, shall inform the appropriate professional authority. (Ross, 1996: 199)

This is precisely how the Webster Hubbell case was prosecuted the first time. His fellow partners reported his unethical billing practices.

One legal auditor, James P. Schratz, cites that in his experience "30 to 50 percent of entries are questionable in 80 percent of the bills that he audits." (Ross, 1996: 30).

Ross states the following in his book:

> Most dishonest billing is the perfect crime. Because there is no practical manner of verifying the accuracy of most time records, every attorney who has billed time knows that hourly billing creates tempting opportunities for fraud. (Ross, 1996: 23)

In fact, an entire legal auditing industry has been created at an average billing rate of $175 and up per hour. Under pressure from these auditors, most law firms will very quickly reduce their bills by 25 percent.

Legal Auditors on Value Pricing

Some of the most vitriolic denunciations of value pricing come from legal auditors. They also reject the fact that the hourly billing method is disappearing. Ross ends his book *The Honest Hour* by saying, "Despite its potential for abuse, time remains the best means of billing clients. Hourly billing therefore ought to be reformed rather than abandoned." (Ross, 1996: 263)

But if the hourly billing method is as good as the legal auditors purport it to be, then why did *their* industry arise in the first place? What makes legal auditors believe that they are the ultimate judge and jury with respect to the fairness of a transaction? Are they simply trying to maintain a billing system that provides for their job security and standard of living? Legal auditors owe their existence to mistrust and asymmetrical information between the lawyer and the customer. Remove these factors and legal auditors become superfluous.

Ethical problems arise in hourly billing due to the misalignment of interests created by the system. Attorneys may not have malevolent motives when engaging in padding their hours; Ross says that "much overbilling is the result of attorneys' failure to understand the real goals and needs of their clients." (Ross, 1996: 53) The problem is that professionals pad their timesheets because they know that the value of the service they provide is worth more than the time spent. If that is the case, then the solution is not to try to cope with the ethical issues of hourly billing but to scrap hourly billing entirely and reach a price agreement with the customer before the service is provided. Unfortunately for attorneys, the ABA and the courts have opted for the strategy of trying to impose standards for time-based billing. Here is a partial listing of the issues on which they are spending an inordinate amount of brainpower to solve:

- Double billing—billing two customers for different work performed at the same time.
- Recycled work—billing customers by the hour for work that was created at another time for another customer.
- Overstaffing of lawyers—assigning too many lawyers to a case or project to fulfill billable hour quotas.
- Excessive research.
- Attorneys performing clerical and administrative tasks and billing at their hourly rates.
- Charging for travel time.
- Attorney conferences—chitchat on the customer's dime or valuable timesaving devices?

- Charging for small units of time—rounding up to the quarter hour or charging for every minute?
- Overhead expenses—charging (and possibly marking up) general overhead expenses such as copies, faxes, phone calls, secretary time, and overtime.

Although this list is not comprehensive, it represents the major ethical issues of hourly billing. Each one is worth examining in greater detail.

Double Billing and Recycled Work

The ABA Committee on Ethics and Professional Responsibility issued its Formal Opinion 93-379, in December 1993, declaring double billing unethical, stating "the lawyer who has agreed to bill on the basis of hours expended does not fulfill her ethical duty if she bills the client for more time than she actually spent on the client's behalf." (*Alternative Billing: The Sequel*, San Francisco, Tab 7, page 8)

Here is what the committee said regarding a hypothetical example of an attorney flying on behalf of one client while preparing a brief on the plane for another client, and an attorney charging for a recycled work product:

> A lawyer who flies for six hours for one client while working for five hours on behalf of another, has not earned eleven billable hours. A lawyer who is able to reuse old work product has not re-earned the hours previously billed and compensated when the work product was first generated.

Thus, the ABA Committee concluded:

> Rather than looking to profit from the fortuity of coincidental scheduling, the desire to get work done rather than watch a movie, or the luck of being asked the identical question twice, the lawyer who has agreed to bill solely on the basis of time spent is obliged to pass the benefits of these economies on to the client. The practice of billing several clients for the same time or work product, since it results in the earning of an unreasonable fee, therefore is contrary to the mandate of the Model Rules. (*Alternative Billing*: *The Sequel*, San Fransico, Tab 7, pages 8–9)

Ross elaborates on the ABA Committee's opinion:

> The Opinion states that when an attorney has agreed to charge clients on an hourly basis "and it turns out that the lawyer is particularly efficient in accomplishing a given re-sult, it nonetheless will not be permissible to charge the client for more hours than were actually expended on the matter. When that basis for billing the client has been agreed to, the economies associated with the result must inure to the benefit of the client, not give rise to an opportunity to bill a client phantom hours." (Ross, 1996: 80)
>
> The ABA Opinion suggests that the lawyer is reaping a windfall from "the luck of being asked the identical question twice," just as the attorney who is able to bill two clients for work performed at the same time is receiving an unfair advantage.
>
> The ABA's condemnation of hourly billing for recycled work is consistent with judicial decisions that have reduced fees when attorneys have billed for work that was developed in previous cases. As one court has explained, "accumulated expertise may be a factor justifying a higher hourly rate, but it is clearly improper to make multiple charges for work that has only been done once." (Ross, 1996: 84)

What is curious is that the ABA could ignore the economic value derived by the customer. The hourly billing method is impeding attorneys from reaping the rewards they deserve for the value they provide. After all, the hourly billing method was adopted because studies found the attorneys who used it were making more money than those who were not. And now, the exact opposite seems to be taking place. Rather than suggesting attorneys now adopt other pricing methods, the ABA is wasting time pondering the picayune issue of attorneys sitting on airplanes not watching movies.

Overstaffing of Lawyers

Legal auditor James P. Quinn contends that overstaffing is "the one factor that has contributed more than any other to excessive legal costs." (Ross, 1996: 99) It has also been the topic of scorn from judges in various cases. But what causes overstaffing? It is the perverse incentive built into hourly billing, which rewards *efforts* over *results*. If everyone in a firm has to meet an hourly quota, then you can bet that bodies will be thrown at work out of proportion to what is necessary. This is perhaps why customers of major law firms have protested and refuse to pay for any associate not employed by the law firm for at least three years. The customer is simply tired of paying for the on-the-job training of inexperienced associates and demands that a case be staffed in accordance with his or her needs, not the billable hour goals of the firm. And rightfully so.

Excessive Research

Excessive research is another deleterious effect of hourly billing. Because firms have no incentive to be efficient, they tend to recreate the wheel on each new engagement in order to bill as many hours as possible. This is the equivalent of Ford redesigning each car before assembling it, thereby ensuring the maximum labor input to meet the hourly goals. This is absurd. Duplication of effort takes place in all professional firms, and it is a consequence of the hourly billing system. Ross cites the policy of Wells Fargo Bank, which "requires its outside counsel to obtain prior approval for any legal research in excess of three hours." (Ross, 1996: 120) Since competition has become so intense, these hourly costs are finally being eliminated. Professionals may not like it, but they need to accept it because the market rules.

Surgeons Piercing Ears

Judge Joseph F. Weis, Jr., wrote in a statutory fee decision in 1983, "A Michelangelo should not charge Sistine Chapel rates for painting a farmer's barn." (Ross, 1996: 137) Courts have recognized that sometimes it is necessary for attorneys to perform clerical tasks, and that in these instances the attorney should bill them out at reduced rates. Once again, this is a result of the Almighty Hour mentality, where work gets hoarded by whoever is on the case (to meet billable hour quotas) rather than being delegated to the level where it can be performed in a most cost-efficient way.

Travel Time

Courts have tended to allow attorneys only a portion of their travel time, and bankruptcy courts have stated that travel time is considered part of the attorney's overhead and thus built in to their hourly rates. Ross relates the following case:

> Rejecting an attorney's argument that he ought to receive full compensation for travel to the local courthouse because he was thinking about the hearing while he was traveling, one court declared that "this is a slippery slope argument. If a court allows compensation for this, then ultimately shower time will be compensable." Even shower time, however, should be compensable if an attorney is thinking about a client's problems. (Ross, 1996: 153)

Would a customer share Ross's opinion? No customer of sound mind would contemplate paying for shower time. This is a clear example of the preposterous line of reasoning that develops when you believe that all value is the result of time. No other business even considers this line of thought, but professionals are mired in it.

Attorney Conferences

Ross conducted his own surveys in 1991, 1994, and 1995, and "inside counsel ranked conferences as one of the most unproductive activities of outside counsel." (Ross, 1996: 157) The social network in any firm represents an enormous asset, and it probably is underused in pursuit of the Almighty Hour. Why should you seek out those in your own firm to see if they have dealt with a similar issue, if you know a project will provide a few days of billable hours and the customer will pay for it? Take away the Almighty Hour as the source of price, and professionals will engage in conferences only when the benefits outweigh the costs.

Rounding Up Time Charges

Is it ethical for a professional to round up to the nearest tenth of an hour? A quarter hour? Bankruptcy courts have mandated six-minute billing increments. Ross takes this issue to its extreme by proposing the following recommendation:

> The use of smaller billing increments would seem likely to encourage ethical behavior by dampening the temptation of attorneys to use liberal rounding techniques. Accordingly, clients would be wise to insist that their attorneys bill in increments of six minutes or less.
>
> Indeed, it might therefore make sense for attorneys to begin billing time in one-minute increments in order to assure maximum accuracy in billing. The use of such small increments would not be burdensome to attorneys because, as we have seen, most tasks are performed in aggregates of many minutes or hours, and it takes the same amount of time to record each task, regardless of the duration of the task or the minimum billing increment. Literal accuracy, of course, would not be demanded of tasks that took more than a few minutes. For example, an attorney who spent 177 minutes on a project might be excused for estimating her time at three hours and billing 180 minutes. (Ross, 1996: 168)

How many practicing attorneys would agree with Ross that accounting for *every minute* would not be a burdensome task? But that's not even the right question. The right question is this: Is there a direct relationship between a minute and the value of a service? The answer is an unequivocal *no.* To go to the absurd extreme of tracking every minute shows that the focus of the Almighty Hour is wrong; attorneys are focusing all their ef-forts on trying to solve these problems rather than on pursuing the opportunities that exist with value pricing.

Overhead Expenses

The ABA Opinion condemns marking up overhead expenses, and states: "In the absence of an agreement to the contrary, it is impermissible for a lawyer to create an additional source of profit for the law firm beyond that which is contained in the provision of professional services themselves." (Ross, 1996: 173) Again, this issue is best settled between the customer and the professional, discussed up front and understood by each party. Firms would do well not to consider overhead expenses as profit centers because that distracts the customer (and the professional) from focusing on the true source of value—the service rendered rather than the number of faxes, copies, and phone calls made. By charging for such items you put the focus on things customers do not value and distract them from the things they do value. This is the wrong approach. You should avoid any charge that is part of your fixed overhead (direct expenses are, of course, an exception). After all, the only true profit center is a customer's check that does not bounce.

Lawyers will freely admit that hourly billing creates a conflict of interest between the attorney and the customer, yet some of them desperately cling to the method as if it were sacrosanct. Other attorneys, however, are leaving hourly billing. Customers are demanding to know the price of legal and accounting services in advance, as shown in this testimonial from Ronald A. Williams, Vice President and Assistant General Counsel for Wal-Mart Stores, Inc.:

Wal-Mart Flat Fee Program

> In regard to premises liability, product liability, truck liability, and pharmaceutical liability litigation, Wal-Mart has entered into flat fee agreements in 35 areas of the country. This program has been in existence for the past 6 years and Wal-Mart has had great success with it.
>
> Under the Wal-Mart arrangement the company and the law firm agree that a set amount will be paid on each lawsuit that is sent to the law firm. It is also agreed that all of the lawsuits received in the area the law firm covers will be sent to that law firm. Under this arrangement this flat fee amount includes all attorneys fees and inside expenses such as copying, telephone charges, fax charges, computer research charges, delivery charges, mailing charges, and auto mileage charges. There is also agreement among the parties that if the matter is tendered to another entity and it takes over the defense of the case within 60 days there will be no flat fee due in the matter. On the other hand, the parties recognize that the arrangement should incorporate a "squeal factor" in which the law firm can request that on a very special case the flat fee not apply. This would be a particular case which is out of the ordinary and would not be considered to be the normal "run of the mill" case. However, such a case must be extraordinary since the whole intent of the arrange-

> ment is that in some cases the firm would do very well in regard to the number of hours spent on the case and in other cases they would not do as well since there would be considerable matter of work to be done, including a trial.
>
> The philosophy of such an arrangement is that this is a long term partnership between the law firm and Wal-Mart and over the period of this long term relationship all of these matters will average out and the law firm will make a profit from the cases in view of the fact that a good number of them will settle or be dismissed without a trial. The distinct advantage to Wal-Mart in these cases is that bills do not have to be reviewed nor does there have to be any discussion between Wal-Mart and the attorney concerning the amount of time spent on a certain matter. Furthermore, Wal-Mart knows exactly how much each case will cost and can budget for those costs. (*Alternative Billing*: Tab 6: 5–6)

This is precisely the solution to the ethical dilemmas that are confounding the ABA, courts, and lawyers. Notice that this is a *customer-imposed change*. Wal-Mart will not deal with firms unless they countenance this type of partnership. How long will it take for other major corporations to adopt the same practices? How long will it take them to adopt these same arrangements with their CPAs? It's already happening, despite what the legal auditors say about the immortality of hourly billing. When you and the customer see things differently, you will only succeed when you begin to view the world the same way they do.

There are signs that the legal profession is getting the message. The Committee of the American Bar Association (ABA) Section of Business Law issued a report in November 1998 titled "Business and Ethics Implications of Alternative Billing Practices: Report on Alternative Billing Arrangements," which proposed the following modifications to the ABA's Model Rule 1.5:

> The Committee believes that the following items might well be added to Rule 1.5 (a) as factors to be used in testing fee "reasonableness":
>
> 1. The size and complexity of the transaction or matter for which the lawyer is retained; and

2. The client's sophistication and extent of experience in business matters.

> The Committee also continues to support the proposition that reasonableness should be presumed "if the client and the lawyer reach an agreement with respect to a billing arrangement after disclosure and understanding" and fees are charged in accordance with that agreement. (*The Business Lawyer*; Vol. 54, November 1998: 204)

Another positive indication that the ABA is finally figuring out the validity of value pricing is its Commission on Billable Hours Report, issued in August 2002. This report is quite comprehensive; it discusses the deleterious effects of the billable hour on lawyer morale, pro bono work, customer relations, and so on. A full copy of the report can be found at www.abanet.org/careercounsel/billable.html.

Fairness and Pricing

The notion of a "fair" or "just" price has bedeviled philosophers, religious leaders, rulers of nations, and businessman for centuries. During the Dark Ages merchants could be put to death for exceeding the communal concept of a "just" price. In A.D. 301, Diocletian, the Roman Emperor, issued an edict fixing prices for nearly 800 items and punishing violators with death. Of course, whenever you fix a price below its market level, you will get shortages, which is precisely what happened.

In ancient China, India, and Rome, and almost everywhere throughout the Middle Ages, all interest charges were called "usury" and were prohibited entirely, making economic progress through lending and risk-taking all but impossible. Even today, "price gougers" are subject to societal condemnation, regulatory harassment, and editorial vitriol. Oil companies are frequently a prime target of public outrage, especially when prices at the pump vary from one location to another. Pharmaceutical companies are held in contempt when they charge $5 to $20 per pill, even if the dosage reduces the cost of medical intervention by other means.

On the other hand, popular movie stars, directors, and entertainment companies (such as TV networks and Disney) can earn above-normal profits without so much as a whisper of public protest. Premium ice creams and chocolates, which are very expensive and yield enormous profits, also escape criticism. Why the different standards? Is the consumer a hypocrite or just emotionally responding to the issue of fairness?

Traditional economic theory has long ignored subjective issues such as fairness, tending instead to rely on the rational man economic model. But there is no doubt that in the real world, the perception of fairness can, and does, influence the purchasing behavior of consumers. This is an interesting economic anomaly, because rational theory would predict that a consumer would purchase a commodity as long as the price was below his or her reservation price. It is simply not rational to refuse to purchase a product or service because the terms of the transaction are perceived to be unfair by the purchaser.

In his book *Passions Within Reason: The Strategic Role of the Emotions*, economist Robert H. Frank posits a "fairness model" to explain this anomaly:

> People will sometimes reject transactions in which the other party gets the lion's share of the surplus, even though the price at which the product sells may compare favorably with their own reservation price. (Frank, 1988: 167)

Consider the following illustration:

> You are lying on the beach on a hot day. All you have to drink is ice water. For the last hour, you have been thinking about how much you would enjoy a nice cold bottle of your favorite beer. A companion gets up to make a phone call and offers to bring back a beer. He says that the beer might be expensive and asks the maximum price you are willing to pay. If the price is higher, he will not buy it. What price do you tell him if (1) the only nearby place where beer is sold is a fancy resort hotel, or (2) the only nearby place is a small, run-down grocery store? (Nagle and Holden, 1995: 309)

The median price stated from the fancy hotel was $2.65 and from the grocery store $1.50. Note that the consumer would be drinking the beer on the beach and not entering the hotel or store where the beer was purchased, and thus—under the theory of rationality—should be willing to pay the same amount no matter where the beer is ultimately purchased. But most people who participated in this survey expressed the feeling they would rather go thirsty than be "ripped off" by the grocery store.

Frank's "fairness model" is certainly influencing the behavior of these consumers. It may be argued that this experiment is not valid because the participants were asked to imagine sitting on a beach in the hot sun, rather than actually doing so. Therefore they are stating how they think they would react under those circumstances but this is different from their "revealed preference."

The example, however, does give insight into the process of negotiating with the customer, a process in which perceptions of fairness are very important to both sides. It is vitally important to understand each customer's perception of fairness and what the customer expects from a professional. Violating those perceptions will lead to irreparable damage to the relationship, even if the perceptions are not rational. Sometimes you can overcome irrational perceptions of fairness by educating the customer; other times you cannot. You must decide whether you can abide by the customer's perceptions of fairness in the transaction, and the more you learn about what those perceptions are, the better you will be able to perform in accordance with them.

The Market as an Arbiter of Value

Professionals naturally look to third parties to solve problems, be it ethical issues or quality issues. Anyone who understands free markets knows that these problems take care of themselves. People are mistaken who believe that the government is effective at ensuring quality. Organizations such as the Contractors Licensing Board are virtually useless in insuring the quality of contractors. The best protection is competition and tort law, not a government agency. All the government agency will do is protect the contractor from the consumer, which is what government licensing is all about. Ask yourself which group of products and services has gotten better in recent decades: automobiles, electronics, computers, and transportation, or public schools, police protection, Social Security, and Amtrak. The best insurance possible against consumers being taken advantage of is to give consumers competition and leave them free to choose among a host of providers.

Summary and Conclusions

The members of the American Bar Association (ABA) should not be disparaged for taking up issues pertaining to ethics in pricing. The problem is that the ABA is applying the labor theory of value to legal services and ignoring the subjective theory of value.

Professionals who are convinced that all value is determined by the number of hours spent face a dilemma. One wonders whether two professionals leaving a movie together would be timid about expressing their opinions on the movie. According to the labor theory of value, the movie should be equally valuable to both because it took the same amount of production time. Obviously, this is faulty reasoning. Yet hourly billing is a direct extension of this labor theory of value.

The value of any professional service—or any other product or service offered in the marketplace—is that which is agreed upon by the parties to the transaction. If both parties do not feel like they are benefiting from the exchange, it will not take place.

The New York State Bar Association had this to say with respect to alternative pricing methods:

> Indeed, subject to the economic realities of the situation and an attorney's professional obligations, virtually any billing method that attorney and client can both agree upon and abide by will result, almost by definition, in a fair fee. (*Alternative Billing*, 1997: 55)

The concepts discussed in this book—ascertaining customer expectations, discussing price up front, entering into fixed price agreements, and involving customers in the design and terms of your services—are the rational alternative to the ethical quandaries discussed in this chapter. Value pricing requires character, integrity, and honest dealings, which are less likely to be cultivated with the use of hourly billing; in value pricing the interests of the professional and the customer are aligned.

17 VALUE PRICING AND SELF-ESTEEM

The greatest danger is not that our aim is too high and we miss it but that our aim is too low and we reach it.

—Michelangelo

CPAs tend to suffer from write-downs and low pricing. One reason is low self-esteem, which directly affects the pricing of a professional's services.

Allan S. Boress, editor of the *CPA Profitability Monthly Newsletter*, offers explanations of why CPAs capitulate so easily:

- The CPA does not have enough quality clients.
- The client doesn't really want to work with a CPA but has to deal with such issues as tax compliance.
- The client sees little value in what the CPA does.
- The client beats up the CPA because it is a negotiation tactic.
- Fee arrangements are not discussed up front.

(Boress, 1996: 5–6)

Confident Pricing and Self-Esteem

These are all good explanations; however they do not really get at the root of why CPAs have not been confident enough to engage wholeheartedly in value pricing. The deeper reasons lie in the issue of self-esteem. Timothy J. Beauchemin's article titled "No More Begging for Work: Self Esteem Is the Key to a Better Practice," which appeared in the August 1996 issue of the *CPA Profitability Monthly Newsletter*, provides the definitive answer to why CPAs are so conservative when it comes to pricing. Here is a portion of what Beauchemin wrote:

> I see too much of what I call "begging" in our industry—begging for work (especially by under pricing) and then

> begging to get paid. I have never really understood why this is, particularly when you consider the training, hard work, and risk that accountants go through. The only explanation I can see is that accountants tend to have rather low self images, unfairly and unreasonably low, but low just the same. (Beauchemin, 1996: 4)

Low self-esteem does go right to the heart of why CPAs question the value of the service they provide. Many participants in one of my seminars have commented that they would "feel guilty" about charging a substantial multiple of their hourly rate. They say this as if they are taking advantage of the customer. This attitude is shocking. Why would they attend a course titled *The Shift from Hourly Billing to Value Pricing* if they did not want to increase their net incomes?

Do you truly believe the benchmark of your value is the hours you spend? What about the years of experience that stand behind that 15-minute tax-planning brainstorm that saves your customer thousands of dollars in taxes? Is the value really one-quarter your hourly rate? CPAs are so imprisoned by the hourly billing method that it has affected their own concept of self-worth and has lowered their self-esteem. Do you think other businesses "feel guilty" about pricing based upon value? Do the airline executives feel guilty about charging the first-class passenger four to ten times the cost of coach, even though it doesn't cost that much more to fly them? Do General Motors executives feel guilty about charging a higher price for a Cadillac than for a Buick, even though they are churned out of the same factory with minimal cost difference?

The lesson is vital, and it is this: **Before you can charge a premium price, you first have to believe, internally, that you are worth it. If you do not think you are worth multiples of your hourly rate, your customers never will believe it either.**

A good example of pricing comes from a customer who owns an industrial coating shop and is very adroit at pricing. He has done all the time and motion studies, cost analyses, and labor overhead allocations on his automated line for purposes of bidding. Yet, every time he bids a job, he considers a myriad of factors, and the price is usually much higher than the "standard cost-accounting rates." He explained his method of pricing by telling of an early business experience. Before he owned his business, he worked as a carpenter, building decks, fences, and so on. As he was working on a deck for a particular customer whom he really did not like, he hit his hand with a hammer, causing it to swell immediately. Just then, the homeowner emerged and asked him how much the deck was going to cost. At that point, he was so frustrated—and in dire pain—he did not care whether or not he lost the job, so he quoted a price three times what he thought the "time and material" cost would be. The homeowner did not blink. He said he learned a valuable lesson that day, and it was this: Pricing = Guts.

Have you ever dealt with a professional, such as a doctor or a consultant, who came highly recommended? When you learned of the price, did you try to negotiate it downward? Most highly recommended professionals will not budge on their pricing, because they know they deserve it and are worth it. They are secure and confident in their worth, and they price above the market as a result. Obviously, not everyone can do this. But the ones who do all possess a common characteristic: *high self-esteem*.

The ultimate treatise on self-esteem is the book *The Six Pillars of Self-Esteem*, by Nathaniel Branden. Branden defines self-esteem as:

> 1. Confidence in our ability to think, confidence in our ability to cope with the basic challenges of life; and
> 2. Confidence in our right to be successful and happy, the feeling of being worthy, deserving, entitled to assert our needs and wants, achieve our values, and enjoy the fruits of our efforts.
>
> (Branden, 1994: 4)

This directly relates to the guilty feelings of CPAs with respect to value pricing.

Branden further points out: "[Self-esteem] is directly affected by how we act. Causation flows in both directions. There is a continuous feedback loop between our actions in the world and our self-esteem. The level of our self-esteem influences how we act, and how we act influences the level of our self-esteem." (Branden, 1994) And please do not think your level of self-esteem is set, once and for all, in childhood. It is not. You can increase it, and you can decrease it as well; Branden's book covers this subject well and is recommended reading for anyone interested in this vital subject.

Pause for a moment and think about how you act with your customers. When they object to your price, what is your first reaction? In the majority of cases, the first thing a CPA will do is to cut the price, in hopes of pleasing the customer. Why? Not only are professionals loss-averse, but they are not convinced they are worth what they are quoting. So rather than educating the customer on the value they are providing, professionals capitulate and cut their price, which cuts the value of the service. Quoting a premium price, and sticking to it, takes a positive self-image and sense of self-worth. As Beauchemin pointed out in his article, most accountants do not possess either. This is attributable to several factors:

- CPAs tend to come from middle-class and blue-collar families.
- The profession is relatively easy to enter compared with law or medicine.
- The profession does not require an Ivy League school to get certified.
- The profession is fairly open in employment, with grades, rather than connections, being the primary determinant for getting hired.
- The profession offers a good salary, even during apprenticeship.

(Beauchemin, 1996: 4)

Like most professionals, CPAs take all customer complaints and defections personally. After all, what CPAs sell is *themselves*, so it is only natural for them to take negative feedback from customers personally. You should not detach yourself from your professional pride and sense of identity; rather, you should understand your own role in determining your attitude and sense of self-worth. All actions start as thoughts in your mind. As Boress points out: "You will never be paid more than what you think you are worth." (Boress, 1995: 27).

In his article, Beauchemin told of the changes he and his partner implemented to get over their "inferiority complex." They enhanced their office, bought a Mercedes, increased their prices to near the top of the market, and told prospects "If you want the best, you have to pay for it." (Beauchemin, 1996: 4) Probably the biggest change they made was to grade their existing clients *A, B, C, D,* and *F,* firing all of the *F* clients, including one that was a large portion of their revenue. The *F* clients were referred to their competition. They also referred to the competition clients who did not pay, clients who were rude to the team members, and clients who were not managing their businesses in an ethical manner. Finally, Beauchemin recommends the following:

> Take any of your weak staff members who just are not cutting it, and send them to your competition. Two things will soon happen. First, the environment in your office will be so

> positive that the work will move quicker and the growth will come sooner as others are attracted to your wonderfully powerful firm karma. Second, your competition will soon be having severe operational problems—making you look even better! I've done all this. I know it works. (Beauchemin, 1996: 5)

By taking such bold—some might even say drastic—actions, your self-esteem is bound to increase. By surrounding yourself only with *A* customers and excellent team members, you will begin to feel better about yourself and your firm.

Branden says "*Self-esteem is the reputation we acquire with ourselves.*" (Branden, 1994: 69) That is profound. Professionals are deeply concerned, and rightfully so, with their reputations: They care what their customers think of them, of their firm, of their integrity. But what about their reputations with themselves? Most professionals were never taught even to ask the question. According to Branden:

> If low self-esteem correlates with resistance to change and clinging to the known and familiar then never in the history of the world has low self-esteem been as economically disadvantageous as it is today. If high self-esteem correlates with comfort in managing change and in letting go of yesterday's attachments, then high self-esteem confers a competitive edge. (Branden, 1994)

Intellectual Capital

In today's world, intellectual capital is the source of all wealth; even the Pope recognized this fact, in an encyclical. When the source of wealth shifts from matter to mind, then the mind becomes more important. And if the mind is important, then self-esteem is critical and will have a substantial impact on what price you can command in the marketplace. When entertainment moguls Steven Spielberg, David Geffen, and Jeffrey Katzenberg formed DreamWorks SKG, they were willing to sell a one-third third stake in their brand new company for $900 million. It doesn't take a CPA to calculate that these three valued their new venture at $2.7 billion. That's not bad for a start-up with rented offices, copy machine leases, and virtually no tangible capital. Do you think they used cost-plus accounting in setting their value?

CPAs often voice objections to value pricing such as, "It will not work in my market; it is too competitive." Or, "I practice in a small town, and my customers talk with one another. I can't engage in price discrimination without losing their trust and confidence in me." These objections, and others, are known as the *fallacy of the exception.* Even after presenting empirical evidence that practically all businesses price discriminate, some CPAs remain unconvinced that it would work for them. Yet when Vidal Sassoon entered the business in the United States, he charged $50 for a haircut. My father's union buddies, the competition, were of the opinion that *nobody* would pay that much for a haircut. They couldn't have been more wrong. The argument of two customers talking with one another about a firm's price carries more weight, but not much more. This is really the exception, not the rule, even in a small town. And if you do not have the imagination and creativity to justify different prices, then you probably do not have what it takes to price discriminate in the first place. If you are truly concerned that two customers are completely identical, then simply charge them the same price. But do not let that type of exception tie your hands behind your back and prevent you from pursuing the opportunities inherent in price discrimination with other customers.

The notion that customers get excited over low prices is not grounded in reality, especially when it comes to professional services. Roy Williams in *The Wizard of Ads* offers this comical (but absolutely true) advice:

> "I WAS CHARGED A FAIR PRICE" is not the statement of an excited customer, yet many business owners mistakenly believe they need only convince the public that they will be treated "fairly" to win their business. Phrases like "Honest Value for Your Dollar" and "Fair and Honest Prices" tempt me to say (with no small amount of sarcasm), "Yippee Skippy, call the press."
>
> If the most your customer can say when he walks out your door is "I was treated fairly," your business is pitifully stale and you have virtually nothing to advertise. Why? Because the expectation of "fair treatment" is such

> a basic assumption in business dealings that most people take it for granted. What we really hope to find is the "delight factor." (Williams, 1998: 88)

Viewing the Success of Others

People with high self-esteem are not threatened by the success of others. On the contrary, they are truly happy for another's success and will go out of their way to learn from them. The man who is not afraid of competition doesn't have any. An example of this is Rush Limbaugh and his Excellence In Broadcasting Radio Network. For years, the political left (Rush's opposition, so to speak), has been searching for its own "Rush" who could make an impact on the airwaves similar to Rush's (more than 22 million listeners in any week tune in to him). Mario Cuomo tried it. Jerry Brown tried it. Others tried it. Each time, Rush would proclaim, "Come on in, the water is warm." He was so confident of his own abilities that he did not see these potential competitors as a serious threat. He turned out to be right. Cuomo and Brown both are off the air. CPAs should have the same attitude about American Express and others entering their markets.

One CPA who uses value pricing should not view others who do as competition. If all CPAs learned value pricing, it would raise the prices for all services across the profession. It is not a zero-sum game. Consider a customer who is used to paying a substantial premium for his accounting and tax services. If this customer moves and becomes *your* customer, will you not benefit from the high price he's used to paying (assuming you provide the same total quality service)?

Summary and Conclusions

Customers prefer to associate with successful professionals. Customers want their professionals to be successful because *they* want to be successful. Do not feel guilty or ashamed of your success. Do not be afraid to show opulence in front of your customers. Harry Beckwith tells a wonderful story about Picasso in his book *Selling the Invisible*:

> A woman was strolling along a street in Paris when she spotted Picasso sketching at a sidewalk café. Not so thrilled that she could not be slightly presumptuous, the woman asked Picasso if he might sketch her, and charge accordingly.
>
> Picasso obliged. In just minutes, there she was: an original Picasso.
>
> "And what do I owe you?" she asked.
>
> "Five thousand francs," he answered.
>
> "But it only took you three minutes," she politely reminded him.
>
> "No," Picasso said. "It took me all my life."
>
> (Beckwith, 1997: 137–138)

Charge by the years, not by the hour.

18 ANTITRUST LAW

Monopoly has become as popular a subject in economics as sin has been in religion. There is a characteristic difference: Economists are paid better to attack monopoly that the clergy are to wrestle with sin. It is to be observed than the economists who defend monopoly in antitrust cases are better paid than the government's economists: Do sinners always earn more than the virtuous who combat them? Probably yes; one must be compensated for bearing the opprobrium of sinning.

—George J. Stigler, *Memoirs of an Unregulated Economist*

After the Civil War, and with the development of better transportation systems that integrated a host of local markets into a national market, business corporations grew to unprecedented size in order to take advantage of economies of scale. As this process unfolded, many small and undercapitalized businesses went bankrupt or were purchased by larger concerns, and the term "Robber Baron" gained currency. The public was suspicious of this concentration of economic power, and politicians responded in 1890 by passing the first antitrust law, The Sherman Antitrust Act. The act was thought the perfect remedy to stop any business from monopolizing its market and to restore efficient competition to the economy.

Over the years, antitrust policy has evolved through further legislative acts and amendments, regulatory guidelines and judicial interpretation. Antitrust laws have implications for various pricing decisions. As professionals consult with customers on pricing, they need to be aware of the major antitrust laws and acts that proscribe certain pricing tactics. Although services are not subject to certain provisions of these laws—for instance, price discrimination—many other business are affected, and the laws need to be taken into account when formulating pricing strategy.

This chapter is not intended to be a comprehensive examination of the legal and strategic ramifications of antitrust law, but rather to serve as an introduction to the cornerstones of antitrust policy: The Sherman Antitrust Act of 1890; the Federal Trade Commission Act (FTC Act) of 1914; the

Clayton Act of 1914; and the Robinson–Patman Act of 1936. Discussion here covers the justifications for the aforementioned acts and the criticisms leveled against them in recent years.

The Sherman Antitrust Act of 1890

Section I

Every contract, combination in the form of trust or otherwise, or conspiracy, in restraint of trade or commerce among the several States, or with foreign nations, is hereby declared to be illegal.

Section II

Every person who shall monopolize, or attempt to monopolize, or combine or conspire with any other person or persons, to monopolize any part of the trade or commerce among the several States, or with foreign nations, shall be deemed guilty.

The first legal action involving the Sherman Antitrust Act to reach the Supreme Court was the E.C. Knight case, decided in 1895. For the Justice Department, the case turned out to be a mild disaster. While the court admitted that the acquisition of the E.C. Knight Company and three other independent sugar refineries owned by the American Sugar Refining Company did tend to create a monopoly in sugar manufacturing, it held that the "sugar trust" was not in violation of the Sherman Act.

In 1904, the federal government won its first case, in *United States v. Northern Securities*, preventing a merger allegedly designed to reduce price competition between two railroads. Energized by its victory in this case, the Justice Department initiated a number of legal actions against large corporate holdings, none of which were as important as the one filed in a St. Louis federal court on November 15, 1906, against the Standard Oil Company of New Jersey.

The modern petroleum industry began in 1846 when Dr. Abraham Gesner, a Canadian geologist, discovered that oil could be distilled from coal, and kerosene could be drawn off and used as an illuminant. By 1880,

John D. Rockefeller was the king of the industry, with his Standard Oil Company holding the dominant market share. How did he achieve such a dominant market position? "Between 1870 and 1885, the price of refined kerosene dropped from 26 cents to 8 cents per gallon. In the same period, the Standard Oil Company reduced average costs per gallon from almost 3 cents in 1870 to 0.452 cents in 1885." (Armentano, 1990: 60)

Legend has it that this was predatory pricing: the act of deliberately underselling competitors in certain markets in order to drive them out of business. Once they are gone, the monopolist raises the price in the absence of competition. History books have immortalized this view of Standard Oil, and predatory pricing has been a major concern of government antitrust lawyers, politicians, and the general public then and now. However, like most conventional wisdom, this theory is more conventional than wisdom, as explained by Dominick T. Armentano in his indictment of antitrust laws, *Antitrust and Monopoly: Anatomy of a Policy Failure*:

> Unfortunately for lovers of legends, this one has been laid theoretically and empirically prostrate. In a now classic article, John S. McGee theorized that Standard Oil did not employ predatory practices because it would have been economically foolish to have done so. In the first place, McGee argued, such practices are very costly for the large firm; it always stands relatively more to lose since it, by definition, does the most business. Second, the uncertainty of the length of the forthcoming battle, and thus its indeterminate expense, must surely make firms wary of initiating a price war. Third, competitors can simply close down and wait for the price to return to profitable levels; or new owners might purchase bankrupt facilities and ready them to compete with the predator. Fourth, such wars inevitably spread to surrounding markets, endangering the predator's profits in his "safe" areas. And last, predatory practices already assume a "war chest" of monopoly profits to see the firm through the costly battles; firms apparently cannot initiate predatory practices unless they already possess monopoly power. But if this is true, firms cannot gain initial monopoly positions through predatory practices.

> Thus. . . Standard's position in oil refining grew rapidly because of the natural decline of small competitors; the increasing capital and innovation requirements of large-scale oil technology; the economic advantages achieved through intelligent entrepreneurship; the ownership of tank cars and pipelines; vertical integration into barrels, cans, glues, exporting; and the consequent lower transportation costs provided by the railroads. It did not grow from any general reliance on alleged predatory practices. (Armentano, 1990: 63–64)

Even though the government won its case against Standard Oil, and tobacco trusts, supporters of antitrust were still not satisfied with the narrow interpretations by the court, and Congress began work on two additional legislative initiatives designed to prevent further anticompetitive business practices.

The Federal Trade Commission Act (FTC Act) of 1914

The Federal Trade Commission was established in order to enforce the provisions of the Sherman Antitrust Act in a more rapid manner than could be achieved by judicial law. Section 5 of the FTC Act reads: "The Commission is hereby empowered and directed to prevent persons, partnerships, or corporations . . . from using unfair methods of competition in commerce." The FTC could ban a business practice merely because of the suspicion that it promoted unfair competition, without the permission of a court.

Also, the FTC has the authority to subject pricing practices to administrative review, not in order to punish past wrongdoing, but to make new law. The FTC is empowered to order a business to cease and desist from any practice it deems unfair, even if that practice would not necessarily be deemed unfair or anticompetitive in a court of law.

The Clayton Act of 1914

The Clayton Act was passed to correct defects and omissions of the Sherman Act. Specifically, it prohibits anticompetitive mergers, tying arrangements, exclusive dealing agreements, interlocking directorates, and the acquisition of stock in competitor companies. Also, Section 2(a), as amended by the Robinson–Patman Act, prohibits predatory price discrimination:

> That is shall be unlawful for any person engaged in commerce, in the course of such commerce, either directly or indirectly, to discriminate in price between different purchasers of commodities of like grade and quality, where either or any of the purchases involved in such discrimination are in commerce, where such commodities are sold for use, consumption, or resale within the United States or any Territory thereof or the District of Columbia or any insular possession or other place under the jurisdiction of the United States, and where the effect of such discrimination may be substantially to lessen competition or tend to create a monopoly in any line of commerce, or to injure, destroy, or prevent competition with any person who either grants or knowingly receives the benefit of such discrimination, or with customers of either of them: *Provided*, That nothing herein contained shall prevent differentials which make only due allowance for differences in the cost of manufacture, sale, or delivery resulting from the differing methods or quantities in which such commodities are to such purchasers sold or delivered: *Provided*, however, That the Federal Trade Commission may, after due investigation and hearing to all interested parties, fix and establish quantity limits, and revise the same as it finds necessary, as to particular commodities or classes of commodities, where it finds that available purchasers in greater quantities are so few as to render differentials on account thereof unjustly discriminatory or promotive of monopoly in any line of commerce; and the foregoing shall then not be construed to permit differentials based on differences in quantities greater than those so fixed and established: *And provided further*, That nothing herein contained shall prevent persons engaged in selling goods, wares, or merchandise in commerce from selecting their own customers in bona fide transactions and not in restraint of trade: *And provided further*, That nothing herein contained shall prevent price changes from time to time where in response to

> changing conditions affecting the market for or the marketability of the goods concerned, such as but not limited to actual or imminent deterioration of perishable goods, obsolescence of seasonal goods, distress sales under court process, or sales in good faith in discontinuance of business in the goods concerned. (Armentano, 1990: 281–282)

The Robinson-Patman Act of 1936

After the passage of the Clayton Act in 1914, chain stores grew rapidly and increased their buying power, and this type of price discrimination was thought to threaten the survival of independent wholesalers and retailers. Therefore, in 1936, Congress passed the Robinson–Patman Act in order to strengthen the Clayton Act. This was in the middle of the New Deal and protecting small businesses was viewed as a legitimate goal of antitrust policy. During the Great Depression, government policymakers were averse to price competition, believing it to be a major cause of the economic stagnation during the 1930s. Small business interest groups, in fact, were the impetus behind the passage of the Act, which was actually drafted by the U.S. Wholesale Grocers' Association. The Act contained the following major provisions:

> Deleted the exemption, which existed in the original Clayton Act, that allowed firms to price discriminate among buyers who purchased different quantities of a good.
>
> Forbade price rebates to selected buyers in the form of fees for brokerage, handling, processing, or any other services when those same fees were not offered to all buyers equally.
>
> Made it illegal for buyers (that is, the large chains) to solicit lower prices from manufacturers if those prices would be discriminatory under the amended Clayton Act. (Nagle and Holden, 1995: 365)

The foregoing acts are the major foundation of antitrust policy today. They have been amended many times by later legislative acts and special exemptions have been granted to interest groups, such as labor unions, insurance companies, and farm cooperatives.

Price Discrimination as Prohibited by the Acts

Since so much of this book has dealt with price discrimination, it is worth exploring the judicial interpretations of this ubiquitous practice and to ensure, if you are advising a customer on pricing strategy, that you don't run afoul of these laws.

The term *commodities of like grade and quality*, as used in the Clayton Act, has been interpreted narrowly by the courts to mean tangible goods; the Act does not apply to discrimination in services. Price discrimination among final consumers is prohibited under the Civil Rights Act if the basis for such discrimination is the race, religion, or sex of the purchaser. Further, any tangible difference in the materials, workmanship, or design is recognized as a difference in grade or quality, and thus a manufacturer can sell a deluxe model (think of Buick vs. Cadillac), or a customized model, at a premium price that more than reflects the cost of production, without violating the law.

One of the landmark legal cases in the price discrimination area is *The Borden Company v. Federal Trade Commission,* 339 F. 2d 133. In April of 1958 the Federal Trade Commission issued a complaint against the Borden Company, accusing it of selling goods of like grade and quality to different buyers at different prices with the effect of reducing competition. The goods in question were Borden's private label evaporated milk and "identical" milk that it made and sold under private label. The price difference between the two milks was substantial, and the FTC charged that this difference violated the Robinson–Patman Act. On November 28, 1962, the FTC ordered the Borden company to cease price discriminating on goods of like grade and quality sold to different buyers at different prices.

On December 4, 1964, a Circuit Court of Appeals dismissed the FTC's cease-and-desist order against Borden. As Armentano documents in *Antitrust and Monopoly*:

> Circuit Judge Joseph C. Hutcheson, Jr., reviewing the undisputed facts in the case, argued that the first issue was "whether or not the Commission applied the correct legal test in deciding that the commodities sold at different prices were of like grade and quality."
>
> Judge Hutcheson indicated that the record clearly showed that Borden's own brand of evaporated milk did command a

premium price in the market, and that the Borden product was recognized as a premium product by both consumers and dealers who sold evaporated milk. To support these conclusions, the court quoted testimony of grocers that had stated that consumers asked for the Borden brand by name, and could not be convinced to accept some other brand. Significant price differentials had to exist, apparently, before dealers would even stock and sell other brands. That dealers continued to purchase both products and the different prices indicated, to the court, that one was a "premium line" and one was not.

But was the "demonstrated consumer preference" for the Borden brand to receive legal recognition? The Circuit Court thought it should. Contrary to what the FTC declared, there was no clear Congressional intent on the matter of "private brands" and price discrimination. In fact, if the intent of the Robinson-Patman and the rest of the antitrust statutes generally was to avoid price rigidity and price uniformity, then "commercial factors" had to be considered in pricing . . .

[Armentano then quotes from the Court's opinion:]

An established brand name may have a large following among purchasers. This fact can be of great economic significance in a competitive market. We do not believe it was the intention of Congress that such clearly demonstrable consumer preference should simply be ignored in determining when products may be priced differently. As a practical matter, such preferences may be far more significant in determining the market value of a product than are its physical characteristics. (Armentano, 1990: 189)

The Court ruled in favor of Borden and set aside the FTC order. Subsequently, the Supreme Court reversed the Circuit Court of Appeals decision on the issue of "like grade and quality," and remanded the Borden case back to the Appeals Court. Also, the Supreme Court hypothesized that if a manufacturer sold its branded, higher priced milk to a retailer, but refused to sell the private-label brand to him:

> the retailer who was permitted to buy and sell only the more expensive brand would have no chance to see to those who always buy the cheaper product or to convince others, by experience or otherwise, of the fact which he and all other dealers already know—that the cheaper product is actually identical with that carrying the more expensive label. (Armentano, 1990: 190)

Justice Stewart and Harland dissented from the majority, and Stewart wrote, rather disgustedly:

> In the guise of protecting producers and purchasers from discriminatory price competition, the Court ignores legitimate market preferences and endows the Federal Trade Commission with authority to disrupt price relationships between products whose identity has been measured in the laboratory but rejected in the marketplace. I do not believe that such power was conferred upon the Commission by Congress. (Armentano, 1990: 191)

The Circuit Court again considered, and again dismissed, the FTC cease-and-desist order, ruling that "the record does not contain substantial injury to competition at the seller's level." Recall the discussion in Chapter 5 about the price difference between Lancôme and L'Oréal cosmetics. The brand is far more important to customers than the actual ingredients of the makeup, and thus a higher price is charged for Lancôme than for L'Oréal.

Another key phrase in the Clayton Act quoted above is *in commerce*, which has been interpreted to mean an injured party has to be a business whose ability to compete has been hampered by a discriminatory price. Consumers can always be charged different prices because they are not using the products in commerce. A wholesaler, however, may be found in violation for charging different retailers different prices because the retailers are engaged in commerce.

The term *substantially to lessen competition* has two interpretations:

> Price discrimination will be found to violate the law if it harms competition at either of two levels. *Primary-level*

> competition is between the firm that price discriminates and its own competitors. *Secondary-level* competition is between two firms that are customers of the firm that price discriminates (or are customers of a middleman who is, in turn, a customer of the price discriminating firm). The courts do not want to discourage price-cutting at the primary level, even when it is discriminatory, unless competition is clearly harmed. (Nagle and Holden, 1995: 376)

There are three specific affirmative legal defenses a company can invoke to protect itself from prosecution for illegal price discrimination: (1) meeting competition, (2) changing market conditions, (3) cost justification.

Criticisms of Antitrust Policy

Antitrust policy has come under intense scrutiny in recent decades, especially by the economics profession. As the Nobel Prize–winning economist Gary S. Becker points out in his book, *The Economics of Life*:

> During the 1980s both the government and private antitrust cases have declined dramatically, while malpractice, product liability, and other business litigation has boomed. Specialists in antitrust law have shifted to other business areas as the once-prosperous antitrust field has fallen on difficult times.
>
> The immediate cause of the decline has been the growing influence of economic analysis of competition and business practices on the thinking of judges and government officials. That analysis shows that competition usually promotes efficiency and the well-being of consumers and that anticompetitive behavior arises mainly from unwise public policies and a natural tendency for rival producers to collude on prices and production.
>
> Conspiracies in restraint of trade tend to break down eventually without an active antitrust policy. Companies that are part of a conspiracy cheat on their output quotas, and high

> prices attract new companies into their industry. The experience of OPEC illustrates the spontaneous breakdown of an open conspiracy outside antitrust laws. However, antitrust policy can certainly discourage business conspiracies by imposing large fines and other punishments.
>
> Competition will weed out inefficient behavior without government intervention. Antitrust action should only challenge behavior that obviously encourages collusion, such as agreements among rival producers to divide a market into exclusive territories.
>
> Since domestic producers try to use their political clout to reduce foreign competition through tariffs or import quotas, an open trade policy is as valuable as antitrust laws in the fight against collusion and anticompetitive behavior. (Becker and Becker, 1997: 162–63)

Another Nobel Prize–winning economist, George J. Stigler, began his career as a proponent of vigorous antitrust laws and enforcement. After studying the issue most of his professional life, however, he came to doubt the efficacy of antitrust policy. Here is how he summed up his opposition to the Robinson–Patman Act in 1969, before the Subcommittee on Small Business and the Robinson–Patman Act of the House Select Committee on Small Business:

> The Robinson–Patman Act is opposed by virtually all economists. I hope the Subcommittee will reflect upon the fact that if all the prominent economists in favor of the Robinson–Patman Act were put in a Volkswagen, there would still be room for a portly chauffeur. (Stigler, 1985: 127–28)

Perhaps the best indictment of antitrust policy is Dominick T. Armentano's *Antitrust and Monopoly*. His work is a major exploration of the economic theories underlying antitrust law, and how those theories are flawed, as well as the major court cases and regulatory actions in the antitrust area. He concludes that both "antitrust theory and history are an elaborate mythology with no solid foundation in either logic or fact." Here is a partial summary of his more scathing conclusions:

In many of the classic antitrust cases, both public and private, the indicted defendant firms had lowered their prices, expanded their outputs, engaged in rapid technological change, and generally behaved in ways consistent with an efficient and rivalrous market process. Indeed, it was precisely this rivalrous behavior that may have precipitated the antitrust legal action. There is now wider recognition among antitrust specialists that competition is a process—not an equilibrium condition—and that antitrust (especially in the private cases) has been employed often as a legal club to thwart competitive behavior and protect existing market structure.

Government, and not the market, is the source of monopoly power. Government licensing, certificates of public convenience, franchises, tariffs, and other legally restrictive devices can and do create monopoly, and monopoly power, for specific business organizations protected from open competition. Thus, ironically or intentionally, the bulk of the abusive monopoly in the business system has always been beyond the scope of antitrust law and antitrust policy.

Various scholars have demonstrated that these particular "antitrust" statutes were often supported and employed by established business interests in an attempt to restrain and restrict the competitive process. Unable to compete effectively with more efficient business organizations, certain special interests sought political and legislative restrictions in an attempt to secure or enhance existing market positions.

In many and important and embarrassing ways, the Borden controversy is a fitting climax—a climax of absurdity—with respect to price discrimination under the antitrust laws. It is the theoretical dead-end to which a mechanistic, demand-ignoring, "costs (should) determine prices" theorem can be pushed. The products under discussion were clearly distinguished in the mind, and in the market behavior of the consumers; the products did not really compete directly with each other; the products had different brand names, sold in different ways and at different prices, to different buyers. Yet they were declared by an "expert" regulatory commission and by the highest court in the land to be "equal" and of like grade and quality. Declaring it, apparently, would make it so.

What was the Borden Company to do under the circumstances? Were they to adulterate the production of private-brand evaporated milk in order to make it chemically "unequal"? Or were they to raise the price of the private-label milk to the Borden brand "equivalent"? The latter proposal would surely end the alleged "discrimination," although it could bring a huge loss in the sales to Borden on their private-label accounts. Of course they could lower the price of the Borden brand to the private label rates; but this action could bring the Justice Department down upon Borden for attempting to eliminate competition from the market. One would also have to assume, since Borden had not voluntarily adopted this policy, that such a reduction in price would lower, rather than increase, Borden's profits. In summation, therefore, Borden was illegally discriminating in price, and no change in its prices could have, it appears, been wholly consistent with the antitrust laws. Any change Borden might have made, other than giving up its private-label business altogether (a refusal to deal?), might have tended to "injure" someone in violation of the law. (Armentano, 1990: 2, 3, 6, 191–192)

The Case against Microsoft

In 2000, a federal judge found Microsoft Corporation to be in violation of the antitrust laws. In 1990 the Federal Trade Commission investigated the company's software licensing practices and decided to close the case in 1992 without filing any charges. In 1998, under pressure from Microsoft's competitors, Senator Howard Metzenbaum (Democrat, Ohio), and Senator Orrin Hatch (Republican, Utah), the Department of Justice, and twenty state attorneys filed an antitrust suit against the company. It is interesting to note that 90 percent of all antitrust litigation is brought by private parties, usually competitors of the alleged monopolist. (Armentano, 1999: xi) This case is unprecedented in American history, in terms of attacking a successful and innovative private company without any evidence of harm to the consumer (or high prices, for that matter, as prices in the computer industry have been falling rapidly for the past two decades). In addition, in an industry that operates in dog years (i.e., one year is like seven), the ultimate decision will be obsolete by the time the ink dries. Obviously, nothing was learned from the decade-long IBM antitrust suit, which wasted millions of dollars with no measurable benefits to the company or the consumer.

The offense is serious. Any time the government interferes with the pricing mechanism of the free market, unintended consequences are sure to follow (discussed further in the next chapter). It needs to be emphasized that "monopoly" isn't illegal under the Sherman Act; "monopolization" is. In many economists' opinion, monopolization was never proved against Microsoft. The case against the company was premised on the assumption that Microsoft was expanding its monopoly in operating systems to the Internet browser market. This is an interesting claim, since Microsoft gave away its browser for free, and Netscape reportedly distributed more than 100 million copies of its browser, Navigator, during 1998. (*The Wall Street Journal*, November 6, 1998, p. A3) In fact, as in most antitrust cases, the Department of Justice actually sought a preliminary injunction to require that Microsoft offer Netscape's browser with Windows or, alternately, sell its browser separately. (*The Wall Street Journal*, May 19, 1998, p. A3) It is an interesting question how selling a product once given away for free benefits consumers; but this is precisely the result in the majority of antitrust cases brought by the government—that is, the end result is usually a price increase to the consumer. Moreover, the Justice Department itself is a major purchaser of Windows, because they claim it was the best deal for the taxpayers. Most economists believe that an independent determination of a "competitive price" in a free market is impossible. Free markets contain only free-market prices, as the late economist Murray N. Rothbard (1926–1995) argued.

It was further alleged that Microsoft's agreements with Internet service providers were restrictive of competitors. This is stating the obvious: All business contracts are restrictive, limiting options and excluding options to both parties to the agreement. Had Microsoft restricted the licensing of its operating system to a few select businesses, it could have been accused of monopolizing in restraint of trade.

Dominick T. Armentano provides the crucial critique of the inherent contradictions of antitrust laws:

> The enforcement of the antitrust laws is predicated on the mistaken assumption that regulators and the courts can have access to information concerning social benefits, social costs, and efficiency that is simply unavailable in the absence of a spontaneous market process. Antitrust regulation is often a subtle form of industrial planning and is fully subject to the "pretense-of-knowledge" criticism frequently advanced against government planning. (Armentano, 1999: 19)
>
> The problem with these "calculations" is that they cannot actually be made; because individual costs and benefits are ultimately subjective and personal, they cannot simply be added up or subtracted to determine net social efficiency or welfare.
>
> A metaphor can illustrate the inherent difficulties of aggregating personal costs and benefits. Assume a temperature of 70 degrees in a room. It is apparent that different people in that room can feel either warm or cold; the 70-degree figure does not actually measure how cold or warm individuals feel but only the level of mercury on an objective scale. The subjective states of warm and cold are not themselves directly knowable or measurable by others, and they are not susceptible to addition, subtraction, comparison, aggregation, or any other mathematical manipulation. Temperature readings can be averaged, but feelings of comfort or discomfort on the part of different individuals cannot be manipulated mathematically. Neither can their individual costs and benefits. (Armentano, 1999: 102–103)

In studying the history of antitrust cases and policy, one is left with the conclusion that almost any type of pricing behavior by a company is in violation of the law. If a company raises its prices above its competitors, it must be a monopoly. If a company lowers its prices below that of its competitors, it is obviously engaging in predatory behavior. If a company maintains its prices for any period of time, it must be colluding with its competitors to fix prices.

Summary and Conclusions

Antitrust has a rich and fascinating history, rooted firmly in economic theory, as well as emotional appeal among the public, politicians, and the media. The so-called Robber Barons have an infamous reputation among American culture, even though many would argue that it is a misapplied name for entrepreneurs who brought needed goods and services—at constantly lower prices—to the masses.

In any event, professionals need to be cognizant of the law and its implications for devising pricing strategies and tactics. And although the laws don't apply to services, if your customer is in manufacturing, or deals with distributors, then appropriate legal advice needs to be obtained to ensure that you are complying with all applicable federal and state antitrust laws.

19 ADVANCED PRICE THEORY

Pricing is the moment of truth—all of marketing comes to focus in the pricing decision.

Raymond Corey, *Industrial Marketing: Cases and Concepts*, 1962

This chapter provides additional theories and concepts regarding advanced price theory that can be used not only in the pricing of professional services, but also when professionals consult with their customers on pricing strategies and tactics. Although the information in this chapter is not necessary in order to implement value pricing inside your professional firm, if you are interested in price theory, the material will help you advance to the next level. The concepts presented here are broad and apply to a wide range of pricing scenarios beyond those encountered in a professional service firm.

The Three Functions of Price

Before the microeconomic ramifications of price are explored, it is essential to understand the macroeconomic function that prices perform. In any economy—from a planned, centralized structure, to a free market—prices perform three critical functions:

1. Prices transmit information;
2. Prices provide an incentive to adopt methods of production that are least costly and therefore use available resources for the most highly valued purposes; and
3. Prices determine who gets how much of the product—the distribution of income.

(Friedman and Friedman, 1990: 14)

Prices are a form of economic speech, and as such should be protected with the same force and vigor offered by the First Amendment in its protection of the freedom of political and religious speech. Milton and Rose Friedman proposed such a constitutional amendment, in their book, *Free to Choose*: "Congress shall make no laws abridging the freedom of sellers of goods or labor to price their products or services." (Friedman and Friedman, 1990: 305)

When a government tries to suppress the freedom of prices to perform their functions, disaster usually develops. Whether it is the inability of the former communist countries to feed themselves (through the forced collectivization of agriculture) or wage and price controls (leading to chronic shortages of goods and services), trying to control prices by any mechanism other than the voluntary transactions between consenting adults is an abject failure. Corruption, black markets, violence, and endemic crime are usually the results of suppressing economic freedom.

There is little understanding, even among professionals, of the role that prices play in any economy, be it communist or capitalist. The major theme running through this book is that ultimately it is the consumer who determines the value of anything in this world. In *Planned Chaos*, the great economist Ludwig von Mises writes

> In the market economy the consumers are supreme. Their buying and their abstention from buying ultimately determine what the entrepreneurs produce and in what quantity and quality. It determines directly the prices of the consumer's goods and indirectly the prices of all producers' goods, e.g., labor and material factors of production. It determines the emergence of profits and losses and the formation of the rate of interest. It determines every individual's income. The focal point of the market economy is the market, i.e., the process of the formation of commodity prices, wage rates, and interest rates and their derivatives, profits, and losses. It makes all men in their capacity as producers responsible to the consumers. This dependence is direct with entrepreneurs, capitalists, farmers and professional men, and indirect with people working for salaries and wages. The market adjusts the efforts of all those engaged in supplying the needs of the consumers to the wishes of those for whom they produce, the consumers. It subjects production to consumption.
>
> It is the consumers who make poor people rich and rich people poor. It is the consumers who fix the wages of a movie

> star and an opera singer at a higher level than those of a welder or an accountant. (Mises, 1947: 25–26)

To the often-made charge that a free market ends in complete chaos, with no central direction or unifying goals, Mises directs this stinging missive:

> No "automatic" and "anonymous" force actuates the "mechanism" of the market. The only factors directing the market and determining prices are purposive acts of men. There is no automatism; there are men consciously aiming at ends chosen and deliberately resorting to definite means for the attainment of these ends. There are no mysterious mechanical forces; there is only the will of every individual to satisfy his demand for various goods. There is no anonymity; there are you and I and Bill and Joe and all the rest. And each of us is engaged both in production and consumption. Each contributes his share to the determination of prices.
>
> The dilemma is not between automatic forces and planned action. It is between the democratic process of the market in which every individual has his share and the exclusive rule of a dictatorial body. Whatever people do in the market economy, is the execution of their own plans. In this sense every human action means planning. What those calling themselves planners advocate is not the substitution of planned action for letting things go. It is the substitution of the planner's own plan for the plan of his fellowmen. The planner is a potential dictator who wants to deprive all other people of the power to plan and act according to their own plans. He aims at one thing only: the exclusive absolute preeminence of his own plan.
>
> There is no such thing as an "excessive" advocacy of economic freedom. Men must choose between the market economy and socialism. The state can preserve the market economy in protecting life, health and private property against violent or fraudulent aggression; or it can itself control the conduct of all production activities. Some agency must determine what should be produced. If it is not the consumers

> by means of demand and supply on the market, it must be the government by compulsion. (Mises, 1947: 29, 34)

It is hard to argue with Mises' logic, especially given the abject failure of planned economies throughout the world. Using this background of the macroeconomic importance of price, the discussion can move on to the microeconomics of pricing and how this integrates with the marketing function in business firms.

Pricing and Marketing

Pricing is an art. But art is not above scientific analysis or critical judgment. No matter how creative and beautiful an engineer designs a bridge, it still must be structurally sound. And while economic theory, especially "price theory," has great insight into the role prices play in an economy, it doesn't offer much guidance on how those prices are set, at the margin, in the day-to-day running of a business enterprise.

Pricing is also a multidisciplinary and multifunctional subject, with conflicts between economists, accountants, financial management, marketing management, legal advisors, and government regulators. Pricing is seldom taught, in any great detail or systematic way, in the business schools, even among MBA and graduate students. Surveys conducted in the 1950s indicated that prices were set rather mechanistically, based upon cost-plus methods or simply imitating competitors.

With the arrival of a global economy, by the 1980s, this attitude began to change. "A 1984 survey revealed that top marketing executives considered pricing the most critical issue with which they had to contend." (Nagle and Holden, 1995: 14) In today's business environment, all but the most naïve companies set their prices based on cost-plus formulas, or the me-too pricing of their competitors. If the business world has paid little attention to pricing, then professionals have been downright negligent in heeding this all-important marketing function.

Cost-Plus Pricing's Epitaph

In the past, cost-plus pricing was the most popular way to set prices. The method appears to have achieved this status because it is financially prudent and is seen to be "fair." You mark up your costs by a reasonable return and you achieve a reasonable profit. This is simple, in theory, but in practice it is a prescription for mediocre financial results. As Thomas Nagle and Reed Holden point out in their excellent book *The Strategy and Tactics of Pricing*:

> The problem with cost-driven pricing is fundamental. In most industries it is impossible to determine a product's unit cost before determining its price. Why? Because unit costs change with volume. This cost change occurs because a significant portion of costs are "fixed" and must somehow be "allocated" to determine the full unit cost. Unfortunately, since these allocations depend on volume, which changes with changes in price, unit cost is a moving target. (Nagle and Holden, 1995: 3)

If one follows the internal logic of cost-plus pricing versus value pricing, it would look like this (adapted from Nagle and Holden, 1995: 5).

Cost-Plus Pricing

Product ➔ Cost ➔ Price ➔ Value ➔ Customers

Value Pricing

Customers ➔ Value ➔ Price ➔ Cost ➔ Product

Notice how value pricing completely reverses the order of the strategic decisions necessary in offering products and services to the marketplace. The traditional cost-plus theory (and the theory that guides most professional firm's pricing policies) starts with a product and asks, "How much does it cost us to produce this product?" The answer dictates the price, which, it is hoped, is less than the perceived value to the ultimate customer. Alternatively, value pricing turns this process inside out, asking "How much does the customer value this offering?" Only then is the price determined, and that price also dictates the costs that will be incurred in producing the final product. The target price is not an estimate of internal costs to the firm but an external value to the customer. As Nagle and Holden point out:

> Strategic pricers do not ask, "What prices do we need to cover our costs and earn a profit?" Rather, they ask, "What costs can we afford to incur, given the prices achievable in the market, and still earn a profit?" Strategic pricers do not ask, "What price is this customer willing to pay?" but "What is our product worth to this customer and how can we better communicate that value, thus justifying the price?" When value doesn't justify price to some customers, strategic pricers don't surreptitiously discount. Instead, they consider how they can segment the market with different products or distribution channels to serve these customers without undermining the perceived value to other customers. And strategic pricers never ask, "What prices do we need to meet our sales or market-share objectives?" Instead, they ask, "What level of sales or market share can we most profitably achieve?" (Nagle and Holden, 1995: 2)

This is precisely how Lee Iacocca derived his success with the Ford Mustang in 1964. Iacocca didn't start with a group of costs in order to compete against the successful General Motors Corvette; he began, instead, by learning about what the customers wanted, and how much they would be willing to pay for it. This response determined what the car would have to sell for, which in turn dictated the amount of internal costs that could be justified to produce it. In April 1964, Ford introduced the Mustang at a base price of $2,368 and more were sold in the first year than any other car Ford had ever built, with net profits after the first two years of $1.1 billion, in 1964 dollars, "which was far more than any of Ford's competitors made selling their 'good' sports cars, priced to cover costs and achieve a target rate of return." (Nagle and Holden, 1995: 6–7)

This is not to say that internal costs are unimportant or irrelevant to the pricing decision. But the effective pricer will invest only in those costs that can be recouped through the value offered in the market, not the other way around. Costs do not dictate quantities produced, but rather the price acceptable to the market will dictate which markets can be adequately served, and what quantities they demand. When the cost of jet fuel rises, airlines are not naïve enough to try to pass on the entire cost increase to their customers while at the same time maintaining their existing flight schedules. Instead they do something such as reduce or eliminate discount fares or reduce the number of flights.

More significantly, not all costs are relevant for every pricing decision. One of the disservices that cost accountants foisted upon service industries was the idea of fixed versus variable costs. Because costs need to be fully allocated over a given quantity of units, this procedure of determining fixed and variable costs often results in a completely arbitrary allocation. One of the concepts that activity-based costing, and marketing managers, use is that of the avoidable cost—that is, those costs that either have not yet been incurred or that can be reversed. The opposite of avoidable costs are sunk costs (costs that are irreversible). Only avoidable costs are relevant for pricing decisions.

Avoidable costs deal mostly with the future costs, not the historical costs, of making a sale. In 2004, gas prices in various parts of the United States jumped to more than $2 per gallon, causing much public outcry and consternation, not to mention political posturing among politicians. If you were to inquire of people how much it costs an oil company to sell a gallon of gas, they would most likely respond with the cost of the oil, plus refining it and distributing it to the stations. But oil company executives understand that these historical costs are irrelevant and that it is the replacement cost that is important in determining the sales price. Conventional accounting ignores this reality. Even last-in, first-out (LIFO) doesn't capture the true essence of the pricing dilemma. Actually, one needs to calculate the next-in, first-out (NIFO) cost in order to determine the sales price at the pump. Since each gallon sold of the old gasoline has to be replaced with a new gallon, it is the replacement cost that is important, not the historical cost.

The other difference between basing pricing on avoidable costs rather than on traditional cost-plus methods is deciding when certain costs are to be considered. At some point—especially in the long run—every cost is incremental and therefore avoidable. The importance of this concept is that it is customers, not costs, that determine what a product or service can sell for, and this drives which costs can be profitably incurred, given the expected revenue.

The Limitations of Economic Demand Theory

In Chapter 5, the law of demand and demand elasticity was discussed. It was stated that before buyers were considered to be on the demand curve, they had to be both willing and able to purchase the product. These are not the only assumptions made in that particular model. The model also assumes rational behavior among buyers, and to the economist that means perfect information about prices, being able to process that information perfectly, prices that do not affect subjective wants or satisfaction, and perfect information about tastes and preferences.

These are big assumptions, and may not actually be realistic in the marketplace, where information is often imperfect or not readily available, though the Internet is changing this dramatically. Given this level of imperfection among buyers, perception becomes very important. If customers do not possess perfect information with respect to a product or service, they tend to resort to reference prices. This could be what they have paid in the past, the perceived average market cost, or a perceived "fair" price. This is why buyers experience sticker shock when they haven't purchased a car in four to six years, even though the price of cars may not have increased as much as food or other consumer products. It also explains why seniors react more negatively to prices; they have reference prices from an earlier time that are much lower. Usually, buyers don't have any one specific acceptable price, but rather a range of prices they might be willing to pay for an item.

This leads to an interesting phenomenon. Not only do customers refrain from buying if the price is far above their reference price, they also refrain from buying if that price is too far below their acceptable range. This latter phenomenon is not considered in the traditional law of demand. Customers' responses to prices are based on more than simple rational calculation, as assumed in traditional economic demand models. Yet most pricing experts agree that the mental behavior governing a customer's response to price is too little understood. In a purely rational sense, a difference of $400 between two products is the same no matter what the product price is. However, that same $400 is perceived to be a much larger difference for a $1,000 purchase than it is for a $20,000 purchase. In one study, 68 percent of the respondents said they were willing to drive to another store to save $5 on a calculator selling for $15; but if the same calculator costs $125, only 29 percent of the respondents were willing to do so. (Nagle and Holden, 1995: 300)

The tendency of buyers to engage in this type of calculation is known as the *Weber-Fechner Law*, which states that *buyers perceive price differences in proportional terms, not absolute terms*. This refers to the percentage change in price, and not to the absolute level, and indicates that there is an upper and lower threshold of price in the mind of each customer. If the price falls outside of that band, customers ignore the offering.

The notion of perceived value is difficult for even a customer to determine, let alone a firm trying to market to that customer. Part of the marketing department's job is to raise the price customers are willing to pay for their offering. The calculation of perceived value looks something like this:

$$\text{Perceived value} = \frac{\text{perceived benefits}}{\text{perceived price}}$$

> Perceived price = perceived total cost to the buyer: purchase price + start-up costs (acquisition costs, transportation, installation, order handling) + postpurchase costs (repairs and maintenance and risk of failure or poor performance)
>
> Perceived benefits = some combination of physical attributes, service attributes, and technical support available in relation to the particular use of the product, as well as the purchase price and other indicators of perceived quality (Monroe, 1990: 88).

All of these perceptions are relatively difficult to quantify, and this complicates the marketer's job even further. Even how the product is going to be used affects the customer's perception of its value. "In one study, it was determined that buyers were willing to pay significantly more for a pair of pants to be worn to a symphony or cocktail party than if the pants were to be worn at a football game or rock concert." (Monroe, 1990: 62) In fact, perception plays such an important role in the minds of customers, it might be deemed the fifth "P" of marketing. The topic of perceptions and psychology and their effect on pricing is covered later in this chapter.

Consumption Values

Goods and services are purchased because they satisfy certain needs and wants, either by individuals or by businesses. Both individual and business purchasers are restrained by their limited resources and therefore must make value judgments on competing offerings. These types of choices are called *consumption values*: the perceived value, or utility, an individual or business believes a specific choice will provide. The five consumption values that influence purchasers, as outlined in *Services Marketing*, are as follows:

> **Functional value** is the perceived utility acquired when a particular choice provides utilitarian or functional benefits for the customer. These benefits are based on the attributes a particular choice possesses and the benefits those attributes will provide the consumer.
>
> **Social value** is the perceived utility acquired from making a purchase decision that is associated with a particular reference group. This group could be friends, or it could be a group based on demographics such as age, sex, ethnic origin, or religion.
>
> **Emotional value** is obtained when the choice stimulates feelings and emotions within the consumer. For many services, especially entertainment-type services, perceived emotional utility is an important motivating factor in the purchase decision.
>
> **Epistemic value** is acquired when a purchase decision is perceived to satisfy a desire for knowledge, provide novelty, or arouse curiosity. This value is often the motivation behind a senior citizen going back to college or a homemaker taking a painting or art course. Most museums, historical sites, zoos, and botanical gardens are visited because of the epistemic value provided.
>
> **Conditional value** is the perceived utility provided when an alternative is chosen because of temporary situational factors that will enhance one of the other consumption values. Finances may be a temporary situational factor that would alter a purchase decision. (Kurtz and Clow, 1998: 32–34)

None of the values listed above are mutually exclusive, as a particular choice may provide more than one consumption value.

Three Generic Pricing Strategies

As discussed in the chapter on total quality service (Chapter 14), the value proposition of any firm is price, quality, and service. For some companies price is an effective way to compete. Think of Wal-Mart, Southwest Airlines, Costco, Dell Computers, or Timex watches. All of these companies have used price as an effective competitive differentiation and have relentlessly driven needless costs out of their operations. On the opposite side of the spectrum there is Nordstrom, Cadillac, Mercedes, FedEx, and Disney, all of which command premium prices because they offer premium service. In the middle are companies such as Buick and Casio watches, in which price plays a more neutral role.

Any business has to decide between three generic pricing strategies: skim pricing, penetration pricing, and neutral pricing. Selecting one of these strategies is a major marketing decision, not to be taken lightly, and must be adopted by the leaders of the organization because it transmits a definitive message to the marketplace regarding the firm's offering.

Skim Pricing

In any market, a certain segment of buyers is relatively price insensitive because they value the offering so highly. Think of early adopters in technology, who rush to purchase the latest and greatest gadgets or newest high-speed computers and printers. Skim pricing is a conscious decision to sell to this certain segment at prices above market-level, thereby earning more profit for the firm than could be made selling at a lower price to an albeit wider market. The firm isn't so much interested in market share as it is in extracting the perceived value from this smaller segment of the market. Polaroid, for example, knew that a certain group of customers valued highly the ability to see their pictures immediately (real estate agents, insurance claims adjusters, grandparents with discretionary income) and thus engaged in skim pricing for this segment of the market even though this strategy severely limited its penetration into the wider market. Apple Computer maintained the same strategy by forbidding cloning and keeping its gross profit margins from devoted Macintosh users higher than the industry average.

While many business consultants argue that market share determines profitability, this is patently false if one examines the empirical evidence in the marketplace. Sears certainly has a larger share of the retail market than does Nordstrom, but it would be nonsensical to argue that Nordstrom is not profitable or not as successful as Sears.

Penetration Pricing

Penetration pricing is when the firm decides to set the price below the product's value to the customer, thereby ensuring a larger customer base. It is the trade-off of higher sales volume vs. higher margins and can be a very effective strategy, especially for new entrants into a particular market.

Penetration prices are not necessarily cheap, but they are low relative to the perceived value. For instance, Lexus used a penetration pricing strategy in order to compete successfully with Mercedes, Audi, BMW, and Porsche in the early 1990s. The Lexus wasn't necessarily cheap, but it was less expensive than its competitors and thus was perceived to offer a higher value. MCI and Sprint used penetration pricing to great success against AT&T after the telecommunications market was deregulated.

Neutral Pricing

In effect, neutral pricing strategy minimizes the role of pricing in the marketing mix by not using price to gain or to restrict market share. A company might select this strategy when it knows its product, promotion, or distribution offers other powerful advantages to the customer. The neutral price doesn't mean a price in between that of competitors; rather it is neutral in relationship to value. Toshiba laptop computers, for example, are consistently priced above market level, but because they offer such excellent value, the market still perceives the price as neutral.

Another reason to adopt a neutral price is to maintain the coherence of a product line. General Motors, for instance, prices the Chevrolet Camaro at a level that makes it affordable to a wider market, even though there is a certain segment of that market willing to pay more for its sporty appearance and performance. Because GM already had a skimmed price product in its lineup (the Corvette), it didn't want to be redundant by offering another one.

Market Segmentation

One of the mistakes made by many companies, especially professional service firms, is their tendency to think of the "market" rather than the individuals who make up the market. As such, they develop pricing strategies based upon averages, even though this is woefully inadequate and seriously flawed and leads to extreme pricing errors. After all, there is no such thing as an "average" customer. This is why it is so important to segment a company's customers into different markets and price according to the value offered in each segment, which is called *market segmentation.*

In Chapter 5 we studied how various businesses employ market segmentation in order to capture the consumer surplus. Cosmetic companies and airlines all engage in market segmentation in order to charge different prices to different customers. Book publishers offer hardcovers and softcovers. This is an extremely important pricing tactic, especially when you are trying to serve multiple segments within a given market. Following is a list of some of the many ways to segment a market among buyers and charge different prices to different customers.

Segmenting by buyer identification Senior discounts, children's prices, college students, and coupons are all examples of ways to identify different buyers.

Segmenting by purchase location Dentists, opticians, and other professionals sometimes maintain separate offices, in different parts of the same city, or in different cities, that charge different prices based upon the economic and demographic makeup of each. With the increasing use of the Internet to make purchases, being able to segment by location will become more and more difficult.

Segmenting by time of purchase Theaters offering midday matinées, restaurants charging cheaper prices for lunch than dinner, and cellular and utility companies offering pricing based upon peak and off-peak times are all examples of segmenting by time of purchase.

Segmenting by purchase quantity Quantity discounts are usually based on volume, order size, step discounts, or two-part prices. Customers who buy in large volumes tend to be more price sensitive but less costly to service, and they have more incentive to shop for a cheaper price. Thus, they are offered volume discounts. When offering discounts to business buyers, one must be careful not to violate the antitrust laws against price discrimination, as discussed in Chapter 18.

Two-part pricing involves two separate charges to consume a single product. Amusement parks might charge an entrance fee and then price tickets extra for certain attractions. Rental car companies use a flat price plus a price per mile, health and country clubs charge both membership fees and monthly dues. Night clubs charge a cover at the door as well as for drinks and food.

Segmenting by product design Offering different versions in a product or service is a very effective way to segment a market. Premium gasoline, for instance, only costs the oil companies approximately $0.04 more per gallon to refine but sells at the pump for anywhere from $0.10 to $0.15 more.

Segmenting by product bundling Restaurants bundle food on the dinner menu as opposed to à la carte, usually at cheaper prices. Symphonies, theaters, and sports teams bundle a package of events into season tickets (See the discussion of menu pricing in Chapter 12, and how this type of bundling applies to the professional service firm.)

Segmenting by tie-ins and meterings Before the Clayton Antitrust Act of 1914, tie-in sales were common. American Can, for instance, leased its canning machines with the requirement that they be used to close only American's cans. Since the passage of the Clayton Act, the courts have refused to accept tying agreements, except for service contracts where it is essential to maintain the performance and/or the reputation of a new product. While using the tying method with a contract may be illegal, opportunities still exist to use this tactic without a contract. For example, razor blade manufacturers design unique razors that require customers to purchase their blades for refill.

Segmented pricing is among the most effective pricing tactics that a business can employ, and it also among the most difficult. It takes enormous creativity and market and customer research in order to be effective. With the increasing propensity for customers to utilize the Internet to make their purchases, market segmentation is taking on a new dynamic: While it will become easier to segment potential customers based upon their profiles and buying habits, it will also require experimentation with different pricing policies. Nevertheless, customer segmentation is a part of any effective marketing strategy, and its potential to add to profitability should never be ignored.

Search, Experience, and Credence Attributes

From a marketing perspective, products and services can be separated into three classes: search products, experience products, and credence products. Search products or services have attributes customers can readily evaluate before they purchase. A hotel room price, an airline schedule, television reception, and the quality of a home entertainment system can all be evaluated before a purchase is made. Well-informed buyers are aware of the substitutes that exist for these types of products and thus are more likely to be price sensitive than other buyers. This, in turn, induces sellers to copy the most popular features and benefits of these types of products. Price elasticity is high with respect to products with many substitutes, and since most buyers are aware of their alternatives, prices are held within a competitive band.

Experience products or services can be evaluated only after purchase. Dinner in a new restaurant, a concert or theater performance, a new movie, or a hairstyle all must first be experienced before judgment can be passed on their relative value. These types of products and services tend to be more differentiated than search products or services, and buyers tend to be less price elastic, especially for their first purchase. However, since they will form an opinion after the experience, if it is not favorable, no amount of differentiation will bring them back.

Credence products or services have attributes that buyers cannot confidently evaluate, even after one or more purchases. Thus, buyers tend to rely on the reputation of the brand name, testimonial from someone they know (or respect), service quality, and price. Credence products include healthcare; legal services; and accounting, tax, and consulting services. Credence products and services are more likely than other types to be customized, making them difficult to compare to other offerings. Because there are fewer substitutes to a customized product or service, and there is more risk in purchasing these types of products and services, price elasticity tends to be relatively low—that is, the majority of customers purchasing credence products and services are relatively price insensitive.

One of the lessons of categorizing products and services in this fashion applies to menu pricing, or bundling various offerings. In order for price bundling to be effective, at least one of the bundled offerings should be a search product because buyers of that product will tend to be more price sensitive and then can be induced to move up—in price—to the more valuable credence offerings.

Understanding Customer Risk

Any purchase entails risk. Consider this story by Anne Naujeck, of the Associated Press, that appeared May 12, 2000, "Surgical Procedures Bought Online":

> Consumers who like to surf the Internet for good deals now have the chance to shop the Web for surgical procedures—from facelifts and tummy tucks to eye operations and even heart surgery.
>
> While some doctors and patients raise ethical questions about the idea, a handful of companies are setting up shop online to let consumers compare physicians' bids for their business.
>
> Consumers can log on, enter their medical profile, and list what procedures they want. The online services match the requests with participating doctors, who submit proposals, including cost, for the patient's review.
>
> Some sites match bids only for elective surgeries. But Kenosha, Wis.-based PatientWise will accept requests for nearly 100 procedures, including major procedures such as hip replacement, heart surgery, and brain surgery, said chairman Bradley Engel.
>
> Although PatientWise's online site is up, the company won't be ready to serve customers until later this year, Engel said.
>
> Medicine Online Inc. of San Diego launched its site in March, offering 36 procedures, including breast augmentation, nose jobs, liposuction, hair replacement, dental surgeries, and laser corrective eye surgery. The company has matched 250 patients with its care providers, said CEO Kevin Moshayedi.

Dawn Buchanan shopped Medicine Online when she was contemplating cosmetic eye surgery. Buchanan, 43, of Orange County, Calif., got five bids from different surgeons, ranging from $1,500 to $3,000, to remove bags under her eyes and tighten her brows.

She had the surgery Monday and said she'd use the service again.

"It's the wave of the future," Buchanan said. "It was like shopping for a car but I didn't have to leave the house."

But another surgical patient said she wouldn't trust doctors she only knew from their computer profiles.

"I am very curious as to why a doctor would go online advertising for this kind of business," said Joanne Vaughan of Beaver Dam, who has had two wrist surgeries and two abdominal surgeries.

"Credibility plays an awfully big role," she said. "I wouldn't go through surgery and put my life in the hands of somebody I don't know or wasn't referred to me. It's too risky on my end."

Buchanan said she, too, had reservations, so she asked her own doctor for advice.

"I chose the one with the most credentials and the one who was most highly recommended by my doctor. I didn't want to end up a statistic," she said.

The medical establishment has given online doctor-patient matchmaking a cool reception.

"This seems an excessive commodification of healthcare. This is not the stock exchange. It is irresponsible for surgeons to even discuss the cost before seeing the patient," said Dr. Joseph J. Fins, director of medical ethics at New York Presbyterian Hospital-Weill Cornell Medical Center.

Dr. Donald Palmisano, a New Orleans surgeon, had a similar view.

"Healthcare is not a commodity to be traded on the Internet," he said. "Why would you trust your life to the lowest bidder?"

Medicine Online said it does not encourage patients to pick doctors solely on price.

> Engel, of PatientWise, said quality care, not cheap medicine, is the company's goal, although he said using the service can mean significant savings.
>
> "For some, the focus will be on price, but the objective is to give people side-by-side comparisons of statistics on quality," Engel said.
>
> Engel said PatientWise consumers must submit a bona fide diagnosis and treatment recommendation from a referring doctor. The company will verify all patient and doctor information.
>
> But critics questioned the diligence of such services.
>
> "A lot of people are influenced by price and these services do little to screen the patients or the providers," said Dr. Michael McGuire, president of the California Society of Plastic Surgeons, which is asking the state attorney general to investigate online medical bidding.
>
> McGuire said he joined one site as a psychiatrist and successfully bid to perform a breast implant. The site had a disclaimer saying it could not verify doctors' credentials.

The trend of offering professional services online is interesting. Some segments of an industry or profession will run to the government—all in the name, of course, of protecting the consumer, as if consumers aren't smart enough to perform due diligence and spend their own money on themselves wisely. A relevant question to ask the critics is: "Are you suggesting that doctors have to be highly compensated in order to be ethical?" The online trend is the market exerting its sovereignty, and no doubt it will be resisted by members of the professions. The buggy-whip manufacturers didn't have much affection—or use—for Henry Ford. Of course, any time that risk is present, an opportunity to socialize that risk exists. Perhaps insurance companies will start to insure online services by offering credential information, performance statistics, success and failure rates, and so on. This trend also underscores the importance of differentiating your business from the competition so as not to compete solely on price.

In light of Naujeck's article, let us discuss the elements of purchase risk. Bear in mind that services are relatively more risky than products, because there are more unknown factors involved, which in turn leads to higher loyalty to service providers. The seven types of risk, again from *Services Marketing*, are the following:

> **Performance risk** is the chance that the service provided will not perform or provide the benefit for which it was purchased.
>
> **Financial risk** is the amount of monetary loss incurred by the consumer if the service fails. Purchasing services involves a higher degree of financial risk than the purchasing of goods because fewer service firms have money-back guarantees.
>
> **Time loss risk** refers to the amount of time lost by the consumer due to the failure of the service.
>
> **Opportunity risk** refers to the risk involved when consumers must choose one service over another.
>
> **Psychological risk** is the chance that the purchase of a service will not fit the individual's self-concept. Closely related to psychological risk is **social risk**. Social risk refers to the probability that a service will not meet with approval from others who are significant to the consumer making the purchase. Services with high visibility will tend to be high in social risk. Restaurants and hair stylists are examples of service industries that are perceived to have a high level of social risk. Even for business-to-business marketing, social risk is a factor. Corporate buyers are concerned that a service they purchase will meet with approval of their superiors [thus, IBM's famous slogan: "No one ever got fired for choosing IBM"].
>
> **Physical risk** is the chance that a service will actually cause physical harm to the consumer. (Kurtz and Clow, 1998: 41–42)

It must be emphasized that the above are perceived risks, and the perception is in the mind of the customer. The actual probability of service failure is immaterial. Consider earthquake insurance; the best time to sell such policies is right after a quake strikes. Any actuary will tell you that fault lines—like dice on a Las Vegas craps table—don't have memories, and the chance of another quake striking hasn't changed. Nonetheless, due to the perceived risk by the customer, the purchase is made. Usually, all things being equal, the service provider that offers the lowest perceived risk will be chosen. FedEx's guarantee of "absolutely, positively overnight delivery" was a strong factor that led to—and maintains—its dominant share of the overnight delivery market. H&R Block has offered a guarantee of satisfaction that lowered the perceived risk to the customer, by stating:

> If we make any error in the preparation of your tax return that costs you any interest or penalty on additional taxes due, while we do not assume the liability for the additional taxes, we will pay that interest and penalty. Furthermore, if your return is audited, we will accompany you at no extra cost to the Internal Revenue Service and explain how your return was prepared, even though we will not act as your legal representative.

The response to this guarantee from members of the accounting profession was basically, "So what?"—joking that you might as well bring your dog along to the IRS for all the help H&R Block was going to be. But that misses the point. The success of Block's guarantee is that it made overt a policy that many CPAs keep covert, thus lowering the perceived risk in the customer's mind. This highlights the importance of making the service guarantee an instrumental part of your firm's marketing offering, as discussed in Chapter 9. Consider this thought experiment: You want to build a pool for your home. You go online and comparison shop, securing four bids: $50,000, $49,000, $48,500, and $42,000. Which would you choose? Would your decision be influenced if one of the companies provided a satisfaction guarantee? Would you, like most customers, automatically throw out the low bid?

Whether you are dealing with your firm or consulting with a customer on their business, be sure to perform a risk analysis using the above seven factors and find ways to mitigate those risks, keeping in mind that it is the perceived risk to the customer that is important.

Confusing Costs with Value

With the increase in e-business taking place, one tends to infer that prices will continue to decrease, products and services will become more commoditized, and consumers will be able to shop based on price comparisons in a global market. Some of these trends are encouraging, because anytime the consumer is better served, the free market is functioning properly. That being said, are all consumers interested in the lower price? Will value become irrelevant in a world of e-commerce? In the March-April 2000 issue of *Harvard Business Review*, Indrajit Sinha posits the following theory in his article, "Cost Transparency: The Net's Real Threat to Prices and Brands":

> The vast sea of information about prices, competitors, and features that is readily available on the Internet helps buyers "see through" the costs of products and services. That's bad news for manufacturers and retailers, but there are ways to fight back.
>
> The real threat is what economists call *cost transparency*, a situation made possible by the abundance of free, easily obtained information on the Internet. All that information has a way of making a seller's costs more transparent to buyers—in other words, it lets them see through those costs and determine whether they are in line with the prices being charged.
>
> As cost transparency increases, so will the problems it causes for companies. These problems usually take four forms:
>
> **First, cost transparency severely impairs a seller's ability to obtain high margins.**
>
> **Second, cost transparency turns products and services into commodities.**
>
> **Third, cost transparency weakens customer loyalty to brands.**
>
> **Fourth, cost transparency can damage companies' reputations by creating perceptions of price unfairness.** (Sinha, *Harvard Business Review*, March-April 2000: 43–45)

There are several problems with Shinha's analysis. The first is the notion of the reality of cost transparency. Having read an enormous amount of literature from the economics profession—and being especially influenced by the Austrian school—I have never seen the term "cost transparency" used by an economist. The Austrian theory is that value is subjective, in the mind of the buyer, not the costs of the seller, no matter how transparent those costs may be. I believe Mr. Sinha makes a rather fundamental error endemic to a lot of business managers and professors, which is to confuse the internal functions of a business—costs and efforts—with the external value as perceived by customers. The results—and value—of any business are created in the external marketplace, not in the internal costs and efforts of a business. As Peter Drucker says, "Quality in a product or service is not what the supplier puts in. It is what the customer gets out and is willing to pay for. A product is not quality because it is hard to make and costs a lot of money, as manufacturers typically believe. This is incompetence. Customers pay only for what is of use to them and gives them value. Nothing else constitutes quality." This is precisely why one cannot study price theory without studying economics, because so much that is written in the business community on pricing is so inward focused.

Customers don't spend an inordinate amount of time worrying about or comparing the internal cost structures of various sellers. So, many of Sinha's premises are based on flimsy evidence and can easily be refuted by observing the behavior of consumers in the marketplace. For instance, if customer really cared about internal costs, how have the automobile manufacturers been able to command a premium price for sport utility vehicles (SUVs) when the cost structure of building these is not much different from that of an automobile? How can United Airlines and Delta Airlines continue to be price leaders—especially among business travelers, who contribute the majority of their profits—and price seats at radically higher prices than the competition, even pricing differently among customers on the same flight, and even list the lower-price flights right on its own Web sites? If cost transparency was a real concern of customers, not to mention perceptions of "price unfairness," who would ever purchase a business-class or first-class ticket knowing that they might be paying ten times what leisure travelers paid even though the cost to the airline of flying different classes of passengers is not marginally different? All of the examples of price discrimination listed in Chapter 5 empirically refute the idea of "cost transparency."

The evidence that customers who shop over the Internet are price-sensitive is mixed, at best. A case may even be made that in the virtual world, service, brand, and trust take on increasing significance in the mind of the buyer. While it is true that Amazon.com discounts books—among other products—the only possible way the company could have achieved the growth it has is through offering premium service. If word-of-mouth can build a business, think how devastating bad word-of-mouth can be over the Internet, where information can be transmitted to millions of people at virtually no cost (witness the growth of Web sites, such as sucks.com, that are highly critical of companies). To discount the value of the Amazon brand is to ignore the realities of marketing. In the same issue of the *Harvard Business Review* in which Sinha's article appears, it is noted that "Ten years ago, only 3% of all coffee sold in the United States was priced at a premium—at least 25% higher than value brands. Today, 40% of coffee is sold at premium prices" (the so-called Starbucks Effect). Has any customer of Starbucks ever considered the company's internal cost structure and asked to see an activity-based costing analysis on the efficiency of preparing an espresso macchiato so they may compare the cost per ounce to that offered by Folger's (over the Internet, of course)?

Sinha even admits later in his article that there are three strategies available to overcome his notion of cost transparency: "price lining" (which is a fatuous description of price discrimination, as discussed in this book); bundling (which is the strategy embodied in the fixed price agreement, derived from the value curve); and finally innovation.

Although it is relatively easy to dismiss the notion of "cost transparency" by observing real-world behavior, one trend that is certainly taking place because of the Internet is disintermediation—the reality that sellers will be able to deal directly with vendors, thereby eliminating the middleman from the value chain and lowering the overall price to the customer. One of the most controversial issues about disintermediation, and one that will be fought aggressively and bitterly, is the $360 billion new-car market. Auto manufacturers have been studying the Dell, Gateway, and other computer retailer models and have concluded it is time to revamp the distribution model for automobiles. Almost 7 million Americans (myself among them)—more than 40 percent of the 16 million new car buyers last year—kicked tires online before purchasing. Harold Kutner, worldwide purchasing chief for General Motors, promises that by 2003, 80 percent of new car buyers will be able to custom-order vehicles online.

As with any wave of "creative destruction," the entrenched businesses won't give up without a fight, and they run to the government to assist them in postponing the inevitable. The barrier to selling cars directly to the customer is not the free market; it is the government, in the form of franchise laws, which grant a restrictive license over every new car sale. Forty-eight states currently regulate who can sell a new car and where they can sell it. The National Automobile Dealers Association (NADA) has lobbied hard to restrict auto sales online and in recent months has convinced nine states to pass such legislation, with bills pending in several more. Texas even restricted online brokers, imposing a $10,000 per violation fine and ordering Los Angeles–based CarsDirect.com to cease offering services online. A bill pending in Washington State prohibits manufacturers from owning dealerships, and one in Arizona would restrict outright sales directly to customers and would not allow manufacturers to own even a percentage of a dealership. In Nebraska, a pending bill would require all car sales to be delivered through a dealer. With all of this economic rent seeking—that is, what economists call behavior that tends to benefit one party at the expense of another, especially with the aid of government coercion—one wonders where the Department of Justice and state attorneys general are who claim to be mindful of the concerns of customers and have attacked Microsoft on such grounds. As argued by Diane Katz and Henry Payne in the July 2000 edition of *Reason* magazine:

> Michigan, the heart of the U.S. auto industry, provides perhaps the worst-case scenario of overambitious franchise law, with the statutory fine print running 19 pages long. But it is indicative of the anti-competitive restrictions built into most states' franchise laws.
>
> Michigan's dealership laws cover everything you can think of, ranging from allowable sales territory (in counties with more than 25,000 people, there can only be one dealership per six-mile radius) to which family members can inherit a franchise ("the spouse, child, grandchild, parent, brother, or sister of a deceased new motor vehicle dealer"). Back in the 1950s, dealers secured franchise laws after convincing legislators they needed protection against bullying manufacturers, who otherwise might impose costly dictates on dealers and demand sales and

> service concessions in return for advantageous inventory. Some states also banned automakers from directly competing in sales to ensure that distribution was "fair."
>
> In a 1997 study, Hillsdale College's Gary Wolfram and Michigan State's Lynn Jondahl pegged the cost of franchise regulation at $800 million annually in Michigan alone—a huge transfer of wealth from consumers to dealers. Supply restrictions increase vehicle price and search costs. And Wolfram and Jondahl's calculations included the cost to consumers of dealers using their market power to restrict product choices to mostly option-rich vehicles. (Katz and Payne, July 2000: 48–50)

J.D. Power and Associates report that more than half of respondents to one survey indicated they would rather purchase a new car directly from the manufacturer, *even if there was no price advantage.* The response increased to 70 percent if a price savings was included. Most customers indicated they simply want more freedom in choosing options, and color and to avoid the unpleasantness of haggling with a dealer over price.

It is truly a sad situation when market forces are not allowed to prevail because of political influences. No doubt automobile dealerships are important members of any community's economic sector, which doesn't go unnoticed by state legislators. States recognize that it is much easier to collect taxes from fixed-location dealers than from virtual dot-com companies. But if the franchise laws were eliminated, would this also be the death knell for the dealer? Not at all. Cars would still need to be serviced, some customers would still no doubt prefer to deal with local businesses, and the used-car market is burgeoning. Ultimately, the dealers will have to change with the new realities, but they should not overlook the opportunities that this presents. For instance, inventories and financing costs would be reduced because cars would no longer sit on lots awaiting buyers. Dealers will simply have to find alternative ways to add value in the auto market, much like every other business trying to adjust their value propositions in an increasingly virtual world.

Price Sensitivity

The three categories—search, experience, and credence—discussed above help marketing managers determine a customer's price sensitivity to products and services, as well as the customer's perceptions of value. Other methods also help to determine the price sensitivity of the customer. One might get the impression, given the sophistication of economic research techniques and marketing studies (especially with modern-day computers), that measuring price sensitivity among customers would be more of a science than an art. That impression, however, would be incorrect. Here is how Nagle and Holden explain this misconception:

> The implication that somehow soft managerial judgments about buyers are actually more fundamental to successful pricing than are numerical estimates based on hard data may come as somewhat of a surprise. Managerial judgments are necessarily imprecise, while in contrast, an empirical estimate of price sensitivity is a definite, concise number that management can use for profit projections and planning. However, the fact that empirical estimates of price sensitivity are concise does not imply that they are accurate. The history of marketing research reveals that estimates of price sensitivity are frequently far off the mark. . . . Accuracy is a virtue in formulating pricing strategy; conciseness is only a convenience.
>
> If one were forced to choose between estimating price sensitivity by informed judgment or by concise empirical estimation, judgment would be the better choice. No estimation technique can capture the full richness of the factors that enter a purchase decision. In fact, measurements of price sensitivity are concise precisely because they exclude all the factors that are not conveniently measurable.
>
> Managers deceive themselves into thinking that an estimate of price sensitivity based on hard data is as precise as it is concise. (Nagle and Holden, 1995: 349–350)

The above is certainly true with respect to the purchase of credence products and services, and perhaps less true with search products and services. Many factors influence a customer's price sensitivity, and managers need to understand these factors long before setting a price for various market segments.

Nagle and Holden identify the following ten factors affecting price sensitivity:

1. Perceived substitutes effect

The perceived substitutes effect states that buyers are more price sensitive the higher the product's price relative to its perceived substitutes. New customers to a market may be unaware of substitutes and thus may pay higher prices than more experienced buyers. Restaurants in resort areas face less pressure to compete based upon price (which locals may describe as "tourist traps"). Branding can also overcome, to a certain extent, the substitute effect. Woolite, for example, has maintained a relatively expensive price because it positions itself as an alternative to dry cleaning. Customers have a reference price when there are many substitutes, and as long as the offering is within that range it will be considered acceptable.

2. Unique value effect

Buyers are less price sensitive the more they value the unique attributes of the offering. This is precisely why marketers expend so much energy and creativity trying to differentiate their offering from that of their competitors. Heinz ketchup, for example, developed a secret formula for making its product thicker and was able to increase its market share from 27 to 48 percent while maintaining a 15 percent wholesale price premium. The Volvo automobile has a reputation as the safest car, an attribute many find desirable and are willing to pay a premium to acquire (not just in price but lower fuel economy and performance).

Auction houses rely on the unique value effect in order to command the prices they do among their bidders. Rare artifacts from the John F. Kennedy estate are known as "positional" or "expressive" goods, since the people who purchase them are trying to position themselves in society, or express who or what they are (art collectors, for example).

3. Switching cost effect

Buyers are less price sensitive the higher the costs (monetary and nonmonetary) of switching vendors. Airlines that have a fleet of Boeing airplanes may be reluctant to switch to Airbus because of the enormous investment they have in their pilots, flight crews, and the mechanics of operating a certain plane. Many people are unwilling to give up certain software products due to the learning and familiarity they have with their existing product. Personal relationships are most susceptible to this type of perceived cost, due to the emotional investment the customer has made in the relationship. Childcare providers, doctors, lawyers, and accountants all can benefit from this effect, especially if they provide total quality service.

4. Difficult comparison effect

Customers are less price sensitive with a known or reputable supplier when they have difficulty in comparing alternatives. People eat at McDonald's, continue to use AT&T, lodge at Marriott, and shop at J.C. Penney because they are familiar with these offerings and perceive them to be less risky than unknown alternatives. Stockbrokers price based on different criteria (shares of stock traded or value of shares traded), making it difficult for the customer to compare one with the other.

5. Price quality effect

Buyers are less sensitive to a product's price to the extent that a higher price signals better quality. These products can include image products, exclusive products, and products without any other cues as to their relative quality. Rolls-Royce is an example of an image product because it would be hard to argue it offers more superior value to, say, a Lexus or Mercedes. A Rolex watch is another example. Certainly one does not buy it for accurate timekeeping. These type of prestige products are an important form of marketing. Witness designer clothing and accessories, American Express Gold and Platinum Cards—which command enormous premiums over alternative cards—and first-class travel, which many people use not because of more leg room but because of the reduced probability of sitting next to loud children or talkative sightseers when they are trying to get work done.

Some products might even be judged solely on price. A synthetic car wax failed in the market at a price of $9.69 until the price was raised to $39.69. Many consumers still have a common visceral reaction that high price equates to high value (and quality). Marketers have discovered that utilizing a high price for new products is quite effective for signaling quality to the marketplace. Other marketing research has shown that while discounting familiar brands can increase sales, the same strategy for unknown brands can actually reduce sales.

6. Expenditure effect

Buyers are more price sensitive when the expenditure is larger, either in dollar terms or as a percentage of household income. A one-office accounting firm may not pay much attention to the price of paper clips, but an international firm that buys in large quantities will. Business purchasers look at the total amount of the purchase, while households compare the expenditure to total income. Many people won't expend much energy shopping for the lowest price of gum, but they will put more effort into searching for an automobile or a home. Higher income customers often will pay higher prices because they do not have the time to shop as thoroughly as low income individuals.

7. End-benefit effect

The end-benefit effect is especially important when selling to other businesses. What is the end benefit they are seeking? Is it cost-minimization, maximum output, or quality improvement? The fulfillment of the end benefit is often gauged by its share of the total cost. For instance, when steel suppliers sell to auto manufacturers, the price of the steel is a large component of the cost of the car; when steel is sold to a luggage manufacturer, the steel cost is relatively minimal compared to the other material used. High-end auto wax, marketed to luxury car owners at $40 and up is not a significant cost to operating a $80,000 automobile. "AOG," in the airline industry, stands for Airplane On Ground, and usually an AOG is awaiting some small replacement part. How price sensitive is an airline with respect to a $100 electrical switch that could get its plane back in the air and save countless thousands of dollars?

The end-benefit effect also is psychological. Think of going out for a romantic anniversary dinner and paying with a two-for-one coupon. Most people view price shopping as tacky when the purchase involves something emotional. Wedding florists, caterers, and bands certainly understand this principle. The larger the end benefit, the less price sensitive the buyer. Think of the Michelin tire ads showing a picture of a baby in diapers next to its radial tire proclaiming: "Michelin. Because so much is riding on your tires."

8. Shared-cost effect

Chapter 4 looked at the fact that when you spend someone else's money on yourself, you are not prone to be price conscious. This is why airlines, hotels, and rental car companies can all price discriminate against business travelers, because most of them are not paying their own way. This also explains some of the success of the frequent flyer and other reward programs. Many business travelers value these rewards and won't accept alternative offerings, especially since they are reimbursed anyway. Also, publications, educational seminars, and other business expenses are tax deductible and this reduces the buyer's price sensitivity relating to various business expenses.

9. Fairness effect

Notions of fairness can certainly affect the customer, even when they are not economically (or mathematically) rational. If a gas station sells gas for $1.30 per gallon and gives a $0.10 discount if the buyer pays with cash, and another gas station offers the same gallon at $1.20 but charges a $0.10 surcharge if the customer pays with a credit card, which station will sell more gas to credit card users? The economic cost is exactly the same, but most people will psychologically prefer to deal with the first station and not the second because there appears to be something inherently unfair about being assessed a surcharge.

In the past, rental car companies charged their customers if they brought back the car with less than a full tank of gas, and the price was usually two to three times the market rate. Many business travelers, who value their time more than vacationers, viewed this as being completely unfair, so they took the time to fill the tank before returning the car. Finally, the rental car companies figured out that fairness was an issue, and now they price their "gas options" at less than the prevailing market price, inducing a large percentage of the business travelers to opt to pay them for the gas. This has turned into a nice profitable service for the rental car companies, now that it is perceived as being fair.

Perceptions of fairness are differentiated based upon whether the product or service is a necessity or a luxury. This is why the pharmaceutical industry can receive such public condemnation when it prices new wonder drugs at a premium, even if these drugs prevent other, more costly, medical interventions. It is also why people will boycott stores that hike up the price of needed food, water, and building materials after a natural disaster. Companies that price based on capacity or season are careful to maintain relatively high regular prices so that they can be seen as giving discounts to most customers, which is perceived as being "more fair" than charging a premium above a lower "regular" price. Insurance companies emphasize peace of mind and security, rather than preventing a loss, which most customers resent having to pay for.

10. Inventory effect

The ability of buyers to carry an inventory also affects their price sensitivity. Amateur cooks with large pantries will stock up on a good deal but a single person living in a small apartment will not. The perishability of the item in question is another factor to consider.

Analyzing price sensitivity is certainly an important task for any business that wants to maximize the value it receives from its offering. Taking into account the ten factors above that affect price sensitivity is a good start. Nagle and Holden offer the following set of questions that should be asked about each of the above factors in preparing a managerial analysis of price sensitivity (Nagle and Holden, 1995: 95–99):

1. Perceived substitutes effect

- What alternatives are buyers (or segments of buyers) typically aware of when making a purchase?
- To what extent are buyers aware of the prices of those substitutes?
- To what extent can buyers' price expectations be influenced by the positioning of one brand relative to particular alternatives, or by the alternatives offered them?

2. Unique value effect

- Does the product have unique (tangible or intangible) attributes that differentiate it from competing products?
- What attributes do customers believe are important when choosing a supplier?

- How much do buyers value unique, differentiating attributes?
- How can one increase the perceived importance of differentiating attributes and/or reduce the importance of those offered by the competition?

3. Switching cost effect

- To what extent have buyers already made investments (both monetary and psychological) in dealing with one supplier that they would need to incur again if they switched suppliers?
- For how long are buyers locked in by those expenditures?

4. Difficult comparison effect

- How difficult is it for buyers to compare the offers of different suppliers? (Be sure to account for the Internet in your answer).
- Can the attributes of a product be determined by observation, or must the product be purchased and consumed to learn what it offers?
- What portion of the market has positive past experience with your products? With the brands of the competition?
- Is the product highly complex, requiring costly specialists to evaluate its differentiating attributes?
- Are the prices of different suppliers easily comparable, or are they stated for different sizes and combinations that make comparisons difficult?

5. Price-quality effect

- Is a prestige image an important attribute of the product?
- Is the product enhanced in value when its price excludes some consumers?
- Is the product of unknown quality and are there few reliable cues for ascertaining quality before purchase?

6. Expenditure effect

- How significant are buyers' expenditures for the product in absolute dollar terms (for business buyers) and as a portion of income (for end consumers)?

7. End-benefit effect

- What end-benefits do buyers seek from the product?
- How price sensitive are buyers to the cost of the end-benefit?
- What portion of the end-benefit does the price of the product account for?
- To what extent can the product be repositioned in customers' minds as related to an end-benefit for which the buyer is less cost sensitive or which has a larger total cost?

8. Shared-cost effect

- Does the buyer pay the full cost of the product?
- If not, what portion of the cost does the buyer pay?

9. Fairness effect

- How does the product's current price compare with prices people have paid in the past for products in this category?
- What do buyers expect to pay for similar products in similar purchase contexts?
- Is the product seen as necessary to maintain a previously enjoyed standard of living, or is it purchased to gain something more out of life?

10. Inventory effect

- Do buyers hold inventories of the product?
- Do they expect the current price to be temporary?

Pricing and the Competition

Pricing does not take place in a vacuum. It is more akin to a game of chess, where one player will make a move, alter the dynamics of the game, and the opponent will try to counteract that move. Frequently managers complain about pricing problems and pressures, but these are rarely mere pricing problems. They usually deal with communication, branding, image, product, distribution, segmentation, and other ill-conceived, or often ignored, functions of a cohesive marketing strategy.

Managers also let capacity utilization play a devastating psychological game with their pricing, especially when they are underutilized. Their logic is always "better some job (at a low cost) than no job at all." This could have very serious long-run consequences, such as sending a message to the market that you will capitulate on your pricing policies.

Almost all companies claim to want to sell a differentiated product or service to the market, but often the sales force is not given the proper training or incentives. Pricing on value takes time and energy, and many salespeople will resort to their comfort zone and cut price in order to make the sales quotas. Price is perhaps the quickest way to influence sales volume, and it is certainly easier than branding, image, distribution, packaging, marketing, and product changes, not to mention cheaper.

It must be constantly remembered that pricing can only capture value—it does not create it. Value is created based on a company's competitive advantages. If a company is not attaining its desired price from the market, usually more is wrong than simple cutthroat competition.

A business should be cognizant of its competitors' pricing strategies; customers certainly will be, especially through the Internet. But don't fall into the often repeated error of thinking that your competitors set the upper boundary of your price. Your customers set the boundaries of your price, both the lower and the upper end. If you listen closely enough, your customers will always communicate to you—both in words, and more importantly, in actions—what price they are willing and able to pay.

Summary and Conclusions

Pricing cannot be reduced to neat mathematical formulas and checklists. To be successful, pricing must be adapted to both the internal and external environments of the business. Pricing is a strategic marketing decision and deserves just as much attention as packaging, distribution, advertising, and promotion. Pricing decisions need to be made with a full understanding of the long-term ramifications of those decisions. Lowering price to make the next sale should never be permitted, unless it is part of a coherent marketing strategy.

The four cardinal rules of strategic marketing are: Know your costs; know your demand; know your competition and your customer; and, most importantly, know your value proposition. Anything less will subject you to the vagaries and whims of your competition and sales force. Following the strategies outlined in this chapter will help you achieve your pricing goals, and hence your profitability goals.

20 MAKING THE TRANSITION TO A TIMELESS CULTURE

The rewards and refreshments . . . come from the courage to try something, all sorts of things, for the first time. An enamored amateur need not be a genius to stay out of ruts he has never been trained in . . . Adventuring amateurs reward us by a wonderful vagrancy into the unexpected.

—Daniel Boorstin, historian

The secret of life is to have a task, something you bring everything to. And the most important thing is—it must be something you cannot possibly do.

—Henry Moore (1898–1986), sculptor

In the April 2000 issue of *The American Spectator,* Ben Stein, author, actor, lawyer, economist, and game-show host, recounts his meeting with Bill Porter, founder of E*TRADE. It is an inspirational illustration of the importance of entrepreneurial creativity and dynamism, as well as a lesson in the value of challenging prevailing wisdom and altering the status quo:

> At the dinner, I sat next to a man named Bill Porter. He had an amazing tale to tell. He basically invented online trading and founded E*TRADE, but his back story is even more astounding. He grew up in Colorado. He was a young teenager during World War II. To help with agricultural production, as a boy of 14 and 15 he had worked as a ranch hand on a large spread near Glenwood Springs—coincidentally quite near Aspen, which was a small town then. He rode fences, which means he rode on a horse along

the borders of the ranch, making sure the fences were up so that cattle would not walk away. He did this alone, for weeks at a time, carrying food with him and sleeping out of doors. Once he was attacked by a swarm of hornets. They stung him so much he went blind temporarily and was covered with blood. He had the presence of mind to recall a pond and a spring, which he found without sight. He bathed his eyes and eventually his sight returned. He was also alone in cold and rain and with wild animals nearby. "It was incredibly hard work," Dr. Porter said, "but it shaped me more than anything else ever has. I learned that if I could do that work by myself I could do anything. That helped me when everyone was telling me trading online would never happen and when we were running out of money and people said it would never work."

At age 16, Dr. Porter in wartime lied about his age and joined the Navy. After very little training, he was put in the fire room of the carrier *Bunker Hill.* He was in the engine room when the Battle of Okinawa took place and the ship was struck by six kamikazes. (I later read that 650 men died in that attack on the *Bunker Hill.*) "I thought we were done for," he said. "I was scared."

In fact, he said, he cannot talk about the ordeal without getting overcome—and I can easily believe it. Seeing your friends around you dying in flames is beyond imagining for the human mind.

After the war, he studied physics and became an inventor. He invented a horizon-sensing device that stabilizes satellites, and an endoscopic light for doing colonoscopies and endoscopies. He invented other things, too, and then he turned to using the Internet for stock trading.

"When I went to the people who ran the Net years ago, they said, 'Oh, no, it'll never be used for commerce. It's for science.' When I went to the New York Stock Exchange and asked them about posting prices on the Internet they said that would never be allowed. But I knew it would happen."

> Dr. Porter looks like a very prosperous rancher, not at all like a man who revolutionized stock trading. . . . "There are a lot of people out there who have done feats on a daily basis that exceed in importance and bravery everything I have ever done in my life put together."
>
> "I guess I have about half a billion dollars," Bill Porter said at one point in the evening. "It's what you do for other people that makes life work." When I think of what he's done to serve his country, let ordinary people take charge of their financial lives, and how brave he was when he was a kid, I feel as if it should be a billion. (Stein, 2000: 45–46)

Porter's story is an excellent example of the advice of noted historians, Will and Ariel Durant: "If you want the present and the future to be different from the past, Spinoza tells us, find out the causes that made it what it was and bring different causes to bear." Since the first publication of this book, I have had the good fortune of presenting its ideas and concepts to thousands of professionals around the world. Being an enthusiastic student of price theory, I have easily learned more than I could ever have hoped to teach. Usually, when I posit to an audience of professionals the possibility of operating a firm without timesheets, I am greeted with a staring ovation. Many professionals just don't see how it would be possible to run a firm profitably without timesheets—just as Bill Porter was told that online trading would never work. After talking, corresponding and visiting with thousands of professionals from all over the world, I am convinced now, more than ever, that the preparation, tracking, and recording of time by accountants and attorneys has far more costs than advantages.

That being said, let me also say that the perfect replacement for timesheets has yet to be found. I am constantly challenged by accountants to offer the replacement mechanism and tools for timesheets. My first instinct is to wonder, If you put out a fire destroying your home, would you feel obligated to replace it with something? Finding an alternative to leading a professional practice without timesheets is a tall task, and one that—like any new technology—cannot be mapped out with precision. If you follow the pricing procedures outlined in this book—that is, utilizing fixed price agreements, change orders, and the unlimited access clause; offering a service and price guarantee; always establishing a price before any engagement; and being cognizant of the customer's pricing emotions and expectations—making the transition to a timeless culture is feasible. There are four essential areas to focus on in order to eliminate the burden of timesheets in your practice:

1. Human capital
2. Firmwide key performance indicators (KPIs) and team member performance and evaluation
3. Customer selection
4. Leadership

Very few firms have tossed out their timesheets; therefore, empirical evidence is sparse, as it always is with any new paradigm shift. The foregoing list is offered in the hope that further thinking, research, and protocols will be developed in order to create a professional culture more conducive to focusing on human capital and results provided in the external environment. This chapter, as well as the pricing protocols set forth in this book, will assist firms that choose to be among the leaders in the profession by making the transition to a timeless culture—a meritorious culture focused on the external results provided to the customer by motivated professionals who are dedicated to improving the lives of those whom they serve.

Human Capital

Almost every executive and annual report will remark, "People are our greatest asset." Certainly in companies that innovate and create, and sell intellectual capital, this appears to be true. One managing partner told me, "The difference between an accounting firm's assets and other businesses is our assets get in the elevator every evening." When you analyze it, though, people are not assets, and whether or not companies truly practice what they preach is debatable. Michael Hammer, renowned reengineering expert, has called the people-are-our-greatest-asset comment "the biggest lie in contemporary American business." In all fairness, the problem may not be that companies don't value their team members but rather that they don't know how to value them. Generally accepted accounting principles certainly don't help this process; by expensing all current salaries and wages and not reflecting the value of intellectual capital on the balance sheet, businesspeople are not forced to appraise the worth of their associates.

Knowledge workers are not assets. People deserve more respect than assets such as phone systems and computers. In order to value their team members, firms have to distance themselves from the notion of "human resources" and move instead toward the concept of "human capital." The term "resource" is from the Latin *resurgere*, "to rise again," as if people were oil under the ground or timber to be harvested when needed. The term "human capital" first appeared in a 1961 *American Economic Review* article, "Investment in Human Capital," by Nobel Prize–winning economist Theodore W. Schultz. Human capital comprises skill, experience, and knowledge. Nobel Prize–winning economist Gary S. Becker describes human capital as personal capital (education, skills, experience, etc.) and social capital, which is the influence of past actions by family, friends, peers, and others in an individual's social network and control system. "Human" is from the Latin *hominem*, for "man," and "capital," is from the Latin *caput*, for "head." This makes more sense in describing knowledge workers, because in today's economy wealth is created not from physical resources and brawn but from ideas and brains.

The behavior of individuals is not analogous to machinery and equipment; people do not act in isolation but affect each other in complex ways. The behavior of workers in an intellectual environment can never be understood by mechanistically adding together their component parts. Any professional service firm is more than the simple summation of the individuals who inhabit it. In the past, firm managers and partners believed in the checklist mentality, which said do A, B, and C, and the consequences will be X. This is not control but rather the illusion of control. As the Chinese philosopher Lin Yutang puts it, man:

> does not react to surroundings mechanically and uniformly as animals do, but possesses the ability and the freedom to determine his own reactions and to change surroundings at his will. This last is the same as saying that human personality is the last thing to be reduced to mechanical laws; somehow the human mind is forever elusive, uncatchable and unpredictable, and manages to wriggle out of mechanistic laws or a

> materialistic dialectic that crazy psychologists and unmarried economists are trying to impose on him. Man, therefore, is a curious, dreamy, humorous and wayward creature. (Yutang, 1937: 12)

A better paradigm for measuring human capital is from the side of the owner, not the purchaser. At the end of the day, knowledge workers are investors—that is, they own their intellectual capital and will seek the highest return on investment for it. Knowledge workers will produce the greatest value for employers when, and only when, the company generates the greatest value for workers. In his fascinating and thought-provoking book, *Human Capital: What It Is and Why People Invest It,* Thomas Davenport offers the following equation to define the elements of human capital (HC):

Total Human Capital Investment = (Ability + Behavior) × Effort × Time

Davenport explains that the formula is multiplicative because increasing one element can dramatically raise the amount invested and, conversely, a higher level of one factor cannot make up for a low level of another. Further, Davenprot defines "Ability" as knowledge, skill, and talent; "Behavior" as the observable ways of acting that contribute to the accomplishment of a task; "Effort" as the conscious application of mental and physical resources toward a particular end; and "Time" as the chronology of investment: hours per day, years in a career, and so on.

A Brain Surgery Example

To illustrate how the equation works, Davenport describes a brain surgeon about to operate. Assume a scale of 1 to 10, where 1 is a low level of each HC component and 10 is a high level. Time is expressed in terms of hours and effort as a percentage ranging from 0 to 100 percent. The surgeon has excellent mechanical skills (9 on the 1–10 scale), strong medical knowledge (8), and exceptional physical dexterity and coordination (9). She exhibits moderate bedside sensitivity, a 6 on the behavioral scale. She is about to operate on her favorite cousin, so investment of effort is high, at 100 percent. The operation is expected to last 6 hours. The equation is as follows:

$$\text{HCI} = [(9 \text{ skill} + 8 \text{ knowledge} + 9 \text{ talent}) + 6 \text{ sensitivity})] \times (100\% \text{ effort}) \times 6 \text{ hours} = 192$$

Obviously, increasing any element raises the brain surgeon's HCI. If medical knowledge increased to 9 from 8 (she took more courses, for example), her HCI would increase to 198, a 3 percent increase, not insignificant if you are the person under the knife. Improving her behavioral skills, perhaps by working more with her medical team, from 6 to 8 would raise her HCI from 192 to 240, a 25 percent increase. Changes in effort can also produce dramatic leverage. Suppose, instead of operating on her cousin, it's her cousin's cat, and she is no cat lover, so effort drops to 20 percent. Her HCI then drops to 154, a 20 percent decrease. (Davenport, 1999: 22–24)

While this formula is not perfect (human behavior can never be calculated with such precise results), it does illustrate the concept that knowledge workers have far more control over their intellectual capital than their employers do and that small changes in the elements can have a dramatic impact on final results. One serious misgiving I have with the formula is the emphasis on efforts. However, we must distinguish between efforts invested by team members and efforts spent on behalf of customers. Customers buy results, not efforts. Those results are created by the efforts of team members. While employers, in the long run, pay team members for results, with proper training, supervision, and leadership, directed efforts will translate into effective results for customers.

The real breakthrough of Davenport's thesis is the concept of having to make your firm an attractive investment option for the knowledge worker of the future. By focusing on team members as investors, rather than assets and resources to be used and discarded as needed (or worse, as costs and drivers of costs), firms will be forced to create an attractive business and to constantly innovate in order to retain their team members' intellectual capital. In other words, human capital will gravitate to those firms that treat it best, offer the best chance for solid returns, and are dynamic and innovative enough to offer excellent growth potential. This is more analogous to an investor's selecting which company's stock to buy on the stock market than to a company's selecting which machine produces widgets most efficiently. Yet, as Professor William Halal of George Washington University noted, "The biggest problem in most organizations is that they are centrally planned economies." (O'Dell and Grayson, 1998: 77)

One lesson that was learned from the death of socialism and communism around the world is that centrally planned economies don't work. There is no dynamism, creativity, or surprise to spur growth and innovation. The same argument can be made for companies. It is as if we want capitalism everywhere except in our own firms. Rewards, compensation, and bonus structures are geared toward a top-down, command-and-control environment rather than an entrepreneurial and meritorious culture where performance is the main evaluation. As Steve Jobs said about Apple Computer during its most creative years: "It doesn't make sense to hire smart people and then tell them what to do; we hired smart people so they could tell us what to do."

Peter Drucker, who coined the term "knowledge worker," has made insightful observations about this new type of worker. In his book, *Management Challenges for the 21st Century,* Drucker had this to say:

> Altogether, an increasing number of people who are full-time employees have to be managed as if they were *volunteers.* They are paid, to be sure. But knowledge workers have mobility. They can leave. They own their "means of production," which is their knowledge. We have known for fifty years that money alone does not motivate to perform. Dissatisfaction with money grossly demotivates. Satisfaction with money is, however, mainly a "hygiene factor," as Frederick Herzberg called it all of forty years ago in his 1959 book *The Motivation to Work.* What motivates—and especially what motivates knowledge workers—is what motivates volunteers. Volunteers, we know, have to get *more* satisfaction from their work than paid employees, precisely because they do not get a paycheck. They need, above all, challenge. They need to know the organization's mission and to believe in it. They need continuous training. They need to see results.
>
> [They cannot] be ordered. They have to be persuaded. Increasingly, therefore, management of people is a "marketing job." And in marketing one does not begin with the question: "What do *we* want?" One begins with the question: "What does the other party want? What are its values? What are its goals? What does it consider results?" And this is neither "Theory X" nor "Theory Y," nor any other specific theory of *managing* people.

> The starting point may be a definition of results—just as the starting points of both the orchestra conductor and the football coach are the score. . . . One does not "manage" people. The task is to lead people. And the goal is to make productive the specific strengths and knowledge of each individual. (Drucker, 1999: 20–22)

Certainly Drucker's explanation applies to professionals in the accounting and legal professions. Yet how many firms do you know that have this type of philosophy and attitude when it comes to their "most important assets?" Drucker offers the further analogy between the traditional "boss" and "subordinate" as one between the conductor of an orchestra and the instrumentalist. The instrumentalist depends on the conductor for direction, values, performance measurements, results, and the score for the entire orchestra. As my friend Paul Dunn loves to say, in the traditional accounting firm, "The partners don't trust the team members enough to play the triangle." Benjamin Zander, conductor of the Boston Philharmonic Orchestra, said it best: "I make myself a relentless architect of the possibilities of human beings."

In order for the partners in a professional service firm to change their present focus from a human resources mentality to one of intellectual capital investors and volunteers, here are questions you can have your team members answer to help guide you through the process:

- What should my contribution be?
- What should you be expected to contribute?
- How fair are those expectations?
- How could I make the greatest contribution utilizing my strengths, my ways of performing, my values, to what needs to be done?
- What results have to be achieved to make a difference?
- What hinders you in doing your task and should be eliminated?
- What progress are you making in your career?
- How is the firm helping you to achieve your professional goals and aspirations?
- What does the firm do right and what should it continue doing?
- What are the firm's weaknesses and what should it stop doing?
- What critical things should the firm start doing?

The above list of questions is not about giving team members freedom to do their own thing, their own way. That is not freedom, it is license. Doing one's own thing does not take into account results, and it does not necessarily contribute to the objectives of the organization. Asking, instead, "What should I contribute?" gives freedom and responsibility to someone for creating results.

Microsoft is the premiere intellectual capital organization; it has virtually no assets other than what exists in people's minds. How does it attract the best and brightest software engineers, programmers, and developers? How does it create an environment conducive to attracting investment of intellectual capital? There are many similarities between high-technology companies and professional service firms. Both create, innovate, and trade in intellectual capital. It is time to assign the antiquated paradigm of human resources management and a top-down, command-and-control environment to the dustbin of history and replace it with one that unleashes the creativity, dynamism, and wealth-building potential that exists at all levels in the professional service firm of the future.

KEY PERFORMANCE INDICATORS

About half.

—President Calvin Coolidge's response when asked how many people in the government worked for him

In early May 2000, Paul Dunn, founding chairman of Results Accountants' Systems, received the following e-mail from an Australian Chartered Accountant:

> Good day, Paul,
>
> I'm interested in your opinion on the value of timesheets. I have filled them out for ten years now and still find them a nightmare. They are used in our firm as the obvious basis for

a client's bill, but in my opinion are the ultimate stand-over tactic for the owner: How many minutes have you billed? And there is always pressure to keep your charge percentage up. They also act as the way staff get paid, especially casual staff. You bill the hours, fill out the timesheet, and you get paid. While there is no direct pressure put on you to charge time, the timesheet is always there. And when staff are responsible for their own billings, there is no scope to fudge time or working hours. A partner could, say, go away for one month on vacation and still know his staff is flat out working and billing. Otherwise, no pay.

In my opinion, the timesheet is very stressful on staff and causes shortcuts to be taken because you know the approximate fee for the client and you need to keep the client's fee reasonable. Also, currently there is a lot of downtime with the General Services Tax [a new VAT tax in Australia, effective in 2000]. You get to the end of the day, and you have been flat out all day, and you have only four hours to charge, it's very demoralizing. Sometimes you can't help clients because you are frightened to open the file because you don't want to load the client with any more time. There is no doubting it causes shortcuts to be taken, you push it through, get the job out, and bill it. The problem being we deal with a very complex and gray system, and in a lot of cases the client's records are poor.

The timesheet is the main reason I'm currently studying in another related area, because I won't be filling them out when I'm 40 years old. Under the timesheet method, your value as an accountant is how many hours you can bill and recover, not how you have helped over 400 people and their businesses.

In short, they are painful and time-consuming. [Expletive deleted], who can I bill the time it took to write this to?

This e-mail raises interesting points relative to timesheets, issues I am sure resonate with most of the readers of this book. It would be easy to reject the letter, as Ric Payne does, by accusing its author of not wanting to be held accountable. However, I have heard these charges leveled against the timesheet from accountants around the world—there must be something to them.

Ever since Frederick W. Taylor searched for the "one best way" to use labor and material in order to control their efficiencies (not to monitor financial costs), management has been obsessed with recording, allocating, and measuring time. Indeed, the Electric Signal Clock Company's 1891 catalog touted the benefits of its best model of time clock, the Autocrat: "Gives military precision, and teaches practicality, promptness and precision wherever adopted. A school, office or factory installing this system is not at the caprice of a forgetful bell ringer, nor anyone's watch, as the office clock is now the standard time for the plant," thereby offering supervisors a means for extending their disciplinary reach beyond their vision. The 1914 catalog of the International Time Recording Company [which eventually became IBM] argued that time clocks would "save money, enforce discipline and add to the productive time." Also, "the time recorded induces punctuality by impressing the value of time on each individual" (Levine, 1997: 67–8).

At first glance, it may seem the height of absurdity to claim that partners and managers are using timesheets as an autocratic tool to control associates or as a mechanism—in the spirit of Frederick Taylor—to conduct time and motion studies to increase a professional's efficiency. But first appearances can be deceiving. Dozens of partners and managers have asked me, "If we didn't have timesheets, how would we know what our associates are doing and how efficiently they do it?" This appears to be an issue of trust, not productivity. Never one to let me get away with sloppy or illogical thinking, Ric Payne has challenged me on this point: "Are you suggesting that if you eliminate timesheets, trust will increase?" My reply: "Yes!" Timesheets, time clocks, and factory whistles may have been an effective way to control workers and children in the emerging Industrial Revolution, but they are absurd as a way to control knowledge workers in the twenty-first century.

It has become a cliché in the business world to say that what can be measured can be managed and what gets measured gets done. As Jeffrey Pfeffer, the Thomas D. Dee Professor of Organizational Behavior at Stanford Graduate School of Business, said in an interview in *Fast Company,* in June 2000 (www.fastcompany.com/online/35/pfeffer.html):

> There's an old saying in business: What gets measured is what gets done. What's happening today is the flip side of that. Measurement has become a tyranny that makes sure that nothing gets done.
>
> I've developed what I like to call the Otis Redding Theory of Measurement, which is named for his song "(Sittin' on) The Dock of the Bay." In that song, Redding sings, "I can't do what ten people tell me to do, so I guess I'll remain the same." That line sounds as if it could be about companies' misconceptions about measurement.
>
> Companies have managed to convince themselves that, since what gets measured is what gets done, the more they measure, the more stuff will get done. Last summer, I met a woman who works for a large oil company, and she told me that the company has 105 measures for which she is responsible. So I asked her, "How many of those 105 measures do you pay attention to?" Her answer? "None." Because in the end, she's measuring so many things that she doesn't pay attention to any of them—105 equals zero.

Albert Einstein had a sign hanging in his office at Princeton that summed up this conundrum nicely: "Not everything that counts can be counted, and not everything that can be counted counts." In a day and age when the average American spends the equivalent of five years of life standing in line, six months sitting at traffic lights, and two years trying to return phone calls (according to a 1988 series of field studies conducted by researchers for the consulting firm Priority Management Pittsburgh, Inc.), it is ludicrous to have professional knowledge workers account for every six minutes of their day. The United Kingdom tax newswire circulated this memo regarding timesheets, most likely written by someone who works in a professional service firm:

> **Staff Note: Timesheets**
>
> It has come to our attention recently that many in the tax department have been turning in timesheets that specify large amounts of Miscellaneous Unproductive Time. To our department, unproductive time is not a problem.

What is a problem, however, is not knowing exactly what you are doing with your unproductive time. The newly installed Activity Based Costing Financial System requires additional information to achieve its goals. Attached below is a sheet specifying a tentative extended job code list based on our observations of employee activities.

Extended Task Code List

5000	Surfing the Net
5001	Reading/Writing Social e-mail
5002	Sharing Social e-mail
5003	Collecting Jokes and Other Humorous Material via e-mail
5004	Forwarding Jokes and Other Humorous Material via e-mail
5316	Meeting
5317	Obstructing Communications at Meeting
5318	Trying to Sound Knowledgeable while in Meeting
5319	Waiting for Break
5320	Waiting for Lunch
5321	Waiting for End of Day
5500	Filling Out Timesheet
5501	Inventing Timesheet Entries
5502	Waiting for Something to Happen
5504	Sleeping
5510	Feeling Bored
5610	Searching for a New Job
5701	Not Actually Present at Job
5702	Suffering from Eight-Hour Flu
6200	Using Company Resources for Personal Profit
6203	Using Company Phone to Make Personal Calls
6206	Gossiping
6207	Planning a Social Event
6221	Pretending to Work While Boss is Watching
6222	Pretending to Enjoy Job
6601	Running Own Business on Company Time
6602	Complaining
6603	Writing a Book on Company Time

6604	Reading a Book on Company Time
6605	Planning a Vacation on Company Time
6611	Staring into Space
6612	Staring at Computer Screen
6615	Transcendental Meditation

The foregoing memo should be read as a rebuff—albeit tongue-in-cheek—to those partners and managers who believe you can measure productivity on the basis of hours logged on a timesheet. As Justin Barnett, my partner of more than ten years, points out, "Timesheets can actually obfuscate productivity." In other words, partners can gleefully view a team member's 90 hours recorded in one week's time and miss the fact that the person is woefully inefficient, has a bad customer service attitude, and is destroying the morale of the firm's associates. Today's knowledge worker has total control over just how much effort is expended on the job—as the above categories illustrate.

No two hours are of equal value. Characteristics such as passion, obsession, motivation, desire, innovation, interpersonal skills, and knowledge are critical in creating products and services as well as relationships with lifetime loyal customers. These traits cannot be measured by time but must be observed based upon results achieved in the external environment—that is, for the firm's customers. As Kenneth Atchity points out, "Every human being has exactly the same amount of time, and yet consider the output of Robert Louis Stevenson, John Peabody Harrington, Isaac Asimov, Agatha Christie, and John Gardner. How did they accomplish what they have? . . . When people ask them, 'Where do you find the time?' they wonder, 'Where do you lose it?' It is extremely difficult for firm leaders to inspire ordinary professionals to do extraordinary things without the further obstacle of making them account for every six minutes of their day." Tom Peters asks, "Was Einstein 'on budget' for his research? Who knows? Or cares?"

Firmwide Key Performance Indicators

Paul Dunn received the following e-mail in May 2000:

> Greetings, Paul,
>
> After studying Ron Baker's book during the year we stepped off the plank and eliminated timesheets 100% in

> January. This has forced us to rely solely on Fixed Price Agreements and dramatically increase our communication skills. The only mathematical performance measure we look at is the antidonkey strategy. Our percentage of salaries to turnover [gross revenue] should be reducing. The other is simply customer satisfaction. The Team are in total support and no one can remember what benefit timesheets were!

Dozens of firms have stepped off the plank and eliminated timesheets. This can be done, but only in tandem with the value pricing policies discussed in the book—FPAs, change orders, and so forth—have been planted firmly into the firm's marketing culture. Is it enough to simply measure labor costs as a percentage of gross revenue and customer satisfaction, as the above firm has decided? There is more to it than that. Other measures—what are known as key performance indicators (KPIs)—can be used by a firm's leaders and managers to measure the productivity of its team members. Peter Drucker provides the context for measuring the productivity of the knowledge worker:

> Work on the productivity of the knowledge worker has barely begun. In terms of actual work on knowledge worker productivity we are, in the year 2000, roughly where we were in the year 1900, a century ago, in terms of the productivity of the manual worker. But we already know infinitely more about the productivity of the knowledge worker than we did then about that of the manual worker. We even know a good many of the answers. But we also know the challenges to which we do not yet know the answers, and on which we need to go to work.
>
> SIX major factors determine knowledge-worker productivity.
>
> 1. Knowledge-worker productivity demands that we ask the question: *"What is the task?"*
>
> 2. It demands that we impose the responsibility for their productivity on the individual knowledge workers themselves. Knowledge workers *have* to manage themselves. They have to have *autonomy.*

> 3. Continuing innovation has to be part of the work, the task and the responsibility of knowledge workers.
>
> 4. Knowledge work requires continuous learning on the part of the knowledge worker, but equally continuous teaching on the part of the knowledge worker.
>
> 5. Productivity of the knowledge worker is not—at least not primarily—a matter of the *quantity* of output. *Quality* is at least as important.
>
> 6. Finally, knowledge-worker productivity requires that the knowledge worker is both seen and treated as an "asset" rather than a "cost." It requires that knowledge workers *want* to work for the organization in preference to all other opportunities (Drucker, 1999: 142).

The advantage of KPIs over timesheets is that they measure results, not efforts; productivity, not activity; outputs rather than inputs. The more common KPIs being used as firmwide measurements in practices where timesheets have been eliminated are as follows:

Job Turnaround When did the work come into the firm, when is it statutorily due (tax returns, etc.), when was it promised to the customer, and what percent of the time does the firm fulfill its promise?

Labor as a Percentage of Gross Revenue What is the total labor cost percentage? How does it compare to prior periods? What is the trend (increasing or decreasing)? Why? How does it compare with other firms of comparable size?

Revenue per Person Total firm revenue divided by number of professionals (or total team members). How does it compare to prior periods? What is the trend (increasing or decreasing)? Why? How does it compare with other firms of comparable size?

Customer Yield What is the firm's average revenue per customer? Is this consistent with the firm's marketing plan and image? Is it consistent with the firm's minimum price guidelines? Should the firm consider firing low-value customers in order to make room for offering higher value services to more valuable customers?

Customer Loyalty What is the firm's customer retention rate? Customer defection rate? What is the trend (increasing or decreasing)? Why?

Share of Wallet What is the firm's share of each customer's wallet—that is, what percentage of each customer's tax, audit, accounting, and consulting dollar goes to the firm? What is the trend? Why?

Customer Churn Divide customers lost by customers acquired. Also, divide revenue lost by new revenue acquired. What is the trend? Why? How does it compare with firms of similar size?

Percentage of Revenue Derived from New Services What percent of the firm's total gross revenue is from services not offered last year? Three years ago? Five years ago? This measures the innovation and creativity of the firm's value proposition.

Net Income Percentage and Profit Per Partner What is the trend (increasing or decreasing)? Why? Compared with firms of similar size?

This list is a starting point for firms to develop their own specific KPIs. Some of the above KPIs can be gleaned from the firm's basic income statement. Engage in this thought experiment: Assume that timesheets were not available to measure and compare the profitability, productivity, and efficiency of your firm. If that were the case, what measurements would you look at? If time were no longer needed for pricing purposes, what indicators would you look at to measure the effectiveness of the firm's ability to fulfill its mission? This is precisely what many consultants do when they enter a firm from the outside. One of the last pieces of information they require is billable hours; it simply transmits no useful information about the effectiveness of the firm.

When developing and tracking KPIs, don't boil the ocean—in other words, don't try to analyze everything. Have the partners and team members agree upon the essential KPIs and make sure they measure results and productivity, not efforts and activity. Be prepared to do a cost-benefit analysis on any tracking and monitoring of KPIs and require the benefits to justify the costs. It is very easy to imagine a firm developing and tracking so many KPIs that they become more cumbersome than the timesheets they are designed to replace. Three or four firmwide KPIs that measure the right things—even if imprecisely—are a much better tool than precise measurements of the wrong things. What we witness in professional service firms today, as Viv Brownrigg, a Chartered Accountant in New Zealand, pointed out to me, is that the time and billing system tends to be the number-one customer of the firm in terms of the resources and maintenance it requires. We certainly do not want the KPI measurement simply to replace the complex and tedious time and billing system—its benefits must justify its costs.

Team Member Performance and Evaluation

Most professional service firms already have specific KPIs and evaluation tools to measure the productivity and job performance of team members. Any standard evaluation form (such as those published in *How to Manage Your Accounting Practice,* by Roy C. Thornton and Jayne E. Osborne) grades team members on technical knowledge, job performance, communication and interpersonal skills, approach to customer relations, supervisory skills, management skills, and the like. These evaluations provide more meaningful performance indicators than do timesheets. The act of completing these evaluations forces supervisors, managers, and partners to consider those traits and qualities that are most important in terms of providing results to customers. I will assume that readers have already developed these types of tools for use in their firms. Here I focus on KPIs that are not in common usage for evaluating team members.

Team member KPIs Obviously some of the firmwide KPIs mentioned previously can be used for any one team member, such as job turnaround, revenue per person, and percentage of revenue derived from new services. Most of these KPIs are self-evident, but revenue per person can become an issue in a fixed price environment. How do you track any one team member's revenue contribution on a fixed price audit, for example? Some firms that have discontinued the use of timesheets but still prefer to track revenue per person have developed some innovative ways around this issue. One is to simply agree, in advance, what the job is worth to the various team members. For instance, a firm conducting a $25,000 audit required one manager, two team members, and a partner. Since the price was set in advance, the team members knew exactly what the revenue contribution was going to be to the firm. They then agreed to a revenue split based upon their relative contributions to the job. For this firm this is an effective method. However, in other firms, the partners don't like team members focusing on their specific revenue and would rather work as a true team, measuring the overall performance. Each method has its advantages and disadvantages, with the culture of the firm being the most important determinant. Some firms have simply given up on the idea of revenue per person, choosing to focus on the overall revenue of the firm. Unless your firm derives a significant portion of its revenues from cross-selling additional services, from offering new services, or from the marketing activities of your team members, this may be the preferable path to follow, which leads us to another potential KPI.

Contribution to firm revenue The contribution to firm revenue KPI, suggested by Ric Payne, tracks the cross-selling of marginal services to existing customers and the acquisition of new customers for the firm. Many firms already provide bonus and compensation plans to reward this type of activity (e.g., 10 percent of revenue generated over the life of a new customer). In order for firm leaders to develop an entrepreneurial culture, these types of KPIs should be monitored and rewarded. One caveat, however, should be noted: The goal is not just more business, but better business. Make sure all team members are cognizant of the overall marketing plan of the firm, minimum pricing structure, and so on. It is relatively easy to attract new customers by severely discounting your price; this is not, in the long run, an effective strategy for building a high-profit business.

Customer feedback The results of any organization exist externally—happy customers who return. Soliciting customer feedback on team member performance is a critical KPI, and one that is used far too infrequently. In the old days, the pressure to bill hours kept team members from becoming effective customer service providers. As UPS discovered, requiring drivers to enter and leave each customer location as quickly as possible may have increased efficiency but the customers didn't like it. They wanted to talk with the drivers, get shipping advice, and handle specific problems that arose. UPS finally got the message by letting its drivers spend more time with each customer. The results have been impressive in terms of customer loyalty and retention, as well as share of wallet. Feedback from customers can be gathered from formal surveys and casual conversations by the managers and partners. One of the most effective methods for gathering customer feedback is conducting Customer Advisory Boards, whereby the firm hires an outside facilitator and holds a focus group with six to eight of the firm's best customers.

Effective listening skills Part of being a true professional is the ability to actively listen to customers and to seek to understand what they are saying, what they need, and what they want. The best rainmakers in firms around the world have one trait in common: They are the best listeners. This skill can be developed by education and on-the-job training. Team members should watch the best listeners in the firm interact with customers and accompany them on sales calls. Human beings learn far more from their leader's actions than they do from their words. A proper mix of formal training and learning by doing will pay off handsomely in increased revenue and profitability.

Risk-taking, innovation, and creativity Profits ultimately come from risk. Most firms, unfortunately, stifle risk-taking and reward the status quo. Having team members take risks, innovate new and creative ways to solve customer problems, and pursue opportunities is one way to differentiate your firm from the competition. Developing a novel tax strategy or solving a complex internal control problem is far more important to the customer than how many hours a team member spends. Encouraging this type of culture no doubt requires partners to tolerate a higher level of errors and failures; however, think of the hidden costs of stifling this type of behavior.

Knowledge elicitation A professional service firm trades in intellectual capital. How well that knowledge is gathered, put into a specific context, and delivered effectively back to the customer will ultimately determine the success of the firm. In today's competitive environment, it is no longer enough for the firm to act like a black box, wherein work is brought in and solutions are put out. Increasingly, customers are demanding to be taught so they can make better decisions in the future and increase their capabilities. How well your team members can transfer knowledge to the customer will determine your ability to secure future engagements, especially high-value business development and consulting work.

Ability to deal with change In today's environment, yesterday's best practices are today's rut. Firms must continuously innovate and change to keep up with the environments in which their customers operate. Technology has had an obvious and dramatic impact on this aspect of providing professional services. Those firms that are best able to handle change internally are also the best firms to help their customers deal with change in their businesses. Team members need to be aware of the importance of embracing change.

Continuous learning As David Maister has pointed out in his work, the income statement may determine your annual income, but your balance sheet determines your future. The most significant way any professional can make an impact on his or her balance sheet is to enhance his or her knowledge base. This requires a substantial investment in Continuing Professional Education, and not just the technical courses dealing with accounting, auditing, and tax. Courses should also be attended that deal with general business issues (specifically related to your customers' industries), management skills, total quality service, marketing, leadership, listening, and other personal relationship skills critical to a true professional. Recall from Chapter 15 the fact that Accenture spends 6 percent of its gross revenue on training, and that the average Accenture team member spends 135 hours each year in a classroom, compared with the average company's 1.8 percent of payroll spent on educating the workforce. Most of the value any professional service firm creates exists in the heads of its team members, and thus it would seem self-evident that lifelong education and training is necessary to enhance the firm's balance sheet. Unfortunately, most firms have a myopic view of training, reluctantly spending the bare minimum to meet state licensing requirements. The conventional wisdom seems to be—and I have heard this from professionals around the world—if we train our team members, they will leave and become our future competitors. "Why should I invest in building the skills of my competition?" This attitude may have worked twenty to thirty years ago, when there existed an ample supply of labor coming into the professions; it is disastrous in a labor market plagued by chronic shortages. Even companies with relatively high turnover now understand the importance of training and education, as is attested by the creation of McDonald's Hamburger University and Disney University. Yes, your team members may leave after you train them, becoming your competition, but I believe the more critical question is: What if you don't train them *and they stay?*

Developing KPIs for continuous learning is more than just tracking hours sat in CPE courses. Think about how the team members will demonstrate and use the new skills they have learned to enhance the opportunities of the firm. Some firms have implemented something as simple and inexpensive as requiring team members to read specific books and share what they have learned with their colleagues over a breakfast or lunch meeting. Having customers come in and conduct "reverse seminars" and train the firm on what is going on in their industries is a very effective (and flattering) way to learn more about the opportunities that exist to sell more services to your customers. There is virtually no limit to the ways in which learning can take place. The main message is to create a culture that encourages and rewards the sharing and transmission of knowledge, the cornerstone of any firm's value proposition.

Mentoring and coaching skills In the mid-1990s, Price Waterhouse added knowledge sharing to its evaluation and appraisal system to ensure its associates were recognized for evidence of tutoring, training, publishing and presenting, coaching, and mentoring. Much of a firm's knowledge is tacit, as defined by Michael Polanyi, the philosopher who first articulated the concept of tacit versus explicit knowledge. Explicit knowledge exists within the firm's infrastructure, processes, procedures, protocols, databases, and so on. Tacit knowledge is "sticky," existing in the minds of team members. An example of the difference, and the difficulty, in communicating the two types of knowledge can be illustrated with a thought experiment: Try explaining, in detail, how to ride a bike or how to swim. This is precisely why so many of the larger professional service firms have created a director of intellectual capital or chief knowledge officer. One of the main functions of these professionals is to capture tacit knowledge and make it explicit. A difficult task, to be sure, but one that is starting to pay dividends in firms that rely so much on what is between their team members' ears. The old paradigm might be described as "Stop talking and get to work." The new paradigm, in an increasingly knowledge-driven economy, may very well be "Start talking and get to work." Tacit knowledge is best delivered in a social setting, usually through stories and simply talking among colleagues. Firms should encourage this type of knowledge transmission.

Personal development (or marketing) plan Have the team members develop, in conjunction with their coaches or mentors, a personal and professional development plan, outlining goals, plans, resources needed, and so forth, in order to enhance their professional development within the firm. Areas might include practice development, acquisition of new skills, areas of interest, initiatives to be performed to assist the firm in meeting its goals, and so on.

Let the Team Select KPIs

Trying to build the model for the timeless culture is no easy task. Old habits die hard. One innovative way some firms have replaced timesheets is to have their team members help them develop the KPIs to measure results. Professionals are smart people. They know how the firm operates, and they want to do a good job for both the employer and the customer. They also know the correct measurements that are needed to define success. People also tend to give you what is being measured and rewarded. So even if you define success correctly, if you measure and reward the wrong things, the team will give you precisely that; the wrong things. Therefore, it is much more advisable for the team to have a sense of "ego investment" in the measures and definition of success.

The partners in one firm gathered the team members together and made a covenant with them. They agreed to remove timesheets, and in return the team members would define four to six KPIs that would measure their specific contribution to the firm's success. They decided on job turnaround, customer feedback on team member performance, contribution to firm revenue, and customer yield. The partners also reported that the team members are much harder on themselves than the partners would have been in terms of measuring their success. This should not be surprising, as most people will more readily adopt change when they have had a say in how it is going to be implemented. People may hate change, but they love to experiment. This firm decided to test the hypothesis that an accounting practice could operate efficiently and profitably without timesheets. So far, the results have been impressive, and the partners have not felt the need to bring back timesheets.

Team member morale has also increased (I have yet to meet a professional who enjoys completing timesheets). This is no small change. Not requiring timesheets is an enormous competitive differentiation that will help attract new talent to your firm. Dale Dauten, in his book, *The Gifted Boss: How to Find, Create and Keep Great Employees,* points out that a "gifted boss" and a "great employee" want the same things from a workplace:

- Freedom from . . .
  management,
  mediocrity, and
  morons
- A change
- A chance (Dauten, 1999: preamble)

It is much easier to accomplish these things in a timeless culture than in one that makes every employee feel they have to account for every six minutes of their workday. Any one of the KPIs this firm has selected is a more effective measurement than hours logged on a timesheet, because the KPIs focus on external results, not internal efforts. They provide incentive for team members to focus on creating value, not controlling costs. The KPIs are not redolent of the antiquated—and incorrect—labor theory of value, as discussed in Chapter 6.

Many professionals vigorously defend timesheets on the grounds that there is no better way to measure the efficiency and productivity of team members. I challenge this assertion. In fact, I will go one step further and say the burden of proof is on those professionals to prove that timesheets are an effective—and correct—measurement of productivity. This is a logical shift of the burden of proof, since most businesses do not use timesheets to measure productivity. How does an airline or a software company measure the productivity of its team members? Let us be honest, most professionals are not using timesheets in order to gauge the efficiency and effectiveness of their people; they are using them for pricing. Once you have broken the nexus between time and price, using other KPIs to measure output is a more effective mechanism for measuring the external results created by your firm.

Nonetheless, if you are still skeptical, consider this a testable hypothesis. Involve your team in developing some meaningful KPIs, hold them accountable for them, and examine the results. If I am proven wrong, go back to timesheets. If it works, I know you will be pleased with the results. Either way, contact me and let me know of your experience.

CUSTOMER SELECTION

It's axiomatic: You're as good—or as bad—as the character of your Client List. In a very real sense, you are your Client List!

—Tom Peters, *The Professional Service Firm 50*

If there is one lesson to learn from successful professional firms around the world, it is this: Customer selection is arguably the most important criterion a business can establish for long-term success. In a world of increased competition, customization, and specialization, professional service firms can no longer be everything to everybody. It is critical to define your target customers, what they want and need from you, and the value proposition you will offer them. The most successful firms turn away more business than they accept because they are diligent in prequalifying potential customers. Recall from Chapter 14 the corollary to Gresham's Law: *Bad customers drive out good customers.*

There has been a lot written over the past decade about grading customers, firing your C and D customers, getting your B customers to become A customers, and concentrating on the As for cross-selling top-of-the-value curve services. All of this makes sense, especially in light of the Pareto Principle, as discussed in Chapters 5 and 14. It is important to reiterate, however, that your customers will not get better until you do. Customer loyalty is a two-way street, and professionals must give their customers a reason to be loyal.

Let us examine the quantitative and qualitative characteristics of good customers. What do your best five or ten customers have in common? Why do you enjoy working for them? As David W. Cottle points out in his book, *Target Marketing: How to Gain Profitable New Business,* "The best way to grow in your business is to 'clone' your best clients" (Cottle, 2000: 33). Your marketing success should be defined not just as getting more business but getting better business. Growth for the sake of growth is the ideology of the cancer cell, not the successful professional service firm. Here are quantitative traits you can consider before accepting a new customer, or for grading an existing one, again according to David Cottle:

- Amount of annual purchases
- Promptness of payment
- Growth potential
- Referral potential
- Actual referrals
- Profitability of serving client (write-downs/write-ups)
- Risk of litigation or damage to your reputation
- Fiscal year or time of year you do the work (ibid.: 33).

The above traits are the most common grading criteria. However, if you are interested in attracting above-average customers—that is, those who are willing and able to pay for services located at the top of the value curve—then the above criteria need to be expanded. Ric Payne and Paul Dunn advocate the following eleven criteria in order to select those customers who are likely candidates for value-added services:

1. **In business for at least three years** This is generally enough time for the client to become established, prove he or she has some management skill, and appreciate the importance and need for professional assistance.

2. **Pleasant, outgoing personality** There's no point in spending time with unpleasant people. In our experience, pleasant, outgoing people seem to have more successful businesses. Their personalities are unquestionably a contributing factor to their success.
3. **Willing to listen to advice** Even nice people don't always listen to advice. You will be wasting your time if the person you're working with "knows it all" or refuses to take your recommendations. Be careful not to use this to rationalize your inability to sell your service potential. More often than not, a person doesn't listen to advice because it hasn't been communicated in an understandable manner or the payoff hasn't been clearly stated.
4. **Positive disposition** Unfortunately, the business world is full of people who have had such a hard time that the only way they can live with themselves is by blaming everyone else for their problems. If a client refuses to take personal responsibility for the condition of the business and is unwilling to look positively at the environment and existing opportunities, you would be well advised to look elsewhere for clients. Of course, your ideal client will be a positive person who is not simply an ambitious dreamer. It's important to maintain a balance between ambition and potential. Rome wasn't built in a day, they say. Nor are great businesses.
5. **Technically competent** It goes without saying that all the fancy marketing, management, and performance standards will come to nothing if the client's product or service is technically flawed.
6. **Business is profitable** Accountants typically are called in to assume the role of company doctor for an ailing business. Naturally, many of the approaches and skills required to turn a business around are the same tools used to make an already sound business better. However, it is much smarter, in terms of the success probability, to work with businesses that are already profitable—but underperforming—than with businesses in a loss situation (unless that is your specialty). Clearly you need to consider this criterion individually for each potential client.

7. **Business is not chronically undercapitalized** This will generally apply only to relatively new businesses that have experienced rapid, uncontrolled growth or to businesses that have experienced several periods of sustained losses. Again, you need to consider this criterion individually for each potential client. But, other things being equal, pass up this opportunity for an easier one.

8. **Business is not dominated by a small number of customers or suppliers** This is a strategic issue. If a business is subject to severe buyer or supplier dominance and it does not otherwise have any significant competitive strength, you might be less than excited to take it on. In these circumstances, it is very difficult to do much because margins are often dictated by the supplier or the buyer. Unless there are immediately obvious ways for the firm to create and retain value, it's hard to do much for the business.

9. **Clearly established demand for the product or service** There is no question that new products or services have the potential for very substantial rewards. The first successful entrant into the industry usually has a big payoff. But statistics speak for themselves. New product or service ventures have a high failure rate. Furthermore, innovative entrepreneurs generally commit all their resources to the design concept. So there's not likely to be much left over to cover your investment and the costs involved in creating a market. As with the other criteria, assess this one individually for each potential client. You may decide to take such an assignment as an entrepreneurial investment of sweat equity (e.g., stock options), but limit this type of investment in your client portfolio (and be sure it doesn't detract from your firm's overall mission).

10. **Business has a scope for product or service differentiation through innovative marketing** Another strategic issue. If you believe you could significantly affect margin or volume through a sound marketing strategy, the client would be ideal—given other factors, of course. If, on the other hand, you're not really sure where to start, then you may want to pass up the opportunity.

11. **Business has scope for improved productivity through innovative management planning and control** A business that fails criterion #10 could score well on this one. Think about what you could do to improve internal efficiencies. Specifically, note that where performance is not being systematically measured, there's almost always scope to improve it. A cursory review of your potential client's internal management information system will give you a very good idea of the potential here.

The foregoing eleven criteria are excellent for evaluating and prequalifying new customers before accepting an engagement. It is also important to analyze existing customers for their ability and willingness to pay for value-added services. The American Institute of CPAs says it costs eleven times more to acquire a customer than it does to keep an existing one. Obviously, the best potential candidates for value-added services are existing customers. An effective method to begin the dialogue process with them, in order to cross-sell business development and consulting services, is to use the following questions adapted from the Results Accountants' Systems Business Development Assessment Questionnaire. These questions are also written so they can apply to new customers as well:

1. What industry is your business in?
2. How many years have you been running this business?
3. How many years have you been involved in owning or managing any business?
4. Did you start this business or did you acquire it?
5. Are you happy with the financial return you're getting from the business? If you answered "no," what return would you like to be getting?
6. On average, how many hours in a typical week do you spend working in your business?
7. How many hours would you like to spend working in your business?
8. What do you consider to be the biggest problems in your business? (Rank in order of importance from 1 to 16, where 1 = most critical

problem and 16 = least critical problem). Ignore it if it isn't applicable or a problem.

- Lack of capital for expansion
- Lack of sales
- Cash flow
- Slow-paying customers
- Lack of skilled people
- Difficulty getting employees focused
- Difficulty hiring suitable employees
- Taxation
- Price competition
- Lack of time to do what needs to be done
- Not enough customers
- Supplier problems
- Production problems
- Government regulations
- State of the economy
- Other (specify)

9. If you had access to unlimited finance, what would you do to improve the business?
10. What key performance indicators do you use to monitor the progress of your business?
11. Do you set targets as a reference point for managing your business?
12. Do you have a Business Action Plan that sets out precisely what you need to do to achieve your profit target?
13. In the following list, check off those whom you involve in critical decision-making in your business:

- Investors
- Board of directors
- Employed managers
- Other employees

- Your accountant
- Your attorney
- Your banker
- External business consultant(s)
- Spouse
- Friends
- Other (specify)

14. What was the main reason you went into business for yourself?
15. Do you feel you are achieving this? If you answer "no," please explain why.
16. When we work with each customer on business development, our primary focus is to increase the value of the client's business and, as a result, increase your net worth. As part of this process, we ask our customers to think into the future and imagine where they would like their business to be in 5 years.

    (i) In 5 years, what is your target for: Revenue, Net profit, Number of employees?

    (ii) What is the value of your business now?

    (iii) What would you like your business to be worth in 5 years?

    (iv) Do you have a strategic plan to help you achieve that goal?

    (v) How much money do you have invested or at risk in your business?

    - Equity capital
    - Loans to the business
    - Value of personal property mortaged to secure business loans
    - Total exposure

17. To help us to assess your profit improvement potential, please provide us with the following information. (Note: If you do not know your exact average transaction value, an estimate is fine

at this stage. Give a reasonable estimate by picking 20 sales invoices at random and calculating the average. If you feel comfortable that the result is about right, enter the value in the space provided below. If you're still unsure, select more invoices until you're confident that your estimate gives a fair indication of the true average.)

(i) What is your average transaction value?

(ii) Do you have a system to measure this or is it estimated?

(iii) How many times a year do your average customers buy from you? Once a year, quarter, month, week, day (other)?

(iv) How many active customers do you have? Do you have a system to measure this or is it estimated?

(v) So that we can complete a preliminary analysis of your financial performance, please attach a copy of your financial statements from the past two to three years.

It might appear to be a contradiction to have this questionnaire in a section on customer selection. But one of the most important lessons you can learn from the best salespeople in the world is the importance of prequalifying your customers. If you get a sense from the above questions—whether you complete them with a new customer or they answer them on their own—you will get a feel for the opportunity to cross-sell value-added services. This is by no means discounting the value of basic compliance services—tax returns, write-up work, reviews, and so on—since they are usually the "foot in the door" that will lead to higher value services. Nonetheless, you have to gauge, at the beginning, the customer's ability and willingness to use your firm for those services. Furthermore, and perhaps more importantly, you have to position your firm in the mind of the customer as one that can help them grow their business; in other words, your firm will not just record history but help make it.

The economics of this are quite rational. Businesses tend to stay with accounting firms that are of approximate size to theirs. If all you are doing for a customer is bottom-of-the-value-curve services, once the customer begins to grow, they will feel they have outgrown your capabilities and will select another provider. However, if you have helped that customer grow their business, you will lock them into a solid relationship, raise their switching costs dramatically—because you know so much about them and have a proven track record—and they will be more likely to retain you, even if you have to outsource some of the services they desire.

Moreover, from a marketing position, the foregoing questions differentiate your firm from the average service provider—not to mention that, in the minds of the customer, they will be less price-sensitive if they believe you have the capabilities to help them grow and achieve their business objectives. As Ric Payne points out: "It is much easier to differentiate your firm with a price of $25,000 than it is at a price of $1,500." This is true because at the price of $25,000 your firm is obviously doing more for the customer than compliance work, and the customer's perception of the value is much greater.

In the discussion on "firing customers" in Chapter 14, where we discussed David Maister's personality grading system from his book *True Professionalism* (a book every professional must read), Maister states that you should work only with customers whom you enjoy, and that should be the primary qualification before taking on a new customer. According to his surveys, when asked to divide all the customers they have worked for in the past year into three categories, professionals around the world told Maister:

1. I like these people, and their industry interests me (30–35%).
2. I can tolerate these people and their business is OK—neither fascinating nor boring (50–60%).
3. I'm professional enough that I would never say this to them, and I'll still do my best for them, but the truth is that these are not my kind of people, and I have no interest in their industry (5–20%). (Maister, 1997: 23–24)

Why do professionals spend the majority of their time with people they are indifferent to or don't like? Maister points out:

> Supposedly, professionals are among society's most bright, educated, and elite members—people who are supposed to have more career choices than anyone else. Yet they seem

> to be willing to accept a work life made up largely of "I can tolerate it" work and clients, and they feel that they cannot safely do anything about all that. (Maister, 1997: 25)

The fact is, you can do something about it, and you do have a choice of whom you work with and whom you accept as a customer. There is no justifiable reason for accepting—or retaining—customers whom you or your team members personally do not like. Toxic customers can have a negative effect on team morale, and that will ultimately have a deleterious effect on the firm's financial results. If, on the other hand, you work with people you enjoy, not only will you do better work, be a more effective marketer, cross-sell more services, and attract like-kind customers, you will meet Maister's definition of a true professional—a "technician who cares" and one who seeks excellence in the service of others.

LEADERSHIP

The task of the leader is to get his people from where they are to where they have not been.

—Henry Kissinger

There ain't no rules around here! We're trying to accomplish something!

—Thomas Edison

Imagine for a moment you are bowling, with one difference: There is a big black curtain draped about three-fourths of the way down the alley. You do your best to hit your mark, as indicated by the arrows on the lane, but you never really see the end result of your throw. After each shot, a person ducks his head out from behind the curtain and says, "You missed four pins." There is a another person who is standing behind you, and she says, "You hit six pins." Which one is the manager and which is the leader? Which one is more likely to act as a coach in enabling you to get better and reach your potential?

There has been a plethora of writing on leadership and how it relates to business. This is nothing new. The history of nations is rich with the sagas of great leaders, and thus you see book titles espousing leadership wisdom from a diverse group of individuals, from William Shakespeare and Attila the Hun to Abraham Lincoln and General George S. Patton. There is no doubt that leadership is essential to building a successful and lasting business. Think of the rich legacies and cultures that Henry Ford, Ray Kroc, Walt Disney, the Nordstrom brothers, Conrad Hilton, Stanley Marcus, and J. W. Marriott built. Some of these individuals, no doubt, may have been effective managers; all were great leaders and visionaries. According to Warren Bennis, a student of leadership for decades, leaders of all different personality types share these traits:

- Guiding vision
- Passion
- Integrity (self-knowledge, candor, maturity)
- Trust (earned, not acquired)
- Curiosity and daring (Bennis, 1994: 39–41)

All leaders need followers. What do followers seek in a leader? Essentially, three things:

1. Direction
2. Trust
3. Hope

Think of these three qualities as they relate to presidents of the United States. Did Franklin Delano Roosevelt offer the country direction, hope, and trust? How about Ronald Reagan, George H. W. Bush, or Bill Clinton? It doesn't matter whether you agree or disagree with any of these presidents' policies and visions. The point, rather, is that the voters are essentially grading the occupant of the White House on these three criteria. No nation, let alone business, can rise above the level of its leadership.

What difference can effective leadership make? The difference between success and failure. Ask Gordon Bethune, CEO of Continental Airlines. When he took over the airline in late 1994, Continental had filed for Chapter 11 bankruptcy protection twice in the preceding decade, and the stock was trading at $3.25 a share, with a net loss in 1994 of $204 million. Employee morale was low, turnover was high, planes were perpetually late, and baggage losses were among the worst in the airline industry. By 1995, under the effective leadership of Bethune, the company turned a profit of $202 million, and in 1996, it made $556 million. Today, Continental is one of the few airlines in the black.

What was the difference? The same planes were flying, the same employees on the payroll, the same destinations served and the same infrastructure was in place. The difference was leadership. Bethune outlines his turnaround strategy in his book, *From Worst to First: Behind the Scenes of Continental's Remarkable Comeback.* This book is full of practical, commonsense leadership wisdom from someone who turned around a nearly bankrupt company to one of extraordinary success. He didn't do it by more control and management—in fact, he burned the employee manuals in the company parking lot—but, rather, through the three traits of an effective leader previously mentioned. Here are more nuggets from Bethune's book:

> I'm not saying everybody has to be marching in lockstep—in fact, that's exactly what we *don't* want. We want people doing their jobs with a minimum of interference from their bosses. That's why we burned the employee manual. But that doesn't mean you're not the leader.
>
> In fact, that's what leadership is. Your real job as boss—my real job as chief executive—is to *let* people do their jobs. It's to assemble the right team, set the big-picture direction, communicate that, and then *get out of the way.* If employees have a problem or if something is really bothering them, you help them with that. You say, "Okay, you go back to work and I'll get this straightened out for you." That's what bosses are for. A boss' job—a leader's job—is to facilitate, not to control. You have to trust people to do their jobs. That's the strongest leadership there is. (Bethune, 1998: 43)
>
> When we're looking for goals for an entire company, we make sure our employees know what we're going for: to get the planes on time, not to aim for a certain return on investment. Goals such as certain equity or debt ratios or interest percentages work fine for the accountants, just as striving to repair a specific number of engines or reduce the number of seconds before the phone gets answered are goals set for particular departments. But when it concerns

the whole company, we need a companywide goal—something that employees can immediately identify. (Bethune, 1998: 208)

At the risk of oversimplifying, this is basically the key to running a successful business. You have to decide what constitutes success. If it's a fishing contest, are we trying to catch the heaviest fish or the longest fish? If it's a baseball game, what makes an out and what scores a run? If it's an airline, what are the indications that it is doing well? You have to explain to the people who work with you what those are, and the people have to buy into that. You have to measure that, and let them know how you're going to measure it. And you have to reward them if they succeed. That's it. (Bethune, 1998: 232)

This is one of the most common problems in businesses. Businesses fail because they want the right things but measure the wrong things—or they measure the right things in the wrong way, so they get the wrong results. Remember? Define success the way your customers define it.

Before I came to work at Continental, the company wanted to be a successful airline. But it measured only one thing: cost. That made Continental an airline that ran on low cost, paid its employees poorly, and delivered a really, really crappy product. Amazingly enough, that did not turn out to be the way to success any more than throwing all balls and no strikes is. That was not what our customers wanted.

Don't forget, Continental got what it seemed to want at the time: By saying that cost was the thing that defined its success, Continental's management got everybody to focus on cost. That turned out to be the wrong thing to focus on, though, and they just couldn't get that through their heads. It was what they focused on, it was what they measured, and they simply believed that somehow it would lead to success. That's why, even before the organization almost gave up the ghost, even when it was still trying as hard as it could, Continental just couldn't find the key to success—because the key didn't reside

> in cost, and cost was the main thing Continental focused on. (Bethune, 1998: 233)
>
> Well, you can make a pizza so cheap nobody wants to eat it. And you can make an airline so cheap nobody wants to fly it. (Bethune: 50)

Does this sound familiar? What do professional service firms tend to focus on and measure? Billable hours, which is redolent of cost accounting. Yet, is that how our customers define success? Is that what makes them select one firm over another or pay a premium price? Why do the accounting and law professions insist on tracking, measuring, and benchmarking a metric that has little, if anything, to do with the external results provided to the customer? To borrow an analogy from Bethune, if professionals ran fishing boats, they would define success not by how many fish were caught but by how many hours the boats spent on the open seas. There is no doubt that spending time is the means to a particular end, but there is more to the means than simply the time spent.

Perhaps one of the reasons morale is so low in the legal and accounting professions is an overemphasis on efforts, rather than external results. You can't inspire people with billable hour quotas and yield-per-hour statistics. There is no doubt that you can measure these things, but are they the right things to measure? Leadership is not about doing things right; it's about doing the right things. Managers can run a company, but leaders can take it somewhere, hopefully to a preferred vision of the future. Peter Drucker has never made efficiency one of his primary goals, taking this shot at the accountant's vision: "The last buggy whip factory was no doubt a model of efficiency."

At the time Bethune wrote his book, Continental Airlines had 48,000 team members, has 2,100 flights per day, and carried approximately 3 million passengers around the world per month. They accomplish this—as do most other airlines—by focusing on a few key performance indicators, such as on-time arrivals, luggage losses, complaints from customers, and measurements provided by the Department of Transportation on customer satisfaction. Does this sound more complicated than running the average professional service firm? How do they manage without timesheets?

In the May 1990 issue of *Training* magazine, Warren Bennis delineated the following differences between a manager and a leader:

Manager	**Leader**
Administers	Innovates
Short-range view	Long-range perspective
Asks how and when	Asks what and why
Eye on the bottom line	Eye on horizon
Accepts the status quo	Challenges the status quo
Does things right	Does the right thing
Focus on efforts/activity	Focus on results
Manages within paradigm	Leads between paradigms

Even Peter Drucker, the inventor of management, has grown uncomfortable "with the word *manager* . . . I find myself using executive more, because it implies responsibility for an area, not necessarily dominion over people." (Beatty, 1998: 163) When you are dealing with professional knowledge workers, the idea of managing them is ludicrous.

One thing is certain: If you want to create a timeless culture in your firm, it has to be set by the firm's leader. I trained partners of a national CPA firm in value pricing, who in turn trained their fellow partners. In one session, a partner raised his hand and asked the managing partner of his office—who was conducting the seminar—the following question: "Come now, Debbie, you know as well as I do that we have many alumni in our customers' businesses in the role of controller or CFO. If we start talking about fixed prices, fixed price agreements, and change orders, their response is going to be: "Cut the nonsense. We know how the game is played, how many hours will it take?"

I sat in the back of the room, not even sure how I would have answered that question (it's a good one). Debbie walked down to the back of the room, stuck her face right in this partner's face, and said this: "You tell him the game has changed and we don't talk hours, we talk value."

Does anyone doubt that the pricing culture in that office changed? My guess is Debbie would have no compunction about letting that partner go if he didn't conform to the culture. That is leadership by example. That is passion. That is setting a direction and showing your team you mean to stick with the preferred vision of the future. Margaret Thatcher, a dynamic world leader if there ever was one, always says: "Consensus is the negation of leadership." Your practice will not rise above the level of its leadership.

STEPS TO A TIMELESS CULTURE

No matter how far you have gone on the wrong road, turn back.

—Turkish proverb

Nothing will ever be attempted, if all possible objections must be first overcome.

—Dr. Samuel Johnson, 1709–1784

If you are a student of business, you know how important innovation is in the life of any enterprise. But it is not enough to build a culture that encourages innovation and change. You must also be willing to change the way things are currently being done. Peter Drucker, offers sage advice on this point:

> The *first policy*—and the foundation for all the others—is to *abandon yesterday*. The first need is to free resources from being committed to maintaining what no longer contributes to performance, and no longer produces results. In fact, it is not possible to create tomorrow unless one first sloughs off yesterday. To maintain yesterday is always difficult and extremely time-consuming. To maintain yesterday therefore always commits the institution's scarcest and most valuable resources—and above all, its ablest people—to nonresults. Yet to do anything different—let alone to innovate—always runs into unexpected difficulties. It therefore always demands leadership by people of high and proven ability. And if these people are committed to maintaining yesterday, they are simply not available to create tomorrow.

> The first change policy, therefore, throughout the entire institution, has to be *Organized Abandonment.*
>
> The change leader puts every product, every service, every process, every market, every distribution channel, every customer, and end-use on trial for its life. And it does so on a regular schedule. The question has to be asked—and asked seriously—"if we did not do this already, would we, knowing what we now know, go into it?" If the answer is "no," the reaction must not be "Let's make another study." The reaction must be "What do we *do* now?" The enterprise is committed to change. It is committed to *action* (Drucker, 1999: 74).

Dozens of firms have eliminated timesheets around the world. I will continue to make the case that this is the direction the profession needs to move toward. There are a number of similarities between the firms that have trashed their timesheets: innovative and creative leadership; willingness to take risks; a meritorious culture committed to total quality service; high self-esteem; and most importantly, stringent customer-selection criteria. The following is a checklist of steps that your firm can take to become a Timeless Culture:

- **Establish a pricing cartel** This will place pricing authority in a central location and help to ensure the firm is consistent with its pricing signals to the marketplace. It will also assist in commanding prices commensurate with value, not hours.

- **Appoint a traffic manager** This person will be responsible for tracking all engagements flowing in and out of the firm and for knowing who is responsible for them and whether they are being completed by the internally-set deadline. Usually, the traffic manager can be the same person who used to hunt people down to get their timesheets.

- **Establish a minimum price for all new customers** Do not take on new customers below this price, and be sure to inform your referral network of this policy so they can act as pre-qualifiers for you. Also, review this price annually and adjust it upward.

- **Enter into a covenant with team members for KPIs** Let the team members decide on the firm-wide and specific team member KPIs that will be used to measure and assess the performance of how the firm is carrying out its mission to enhance the wealth of its customers. Your people are professionals who want to do a outstanding job for the firm and its customers. Trust them to select measurements that grade the success of the firm the same way customers do.
- **Track percentage of Walk-Away, Hope For, and Pump Fist price realizations** This will enable the firm to learn from its failures and successes.
- **Track percentage of FPAs written above the minimum price** This metric will show how effective the team is at cross-selling additional services. Be sure to combine this metric with some type of reward in order to assure the behavior is repeated.
- **Reward and celebrate pricing successes** Celebrate the successes so they become part of the firm's pricing culture, and develop rewards for team members who price commensurate with value.
- **Perform a postmortem analysis on all FPAs and change orders** There is a wealth of information in a closed customer file. By brainstorming with the team members who serviced the customer, you will be able to better spot "value drivers" in the future, ascertain customer price sensitivity, and become a firm that prices on purpose. Pricing is complex, and it deserves more resources and brainpower than the average firm currently devotes to it. A Timeless Culture demands this investment.
- **Align KPIs to team member compensation** You will get the behavior you reward. Make sure KPIs are aligned with the compensation, bonus, raise, and promotion system. Don't make the mistake many firms have by stating how important the new KPIs are but then rewarding and measuring based on hours and efforts.
- **Consider implementing a "forced churn" KPI** Because many firms are reluctant to fire up to 80 percent of their customer base, a forced churn allows the firm to implement this strategy incrementally. For every new customer acquired, consider firing between one and four of your old ones. This ratio, obviously, will depend upon how many "D" and "F" customers your firm has.

The forced churn provides an excellent way to upgrade your customer base.

- **Use "No timesheets" as a lighting rod to attract top talent** Not many professionals enjoy filling out timesheets (think about the individuals you know who have left the profession for private industry who usually remark they love not having to do timesheets). A Timeless Culture is an enormous competitive differentiation when competing for talent in the competitive marketplace. As with customers, it sets your firm apart from the competition and provides a compelling reason to work for your firm. In other words, it becomes part of the firm's value proposition in attracting (and retaining) human capital.
- **Continuously study the art of pricing—it's a marathon, not a sprint** Have your team read some of the books on pricing in the "Suggested Reading" section of this book. Have them share what they learned with the firm. Pricing is an art and a skill; the more you learn about it, the better you become at doing it.

Why Your Firm Should Establish a Pricing Cartel

The greatest improvement in the productive powers of labour, and the greater part of the skill, dexterity, and judgment with which it is anywhere directed, or applied, seem to have been the effects of the division of labour.

—Adam Smith, *An Inquiry into the Nature and Causes of the Wealth of Nations*, 1776

You can judge a firm's commitment to value pricing by how it is implemented, and how the competency of pricing is developed over time. One of the most effective ways to implement the ideas in this book is to establish a pricing cartel.

In spite of present-day management gurus who claim to have discovered the concept of core competency, in reality it is a very old principle. Adam Smith's famous example illustrated how a pin factory could produce up to forty-eight thousand pins in a day if it *divided* and *specialized* the labor in such a way as to assign a particular task to each worker, whereas perhaps not one pin a day could be manufactured if each person made a whole one on their own. Smith demonstrated that the division and specialization of labor was a central cause of the wealth of nations. It is also the central cause of the success of a business. Not everyone is good at everything.

Despite this, many professional firm partners behave as if the firm is a household, in which all of the chores have to be divided equally. Pricing is a prime example. It seems as if just because you are a partner, you are responsible for pricing your engagements. But ask yourself if a commercial airline pilot also sets the airfares? Do General Motors' plant managers set the sticker prices of the cars? The answer, of course, is no. Pricing is considered a *function* in the business world; an individual (or specific group) within the company is responsible—and has final authority—for it.

Nonetheless, I have yet to encounter a professional firm where the majority of partners do not believe they are quite competent at pricing, despite overwhelming evidence that this is not the case. Furthermore, everyone in the firm already knows who the best and weakest pricers are, yet every partner is responsible for the function. This is not *pricing on purpose*, and it is a serious violation of the division and specialization of labor, not to mention a barrier to firm profitability. In golf, the lesser-skilled players receive a handicap; with respect to weak pricers, the handicap is less profit in every partner's pocket.

Pricing is far too important to the viability of the firm to be left to mediocre pricers. No other area—not cost-cutting, productivity increases, or rainmaking—can have as large an effect on profitability as does pricing. Which is why it is time for firms to recognize that if they are serious about pricing commensurate with the value they create, they need to establish a core group of enthusiastic pricing students in order to make pricing a core competency within the firm.

Many partners will argue they already do this, by, for example, discussing pricing amongst each other and bouncing different pricing scenarios off of one another. That is not enough—it is too informal and ad hoc. In successful businesses, pricing becomes a *function* within the firm, delegated to a team that develops an intellectual capital base of skills in this vitally important area, and acts in the interest of the entire firm, not just each partner's individual book of business.

Establishing the Cartel

This group will have final authority to set prices in order to maximize profits for the entire firm, while also acting as an educational unit and resource in order to assist all members in capturing prices commensurate with value. I recommend a group of between four, with no more than six, self-identified individuals who have demonstrated competency in creating value for the firm's clients, and capturing that value through price. The cartel should not consist solely of partners but should have managers and team members in order to spread the competency throughout all levels of the firm. Some firms have made half of the positions rotate, perhaps on a two- or three-year basis, in order to bring in new perspectives.

The final determination of the cartel's membership should be made by the managing partner, who should begin by asking for volunteers, thereby self-identifying team members with an interest in the art of pricing (volunteers not selected may be eligible for future terms).

I have seen two reactions from this selection process—relief and frustration. Recognizing they are not the most aggressive pricers, some partners feel better knowing a pricing cartel will assist them in setting a proper price. The other reaction—frustration—is more difficult, because some partners will inevitably believe they should be on the committee but were passed over. My response to those who whine and pout over not being chosen: *grow up*. This is a business and only those with demonstrable skills should be allowed to price, for the benefit of the entire partner group. This is a not a popularity contest, it is a skill set, and responsibility and final authority should be given on the basis of ability, not status or seniority. It is the leader's job to put individuals in positions that accentuate their strengths, not their weaknesses. Leadership demands tough choices, and sometimes individual egos have to be sacrificed for the good of the firm.

The Cartel's Mission

Examples of mission statements for the pricing cartel are:

> *To ensure [firm name]* Prices on Purpose, *according to the value received by the customer, not the hours spent.*
>
> *To make* Pricing for Value *a core competency within [firm name].*

To change the marketing culture within [firm name] to one that comprehends, creates, communicates, convinces, and captures the value of the services we provide to our customers.

The cartel should meet as needed in order to assist firm members in setting prices above some specified minimum (routine work need not be submitted to the cartel, but it should be responsible for setting minimum firm-wide prices). Because the team would see pricing from a firm-wide perspective, they are in the best position to ensure work is not priced below value. This may require someone from the cartel to assist in the sales process with partners who may not be the most competent pricers, because those partners will still be dealing directly with the customer, and will have to communicate and capture the price from them. After all, it is the partner who has the relationship that ultimately has to get the price from the customer. The pricing cartel, however, can be a very effective method for achieving this objective.

It will also slow the process of quoting prices, and although most partners treat this as a disadvantage, it is in fact an enormous advantage. Why? *The sooner the firm quotes a price, the lower it will be*, because most likely you have not given enough thought, creativity, or innovation to the value proposition being offered to the customer. It is much better to step back and have four or six minds come together to make sure the firm is offering the maximum value to the customer, and pricing it accordingly. The pricing cartel will be *obsessed with value*, which is exactly where the focus needs to be when it comes to marketing—externally on the customer value, not internally on the process, labor hours, and costs.

The Cartel's Functions

Establishing minimum prices for tax work, accounting, auditing, consulting, various legal services, etc. A growing firm needs to set a cut-off price for all new customers, recognizing it should not take all comers. One of the most effective ways to pre-qualify low value customers is through minimum prices. These are, of course, increased annually.

Pareto analysis and grading customers. Baker's Law: Bad customers drive out good ones. Twenty percent of your customers generate eighty percent of your revenues. Should the firm "outplace" some of its customers in order to focus on providing more value-added services to better customers who are less price-sensitive and more valuable to the firm? Should the firm consider outsourcing to India, or another foreign country, work on low-value customers?

Develop the firm's standard Fixed Price Agreement and Change Order. With a pricing cartel, all work is priced *before* it is done, period, just like every other business (would you fly on an airline that charged you $4 per minute?). A team member is not allowed to do anything on behalf of a customer without a signed FPA or Change Order. This ensures the firm is pricing when it has the leverage, and ensures the customer will never be surprised by an invoice from the firm. It also eliminates write-downs and write-offs. When do you want to learn the customer doesn't like your price, *before* or *after* you do the work?

Establish the firm's 100 percent money back guarantee. Why should your customers bet on you if you won't? Offer an unconditional service guarantee to all customers, thereby gaining a competitive differentiation, and an opportunity to command premium prices. You do this already, why not get some marketing advantage from it?

Select Key Performance Indicators for pricing. As discussed earlier in this chapter, pricing KPIs can be quite valuable to track, such as what percentage of FPAs are written above the firm's minimum price; what percentage are rejected; track the percentage of reservation, hope-for and pump-fist prices the firm realizes on each engagement; how many Change Orders is the firm capturing. These KPIs help change the focus of the firm from internal processes and efforts to external results and value.

Post-mortem analysis. Every large engagement under the authority of the cartel needs to be reviewed once the engagement is finished in order to assess what was learned, how adequate was the price, what was the value created, and how could the firm have priced it better. This process will, over time, build an intellectual capital base of skills that will turn pricing into a core competency.

Continuous teaching. The pricing cartel is not just an effective group of pricing warriors; it is also a teaching organization, responsible for reading books, articles, and other information on the art of pricing. Further, it continuously teaches every team member the importance of pricing for value. Because pricing is a self-esteem issue—you have to believe you are worth it before your customer will—the cartel can enhance self-esteem by achieving pricing excellence and sharing success stories throughout the firm.

(Not) Final Thoughts

All partners have heard pricing objections from their customers, they are to be expected. After all, it is the customer's job to push down prices. That said, it is the firm's job to *push back*, which is done most effectively by focusing on value, not capitulating on price. At the present time, it seems the only competency most firms have with respect to prices is *lowering* them.

The pricing cartel will be the group responsible for keeping the firm obsessed with value and wealth creation for the firm's customers—the main purpose of any business. It is a group of professionals who see pricing as an enormous opportunity, not a limitation. It is a group that will force the firm to work *smarter*, not *harder*, because pricing is the single largest driver of profitability in a professional service firm. Like the division and specialization of labor, it is an old idea whose time has come.

SUMMARY AND CONCLUSIONS

Wandered, there is no path. You lay a path in walking.

—A. Machado, Spanish poet

In this chapter, we have put a fifty-year-old practice on trial for its life: maintaining, measuring, and monitoring hours. Any enterprise—be it a government entity, a not-for-profit agency, or a private company—exists for the sole reason to create results external to itself. All of the firm's resources—land, labor, capital, and entrepreneurship—have to be organized in such a way as to produce those desired results. The fact of the matter is that any enterprise exists to create wealth, not to control costs. Generally accepted accounting principles do an abominable job at measuring this wealth-creating activity. For instance, the balance sheet tends to report the liquidation value of a business. But businesses are not established in order to be liquidated. They have to be operated by leaders as a going concern and for wealth creation.

I offer an alternative model to the time-based culture of most professional services firms, one grounded on four essential elements: human capital, key performance indicators, customer selection, and leadership. This is not a complete model; I am acutely aware of its shortcomings and the many misgivings some have about implementing it. This is not unusual, as any new paradigm offered can never satisfy the most trenchant critics. Accounting and law firms measure the wrong things by focusing on hours (or worse, minutes). No customer buys hours. That means we don't sell time, which means time is not a measure of any firm's success. We need alternative metrics to measure the right things, as defined by our customers, not merely by our temptation to control costs and follow a habit that can no longer be justified in a knowledge-based economy. I am not saying measurements are not important—indeed, the KPIs offered here are a critical component of replacing the time-based culture—only that the measurements need to be of the right things.

Much more work needs to be done in this area. The final chapter on this topic has yet to be written. I offer this chapter as a way to focus attention in the profession on this issue and to challenge the necessity of timesheets. All revolutions require both thinkers and doers. It has been said that while George Washington fought in the American Revolution, Thomas Jefferson *thought* for it. Timesheets can be discarded, and we can once again focus professionals on the one task for which they exist: Creating wealth for their customers. As Benjamin Disraeli wrote, "Man is not the creature of circumstances. Circumstances are the creature of man." We have it within our power to create the timeless culture in the professions. Let us forge a Declaration of Independence and free ourselves, once and for all, from the tyranny of time. To paraphrase from Karl Marx: Accountants of all countries, unite! You have nothing to lose but your timesheets. [I am indebted to Paul O'Byrne, a Chartered Accountant in the United Kingdom (and a slight admirer of Karl Marx), for coining this phrase and for giving me a T-shirt with the following imprinted on the front and back: "You have nothing to lose but your timesheets," and "Timesheets are the opium of the professions." Paul was also kind of enough to take me to Highgate Cemetery in London to visit the tomb of Karl Marx.]

The road ahead is long, and much work remains to be done. An author must be content with the knowledge that what is false in what he says will soon be exposed and as for what is true, it might someday be ultimately accepted, if only he lives long enough.

21 THE TIMESHEET DEBATE CONTINUES

When two men in business always agree, one of them is unnecessary.

—William Wrigley, Jr., 1861–1932

A certain amount of opposition is a great help to a man. Kites rise against, not with the wind.

—John Neal, 1793–1876

One of the great pleasures I have enjoyed since the publication of the first edition of this book is meeting with leading members of the accounting profession around the world. Not all of them agree with the premises I set forth in this book, however, and it has ignited quite a debate. In the arena of ideas that is important, because ideas have consequences. As Samuel Johnson wrote, "It is advantageous to an author that his book should be attacked as well as praised. Fame is a shuttlecock. If it be struck at only one end of the room, it will soon fall to the ground. To keep it up, it must be struck at both ends."

One of the individuals who have struck is Ric Payne, founder of Principa. Ric is a towering intellectual in the profession, a Chartered Accountant from Australia as well as a former professor of accounting and economics.

From February through April 2000, I had the great good fortune of taking the value pricing message to Australia, New Zealand, and the United Kingdom, along with Paul Dunn. During these tours, one issue that always came up was the relevance of timesheets. Ric Payne and I began a debate, via email, which was published in its entirety in the Third through Fifth Editions of this book. It is my belief that the no timesheet theory has been validated by the approximately 300 firms around the world that have discarded them. Some of these firms have contributed their profiles in the Case Studies chapter which follows.

One of the interesting questions regarding new ideas and theories is how do they diffuse throughout a population? Value pricing—meaning FPAs and change orders—has now been implemented in approximately 5–10 percent of the accounting firms in the world, while the number of firms that have gotten rid of timesheets has been a much smaller percentage (less than 1 percent). The question is, why? Why have these ideas taken so long to diffuse through the professions? I set out to answer that question in an editorial that was published in the June 21–July 11, 2004, edition of *Accounting Today*. A longer version of this editorial is included below, as well as some of the issues brought up by responses to the editorial by various consultants to the profession.

Finally, also included in this chapter is an essay from Paul Kennedy, a Chartered Accountant from the UK, who used to be a staunch believer in the necessity of timesheets but who now runs his firm without them (you can read his profile of his firm, O'Byrne and Kennedy, in the Case Studies chapter). I thought this essay was so compelling that I should share it with readers who still are skeptical about getting rid of their timesheets.

The Diffusion of an Idea—An Editorial

Whenever anything is being accomplished, it is being done...
by a monomaniac with a mission.

—Peter Drucker

Winston Churchill once said America will do the right thing—once it has exhausted the alternatives. One could say the same about the accounting profession, which has the puzzling tendency to circle the wagons and fire *inward*, snatching defeat from the jaws of victory.

At present, there are two particular practices that are killing our profession: pricing by the hour and maintaining timesheets. These practices are stifling growth, wealth creation, and innovation. They inhibit customer service and enthusiasm and destroy morale and the professional's quality of life, not to mention making the accounting profession less attractive to potential students. Most disturbing of all, consultants to the profession—those who should know better—play a significant part in this death spiral.

Any profession or industry has a natural resistance to new ideas. Of course, sometimes we are resistant to change for good reason. If every crackpot idea were tested, the costs would be astronomical while the benefits minimal. Yet we must strike a healthy balance between resistance and experimentation—if no new ideas were ever tried we'd still be in the Stone Age.

Fortunately, history is replete with renegades who were ridiculed yet eventually triumphed. Yesterday's cranks frequently are tomorrow's conventional wisdom.

The Diffusion of an Idea

The diffusion of an idea is the process whereby an innovation is communicated through certain channels over time among the members of a social system. Diffusion essentially is a social process, and often it takes a substantial amount of time for an idea to become accepted by a majority of a population.

Consider, as evidence, germ theory—the idea that diseases are transmitted by specific germs, or microorganisms, as has been proven for many infectious diseases. Scholars have traced the development of this theory back to the sixteenth century, though it was generally ignored until Jacob Henle revived it in 1840. Still, germ theory remained on the fringes of medical science until 1865, when it reached a critical mass of acceptance, and it became conventional wisdom by 1914. It is one the most significant ideas to have bettered the human condition; prior to its acceptance a trip to the doctor, on average, didn't do much good—and sometimes did harm.

Another example is the facsimile machine, invented in 1843 by Alexander Bain, a Scottish clockmaker, who called it a recording telegraph. In 1948, RCA introduced a machine that transmitted messages via radio waves, yet the fax machine did not diffuse through the general population until 1987—it took 150 years to become an overnight success! Books on history, science, economics, and others, are filled with similar stories.

A Radical Idea

Attempting to diffuse an idea throughout a social system can be a frustrating and tiring task. It is a mission I have been on since 1995, and simply stated, it this: *To bury the billable hour (and timesheets) in the accounting profession.* Why? Because—to reiterate—timesheets and the billable hour are killing our profession. The billable hour has nothing to do with what customers buy—it measures efforts and activities, not results. Because there are only so many hours in any one person's life, the billable hour is an artificial ceiling on the income potential of the profession. As for timesheets, nobody joined this profession to bill the most hours and become a galley slave on the *SS Billable Hour*. To measure a knowledge worker's value and efficaciousness in six-minute increments is a form of degradation, making modern day accounting firms redolent of the sweatshops of yore.

There are approximately 80,000 accounting firms in the English-speaking world and approximately 5–10 percent of them have successfully implemented some form of value pricing (quoting fixed prices up-front to the customer, using fixed price agreements and change orders). However, less than 1 percent of accounting firms have gotten rid of their timesheets.

Usually, a critical mass is achieved when 17 percent or so of a population adopts an idea; then it becomes a question of time before the remaining percentage follows. Yet when one studies the history of idea diffusion, you quickly realize reaching that 17 percent can be an extremely long process. Why hasn't the idea of value pricing diffused more quickly throughout the accounting profession?

Obstacles to Diffusion

What are the major obstacles inhibiting the diffusion of the ideas of value pricing and no timesheets?

DNA The accounting profession learned the billable hour from the legal profession approximately two generations ago, and the practice has had time to become part of the molecular structure of every CPA. When I entered the profession in 1984, I was told "You sell time." It took me more than five years to challenge this assertion. How can we sell something the customer doesn't buy?

Metrics Peruse any Management of an Accounting Practice (MAP) survey, study any benchmarking report, read any trade journal, visit any Web site, attend any seminar, listen to any consultant, or read any book on the profession, and you will find metrics related to billable hours, realization and utilization rates, revenue per hour, *ad nauseam*. The billable hour is the yardstick every firm uses to measure, and no one ever bothers to ask if the measurement means anything. Firms then compare their hourly metrics with each other, thereby benchmarking mediocrity and never rising to new levels.

Job security Accountants aren't starving, and they certainly are not being threatened by any significant external shocks. Indeed, the more complicated the tax code and regulations such as Sarbanes-Oxley become, the more accountants earn. Contrast this with the barbering profession in the 1960s when it was confronted with the British Invasion. Barbers always had a predictable and steadily rising income in good times and bad, but that changed with the Beatles and men growing their hair longer. They were forced to change or become extinct. No such imminent threat faces the profession or even any one firm (Arthur Andersen, perhaps, being the most recent exception, though many would argue they set fire to their own platform).

Partnership structure Margaret Thatcher was fond of saying "Consensus is the absence of leadership." Nothing is more illustrative of this view of consensus than a group of partners sitting around a table taking days to decide which photocopier to purchase. Whenever a new idea is introduced, inevitably one (or a few) partner(s) will rise and assert, "We tried that idea during the Coolidge administration and it didn't work." Then and there, the initiative dies. Can you imagine the same thing happening in a meeting at General Electric when Jack Welch was CEO? If you were an investor, would that be a *buy* or *sell* signal?

Lack of leadership Most accounting firms are over-managed and under-led. A firm without timesheets requires leadership and vision. It requires knowing you are doing the right things, not just doing things right. It requires focusing the firm on the external results and wealth it creates for the customer while building the type of firm people are proud to be a part of and contribute to. It requires a sense of dignity and high self-esteem that you are worth every penny you charge. It requires an attitude of experimentation, not simply doing things because that is the way they have always been done. It requires less measurement and more trust.

Disdain of theory Pick up any book, or attend any seminar, and one of the first things you'll read is "This course is not based on ivory tower theory, but practical steps you can take back to the office Monday morning and implement." Any time you read that, you are about to read a bunch of discombobulated facts (like reading the phone book) and learn nothing of lasting value. All learning starts with theory. As the great mathematician David Hilbert once said, "There is nothing more useful than a good theory." Man is ruled by theories, they keep planes in the air, bridges and buildings standing—and, by the way, theory is also the reason you bill by the hour and maintain timesheets. The positing and falsification of theory is the cornerstone of all scientific progress, but you'd never know it in the accounting profession, where we avoid theory as if it were a type of plague.

Truth is not determined by popular vote At one point in history, the majority of learned people thought the earth was flat, which, of course, didn't make it so. One of the most puerile objections to the value pricing and the no-timesheet argument I hear is "If these ideas are so good, why aren't more firms using them?" Because, quite frankly, an idea is not validated simply because a substantial portion of a population engages in its practice. That is not how science progresses. The Scientific Method, established in Europe between 1589 and 1687, gives us concepts such as hypothesis, falsification, parsimony, and the experimental method. This is the rational way in which new ideas should be tested, not by an opinion poll.

Consultants Consultants are perhaps the most disconcerting obstacle because they usually are the "change agents" in the population, spreading new ideas. Yet some of the most obtuse opposition I encounter is from this sect, reminiscent of the guilds of yesterday that degenerated into technologically conservative organizations. With respect to the ideas of value pricing and no timesheets, some of the profession's most notable consultants are arguably modern day Luddites. Even though the value pricing idea has managed to be diffused among them, many consultants do not attempt to scientifically falsify the idea of running an accounting firm without timesheets. Simply put, they are helping to keep the profession mired in the mentality that there is a correlation between measuring efforts and activities and results and wealth creation. Even worse, their attitude seems to be "I would not believe it even if it were true."

To categorically reject a posited idea rather than scientifically refute it is inexcusable. Given that the idea is now being tested in many firms around the world, one would expect this group to show the most intellectual curiosity. Yet, up until now, Ric Payne has been the only one to offer an intellectually cogent counter argument to mine.

My open question to the consultants is: What will you be known for 50 years from now? Are you simply going to perpetuate the current orthodoxies in the profession and create better, more efficient ways to do the *wrong* thing, or will you have the courage to explore new and innovative ideas—whether tested or not—and help the profession remain dynamic and relevant? Will consultants stand by while an entire industry becomes irrelevant?

The physicist Max Plank wrote, "A new scientific truth does not triumph by convincing its opponents and making them see the light, but rather because its opponents eventually die, and a new generation grows up that is familiar with it." This is an incredibly pessimistic view of human nature—and one which I reject—as it implies that people are incapable of intellectual adaptation or change, and the only way to make progress is to wait for older members of a society to die. And yet, as Charles Murray documented in his book *Human Accomplishment*, the peak age for almost all significant accomplishment is 40, and as my colleagues Paul O'Byrne and Paul Kennedy (whose firm dumped timesheets two years ago and who now are bigger zealots about these ideas than I am) recently asked me in a London pub—where such issues tend to contemplated—"Why do intelligent people stop learning?"

Not Final Words

For a profession to be truly innovative, it not only must do new things, it must stop doing old things. It is not possible to create tomorrow unless one first gets rid of yesterday. Maintaining yesterday is always difficult and time-consuming, and wastes resources on non-results. Instead, every policy, procedure, service, and activity should be put on trial for its life, every two to three years, by asking "If we didn't do this already, would we go into it the way we are now?" If the answer is no, then the question is, "What would we do?"

I should not be the lone voice in the wilderness attempting to answer these questions with respect to value pricing and "Trashing the Timesheet." I welcome each of you—especially the consultants—to join me in the search for truth. In the meantime, I will continue on my quest, and continue to argue, debate, defend, and confront anyone who challenges my theories in the arena of ideas, which is the way better ideas emerge.

Victor Hugo wrote, "No army can withstand the strength of an idea whose time has come." The billable hour and the timesheet are ideas from the day before yesterday, and they will be eliminated. Good ideas may be neglected, but they seldom die. My only hope is to live long enough to see it happen.

Responses to the Editorial

Ron,

I read your excellent article in *Accounting Today*, and I agree with you wholeheartedly, as you know from the book that August and I just finished (*Client at the Core: Marketing and Managing Today's Professional Services Firm*, by August J. Aquila and Bruce W. Marcus).

About five years ago, I argued your argument with a law firm client, who pointed out that there is too much advantage to partners to ever change it. "You're absolutely right," I told him. "But it won't be the professionals who change it—it will be the clients who revolt against being shafted by the professionals."

I still believe that, and we've seen evidence of it. My point is that first, the short-sightedness of the professionals doesn't allow them to see the ultimate advantages of value-based pricing, and second, if you want a crusade that works, aim it at the clients. That, I believe, is where the revolution will start.

Next we go after the obsolescent partnership structure.

Bruce W. Marcus
www.marcusletter.com

Hi Bruce,

Thank you so much for your kind words—they truly mean a lot to me. As you can see, I'm very frustrated with the supposed "change agents" in this profession and really believe they are now doing more harm then good. This Op-Ed was an opening salvo aimed right at them, and I will continue to battle in the arena of ideas. It will be interesting to see if any of them have the intellectual sophistication to defend their ideas.

You are so right about the customer being the driver of change, which has already happened in the legal profession. I wish it didn't have to be that way, as I'm furiously committed to bettering the CPA profession, but I'm realistic enough to know change doesn't happen without some driving force.

You have already taken on the partnership structure (I've learned much from your writings on that issue), and I will follow your lead in that battle.

Sincerely,
Ron

Ron,

I just finished reading your article in *Accounting Today*. We met at one of the consulting conferences a couple of years ago in Seattle.

I have given up the billable hour over the last five years, with much success. I am now 99 percent fixed price agreements. I still bill hourly for a few tax clients who want some questions answered. ALL ongoing clients have a fixed price agreement with me.

The success of this (motivated again by your book, *The Firm of the Future*) has only increased my gross fees by over 30 percent per year each of the last three years, with NO INCREASE in expenses. Needless to say, it's a lot more fun going to the bank!

Don't get frustrated and quit, because what you present has so much going for it. Clients ABSOLUTELY LOVE FIXED PRICE AGREEMENTS, because they don't [care] about time, they want value.

Just thought I would write to tell you to keep at it, some of us know you are on to something. The remainder get to work more to make more....

Charley Kanieski
Business Guide
Guiding Business Owners to Financial Freedom
charley@learninguide.com

Hi Charley,

Thanks so much for your e-mail, it means a lot to me. I know there's a group of my colleagues out there who get it, and have produced great results like you. I just wish the consultants to the profession were among that group. Sadly, they are not, and that is why I wrote that Op-Ed piece. It was directed at them, not CPAs.

It has produced a response from some of the more notable consultants, and touched off quite a debate. Anyway, thanks again Charley for your kind words. I really appreciate them and it inspires me greatly to keep up the quest.

Sincerely,
Ron Baker

Sir Ron,

My reference of course is to the movie *Braveheart*. Hopefully, you will not have your intestines flayed out of you in order to win the freedom of the accounting profession from the wicked rule of Sir Charge-hour and his evil mistress, Madame Timesheet. However, you may be up against the same sort of challenge that Scotland faced to secure her freedom from England.

I just finished reading Jay Nisberg's "A response to Ron Baker" in the July 26-August 8 issue of *Accounting Today*, which was in response to your editorial, "The Diffusion of a New Idea," in the June 21-July 11 issue.

I think the conflict you may have inadvertently, or purposefully, created with your indictment of the consultants to the CPA profession is a good thing. Dissension and conflict are wonderful attention getters. Dissension and conflict are absolutely essential in democratic societies if those societies are to constantly strive for improvement in the lives and functionality of their members. The more conflict you can generate around an idea, the better for the future of the idea and, in this case, our profession.

I know of you very well, as I am sure many CPAs do. I read your book, *The Professional's Guide to Value Pricing*, in 2000. I also attended The Value Pricing Seminar, presented by Danny Morriss, in November 2002, in Cincinnati. And, many CPAs and firms also know of Jay Nisberg. No matter who gets the credit for the idea, it is a good one. I have been a proponent and practitioner of your ideas in my part of the practice for several years. However, when I propose doing away with timesheets and universally adopting fixed-fee pricing, service/money-back guarantees, and related Bakerisms, both within my firm and with other CPAs, only a rebellious few sign on. Certainly, I think CPAs are not passionate about it. They do not fall in love with the idea. I was once told, "the opposite of love is not hate, the opposite of love is indifference." It takes a lot of love to change the DNA of an old idea.

Just as Sir William Wallace had the passion to fight to break the shackles of British rule during the thirteenth century in Scotland, you will need to continue to be the passionate voice for our profession to free it from the evil rule of Sir Chargehour and Madame Timesheet. To be sure, there is a "band of brothers" within my hamlet here in our Covington office—ok, only two of us really—who believe. Nevertheless, I urge you to carry on. Sir Ronald, carry on and fight the good fight!

With highest and best regards,

Scott J. Malof CPA/PFS
Covington, Kentucky

> Hi Scott,
>
> Thank you for such a great email—it literally made my month. It is easy to become discouraged when you're trying to change a profession, but people like you keep me going, and help sustain my hope and passion.
>
> At the risk of overloading you, I'm attaching my article on establishing a Pricing Cartel.
>
> Thanks again Scott. I hope I have the chance to work with your firm in the future. Maybe we can't get rid of Madame Timesheet, but we can certainly improve your pricing.
>
> Keep in touch,
> Ron Baker

Jay Nisberg also responded to my editorial, which response was published in *Accounting Today* online. His response included, "For the most part, I enjoyed what you wrote until I felt this unwarranted attack upon myself…. Let me suggest that, before you ubiquitously accuse 'all' consultants of anything, you do your homework." I do not have permission to reprint his response in full, which is unfortunate because he is a member of The Advisory Board, self-identified as a "Think Tank to the Professions." Think tanks battle in the arena of ideas, and usually members don't deny permission to publish their works.

Here is my reply to Jay:

> Thank you for your letter, Jay, and reading my article. The intent was to begin a dialogue with the supposed "change agents" to the profession, and it appears from your passionate response that I was successful.
>
> This is a debate about ideas, not egos or personalities. I am leading a revolution and in the process eggs—and egos—do break. Your letter of reprimand was a gallant effort, but results are what matter. I believe in the theory of Revealed

Preference—that is, watch what people *do*, not what they *say*. You have offered no empirical evidence that refutes the central claim in my editorial, i.e., that consultants continue to perpetuate the timesheet in the profession. Ideas have consequences and the timesheet is a bad idea with bad consequences.

I have done "my homework" on all of the consultants; I've listened to and read just about everything they've said and written. You protest that you have advocated "value billing" for longer than I've been consulting to the profession, and this may be so. Although judging from the number of firms that are out there doing it right, your message appears not to have been heard. Furthermore, you are not advocating value pricing as I have posited it in my work (i.e., quoting prices on work *before* it is begun, as well as utilizing fixed price agreements, change orders, etc.). This is the methodology I described in my book, *Professional's Guide to Value Pricing*.

I, too, have fond memories of our dinner last December in Nashville (with our mutual colleague, Troy Waugh) and enjoyed the food and the conversation. My recollection—in addition to the food—was your admission to Troy that you had not read either of my books, and upon returning home I sent you one. I found it unbelievable that a leading consultant to the profession had not read the leading books in the profession relating to pricing and the no-timesheet theory. It is ironic, since you admonished me to do my homework and yet it appears you have not done yours. Then again, it just proves the point in my article: Not many change agents lead a profession to a new paradigm past the age of 40. Most people simply are born and die within the same paradigm.

As far as "touching base" with the hundreds of firms you have consulted with, please name for me *one* firm that has eliminated timesheets due to your consultations? Show me one talk, or one article you have written, that calls for the complete elimination of timesheets and all firm metrics revolving around billable hours and realization rates.

In fact, name for me one firm in the Top 100 that any consultant has been successful in removing timesheets from? How about the Top 500? How about a sole proprietorship? I have removed timesheets from dozens of firms so far around the world, and it would be a lot more if any of the change agents were to join me.

Many consultants do preach "value billing," but they know very little about the economics of pricing, and unfortunately what they do know is wrong. On the issue of eliminating timesheets, the consultants have shown no intellectual curiosity whatsoever. Not one of them (except Ric Payne) has tried to empirically refute my theory for no timesheets (and Ric lost the argument, as the theory has been validated). The silence has been deafening from the rest of you. I welcome the debate, and want you to know it is not personal. This is a battle in the *arena of ideas*, and we should be able to conduct it with civility and respect, and keep the end-goal in mind—the betterment of the profession we are proud to serve.

Until we remove the cancer of the timesheet from our profession we will not soon see CPAs earn what they are truly worth (a goal we both share). The consultants have not called for the elimination of timesheets; rather they continue to advocate incremental moves up the value curve by measuring hourly realizations. I have left the curve.

I welcome you to join me by signing the Declaration of Independence at www.verasage.com. If you believe in this revolution then pledge your sacred honor. I eagerly await your participation—I have been holding my breath for nearly ten years.

Respectfully,

Ron Baker, Founder
VeraSage Institute

Troy Waugh then replied, in a mediating fashion, to Jay and me. He was concerned that the tone of the conversation had become uncivil, unprofessional. He helpfully fleshed out the points on which we disagree, the different approaches Jay and I have to addressing the present needs and the future growth of our profession. He drew comparisons between small and large firms' realization of profit growth, drew attention to the difficulty of the profession, and the difficulty of pleasing all clients while implementing change. Troy Waugh recognizes the importance of pricing in our profession and realizes, as I do, that what we want in common is to help clients reach their maximum potential.

I felt it incumbent upon me to reply to Troy and have included my response below:

> Hi Troy,
>
> I certainly appreciate you taking the time to compose such a thoughtful letter, and especially the spirit in which it was offered. There are so many issues in your letter I feel I must address, but let me begin with your major one.
>
> It was certainly never my intent to show any disrespect to Jay. I have a very high of opinion of Jay, as I do you. I wouldn't be engaging in this debate with either of you if that were not the case. I learn from intelligent debate, and I place my ideas in the arena of debate to test them. I will be the first to apologize to Jay if he felt any disrespect on my part.
>
> I thought both of our letters contained some personal barbs, and I'm used to that and ignore them (though they spice up any debate). Please remember, I've debated this entire topic with Ric Payne, whom I also consider a towering intellectual (the debate can be found in its entirety in the Third through Fifth Editions of *Value Pricing*, and I continue to debate with Ric to this day). He landed many blows to me, and it probably has made my debating style more aggressive, as well as sharpened my thinking. Nonetheless, I can't emphasize this enough: This is not about personalities or egos, this is about ideas, and that is where I will keep the focus. Thanks for assuming the role of Marquess of Queensberry.

I certainly do not agree that eliminating timesheets is a "minor element" in achieving a better quality of life, or better profits. The timesheet is the ultimate artificial ceiling on our profession, and we put it there. It is one of the major reasons the accounting profession does not have a Larry Ellison or Bill Gates (though one could point to Henry Bloch as a successful entrepreneur in the profession, but he wasn't a CPA). Both Gates and Ellison don't have a ceiling on their income or wealth-creating abilities. With value pricing, I have taken the ceiling and made it a floor, and propose that, in the real world, there is no ceiling.

With any change, it's always easy to point to the status quo and say it's not necessary, the big firms haven't done it, etc. This keeps us prisoners in the moment, and less prone to experimentation and innovation. I truly believe it is coasting on the path of least resistance. None of which I find at all persuasive. Revolutions always happen from the outside, and I wouldn't expect to find a Top 100 firm engaged in testing this idea.

As for the law firm partners making over $1 million, it doesn't surprise me they use timesheets. If they do litigation work, the courts still require price to be anchored to time. Accountants don't suffer from this restriction, unless they, too, are doing litigation, bankruptcy, or governmental-type work.

I have never claimed eliminating timesheets will make a firm more profitable (I would never claim wet streets cause rain). What I have said is this: Their costs exceed their benefits. Yet, because so many of their costs are not measurable—the deleterious effects on morale, entrepreneurship, customer service, innovation and dynamism, etc.—I will never be able to prove my case with numerical certainty. That does not mean those costs do not exist, it merely demonstrates we do not have the sophistication to measure them.

There is a big firm that has eliminated timesheets, and I would put it in the top 15 percent of profitability. Now this firm is pricing on purpose, using fixed price agreements, change orders, etc. (You can read the profiles of firms that have transitioned fully to value pricing, and some that have also eliminated timesheets, in the Case Studies chapter in both the fifth and sixth editions of *Value Pricing*, written in their own words. To me, this is the beginning of verifying that the theory works.) Other firms have begun to establish a Pricing Cartel, delegating the pricing function to a group of people who have sole responsibility for it. Establishing a pricing cartel is what the Fortune 500 companies do (e.g., your airline pilot does not set your airfare), and I believe assigning this important driver of profitability to a committed group of people will have a salutary effect on any firm's pricing competency. There may well be firms that don't have timesheets that are not more profitable, but it's not because they trashed timesheets, it's because they are not competently pricing on purpose.

But there is a larger issue here, and one that I believe doesn't have a voice. My yardstick for the success of this revolution is not just the impact on existing firms' income statements; it's the betterment of the profession as a whole. Who is in charge of making this profession better for posterity if not its leaders? I see the morale in our profession going the way of the legal profession, and that scares me. Law firms burn out young associates with ridiculous billable hour quotas that everyone recognizes have no correlation with the characteristics of a successful lawyer. The ABA has written a report on the debilitating effect of the billable hour treadmill, and in fact, the Foreword to the report is written by Supreme Court Justice Stephen Breyer (a copy of which is in *The Firm of the Future*).

Is this the best future we can offer new and potential members to the accounting profession? I think we can—indeed, must—do better. It is up to the leaders to take the profession to a new level, and develop metrics, measurements, and judgments that actually correlate with the successful traits of a knowledge worker. We are working with the ultimate knowledge workers, and the timesheet is a relic from the days of Frederick Taylor, who studied manual laborers. I have laid the groundwork for this in *Firm of the Future*, positing that many Key Performance Indicators (KPIs) do a better job than the timesheet. After all, the timesheet is a *lagging* indicator, and what all firms need are *leading* indicators that define success the same way the customer does. No customer judges the success of their CPA firm based on the number of billable hours. This is not some fad or fantasy world, this has been tested empirically around the world. If we are what we measure, isn't it time we start to measure what we want to become?

I applaud Jay's results for firms by creating an income stream (financial services) not dependent on billable hours; I only wish we all would do the same for the major income stream in the profession. I don't see how that can happen while the timesheet exists, because it keeps the firm mired in the mentality that it sells time. After all, that is what is measured in 6-minute increments, every single day, day in and day out. Private industry doesn't use timesheets, and we should ask ourselves why not.

This idea is not just "revolutionary" to me, but to every firm and conference I speak to. If there weren't something fundamentally wrong with the timesheet, people wouldn't have listened to me for as long as they have, and the message would not resonate as strongly as it does. I do live in the real world, this is where I test all of my ideas. But I do it by positing falsifiable theories and then following the scientific method to either refute them or confirm them (and then, hopefully, develop better theories). You claim you cannot "change a technician to an entrepreneur by having them eliminate timesheets," and I never said you could. But I can guarantee one thing: as long as the timesheet culture remains, we will never have true entrepreneurs.

Also, the three defenses of timesheets—that they are a pricing tool, a productivity tool, and a cost accounting tool—

have been refuted in my books. Take cost accounting—the billable hour realization is *profit forecasting*, not *cost accounting*, as it contains the desired net income of the partners in the rate. Cost accounting has never been about allocating profit, or opportunity cost as defined by economists. I believe the cost accounting tool is the strongest defense of timesheets, but I still have successfully argued it away. Just quickly: Toyota has never had a standard cost accounting system, and we certainly cannot say they are not profitable, dynamic, innovative, etc. This is well documented in *Profit Beyond Measure,* by H. Thomas Johnson, an accounting professor. You can read about the intellectual feud he is having with his former co-author Robert Kaplan, of Balanced Scorecard fame, in *Firm of the Future*.

Our colleagues are not going to become better pricers by becoming better cost accountants. We already have that skill, and 95 percent of our costs are fixed anyway (at least in the short and medium run), so how hard is it? And anyway, firms are using timesheets for pricing, not cost accounting. What better pricing decisions do they make as a result of maintaining timesheets? I'm afraid not many, since the profession still writes down and writes off more than it writes up.

I am a member and speaker at the Professional Pricing Society, comprising many of the Fortune 500. These companies have established the role of Director of Pricing because they realizes the impact better pricing can have on profits (supported by studies from McKinsey to Accenture, and many others). None of these folks are cost accountants, and in fact, they don't like cost accountants much because the information they get from cost accountants is late and irrelevant. Cost accountants look inside a company, and pricers look outside, just like any good marketer.

I understand that the process of change—and idea diffusion—is slow and incremental. I made this very point in my Op-Ed piece in *Accounting Today* that touched off this whole debate. But change will be much slower if the change agents in the profession don't see the logic in it and don't spread the word and advance the methodology. You claim that firms need a "detailed method" and I agree. I have provided them one comprising pricing strategies and methodologies, as well as Critical Success Factors and KPIs. What else can we do? Ultimately, the profession will have to change because it is the *right* thing to do. Firms have to be committed to being excellent environments for the knowledge workers of the future to work and invest, not sweatshops that are going to hold them accountable for every six minutes of their day. For the amount of work that all of us do with firms, we still affect a very small minority of the total population; hence being a change agent means disseminating ideas beyond our immediate sphere of influence if we are to have a long-lasting impact on the profession.

As for firms with an entrepreneurial leader and other partners who cannot function in a fully value priced environment, this is precisely why I now advocate a Pricing Cartel. Remove the pricing function from people who are poor or mediocre at it (and every firm already knows who they are). I can't imagine GE or General Motors allowing people to price simply because they have a title. Part of a leader's job is to use people's strengths and to eliminate or downplay their weaknesses. Yet many partners believe they should be pricing simply because they are partners. I disagree. Form a Pricing Cartel and let those who see pricing for what it is—the number one driver of profitability in the firm—develop a core competency in the firm. The only competency we seem to have now is in cutting prices. The root cause of this problem, in my opinion, is the partnership model, where everyone has an equal voice in everything. This does not capitalize on the specialization and division of labor so essential to creating wealth. Of course, that is an entirely different topic that also needs to be addressed and debated.

I actually agree with your method in the Rainmaker Academy of introducing pricing later rather than sooner (though I think the third year is too late). A firm must have a strategy and a value proposition before it can set premium prices. It also must provide—to borrow a phrase—Five Star Client Service. I realize many steps precede taking on the challenge of eliminating timesheets, but when is the time right to bring up fundamental measurements, metrics, and judgments that better reflect the wealth-creating abilities of knowledge workers? After ten years? Twenty? It's like having kids—the time will never be right, so just do it. If a firm is committed to it, it will happen. I had a no-timesheet firm partner recently tell me, "Ron, I'd sleep under a bridge before I went back to the old way of operating a CPA firm." Now that's commitment, and willingness to pay the price for making genuine change.

I can't imagine the signers of the Declaration of Independence asking, "How do you do it? How long will it take? How much will it cost? How do we get those other people to change? How do we measure it? How have other people done it successfully?" These are the wrong questions. The right questions are: What type of future do we want to create and what price are we willing to pay to create it? (These questions are from a book all consultants should read: *The Answer to How is Yes,* by Peter Block.) Developing a competitive advantage is never free.

Let's be honest, part of the problem is that every consultant has a certain investment in the status quo, and when you are selling advice and other methods, it's imperative to demonstrate they work. I have no investment in the status quo; I am offering the automobile in a buggy whip world. Simply, we need to test new ideas to move our profession forward. This is not easy (and sometimes I want to just throw up my hands and walk away); it often feels like jousting at windmills. But I'm also tilting at the consultants, which makes my job doubly frustrating.

Troy, I've never doubted your track record, and $300 million is impressive. However, I would also suggest that bringing in new clients at the wrong price doesn't make a major improvement in a firm; it could just add layers of mediocrity. I'm *not* suggesting you are doing that, I know you preach value pricing, but we've both seen firms churn through customers, and it's very easy to report on acquisition numbers without reporting on defection numbers, not to mention the actual profitability of the acquisitions.

I have added millions of dollars of pure profits to firms with the TIP clause pricing strategy alone, which goes straight to the bottom line by pricing smarter, not working harder. The largest single example being $1.1 million from Texas (for work he was going to price at $180,000 at standard hourly rates). I'm not saying this to boast (it's the firm that *created* the value, I just helped *capture* it with better pricing strategies), I'm making the point that pricing smarter is the number one driver of profit in a firm (of course, TQS is critical in getting and keeping clients as well). Firms will never capture that type of value if they have a timesheet mentality strapped around their necks. As one partner retorted to Ric Payne, who claimed you could receive a TIP like that even while maintaining timesheets, "That's true, but we *never did*." And that is my point—it's a *mental* barrier, not a *physical* one (much like Roger Bannister and the four-minute mile—once he broke it, high school kids began to break it).

Our metrics don't capture money left on the table. In the case of the $1.1 million TIP, if he would have charged $180,000, the realization would have shown 100 percent (or maybe a bit more), thereby earning him accolades from his partners. But the $900,000 left on the table would not show up in the cost accounting or realization reports. This is why I'm adamant that benchmarking against an arbitrary hourly rate is not just useless, it's self-limiting. There are simply no metrics that capture lost pricing opportunities (or mistakes) and these losses dwarf any gains you can make from efficiency, better cost accounting, or rainmaking. Further, as Yogi Berra said when asked why his team lost the World Series, "We made too many wrong mistakes." Firms leave money on the table and never learn from it because the metrics they are using can't capture external value. So much for better pricing through better cost accounting.

I probably would advocate eliminating timesheets even if a short-term effect were lower profitability because I believe it is the *right* thing to do. But because I can't quantify the costs and benefits precisely, perhaps it is the firms who are being myopic, since they are just chasing a fast buck and not investing in their future. I understand the gap between potential and reality, but I'm not about to dumb down expectations and hand our colleagues *Dick and Jane*. I want to hand them Dickens, and challenge them intellectually and emotionally to be all they can be. What does it say about the change agents to the profession if their expectations are that low?

This debate is public and that is precisely where it belongs (conducted with the utmost respect and civility). But it's not about individuals such as Jay, Troy, myself, or any of the other consultants. It's about our profession and moving it forward into a better future. It's simply too important to the profession not to debate in public, and I will continue to write, speak, rant, and rave against the billable hour and the timesheet—in public, private, and anywhere else. I may alienate everyone I know, but I simply must state what I believe to be true and accept the consequences. I've never seen the book *Great Moderates in History*. Revolutionary change is accomplished by those on a mission with firm convictions.

For example, I think if one disagrees with those consultants that advocate firing customers, it should be made public. I may very well be one of those consultants, though my definition of an "F" customer is someone with a toxic personality. I've also offered an Adaptive Capacity Model that says some "priceline.com" customers are acceptable, as long as the firm doesn't *add* capacity to accommodate more of them (something an airline would never do). One wonders, though, where do you draw the line? Was Enron an "F" client that should have been fired? Or was it simply a big risk with the wrong premium (as an actuary would say)?

> Thanks again for your letter Troy. I have always held you in the highest regard, and none of these words change that opinion at all. I, too, have the abundance mentality, as this profession needs all the help it can get. I hope we can collaborate more in the future because I think the amount of intellectual capital we all possess is awe-inspiring and is the ultimate lever to bettering the profession we are proud to serve.
>
> Sincerely,
> Ron

Troy Waugh was kind enough to reply to my direct letter, and he again emphasized our mutual desire to help our clients succeed, and praised the challenging way in which I evangelize pricing concepts. I consider it a success to get people engaged in debate, to get their juices flowing, as it were. The fixed ideas of the billable hour and timesheets comprise a formidable wall to bring down. Nonetheless, I intend to bring it crashing down like the Berlin Wall.

An Essay on Timesheets, by Paul Kennedy, O'Byrne and Kennedy, Great Britain

I write as reformed sinner.

Once, not only did I believe a firm could not be managed without timesheets but thought our profession privileged to have such important information!

I now write with all the vile and evangelical passion of a reformed sinner. My conversion probably went through various stages, not unlike the development of mankind from Neanderthal to modern man.

The Five Stages of an Accountant

The development of the thought process of an accountant regarding pricing can be broken down into five stages:

1. "We need timesheets to price and to monitor team performance otherwise we wouldn't make any money"

2. "Timesheets are not relevant to pricing but they are an essential tool to monitor job and client profitability and team performance"
3. "Timesheets are not the only way of monitoring client, job and team performance, *but are still relevant* and they don't do any harm"
4. "Timesheets are not the only way of monitoring client, job, and team performance, they are *not* relevant, but they don't do any harm"
5. "Timesheets are dangerous and lead to massive sub-optimisation but how do I run a business without them?"

I now run an accounting practice without timesheets and I am so glad I found a way to do it. Any reader who thinks that price is in any way related to cost needs to find a more basic article to read. This essay addresses readers who are at stage two or beyond!

Our Focus Determines Our Destiny

If timesheet measurements were a small part of an overall Management Information System, their impact would not be so insidious. The fact is they are the main (only?) tool for managing accounting practices. The problem with this is they focus our attention on the wrong things—and what we focus on is what we get.

Take the true story of the supermarket cashier: A customer at a supermarket asked the cashier if the cashier could help him pack his purchases in his bags. The cashier just shook his head and kept scanning the goods and passing them along the conveyor. Only after scanning the last item and ringing up the till did the cashier turn to help the customer, who by this time was swamped with the purchased items. The cashier apologised for not helping before and explained that the management measured his scanning speed against benchmarks. This story illustrates the dangers of measuring the wrong things. What the supermarket really wanted was happy customers who kept coming back. By measuring productivity they unwittingly cultivated a behaviour that was inconsistent with this main aim. Timesheet metrics do the same thing in our profession.

Metrics must be aligned to our main aim. If accountants typically pursued a cost leadership strategy (Porter) or a operational excellence model (Treacy & Wiersema) than cost related, short term resource allocation KPIs like yield and productivity may be more important metrics in an overall Management Information System dashboard (although only partly as every organisation exists to create value outside of itself, to quote Drucker); but accountants are not these sort of businesses or shouldn't be!

Accountants are in a mature, fragmented industry and a more appropriate strategy involves differentiation through customer intimacy. Management and management metrics therefore need to focus on the customer's view of the business.

Profits come from our ability to create value for our clients and from our ability to capture some of that value (and of course risk). We create value by delivering benefits that satisfy their needs. We capture that value by pricing those benefits over the resource costs of creating those benefits. Our long-term profitability therefore depends on:

1. Our ability to understand our target customers' needs.
2. Our ability to target those customers most likely to value those things we can do well (customer segment selection and selection criteria within segment).
3. Product/service design and mix.
4. Our ability to develop our clients needs in their minds (selling).
5. Our ability to generate and convert leads of the type we want.
6. Our ability to value price our services.
7. Our ability to select and manage appropriate intellectual capital (mainly people).

If timesheets were part of a range of feedback metrics covering all the points above, and the information was properly put in context of the main aim of the firm, then arguably the data could contribute to the overall view. However, in many accounting practices timesheets are the dominant (sometimes only) feedback system and are not put into any proper context. As a result, they lead to behaviours that contradict the firm's main aim (not that many firms have a consensus as to what their main aim is).

For the purposes of this discussion, let's assume the firm's main aim is long term profitability with a wish to pursue a customer intimacy strategy.

Ironically the first problem lies with our profession's failure to understand all the dimensions of profitability. You cannot maximise profits without asking the question "Over what period of time?" If you wanted to maximise profits during the current hour you should probably not be reading this essay. The fact is long term profitability requires investment. It requires investment in fixed and current assets but also intangible assets including relationship capital, structural capital, and human capital. These intellectual capital investments are particularly significant to the knowledge economy and to accounting firms.

Timesheet data gives us crude (some would say inaccurate) data about productivity, yields and recovery rates. Problems with timesheets include:

1. They measure quantity of time spent not quality.
2. They assume time spent is a cost not an investment.
3. They do not consider longer term profitability issues, for example, lifetime value of a customer (see Frederick Reichheld's *The Loyalty Effect*).

Not All Hours Are Equal

Take the example of Accountant A and Accountant B in Figure 1, below. In Job 1, Accountant A performed well using the traditional way of measuring performance. The average yield per hour was above target with a recovery rate in excess of 1 (1.05).

Accountant B, by contrast, wasn't watching the timesheet reports. He was thinking about the client. He recognised client expectations could be greatly exceeded if he put some additional thought (and, in this case, some extra hours) into the job. As a result, the job added value to the client in such a way that the client became a "raving fan." The client's trust was enhanced, his price sensitivity eased, and he was more willing to spend more money with his accountant. Job 2 represents the long-term numbers for this client.

In this example, Accountant B put additional work into delighting the customer when he spotted the opportunity. The question is, had he been looking at his timesheets, would he have done so? Would he have done so if he had to explain the recovery rate to his boss?

Adding value doesn't always mean working more hours. Indeed, the *quality* of the hours is what counts, not the *quantity*. However client relationships do need investment especially in the early days of the relationship when trust is being established. Timesheets militate against such

Figure 1

Recovery Trap

Job 1 for Client Alpha

Accountant	Max. Avail. Hours	Fee	Hours	Target Hourly Rate	Productivity	Yield per Hour	Recovery Rate	Client Value Index**
A	150	10000	100	95	67%	100	1.05	73
B	150	10000	130*	95	87%	76.92	0.81	94

Job 2 for Client Alpha

Accountant	Max. Avail. Hours	Fee	Hours	Target Hourly Rate	Productivity	Yield per Hour	Recovery Rate	Client Value Index**
A	150	10000	100	95	67%	100	1.05	73
B	150	18000	70	95	47%	257.14	2.71	94

Traditional P&L

	Accountant		
	A	B	Difference
Income	20000	28000	8000
Costs	same	same	n/a
Profits			8000

Intangible Balance Sheet

	Accountant	
	A	B
Relationship Capital Index	73	94

* Not all hours are equal; the last 30 hours relate to adding value the client really wants. These hours wouldn't have been worked if looking at recovery rates. We see hours worked as costs when really they are, at least in part, investments.

** Impacting on client trust, price sensitivity, and willingness to invest more with accountant.

Figure 1 (cont.)

Impact of investments of time (quality rather than quantity) on long term value captured

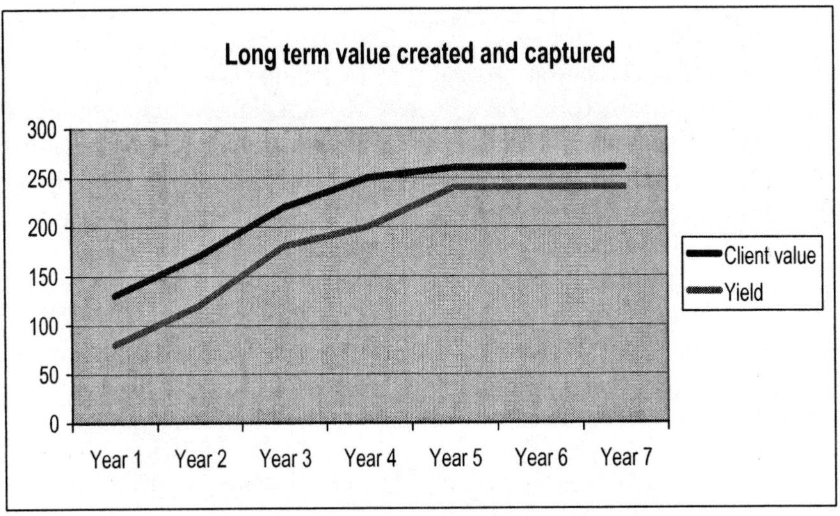

	Year 1	Year 2	Year 3	Year 4	Year 5	Year 6	Year 7
Client A							
Client value	130	170	220	250	260	260	260
Yield	80	120	180	200	240	240	240

investments because time is seen as a cost, not an investment. The long-term benefits of such investments are represented in Job 2 (in Figure 1). By focusing on client value and not on short-term profitability metrics, Accountant B became more profitable in the long term. Long-term profits will *only* come from focusing on client value.

In Figure 1, the additional work is reflected in the higher rate of productivity. If productivity was already very high, this could not have happened, which is why we should always leave room in first class.

Also, the example in Figure 1 should not be confused with discounting, scope creep, or being cheap. If you have selected a customer who recognises that he or she is paying a price premium in the first instance, then you have all the more reason to do whatever it takes to delight the customer and keep them for the long term. It amazes me that firms are prepared to budget for "lost time" to win new clients and then think the marketing and selling to that client finishes once the lead becomes a client.

Strategy/Positioning Is Everything.

Delighting the customer must be our aim. In the long term this is what will lead to profitability. Timesheets do not measure relationship capital or consider any long-term issues, however. They focus our attention on short-term profitability and force us to behave in a way that contradicts our long-term aim.

As I have illustrated, Figure 2 represents the variability of the value clients receive over time compared to the relatively invariable nature of a typical accounts prices. Area *x* represents the additional value the client received, some of which could have been captured through higher prices. Area *y* represents the work from which the client did not perceive any value and for which the client resents paying (whether articulated or not).

A number of observations on this diagram.

Do clients tolerate *y* because of *x*? In other words, do clients console themselves that in the long term they get value, if not from every job? Or does *y* make the client very cautious about using the accountant? Does it make him query the price (which in reality is value) of future work? Does *y* erode the trusted status of the accountant?

Also, we must not ignore the impact of pricing on the perception of value effectively taking the perceived value line higher.

As I have illustrated, Figure 3 assumes the firm's pricing policy is aligned to the client's perception of value received. By pricing to value in this way the firm and the client can choose whether the work in area *y* is done or not. If the price at which the client would value it is too low for the accountant to want to do it, other options can be explored. It may be that doing the work at a loss is better than doing it at a profit because of the impact on long-term relationship capital. By constantly ensuring the client receives value—by understanding the client's needs *whatever the cost*—the firm builds trust, which translates into premium pricing, value-added work, and a bigger share of the client's wallet.

Once again, we cannot ignore the importance of good strategy. Good positioning, client selection and value added product design all make the difference. If a firm takes the "whatever the cost" approach to a mixed bag of clients, some of whom are never going to value what their accountant

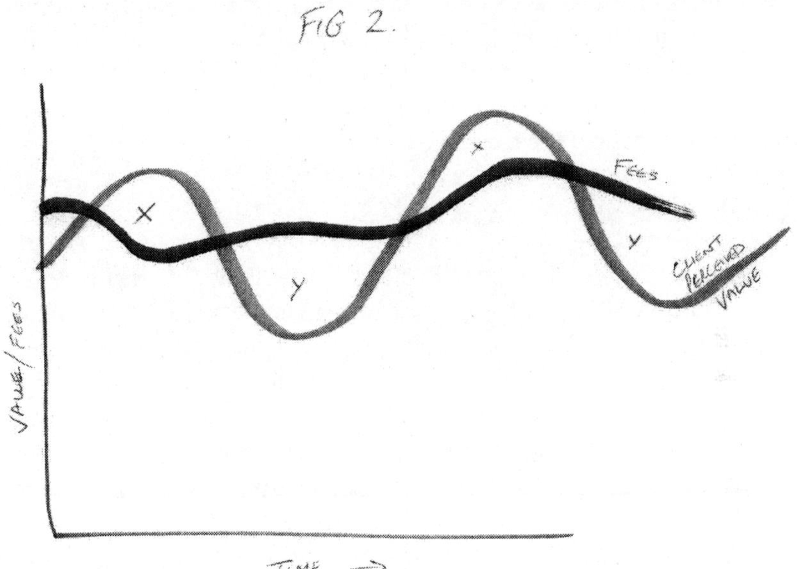
FIG 2.
X
Y
X
Y
FEES.
CLIENT PERCEIVED VALUE
VALUE / FEES
TIME →

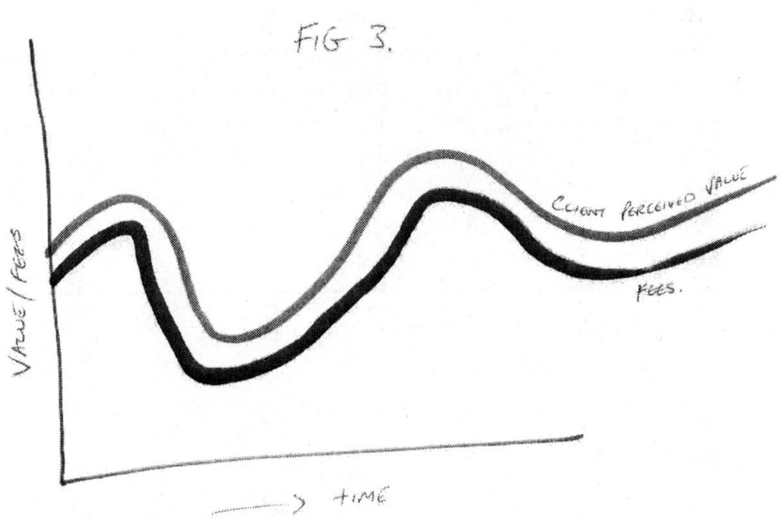
FIG 3.
CLIENT PERCEIVED VALUE
FEES.
VALUE / FEES
→ TIME

does, then they are going to have problems. The fact is most accounting firms are over servicing some clients (those they should not have as clients) and under servicing others. The cost of under servicing our better clients is huge and the rewards of addressing this are similarly large. By focusing on short-term profitability, timesheets systemically prevent us from tapping this potential.

Mismanaging with Timesheets

Take a typical write-off report. For example, a write-off report tells you that you have worked ten hours at an average hourly rate of £100 and your work in progress is £1,000. Let's say your fixed price was £800. What does this mean? Does it mean that £200 was lost on this job? How would you use this information to manage the business? The answer in most cases is that the accountant would charge a higher price to this client next time. But price has nothing to do with cost! If the client will pay the higher price next time, shouldn't the higher price have been charged in the first place? Even firms that have made the intellectual leap of fixing prices in advance and believe they are not using timesheets to price still are. Only now they are making pricing adjustments on future contracts based on historical timesheet records. Accountants even use it for client self-selection: "We will put our price up on this job so that we will make a profit (as defined by them) and if client won't pay then they can go somewhere else." In this way, the client is given the choice, which is better than not giving him the choice by after-the-event billing. Clients must always be given the choice; however, this form of marginal pricing is an abdication of our responsibility to choose our market in the first place. And maybe the price wasn't wrong. Maybe the problem was the cost. But timesheet data looks at the *effect* of cost, not the *cause*. To control cost at the source, you need to consider:

- Product/service selection and scope.
- Target market selection and scope.
- Customer selection criteria.
- Internal process design.
- Recruitment and training.

What if the write off report shows time costs at £800 and the fee at £1,000? How would this information be used? Is the inclination to pat ourselves on the back and say "well done"? But what if the fee could be £3,000, not £1,000, based on client perception of value? In short, timesheet feedback tends to punish professionals who think about long-term relationships and reward those who are failing to capture real value. Truly we are a profession intent on not making job losses while not making (too much) profit. The argument given is often, "Yes, but how do know whether you are making money on a job/client?" Timesheet data doesn't tell you. The problem is that accountants think it does and this is why timesheets are so dangerous. The truth is the typical job cost report does not measure profit (see "Not All Hours Are Equal," above) but focusing on this false information we make decisions that take us further away from our objectives of higher real profitability.

Firms spend huge amounts on maintaining this irrelevant and misleading information. Software, time taken to do time recording, write offs, report production, erroneous decision making are just a few of the costs. That said, the real costs are performance sub-optimisation, degraded team morale, and loss of strategic focus.

An Alternative Value-Based Management System

Instead of looking at cost and time data at the end of a job, consider the following checklist (see also the Checklist for Examining Closed Files):

- Did we add value with this job?
- How could we have added more value?
- Could we have captured more value through higher price?
- If we were doing this type of job again, how would we do it?
- What are the implications for product/service design?
- How should we communicate the lessons on this job to our colleagues?
- How could we have enhanced our client's perception of value?
- What other needs does this client have and are we addressing them?
- Did this job enhance our relationship with this client?
- What impact has this job had on developing our client's trust in us?
- How would you rate our client's price sensitivity before and after this job?

These questions force actions—actions that are prompt and consistent with long-term profitability.

How to Run a Practice without Timesheets and Live Happily Ever After

The practical issues surrounding ditching timesheets include:

- How do we measure revenue, WIP, and prepaid income for the purposes of our monthly and annual practice accounts?
- How do we know how well our team members are performing?
- How do we plan and monitor jobs?

Our firm has designed its own systems for doing these things. Our system also gives us a forward view of value creation and pricing and allows us to plan capacity looking ahead, rather than looking backward with timesheets. The benefits of working this way include:

- We have become a value-focused business.
- We price based on client perceptions of value (we have no choice!).
- We fix all prices and arrange standing order payments for invoices.
- We no longer have damaging and time consuming price disputes.
- We have prepaid income in excess of our work in progress.
- We have no credit control function.
- We have no timesheet management processes including:
  —No timesheet completion and input
  —No write-off processes
  —No after date invoicing processes (we do all our invoices at the outset of the contract)
- We have no timesheet software (we have our own value and job tracking software).
- We have a happier team, which makes it easier to attract better talent.
- We have happier, less price-resistant clients.

Fear of Change

Having moved from a timesheet/cost culture to a value culture I now wonder what stopped us from taking this step before. I think the answer was fear. Winning the intellectual argument may do it for some. But change is usually about emotion. To paraphrase Anthony Robbins, "You intellectually know chocolate cake is not good if you are trying to lose weight, but you will only stop eating it when you mix it with tuna casserole in your gut." Ron Baker has started a true revolution. The value-based accounting firm has been born. The market place has been destabilised, the dominant business model challenged. If you fear change, be afraid. Be very afraid.

A Decade of Pricing Wisdom

In April of 2004, I had the good fortune of conducting a five-city tour of New Zealand, spreading the value pricing message to professionals in that lovely country. On the flight over, my brother—Ken Baker, a marketing person with Procter and Gamble—asked me what I have learned about pricing over the past decade. Some of the lessons have been previously mentioned in this book, but are included here again in summary. Although I'm certain—or is it hopeful?—that the text below does not contain all that I have learned, it does summarize some of the major lessons in the infinitely fascinating field of pricing.

Establish a pricing cartel. In order for pricing to become a core competency within professional service firms, it has to be allocated the intellectual capital it deserves. Pricing is far too important to be left to those who are poor—or just mediocre—at capturing the value the firm provides. By centralizing the pricing decisions, the firm will be able to develop intellectual capital in this vital skill, capital which then can be leveraged throughout the firm. Some firms inform their customers about the existence of this function, most do not. My preference is to not disclose the existence of a pricing cartel, but perhaps to disclose the next level.

There is a level beyond the pricing cartel, which can be adopted by those firms that have had a cartel in place for a period of time. I believe someone in the firm should be in charge of value—external value created for the customer. One of the disadvantages to a pricing cartel is it can become too focused on the firm, rather than focused on value for customers. When asked who in your firm is in charge of value to the customer, almost everyone answers "Everyone." Well, if everyone is in charge, no one is. A value cartel is the next step in the revolution of value pricing.

Discuss value, not price. Buyers have a natural incentive to lower the price they pay, but they do not have an incentive to lower the value they receive. If the firm structures its value proposition in order to maximize value, this will reduce price sensitivity. For those Customers who want a lower price must sacrifice value in return. The airlines are a good example of this, offering many different fares, each with different value propositions. For those customers only willing to pay the lowest fares, they may have to sacrifice getting the flight time they desire, fly standby, or not get the nonstop route. Professional service firms, with some creativity, also have the opportunity to make similar value-price tradeoffs in their service offerings.

Supply always exceeds demand. Many of pricing mistakes are made because of excess capacity considerations. Especially in slow and non-peak periods, it is easy to believe that any dollar in the door is better than nothing. This is clearly false. When firms offer discounts to certain types of customers, or in certain periods, this degrades their pricing signal to the rest of their customers, and sends a mixed signal into the marketplace. Because a firm's capacity always exceeds its demand, it doesn't make sense to price at premium levels only when the firm is operating at maximum capacity. The strategy is to allocate the capacity appropriately, while offering different value packages to different customers. Remember, the airline's goal is not to maximize the number of seats occupied per flight, but rather to maximize the revenue per flight. This can sometimes be done by reserving capacity for high value customers, even at the risk some seats remain vacant at takeoff. In today's world of offshoring and alliances, firms can almost always find the capacity they need. Capacity decisions should not have a major influence on your pricing strategies, given that they do not affect the external value you create for customers.

Customers want to compare value with price *before* they buy. Professionals violate this basic law of economics, price psychology, and customer behavior at their own peril. There are few items purchased in the marketplace today where the customer doesn't know the price before they buy—legal and accounting services being major exceptions. Why? Because of the billable hour method, you can't price until you know the exact time. The goal is to have the customer decide on the price versus value comparison *before* they buy, not with each additional hour spent. From the firm's perspective, when do you want to learn the customer does not like your price—before or after you do the work? Pricing up front maintains your price leverage and allows the customer to decide to buy based on value, not to mention that every other business prices in this manner.

Focus on benefiting the customer. Marketing is all about the customer, about the results that are created outside the walls of the firm. All engagements and RFPs should focus on how the customer will benefit from the services being delivered, not how those services are going to be performed. Customers are interested in—and pay for—results, not efforts. Do not bore them with your internal processes and procedures; rather, excite them with the results of your services.

Establish criteria for success. All customers make judgments. When you walk into a Starbucks, you make judgments regarding the facility, friendliness of the servers, displays, etc. Isn't it a good idea to know how customers judge the effectiveness of their professional relationship? What are their criteria for prompt response? How often do they want to meet with you? The more customer expectations are determined upfront, the higher the probability of a successful service experience, which translates into higher prices for the firm (because perceived value increases). For an excellent questionnaire to determine each customer's success criteria, go to www.cpadudes.com and download my colleague Dan Morris's Prospective Customer Questionnaire. Of course, you will need to modify it to fit your firm's culture and personality.

Nothing raises your price like being willing to walk away from work. Your ultimate negotiation position is value, not price. That said, it is sometimes necessary to walk away from customers who do not value what you are offering. Establishing a policy of minimum and reservation prices is a critical task for the pricing cartel. Do not get caught in the mentality that all growth is good growth. Not all customers are equal, and most firms could shrink their customer base and actually increase their profits. It is almost always easier—and more profitable—to cross-sell more services to existing customers than to acquire new ones.

When you move forward, you leave some things behind. Leaving behind, or "firing," customers is an important part of your firm's capacity allocation process. If you have too many D and F customers, it is better to let them off your airplane so you can allocate more capacity for your full fare coach, business, and first class customers. There are many ways to accomplish this, as discussed in Chapter 14.

New customers love value pricing. In the transition phase of implementing the ideas in this book, you will not encounter resistance from new customers by offering them fixed prices and change orders. Customers want certainty and less risk; the billable hour shifts the risk to the customer, fixed prices put more of the risk on the firm. In return, you get a risk premium (consider fixed rate mortgages versus variable rate mortgages—customers will pay a premium for certainty). If new customers prefer fixed prices, you would be remiss not to offer them to your *existing* customers. In addition to educating them that fixed prices reduce their risk, you can also explain that new customers are being priced in this manner.

Never discount unilaterally. If you do, you are rewarding your worst customers for challenging you on price, thereby subsidizing your worst customers at the expense of your best ones. If you make a price concession, be sure the customer gives up something in return. This should be value (reduced services, scope, etc.) or accelerated payment terms. There are only two exceptions to the no discounts rule: (1) if you offer a discount for advance payment (usually 5–10 percent) or (2) if you offer a loyalty program, in which the customer may earn a discount from the price of change orders above a certain threshold or annual yield.

Price complicated engagements in phases. For projects you cannot price in total up-front because you are unsure of the scope, you can always break the project down into various phases, with an appropriate scope, price, and payment terms for each phase. "Phase pricing" is an effective method and it has been used on engagements ranging from complex estate planning, computer training and installation, consulting projects, and IRS audits, among others.

There is one more important point with respect to phasing: Be sure to price phase two—and have the customer agree to the price, scope, and payment terms—*before* you complete phase one. You should be able to determine phase two by the time you are 80–90 percent done with phase one, and you want the customer to agree to the terms before phase one is complete in order to maintain your price leverage.

We've heard all the price objections before. There is nothing new under the sun, at least when it comes to price objections. If your firm is going to charge premium prices, you will no doubt induce sticker shock and confront your share of price objections. Keep in mind, however, that when a customer questions your price, it is usually because they do not see the value of your offering. This is where the pricing cartel (or the value cartel) can enable the firm to effectively communicate the value it is providing.

What's my budget for this? There are two main reasons a fixed price might result in a lower total amount than hourly billing. First, the firm might have quoted too low of a price from the outset. This is the result of not pricing on purpose and not developing a competency in pricing. Second, the firm might have missed change order opportunities. Change orders are an essential component of offering fixed prices because they greatly reduce the firm's risk while offering a pricing strategy, whereby the firm maintains its price leverage and the customer stays in control of the purchase decision. Change orders are simply one of the best pricing strategies ever invented.

Simple to moderate projects can be scoped with the input of the customer. For the change orders that are basic to moderate in complexity—for example, relatively simple projects such as some tax research, lease versus buy analysis—one question has been found to be very effective in helping to set the price: "[Client], what's my budget for this?" (I am indebted to my colleague Daryl Golemb for this eloquent, non-threatening, brilliant and effective question.) For more complex change orders, obviously, this method will not be as effective, but those change orders should be priced by the cartel.

Never submit a proposal without options. Whether you are offering an FPA or an RFP to a potential customer, you will increase your success if you offer a variety of options. (This was discussed under "Menu Pricing" in Chapter 12.) Customers today are sophisticated; they can select the type of value/price offering they want and most customers will not select the cheapest offering. By offering three (sometimes four) different service bundles, you put customers in control of the trade-off they want to make. It's an effective pricing strategy because, over time, it usually results in the customer trading up among the levels.

Some firms offer three value bundles and a fourth option will be a low-price, basic service that enables the potential customer to "test drive" the firm to determine compatibility. Usually this service is something relatively easy and inexpensive for the firm to provide, but highly valuable to the customer, such as a benchmarking report or a tax or legal review.

The more quickly you quote a price, the lower it will be. This is an axiom of value pricing, and the reason for it is if you quote a price too soon, chances are you have not thought enough about creating value for the customer. This is part of the logic behind the pricing cartel, to slow the process down and make the firm think harder about the value proposition. Some professionals have objected to the pricing cartel, charging it is too bureaucratic and slow, but that is precisely its function. There is nothing urgent about quoting a price, and the longer the firm thinks about it, the higher it will be (commensurate with value, of course).

Formulas lower prices. Value, like beauty, is subjective and in the eye of the customer, therefore, if a firm tries to make pricing formulaic it will miss myriad factors that cannot be quantified when determining value. The billable hour is an excellent example of this formulaic mentality. Not only does it violate the Subjective Theory of Value, but it also places an artificial ceiling on the income of the firm. Any formula will do this. If you follow the methods in this book, you quickly will discover that the hourly rate becomes a *floor*, not a ceiling. Further, if you subscribe to the Subjective Theory of Value, you soon realize there is no ceiling, except that which you impose on yourself.

You control when price is discussed. Many professionals become nervous when a customer insists they quote a price, and wanting to please is one of the cornerstones of all good professionals. You should never quote a price, however, before you fully understand the customer's expectations, criteria for success, needs, wants, and the scope and value of the services. You have absolute control over when to discuss price, and you should never let the customer force you into a premature price quote (another advantage of the pricing cartel).

Only discuss price with the economic buyer. When pre-qualifying a new customer, or when submitting an RFP, it is essential to deal with the person who actually will authorize hiring your firm. If you cannot get past the gatekeepers to the economic buyer, this may be a signal the company is not serious about switching professionals, and your quote may just be used as price leverage with their existing provider. Unless you know something that contradicts this advice, it almost never pays to submit an RFP unless you have had the chance to communicate with the actual economic buyer.

22 CASE STUDIES

Introduction

You are about to read nine case studies of firm leaders—in their own words—who implemented value pricing. Some began this process long before we had the details and methods worked out, and some innovated their own best-practice methods. I thank these individuals—and their teams—for contributing these case studies. The studies are a wonderful exposition of experiences and knowledge that readers will be able to leverage. I have learned from their failures, and learned more from their successes; there is no greater pleasure than watching your colleagues do better for their customers—and, in turn, themselves—than even they thought was possible.

Bradley, Allen & Associates, LLP, Lakewood, Colorado

Tim Bradley, of Bradley, Allen & Associates, LLP, Lakewood, Colorado, describes his firm's experience with value pricing as follows.

If you're reading *Professional's Guide to Value Pricing,* you probably didn't choose it to take with you on vacation. Someone in the profession probably recommended it to you. That's how it went in our firm, anyway—but what an amazing return we've realized on that small investment of a few dollars to buy the book and the time to read it.

Directly and indirectly, value pricing has changed the way Bradley, Allen & Associates, LLP, does business. We were a good firm before we ventured down the value pricing path, but we're a better firm today because:

- We are a more valuable resource to our clients.
- We now operate less like a practice and more like a business.
- Our profit per partner has increased dramatically.

I'll bet that last one got your attention. I'll address all three points here, but first, to help you understand how we got from here to there, a little background is in order.

In 1998, the partners of Bradley, Allen, in business for about 15 years, enrolled in the Results Accountants' Systems Boot Camp, a four-day, very intense workshop conducted by Paul Dunn. That Boot Camp and our subsequent affiliation with RAS helped us realize that to do the kind of work we wanted to do with the kind of team we aspired to have, and to have the kind of professional and personal lives we desired for ourselves and our team, we had to do some serious work on our focus, systems, and even our clients. So the partners and key team members got to work improving our firm's team and systems, developing our services, and analyzing our client base—including reading Ron Baker's *Professional's Guide to Value Pricing* at the recommendation of RAS and at the urging of fellow Boot Campers.

I've made that sound a little too easy. Improving was very hard, and it continues to be very hard. But we were fortunate to get to a point in our re-engineering process where we could be receptive to the value pricing message Ron delivered at a conference in September 2000. Ron was the keynote speaker at the conference, and never before or since have I seen a ballroom full of accountants jump to their feet with such enthusiasm and appreciation as I did at the end of his presentation. We were inspired and excited—and came back to the office convinced we could do this value pricing thing.

Implementation

Book Club

The very first thing we did when we got back from the conference was start a "Value Pricing Book Club." We ordered enough copies of Ron's book for every person in the office and asked one of our supervisors to facilitate a discussion group. She provided reading assignments, timelines, discussion questions, and fun quizzes. She organized role plays so we could practice asking the right questions in client meetings and prepare ourselves for resistance. The Book Club met in the conference room for about 1½ hours every other week for seven weeks. One member took notes on a laptop during the discussion so that we could capture decisions and action items. The notes also provided a reference for those who missed a session (although we had nearly perfect attendance throughout). Our facilitator announced the following guidelines at the beginning of the first meeting, and they were honored throughout the seven-week Book Club period:

- Participation is mandatory.
- Sharing is encouraged.
- All opinions are valued.
- Cooperation is essential.
- Misery is optional.

We found tremendous value in this process. Our decision to ask a supervisor to facilitate provided her with a leadership opportunity while minimizing the potential for members of the team to feel that the partners were shoving this initiative down their throats. Having everyone from the wet-behind-the-ears staff accountant to the senior partner participate in the Book Club (and be held accountable to the same timelines and guidelines) created a feeling that we were all in this together. Although the initial goal of the Book Club was to make sure everyone actually read the book, the real result was that we got buy-in of the value pricing philosophy at all levels.

Lingo

One thing we've discovered about implementing processes over the years is how important it is to be consistent in the use of key words. Nowhere has this proved to be more true than in our value pricing implementation. For example, Ron explains in an earlier chapter that the word "pricing" is a more friendly term than "billing." In our firm, "invoicing" (creating a piece of paper for the client) became different from "billing" (relieving work in progress [WIP]). We began to use many new terms—FPA, change order, contract administration, Pareto Principle—and eventually captured and defined them in a document that we use to help new team members assimilate more quickly into our value pricing culture.

One bit of lingo we did not adopt was "customer" to replace "client." Ron offers a convincing argument as to why a firm would want to make this choice, but after a long and lively discussion in one of our Book Club meetings, the team elected to stick with "client." I think the lesson here is that it's important to make it your own when implementing change. As much as we bought into the value pricing philosophy, the decision to maintain the use of "client" was one small way we could still feel in control amidst the major firm-wide changes that were occurring.

Fixed Price Agreements

The Book Club had created enthusiasm for value pricing, but our next challenge was to turn that into action. We were innately cautious (or fearful) enough to realize that we weren't ready to value price all of our clients in one fell swoop. The question became, "How do we decide who to try this on?" Being accountants, we started with a numbers approach. We performed a Pareto analysis to identify the top 20% of our clients, and in early November 2000 established an initial goal of getting all of the businesses in this group on fixed-price agreements (FPAs) by the end of the year. This proved to be a far too aggressive goal. We extended the deadline first to mid-January 2001 and ultimately to the end of February.

From the top 20% of our business clients, we chose to introduce FPAs to those with whom we had the strongest relationships. Our partners and service providers (our lingo for "in charge") identified those clients and then began setting up meetings with them to present the concept of selecting services for the coming year and agreeing to a price and terms up front. Partners and service providers scheduled these client meetings with great trepidation. As much as we believed in the process, as much as we'd studied and planned and role played, we anticipated resistance and feared rejection. We weren't yet convinced that our clients would be receptive to a fixed price and worried that the sticker shock of a year's worth of services would be a deal killer.

We were wrong. Most clients really appreciated the meeting to talk about their needs for the coming year and were delighted to have the opportunity to negotiate terms other than "Payment is due upon presentation of invoice." Confidence among the partners and service providers grew as they shared their victories at our Monday morning staff meetings, and we kept a running total of signed FPAs so we could all track—and celebrate—our progress.

In terms of dollars and cents, the result of all this effort was remarkable. In the first six months of our implementation (October 2000 to March 2001), we sold $981,000 in FPA services to our business clients and $164,000 in fixed-price 1040s. In 2003, our business and individual FPAs will be around $1.4 million, or 59% of revenue.

Unlimited Access

Using Ron's FPA letter template, we include an Unlimited Access section in every annual FPA. The FPA letter tells the client they are "entitled to unlimited consultation with us." Clients are then free from being nickled and dimed for phone calls and meetings. This makes clients more likely to call when facing an important financial decision, and opportunities for us to deliver additional services often present themselves in the course of these conversations. So far, none of our clients have abused this service. The Unlimited Access element of a FPA often seals the deal for a reluctant client. Clients find it reassuring, and it opens the door for service providers to be more proactive about contacting clients to find out what's happening in their world. We get to invite ourselves into a client's business, and it almost always results in an improved relationship between client and partner or service provider.

Scoping Services

Perhaps you've been in a situation in which at the end of an engagement, the client's expectations were beyond what you had expected to deliver. We've been caught in that scenario a time or two, particularly in engagements that are nontraditional and complex. Defining the entire scope and process up front can be daunting, so we try to organize and price these kinds of engagements in phases. This approach affords an opportunity to spend a few hours meeting with the client to clarify the expectations while explaining the value of the engagement and, ideally, creating enthusiasm for proceeding with future phases. This first phase is typically priced at $750 to $1,000. The value to the client is in an improved definition of the project, better communication, and fewer change orders.

Change Orders

We've been lousy at writing change orders. While logic tells us it makes sense to notify the client when a change order is warranted and to agree on the scope of the services and the price before work begins, the difficulty stems from the fact that most accountants don't like to talk to a client about what we should be paid. We're even less inclined to explain our value in the context of delivering a specific service. Whether it's humility or stupidity, we've walked past many pricing opportunities because we were reluctant to propose a change order. We're slowly getting better at it, but we have a long way to go before we see change orders as an opportunity rather than a necessary evil.

One way we've dealt with making change orders more palatable to ourselves and our clients is by swapping services. For example, we have a client who is in the business of providing disaster restoration services. In 2003, this client's FPA included quarterly strategic planning meetings, but early in the year we identified a marked decrease in production and needed to discover the cause. Knowing this client is very price conscious, we offered to swap a strategic planning meeting for a time and motion study. The client found the study to be more timely and valuable and was appreciative of our response to his needs. Did we miss a pricing opportunity? Probably, but our gain was in a strengthened relationship with the client.

Products

In the process of determining how to present the FPA concept to our clients, we realized that although we had the resources to deliver quite a variety of services, we hadn't defined or developed them to the point where any team member could sell any service regardless of whether he or she would be the one to actually deliver it. We solved that problem by developing a menu of services that can be used as a generic handout in an initial meeting and can later be customized to scope specific services associated with an FPA.

More importantly, we began to focus on improving existing services and developing new ones that our clients might need. For example, we had been working on a Cash Management Plan product that we felt most of our middle market clients could benefit from. The product is a process whereby we help clients set goals and define them in an annual budget. We then use specialized software to produce a cash flow projection and pro forma monthly balance sheets. We then meet with the client to discuss the results. Once we began selling cash management plans as an FPA service, we standardized its production and delivery and established pricing for the initial plan and for periodic updates. At $2,500 to $4,000 each, we sold about $36,000 in cash management plans in 2002.

Easily the most popular consulting service we've developed is Strategic Planning. Clients loved the sound of it from the get-go, and we were selling it before even we knew exactly what it would be. Although we continue to improve the product, it is now systematized to the point where partners and service providers have a process for planning and documenting the meetings while maintaining the flexibility to customize them according to the client's needs and interests. These monthly, quarterly, or semi-annual meetings keep us in touch with the client and often generate new projects and pricing opportunities. Strategic planning services came in at about $100,000 for 2002.

Systems

Because we were moving so fast at the end of 2000 and the beginning of 2001, we had to create and modify certain systems on the fly. We needed new internal forms for pricing, contract administration, and templates for FPA letters. We had to incorporate value pricing into our time and billing system and figure out when to relieve WIP and when to recognize revenue. We needed to train. We had to redesign management reports. If we had taken the time to make it all perfect before we took the plunge, we never would have gotten it done. The moral of the story is just do it! The progress we made by forging ahead far outweighed the effect of minor stumbles along the way.

Cash Flow

One issue we thought would be a stumbling block actually turned out well. We expected that because we'd made monthly, quarterly, and semi-annual terms available to our business FPA clients, cash flow would be spread out over the span of a year as opposed to getting the bulk of it from March to June, the pattern we were accustomed to. What we had failed to anticipate was that by invoicing monthly, quarterly, and semi-annual clients on January 5 and our quarterly clients again on April 5, we were actually accelerating cash flow such that by the fourth month of the year, we had invoiced 50% of the FPAs with quarterly and semi-annual terms and 33% of those with monthly terms.

Another factor in this acceleration of receivables was that we sent the last rate × hour invoices to FPA clients on December 31, 2000, and then sent their first FPA invoices just after the first of the year. (We were proactive about contacting clients to make sure they understood they weren't being double billed.) So we were in cash flow heaven for a while before realizing that the bump in collections was simply due to timing, and part of that bump was a one-time occurrence resulting from clients converting to FPAs.

Although we can't claim it as our own brilliant strategy and didn't recognize it as part of Ron's, since we began value pricing we've reduced our A/R turn from 60 to 37 days.

Ongoing Challenges

Marketing

Most of us at Bradley, Allen & Associates aren't very good at marketing. We've built our business on referrals and until the economy got so tough, we had as much new business as we could handle. We've begun to realize the need for growth to make our succession plan work, and to understand that building our relationships with clients and referral sources makes us more valuable to all of them.

Training

New team members who come from more traditional CPA firms have to quickly absorb what the rest of us have been learning over the last several years. We require them to read *Professional's Guide to Value Pricing,* but we haven't reconvened the Book Club. We show new team members where we saved many of the computer files they'll need. But we haven't figured out how to inspire the enthusiasm for value pricing or instill the confidence it takes to embrace it.

In fact, training is a necessity even for those of us who've been here all along. We perform a value pricing review each fall, for which everyone rereads several chapters of Ron's *Value Pricing*. We meet to talk about pricing strategies, review processes, and address concerns. Shortly before we began negotiating our 2003 FPAs, we held weekly lunch meetings to which partners and service providers could bring their proposed FPAs to have the group critique their pricing and/or strategy and to get ideas for addressing price resistance, moving clients up the value curve, and so on. Staff accountants were also invited. It proved to be a great way for our less experienced people to learn from real-life examples, and for the more experienced folks to brainstorm with each other in a way they might not have taken the time to do otherwise.

Client Retention

I hesitate to talk about lost clients because client retention hasn't been a problem. The few clients we've lost have been due to price resistance, and we should have known better than to try to get a premium from clients who did not fit our criteria for either client selection or fixed pricing. Our fixed pricing criteria are pretty simple; clients either (1) want or need the consulting services we offer or (2) present a pricing opportunity. The clients we lost were unwilling to pay premium prices for compliance work and we were unable to convince them of the value of our consulting services. We've also lost some of our low-end 1040 clients—and see that as healthy for the organization. We have a number of individual clients who would be phased out if we followed our internal guidelines to the letter; however, they have been with us for many years, we're emotionally attached to them, and we will continue to keep them in our fold.

Where We Are Now

Value pricing has made us a better firm. How much of our success can be attributed to the influence of Ron Baker and RAS versus our own sheer will is impossible to determine, but this much is true: this change could not have happened in our firm without the passion and creativity of some of the great minds in our profession and the hard work of a dedicated Bradley, Allen team. Our implementation of value pricing has resulted in tangible and intangible benefits of this shift in paradigm:

- Our client service has improved because we've focused on creating more "touches" with our clients. We spend less time regurgitating historical financial data and more time helping our clients achieve their strategic and financial goals.

- We've become better at running our business. So much of what we were doing before was brainless. Wait for a call from a client, do the work, send an invoice. Now we approach our business in the way of good businesses everywhere. We plan, market, identify needs, develop products, sell, and deliver. Best of all, we control our destiny because we're not sitting at our desks waiting for a client to call and tell us what to work on next.
- We've begun to measure the right things. We use concrete information rather than relying on gut instinct to determine our best clients. We know which of our services generate the most revenue and which are the most profitable. We're paying attention to industry niches in our client base.
- We're making more money. Revenues increased more than $700,000 between 1998 and 2002 and profit per partner increased 75%. In any practice survey you'll see for a firm our size (15 to 17 team members, about $2.3 million in revenue), we're now at the top of the heap in that category. And because we recognize the contribution of our team to this success, we've established a bonus pool to share the profits with those who continue to make it happen.

Where We Are Headed

So where do we go from here with value pricing? New clients are easy. Establishing pricing up front is usually perceived by prospects as progressive and client-friendly, and they're quite ready to jump on board. Existing clients can be more challenging, but the better the relationship, the easier it is. We'll continue to convert existing clients from rate × hour to the extent they have the potential to add consulting services to their compliance needs. But after three years of value pricing, we still feel like rookies when pricing certain types of engagements (merger and acquisition work comes to mind) and have yet to muster the courage to write a TIP clause. I predict we'll get there one day.

Though we've always considered ourselves to be very customer service-oriented, we now have a better understanding of what that really means: making sure we're truly providing value to our clients. And with that, we can feel good about being compensated for our years of experience, our resources, and our ability to help clients reach their goals. This shift in paradigm has been the single most important development in our firm's 20-year history.

For the last couple of years we've been working with an industrial psychologist who coaches our team on developing customer-centric service and positive management skills. He tells us that change is "slow, incremental, and painful." As applied to our firm's move toward value pricing, I would add "rewarding" to that list. Of course we're all enjoying the financial benefits of value pricing, but the most rewarding aspects of this change are seeing the professional growth of my partners and team, and knowing that our clients are getting better service than they were before we embarked on this journey. Making the shift to value pricing is not for the faint of heart, but good firms with strong leadership and a willing team can absolutely make it happen.

Peter Thorby, Christchurch, New Zealand

Peter Thorby, a Chartered Accountant in public practice in New Zealand, describes the experience of trashing his timesheets as follows.

The Beginning

I'd like to take to take you on a journey—a journey that took me from a time-and-cost mind-set to freedom and rewards. I am going to tell you how I trashed my timesheets.

I went to University of Canterbury, the local university, to gain my qualifications so I could hang my shingle somewhere in New Zealand. I chose the lovely anglicized city of Christchurch, which has a population of about 350,000 people and serves a very wide provincial area that supports rural, manufacturing, and service industries.

My personal interest was in manufacturing, as my family owned a furniture manufacturing business. My interest in the furniture business was to become crucial in my views and assessment of business fundamentals, be it for manufacturing or service industries.

My first foray into the workforce saw me working for a four-partner accounting practice. This was my first look at chartered accountancy business fundamentals, and the experience is still crystal clear in my mind. The first function I was indoctrinated to was the filling out of the timesheet.

The skill required to do it was horrific. Timesheets had to be maintained in 10-minute blocks, and every 10-minute block had to be accounted for. I had to account for every block with a client code, and I soon learned that "unproductive" codes were really frowned upon.

The daily timesheet was then transferred to a weekly timesheet and the weekly timesheet punched onto a client job card by ladies who could make the infamous Burroughs bookkeeping machines play songs and do dances. I used to be amazed at this process.

Creative Accounting Begins

The skills I had to balance my timesheets in those early days were relatively limited. I guess I can fess up to the fact that my first exposure to creative accounting was here. The biggest skills I learned at this time were creativity in giving the partners what they wanted to know and adeptness on a calculator.

I quickly realized that "excess time" over last year's time billed was not acceptable. So I used to put "excess time" down to the biggest client I did work for so he could carry that excess, unquestioned.

This first job was also my first experience describing my time utilization as "productive" and "unproductive." I assumed I was employed to add value to the partners, but somehow I was "unproductive" from time to time. If I was too "unproductive" then questions were asked.

Of course we all know that the categorization really meant to distinguish between a possible billable hour and an unbillable hour. But the hourly rate took that into account, didn't it?

My point is that everybody is employed to do good job. The billable hour measure does nothing to add value because the times are masked to produce what the partners want to hear.

The whole issue of time, recording of time, time as a measure, and useful data was to rear its head again in our manufacturing business in 1999, but more about this later. (Here's a clue: have you read Eliyahu Goldratt's book *The Goal*?)

It was difficult back in 1976 to trap the really good data that we can trap today, such as all the partner statistics, employee statistics, billable hours, recovery rates, write-offs, and disbursements to be recovered. Now, I can say for sure that Bill Gates has a lot to answer for. The arrival of the personal computer heralded a new era of data. As we tried to grapple with the early general ledger and timesheet systems, we imagined the load the biggest clients carried. The first applications were practice management systems, which were ripe for the picking due to their high data-entry content and the analysis that went with it.

The arrival of the PC represented an opportunity for service industries that charged by the hour to make lots more money due to the increased efficiency of billing out "the true cost of supply."

We have now had 30 years of this prime measurement tool. I guess it is fair to ask the question, "Does it help us make more money?" Is anyone prepared to answer?

Moving On

After about one year with my first firm, I moved to another that had three partners. Again the first task to learn was "completing the daily timesheet and transferring it to the weekly timesheet." This firm was ahead of my previous employer. I mean, we had a golf ball IBM typewriter and it wasn't long before we had two of them. All our data entry, timesheets included, was coded onto paper tape and sent to a computer bureau, which then processed the paper tape and sent us the printouts. Again, the time and cost was the prime measure for practice management.

By this point such measures were everywhere. There were actually courses held by the New Zealand Society of Accountants to educate accountants on how it all worked.

Then the repercussions really came. The underrecoveries, the write-offs, the accountability for the write-offs, the recovery rates, the total billable hours, and the ability to compare one partner with another all needed to be measured. Fudging started as partners began to learn how to bill "unproductive" work to other partners or other offices or manipulate hourly rates as a form of "cost recovery."

People hated timesheets and the process with an absolute passion.

But it didn't stop there. As Windows went from 3.2 to 95 to 98 to 2000 to XP over the years, so did the ability to trap additional data with more accuracy. We now have computers attached to telephone systems to catch toll charges that can be billed to clients. We have computers attached to photocopiers to catch charges that can be billed to clients. As accountants find easier ways to trap data electronically, the list of what can be trapped seems to be endless and so does the capital resource needed to fund such electronic processes.

Of course it's all in the name of efficiency and the quest to make more profits. But is it working? Are we more efficient and are we making more profits?

Take a break for a moment and consider the cost of running the current time and cost processes. Consider the value of the endless reports that these systems produce. These systems can slice and dice data in endless ways. One person wants it this way, someone else wants it another way. Where is all this heading?

How many of you have thought privately or publicly, "Wouldn't it be great to not have to fill out timesheets? They are the bane of our existence. They do nothing to improve the way I work, they only teach me to find ways to increase my recovery by foul means or other. They add no real value to the business and they are the root cause of the conflict."

What conflict? For me, this was the conflict between the measure imposed on us by the timesheet mentality and the real value of what the measure produced. There had to be a better way. Consider bills like this ($10,000 as per the time and cost, say $9,100):

Disbursements:

Tolls	5.50
Photocopying	10.00
Travel	5.33
Paper	9.37
Total	30.20
Total Due	$9,130.20

It's exactly what we did, and it's bizarre to the point of absurdity. We never asked the client what he thought.

No wonder clients were miffed. It was hardly a customer-focused statement. They certainly didn't feel better because they received a discount. Clients even felt guilty that their job must have been too messy, which reflected on them, and the accountant could not fully recover the time.

A Different Approach

What I could never understand was the difference between manufacturing and the service industry. In our furniture business, we had fixed pricing. A bedroom suite was priced and that was that. The price was set for the next 6 months at least. To make money we had to process and sell as many bedroom suites as possible in a given period. It was a system that haunted me for years to come.

In 1988, I purchased a part of the accounting firm I was working for, and along with that came "time and cost." Well almost. The thinking came with me. I purchased time and cost software and began the tedious task of building catching systems to trap:

- Time
- Tolls
- Disbursements
- Stationery
- Other

I had four staff and away we went. Another practice, just like all the others. Almost. I became a wee bit of a rebel in the local branch of the accountants society. I began to dress casually at work. The clients thought it was fantastic, but my fellow accountants thought I was a bit flippant. I have a photo of the local branch committee, with me the only one not wearing a tie.

My practice grew, and I began to do the time and cost and billing on the first Saturday of every month. Frustration grew. I began to hate the process even more. I had a young family and going to work on a Saturday began to get at me.

Then there was a defining moment. A new prospect came to see me. He asked me what my hourly rate was. I replied "about $100 per hour." He said that it was too high. I agreed to $80 per hour but privately I knew I would load the timesheet. I then gave him my business card and he pointed out correctly that it did not have my private phone number on it. I told him that this was correct, it didn't. He demanded to know what it was. I refused to give it. I told him I wasn't a funeral director, and there was nothing that couldn't wait until Monday. If he wanted my services in the weekend he could look up the phone book and the chargeout rate would be $300 per hour. And yes, the phone never rang. But the episode alerted me to different prices for different conditions and started me thinking about value pricing. In another year or so it hit me: I had had enough of the whole process of accountancy services and timesheets.

Leaving Timesheets Behind

One morning, in April 1993, I woke up and decided to sell my practice. I found a buyer within 2 weeks for the complete practice minus 10 of my choice clients.

At the same time I chose never to employ staff again, and I haven't to this day. It wasn't because I had had a bad experience with staff, it was just a choice I made. So I was everything: accountant, secretary, and stamp licker—and my wife, who is also an accountant, helps from time to time.

Interestingly, I discovered how much secretarial work was unnecessary (i.e., small letters that stated the obvious when a quick phone call would get the same result much faster).

Then I approached my 10 clients with a deal—the fixed price agreement. The deal was this:

1. I presented an oral quote.
2. There was to be no adjustment either way at the end of the year.
3. The next year's fee was to be negotiated with the past as a guide.
4. There was to be no time and cost record.
5. There was only one invoice.
6. There were to be 12 equal monthly payments.
7. There were to be no disbursements, tolls, stationery, etc. charged.
8. The fixed price agreement was to be flexible so any big project that fell outside the scope would be quoted separately.
9. So I could be at my existing clients' disposal, I guaranteed not to take on any new clients.

Of course I knew that those handpicked 10 could only grow. After 9 years, only one had left, by mutual agreement. The other 9 have grown and grown and grown.

What my clients wanted was a fast turnaround. I can give my monthly management clients same-day turnaround. It's what I try to achieve, and I have an 80% success rate. See how the measurement set begins to change to a customer focus perspective? It's why my clients hire me. Hassle-free assistance. Do they demand discounts? No. And every client that was approached signed the bank authority without question. My clients win:

- An agreed amount that they can control and are happy to pay
- No more invoices for varying amounts of unexplained value
- No more silly disbursement invoices
- Painless payment by automatic bank authority
- Unimpeded access to my services

My clients didn't feel silly about making telephone calls for what seemed like trifling questions, and their staff began to ring me about issues because they knew only a "rent" was being paid. My clients didn't care anymore about how long a job took and the cost. They just wanted a response as fast as possible.

I win:

- Known fixed income
- No more account queries
- No more Saturday mornings doing timesheets and invoicing
- No more write-offs and the negative connotations
- Having fun servicing my clients again

As a result, I got more involved in my clients' businesses—because spending a couple of hours on their sites didn't involve a "cost" to them. They saw it as real value. And I could spend as much time as I liked with my clients' staff at no "cost" to my client.

The pitfalls of my setup? There are absolutely no pitfalls in the fixed price agreements. I would not do work any other way. No quote, no work. My only comment is that because I have chosen to work on my own, sickness and holidays do not stop the phone ringing or the commitment to the IRD (Inland Revenue Department). Financially, all I want is for my prices to be above my expenses and for my return to give me a good life. I have achieved this.

If a client ends up consuming too much time for too little a price, I simply adjust it the next year to a higher amount. Common sense prevails. There is no niggle or issue. Of course there is no time record; it's all done on the basis of selling value and the perception of value to the receiver.

An Easy Transition

The transition for me was very easy; it was only a head shift. I didn't have partners to consult. I didn't have to achieve any "buy-in." I just woke up in the morning and did it. My satisfaction at work was much higher because my clients were happier. I enjoyed the personal contact with my clients, and I could spend all day debating issues with them. I have never again felt the pressure of the time clock. It's fantastic. If I work on the weekend, it is because I want to, not because I have to. And that is a significant difference.

Back to The Factory

As for production issues in the furniture factory, in reality they were no different from those of the accounting model. We had job cards controlling the use of time. We had back costing. We had inventory systems. We had the lot.

What a gigantic waste of money, time, and energy. The result is the same. The cards are fudged by the workforce to reduce the negative impact of the management reaction. The resulting data is meaningless. How management makes useful decisions from this I will never know. The bottom line is they cannot and no one will convince me otherwise. Of course with the advent of computerization the whole process became even more technical and complex, with bar coding and so on. That will fix it, said the management.

How often can we rely on any bill of materials (BOM) costing? I have spoken to hundreds of cost accountants in New Zealand on this issue. The trapping systems in manufacturing are huge. The questions I ask are:

- Of the raw material component in a BOM, how much are the variances? Answer: About +/- 0% to 10%, with most about 5%.
- Of the labor factor in the BOM, how much are the variances? Answer: About +/- 20% to 40%.

What hope have we got? The measurement of time has to be the biggest issue facing us. How do we control time in processing, be it manufacturing or the service industries?

What I do know for sure is that "time and cost" systems will not do it. I've been there and they do not work as an effective tool. I've had the accounting and the manufacturing experience.

The Answer

The good news is there is an answer. To solve the issue in our furniture factory we need to look to the solutions Eliyahu Goldratt described in his book *The Goal,* which describes a production environment. *It's Not Luck* is a solution to distribution and marketing, and *Critical Chain* is a solution to project management timing issues. Goldratt's solutions build a radar system around a business so that people work the model proactively. The mission is to expose idle capacity and to use that capacity to achieve the best possible course to guide the entity toward its goals.

What Goldratt exposes is the basic uselessness of the typical measurement sets that entities use. They are full of micromanagement rather than the global management that would help the whole business to move forward. Goldratt exposes illogical business logic that we use every day and that we take as a given.

Goldratt's Theory of Constraint

In November 1999 we fully implemented Goldratt's TOC (Theory of Constraint) logic in our furniture business. Today, we have no timesheets, general efficiency measures, no department managers, and no supervisors. What we have is a business that is rapidly approaching autopilot status. The guys on the floor run production. We measure the "money flow" through the slowest part of the business and everything else runs to its tune. The rest of production is subordinated to that slowest process.

Output is rising dramatically. The cost of achieving that output is falling. We have a meaningful measurement set. The guys on the floor use the same measure as management. They are exactly the same numbers. The guys on the floor are helping management and management is helping the guys on the floor. Everyone has a skill to contribute. We quickly learned that management generally stuff it up.

If we want to fix something, just ask the guys on the floor. They generally know best.

Fixed price agreements are not the end of the accountancy issue or a movement from chaos to calm. Goldratt's theory also deals with marketing and pricing of services. To achieve "calm" within the accounting workflow, we need to look at the common sense logic of constraint management to control the workflow in the absence of timesheets and the associated paraphernalia. The question everyone will ask is, "If I haven't got timesheets, what do I do and how do I do it?" The move from no timesheets to fixed pricing is too big. Something must bridge the gap.

Constraint management brings with it a management and measurement tool set to manage time to get the best out of the business. I strongly recommend reading Ron Baker's and Eliyahu Goldratt's books as a starting point in acquiring the logic to work with. Goldratt's book *The Haystack Syndrome* is a great read for the accountancy minded and it explains the measurement set needed to give your business the tools to move it toward its goals.

A consultant who has done work for a "really big" international accounting firm told me that the firm managed work flow by continually assessing the time and cost with the budget. When cost was beginning to match the budget, expensive labor such as managers was moved to other jobs. Lower cost labor was then allocated to the jobs. This saved cost on jobs.

I wonder how much money they saved. The consultant was mum on this. I'd guess probably none, because they still pay the same people the same salaries. The total income received and the total money paid out is probably the same, with or without people being moved from one job to another, despite what the "time and cost" says.

This is another example of the perception of "profitable and unprofitable" jobs according to their time and cost. Time and cost systems promote cost allocation, which distorts every measure that management traditionally uses, be it in manufacturing or service industries.

MKF Group, St. Helena, California

John Heymann, CEO of the MKF Group, of St. Helena, near Napa, California, describes his firm's experience with implementing value pricing, trashing timesheets, and changing culture as follows.

Background

For most of its 20-year existence, MKF has been a single-niche firm focused exclusively on the wine industry. Although it began life as a traditional CPA firm, it has now become the leading firm of business advisors to the wine industry, and it did so by providing high-value services across a broad range of practice areas, including consulting, mergers and acquisitions, wine industry research, and CPA services.

For many years, individual consultants within the firm had experimented with value-based fees, but for the most part the firm's culture, structure, processes, and reporting revolved around the familiar professional firm practices of time and billing. In the mid-1990s MKF reorganized, moving away from the staffing structure of a typical CPA firm and focusing on building a much flatter organizational model. Instead of trying to leverage less expensive junior staff, with a reliance on volume compliance and attest work, our manager-level CPAs were encouraged to develop their skills for providing higher value advisory services. We moved away from hiring junior staff, replacing those positions with paraprofessionals, and helped our clients make the transition to performing more of their own basic accounting work in-house. This concept, supported by the strength of our brand and the expertise we had developed over 20 years, was an important goal of our initial reorganization.

Implementing this type of change is not without difficulty. CPAs who have spent years in organizations where billable hours rule, and where effort is often appreciated and rewarded more than results, do not instantly transform into consultants providing higher level services to their clients. Many of our managers had good relationships with their clients' controllers and CFOs but not with the real the decision makers—owners and CEOs. It was obvious that more effort was needed.

We started by more consistently incorporating the concepts of value pricing into our engagements, using fixed-price agreements and extolling the virtues of results over efforts. We clarified our firm's vision, clearly articulating our core values, goals, and strategies—especially as they related to innovation, professional development, and high specialization. We provided training in presentation and consulting skills, held case study workshops, and delivered briefings on wine industry issues and trends. The principles were sound, the theory was terrific, but the execution turned out to be much harder to achieve than expected. For example:

- The focus on value-based prices is a great concept and, in its most basic form, is not too difficult to grasp. While we expected the professional staff to transform themselves into consultants providing high-value services—focused on achieving results that met our clients' needs—all of our systems and performance measures remained geared primarily toward encouraging effort. We still counted hours worked in 15-minute increments. Budgets and revenue goals were still based on hours × billing rate. In spite of all our proselytizing about value, performance was still in actuality being evaluated based on effort (chargeability and realization) rather than on results (customer satisfaction and revenue).
- Fixed price agreements worked well for introducing many of our clients to higher-value services, but internal tracking and invoicing of cross-functional contributions using our traditional time and billing software was contentious and difficult.
- In focusing on higher-value advisory services, we vilified compliance and assurance work, inappropriately making some professionals who had not taken to it as quickly feel like second-class citizens.

So, after several iterations of the original reorganization, filled with false starts and a certain amount of frustration, we had learned some important lessons: clearly, embracing value-pricing concepts alone was not going to be enough for the firm to fully achieve its goals of providing the highest levels of advisory services across the broad range of our distinct practice groups. In order to reinforce the principles and theories that supported our core values, we needed to get rid of the vestiges of all the internal systems that daily contradicted our professed message of results over effort. Timesheets, for one thing, had to go.

Tracking and reporting had to be changed to de-emphasize effort and clearly put the focus on results. We had been talking about this conceptually for quite a while; so, when the proposal was presented to the partner group, the discussion was brief and reaching consensus was relatively swift. We announced to the staff that, as of the start of our upcoming fiscal year, timekeeping would no longer be required. The decision caused quite a stir, prompting a lot of questions and debate over what metrics should be used to replace timesheets, what the reporting process would look like, whether or not it could or even should be attempted, and how personal performance would be evaluated without hours and realization.

Not surprisingly, the reactions were mixed and acceptance of the change was directly related to how evolved each person was in their own professional development and approach to work. Those who already thought in terms of results, immediately accepted trashing the timesheets as a good idea, with just a few concerns expressed about how results would be reported. Others, more vested in the concepts of effort, were skeptical and tended to list all the reasons why the whole process would be impossible to implement and impractical to sustain. Their fears and concerns centered on a few main points:

- How will I be evaluated fairly if not by effort (as revealed by chargeability)?
- How will this affect paraprofessionals who don't control the jobs they work on?
- How will we account for WIP?
- How will we be able to schedule jobs if we don't know how many hours are required?
- How will we generate invoices from our time and billing software?
- How will we know the costs of our jobs?
- How will we share revenue from cross-functional fixed price agreements?

Notice that all of these fears were, without exception, internally focused. Not one of them had anything to do with client needs or any of the things clients might value.

The objections only confirmed the correctness of the decision, though in retrospect, we definitely underestimated the difficulty of breaking such a closely held habit. Even partners who had embraced and encouraged the trashing of timesheets lost some heart when faced with the reality of day-to-day implications of actually having to change some of their routines. In fact, when it comes time to allocate shared revenue, some partners still ask staff about how many hours they worked on a project.

We solicited input from all levels in designing the new process. We studied several feasible KPIs and approaches for tracking them, but in the end opted for the simplest approach: we would start by just replacing our traditional time entry and reporting with a simple monthly spreadsheet showing individual revenue, revenue per practice group, and total firm revenue, all benchmarked against budget.

The process also had to be simple to allay fears that an onerous Rube Goldberg system might emerge. We continued to use our time and billing software, opening each new project as usual. Each engagement was assigned a single biller (usually the main client contact or regular project manager) who would enter one hour at the start of the job to mark it as active. At the end of each month the firm's internal accounting manager would call for details of all active engagements, and the billers responded with an invoice amount based on their knowledge of the percentage of the work completed or the agreed upon client billing schedule. When the engagement was completed, the responsible biller would simply indicate that it was a final billing and the accounting manager would close out the job.

This worked very smoothly for the consulting group, whose engagements were mostly single projects that they worked on individually. For the engagements on which they collaborated with someone else, the revenue generated was simply divided by mutual agreement, with reporting instructions to the accounting manager indicated along with the monthly invoicing information.

The process turned out to be more difficult with the tax and audit group because their work was mainly recurring, tended to be sold as a combined-task fixed price agreement (audit, tax, consulting), sometimes contained special periodic billing arrangements, and often required several people to work on an engagement, including paraprofessionals who were not assigned individual revenue goals the first year.

One of the serious mistakes we made the first year was to give in to pressure from the CPA services group, whose members strongly resisted because they felt the process of tracking and accounting for their cross-functional work would be too difficult. As a compromise, and because we couldn't yet see the full picture of implementation clearly, they were allowed to report only their monthly combined group results during that first year. That decision, among other factors, contributed to a significant drop in revenue the first year, because no one was held individually responsible for his or her own contribution to the total.

After the first three or four months, anxiety about our ability to implement the new system dissipated, but by the end of six months, concerns about revenue shortfalls in CPA services brought out new doubts about the wisdom of the changes. After nine months, there was even murmuring about going back to timesheets, but after additional discussions, everyone realized that it was our reporting system that needed tweaking, rather than their being some fatal flaw in the concept.

Ultimately, the breakthrough in the individual reporting dilemma was developed by the CPA services group themselves. They came up with a simple but elegant way of having all the professionals enter their own billings at the end of each month, and to give and receive allocated revenue to and from others based on mutually determined amounts. Their individual monthly revenues were then automatically imported to the firm's monthly aggregate report, and the results were compared with invoices sent to clients to make sure nothing fell through the cracks. The entire billing process now takes each person just a few hours at the end of each month. There is no longer any talk about bringing back timesheets.

This enhanced system worked much better in the second year. Revenues were tracked against budget during the entire year, and everyone could not only see the results of their own revenue generated, but the revenue of their colleagues, their functional group, and the firm as a whole. Without the onus of tracking and reconciling billable and nonbillable hours, and all the attendant games that are played to finesse that whole system, everyone became more focused on considering what their clients valued instead of on the process of getting the work done. The need to discuss equitable revenue allocations engendered more cooperation among members of the engagement team than competition, as some had feared, although the process still generates competitive tension. Cross-selling services became the norm, rather than the exception, as the professional staff realized that it now worked both ways.

As we enter our third year without timesheets, we've already designed the next iteration of reporting, which for the CPA services group will separate revenue generated by advisory services from that generated by recurring compliance and assurance work. We are also introducing several new individual KPIs, such as number of client contacts, key relationship development and cross-selling efforts, as well as individual and firm practice development activities. These will be cooperatively set goals that will all be self-reported in the manner of the revenue reporting process, and the concepts have been readily accepted because they support the activities that everyone now agrees are the most critical for success.

It is important to distinguish that these are tools that we use to help us determine the progress we are making toward our firm goals. The revenue against budget tracking is a helpful tool for individuals to gauge their results throughout the year, but these additional KPIs will not be used directly as determinants of compensation. Because we feel we have built a high-trust organization with very little traditional supervision, strict metrics are not required—everyone knows intuitively who is performing and who isn't. When performance becomes self- and peer-enforced, there is a vastly reduced need for quantitative measurement and other traditional methods of management.

This sort of fundamental transition requires a lot of hard work. Along the way, we've encountered many tough issues. Some had relatively easy fixes; for others the solutions were quite painful and often entailed implementing fundamental changes to the business. Lessons learned include the following:

- To successfully effect such fundamental cultural change, partners must first be aligned in their thinking, action, and messaging. Eventually, everyone in the firm—from administrative to professional staff—has to be on board with the concepts. And although passive skeptics can be trained with difficulty, active resisters at any level will poison the process and have to be transitioned out.
- Job descriptions, skills, and tasks changed at all levels of the firm—from administrative staff to managers—because basic accounting work was no longer valued or taken on, and clients who required it were transitioned out. Some longtime employees who were unable or unwilling to adjust became disgruntled and left, taking a toll on office morale in the process.
- We have learned the absolute necessity of patience and discipline in hiring. Our standards and requirements have become even more stringent as a result of this transition. The more qualified the firm's staff has become, the higher their own standards and demands have become for colleagues of equal measure. One corollary of this is that having a progressive, innovative environ-

ment with high standards for excellence draws top talent to it, making recruiting and retention that much easier.

- A real investment in effort and dollars was required because accounting and software systems had to be rethought, modified, or replaced. Flexibility in problem-solving was also critical. For instance, to deal with the difficulty of tracking work-in-process without entering hours, we simply stopped tracking it. Revenue was recognized only when it was invoiced—potentially a major change in the timing of revenue and cash flow. During the first year, we had to perform some additional analysis so we could more accurately understand our productivity compared to prior-year results, but after the first year's cycle it all washed out.
- Changes of this magnitude always take longer than expected; ingrained habits must be changed, untested concepts need time to evolve and become accepted, new systems must be developed and then improved, and all this done while there is a business to run and clients to please.
- It's O.K. if people want to continue tracking hours or effort on their own for whatever purpose they may have—self-discipline, scheduling their time and resources, tickler files, engagement records, understanding costs, or litigation engagements. The important thing is that the organization doesn't require it for any purpose.

Now that we are comfortable with the process for reporting the basic results for individuals and the firm, we have been able to use the base revenue data we capture to track all kinds of relevant KPIs—the ones that really tell us whether or not we're making progress toward our goals.

Among the KPIs we currently review or are considering are:

- Individual revenue against budget
- Practice group and firm revenue against budget
- Contribution rate ($ and %)
- Revenue per client
- Revenue per staff
- Revenue to salaries

- Revenue by engagement types
- Value gap analysis (current client revenue versus what could be generated through additional services). This is determined at beginning of each year and measured by how much the gap is closed by end-of-year.
- Growth of revenue generated from higher-value advisory services versus traditional compliance and assurance work
- Client satisfaction surveys conducted on an annual basis

Although this is still very much a work in progress, finally, after a few tough years, we are beginning to see positive results from this change process. Was it worth all the trouble? Absolutely. We're a different firm today: more customer-focused, team-oriented, innovative, less-stressed from January to April, and buzzing with more energy than ever before. Our revenues are up 25% this year, and the bottom line grew even more vigorously. We're taking advantage of the synergies inherent in the diversity of our various specializations, strengthening our brand, and providing new professional growth opportunities for our very smart, very passionate, very enthusiastic staff and partners.

Stratagem, New Plymouth, New Zealand

Stratagem is a four-partner accountancy practice with 30 team members based in New Plymouth, New Zealand. The firm has developed novel systems for practice management based on providing certainty to clients—certainty of price, certainty of on-time delivery, and certainty of availability. Here Marketing and Business Development Manager John Haylock tells the story.

Stratagem's directors attended the Accountants Boot Camp conducted by Results Accountants in 1996. Their experiences at Boot Camp opened their eyes to the stronger relationship that was possible for accountants to have with their clients, and the value that accountants could add to their client's businesses. After Boot Camp there was a new focus at Stratagem, away from traditional compliance work and on helping clients improve the performance of their businesses.

Despite this new focus, the firm didn't change that much. Every year, during compliance season (which in New Zealand runs from around May to October), we were sucked back into preparing sets of annual accounts and tax returns. There was more than enough compliance work during that season and not enough people to do it. The result was that the added-value services the directors had learned about at Boot Camp were implemented in a stop-start fashion. We could provide these services for six months, then we couldn't, then we could provide them again and then we couldn't.

We recognized that clients wanted consistency of delivery, not an on-again off-again approach. Clients wanted these marketing and business development services all year round. They wanted certainty of availability.

In 1999, our directors decided we needed to change. They wanted a fresh approach to take the firm forward. At that stage, Stratagem was still called Cottam Cave Evetts and Fah. The firm was, like most accountancy firms, named after its owners. The directors took the bold step of rebranding and repositioning the firm.

During 1999, an internal project team met regularly to develop the new brand and a new business strategy to go with it. Development of that new strategy started with three Client Advisory Boards. Groups of clients were asked what they did and did not like about us and what services and standard of service they wanted. Several very clear messages came back from our clients. Top of the list were:

- We don't like not knowing how big the bill is going to be.
- We don't like not knowing when we're going to get our completed set of accounts back from you.
- We don't like ringing you up and getting a $100 invoice for a five minute phone call.
- We don't like you not being available when we call and then taking days to get back to us.

Although there were plenty of things they liked about us, we recognized that there were some significant shortcomings in our service. So, we asked the clients, "Why do you stay with us?" The response was very straightforward: "You accountants, you're all the same. You're just as bad as each other." In other words, our clients stayed with us because there was no better alternative. This was a very important lesson for us. Despite our technical excellence (which was never questioned), our expert advice and our friendly service, many of our clients would leave if another accountant had an improved service offering. We recognized that it's not what you do, it's how you do what you do that counts. Just being great accountants wasn't enough. We had to provide standout service as well.

To our clients, our technical ability was a given. We were, after all, members of the Institute of Chartered Accountants of New Zealand, along with most other accountants in New Plymouth, and that was enough proof that we knew what we were doing. We recognized that most clients have no idea about the technical ability of their accountant. So they judge us on other criteria. As we discovered when we met with our Client Advisory Boards, these other criteria included the ability to provide:

- Certainty of availability
- Certainty of delivery
- Certainty of price

Many of our clients commented along the following lines:

> We're only asking you to provide what we have to provide to our own customers: We provide certainty to our customers, so why don't you? What make accountants think they're so special that they can get away with this lack of certainty?

Such comments forced us to ask some very serious questions about the nature of our business and our relationship with our clients.

Rather than looking inward, as most accountancy firms would do, and coming up with excuses for why providing certainty is impossible, we looked outward. By doing so we learned what was possible from other firms and more importantly from other industries.

Three books had great impact on us as we developed our new service offering. Christopher Hart's book *Extraordinary Guarantees* started us thinking about the importance of guarantees in a service-based business. This led us directly to the idea of providing a four-week turnaround guarantee on preparation of annual accounts. After all, our clients said they wanted certainty of delivery.

What prevented us from providing certainty was that during May, June, and July our clients would drop their records into our office. We would end up with a huge pile of work that we gradually chipped away at over the following months. When there was a problem with a job (say, some records were missing), it was easier to start another job than complete the first job with the problem. So, every year, we ended up with lots of jobs started, all progressing very slowly. We had no idea when individual jobs would be completed. Our productivity (as a measure of chargeable hours as a percentage of total available hours) was high but our output of completed work was low.

In his book, Hart notes that although guarantees are a great marketing tool, the real reason for a guarantee is to drive internal process improvement. This is so that the costs of occasionally paying out on a guarantee are lower than the value of the benefits your business gains. We recognized that we needed to make major process improvements, so we challenged ourselves with the idea of providing a four-week turnaround guarantee.

Our team came up with a lot of excuses why the guarantee could not be made—mostly related to problems "out of our control" such as the quality of records provided by clients and the time it took clients to respond to our queries. Despite these excuses, we recognized that most of our annual accounting jobs for our typical owner-operated business clients took only 10 to 20 hours to complete. We figured we had to be able to do a 10 to 20 hour job in four weeks. After all, having four weeks to complete a 20-hour job means the job is still sitting idle doing nothing for 87.5% of the time.

The second key book was Eliyahu Goldratt's *The Goal,* a novel about process improvement in a manufacturing plant. Goldratt introduced us to the Theory of Constraints and a methodology that we could implement to provide our goal of a four-week turnaround guarantee. We learned why our directors were bottlenecks, who held up the completion of work on time. For example, they were so busy that jobs sat in their in-trays for several weeks waiting for review and they were too busy to return client phone calls. To remove these bottlenecks, we put in place much improved systems for delegating work to free up our directors' time.

We learned why it is a mistake to measure productivity by how busy people are. After all "productivity" should be based on what people produce, not what they put in. So, we developed a performance management system based on completing set work on time. Our team is now much more focused on outcomes than inputs.

We learned about how managing capacity and scheduling work between the various people involved on a job can make work flow through a business much quicker. Rather than letting our clients drop their records off when they wanted to, we scheduled when all work was to be completed. At the same time, we made sure we had spare capacity so that we could cope with the jobs that had to be brought forward for valid reasons—such as someone selling their business. Deadlines were also set for several steps in each job to ensure jobs were being completed on time.

We also developed a workflow management application that allowed us to schedule work, manage capacity, and then track each job on its way to being completed inside four weeks. The application helps coordinate all the people involved in the completion of each job.

We also learned about the importance of controlling the quality of our raw material (our client's records) and of putting performance standards on our suppliers (our clients). As a result, we provided our clients with standard folders to keep their (nonelectronic) records in. Then, in exchange for providing a four-week turnaround guarantee, we set performance standards for our clients to provide us with the information we needed to prepare their accounts. The result was much improved records and less opportunity for stopping a job once it was started. We recognized that excessive pickup and putdown time on each job was a major cause of wasted time.

Goldratt taught us that profitability depends on capacity. For example, at Stratagem we usually have spare capacity in February. Therefore any work we do in February on top of our existing workload is profit because the revenue goes straight to the bottom line. We don't need any extra resources to do more work in February. In contrast, adding work during our busy season, when there is no spare capacity, means we need extra resources. Although a specific job may appear profitable based on traditional measures (i.e., we achieve our target chargeout rate for all the hours spent on the job), this way of measuring profitability does not take into account the cost of carrying those extra resources through the quieter periods of the year.

After recognizing this seasonal variance in potential profitability, we concentrated on moving our existing clients to receiving services year-round and made sure that the majority of our new clients also require services year-round. This understanding of the extra profit from providing year-round services for clients was complemented by reading a third key book, Ron Baker's *Professional's Guide to Value Pricing*. We had already been thinking about providing certainty of pricing when we read this book. It opened our eyes to the value created simply from providing certainty. Not only could we have happier clients by providing certainty, we could charge more as well.

We recognized the relevance of what we now called Baker's Law: "bad clients drive out good clients." We have developed processes for ending our relationships with poor clients (i.e., the ones who don't pay on time, who provide bad records, or who are unpleasant to deal with). We have also developed an excellent screening process to make sure that new clients are better than our average existing client.

Based on the templates in this book and ideas provided by Results Accountants, we developed a fixed-price-agreement system suitable for our firm and a complementary levels of service structure. One of the key ideas was including phone calls to encourage our clients to call us when needed rather than holding back out of concern for what we would charge them for the call.

On February 29, 2000, we launched our new brand and new suite of services. Since then, every performance measure of the business has improved bar one. From 2000 to 2003 we grew our gross revenue by 18% while we reduced our number of clients. That means our average revenue per client had increased—up by 30%. Net profit before partner remuneration has increased by 39%.

A key reason for the percentage increase in net profit being greater than for gross revenue is that the cost structure of the business has stayed much the same. We're getting more output from the same or fewer resources. Overheads have not increased. The average salary per team member has increased but at the same time the number of team members has gone down slightly. When some people left, the team recognized there was no need to replace them because they could absorb the work the former team member had done. In 2002, we introduced a profit-sharing scheme that gave everyone a direct interest in making the business more profitable.

Through changing to a workflow management system based on throughput, we're getting our work completed much quicker and on time. We're both more effective in our client's eyes and more efficient. Time written off has vanished. The average New Zealand accounting firm writes off time equivalent to around 8–9% of its gross revenue. In 2003, we had a firm-wide write-on of 1%. That time is now available to be sold to other clients to increase profits.

The change to a throughput-based system and a four-week turnaround guarantee also means we're getting jobs in and out quicker. Work-in-progress has dropped by 30%.

Our debtor situation has also improved. There are three reasons for this. We stopped working for the worst of the bad payers. Our remaining clients have little reason to ever question our prices or our standard of service, so they pay on time. We also put in place many fixed price agreements with automatic payment clauses.

In New Zealand, the term "lockup" is used for the combination of work-in-progress and debtors. This is because it is the working capital that is "locked up" in the business. Our "lockup" has dropped by 19%. So we're getting more profit out with less working capital required.

Since we implemented these changes we have also noticed a genuine reduction in stress levels in the firm. That's partly because our team now has more certainty about what they're doing and are expected to do on a day-to-day basis. And it's partly because we're getting through our work in less time meaning there's less pressure.

We've also held three more Client Advisory Boards with our clients. The generic problems with uncertainty that were present in 1999 were gone. Overall, our clients were happier. The issues they did raise were usually specific to them and their business.

As I mentioned, one measure did not improve—at least not in the way most accountants view this measure. This measure is "productivity" or the chargeable hours as a percent of total hours available. Our "productivity" has dropped by 5% of total available hours per person. We suspect most accountants would be really disappointed by this reduction because one way most firms aim to grow is by driving productivity to ever higher levels.

We're not at all upset by this 5% drop. Rather than view it as a reduction in productivity, we view it as an increase in "spare capacity." In other words, we've improved all the measures that really matter and we've got the capacity to do even more work if we want to. And remember, because our costs are fixed, that extra work, if we choose to do it, will be virtually all profit.

You can probably tell from this summary that we still use timesheets at Stratagem. If we didn't, we couldn't tell you about the improvements in the traditional performance measures mentioned above. For now, we will probably still keep using timesheets because we're selling our workflow management systems to other firms. Having the hard evidence of these improvements that traditionally managed firms can relate to is an important selling tool for us.

If we wanted to stop using timesheets, we could do so tomorrow. We base our performance management around completing work on time. If that is done, we know we will be profitable. As part of our system, we do use a time budget for each job and compare it to actual hours once the job is completed. We need to do that to manage our overall capacity to ensure we can complete our agreed work on time.

Joe Gallardo, CPA, Arcadia, California

Joe Gallardo, CPA, of Arcadia, California, explains how value pricing has had an impacted on his business and on himself as follows.

To begin, you need understand where I was and how I felt about being a practicing CPA prior to embracing the principles of value pricing. My business was fledgling and I found myself trying to justify to prospects why I was asking for $125 per hour (now I can't believe I was asking for such a low price.). Anyway, I was constantly being turned down. On that rare occasion, when I did get the full price, I was ecstatic. Most of the time I was settling for a fraction of my price.

Back then I knew nothing about concepts such as wealth creation, capturing value, buyer's emotions, climbing the value curve, and so on. I was focused strictly on doing compliance work. I worked very hard at it but just couldn't seem to make much progress. My annual revenue growth was minimal; I was experiencing frequent write-offs, not to mention write-downs. I was often forced to justify my hours even though I provided details on my invoices. All these factors created for me a deep feeling of frustration and lack of satisfaction. There were times when I told myself that it would be easier for me if I went to work for someone else.

The facts that I'm open-minded, have a strong level of determination, and am willing to experiment with new ideas are what kept me going. Naturally, when I read Ron Baker's course syllabus I was intrigued. I took the course with a lot of anticipation.

I attended Ron's value pricing course in the fall of 1997. Ron presented a lot of thought-provoking information; who else but Ron would ask "Why is movie theater popcorn so expensive?" in the context of pricing professional services? In listening to the presentation about the value curve, what people buy and how they buy, capturing consumer surplus, and the deleterious effects of hourly billing, I was intrigued, trying to absorb every concept being presented.

Some of the concepts I vaguely understood, for others I had to later re-read the course manual several times before they sank in. During the afternoon break, Ron identified for me all the books he referenced in the course manual that were worth reading. In the subsequent years, I have read almost all of those books. Ron's novel ideas on pricing specifically and success in general gave me the impetus to try something new.

I immediately began implementing the concept of fixed price agreements (FPAs) and change orders. Unfortunately, I really should have developed a more solid theoretical foundation before venturing into something new. Needless to say, my first several FPAs and change orders were abysmal failures. I would have been better served sticking with the hourly rate. But this was a risk I was willing to take; I saw it as an investment and I was determined to make it successful.

It wasn't until I performed my own informal "After Action Reviews" (AARs), as the U.S. Army calls them, and learned further from Ron that I got a better understanding of my mistakes. I was still a rookie at value pricing, making numerous errors, sometimes repeating them. For instance, I wasn't asking the right questions to determine what customers did and did not value before I set a price. I rarely asked them what they expected of me and what bothered them the most. I never asked them what they thought was a fair price. I didn't sit down with them to review the FPA in depth so I could continue building my value before quoting them a price.

Boy, did I learn a lot. I really needed to be more consistent. I needed to understand the why before the how. My customers did like the fact that I quoted them a price up front, was willing to guarantee my work, and offered a flexible payment plan. They had never heard that before from a professional.

I was hooked on the value pricing concept; I just needed to get better at it. Fortunately, Ron was gracious in answering my numerous questions, which is probably how I got the nickname "the question man." I was constantly asking questions and seeking opinions, sometimes on the most minute of matters, just to learn as much as I could. Unfortunately, real-world experience is often the most effective—and cruelest—teacher.

Some of the mistakes I made cost me plenty. For instance, I think the service guarantee is a fabulous concept. Sometimes, however, you will deal with unscrupulous people who abuse this concept. Without going into specifics or naming names, some people I dealt with used this brilliant marketing concept as a convenient way not to pay. This was at a time when the concept of customer selection and retention was foreign to me. I was accustomed to taking all comers. Live and learn.

Looking back, I now understand what Ron meant when he said, "Value pricing is an art, not a science." Like any art, to get good at it you must practice often; you must be a good student. This I've tried to do.

I can honestly say that since fully embracing the concepts of value pricing my quality of life has improved dramatically. This is not to say that my life was miserable or that I was completely unhappy before. Far from it. I wanted an improvement in my life and in my work and I got it. For example, I no longer have an arduous tax season. Before I implemented value pricing, I worked almost every day from about the middle of February through April 15th. Yes, this is why it's called "tax season," but why must this require working until the late hours on weeknights and sometimes all day Saturday and Sunday? Why not have an enjoyable tax season, without feeling like your head is going to explode with one more tax return?

I followed the concept of focusing on the better customers. I got rid of customers that I didn't like dealing with or who were unwilling to pay a higher price. Granted, I didn't double or triple my price; I may have increased it by 20% to 25%. My revenue from tax preparation increased. But the biggest benefit came from having the opportunity to leave work at a decent hour and not working all day on Saturdays and Sundays. I now have more free time to enjoy myself. Amazingly, the customers for whom I raised my price stayed with me.

Another example came in my new focus on looking toward the future rather than always at the past. Accountants are trained to be meticulous historians. In fact, there is a lot of opportunity to help customers spend time looking at the future. It is even more rewarding and fun when you can help them go from where they are now to where they would like to be. Yes, this requires a completely different skill set. But when you combine forward-looking services with typical compliance-type work, tax return preparation, financial statements, etc., you can generate some nice revenues.

A final example of how I've benefited from value pricing happened in August 2001, just after I returned from Ron's "Trashing the Timesheet" seminar. A customer called me at home and said he wanted to meet with me on Monday. The customer was a couple who owned an advertising agency specializing in servicing auto dealerships. The couple was bidding on a huge contract for a dealer's association. If they were successful, the contract would more than double their annual revenues. They wanted my assistance in proving to the dealer's association that they were financially capable of handling such a large contract.

We met that Monday for about an hour and half. I agreed to prepare a compiled financial statement on the advertising agency, a personal financial statement for the couple, and meet with the CPA of the dealer's association to convince him that my customer was financially stable—and I was to have the financial statements ready the next morning.

That sounds worse than it was; the compiled financial statement had only two footnotes, one on the significant accounting policies and the other on a car loan. The personal financial statement was also a breeze because the couple's only investments were their home, their business, and a retirement account. Total time to complete the entire engagement, including the initial meeting with my customer, the two financial statements, and meeting with the CPA of the dealer's association to review the financial reports including faxing some documents, answering follow-up questions, and keeping my customer abreast was about 15 hours (for two people: my assistant helped me prepare one financial statement while I did the other). Had I billed by the hour using an average rate of $200, the price would have been $3,000. I charged $6,000 for the entire engagement and the customer gladly paid it. I would have left $3,000 on the table. Or as Ron might say, I would have made the ultimate accounting entry: debit Experience $3,000 and credit Cash $3,000. The funny thing is that I could have gone even higher on the price. Do you think they were price sensitive?

Since implementing value pricing back in 1998, my firm revenues have increased 100%. My quality of life has improved immeasurably. My confidence level to quote higher prices has jumped. I haven't yet reached the point where I, as Ron Baker says, "quote a price that will make their head snap back," but I'm a lot bolder than I was. With value pricing the scary thing is that I feel I can continue to grow my revenues by using Ron's concepts.

To those still not sure about making the change, my recommendation is to try it gradually. I was looking for something new to try. Perhaps I made the transition too fast and could have avoided some of my mistakes. The only certainty is that I made the transition and I'm never going back.

O'Byrne and Kennedy, United Kingdom

Paul O'Byrne, of O'Byrne and Kennedy, chartered accountants and business specialists, in the United Kingdom, describes his firm's experience as follows.

We were frightened of trashing our timesheets. As was the usual practice in owner-managed businesses, everyone in our practice of ten professionals had grown up with them; it was what people in practice did. Over the years, we had developed very good patter explaining how time-cost billing worked, why it was best, and—we were very good at this—why fixed prices were bad. I had often told other accountants the single best investment we had made was our time and fees software. We even persuaded certain clients that they needed to record time, otherwise how could they know what the profitable jobs were and who was and wasn't pulling their weight?

So, when I was first introduced to Ron Baker in March 2000, when I read *Professional's Guide to Value Pricing* and shortly afterward saw him speak at an accountants Boot Camp event, I was deeply unsettled. Ron was very persuasive and made sense as he described a world of fixed prices, guarantees, and—horror of horrors—no timesheets.

We didn't see why we had to adopt everything he advocated. He seemed to be right about fixing prices in advance. Because we had long noticed clients' resentment of the blank check approach that professionals use in pricing, we introduced fixed prices and adapted Ron's example fixed price agreement (FPA). However, we kept our timesheets so we could track the success of this experiment. It took us a while to even try FPAs, initially just using them on new clients or on single assignments. But once we committed to using them firm-wide, all but a handful of clients were on FPAs within a year. Some clients were suspicious of FPAs, partly as a result of our training them on the benefits of time-cost billing. The overwhelming majority welcomed fixed prices for agreed on assignments—and our turnaround times. "About time, too" was the single most common reaction when we told them we were going to fix all these things in advance.

We had been using FPAs for around 18 months before we decided to discard timesheets. We had some successes but also several failures—or losses—on jobs with FPAs. Being accountants and never wanting to take a loss on anything, we scrutinized the losses and found three causes:

1. Outrageous optimism/myopia on our part
2. Not holding clients to what they said they would do
3. Scope creep, being of two types:
    - Misunderstanding the client's expectations of what we were to do and then being made to meet them
    - Blithely doing more than we contracted to perform

Of course, the way we recognized our losses (especially the blithe ones) was by looking at our time records and wondering how on earth jobs cost so much.

The big revelation ("epiphany" in Baker-speak) was our abject disappointment that one particular "good job," a £25,000 management advisory, training, and accounts job, made a £2,000 loss. Our postmortem analysis showed willful scope creep ("this is such a profitable job, I'll just do this one more thing") poured time onto the job needlessly. This extra work did add value to the client, but we did not capture any of the value created by utilizing "extra work orders," our term for Baker's "change orders." But even that did not cause the loss, it just stopped us making a profit.

At the root of the loss was that a qualified manager performed work that a junior could have and should have done. This may never happen in your firm, but sometimes we misschedule, have insufficient resources of the right type available, and so on. Thirty or forty hours were recorded on this job at £96 per hour that should have been less. The fact is, we do not actually pay our managers £96 per hour. The whole "loss" was spurious, as Baker would point out, because it included a "desired net income" factor. We made money on the job—of course we did—but the timesheets led us to believe otherwise.

Holding on to timesheets after introducing FPAs allowed us to recognize scope creep—albeit after the fact—and to be attentive to client's expectations and their obligations to provide us information. But it finally dawned on us that all of those factors should be dealt with *before* work is performed. Timesheets were a crutch, one that was holding us back.

We now understood we should price independently of timesheets. What surprised us was that timesheets did not help us with our profit forecasting or revenue recognition. Once FPAs were in place firm-wide, we realized just how inadequate a measure of value timesheets were. They were also inadequate measures of costs. Accountancy firms have fixed costs. Our task is to consider how to allocate the resources bought by those fixed costs. The introduction of FPAs taught how to discuss value with clients for a given outcome. We recognized that it was our task to design the cost structure to meet the price—the opposite of the blank check approach.

The last possible reason for holding on to timesheets was for the valuation of work in progress (WIP). Timesheets and time recording had given us something to fix on as the amount of value created in a given period, be it a day or a year. They provided a way to assess work in progress at the month end, which we then adjusted for known write-downs (never write-ups, of course, timesheets don't help capture the extra value you create).

We realized that we had to talk with our team about what work was going to be done, by whom, and when we could expect it to be completed. Otherwise, how could we be sure of when to recognize revenue? We went so far as to suggest that if we wanted to make life easy for ourselves, it would be best if we could start and finish any given assignment within a calendar month, thus assisting revenue recognition. This, serendipitously, gives clients exactly what they want: predictable and (compared with the past) quicker turnaround times. Our firm decided to track the following KPIs:

- Value expected to be created in the month
- Total contracts WIP at start and end of the month
- Average turnaround time of jobs

We were severely tempted to do more, but resisted. Now we fill out our timesheets in advance: "XYZ company audit to be finished this month? O.K., let's put the resources on it so by month-end it's 100% complete." Of course, the more we do this the more we recognize our work for clients as being the fulfillment of contracts, for which we require certain resources at certain times.

We learned from experience and mistakes somewhat slowly, but now we are so confident in our ability to plan our work and capacity sufficiently in advance that we could abandon timesheets. We complete our timesheets before we do the work and then use the turnaround time KPI to track—on a real-time and leading basis—our firm's velocity. On July 1, 2002, we became a firm of accountants that did not use timesheets for pricing or project or team evaluation (not that we ever did, but we always thought we could).

We are now in a position where our "no timesheets" culture attracts clients and prospective recruits (think about it), and the partners, team members, and bank manager love it. Our clients welcomed fixed prices so much that we arrange the payment terms so we are paid almost entirely in advance. We now have negative lockup (20% —73 days—of our annual income is prepaid), and at the start of the month the team agrees on what jobs will be completed in the month and thus what income earned.

I know that what you've read in this book sounds unsettling, even scary. I've been there, went through it, and have now emerged on the other side. I had the benefit of Ron Baker constantly berating me for holding on to the antiquated timesheet, and he and I had some major arguments over this issue. Once Ron had developed the KPIs presented in this book, we decided to take the leap of faith and abandon timesheets.

You now have the same opportunity. I have yet to meet an accountant who likes completing his or her timesheet. If no customer buys time, and does not measure the success of their accountant based on time, why do we all continue to hold on to a practice that is not relevant to our success—and is injurious to our relationships with our customers? I commend Ron Baker and recommend his ideas to you. He has helped our firm with his insights, logic, and passion. We had no way of being sure in advance that we were right to abandon timesheets. We took a leap of faith. Not a very big leap, because we could always bring them back, but it was uncomfortable abandoning something everyone else was doing. Now we scoff at timesheet-padding scandals, we tell clients and referral sources that we don't do timesheets, and we certainly tell recruitment agents and potential recruits.

We love not having timesheets and will never look back.

Daryl B. Golemb, An Accountancy Corporation of CPAs, San Diego, California

It Began with Total Quality Service

I have always had a service ethic that centered on the customer, an ethic that began with my first position as a staff accountant, and it is who I am today. I had no peers who shared this philosophy, until June of 1996, when I met Ron Baker. His teachings confirmed my philosophies, and together over the years we have shared many ways of implementing TQS into a financial services business.

I look at each customer in a holistic way and our philosophy is illustrated in our mission statement, which we proudly live by:

Our Mission

Our mission is to render services, implemented through close relationships that will accomplish our clients' objectives and goals. By delivering these services proactively, we will exceed, not merely meet, our client expectations.

We will accomplish this by being client focused—being sensitive to our clients' needs and expectations—listening to our clients.

When faced with a customer situation where we are deliberating on how to best act, we first ask ourselves, "If we were the customer, what would be our expectation?" Placing ourselves in the shoes of the customer, thinking and acting like the customer, we come up with the solution. In this way, Total Quality Service creates very satisfied customers.

Fixed Price Agreements

Our first step down the path of Value Pricing was to simply adopt fixed price agreements as our primary method for invoicing customers for services. The sales pitch we made to our customers was this: let's come to an agreement on an annual price for the services we are currently providing. These agreements were an immediate hit. No one really liked the uncertainty of invoicing under an hourly rate system. In a sense, even with billing by the hour, we had been fixing our prices all along without formalizing the fee amount or the payment terms. For instance, unless there were unusual circumstances, this year's tax returns were priced approximately 10% over last year's. This year's tax planning consultations and calculations were priced approximately as last year's, and so on. Our standard hourly rates did not matter to the customer. The time spent on a project did not matter to the customer. The only thing that mattered to the customer was value exceeding price.

Initially, we simply came to an agreement to fix the amount of the compliance services our customers were receiving. We didn't have the courage to discuss payment terms or expand the services we were providing. As we grew, so did our fixed price agreements. We started discussing payment terms, and putting them right into our agreement. Again, this was a relatively simple process. I don't know what we were afraid of. We asked our customer their preference for paying our services—"would you like us to bill you monthly, quarterly, or annually?" We were establishing the price of our services, and the payment terms up front. Allowing the customers to design the scope of their engagement, as well as the payment terms, almost guarantees customer satisfaction from the onset.

Adding Value to Our Customers

Our philosophy for keeping our customers' objectives in the center of our thoughts made for an easy transition to increasing our fixed price agreements by adding customer value. We had already been looking out for our customers' best interests, so why not let them know it and formalize it into our agreements?

How do you add value to a customer? Ask them, and listen carefully. They'll tell you very clearly. Here are some common examples:

- Unlimited telephone conversations—anytime, any topic, any length.
- Unlimited e-mail communications
- Unlimited telephone and e-mail communications with other professionals, e.g. financial planners, attorneys, real estate brokers, etc.—creating a team approach to customer service.
- Year-end tax planning
- Regularly scheduled meetings
- Keeping customers accountable

We tell our business customers "We would like to work with you to help you achieve these goals:"

1. Develop your accounting and reporting systems to their fullest potential.
2. Increased business profit and cash flow.
3. Develop a strategic plan, and assist you in implementing it.
4. Minimize taxation.

Today's Engagements

Our engagements today are exclusively on a fixed price agreement basis. The only exception to this policy are engagements that come under court supervision, which insist on detailed invoices showing time spent times our standard hourly rate.

We have several basic Value Added Fixed Price Agreements. We always begin with the customer's objectives, and build from there. Here are a couple of prototype engagements for business entities (prices shown are minimums).

Level One—$500–$750 per month

- Compliance services—to reduce your worry. This includes the basic tax services that every business has to have done. This level will also include the personal tax returns for the company's owners.
- Tax planning—to minimize your burden. We review your financial performance after six and nine months in order to provide

you with taxation planning advice before the end of the year. Action taken here will allow us to proactively plan to maximize your after-tax profits.

- Unlimited telephone conversations—any time, any topic, any length.
- Unlimited e-mail communications.
- Unlimited telephone and e-mail communications with other professionals, e.g. financial planners, attorneys, real estate brokers, etc.—to create a team approach to serving you, our customer.

Level Two—$1,000 per month

You receive all of the Level One service, plus:

- Management accounting—to put you in control of your business. This is where we help you prepare budgets for cash flow and profit planning purposes.
- Management advice—action on strategies to improve profit and cash flow. This is where we go beyond the budgeting process and proactively help you interpret your periodic reports, such as financial statements, employee productivity reports, project productivity reports, and other key performance indicators.
- Quarterly meetings with you to review the company's financial performance. We will review the results of the quarter—what went right, what went wrong, and look for developing trends.
- In addition to reviewing the company's financial performance, our quarterly meetings will be used to develop and monitor systems for projecting cash flow, employee productivity, and job/contract productivity. We will help you set up company budgets and forecasts, then discuss and analyze any variances that occur. We will also cover current issues in your business and any other topics of interest to you.

Level Three—$2,500 per month

You get all of Level Two service, plus:

- Monthly meetings with you to review the company's financial performance. We will review the results of the month—what went right, what went wrong, and look for developing trends.

- In addition to reviewing the company's financial performance, our monthly meetings will be used to develop and monitor systems for projecting cash flow, employee productivity, and job/contract productivity. We will help you set up company budgets and forecasts, and then discuss and analyze any variances that occur. Then we will discuss strategic planning topics of interest to you, such as ways to grow your business, ways to develop and monitor a marketing system, etc. We will also cover current issues in your business and any other topics of interest to you.
- Semi-annual meetings (independently) with you to discuss personal planning topics of interest, such as household budgeting, retirement planning, investments, etc.
- Business development—to improve the value of your business. This is where we are involved in helping you with the development of your strategic plan. Our specific focus is on helping you discover the potential that lies within your business. Our aim is to help you make your business even more profitable, and therefore more valuable. This will include non-accounting aspects of your business, such as team training and customer service strategies. We will help you develop your strategic plan and assist you in implementing it.

Consequences

Today, we have no accounts receivable collection issues. We usually are paid in advance of the services we render. This fact alone should convince practitioners to adopt the fixed price agreement concept.

We do not accept customers willing to purchase only tax compliance services. Our minimum fixed price agreement includes tax return preparation, tax planning strategies, and unlimited telephone/e-mail communications. During the fixed price agreement discussions, customers become aware of the various services we offer. Analogous to a buffet, customers can select new services that they have not previously used. We thereby can provide more services per customer than we did before.

In setting the payment terms of our fixed price agreements, we are more likely to negotiate payment before the services are rendered than to accept an installment arrangement after the work has been done.

The evolution of our fixed price agreements and value pricing has led us to establish minimum prices for all services, which was an important concept in our growth. Establishing minimum prices established confidence in the services we were delivering, as well as set the bar for customer selection.

Value Pricing (and Total Quality Service) has had a dramatic impact on our quality of life, and I would strongly urge everyone reading this book to implement the ideas set forth by Ron Baker.

Morris + D'Angelo, San Jose, California

Daniel D. Morris, CPA, of Morris + D'Angelo, San Jose, California, describes the experience of his firm in implementing value pricing and discontinuing the use of timesheets as follows.

The Morris + D'Angelo venture into the timeless culture might have ultimately happened simply because the firm's founders despised hourly pricing and timesheets; but we took the plunge because of the groundbreaking work of Ron Baker. Ron's influence on our firm has been both good and bad. Good in that it propelled us to be innovative regarding our pricing structure and service offerings and bad in that it wasn't painless to achieve our objective.

The transformation of an hourly pricing/timesheet firm into a timeless culture where value pricing dominates is a true metamorphosis. As in the transformation of the caterpillar to the butterfly, what was, ultimately, no longer exists.

I was the driver behind our firm's transformation, with my partners concurring and actively supporting the vision. If we had the opportunity to repeat the process, we wouldn't repeat some steps, but we are convinced beyond any doubt that the transformation was worth the effort.

Firm Background

Our firm was founded by two partners in December 1994 in California's Silicon Valley. We perform no work that requires independence (although a third partner was admitted in 1999 who brought with him some reviews). Approximately 40 percent of our revenues are generated by consulting projects, 40 percent from tax services, and 20 percent from accounting. We own our own building and our business plan calls for a firm size of ten or less.

Partners' Attitudes

Like partners in many firms, I (along with my partners and team) dreaded the daily timesheet. The only reason I submitted a timesheet was under threat of not being paid. I recognized that our customers hated our monthly invoices because they never were prepared for their contents. Like many firms, we ended up with net write-downs before we invoiced and we faced subsequent write-downs after our surprise charges were delivered to our customers. Our timesheets were generally late, poorly documented, and omitted many of the important services that we provided, and they certainly included errors of omission and errors of inclusion.

We never suffered a customer revolt against our hourly based pricing, but the deep current of dissatisfaction was evident. This was especially true because we operated in Silicon Valley during a time of great market upheaval, and our primary customer base was constantly attempting to rewrite the traditional rules.

The partners revolted against timesheets. I informed my partners that I was stopping, and while others continued to write down time, I stood my ground. Tension was strong, especially with our office manager, who grew up in accounting firms of the 1970s, when only time-based pricing existed. Within six months my partners agreed to a one-year experiment with a timeless culture. The firm went cold turkey.

During our partner debates about changing our firm's culture, we discussed how often our customers pressured us to reduce our time-based invoices. Our customers were expressing a value gap between their perceptions and our best-efforts-based pricing.

When we began our effort to value price our engagements, including up-front pricing, we had the constant metric of timesheets staring us in our faces—that is, frequently the time-based price was higher than our quoted price.

Intellectually, we recognized that value pricing was a superior method to evaluate the exchange between our customers and our firm. The challenge presented by daily timesheets compiled monthly was the inherent desire to compare the price charged relative to the "standard" or historical price based upon recorded efforts, which suggests that value pricing doesn't work. This comparison is commonly debated in firms migrating from an efforts-based pricing matrix to a fixed price or value price matrix. When we looked at why the hourly pricing method exceeded the upfront quoted price we learned a great deal: The number-one reason why value pricing appeared on the surface to be less desirable then hourly pricing dealt with pure and simply scope creep.

I refer to scope creep as the Davy Crockett approach. Our term tended to leave the prescribed path to forge their own trail. They followed their instincts and meandered around the job (rather than tapping the intellectual capital of fellow team members) and they simply performed special requests for customers without informing management.

This was both a project management and firm leadership issue. The partners needed to create an environment where team members were responsible for completing deliverables in an effective manner, one where barriers prevented scope creep. As leaders, we concluded that it was our primary responsibility to actually know what our team members were doing on a daily, weekly, and monthly basis.

The project management aspects were accomplished via a number of tools, including a master deliverable tracking system and weekly team meetings in which current, future, and past projects were reviewed and commitments relative to completion dates were made, reviewed, and obtained. Performance-based goals for teams were altered to provide incentives for locating change orders before they were performed, for obtaining their committed deliverable schedule, and for not performing any work that didn't have an agreed-upon deliverable scope, price, payment terms, and approval from both the firm and the customer.

Ultimately our firm converted the manual tools into an integrated software system that today provides real-time project knowledge management. Additionally, the system provides forecasted available capacity. Knowing the probability that our firm has available capacity to complete a proposal assists leaders in making better pricing decisions.

From a leadership perspective, the partners had to come to grips with the fact they could no longer let their team flounder. Hourly pricing, timesheets, and monthly invoicing provided an environment of unaccountability, especially when the ultimate price collected turned out to be less then the standard hourly price.

The firm had lost opportunities when the leadership wasn't actively involved in the firm's entire process. No longer would it be excusable for an engagement partner to suggest that he or she was unaware that a team member had performed a Davy Crockett. We realized we could not wean our way off timesheets. Intellectual and emotional survival required that we go cold turkey.

Immediate Fallout

Our office manager calmly explained she thought we were nuts. Being from the old school she liked the concept of hourly pricing. She didn't like the fact that we didn't have a method for systematically recording efforts. She understood the concept of value pricing—she simply didn't approve of the step. Within 10 months of our transition she resigned from our firm and moved to one of the Big Four, where she continues to record her working life in 6 minute increments.

Our professional team, on the other hand, was thrilled to stop recording their daily efforts. The team environment improved, and immediately team members shared more knowledge and customer care. The team wasn't allowed free rein; they were simply freed from reporting every step they performed for a customer. The team understood the goals were to effectively take care of our customers by performing those procedures requested and agreed upon by both the firm and the customer relative to price, scope, and payment terms.

Change orders were identified more frequently, and they provided the firm with the opportunity to cross-sell additional services—and the customer with the opportunity to cancel their request prior to initiating the service because they could not agree on scope, price, and terms with the firm.

Operating in a timeless culture requires a firm to face the fact that not all services requested by a customer should be performed by the firm, if ever at all. A firm has a fixed capacity to provide services; so, it is imperative that the firm balance its opportunities with the desires of its customers.

After serious debate, the partners agreed that it is far superior to decline work and forgo short-term opportunities and profits if we could not achieve a desirable price for the firm. Customers understand this, even if they are disappointed. Being business owners themselves, they recognize the lessons we are teaching. In fact, oftentimes our customers hire us to advise them on their pricing and capacity-allocation issues. Turning them down can lead to a better, more enjoyable, and ultimately more profitable engagement for our firm.

Do we still have cases of Davy Crockett? Yes, although fewer today then when we started. It is easy to react to a good customer's request for help. As human beings, we are innately interested in helping others and mistakes will happen. The firm can recover from its Davy Crockett adventures by informing the customer of the scope creep and requesting a voluntary payment of what they feel is fair. We are always prepared to quote a price; however, we offer our customers a covenant stating that no customer will receive an invoice for work they do not preauthorize and at a price they preapprove. Failure on our part does not create an obligation on their part. Repeat performances of scope creep are not tolerated.

Benefits of Dropping Timesheets

We identified several benefits when we dropped timesheets. First of all, we are now unable answer the question "how long did it take you complete this project?" We don't know and better yet, I don't believe we really care. We are able to redirect the question to determine the true customer concern: Are they really looking for the efforts? Or are they concerned that the price paid for the service received was fair? And when they preapprove the price along with our unconditional unilateral satisfaction guarantee, we are able to focus on the root of their question—and it isn't the efforts.

Our team members—and in our firm our team members are frankly more important than our customers—love not having the ghost of Frederick Taylor standing over them and asking what they are doing each and every 6 minutes of their day. Our customers simply don't care about the efforts: They care about the results.

I had to become a better pricer and I had to share with my partners my pricing knowledge. We had to make pricing a competitive advantage. We had to make pricing something we thought about at the engagement and customer level. We ultimately had to challenge partners to become proactive and aggressive pricers.

We had to learn how to convince ourselves of our value and place our egos on the line. This was frightening yet invigorating. When it works, wow, it feels really good. When it doesn't, you have to reflect and learn how to become better. We learned that our customers wouldn't increase their payments until we communicated the value—

and ego—necessary to stand behind our beliefs. Pricing is an art that requires us to understand the perception and view of our customers: Ultimately it is their perception of value that matters.

Customers Comment about the Timeless Professional

The response of existing customers was different from that of prospective customers. We had trained our existing customers that their price was based upon hours, efforts, time, etc. and we had to explain to them that we were changing the relationship and our pricing mechanism. Some were enthusiastic about the change and dumped upon us their absolute distaste for hourly pricing. Others were confused. They were concerned that perhaps we felt they had not paid us enough (i.e., guilt that the price they paid had been too low) or that they had done something wrong (e.g., guilt that they had not treated us well).

We had to explain why we were changing. We assured our customers that they had not been the reason for the change; rather, we wanted to price our work fairly for them—and for us—based on an agreed-upon value and not efforts. We wanted to remove the barriers between our firm and them, time-based pricing interfered with this. We never wanted our customers to hesitate one nanosecond before contacting us with a question on any subject or at any time.

New customers and prospects simply love it. They love it because they know the price up front. They can budget for it. They know they will never be surprised by the arrival of an invoice that they didn't preauthorize. Value pricing provides a competitive differentiation between our firm and others. It rewards our ability to deliver creative solutions and leverage our unique capabilities without having to rely upon efforts invested.

It finally dawned on us that if new customers love it so much, why wouldn't old ones? Once you educate them properly, it turns out, they love it just as much.

Conclusion

I emphatically believe that a timeless culture is better than timesheets. Our youngest partner was the firm's biggest skeptic. Today he is a leading convert. Is it perfect? No, just better. Should our firm culture and pricing models change in the future? Yes. And when a better model is presented I believe we will adopt it. We have learned that our customers prefer the up-front value pricing model. Our team members prefer an environment where they are able to work and serve customers without recording their every 6 minutes. We focus on metrics that are important, including job turnaround, internal (and external) due dates, and communication with our customers. These aren't perfect metrics, but nothing is perfect.

We solve a vast array of challenges for our customers. We have the knowledge and networks necessary to serve our customers and our value isn't predicated on efforts and time—it is predicated on results and value.

We encourage you to improve your firm's emotional and financial rewards by leaving the timesheet and hourly pricing model behind. You will not regret it.

Peter Byers, Byers & Co Ltd, Chartered Accountants Bay of Islands, New Zealand

About 12 years ago, an elderly female client came into our office to complete her annual tax accounts. Mrs. Watson had weathered tough times; she had lived through the deprivations of World War II, raised two children and worked the family farm by herself after being widowed (due to a logging accident), and despite the trials and tribulations of her life she was still a bright and cheerful person. But all of her life she had been required to watch her money because there was none to spare.

On this particular day she was dressed in her usual (which was as though she was going to a wedding) and sat down and fixed me with her beady eyes, and said, with no further introduction, "Peter, tell me what the tax is then I want to talk to you." I'd known Mrs. Watson all my life, she was many years my senior, so I did what I was told and explained the taxes due, how much and when, which took all of a couple of minutes. Then after a revelation as to why I was privileged to be her accountant occurred, the conversation continued, "I didn't come to see you about my tax, I came to see you because it is your job to see around the corner for me and I've got a few things happening—

how much are you going to charge me?" There it was, although I didn't know it at the time: my introduction to "value pricing."

We chatted away for an hour or so about the matters that were on her mind, we agreed on a fee and she went on her way. I remember the return visit equally well: some three weeks later Mrs. Watson returned to thank me for the discussion we had and to pay me—she would always hand her cheque book over to me (when paying her fee) and I would draw the cheque and then hand the book back for her to sign—and as I was writing out the agreed fee she interrupted (which she was apt to do) and said, "You'd better add a bit on for the advice—you were right." There it was, an old and dear friend and client who didn't have any extra money offering me to write the cheque out to cover the value of the advice. I was deeply impressed by her offer and you can imagine what it did for my office team when the cheque was entered into the receipt book.

So my first lesson in value pricing was introduced to me by a lady, who (1) wanted to know, before the assignment started, what the cost would be and then (2) placed a value on the "conversation" we had shared over the years, a value which had crystallised at the meeting to the extent that she offered a "retrospective price" adjustment to the agreed fee.

Transition

The transition to value pricing from then on has been easy although, in retrospect, too slow in implementation.

Our business is based mainly around the farming industry and our office is located in a small working class service town in the Bay of Islands, New Zealand. The population is about 5,000 and there is probably 15 percent unemployment, so it can be a difficult place to conduct business in—nevertheless it is my hometown and I enjoy every minute of living here. A team of 11 other people work with me and we have differentiated ourselves by being a proactive firm, delivering a wide range of innovative services on time and, of course, on budget. The firm's annual turnover reached $1,000,000 four years ago and we are budgeting for $1,500,000 this year, and at mid-year we are ahead of budget. We now enjoy high value work for a wide range of successful clients.

The reasons for reaching this level are many but can be distilled to the following: we value price with agreed fees; we deliver what the client wants (as well as what they need); we provide clear, easy-to-read reports on time; we provide clients with access to "best practice" by using experts in the fields in which we do not have expertise; we provide "add-on" reports to clients when completing interim reporting; we constantly seek ways to improve our service delivery and the quality of our advice and reporting; and our clients, knowing that their fee is "agreed," use our services fully and do not hesitate to call us on any business-related matter.

In one short sentence, the underlying reason for our success is value pricing.

Implementation

The implementation was relatively easy—we read this book, adopted Fixed Price Agreements (although we call them "Agreed Fees"), did not try to reinvent the wheel of TQS (but adopted it absolutely), and experienced the benefit of clients being able to call us at any time. In effect we improved our clients' access to us, which I think is a fundamental issue of value pricing.

Having agreed fees or an FPA provides the clients with the option of continuing the "conversation" of sound business advice over time, knowing that as their business evolves and develops so too do the services we are able to offer. In effect, as they travel up their "Value Curve" so do we, and the work is so much more satisfying than crunching out the compliance work, although we do have a very sound compliance core to our business which has been developed on the back of proven systems and well-trained team members. This compliance core provides us with much of our Value Curve work and as with value pricing we have found that as we work through the issues of business, whether they are large or small, the ability to improve the net worth of a client's business is underpinned by sound in-house systems and financial data that have integrity.

I have a great deal of fun doing what others often say is impossible or can't be done. Before we adopted value pricing, there was a reluctance to get involved in these matters as "the client wouldn't/couldn't afford it." Really, on reflection, that was nonsense. It is much more ethical to improve a client's in-house system to enable them to improve the quality of their financial data for their own use (and external reporting) than it is to plough through a mess at year's end. Value pricing enables these improvements to be done for all the right reasons—there is a need, a given and required outcome, and an agreed cost with a measurable benefit to the client. Surely this is what we should be about—improving the quality of our client's business and, in turn, the quality of their life.

Value pricing and all that it represents is the method by which we have been able to experience high quality, value added work, while at the same time and as a consequence growing our fees on a sustainable and enjoyable basis.

In implementing value pricing, we have developed the "Baker's Dozen"—practices that are worth repeating here:

1. Have the team members control the workflow—develop a traffic management system (what is where and how is it going).
2. Establish minimum prices—we have and this practice works very, very well (and everyone knows the rules).
3. Don't accept work into the firm that you wouldn't want to do yourself (you are your customer list).
4. Replace timesheets with something meaningful (an activity journal).
5. Share the success of an assignment with the team (including the money, if you receive a premium).
6. Develop a culture of "we can do that" (and don't hesitate to call in backup when you need it).
7. Agree on fees ethically and openly (be honest and use change orders carefully).
8. Continue the "conversation" with your client (be part of their business's success and future).
9. Never, as in never, mention time as a basis of value (bury the billable hour).
10. Always deliver what you promise, on time, at the agreed fee (adopt FPAs for all work).

11. Talk with your team members about the FPAs so they know the value being delivered (the pricing committee).
12. Set your own price—ignore the competition and never let it set your fee (maintain a focus on value delivered).

Because you should always deliver more than is expected and provide options and alternatives for the client, here's an additional one for the "Baker's Dozen: create a mutually beneficial, long-term trusting relationships with your clients that result in them using you as their first port of call for all business-related matters by having a continuous "conversation" with them.

The introduction of value pricing to our firm was gradual and went at a pace set by our clients and the team. We have been value pricing since I went to Ron Baker's seminar in Auckland, New Zealand, four years ago (in 2000).

As a firm, we have adopted value pricing because not only is it the way of the future, it is the way now. The methodology is clearly set out—there is no difficulty in implementing the practice and procedure that cannot be overcome by the logic that value pricing provides to both parties in the business conversation.

When we started the practice of value pricing, we were so busy keeping up with the compliance time lines and filing returns that we did not make any alterations to the recommended systems and processes; we simply implemented the practice and took time to explain to clients the benefits (for both of us) of value pricing and especially how it *removed risk* from them. In retrospect, that was the right approach. It is true that some clients had difficulty with this, especially contractors who traditionally charge by the hour—we simply saw a business opportunity to assist them with their own pricing systems and structure, which we did at an Agreed Fee.

This year (goodness knows why I didn't do it before) I am charging $500 per trust where I'm the trustee of record. I've always done a lot of trustee work and now I refuse to incorporate a company, because I believe the client engages *me*, not some $1 company to hide behind, and wouldn't you know it? Not one objection.

I previously have performed the duties of trustee as part and parcel of the job; now all clients know they can call me at any time on specific trustee issues, given the Agreed Fee. The arithmetic: 115 trusts x $500 = $57,500 straight to the bottom line.

Even the slowest cost accountants will see that just doing that alone, and nothing else, will provide a ROI on your book in excess of anything they have ever seen before!

Receiving TIPs

There are, as you know, many ways to have a Fixed Price Agreement with the client. An agreement that is based on a clear understanding of who does what and who is responsible that is then embodied in a written agreement (although I have been very successful with "hand shake" agreements) and assumes both parties accept the other is in business and the relationship is a true conversation.

The TIP clause ("To Improve Performance," or retrospective pricing, or call it what you will) works best when there is a respect for the skill each party brings to the business. The TIP clause is a natural progression for those clients with whom we have had a long-term relationship and with whom there is a great deal of respect and trust for each other. I have never asked for a TIP clause to be invoked, as I do not believe that you are worthy of receiving a premium payment if you have to ask for it.

The key to making the TIP clause work to the benefit of both parties is to clearly define, at the commencement of the project or assignment, the objectives and the anticipated time lines. From there on it is a matter of devoting your energy and skills to achieving more than the client thought was possible, or, viewed another way, delivering the client's dream.

Of course, you have to have a very close relationship with the client to be privy to what the dream or the expectation is—you call it having a conversation, I liken this phrase to the relationship between old friends who've not spoken to each other for some time and who can continue their conversation where it left off when they were last talking with each other. This level of communication is at the very core of having the courage and energy to care about your client to the extent that you become part of their team.

The success that I've had with TIP or retrospective pricing is attributable in part to the wide business network of business professionals whom I call upon to benefit the position of our clients, which in turn enables me to quickly access the particular skills needed for the project. Whenever I engage another professional, I always agree to pay the fee so that everyone who does business with us knows that, regardless of who our client is, they will be paid in full and on time. This commitment inspires a certain loyalty and allows us to request opinions and assistance on the basis that we are first in the queue, which in turn enables me to deliver responses and advice on a timely basis. I always require clear lines of communication with the principal who has engaged me. Such direct communication is essential, as it is crucial to keep the client informed when decisions have to be made quickly and with skill and determination. I also often have found it beneficial to have an authority level so that when I'm negotiating I'm always able to accept or decline an offer. Negotiating in good faith requires sound briefing and if you are close enough to your client, this should not ever be a problem

I regret that I did not introduce value pricing some 12 years ago when a wise old lady asked, "How much are you going to charge me?"

23 CONCLUSION

There is nothing more difficult to take in hand, more perilous to conduct, or more uncertain in its success than to take the lead in the introduction of a new order of things.

—Niccolò Machiavelli,
Florentine statesman
and philosopher

Things do not change; we change.

—Henry David Thoreau

Rigidity is what most organizations manifest when faced with either superior competition or outdated processes. They blindly cling to "that is the way we have always done it" in defiance of the evidence that this way is no longer relevant to success. Charles F. Kettering, the automotive inventor and pioneer, said it best: "If you have always done it that way it is probably wrong." Edward de Bono explains the phenomenon of change, and how it almost always is imposed from the outside, in his book *Sur/petition: Creating Value Monopolies When Everyone Else Is Merely Competing:*

> The value of being familiar with a field is that both the explicit and hidden patterns are available and applicable, and they cover most situations. It is also possible, however, to become trapped within these familiar patterns. That is where a certain kind of creative innocence comes in. A person who does not have these established patterns can see something in a fresh way.
>
> That is also why industries that have traditionally been inward looking (particularly the auto industry and retailing) are slow to change. A person within the field can never have the freshness of innocence, so creativity has to be obtained in a different way—through the deliberate escape from fixed patterns. (de Bono, 1993: 51–52)

This is the history of business. New ideas, inventions, and experiments from the tinkerer in the garage change the world, while rendering obsolete the existing modes of production, infrastructure, and status quo. The automobile replaced the horse and buggy, the calculator replaced the slide rule, the personal computer replaced the typewriter.

The legal and accounting professions, however, have been slow to adopt and even resistant to adopt the changes taking place in the marketplace today. Never before has this mentality been such a hindrance to success in today's rapidly changing marketplace. *How many CPAs does it take to change a light bulb? Ten. One to change it and nine to talk about how great the old one was.*

Innovation and creativity always come as a surprise from outside the traditional paradigms of the experts. Otherwise, you could plan on it and incorporate it into your existing strategies and processes and the economy could be run simply by governmental bureaucrats and computers. Here are some all-time best blunders on the part of the "experts":

> In 1886, the Gottlieb Daimler Company [DaimlerChrysler today] predicted the ultimate size of the world's automobile market to be an eventual total of one million, rationalizing that there could be no more than one million trained chauffeurs in the world.
>
> "Flight by machines heavier than air is impractical and insignificant, if not utterly impossible." (Simon Newcomb, an astronomer of some note, 1902)
>
> "The horse is here to stay, but the automobile is only a novelty—a fad." (The president of the Michigan Savings Bank to Henry Ford's lawyer in 1903)
>
> "It is an idle dream to imagine that . . . automobiles will take the place of railways in the long-distance movement of . . . passengers." (American Road Congress, 1913)
>
> "There is no likelihood man can ever tap the power of the atom." (Robert Millikan, Nobel Prize winner in physics, 1920)

> "The problem with television is that people must sit and keep their eyes glued to the screen. The average American family doesn't have time for it." (*The New York Times*, 1939)
>
> "We don't need you. You haven't got through college yet." (Hewlett-Packard executive, responding to Apple Computer founders Steve Jobs's and Steve Wozniak's attempts to interest the company in the personal computer they had designed, 1976)
>
> "Get your feet off my desk, get out of here, you stink, and we're not going to buy your product." (Joe Keenan, president of Atari, responding to Steve Jobs's offer to sell him rights to the new personal computer he and Steve Wozniak had developed, 1976)

Engage in this thought experiment: The following go to the government industrial planning board with ideas on launching a new product (or service):

1. A failed haberdasher
2. A Harvard sophomore dropout
3. A junior-college dropout
4. General Motors executives

Which one is the government most likely to invest in? If you answered General Motors, move to the head of the class. Government will always focus on the status quo because that is where the votes are. The employees of General Motors can easily understand that their new project was funded by a certain political party, and therefore they will vote accordingly. However, the government doesn't have much to gain by investing in the other three individuals. But who are they? The failed haberdasher is Sam Walton, founder of Wal-Mart. The Harvard sophomore dropout is Bill Gates, founder of Microsoft. The six-month junior-college dropout is Rush Limbaugh, founder of the Excellence In Broadcasting (EIB) Network. All of these entrepreneurs were scoffed at by the existing establishment. Rush Limbaugh was incessantly told that his format for a call-in talk radio show would never work.

Paradigm Shift

The word paradigm comes from the Greek word *pattern.* A paradigm is nothing more than a mental model of the way the world works. In his book, *Paradigms: The Business of Discovering the Future*, Joel Arthur Barker makes the following points with respect to paradigms:

1. Our perceptions of the world are strongly influenced by paradigms.
2. Because we become so good at using our present paradigms, we resist changing them.
3. It is the outsider who usually creates the new paradigm.
4. Practitioners of the old paradigm who choose to change to the new paradigm early, must do so as an act of faith rather than as the result of factual proof, because there will never be enough proof to be convincing in the early stages.
5. Those who change to a successful new paradigm gain a new way of seeing the world and new approaches for solving problems as a result of the shift to the new rules.
6. A new paradigm puts everyone back to zero, so practitioners of the old paradigm, who may have had great advantage, lose much or all of their leverage.

(Barker, 1993: 198–99)

Changing your paradigms is the equivalent of climbing out of your comfort zones. That is not something routinely done without considerable anxiety. People don't *have* mental models. People *are* their mental models. The models are part of who you are, your experiences, and how you see the world.

An analogy from football is offered by Robert J. Kriegel and Louis Patler in *If It Ain't Broke . . . Break It!*

> A vivid example of the pitfalls of sticking to the conventional game plan in times of change occurred in football just after the turn of this century. In 1905, football was a low-scoring game of running and kicking. Guys in leather helmets and a

> smattering of padding plodded down the field toward the goal line. The offense consisted of formations like the "flying wedge," in which seven players ran together into the middle of the opposition in the hope of gaining three or four yards at a time. It was a tough, gritty game.
>
> Then, in 1906, the forward pass was legalized, making it possible to gain 40 yards with a flick of a wrist. During the first season, however, most teams stayed almost entirely within their conventional, tried and true running game.
>
> Recognizing that they were entering a new era in which the old strategy of "three yards and a cloud of dust" would fast become obsolete, St. Louis University's coaches adapted quickly, switching to an offense that used the forward pass extensively. That season *they outscored their opponents 402 to 11!* (Kriegel and Patler, 1991: 4)

Whenever the concepts discussed in this book are introduced to a firm, certain individuals always act like an organism's immune system and try to kill off anything that is foreign. That is fine, as it prevents organizations from wasting time and resources pursuing panaceas that probably would never work anyway.

However, this book has presented a compelling case for why hourly billing is an antiquated paradigm. All businesses struggle with pricing, one of the most complex, unsolvable enigmas of running an organization. No book, seminar, or consultant can remove the tension that value pricing will no doubt cause you.

Not a Fad

The most frequent comment on my course is something to the effect of: "Timely concepts." However, the concepts discussed in this book are not "timely." They are *timeless*. Most of them come from the great economists of the seventeenth and eighteenth century, who can hardly be characterized as "fad thinkers" or "management gurus."

In his book *Billing Innovations*, Richard Reed cites a survey conducted in 1993 by Altman Weil Pensa on alternative billing (value pricing):

> Of the respondents, 43.4 percent stated they were developing billing and pricing alternatives in response to client requests or demands; 29.5 percent indicated that they were actively developing alternative billing and pricing policies; 22.5 percent said they were not pursuing alternative billing strategies.
>
> The survey indicated that the most commonly used alternative to hourly billing was the fixed or flat fee for defined services. The practice area where alternative pricing strategies was most frequently used was in litigation, notwithstanding the sentiments of litigators expressed in 1987 that hourly billing was the only way to bill. The survey also reflected that other predominant practice areas where alternative billing strategies had been employed included corporate, real estate, estate planning, banking, employment, and personal injury (in that order). The attitude about alternative billing showed that 51.2 percent felt it "somewhat necessary," 24.8 percent "not critical," 20.9 percent "critical to survival/success," and 0.8 percent "unacceptable." (Reed, 1996: 97)

Reed continues to cite other surveys, such as *The National Law Journal's Annual Billing Survey* for 1993, which showed more than "one-third of the respondent firms used methods other than the straight hourly fee." (Reed, 1996: 97) The Mead Data Central survey found that "43 percent of the firms anticipated a decreased use of *standard* hourly billing." Further, "48 percent of America's largest law firms have made operational changes as a result of a shift in their billing methods. Large firms (those with 30 or more lawyers) are the firms most likely to have made these changes." (Reed, 1996: 99)

To counter the charge from professionals that firms that have switched to value pricing have been burned, the Mead Data Central survey offers this analysis:

> Firms that made operational changes in response to changes in billing practices are just as likely to say that profits increased as a result of changes in billing practices (45%) as they are to say their profits remained the same (44%). Fewer than one in ten (9%) large firms reported that profits decreased due to changes in billing practices. Computerization

> is the action most commonly taken to maintain or increase firm profitability. Half (54%) of large firms reported increased profitability due to changes in operations and technology. Even though relatively few firms derive a majority of their income from alternative billing methods, those that rely most on those methods appear more likely than other firms to report increases in profitability.
>
> The Mead Data Central study acknowledges that the business of law is changing. Law firms are beginning to respond to the demands of the market. (Reed, 1996: 99)

For remaining skeptics, the 1993 Altman Weil Pensa survey mentioned above was updated in 1995, with 129 respondents from law firms ranging in size. Reed reports what this recent survey discovered:

- Litigation remains the practice area in which alternative methods are most frequently used.
- 64.3 percent of the respondents use alternative methods for both litigation and nonlitigation matters.
- 36.2 percent of the respondents believe that alternative billing is critical to survival/success, compared to 20.9 percent in 1993.
- In 1995, 79.5 percent of the respondents expect the use of alternative billing strategies will increase. (Reed, 1996: 100–101)

For an excellent case against hourly billing, read the American Bar Association's Commission on the Billable Hour Report, issued in August 2002 (available at: www.abanet.org/careercounsel/billable.html). See Chapter 7 for more on this report.

The shift from hourly billing has now affected the majority of lawyers, and CPAs are next. Just as CPAs followed the attorneys into hourly billing, they will follow them right back out of it. According to Everett M. Rogers, in the *Diffusion of Innovations,* when 13 percent of a population accept a new idea it's only a matter of time before at least 84 percent accept the idea, with *time* being the unknown (it's rare that any idea gets universal, 100 percent acceptance). This is the phenomena of critical mass, which is at the heart of any new innovation diffusion process. Once critical mass is reached, it is often impossible to halt the further diffusion of a new innovation. *The Adoption Model* illustrates how innovators and early adopters are leaders. The majority of the population waits for these leaders to undertake the process of change before joining in:

- **Innovators** are venturesome and willing to try new ideas at some risk. They are the first 2.5 percent to adopt innovation.
- **Early Adopters** are guided by respect from others. They are opinion leaders in their community and adopt new ideas early but carefully. They are the next 13.5 percent to adopt innovation.
- **Early Majority** are deliberate. They adopt new ideas before the average person but are rarely leaders. They are the next 34 percent to adopt innovation.
- **Late Majority** are skeptical. They adopt innovation only after a majority of people have tried it. They are the next 34 percent to adopt innovation.
- **Laggards** are bound by tradition, suspicious of changes, mix with other tradition-bound people, and adopt innovation only because it has now taken on a measure of tradition itself. They are the last 16 percent to adopt innovation, and often only make change when there are no alternatives. (AICPA, 1998: 26)

Risk Taking

Entrepreneurs are society's perennial risk takers, and they almost always disrupt the status quo. According to Steven E. Landsburg:

> Entrepreneurial initiatives are intensely personal. In the 1950s Joseph Wilson (later head of Xerox) had a vision of the copying machine as a tool that would transform American business. At the time, few shared his vision. Most visions fail. Should such visions be pursued? From a social point of view, risk-averse individuals underinvest in risky projects. The existence of corporations helps to solve this problem, since the shareholders, with diversified portfolios, will encourage appropriate risk-taking. However, intensely personal visions cannot always be effectively pursued by large corporations. In such cases

> only the prospect of great personal fortune will induce individuals to take great risks. A society that attempted to limit the amassing of great wealth might be a society without copying machines. (Landsburg, 1996: 652–653)

The future brings risk, and if your future includes implementing value pricing, then it will bring even more risk. But risk is also where profits come from. The more risks you take, the higher your rewards will be. In his comprehensive study of risk, *Against the Gods: The Remarkable Story of Risk,* Peter Bernstein points out:

> The word "risk" is derived from the early Italian *risicare,* which means "to dare." In this sense, risk is a choice rather than a fate. The actions we dare to take, which depend on how free we are to make choices, are what the story of risk is all about. And that story helps define what it means to be a human being. (Bernstein, 1996: 8, 105)

I usually end my value pricing seminars by emphasizing that profits ultimately come from risk and that value pricing entails more risk to the professional. After one seminar in Brisbane, Queensland, Australia, I received the following e-mail from a Chartered Accountant who was in the audience:

> Thank you so much for yesterday's seminar, it was most uplifting. I would, however, take issue with one of the last things that you said, and that is we take on risk by up-front value pricing. I believe that we in fact reduce risk. Let me explain.
>
> For the last three years I have given up-front prices to all new clients as part of our no-surprises billing policy. No surprises for the client when they get our bill with the job, and, hopefully, no surprises for me when I review the WIP. It takes me about half an hour to do this pricing and explain how it works with the client. If they don't like the price, we don't do the work, and we only waste half an hour. Most agree, and we get the job. The risk here is that we don't get the work, but as you correctly pointed out, if they don't like the price, then we don't want their work. If

we had not up-front priced, we could have run the risk of write-offs on this work far in excess of my half hour. I believe here the outcome for us is reduced risk.

By having our no-surprises policy, the clients aren't bad payers, because they agreed to the amount for the work performed. Risk of bad payer reduced. In fact I now insist on cash on delivery (COD) with all new work. We don't lodge returns [filing tax returns with the Australian Taxation Office], etc., until we are paid. Outcome here, reduced risk.

Clients that get bills under the hourly billing process who are shocked at the amount they owe are not only bad payers but also bad-mouth us in the marketplace. They tell others how expensive we are. By up-front agreement on price this risk of being bad-mouthed is removed. Outcome, reduced risk.

There is also the risk that you can underprice a job. We get over this by inserting a clause relating to the state of the client records in our pricing agreement. If the client's records aren't in good shape, we can't guarantee the price. But it doesn't end there.

Our team knows if the records are bad, then they stop work on the job and bring it to my attention. We then contact the client and tell them their records aren't up to standard, then ask them what they want us to do. They can come in and we will show them what needs to be done to bring them into line or we can do it for them at an extra price, which we quote to them. This method reduces our risk of underpricing and gives the client total control of spending their money or not. In most cases, the client accepts our quote and we continue to do the job. At the end of the job we then sit down with the client and show them what we want done in future. Outcome, reduced risk.

I am also pleased to say that I haven't done a timesheet since July 1, 1989, and neither has my partner. We had an ICAA [Institute of Chartered Accountants in Australia] peer review three years ago, and the reviewer was horrified that neither partner accounted for his time. We told him we weren't going to change no matter what he reported.

When we get a new major client, we discuss what to bill them. I'm sure the "Questions We Should Ask Ourselves" will be of great benefit.

We seem to struggle, though, when it comes to eradicating timesheets for our tax team (the audit team does not do timesheets at all). We feel a need to control productivity in the area of tax because of its competitive nature, and timesheets are our best option at this stage, but I'm certainly open-minded about this.

I'd like to keep in touch because I think we are of like minds, and as I have said, I would love to bury timesheets fully but need an alternative for measuring productivity.

Keep up the crusade.

Regards,

Ken Robertson
Robertsons Chartered Accountants
Brisbane, Queensland, Australia

Ken's firm has two partners and employs 15 team members, with a financial planning division, and works mainly in taxation compliance, advice, and audits. He makes several valid points as to why, ultimately, value pricing actually entails less risk than it may at first appear.

A Testable Hypothesis

Some innovations are adopted more quickly than others. It all depends upon the perception of individuals as to whether or not a certain innovation is viewed as superior to the alternatives. According to Everett Rogers in *Diffusion of Innovations*, an innovation has the following five characteristics:

1. **Relative advantage**, as perceived by individuals
2. **Compatibility**—consistency with the existing values, past experiences, and needs of potential adopters
3. **Complexity**—the degree to which an innovation is perceived as difficult to understand and use. New ideas that are simpler to understand

are adopted more rapidly than innovations that require the adopter to develop new skills and understandings.

4. **Trialability**—the degree to which an innovation may be experimented with on a limited basis, which are generally more quickly adopted than innovations that are not divisible.
5. **Observability**—the degree to which the results of an innovation are visible to others. The easier it is for individuals to see the results of an innovation, the more likely they are to adopt it (Rogers, 1995: 15–16).

Value pricing scores well in all five of these characteristics, especially in trialability. It is a testable hypothesis; it is subject to being falsified by your experience in adopting it. Once you have gone through the FPA and change order process, you will then be able to observe objectively whether or not value pricing is an innovation you want your firm to adopt.

The Past Doesn't Equal the Future

When the American Bar Association published its first book on alternatives to hourly billing, they concluded that in all likelihood, hourly billing would always exist as a benchmark to value. Reed had this to say on the transformation in thought that he has witnessed in the legal profession:

> Although in preparing the two earlier books the Task Force on Alternative Billing Methods never contended that hourly billing would completely disappear, it is probable that straight hourly billing (billing by hours spent without limit and without regard for the benefits conferred) will virtually disappear in the years ahead.
>
> Without a doubt, quality and value will be the keys to excellence and success in the years to come. Lawyer-client relationships based on mutual trust and satisfaction are prerequisites. The time has come to say goodbye to time as the *sole* criterion for measuring the value of legal services. (Reed, 1996: xiv)

No doubt all professionals are experiencing tumultuous change. James R. Kurtz, publisher of *Outlook* magazine, wrote in the Fall 1996 issue about the dramatic changes taking place in the accounting profession:

> The CPA profession is unquestionably midstream in unprecedented change. I can say that with the authority of someone who has been a student of the profession for 25 years.
>
> Change is constant, but what we are now experiencing is distinct in three major ways:
>
> 1. The change is much **more comprehensive**. Many disciplines throughout Western culture are undergoing major paradigm shifts. Major transformational challenges in the environment, education, economics, religion, science, and health impact the larger social context in which they reside. Therefore, we must be much more aware of the larger context in order to become aware of changes affecting us.
> 2. The change is **discontinuous**; therefore, it is harder to predict based on past experience. Most of our training is based on past experience. In fact, the process of learning may be described as transforming experience into knowledge. The proper response to discontinuous change is continual learning.
> 3. Multitudes of paradigm shifts are **still in progress**, so it's anyone's guess what the new rules of success will be, and how each one will affect the others. There are no formulae, checklists, or advice to be relied upon in adapting to change this time. We are more dependent upon our *own thinking* than ever before.

Margaret J. Wheatley describes major change in *Leadership and the New Science*. She writes, "The new science cogently explains that there is no objective reality 'out there' waiting to reveal its secrets . . . there is only what we create through our engagement with others and events."

Creating through engagement with others and events is the heart of CPA services. The technical knowledge of the

> profession is not useful until it is applied to real problems or opportunities for clients or employers. Awash in the turbulence of the new changes, they are more in need of innovative services by CPAs than ever before.
>
> Absorbing new principles or views of the world will undoubtedly take some time and will make for lots of doubt about their validity during the next decade. My point here is not to announce a brand new solution, but to point a beacon of light at a very important source of new thinking which is likely to have profound effects on our lives and the CPA profession.
>
> The primary dilemma for individuals and organizations during this period is that the old paradigms have not entirely lost relevance to successful behavior, nor have the emerging new paradigms been completely framed. One has to be aware of the existing rules *and* the possibilities of new rules emerging on a constant basis.
>
> Think about it, because we *are* becoming something distinctly different! (Kurtz, 1996: 5)

The old paradigm of hourly billing is losing relevance to successful behavior. Old strategies rarely produce new results. There is enough empirical evidence from both inside and outside of the profession to convince an observer of this fact. I hope you accept the challenge to help establish a new pricing tradition for the professions, one based on value, and free yourself from the tyranny of time.

According to the German philosopher Arthur Schopenhauer, all truth goes through three steps:

First, it is ridiculed.

Second, it is violently opposed.

Third, it is accepted as self-evident.

The purpose of this book is to encourage you to stretch beyond the traditional dimensions and move to the third level of truth by accepting these ideas as self-evident. Pricing for value will enable you to be paid what you are worth and stop sacrificing profits on the altar of the Almighty Hour.

I am always interested in your successes (and failures) with respect to implementing these concepts. Please feel free to contact me to share your thoughts or discuss a particular issue.

Ronald J. Baker, Founder
VeraSage Institute
Office: (707) 769-0965
Office Fax: (707) 781-3069
Web sites: www.verasage.com
www.ronbakersucks.com
E-mail: ron@verasage.com
E-mail: BandBRJB@aol.com

The Things That Haven't Been Done Before

—Edgar Guest

The things that haven't been done before,
Those are the things to try;
Columbus dreamed of an unknown shore
At the rim of the far-flung sky,
And his heart was bold and his faith was strong
As he ventured in dangers new,
And he paid no heed to the jeering throng
Or the fears of the doubting crew.
The many will follow the beaten track
With guideposts on the way.
They live and have lived for ages back
With a chart for every day.
Someone has told them it is safe to go
On the road he has traveled o'er,
And all that they ever strive to know
Are the things that were known before.
A few strike out, without map or chart,
Where never a man has been,
From the beaten paths they draw apart
To see what no man has seen.
There are deeds they hunger alone to do;
Though battered and bruised and sore,
They blaze the path for the many, who
Do nothing not done before.
The things that haven't been done before
Are the tasks worthwhile today;
Are you one of the flock that follows, or
Are you one that shall lead the way?
Are you one of the timid souls that quail
At the jeers of a doubting crew,
Or dare you, whether you win or fail,
Strike out for a goal that is new?

Declaration of Independence

Action January 1, 2001.

The UNANIMOUS DECLARATION of the FOUNDERS of the VeraSage Institute of the ACCOUNTING PROFESSION ASSEMBLED,

WHEN in the Course of Economic Evidence, it becomes necessary for one group of Professionals to dissolve the Traditional Bands which have connected them with another, and to assume among the Powers of the Free Market, the separate and equal Station to which the Laws of Economics entitle them, a decent Respect to the Opinions of the Profession requires that they should declare the causes which impel them to the Separation.

We hold these Truths to be self-evident, that all Value is Subjective, the Customer is sole arbiter of the Value which we in the Profession create, and Price determines Costs, not the opposite—That to secure these Truths, Policies and Procedures are instituted among members of the Profession, and that whenever any Policy becomes destructive of these Principles, it is the Right of the Profession to alter or to abolish it, and to institute new Policies, laying its foundation on such Principles as to them shall seem most likely to effect their Professionalism, Dignity, Self-respect, and Happiness. Prudence, indeed, will dictate that Traditions long established should not be changed for light and transient Causes; and accordingly all Experience hath shewn, that the Professions are more disposed to suffer than to right themselves by abolishing the Policies and Procedures to which they are accustomed. But when a long Train of Pernicious Effects evinces a Design to reduce them under absolute Despotism, it is their Right, it is their Duty, to throw off such Traditions, and to provide new Procedures for their future Security. Such has been the patient Sufferance of these Founders; and such is now the Necessity which constrains them to alter the former anachronistic Systems of Firm Management. The History of the present Time Accounting is a History of repeated Injuries and Deleterious Effects, all having in direct Object the Establishment of an absolute Tyranny over this Profession. To prove this, let Facts be submitted to a Candid World.

Time Accounting is a descendant of the thoroughly discredited Marxian Labor Theory of Value, which has never adequately explained Value in a Free Market and has no jurisdiction to control the Pricing of Intellectual Capital of which the Profession is engaged in Creating.

Time Accounting has foisted onto the profession the implicit assertion that Time × Rate = Value. This Equation is emphatically false, and is in need of being rejected as without Reason. The Notion that Time is Money is hereby directly rejected.

Time Accounting misaligns the interests of the Professional and the Customer whom it is pledged to Serve.

Time Accounting has focused the Profession solely on hours, not Value, thereby keeping the Professional Mired in Mediocrity at the expense of Entrepreneurial Excellence in the pursuit of opportunities.

Time Accounting places the voluntary transaction risk entirely on the Customer, in direct defiance of the Customer's interests the Profession has pledged to Serve.

Time Accounting fosters a production mentality, not an Entrepreneurial Spirit, thereby hindering the Profession in its attempt to innovate and contribute to the dynamism of the Free Market.

Time Accounting has called together Management and Partners at Places unusual, uncomfortable, and distant from the Professionals and Customers they are bound to Serve, for the sole Purpose of fatiguing them into Compliance with these arbitrary Measures.

Time Accounting creates a subsidy system whereby some Customers will pay for the learning curve of others, and the allocation of Value to any one Customer is completely arbitrary and capricious.

Time Accounting transmits no useful information, as it is definitely not a Critical Success Factor or a Key Performance Indicator for any member of the Profession, as defined by the Customer whom it is Pledged to Serve.

Time Accounting produces information that is Suspect and subject to inaccuracies and nonfeasance.

Time Accounting has made Owners dependent on Its will alone for the Tenure, Promotion, and the Amount of Payment of Professional Salaries rendered, irrespective of the Value they Create.

Time Accounting has erected a Multitude of new Ominous forms, and internal Bureaucracies, and sent hither Swarms of Officers, Nefarious Cost Accountants, and Superfluous Activity Based Costing Neophytes to harass our People, and eat out their Substance, in fifteen minute increments, and sometimes less.

Time Accounting encourages the Hoarding of Hours with no attention paid to the internal efficacious utilization of a Firm's Resources.

Time Accounting has conspired with others to subject us to a Measurement foreign to the Laws of Economics, and unacknowledged by our Self Evident Truths; giving Its Assent to the importance of pretended consequences.

Time Accounting focuses on Efforts, not Results. Customers don't buy efforts, and they don't buy hours, making Time Accounting a measurement of precisely the wrong things.

Time Accounting has become a tool, enhanced by modern technology, already rife with circumstances of Cruelty and Perfidy, scarcely paralleled in any other industry, and totally unworthy of a Proud, and Intellectual Capital based, Profession.

Time Accounting penalizes Technological Advances, as the Profession continues to invest in more and efficient technology, in order to produce more work in less Time, thus lowering Revenue in a Time Accounting Pricing Paradigm.

Time Accounting's Hourly Rates are set by paying attention to competitors, who have no quantifiable interest in the success of any competing enterprise, thereby depriving a Firm's Owners from being compensated for the Value They create.

Time Accounting is a Cost-Plus Pricing method that has been thoroughly discredited throughout its inglorious history, and is no longer relevant in a world where wealth is created by Free Minds in Free Markets. It is not the Customer's duty to provide the Profession with a Desirable Net Income; it is the duty of the Profession to Provide a Service that is so good, the Customer Dutifully Pays a Profit in Recognition of what was done for them. Profit is a Lagging Indicator, at best, and is a Result of a Job well done. In a Free Market, costs do not determine price, rather, price determines costs and value determines price.

Time Accounting defies the imperative rule of private, Free Market Transactions; that is, the Price is known to the Customer before they purchase a product or service. The Profession defies this well-known Law at its Own Peril.

Time Accounting does not Differentiate one firm in the Profession from another. Rather, it transforms the Crown Jewels of any one Firm—the human and social capital, experience, wisdom, professional judgement and intellect—into one completely arbitrary Hourly Rate, viewed as a Commodity by the Public.

Time Accounting imposes an arbitrary ceiling on the Income Potential of the Profession, as there is only a fixed quantity of hours in any given day, week, month, year or life. This ceiling has been imposed by Time Accounting, not the Public the Profession is Pledged to Serve.

Time Accounting diminishes the Quality of Life of the Professional, by viciously segregating His or Her Time into Billable and Non Billable segments. Rather than being a device for tracking the Inventory of Time, Time Accounting has become the Inventory.

In every stage of these Oppressions we have Petitioned, Pleaded and Exhorted the Profession's Leaders and Consultants for Redress in the most humble Terms: Our repeated Petitions have been answered only by repeated Injury and Ridicule. A Master, whose Character is thus marked by every act which may define a Tyrant, is unfit to be the arbitrary Ruler of a free Profession in a Free Market.

Nor have we been wanting in Attentions to Leaders and Consultants of the Profession around the world. We have warned them from Time to Time of Attempts by their anachronistic Practices to extend an unwarrantable Jurisdiction over us. We have reminded them of the Circumstances of our Emigration and Conception of a new Pricing Paradigm and Measurement System. We have appealed to their native Justice and Magnanimity, and we have conjured them by the Ties of our common Knowledge and Interests to disavow these Usurpations, which, would inevitably interrupt our Connections and Correspondence and hinder the Future of our Profession. They too have been deaf to the Voice of Justice, Economics, and of Consanguinity. We must, therefore, acquiesce in the Necessity, which denounces our Separation, and hold them, as we hold the rest of the Profession, wrong in the Marketplace of Ideas.

We, therefore, the Representatives of the VeraSage Institute, in GENERAL CONGRESS, Assembled, appealing to the Supreme Judge of the World for the Rectitude of our Intentions, do, in the Name, and by Authority of the good People of this Institute, solemnly Publish and Declare, That this Institute is, and of Right ought to be, FREE AND

INDEPENDENT FROM THE TYRANNY OF TIME; that it is absolved from all Allegiance to the Past Traditions as they relate to Time Accounting, and that all Measurements and Procedures between them are and ought to be totally dissolved; and that as FREE AND INDEPENDENT PROFESSIONALS, they have full Power to Price on Purpose and for Value, levy Ideas in the Free Market, contract Alliances, establish Commerce, engage in Capitalist Acts between Consenting Adults, and to do all other Acts and Thoughts which INDEPENDENT PROFESSIONALS may of right do. And for the support of this Declaration, with a firm Reliance on the Protection of divine Providence, we mutually pledge to each other our Lives, our Fortunes, our Energies, and our sacred Honor.

Signed by Order *and in* BEHALF *of the* VeraSage Institute,

RONALD J. BAKER, California

JUSTIN H. BARNETT, California

DANIEL D. MORRIS, California

PAUL O'BYRNE, London, England

PAUL KENNEDY, London, England

APPENDIX

FREQUENTLY ASKED QUESTIONS, AND ANSWERS

Here are some of the most frequently asked questions about value pricing.

Q: Isn't price discrimination in violation of the antitrust laws and therefore illegal?

A: The laws against price discrimination don't apply to sales of goods and services to the final user. Price discrimination is so ubiquitous that outlawing it would be impossible. It is simply capitalist acts between consenting adults. Price is a form of free speech in a market economy and should be respected as such. However, you should become educated with respect to the antitrust laws and how they may affect your customer's pricing decisions, especially if you are engaging in any consulting activities related to this topic.

Q: Price discrimination just won't work in my small town, because my customers tend to know one another.

A: I don't think this is as big a problem as it first appears. First, no two customers have the same needs and wants—let alone the same package of services provided by their professional. Second, customers readily understand charging different prices to different people, based upon a myriad of factors. They probably do this in their own businesses. Third, if you enter into an FPA with a customer, that document has been drafted with their involvement and ego investment, and is specifically tailored to them, making comparisons difficult. Finally, if this is truly a concern, and you have two customers who you know communicate about what they pay their professional, then you will need to be able to justify the price differential. However, don't let the tail wag the dog. This is the exception, not the rule, and you shouldn't let it prevent you in engaging in pricing based upon value. Remember Peter Drucker's sage advice: Don't solve problems, pursue opportunities.

Q: How will I know if I am making money on any one customer if I don't keep timesheets?

A: The real answer to this is that the time it takes you to perform a service is absolutely irrelevant to its value to the customer. Services have such a high gross profit that, if you priced based upon value, you would make a profit. The notion of cost accounting doesn't work well in service industries, where there are virtually no variable costs. Most of your costs are fixed—at least in the short run—and this is why most service industries have stopped trying to apply traditional cost accounting techniques to their businesses. Activity based costing is starting to yield more accurate information for service industries, based upon yield and load factors, as in the airline industry. The only reason professionals pay such fastidious attention to time is because it is intimately linked to their pricing. If you price based upon value, hours become superfluous.

Q: If I have two similar jobs in my practice and one is taking much longer than the other, how would I know to price them differently if I didn't record time?

A: Again, this is Marx's labor theory of value raising its ugly head. The time it takes you to perform a job is irrelevant to its price. If each job is priced based upon the value to that customer, and one job is taking more effort than the other, perhaps the firm is not as efficient as it should be. Maybe opportunities for change orders have been missed. Rarely are two jobs exactly alike. This is exactly the trap of hourly billing, and why we need to move away from it. Even thinking about this issue distracts you from focusing on the value delivered to the customer, which is going to be greater than your internal costs.

Q: You say customers don't pay for efforts, just results. How can you reconcile that view with a doctor who gets paid whether his or her treatment is successful or not (whether the patient lives or dies)? Or an attorney who loses a lawsuit? Aren't efforts, too, rewarded in a free market?

A: Absolutely, efforts are rewarded in a free market. But some are rewarded more than others. And it is the ones—in the long run—that produce the best results that are rewarded the most. How else could one explain the difference in pay between Michael Jordan and the average NBA player?

Would you pay for a car that "tried" to work? Lawyers who work on a contingency basis already share the risk of losing the lawsuit. Customers are demanding risk-sharing with their professionals, a trend that will continue.

The medical example is an excellent one, and it really points out the theory of price leverage. When you are ill—especially if you are critically ill—you will value a doctor's intervention, even if there is a low probability of its success. You are, in essence, taking a chance on the treatment. A service that is needed is more valuable than one that has been delivered. And people desire medical care, even if the treatment is not successful. The argument has been made that this is akin to taking advantage of people in an emergency. But how else should medical care be delivered? If people don't pay for it individually, they will pay for it through higher taxes. Then the government will ration the care, not based on price, but on other criteria. There is no such thing as free care. Witness the abject failure of socialized medicine.

Q: How can value pricing possibly apply to all firms, in all markets?

A: There is more than one way to implement value pricing. You will have to apply it to the specifics of your location, your customers, and your firm. But on a broad level, these concepts work. Value pricing is based upon empirical evidence of how the real world works, and it is understood by most business people. Most marketing professionals understand these concepts and it is second nature to them. It is time other professionals caught up.

Q: I wholeheartedly believe in these concepts. How can I get my partners to buy in to this? Some of them are just adamant about the importance of keeping time and pricing based upon it.

A: There are no easy answers to this dilemma. Some people will always resist change or the adoption of a new idea. It is simple human nature. You will need to convince them with empirical evidence. Confronted with facts (and success), most professionals are rational enough to change their minds. But make no mistake, changing a firm's pricing policies requires leadership. And as Margaret Thatcher is fond of saying, consensus is the absence of leadership. The managing partner is going to have to take a strong stand on implementing value pricing and stick to it. Start value pricing on new customers, gain some successes—which will build confidence—and then, gradually, switch your entire firm over to this form of pricing.

Q: How do you see the wave of consolidations that are taking place in the profession? What do you think of the profession's entry into financial services, and how will this affect pricing in the future?

A: It is too early to tell what the ultimate impact on pricing will be with companies such as American Express Tax and Business Services, Century Business Services, and HRB Business Services buying up accounting firms. The same situation exists for the law profession now that multidisciplinary practices are becoming a possibility.

The major impetus behind the consolidations is a mature industry, but other forces are at work. The trend of changing from a CPA firm to a full-service financial organization—offering one-stop shopping—is certainly a factor. Also, many partners near retirement are selling to these consolidators because their team members won't buy the firm and sustain them in retirement.

The interesting dynamic with the consolidators is the fact they will be national firms—which gives them a certain economies of scale—and marketing organizations. Marketers understand the importance of price. Some "loss leaders" may be given away—simple tax returns, for instance—in order to obtain the customer's investment portfolio business. It's too early to tell whether or not the consolidations will spell the death of hourly billing. One thing is certain: when AmEx is conducting marketing during the Super Bowl, the competitive playing field is bound to change.

Q: Why is there so much resistance to ending hourly billing and implementing value pricing?

A: This is due partly to the habit, long entrenched, of billing by the hour. It is due partly to the risk-averse nature of professionals, especially CPAs, and to professionals' desire to be objective about their pricing. You don't get much more objective than counting minutes and hours, even though the standard rate is completely arbitrary. Lack of understanding the role that pricing plays in marketing is also a reason, made more severe by the paucity of literature on the subject within the professions in the past. Further, viewing customers as price sensitive, and cutting prices to obtain and retain customers, is always easier then innovation, offering total quality service, building relationships, and discussing value. This becomes a self-fulfilling prophecy within firms. You cut price to obtain the customer, and end up attracting the very customers who are price sensitive and will leave when they find a cheaper price, despite the level of service. Finally, pricing has always been an uncomfortable topic to deal with for the professional. In fact, in the 1950s and 1960s, lawyers were taught not to discuss price, to the serious discomfort of their customers. Yet the evidence is overwhelming that the customer wants the professional to discuss this sensitive topic up front.

USEFUL CHECKLISTS

DISCOVERING AND FOLLOWING THROUGH ON CUSTOMER EXPECTATIONS

Treat customers *individually,* not *equally.*

Focus on what the customer is *buying*, not what your firm is attempting to *sell.*

Determine whether the customer is buying good feelings or solutions to problems.

Provide *both* good feelings and solutions to problems.

Determine what the customer values most.

Focus on *results*, not efforts.

Emphasize the *benefits* of your services, not their *features.*

Don't focus on *what* you do (or *how* you do it), but on how the customer will benefit.

If the customer's expectations are unreasonable, educate the customer on a more realistic expectation or withdraw from the engagement.

Communicate the expectations you discover to each firm member who serves the customer.

Work to exceed the customer's expectations.

Ask each customer regularly for feedback, using open-ended questions, such as:

- How are we doing?
- How could we do better?
- How do you feel about our level of service?

Have team members ask the above questions of their counterparts at the customer's business and monitor the feedback.

CHECKLIST FOR EXAMINING CLOSED FILES

Customer Name:

Year (or period):

Partner-In-Charge:

Description of services rendered:

Was there a Fixed Price Agreement? ❑ Yes ❑ No

Was there an engagement letter? ❑ Yes ❑ No

Pricing method which was used?

____

____

Were the desired results obtained for the customer? ❑ Yes ❑ No

Explain the value received by the customer:

____

____

How could we have done a better job for the customer?

____

____

What could the firm have done differently in servicing this customer?

____

____

Should any processes, procedures or systems be implemented as a result of this engagement? ❑ Yes ❑ No

Are there any generic forms, letters, memos or other written communications that may be utilized on similar engagements? ❑ Yes ❑ No

Will the firm repeat this engagement for this customer? ❑ Yes ❑ No

Was this engagement profitable for the firm? ❑ Yes ❑ No

Has customer satisfaction been obtained for this engagement? ❑ Yes ❑ No

If Yes, how (formal survey, oral communication, etc.)?

____

Is it documented in the file and in the customer profile in the firm's database? ❑ Yes ❑ No

If No, why not?

____

____

Were any opportunities for cross-selling services discovered? ❑ Yes ❑ No

If Yes, describe the additional services provided:

____

____

Would you use the same pricing method if you had to do over again? ❑ Yes ❑ No

What technology, if any, was used on the engagement?

____

____

Could this engagement have been provided by any other member of the firm more efficiently? ❑ Yes ❑ No

If Yes, by whom?

____

____

Why?

____

____

Did we add value with this job? ❑ Yes ❑ No

How could we have added more value?

____

____

Could we have captured more value through higher price? ❑ Yes ❑ No

If we were doing this type of job again, how would we do it?

____

____

What are the implications for product/service design?

____

____

How should we communicate the lessons on this job to our colleagues?

____

____

How could we have enhanced our client's perception of value?

____

____

What other needs does this client have and are we addressing them?

____

____

Did this job enhance our relationship with this client? ❑ Yes ❑ No

What impact has this job had on developing our client's trust in us?

____

____

How would you rate our client's price sensitivity before and after this job?

____

____

CONSIDERATIONS BEFORE ACCEPTING A NEW CUSTOMER

Make sure the customer is *able* to pay your price.

- Check references (banker, attorney, insurance agent, etc.).
- Contact the predecessor CPA and learn as much as you can about why the customer defected (or why the professional withdrew from the engagement).
- Review a Dun & Bradstreet (or other agency) report on the customer's business and ascertain if it is consistent with the financial information you've received.

Make sure the customer is *willing* to pay your price.

- Discover exactly what this customer expects from your firm.
- Get a retainer up front, before you begin any services.

Remember*: Never discount your price to obtain a customer.*

ITEMS TO CONSIDER BEFORE CONDUCTING A FIXED PRICE AGREEMENT (FPA) MEETING WITH A CUSTOMER

____ Review the *demographic* characteristics (age, sex, income, neigborhood,etc.) of the customer and try to determine the customer's *ability* to pay you.

- Age
- Sex
- Income
- Neighborhood
- Other ______________________________

____ Review the *psychographic* characteristics of the customer and try to determine what the customer is *willing* to pay you:

- Is the customer risk (or loss) averse?
- Does the customer demand a high level of detail or just a summary of your work and the big picture consequences?
- What are the major concerns and problems in the customer's life at the moment?
- What are the customer's expectations of your firm? How can you exceed them?

____ Determine who is paying for the customer's professional services and how price sensitive is the customer (see Chapter 4).

____ Determine where the services are located on the value curve (Chapter 2).

____ Determine where the customer is on your firm's demand curve.

QUESTIONS TO ASK YOURSELF BEFORE YOU SET A PRICE

These are factors to be considered in determining the reasonableness of a price:

1. How much time and labor will be required?

   ____

   ____

   What novelty and difficulty will be involved?

   ____

   ____

   What skills will be needed to perform the services?

   ____

   ____

2. What is the likelihood, if apparent to the client, that acceptance of the assignment will preclude other employment?

   ____

   ____

3. What is the customary price for similar services in the locality?

   ____

   ____

4. What amount is involved for the results obtained?

   ____

   ____

5. What time limits are imposed by the client or circumstances?

   ____

   ____

6. What are the nature and length of the professional relationship with the client?

____

____

7. What is the experience, reputation, and ability of the lawyers or CPAs performing the services?

____

____

8. Is the price fixed or contingent?

____

9. What special expertise or knowledge do you have about the engagement?

____

____

10. What special resources are available to you, such as software, or access to similar engagements completed for other clients?

____

____

11. What special contacts do you have that may facilitate a transaction?

____

____

12. Does opportunity exist to achieve unique results? Why?

____

____

13. What is your firm's risk assumption or credit liability?

____

____

14. What extra effort will you expend, based on deadlines or any form of accommodation for the client?

____

____

15. What is the potential profit or loss to the client?

____

____

16. Is the "nobody else can do it" factor present?

____

____

17. What is the degree of the convenience the transaction involves?

____

____

18. What is your comfort level?

____

____

Adapted from *Innovative Billing and Collection Methods That Work*, by Charles and Joseph Larson, and from The American Bar Association's Model Rules of Professional Conduct.

Here are more questions to consider, preferably with the team that services the customer:

- **Who on the organizational chart am I dealing with?**

____

____

The higher up on the chart, the less price sensitive the person will be. A CEO is not going to take the time to interview multiple service providers and will be more interested in benefits than in price.

- **Who referred the customer to me?**

  ____

  ____

If it was a "warm" referral source, your firm is, most likely, already sold to the customer and you should be able to command a higher price.

- **What is the nature of the relationship with the referral source?**

  ____

  ____

(Same reasoning as the preceding point.)

- **What is the time line on the decision to select a CPA?**

  ____

  ____

The shorter the time line, the greater the probability you will get the business.

- **What are the impending deadlines driving the decision to engage a CPA?**

  ____

  ____

The shorter the time line, the higher price you can command for quick delivery time.

- **Who is paying for the service?**

  ____

  ____

Recall the four ways one can spend money. If the customer is in Category III, you should be able to charge a premium because they will be less price sensitive.

- **Are there any competitors in the arena with you? Who?**

____

____

This may provide you with an opportunity to first achieve parity with any potential competitor and then to focus on your firm's strengths. Never denigrate a competitor! You don't build your firm's value by knocking down your competitors. First achieve parity with them, and then focus on your strengths.

- **Do you have any price information from those competitors (bids, RFPs, etc.)?**

____

____

This is another way of gauging price sensitivity. Don't feel the need to be the low price bidder. Focus on service as part of your firm's value proposition—price, quality, and service. Any professional can match (or beat) your price and quality. But they can't even observe your service—the relationship you have with the customer. And premium service commands premium prices.

- **How profitable is the organization? How long has it been in business?**

____

____

The longer in business and more profitable they are, the less price sensitive they are.

- **Who was the prior CPA and why is the customer changing? [Employ Adverse Selection]**

____

____

Prequalify the customer. Your goal is not just *more* business, but *better* business. Only work for customers who understand and are willing to pay for the value you can provide.

- **If it is a new business, who is the banker, the attorney, etc.?**

____

____

Again, this is part of your prequalifying process.

- **How sophisticated is the customer with respect to my services?**

____

____

The less sophisticated, the more you must educate the customer as to the value of your services.

- **What is the relative price the customer would pay for the service?**

____

____

Relative price is the price the customer would pay for doing the project internally or outsourcing it, or the cost of not doing it at all. Think of it as the opportunity cost of hiring your firm.

- **Is the service you are providing a need or a want?**

____

____

A need is an essential service—a tax return or a compilation for a bank loan. A want can almost always command a higher price.

- **Does this customer add to the firm's skills, or am I simply using existing skills?**

____

____

Developing new skills in new markets with new customers adds to the stock of intellectual capital in your firm.

- **Does this customer open up a new niche or market segment for the firm?**

____

____

(Same advantages as preceding point.)

- **Do I like this customer? Is the customer in a business I am interested in?**

____

____

This is the personality test. In the long run, your firm should only work with people you enjoy, in industries that interest you.

- **What price would I consider commensurate with the value the firm is providing?**

____

____

Three internal prices should be established: (1) a *reservation* price (a price that will provide a *normal* profit to the firm and one you will not go below); (2) a *hope for* price (a price that will return a *supernormal* profit to the firm); and (3) a *pump fist* price (a price that will return a *windfall* profit to the firm). Obviously, you should quote the pump fist price first, because you will never get it if you do not ask for it. Remember, only talk price after discussing with the customer their needs, wants, and the value of your services.

QUESTIONS YOU SHOULD ASK THE CUSTOMER DURING THE FPA MEETING

- What do you expect from us?
- What is your current pain?
- What keeps you awake at night?
- How do you see us helping you address these challenges and opportunities?
- What growth plans do you have?
- If price were not an issue, what role would you want your CPA to play in your business?
- Do you expect capital needs? New financing?
- Do you anticipate any mergers, purchases, divestitures, recapitalizations, or reorganizations in the near future?
- We know you are investing in total quality service, as are we. What are the service standards you would like for us to provide you?
- How important is our satisfaction guarantee to you?
- How important is rapid response on accounting and tax questions? What do you consider rapid response?
- Why are you changing professionals? What did you not like about your former firm that you do not want us to repeat?*
- How did you enjoy working with your former firm?**
- Do you envision any other changes in your needs?
- Are you concerned about any of your asset, liability, or income statement accounts to which we should pay particularly close attention?
- What is your budget for this type of service?

---

* Do not denigrate the predecessor CPA (or attorney). First, this insults the customer and reminds the customer of a poor decision. Second, it diminishes respect and confidence in the profession as a whole and lowers the public's perception of our professionalism.

** Even though the customer is changing firms, it is almost certain that the customer liked certain characteristics of the predecessor. Find out what those were and exceed them. For instance, if they said the prior CPA always returned phone calls within one day, return phone calls within four hours.

- If we were to attend certain of your internal management meetings as observers, would you be comfortable with that?
- How do you suggest we best learn about your business so we can relate your operations to the financial information and so we can be more proactive in helping you maximize your business success?
- May our associates tour your facilities?
- What trade journals do you read? What seminars and trade shows do you regularly attend? Would it be possible for us to attend these with you?

HANDLING PRICE OBJECTIONS

Use the following method for handling objections:

1. **Listen carefully; hear the customer out.** Avoid the temptation to talk or try to solve the objection right then and there.

2. **Confirm your understanding of the objection.** Repeat it back to the customer to ensure you understand exactly what the objection is.

3. **Acknowledge the customer's point of view.** Practice empathy; don't try to impose your view on the customer, but help the customer become convinced of your view.

4. **Answer the objection.** Ultimately, you must answer the customer's objection if the FPA is to be authorized. You may postpone the price objection to the end of the meeting if you are still trying to build your firm's value, but in the end, price must be dealt with.

5. **Confirm that your answer satisfied the concern.**

6. **Attempt to get authorization for the FPA.** If the customer still objects, continue with the meeting until you reach an agreement as to your value.

OVERCOMING OBJECTIONS TO PRICE

Here are some specific methods for overcoming objections to price:

1. Postpone the price objection.

Here are two responses that postpone the price objection until you have had a chance to build your firm's value:

- I can appreciate that you would be interested in the price, and I assure you we will discuss it completely, but before we even consider the price, I want to be sure that our service can satisfy your needs. Will that be all right?
- Mr. Smith, your concern for price is quite understandable. The actual amount paid for the service, however, will depend upon the nature of the services you ultimately select. Let's consider the price for the services after we establish the specific services you will require. Is that fair?

2. Use the lowest common denominator.

Break down the price into the lowest common denominator, usually monthly. That is a much more manageable number to deal with than the total FPA price.

3. Use comparison.

An effective comparison to make is that of your customer's pricing policies with your own, using a statement such as the following:

> Mr. Becker, your own company makes a high-grade product that commands an exceptionally high price, and deservedly so. Your tool-and-die products warrant their outstanding reputation because of the top-quality materials used to make them. Our high-level of service and attention to helping you create more value in your business are naturally suited for you. Sure, you can buy less expensive financial help than ours, but you would not be satisfied with their performance.

Testimonials from other customers can also help prove your case.

4. To get volume up, sell down.

Always present your most expensive price first, and then move down.

5. Use the "bracket up for money" strategy.

Present pricing as follows for the customer:

> Most customers who desire this level of service are prepared to invest $12,000. A fortunate few can invest between $15,000 and $20,000. And then there are those on a limited or fixed budget who can't go higher than $10,000. May I ask which of these categories your company fits into most comfortably?

Begin your pricing at a level that is approximately 20% above your price ($12,000). Then, continue by quoting 50% to 100% above your price ($15,000-$20,000). Finally, give your actual price ($10,000). Psychologically, you are tapping into the instinct of the customer that says: **Expensive = Good**. Most likely, the customer won't want to be in the bottom category, and will opt for the middle or top amount.

6. Focus on the difference.

Perhaps you're trying to price the FPA at $20,000, but the customer wants $15,000. Focus on the $5,000 difference, which is the smaller, more manageable amount.

7. Focus on other terms of the FPA.

If price is an objection, work on the other terms of the FPA first. Perhaps you can change the payment terms; perhaps you can cut some services.

Learn to accept price objections for what they are—opportunities in disguise. They are a sign of an interested customer, and with practice and skill, you will be able to overcome them without cutting your price.

CHECKLIST FOR EXPLAINING EACH SECTION OF THE FPA

Date of the FPA:

- Usually this is the last quarter of the calendar or fiscal year for the next year's services.

Professional services provided:

- Describe each service and the corresponding responsibilities of each party in fulfilling that service.
- Consider using the Unlimited Access Clause, and detail exactly what the firm will provide for this service.

Unanticipated services:

- Include a clause explaining the firm's policy for services not included in the FPA (usually, this is done by using a change order).
- Consider offering long-term customers a discount (10 to 20%, perhaps) on any change orders that arise during the year (a "frequent flyer" program).
- Offer the "frequent flyer" discount on an agreed-upon price. Do not lock yourself into any type of standard hourly rate.

Service guarantee:

- Offer a 100% money back service guarantee in order to command a premium price and overcome price resistance and buyer's remorse.

Price guarantee:

- In order to create a "no surprises" culture in your firm, offer all customers a price guarantee to ensure the firm sets a price when it possesses the leverage, not the customer. This will help to obtain the maximum price and reduce write-downs and write-offs.

Payment terms:

- Detail the exact payment terms in order to overcome payment resistance.

Revision clause (optional):

- Consider using the revision clause as a way to ensure constant communication and customer satisfaction with the entire FPA.
- This clause is helpful for new customers not yet familiar with your firm.
- This reduces the risk of both parties, as the agreement can be revised in light of mutual experience.
- Price resistance and buyer's remorse are reduced by this clause.
- This clause is usually not needed with long-term customers, except in the first year of the FPA.

Termination clause:

- Always leave the customer a way out of the FPA.
- Termination should be required in writing with advance notice (usually 10 to 30 days).
- Be sure that the customer understands that full payment will be required for all services rendered prior to termination. Any amount due is payable immediately upon termination, and any refund due the customer will be paid at termination.

BECOMING A TIMELESS CULTURE

Following is a checklist of steps that your firm can take in order to become a Timeless Culture:

- **Establish a pricing cartel.** This will place pricing authority in a central location, and help to ensure the firm is consistent with its pricing signals to the marketplace. It will also assist in commanding prices commensurate with value, not hours.
- **Appoint a traffic manager.** This person will be responsible for tracking all engagements flowing in and out of the firm, knowing who is responsible for them, and whether they are being completed by the internally set deadline. Usually, the traffic manager can be the same person who used to hunt people down to get their time sheets.
- **Establish a minimum price for all new customers.** Do not take on new customers below this price, and be sure to inform your referral network of this policy so they can act as pre-qualifiers for you. Also, review this price annually and adjust it upward.Enter into a covenant with team members for KPIs. Let the team members decide on the firm-wide and specific team member KPIs that will be used to measure and assess the performance of how the firm is carrying out its mission to enhance the wealth of its customers. Your people are professionals who want to do a outstanding job for the firm and its customers. Trust them to select measurements that grade the success of the firm the same way customers do.
- **Track percentage of Walk-Away, Hope For, and Pump Fist price realizations.** This will enable the firm to learn from its failures and successes.
- **Track percentage of FPAs written above the minimum price.** This metric will show how effective the team is at cross-selling additional services. Be sure to combine this metric with some type of reward in order to assure the behavior is repeated.
- **Reward and celebrate pricing successes.** Celebrate the successes so they become part of the firm's pricing culture, and develop rewards for team members who price commensurate with value.

- **Perform a postmortem analysis on all FPAs and change orders.** There is a wealth of information in a closed customer file. By brainstorming with the team members who serviced the customer, you will be able to better spot "value drivers" in the future, ascertain customer price sensitivity, and become a firm that prices on purpose. Pricing is complex, and it deserves more resources and brainpower than the average firm currently devotes to it. A Timeless Culture demands this investment.

- **Align KPIs to team member compensation.** You will get the behavior you reward. Make sure KPIs are aligned with the compensation, bonus, raise, and promotion system. Don't make the mistake many firms have by stating how important the new KPIs are but then rewarding and measuring based on hours and efforts.

- **Consider implementing a "forced churn" KPI.** Because many firms are reluctant to fire up to 80 percent of their customer base, a forced churn allows the firm to implement this strategy incrementally. For every new customer acquired, consider firing between one and four of your old ones. This ratio, obviously, will depend upon how many "D" and "F" customers your firm has. The forced churn provides an excellent way to upgrade your customer base.

- **Use "No timesheets" as a lighting rod to attract top talent.** Not many professionals enjoy filling out timesheets (think about the individuals you know who have left the profession for private industry who usually remark they love not having to do time sheets). A Timeless Culture is an enormous competitive differentiation when competing for talent in the competitive marketplace. As with customers, it sets your firm apart from the competition and provides a compelling reason to work for your firm. In other words, it becomes part of the firm's value proposition in attracting (and retaining) human capital.

- **Continuously study the art of pricing—it's a marathon, not a sprint.** Have your team read some of the books on pricing in the "Suggested Reading" section of this book. Have them share what they learned with the firm. Pricing is an art, and the more you learn about it, the better you become at doing it.

SUGGESTED READING

How many a man has dated a new era
in his life from the reading of a book.

—Henry David Thoreau

I am regularly asked which books I recommend as "essential reading" out of all the ones I cite. This is always a difficult task, as my first inclination is to answer, "Read them all." However, some are certainly better than others. Therefore, I have put together the following list, by category, which I believe are some of the best books (and publications) by the leading authors on the particular subject matter.

Economics, Marketing, and Price Theory

Far from being the "dismal science," economics is actually the study of human behavior. Many economists have contributed to my knowledge of this fascinating discipline. The ones I recommend the most are the following:

Armentano, Dominick T. *Antitrust and Monopoly: Anatomy of a Policy Failure, Second Edition*. New York: Holmes & Meier, 1990, and *Antitrust: The Case for Repeal, Revised 2nd Edition*. Auburn, Alabama: The Ludwig von Mises Institute, 1999. Among the best books available repudiating antitrust policy and the unfounded economic assumptions that underlie it. It explodes one myth after another, with historical accuracy and empirical data. After reading this volume, you will understand why the majority of economists reject antitrust laws.

Davenport, Thomas O. *Human Capital: What It Is and Why People Invest It*. San Francisco: Jossey-Bass Publishers, 1999. This book is essential reading for understanding how important human capital is and the fact that today's knowledge workers own their own means of production and will only invest it in companies that are attractive and pay a good return for the investment. Another essential volume in order to create the timeless culture.

Dawson, Ross. *Developing Knowledge-Based Client Relationships: The Future of Professional Services.* Woburn, Mass.: Butterworth-Heinemann, 2000. Although not the most dynamic book to read, Dawson makes several valid points about how professional service firms will add value in the future.

Friedman, Milton, and Rose Friedman. *Free to Choose: A Personal Statement.* New York: Harcourt Brace, 1990. This is one of Friedman's classics, in the tradition of his *Capitalism and Freedom.* He is one economist who can make the complex understandable and deserves to be read as widely as possible.

Friedman, David D. *Price Theory: An Intermediate Text, Second Edition.* Cincinnati: South-Western Publishing Co., 1990, and *Hidden Order: The Economics of Everyday Life.* New York: HarperBusiness, 1996. David Friedman is Milton Friedman's son and a distinguished economist in his own right. The first book listed is his intermediate textbook for economic students while the second one is for the general audience. Both are excellent and highly entertaining.

Gilder, George. *Recapturing the Spirit of Enterprise.* San Francisco, California: ICS Press, 1992, and *Wealth and Poverty: A New Edition of the Classic.* San Francisco: ICS Press, 1993. In my opinion, Gilder is the best author on economics, sociology, technology, and anthropology that you will find anywhere. His work has inspired me and changed my vision of the way the world works. These two books are his classics, but he has written others. If you read only two books from this list, read anything by Gilder—twice. Gilder is a senior fellow at Seattle's Discovery Institute. Visit their Web site at www.discovery.org. From there you can link to The Official George Gilder Web site.

Johnson, H. Thomas, and Robert S. Kaplan. *Relevance Lost: The Rise and Fall of Management Accounting.* Boston: Harvard Business School Press, 1991. An indictment of the management accounting profession and how it has lost relevance in terms of helping businesses measure the right things. This book set off the launch into activity based costing, which is much more relevant to the service industries than traditional cost-accounting methods. It is also a historically fascinating read.

Kay, John. *The Business of Economics*. Oxford: Oxford University Press, 1996. An excellent book for understanding how the theoretical world of economics can be practically applied to the business world.

Koch, Richard. *The 80/20 Principle: The Secret of Achieving More With Less*. New York: Currency Doubleday, 1998. A fascinating look at Vilfredo Pareto's principle of the minority controlling the majority of any phenomenon.

Landsburg, Steven E. *The Armchair Economist: Economics & Everyday Life*. New York: The Free Press, 1993; *Price Theory and Applications, Fifth Edition*. Cincinnati, Ohio: South-Western, 2002; and *Fair Play: What Your Child Can Teach You About Economics, Values, and the Meaning of Life*. New York: The Free Press, 1997. In the tradition of David Friedman, Landsburg is another dynamic economist who is an entertaining read. He will challenge, and no doubt persuade, you on many points with his cogent analysis of contemporary issues. Even his textbook is excellent, although very complicated. *Fair Play* relates today's complex economic and social problems down to the child's sandbox on the playground.

Monroe, Kent B. *Pricing: Making Profitable Decisions, Third Edition*. New York: McGraw-Hill, 1990. Along with the one-volume book by Thomas T. Nagle and Reed K. Holden, this is among the best books for understanding, in greater depth, the issues surrounding pricing. For the serious student of pricing, this book offers many insights and is my second choice behind the one by Nagle and Holden.

Nagle, Thomas T., and Reed K. Holden. *The Strategy and Tactics of Pricing: A Guide to Profitable Decision Making, Third Edition*. Upper Saddle River, N.J.: Prentice-Hall, 2002. Simply the best pricing book from an economic and marketing perspective I have found. Nagle and Holden are both professors and are leading experts in the field of economics, marketing, and pricing. For those interested in expanding and deepening their understanding of pricing, this book is a must-read.

Stanley, Thomas J., and William D. Danko. *The Millionaire Next Door: The Surprising Secrets of America's Wealthy*. Atlanta, Ga.: Longstreet Press, Inc., 1996. This book will shatter every myth perpetuated about the wealthy in America and how they live, work, and behave. It is well-researched and a must read for CPAs and attorneys alike.

Young, S. David. *The Rule of Experts: Occupational Licensing in America*. Washington, D.C.: The CATO Institute, 1987. This absolutely demolishes the argument in favor of any occupational licensure, using economic theory and empirical evidence. This is one of those issues on which a majority of economists agree, and yet they are ignored when it comes to the debate.

Hourly Billing (and Its Alternatives)

There is a paucity of books dealing with the shift from hourly billing to value pricing. Nonetheless, a few do exist.

American Bar Association, ABA Commission on Billable Hours Report, August, 2001–2002. (Available at www.abanet.org/careercounsel/billable.html.) The former president of the ABA, Robert E. Hirshon, is no fan of the billable hour. He established this commission, and the report they issued is quite thorough in pointing out the deleterious effects of hourly billing, and it offers alternatives to this anachronistic pricing method. The ABA Web site also has many more resources, as well as discussion boards on the billable hour. Worthwhile reading for CPAs, mandatory reading for attorneys.

Aquila, August J. *Breaking The Paradigm: New Approaches to Pricing Accounting Services*. New York: American Institute of Certified Public Accountants, Inc., 1995. Aquila is the former vice-president of acquisitions for American Express Tax and Business Services. This book was among the first in the accounting profession to challenge the conventional wisdom of hourly billing. To order, contact: American Institute of Certified Public Accountants, Order Department, (800) 862-4272; (800) 362-5066 (fax).

Baker, Ronald J., and Paul Dunn. *The Firm of the Future: A Guide for Accountants, Lawyers, and Other Professional Services*. New Jersey:

John Wiley & Sons, Inc., 2003. Expanding on the concepts presented in this book, this new work—published in April 2003—was co-authored with Paul Dunn, founder of Results Accountants' Systems. This work offers a New Practice Equation model and discusses the importance of intellectual capital, pricing, measuring what matters, leadership, vision, and the future of the profession. It is written in each author's voice, allowing the reader to see different approaches to the same topics.

Calloway, James A., and Mark A. Robertson, Editors. *Winning Alternatives to the Billable Hour: Strategies That Work, Second Edition.* Chicago: American Bar Association, 2002. This is the updated edition of Richard C. Reed's book *Billing Innovations* (mentioned later in this section) and it is an indispensable resource for attorneys making the transition to value pricing. It also comes with a disk full of sample Legal Representations Agreements, used successfully by many law firms around the United States.

Cross, Robert G. *Revenue Management.* New York: Bantam, 1997. This book sheds light on why airline pricing is complex and sophisticated. Written by an attorney, it is one of the best books on the real-world application of price discrimination and yield management.

Larson, Charles B., and Joseph W. *Innovative Billing and Collection Methods That Work*. Burr Ridge, Ill.: Irwin Professional Publishing, 1994. This book is also among the first works to challenge not only the billing methods of CPAs but also their collection methods. Although light on theory, it does offer some illuminating discussion of pricing according to value. Contact Western CPE, The University of Montana, Missoula, MT 59812, 1-800-243-7395.

Reed, Richard C., Ed. *Beyond the Billable Hour: An Anthology of Alternative Billing Methods*. Chicago: American Bar Association, 1989, and *Win-Win Billing Strategies: Alternatives That Satisfy Your Clients and You.* Chicago: American Bar Association, 1992. These two works are the result of a task force put together by the American Bar Association to study alternatives to the hourly billing method in the mid-1980s. The first one offers an excellent historical look at hourly billing and why the law profession was so quick to adopt it as the primary method for pricing its services. The second work gives many examples of how lawyers have implemented value pricing. If you are an attorney, read both books. If you are a CPA, the second one is adequate.

Reed, Richard C. *Billing Innovations: New Win-Win Ways to End Hourly Billing*. Chicago: American Bar Association, 1996. This book was authored by Reed, the leader in the move away from hourly billing in the legal profession. It's very interesting to read all three books in their chronological order, especially for attorneys, as this documents the thought process that Reed went through regarding the shift from hourly billing to value pricing. I also recommend this third work for CPAs, although it is written primarily for lawyers. Contact: Publication Orders, American Bar Association, P.O. Box 10892, Chicago, IL 60610-0892. Or call (312) 988-5522 (Customer Service); (312) 988-5568 (fax); e-mail orders: abasvcctr@abanet.org; Web site: www.abanet.org/lpm/catalog.

Ross, William G. *The Honest Hour: The Ethics of Time-Based Billing by Attorneys*. Durham, N.C.: Carolina Academic Press, 1996. This book, by Cumberland School of Law of Samford University (Birmingham, Alabama) professor William Ross is the most comprehensive volume that I have discovered on the history of hourly billing and the ethical dilemmas of hourly billing and value pricing.

Management Consultants and Consulting

Though the field lacks serious, disciplined thinkers (unlike the economics profession), some consultants do offer intelligent guidance to the businesses of today.

Beatty, Jack. *The World According to Peter Drucker*. New York: The Free Press, 1998. An exposition on the most profound management thinker of our times. A good one-volume read to get the essence of Drucker.

Drucker, Peter F. *Adventures of a Bystander*. Somerset, N. J.: Transaction Publishers, 1994, *Managing in a Time of Great Change*. New York: Truman Talley Books/Dutton, 1995, and *Management Challenges for the 21st Century*. New York: HarperBusiness, 1999. Drucker is the one truly serious thinker that the management consultant industry can point to with justifiable pride. No doubt you should read as many of this prolific writer's works as possible, but I found these three enlightening. His autobiography was the genesis for my thinking on the question, Do you learn more from success or failure? Drucker's main competitive advantage among the management gurus is that he can write intelligently and not bore his reader, a trait lacking in the overwhelming majority of business authors.

Maister, David H. *Managing the Professional Service Firm.* New York: The Free Press, 1993, and *True Professionalism: The Courage to Care About Your People, Your Clients, and Your Career.* New York: The Free Press, 1997. Maister is another of those rare thinkers and consultants to professional service firms worldwide who can write with insight and truly make you think about what it means to be a professional.

Micklethwait, John, and Adrian Wooldridge. *The Witch Doctors: What Management Gurus Are Saying and Why It Matters.* New York: Random House, 1996. This piercing work gave voice to the backlash against the $100 billion profession known as "consulting." Although the authors concede far too much power to the consultants in altering the course of life, referring to them as "the unacknowledged legislators of mankind," their four defects of the "witch doctors" of our age are right on target. The profession has yet to refute successfully the charges against it, so eloquently laid out in this book. For all those who have suffered through many a poorly written business book, Micklethwait and Wooldridge offer a refreshing alternative.

O'Shea, James, and Charles Madigan. *Dangerous Company: Management Consultants and the Businesses They Save and Ruin.* New York: Penguin Books, 1998. Another excellent exposé on the faults within the management consulting business. I have relied on this book for the Customer Bill of Rights and other aspects of hiring consultants from the customer's viewpoint.

Pinault, Lewis. *Consulting Demons: Inside the Unscrupulous World of Global Corporate Consulting.* New York: HarperBusiness, 2000. This book will resonate with anyone who has ever worked in an international accounting or consulting firm. A personal account of one individual's journey and travails; a terrific read.

Reeb, William L. *Start Consulting: How to Walk the Talk.* New York: American Institute of Certified Public Accountants, 1998. One of the best books on making the transition from compliance to consultant by a leading CPA in the field. While I have serious misgivings about his prediction of the trend of generalist versus specialist, his treatment of pricing as an administrative task, and his emphasis on the Almighty Hour, Reeb's outline on how to conduct a consulting engagement is practical and makes enormous sense. A necessary read.

Reichheld, Frederick F., and Thomas Teal. *The Loyalty Effect: The Hidden Force Behind Growth, Profits, and Lasting Value*. Boston: Harvard Business School Press, 1996. This is a seminal work on the economics of customer loyalty. Sure to be a classic, this book focuses on the need for business to concentrate more on customer *retention* than *acquisition*. The book is rooted in economic theory and offers many examples of firms today that understand the bottom-line impact of customer loyalty. Reichheld is a fellow with Bain & Company, the pioneer in customer loyalty economics.

Shapiro, Eileen C. *Fad Surfing in the Boardroom: Managing in the Age of Instant Answers*. New York: Addison-Wesley, 1995. Another critical look at the management consulting industry from a former Harvard MBA and McKinsey consultant.

Marketing, Selling, Leadership

Aquila, August J. and Bruce W. Marcus. *Client at the Core: Marketing and Managing Today's Professional Service Firm*. New Jersey: John Wiley & Sons, Inc., 2004. August Aquila and Bruce Marcus are two of my favorite consultants, writers and thinkers in the professional services field. I was delighted they combined their towering wisdom and created *Client at the Core*, and you will be as well. Client selection and retention is one of the critical success factors for a professional service firm, and Aquila and Marcus do a masterful job at educating us on the necessary ingredients of each. But they don't stop there. I especially found the chapters on firm governance and paying for performance thought-provoking, and certainly challenging to the conventional wisdom. The next item on the Revolution after getting rid of the billable hour and timesheets is to eliminate the partnership structure, since it is a consensus—not a leadership—model. If you want a better understanding of marketing and leading a professional firm in these turbulent times, this book is an essential read.

Beckwith, Harry. *The Invisible Touch: The Four Keys to Modern Marketing.* New York: Warner Books, 2000. More engaging, practical, down-to-earth insights from Beckwith; an excellent sequel to his *Selling the Invisible.*

Beckwith, Harry. *Selling the Invisible.* New York: Warner Books, 1997. This work contains many good marketing ideas for professional service firms, which sell the "invisible."

Bethune, Gordon, and Scott Huler. *From Worst to First: Behind the Scenes of Continental's Remarkable Comeback.* New York: John Wiley & Sons, Inc., 1998. An excellent narrative on how one of the worst airlines was transformed into one of the best in a few years. Bethune's advice is common-sense leadership, with a focus on the customer, not the internal costs of operating a business. Worthwhile reading for anyone trying to change the culture of their business into one focused on the ultimate barometer of success: creating loyal customers.

Boress, Allan S. *The "I Hate Selling" Book: Business-Building Advice for Consultants, Attorneys, Accountants, Engineers, Architects and Other Professionals.* New York: AMACOM, 1995. Most professionals loathe the thought of selling. This book gives practical guidance on how to increase selling success. Boress is a leading consultant to the CPA profession.

Bosworth, Michael T. *Solution Selling: A System for Difficult to Sell Products.* Chicago: Irwin Professional Publishing, 1994. *Solution Selling* emphasizes the customer in the sales process and offers many useful strategies for discovering and emphasizing value-added services.

Cottle, David. *Target Marketing: How to Gain Profitable New Business.* San Diego: Harcourt Professional Publishing, 2000. Cottle offers practical marketing advice that you will be able to implement as part of your firm's culture. I have come to believe that customer selection is the cornerstone to building the timeless culture, and this book will help you target precisely the customers you want. I should note, however, that I have major disagreements with Cottle's advice when it comes to pricing (e.g., the use of "standard rates" and quoting a range of prices).

Dauten, Dale. *The Max Strategy: How A Businessman Got Stuck at an Airport and Learned to Make His Career Take Off*. New York: William Morrow, 1996. An absolutely splendid little book that will make you rethink what it means to set goals ("today's goal is tomorrow's rut") and experiment. This is a very powerful little book.

Dauten, Dale. *The Gifted Boss: How to Find, Create and Keep Great Employees*. New York: William Morrow, 1999. Another book in the spirit of *The Max Strategy* in that it will challenge you on many different levels. This book will help any professional firm think about what it needs to do in order to attract and retain the best people.

Hart, Christopher W. *Extraordinary Guarantees: Achieving Breakthrough Gains in Quality and Customer Satisfaction*. Brookline, Mass.: Spire Group, Ltd., 1998. If this book doesn't convince you to offer a 100-percent unconditional money-back guarantee on your services, then nothing will. Hart has done extensive research on service companies that have offered a guarantee and the financial success they have achieved as a result. Required reading for any firm interested in implementing this significant competitive strategy.

Hopkins, Tom. *How to Master the Art of Selling*. New York: Warner Books, 1980. This is an all-time sales classic.

Rackham, Neil. *SPIN Selling*. New York: McGraw-Hill, 1988. This is, literally, the best-validated sales method available today, developed from research studies of 35,000 sales calls, used by the top sales forces around the world. Rackham presents SPIN selling as a testable hypothesis.

Rackham, Neil, and John De Vincentis. *Rethinking the Sales Force: Redefining Selling to Create and Capture Customer Value*. New York: McGraw-Hill, 1999. Another excellent book by Rackham that will help your firm move from "transactional selling" to "consultative selling" and finally to the most valuable of all, "enterprise selling."

Waugh, Troy. *Power Up Your Profits*. Novato, Calif.: Select Press, 2000. Troy Waugh is one of the leading marketing consultants to the CPA profession. In this book, you will benefit from his accumulated wisdom in increasing your marketing potential with specific and practical strategies on selling, customer selection, offering value-added services, and much more.

Williams, Roy H. *The Wizard of Ads: Turning Words into Magic and Dreamers into Millionaires.* Austin, Tex.: Bard Press, 1998. An absolutely splendid book, well written, with many incisive observations into human behavior. Williams shatters conventional wisdom about effective advertising.

Profits and Morality

At last, this issue is being given the attention it deserves from theologians, politicians, economists, sociologists, the media, and the general public.

Gilder, George, "The Soul of Silicon." This was a speech Gilder delivered to the Vatican in May 1997. It is one of the most profound works I have ever read on why profits are moral. This is Gilder at his best. You can locate this speech at the Discovery Institute (Seattle, Wash.) Web site, at www.discovery.org.

John Paul II. *Centesimus Annus* ("The Hundredth Year"). This is Pope John Paul II's ninth encyclical, and it states positively that capitalism is superior to socialism in solving society's most pressing problems.

Neuhaus, Richard John. *Doing Well and Doing Good: The Challenge to the Christian Capitalist.* New York: Doubleday, 1992. This is an excellent exposition, from a theological perspective, on the morality of making money.

Novak, Michael. *The Catholic Ethic and the Spirit of Capitalism.* New York: The Free Press, 1993, and *Business as a Calling: Work and the Examined Life.* New York: The Free Press, 1996. These seminal works, from another theologian, are well written and are essential reading on current thought among religions regarding the morality of capitalism and business.

Psychology

Branden, Nathaniel. *The Six Pillars of Self-Esteem.* New York: Bantam, 1994. This is the ultimate treatise on self-esteem. The chapter on self-esteem and work is especially relevant to value pricing concepts.

Cialdini, Robert B. *Influence: The New Psychology of Modern Persuasion.* New York: Quill, 1993. Containing many examples from marketing and advertising, this absolutely fascinating discussion of human behavior is entertaining and informative.

Total Quality Service

Albrecht, Karl. *The Only Thing That Matters: Bringing the Power of the Customer into the Center of Your Business.* New York: HarperBusiness, 1992. This book, the bible of the total quality service movement, written by one of its founding fathers, helps the reader to understand the customer service revolution taking place worldwide.

Aquila, August J., and Allan D. Koltin. "How to Lose Clients Without Really Trying." *Journal of Accountancy*, May 1992. This is a masterful article, which won the authors the 1992 Annual Literary award for the best article of the year.

Marcus, Stanley. *Minding the Store.* New York: Dutton, 1993, and *Quest for the Best.* New York: Dutton, 1993. From the son of one of the founders of Neiman–Marcus comes this interesting autobiography on the customer service ethic that made Neiman–Marcus the premiere retailer in the United States.

O'Brien, Robert. *Marriott: The J. Willard Marriott Story.* Salt Lake City, Utah: Desert Book Company, 1977. A well-written, interesting story on the man who built—from a hole-in-the-wall root beer stand and $6,000 in start-up capital in 1927—the empire known as Marriott. Another look at a businessman who put the customer first and understood the importance of loyalty and service.

Rosenbaum, Dr. Edward E. *A Taste of My Own Medicine: When the Doctor Is the Patient.* New York: Random House, 1988. An absolutely splendid book about a doctor who contracts throat cancer and becomes a patient in his own hospital, an experience that profoundly changes how he views his own patients and what it means to be a doctor. If you have ever had a loved one battling with cancer, this book will resonate with you. It is a moving story, passionately told, and is the book that the movie *The Doctor*, starring William Hurt, was based on (which I would also recommend you see). This book helps explain the customer service revolution going on in the medical profession, and especially in hospitals.

REFERENCES

Ailes, Roger, and Jon Kraushar. *You Are The Message: Getting What You Want by Being Who You Are.* New York: Currency Doubleday, 1995.

Albrecht, Karl. *The Northbound Train: Finding the Purpose, Setting the Direction, Shaping the Destiny of Your Organization.* New York: AMACOM, 1994.

———. *The Only Thing That Matters: Bringing the Power of the Customer into the Center of Your Business.* New York: HarperBusiness, 1992.

American Bar Association, Economics of Tort and Insurance Law Practice Committee of the Tort & Insurance Practice Section, *Alternative Billing: The Sequel.* San Francisco: Fairmont Hotel, March 13, 1997 Seminar and Material.

American Institute of Certified Public Accountants. *CPA Vision Project: 2011 and Beyond.* New York: AICPA, 1998.

Aquila, August J. *Breaking The Paradigm: New Approaches to Pricing Accounting Services.* New York: American Institute of Certified Public Accountants, Inc., 1995.

Aquila, August J., and Allan D. Koltin. "How to Lose Clients Without Really Trying." *Journal of Accountancy*, May 1992.

Armentano, Dominick T. *Antitrust: The Case for Repeal, Revised Second Edition.* Auburn, Alabama: Ludwig von Mises Institute, 1999.

———. *Antitrust and Monopoly: Anatomy of a Policy Failure*, Second Edition. New York: Holmes & Meier, 1990.

Armey, Dick. *The Freedom Revolution: The New Republican House Majority Leader Tells Why Big Government Failed, Why Freedom Works, and How We Will Rebuild America.* Washington, D.C.: Regnery Publishing, Inc., 1995.

Baker, Ronald J. "Alternatives to the Federal Income Tax." California CPA Education Foundation CPE Seminar, 1999.

———. "How to Build A Successful Practice with Total Quality Service." California CPA Education Foundation CPE Seminar, 1999.

Baker, Ronald J. and Paul Dunn. *The Firm of the Future: A Guide for Accountants, Lawyers, and Other Professional Services*. New Jersey: John Wiley & Sons, Inc., 2003.

Barker, Joel Arthur. *Paradigms: The Business of Discovering the Future*. New York: HarperBusiness, 1993.

Beatty, Jack. *The World According to Peter Drucker*. New York: The Free Press, 1998.

Beauchemin, Timothy J. *Five Star Client Service System*. Audio Cassette program, Houston, Texas: Enterprise 2000, Inc., 1990.

———. "Thinking About the Future." *CPA Profitability Monthly*, Volume 1995, Issue 12, December 1995.

———. "No More Begging for Work: Self Esteem Is the Key to a Better Practice." *CPA Profitability Monthly*, Volume 1996, Issue 8, August 1996.

Becker, Gary S. and Guity Nashat Becker. *The Economics of Life: From Baseball to Affirmative Action to Immigration, How Real-World Issues Affect Our Everday Life*. New York: McGraw-Hill, 1997.

Beckwith, Harry. *Selling the Invisible:* New York: Warner Books, 1997.

Bennis, Warren. *On Becoming A Leader*. Menlo Park, Calif.: Addison-Wesley, 1994.

Bernstein, Peter L., *Against the Gods: The Remarkable Story of Risk*. New York: John Wiley & Sons, Inc., 1996.

Berra, Yogi with Dave Kaplan. *When You Come to a Fork in the Road, TAKE IT!* New York: Hyperion, 2001.

Berry, Leonard L. *Discovering the Soul of Service: The Nine Drivers of Sustainable Business Success*. New York: The Free Press, 1999.

Bethune, Gordon, and Scott Huler. *From Worst to First: Behind the Scenes of Continental's Remarkable Comeback*. New York: John Wiley & Sons, 1998.

Boress, Allan S. *Building Entrepreneurial People*. New York: Harcourt Brace Professional Publishing, 1995.

———. *The "I Hate Selling" Book: Business-Building Advice for Consultants, Attorneys, Accountants, Engineers, Architects and Other Professionals*. New York: AMACOM, 1994.

———. "Choosing Your Clients." *CPA Profitability Monthly*, Volume 1996, Issue 8, August 1996.

Bosworth, Michael T. *Solution Selling: Creating Buyers in Difficult Selling Markets*. Chicago: Irwin Professional Publishing, 1995.

Branden, Nathaniel. *The Six Pillars of Self-Esteem*. New York: Bantam, 1994.

Brandenburger, Adam M., and Barry J. Nalebuff. *Co-opetition: The Game Theory That's Changing the Game of Business*. New York: Currency Doubleday, 1996.

Buchholz, Todd G. *New Ideas From Dead Economists: An Introduction to Modern Economic Thought*. New York: Plume, 1989.

Buckley, Reid. *Sex, Power, and Pericles: Principles of Advanced Public Speaking*. Camden, S.C.: Peor Es Nada Press, 1996.

The Business Lawyer. "Business and Ethics Implications of Alternative Billing Practices: Report on Alternative Billing Arrangements." The Business Lawyer; Vol. 54, November 1998.

Calder, Lendol G. *Financing the American Dream: A Cultural History of Consumer Credit*. Princeton, N.J.: 1999.

Carlzon, Jan. *Moments of Truth: New Strategies for Today's Customer-Driven Economy*. New York: Harper & Row, Publishers, Inc., 1987.

Cerf, Christopher, and Victor Navasky. *The Experts Speak: The Definitive Compendium of Authoritative Misinformation*. New York: Villard Books, 1998.

Cialdini, Robert B. *Influence: The New Psychology of Modern Persuasion*. New York: Quill, 1993.

Cottle, David. *Target Marketing: How to Gain Profitable New Business*. San Diego: Harcourt Professional Publishing, 2000.

Cowan, Robin, and Mario J. Rizzo, Ed. *Profits & Morality*. Chicago: The University of Chicago Press, 1995.

Cross, Robert G. *Revenue Management*. New York: Bantam, 1997.

Dauten, Dale. *The Gifted Boss: How to Find, Create and Keep Great Employees*. New York: William Morrow, 1999.

Davenport, Thomas O. *Human Capital: What It Is and Why People Invest It*. San Francisco: Jossey-Bass Publishers, 1999.

Davis, Kevin. *Getting into Your Customer's Head: Secrets of Selling Your Competitors Don't Know*. New York: Times Books, 1996.

de Bono, Edward. *Sur/Petition: Creating Value Monopolies When Everyone Else Is Merely Competing*. New York: HarperBusiness, 1993.

deKieffer, Esq., Donald E. *How Lawyers Screw Their Clients: And What You Can Do About It*. New York: Barricade Books Inc., 1995.

Drucker, Peter F. *Adventures of a Bystander*. Somerset, N.J.: Transaction Publishers, 1994.

———. *Management Challenges for the 21st Century*. New York: HarperBusiness, 1999.

——— . *Managing in a Time of Great Change*. New York: Truman Talley Books/Dutton, 1995.

Frank, Robert H. *Passions Within Reason: The Strategic Role of the Emotions*. New York: W.W. Norton & Company, 1988.

Freidheim, Cyrus F. *The Trillion-Dollar Enterprise: How the Alliance Revolution Will Transform Global Business*. New York: Perseus Books, 1998.

Friedman, David D. *Hidden Order: The Economics of Everyday Life*. New York: HarperBusiness, 1996.

Friedman, Milton, and Simon Kuznets. *Income from Independent Professional Practice*. New York: National Bureau of Economic Research, 1945.

Friedman, Milton, and Rose Friedman. *Free to Choose: A Personal Statement*. New York: Harcourt Brace, 1990.

Gilder, George."Civilization Can't Afford to Forget." *Forbes ASAP*, December 2, 1996.

———. "Gilder Technology Report," Volume III, Number 5, May 1998.

———. *Recapturing the Spirit of Enterprise*. San Francisco: ICS Press, 1992.

———. *Wealth and Poverty: A New Edition of the Classic*. San Francisco: ICS Press, 1993.

Gregorsky, Frank, Editor. *Speaking of George Gilder*. Seattle, Wash.: Discovery Institute, 1998.

Gregory, John Milton. *The Seven Laws of Teaching*. Grand Rapids, Mich.: Bake Books, 1995.

Grenier, Ray, and George Metes. *Going Virtual: Moving Your Organization into the 21st Century*. Upper Saddle River, N.J.: Prentice Hall P T R, 1995.

Hagel III, John and Arthur G. Armstrong. *Net Gain: Expanding Markets Through Virtual Communities*. Boston: Harvard Business School Press, 1997.

Hart, Christopher, W.L., and Christopher E. Bogan. *The Baldrige: What It Is, How It's Won, How to Use It to Improve Quality in Your Company*. New York: McGraw-Hill, 1992.

Hayek, Friedrich von. "The Use of Knowledge in Society," *American Economic Review* 35 (September 1945): 519–530.

Hiebeler, Robert, Thomas B. Kelly and Charles Ketteman. *Best Practices: Building Your Business with Customer-Focused Solutions*. New York: Simon & Schuster, 1998.

Hill, Napoleon. *Think and Grow Rich*. New York: Fawcett Columbine, 1987.

Hopkins, Tom. *How to Master the Art of Selling*. New York: Warner Books, 1980.

Johnson, H. Thomas, and Robert S. Kaplan. *Relevance Lost: The Rise and Fall of Management Accounting*. Boston: Harvard Business School Press, 1991.

Johnson, Paul. *Intellectuals*. New York: HarperPerennial, 1990.

Katz, Diane, and Henry Payne. "Traffic Jam: Auto dealers use government to build Internet roadblocks." *Reason*, July 2000.

Kehrer, Daniel. *Doing Business Boldly*. New York: Times Books, 1989.

Kessler, Sheila. *Measuring And Managing Customer Satisfaction: Going for the Gold*. Milwaukee: ASQC Quality Press, 1996.

Koch, Richard. *The 80/20 Principle: The Secret of Achieving More With Less*. New York: Currency Doubleday, 1998.

Kriegel, Robert J. and Louis Patler. *If It Ain't Broke . . . Break It! And Other Unconventional Wisdom for a Changing Business World*. New York: Warner Books, 1991.

Kurtz, David L., and Kenneth E. Clow. *Services Marketing*. New York: John Wiley & Sons, 1998.

Kurtz, James R. "We Are Becoming Something Distinctly Different." *Outlook*, Fall 1996.

Lacey, Robert. *Sotheby's: Bidding for Class*. New York: Little, Brown, 1998.

Lambert, Tom. *High Income Consulting: How to Build and Market Your Professional Practice*, Second Edition. London: Nicholas Brealey Publishing, 1997.

Landsburg, Steven E. *The Armchair Economist: Economics and Everyday Life*. New York: The Free Press, 1993.

———. *Price Theory and Applications, Third Edition*. St. Paul, Minn.: West Publishing Company, 1996.

Larson, Charles B., and Joseph W. Larson. *Innovative Billing and Collection Methods That Work*. Burr Ridge, Ill.: Irwin Professional Publishing, 1994.

LeBoeuf, Michael. *How to Win Customers and Keep Them for Life*. New York: Berkeley Books, 1989.

Levine, Robert. *A Geography of Time: The Temporal Misadventures of a Social Psychologist, or How Every Culture Keeps Time Just a Little Bit Differently*. New York: BasicBooks, 1997.

Levitt, Theodore. *Thinking About Management*. New York: The Free Press, 1991.

Maister, David H. *True Professionalism: The Courage to Care About Your People, Your Clients, and Your Career*. New York: The Free Press, 1997.

Mandel, Michael. *The High-Risk Society*. New York: Random House, 1996.

Marcus, Stanley. *Minding the Store*. New York: Dutton, 1993.

———. *Quest for the Best*. New York: Dutton, 1993.

Marx, Karl. *Wage-Labour and Capital and Value, Price and Profit*. New York: International Publishers, 1995 edition.

Micklethwait, John, and Adrian Wooldridge. *The Witch Doctors: What Management Gurus Are Saying and Why It Matters.* New York: Random House, 1996.

Mises, Ludwig von. *Planned Chaos*. New York: The Foundation for Economic Education, Inc., 1977.

Monroe, Kent B. *Pricing: Making Profitable Decisions*, Second Edition. New York: McGraw-Hill, 1990.

Morgan, J. Harris. *How To Draft Bills Clients Rush to Pay*. Chicago: American Bar Association, 1995.

Nagle, Thomas T. "Economic Foundations for Pricing." Chicago, Illinois: University of Chicago Graduate School of Business: July 1983, Report No. 83-106.

———, and Reed K. Holden. *The Strategy and Tactics of Pricing: A Guide to Profitable Decision Making*, Second Edition. New Jersey: Prentice Hall, 1995.

Neuhaus, Richard John. *Doing Well and Doing Good: The Challenge to the Christian Capitalist*. New York: Doubleday, 1992.

Novak, Michael. *Business as a Calling: Work and the Examined Life*. New York: The Free Press, 1996.

O'Dell, Carla, and C. Jackson Grayson, Jr. *If Only We Knew What We Know: The Transfer of Internal Knowledge and Best Practice*. New York: The Free Press, 1998.

O'Shea, James, and Charles Madigan. *Dangerous Company: Management Consultants and the Businesses They Save and Ruin*. New York: Penguin Books, 1998.

Pacioli, Fra Luca. *Particularis de Computis et Scripturis, 1494, A Contemporary Interpretation by Jeremy Cripps*. Seattle, Wash.: Pacioli Society, Seattle University, 1995.

Payne, Richard A. "The Emerging Competitive Landscape Occupied by the Accounting Profession: Challenges, Opportunities, and Imperatives." Pleasanton, California: Results Accountants' Systems, October 1998. Ras-net.com.

Peppers, Don, and Martha Rogers. *The One to One Enterprise: Tools for Competing in the Interactive Age*. New York: Doubleday, 1997.

Peters, Tom. *The Circle of Innovation: You Can't Shrink Your Way To Greatness*. New York: Random House, 1998.

———. *The Professional Service Firm 50: Transform Your "Department" Into a Professional Service Firm Whose Trademarks Are Passion and Innovation.* New York: Alfred A. Knopf, 1999.

———. *The Pursuit of Wow!: Every Person's Guide To Topsy-Turvy Times*. New York: Random House, 1995.

———. *The Tom Peters Seminar: Crazy Times Call for Crazy Organizations.* New York: Vintage Books, 1994.

Postrel, Virginia. *The Future and Its Enemies: The Growing Conflict Over Creativity, Enterprise, and Progress*. New York: The Free Press, 1998.

Previts, Gary John, and Barbara Dubis Merino. *A History of Accountancy in the United States: The Cultural Significance of Accounting*. Columbus, Ohio: Ohio State University Press, 1998

Rackham, Neil. *SPIN Selling*. New York: McGraw-Hill, 1988.

Reeb, CPA, William L. *Start Consulting: How to Walk the Talk*. New York: American Institute of Certified Public Accountants, 1998.

Reed, Richard C., Ed. *Beyond The Billable Hour.* Chicago: American Bar Association, 1989.

———. *Win-Win Billing Strategies: Alternatives That Satisfy Your Clients and You*. Chicago: American Bar Association, 1992.

———. *Billing Innovations: New Win-Win Ways to End Hourly Billing*. Chicago: American Bar Association, 1996.

Reichheld, Frederick F., and Thomas Teal. *The Loyalty Effect: The Hidden Force Behind Growth, Profits, and Lasting Value*. Boston: Harvard Business School Press, 1996.

Rogers, Everett M. *Diffusion of Innovations.* New York: Free Press, 1995.

Rosenbluth, Hal F. *The Customer Comes Second and Other Secrets.* New York: William Morrow, 1992.

Ross, William G. *The Honest Hour: The Ethics of Time-Based Billing by Attorneys.* Durham, N.C.: Carolina Academic Press, 1996.

Shapiro, Eileen C. *Fad Surfing in the Boardroom: Managing in the Age of Instant Answers.* New York: Addison-Wesley,1995.

Sinha, Indrajit. "Cost Transparency: The Net's Real Threat to Prices and Brands." *Harvard Business Review*, March-April 2000.

Skousen, Mark, and Kenna C. Taylor. *Puzzles and Paradoxes in Economics.* Brookfield, Vt.: Edward Elgar Publishing Company, 1997.

Stanley, Thomas J., and William D. Danko. *The Millionaire Next Door: The Surprising Secrets of America's Wealthy.* Atlanta, Ga.: Longstreet Press, 1996.

Stein, Ben. "Ben Stein's Diary." *The American Spectator*, April 2000.

Stewart, Thomas A. *Intellectual Capital: The New Wealth of Organizations.* New York: Currency Doubleday, 1997.

Stigler, George J. *Memoirs of an Unregulated Economist.* New York: BasicBooks, 1985.

Thornton, Roy C., and Jayne E. Osborne. *How to Manage Your Accounting Practice: A Complete Practice Management System.* San Diego: Harcourt Professional Publishing, 1999.

Will, George F. *Suddenly: The American Idea Abroad and at Home 1986–1990.* New York: The Free Press, 1992.

Williams, Roy H. *The Wizard of Ads: Turning Words into Magic and Dreamers into Millionaires.* Austin, Tex.: Bard Press, 1998.

Winston, William J., Editor. *Marketing for CPAs, Accountants, and Tax Professionals.* New York: The Haworth Press, 1995.

Woods, Earl, and Pete McDaniel. *Training a Tiger: A Father's Guide to Raising a Winner in Both Golf and Life*. New York: Harper & Row, Publishers, 1987.

Wriston, Walter. *Risk and Other Four-Letter Words*. New York: Harper & Row, Publishers, 1987.

Yutang, Lin. *The Importance of Living*. New York: William Morrow, 1937.

ABOUT THE CD-ROM

System Requirements

- IBM PC or compatible computer with CD-ROM drive
- Windows 95 or higher
- Microsoft® Word 7.0 for Windows™ or compatible word processor
- 1 MB available on hard drive

The CD-ROM provided with *Professional's Guide to Value Pricing* contains word processing files of items in "Useful Checklists" as well as a sample fixed price agreement (FPA) and a sample change order.

The word processing forms are intended to be used in conjunction with your word processing software. The word processing forms have been formatted in RTF.

Subject to the conditions in the license agreement and the limited warranty, which is reproduced at the end of the book, you may duplicate the files on this disc, modify them as necessary, and create your own customized versions. Installing the disc contents and/or using the disc in any way indicates that you accept the terms of the license agreement.

The list of the Disc Contents is available on your disc in a file called _contents.rtf. You can open this file and view it on your screen and use it to link to the documents you're interested in, or print a hard copy to use for reference.

1. Open the file _contents.rtf in your word processor.
2. Locate the file you wish to access, and click on the hyperlinked file name. Your word processor will then open the file.
3. You may copy files from the CD-ROM to your hard drive. To edit files you have copied, remember to clear the read-only attribute from the file. To do this, select the name of the file in My Computer, right-click the filename, then choose Properties, and clear the Read-only checkbox.

If you experience any difficulties installing or using the files included on this disc and cannot resolve the problem using the information presented in this section, call our toll-free software support hotline at (800) 835-0105 or visit our website at http://support.cch.com.

DISC CONTENTS

INDEX

A

B

D

E

F

K

L

M

N

O

P

S

T

W

X

Y

Z